D1720772

PROF. DR. REINHARD WILHELM
FACHBEREICH 10 - INFORMATIK

Handbibliothek Nr. 200

PARTIAL EVALUATION
AND MIXED COMPUTATION

IFIP TC2 Workshop on
Partial Evaluation and Mixed Computation
Gl. Avernæs, Ebberup, Denmark, 18–24 October, 1987

Organized by
IFIP Technical Committee 2 Programming
International Federation for Information Processing (IFIP)

Program Committee
D. Bjørner *(Chairman),* A. P. Ershov, Y. Futamura
A. Haraldsson, N. D. Jones, W. Scherlis

Organization Committee
D. Bjørner *(Chairman),* U. Jørring, T. Mogensen
P. Sestoft, H. Søndergaard, A. Rasmussen

NORTH-HOLLAND
AMSTERDAM · NEW YORK · OXFORD · TOKYO

PARTIAL EVALUATION
AND MIXED COMPUTATION

Proceedings of the IFIP TC2 Workshop on
Partial Evaluation and Mixed Computation
Gammel Avernæs, Denmark, 18–24 October, 1987

edited by

DINES BJØRNER
Technical University of Denmark
Lyngby, Denmark

ANDREI P. ERSHOV
USSR Academy of Sciences
Novosibirsk, USSR

NEIL D. JONES
University of Copenhagen
Copenhagen, Denmark

1988

NORTH-HOLLAND
AMSTERDAM · NEW YORK · OXFORD · TOKYO

© IFIP, 1988

All rights reserved. No part of this publication may be reproduced, stored in a retrieval system, or transmitted, in any form or by any means, electronic, mechanical, photocopying, recording or otherwise, without the prior written permission of the publishers, Elsevier Science Publishers B.V. (Physical Sciences and Engineering Division), P.O. Box 103, 1000 AC Amsterdam, The Netherlands.

Special regulations for readers in the USA - This publication has been registered with the Copyright Clearance Center Inc. (CCC), Salem, Massachusetts. Information can be obtained from the CCC about conditions under which photocopies of parts of this publication may be made in the USA. All other copyright questions, including photocopying outside of the USA, should be referred to the copyright owner or Elsevier Science Publishers B.V., unless otherwise specified.

No responsibility is assumed by the Publisher for any injury and/or damage to persons or property as a matter of products liability, negligence or otherwise, or from any use or operation of any methods, products, instructions or ideas contained in the material herein.

pp. 51-64, 65-82, 209-224, 283-298: Work for a Government Agency, not subject to copyright.

ISBN: 0 444 70491 4

Published by:

ELSEVIER SCIENCE PUBLISHERS B.V.
P.O. Box 103
1000 AC Amsterdam
The Netherlands

Sole distributors for the U.S.A. and Canada:

ELSEVIER SCIENCE PUBLISHING COMPANY, INC.
655 Avenue of the Americas
New York, N.Y. 10010
U.S.A.

LIBRARY OF CONGRESS
Library of Congress Cataloging-in-Publication Data

IFIP TC2 Workshop on Partial Evaluation and Mixed Computation (1987 :
  Agernæs, Denmark)
    Partial evaluation and mixed computation : proceedings of the IFIP
  TC2 Workshop on Partial Evaluation and Mixed Computation, Gammel
  Avernæs, Denmark, 18-24 October, 1987 / edited by Dines Bjørner,
  Andrei P. Ershov, Neil D. Jones.
      p.   cm.
    "Organized by IFIP Technical Committee 2 Programming,
  International Federation for Information Processing (IFIP)"
    Includes index.
    ISBN 0-444-70491-4
    1. Electronic digital computers--Programming--Congresses.
  2. Compiling (Electronic computers)--Congresses. 3. Automatic
  programming (Computer science)--Congresses.   I. Bjørner, D.
  (Dines), 1937-   . II. Ershov, A. P. (Andreĭ Petrovich)
  III. Jones, Neil D. IV. IFIP Technical Committee 2--Programming.
  V. Title.
  QA76.6.I1784 1987
  005.1--dc19   88-21268
                                                              CIP

PRINTED IN THE NETHERLANDS

Preface

The *Workshop on* **Partial Evalution and Mixed Computation**, *Gl. Avernæs, Denmark, 18-24. October 1987*, was a "by invitation only" workshop. It featured a geographically very wide spectrum of participants: Belgium 2, Denmark 13, France 2, Great Britain 11, The Netherlands 2, Federal Republic of Germany 2, India 1, Israel 2, Italy 3, Japan 5, Poland 1, Sweden 6, USA 11, and USSR 7.

The volume that you are now reading is one of the final results of the Workshop. It contains the papers of scientific presentations given at the Workshop.

A first **Call for Papers and Invitation** was sent out in October 1986. Response was very wide and positive. Papers submitted by June 1. 1987 were refereed worldwide and a programme committee meeting on August 4. 1987 selected the papers. We take the opportunity here to thank the very many referees (see list of these in this preamble) and the programme committee for their hard work.

During the conference Prof. D. Bjørner, Acad. A.P. Ershov, Dr. K. Furukawa, Dr. Y Futamura, Prof. A. Haraldsson, Prof. N.D. Jones and Dr. W. Scherlis selected among these and other papers, such scientific, full papers which appears here, and such logic programming, technical presentation papers which appears in special issues (*Vol. 6, nos. 2-3, 1988*) of the **New Generation Computing** journal.

The conference was unique in at least the following three ways:

1. It is believed to have been the first international gathering of specialists in the subject field. Hence these proceedings manifest a first comprehensive and generally available collection of state-of-the-art papers on the subject.

2. The number of contributions (12) and participants (7) from the Soviet Union was not only very high, but most exiting and enjoyable.

3. As part of the preparation for this workshop a number of novel actions were taken. These were:

   - A **Literature List** comprising some 200 references to the subject literature was established through the semantic help of *Prof. Alexander Zamulin (Novosibirsk, USSR)* and *Mr. Peter Sestoft (Copenhagen, Denmark)*, and with the initial, syntactic, pragmatic and final assistance of myself and Mrs. Annie Rasmussen. This list was issued in a fourth edition immediately prior to the workshop – and a fifth annotated edition is now part of these proceedings, see pages 589-622.

   - A subject **Terminology** was outlined. Action, on the part of the workshop participants, and lead by *Mr. Torben Mogensen*, eventually resulted in a guide to the scientific and technical, engineering and applications terms of the field – also part of these proceedings, see pages 583-588.

   - A list of **Challenging Problems** of the subject field was also worked out – both prior to and during the workshop. *Prof. Neil D. Jones* lead this effort, and was being helped by *Mr. Anders Bondorf*. We thank those invitees and others who have contributed to this list – finally a part also of these proceedings, see pages 1-14.

The Workshop on *Partial Evaluation and Mixed Computation* was sponsored by the **IFIP** *(International Federation for Information Processing)* **TC2** *(Technical Committee 2 on 'Programming')*, and was financially supported by the *Danish Natural Science Research Council* (SNF) Grant No. 11-6643, the *Danish Technical Sciences Research Council* (STVF) Grant No. 16-4216E, and *Dansk Datamatik Center* (DDC). We gratefully acknowledge their financial support. In addition the *Department of Computer Science* at the *Technical University of Denmark*, and the *Institute of Datalogy* of the *Copenhagen University*, also provided financial and secreterial assistance – for which we likewise thank.

Initiative to the Workshop was first taken by *Acad. A.P. Ershov*, in April 1986, and we thank him for his continuous and enthusiastic support.

Semantical advice on the subject field was continuously given by *Prof. Neil D. Jones*, and I thank him for his likewise support.

Dr. Ulrik Jørring worked out applications for funding to various authorities, and blessed be he for that!

For lots of administrative, strategic, technical and operational help we thank *Messrs. Torben Mogensen, Peter Sestoft,* and *Harald Søndergaard*.

The workshop was held in a "remote" conference center: **Gl. Avernæs**, owned by the *Danish Teacher's Association*. Gl. Avernæs is a lovely place, situated, as it is, on a small peninsula, right on the seashore and with a view of the rolling Danish countryside, a fjord, islands in the sea, and also providing for short strolls in its wonderful park, and long walks in the countryside.

Untiring practical arrangements: travel (airline reservations, train tickets and seat reservations, bus-hires, etc.), banquet (determining the menu and wines), lodging, administrative (literally hundreds of telexes, scores of cables, dozens of computer net messages, phone calls around the globe: in and out), mailings (5-6 bulk mails of various calls, invitations, registrations, tourist brochures, etcetera), and other technical and secretarial assistance (incl. substantial work on post-conference final accounting, extensive LaTeX typesetting of several parts and sections of these proceedings, and, last, but certainly not least, the final assembly of the proceedings) was always available from *Mrs. Annie Rasmussen*, and we all love and thank her enthusiastically for her generous help, initiative and loyal work.

Dines Bjørner
Holte
August 9, 1988

SCIENTIFIC FOREWORD

1. Introduction

The idea expressed by the terms: partial evaluation, mixed computation or program specialization (PE for short) appears to be one whose time has come. After pioneering work by McCarthy, Lombardi, Futamura and others, and important early work in the USSR, Sweden and the USA, the full potential and importance of PE is beginning to be realized, and in recent years much PE-related activity is seen many places in the world. Fundamental concepts and techniques are now beginning to be understood and realized independently in different places - a sure sign that a significant body of ideas is emerging.

In the large, the goal of PE is to construct, when given a program and some form of restriction on its usage (*e.g.* knowledge of some but not all of its input parameter values), a more efficient new or "residual" program that is equivalent to the original program when used according to the restriction. Compiling and compiler generation are but two of its many applications. PE is thus a form of program transformation, but with a greater emphasis on purely automatic methods than traditional program transformation; more will be said in the last section of this foreword. For the reader desiring an overview, two characterizations of PE are presented in another section, and the "Challenging Problems" section is also relevant.

We have here collected a variety of good examples of current work in the field, and hope a commonality will emerge out of our joint efforts. The workshop's papers demonstrate the vitality of this emerging area with contributions at many different points along several dimensions including programming language, application area, degree of automation, degree of formality, technical methods and, of course, nationalities. A major goal was to increase mutual understanding across barriers of language, computer subculture and application area, and here significant success was achieved. Further goals, which we hope will come with time, include transfer of ideas from one subarea of PE to another, stimulation of activity in the field as a whole, and various forms of cross fertilization.

It is still a very young field of endeavour, though, with as yet unstabilized terminology, techniques, algorithms and even basic assumptions. A section on terminology and an extensive bibliography appear at the end, and we hope these will be useful to encourage a more consistent language for use in future works.

2. Why Partial Evaluation and Mixed Computation?

We now relate some themes common to many of the workshop's articles.

Partial evaluation provides a common framework for discussing programming language interpreters and compilers, and means for both compiling and for automatically constructing compilers from interpreters.

A more general reason for interest in PE is the desire for efficient implementation by automatic means of very general, highly parametrized programs. Such programs are strongly desirable for practical reasons, *e.g.* reduction of program maintenance costs, and PE allows high generality without the inefficiency common to very general programs.

Another reason is the movement towards solving complex problems not by writing complex programs, but by designing flexible problem- or user-oriented *programming languages*. But this creates a need to implement such languages efficiently and with minimal human work - another area where PE has shown its utility.

An example: languages that represent programs as data make it natural to bootstrap new languages by *metaprogramming* - using an existing language to extend itself, for example by writing a metacircular (self-) interpreter and the augmenting this to include specialized language features appropriate to a particular problem domain. Again, PE allows the use of such extended dialects without paying the traditional time penalty caused by an extra layer of interpretation.

In recent years we have seen several significant breakthroughs: PE systems have become more powerful, more automatic, more efficient both in their functioning and the programs they produce. They now require much less hand work (and still more important: les human thought) than earlier systems. We have witnessed the emergence of PE systems used in practice to construct not only single programs but also *program generators* that translate certain classes of problem specifications (still fairly limited) into efficient programs able to solve arbitrary instances in the specified problems.

3. Partial Evaluation and Mixed Computation: What is the Common Vision?

Many of the ideas and structure of this section come from a lively discussion led by William Scherlis and Henk Barendregt, in which we reflected on similarities and differences among the starting points and angles of attack of the various contributions.

The obvious first question: why try to recognize or establish a common vision in the field of partial evaluation and mixed computation?   There are several excellent reasons:

(1)   to delineate a scope for our field
(2)   to establish a basis for cohesion among researchers in the field
(3)   to establish a basis for understanding and evaluation of each other's work
(4)   to help fight against compartmentalization in Computer Science

Here are three scope dimensions are relevant to our work. First, *which problems are to be solved?* Some possibilities include

*   program development or synthesis from problem specifications
*   program transformation
*   specialization of general programs to restricted usages
*   more specifically, partial evaluation
*   yet more specifically, compiler generation by partial evaluation

Most workers in partial evaluation and mixed computation put great emphasis on automatic construction of programs by machine, which differentiates our work from much program synthesis (due to the need for "Eureka" steps) and program transformation by interactive methods.   In short, we are willing to do without highly noncomputable problem specifications, and to sacrifice dramatic efficiency improvements, in order to gain more fully automatic program manipulation.

The choice of which goal to emphasize among the remaining problems, program specialization, partial evaluation or compiler generation, has been seen to make large practical differences in the best methods to use and the results obtained.

Second, *which problem-solving approaches are used?* Again there is a spectrum, all points of which are seen in the workshop contributions:

*   pragmatically driven   find a technology that works
*   technique or language driven
*   theory driven   start from abstract requirements

Third, *realizations in computational practice.* Here key issues include:

*   trade-offs between the degree of automation desired *versus* flexibility and efficiency
*   engineering factors: efficiency, scalability to large applications, *etc.*

To cast this last point into clearer perspective, we compare three well-known approaches to computer aided compiler construction.

Degrees of automation in three approaches to compiler construction

	full automation	*heuristic annotations*	*interactive guidance*	*hand craft*
PQCC (Wulf's "production quality compiler compiler")				
• system building				X
• compiler production			X ----- X	
• produced compilers	X			
• fit between semantics and compiler			up to the compiler writer	
Program transformation (Scherlis, Jørring, ..)				
• system building			X ---- X	
• compiler production		X ---- X		
• produced compilers	X			
• fit between semantics and compiler		good: obtained by transformation		
DIKU mix (Copenhagen)				
• system building				X
• compiler production	X (1987)	X (1985)		
• produced compilers	X			
• fit between semantics & and compiler	precise, since mechanically derived			

More can doubtless be said, but attempts to place new results in partial evaluation and mixed computation along such axes can give useful information for evaluating those results. Such comparisons should appear more frequently in published papers - so the reader is not misled into comparing apples and oranges.

Neil D. JONES
Copenhagen, Denmark

Acknowledgement

Every paper was carefully reviewed by (at least) three referees. Their assistances is gratefully acknowledged.

D. Bjørner

A. Bondorf

M. Bruynoghe

H. Christiansen

O. Danvy

D. de Schreye

J. Fischer-Nilsson

D. Friedman

D. Fuller

J. Gallagher

H. Ganzinger

A. Haraldsson

N.C.K. Holst

R.J.M. Hughes

N.D. Jones

U. Jørring

P. Kursawe

K. Marriott

B. Mayoh

T. Mogensen

P. Mosses

F. Nielson

H.R. Nielson

P. O'Keefe

A. Pettorossi

G.S. Port

K.R. Rao

M. Rosendahl

W. Scherlis

D.A. Schmidt

P. Sestoft

L. Sterling

H. Søndergaard

A. Takeuchi

C. Talcott

R.W. Topor

V.F. Turchin

P. Wadler

Contents

Preface
D. Bjørner v

Scientific Foreword
N.D. Jones vii

Acknowledgement xi

Two Charactizations of Partial Evaluation and Mixed Computation
A.P. Ershov & N.D. Jones xv

Opening Key-note Speech
A.P. Ershov xxiii

Group Picture xxx

Challenging Problems
Assembled by N.D. Jones 1

Mixed Computation and Compiler Basis
G.J. Barzdin 15

Towards a Self-Applicable Partial Evaluator for Term Rewriting Systems
Anders Bondorf 27

A Theoretical Approach to Polyvariant Mixed Computation
M.A. Bulyonkov 51

How do ad-hoc Compiler Constructs Appear in
Universal Mixed Computation Processes?
M.A. Bulyonkov & A.P. Ershov 65

Across the Bridge between Reflection and Partial Evaluation
Olivier Danvy 83

A Program Development Methodology Based on a Unified Approach
to Execution and Tranformation
John Darlington & Helen Pull 117

Generalized Partial Computation
Yoshihiko Futamura & Kenroku Nogi 133

Function Inversion
P.G. Harrison 153

Language Triplets: The AMIX Approach
N. Carsten Kehler Holst 167

Backwards Analysis of Functional Programs
John Hughes 187

An Algebra and Axiomatization System of Mixed Computation
V.E. Itkin 209

Automatic Program Specialization: A Re-Examination from Basic Principles
N.D. Jones   225

Pure Partial Evaluation and Instantiation
Peter Kursawe   283

Projections for Specialisation
John Launchbury   299

On the Essence of Mixed Computation
S.S. Lavrov   317

Partially Static Structures in a Self-Applicable Partial Evaluator
Torben Mogensen   325

A Formal Type System for Comparing Partial Evaluators
Flemming Nielson   349

*Implementation of Controlled Mixed Computation in System for
Automatic Development of Language-Oriented Parsers*
B.N. Ostrovski   385

Importing and Exporting Information in Program Development
Alberto Pettorossi & Maurizio Proietti   405

The Generation of Inverse Functions in Refal
Alexander Y. Romanenko   427

*A Compiler Generator Produced by a Self-Applicable Specializer Can
have a Surprisingly Natural and Understanable Structure*
Sergei A. Romanenko   445

Static Properties of Partial Evaluation
David A. Schmidt   465

Automatic Call Unfolding in a Partial Evaluator
Peter Sestoft   485

*Partial Evaluation, Higher-Order Abstractions,
and Reflection Principles as System Building Tools*
Carolyn Talcott & Richard Weyhrauch   507

The Algorithm of Generalization in the Supercompiler
V.F. Turchin   531

A model of Language Semantics Oriented to Mixed Execution of Programs
T.I. Youganova   551

Experience with A Type Evaluator
Jonathan Young & Patrick O'Keefe   573

Terminology
Torben Mogensen & N. Carsten Kehler Holst   583

Annotated Bibliography on Partial Evaluation and Mixed Computation
Peter Sestoft & Alexander V. Zamulin   589

List of Participants   623

Author Index   625

Partial Evaluation and Mixed Computation
D. Bjørner, A.P. Ershov and N.D. Jones (Editors)
Elsevier Science Publishers B.V. (North-Holland)
© IFIP, 1988

TWO CHARACTERIZATIONS OF
PARTIAL EVALUATION AND MIXED COMPUTATION

Andrei P. ERSHOV
USSR Academy of Sciences, Siberian Division
Computing Centre
SU-630090 Novosibirsk, USSR

Neil D. JONES
DIKU, University of Copenhagen
Universitetsparken 1
DK-2100 Copenhagen Ø, Denmark
(e-mail: uucp: ... ! mcvax ! diku ! neil)

The field of partial evaluation and mixed computation can be characterized in a number of ways. Two views held by contributors to the theory and practice of the field are given.

Andrei P. Ershov:

Partial computation is the processing of incomplete information. Mixed computation is the joint processing of a program and its data. Formally, these two activities are defined as follows:

Let $P=\{p\}$ be programs, $D=\{d\}$ be data, and $Sem: P \times D \to D$ be the functional semantics.

Partial Computation *(Part):*

$Part: P \times D \to P$ **such that**
$$Sem(p,(d_1,d_2)) = Sem(Part(p,d_1),d_2)$$

Mixed Computation *(Mix):*

$Mix: P \times D \to P \times D$ **such that**
if $(p', d') = Mix(p, d)$ **then** $Sem(p, d) = Sem(p', d')$

Defining a rigorous semantics of partial and mixed computation gives a unifying theoretical and methodological basis for numerous tools and techniques of program manipulation, especially in compilation, program development and enhancement, all kinds of program adaptation and concretisation, logical analysis and simplification, *etc.*

It also plays an important role in operationalisation of data: in putting knowledge into action with deep methodological and philosophical consequences.

Surviving a period of prophecies and independent insights, partial and mixed computation went, in the late 1970's, into a period of steady and coherent development with a literature now approaching some 100 titles.

After collection a dozen exciting pearls of concepts, ideas and evidence, the field now faces a series of difficult and deep problems that require thoughtful, persistent, hard and coordinated work.

Neil D. Jones:

1. Program specialization, partial evaluation and metaprogramming

Keywords describing the theme of this workshop include *mixed computation, partial evaluation* and *program specialization.* Applications include:

- compiling
- program generation, including compiler generation
- program transformation
- metaprogramming without order-of-magnitude loss of efficiency

Assume that a given program, P, is to be run repeatedly, on various input data. In each run, P is given a single (possibly structured) data value as input argument. Further, assume that the data values for these runs are given a bit at a time:

Stage 1   Where a particular subset of all possible input data values is given, for example by means of common features of elements in the subset

Stage 2   Where the individual data values within that subset are identified

Thus one may at stage 1 name a data subset, *i.e.* a range of applications of P; and at stage 2 give the specific details of data values in that range. In *partial evaluation* one gives *part of* the input at stage 1. Alternatives can also be imagined, e.g. one could give the *shape* of the input at stage 1, and its *value* at stage 2. The main goal is optimization:

Given   P and a stage 1 specification, st1

To produce   A specialized program P_{st1} which is equivalent to P on the range
                 of applications given by st1 and is (by some measure) better than
                 the original P.

1.1   Application to parsing

Program P: A general context-free parsing algorithm, *e.g.* Earley's parser
Stage 1:   A particular context-free grammar G
Stage 2:   A symbol string to be parsed
Program P_G: A specialized *parser* for G, accepting all and only the strings
              in L(G)

Parsing algorithms capable of handling arbitrary context-free grammars are
notoriously slow, but in contrast parsers for specific grammars are efficient
enough to be a standard part of modern compiler technology. In this case
program specialization can, at least in principle, make dramatic improvements in
efficiency.

1.2   Application to compiling

Suppose an interpreter *Int* for some language S is given. The input to *Int* is a pair
of the form (S-program, input data to the S-program). If we regard the
S-program as a stage 1 specification and its input data as a stage 2 specification,
the two together are enough to run *Int*. The result of specializing *Int* to the given
S-program is a program that takes the same input data as that S-program.

What has been accomplished? Answer: the S-program has been *translated,*
from language S into the output language of the program specializer. The result
may be summarized by:

Program P: An interpreter *Int* for some language S
Stage 1:   A source program *s* in language S
Stage 2:   Input data to that source program
Program Int_s: A *target program* for *s*

1.3   Program maintenance

In practice one often faces difficult tradeoffs between program generality and
modularity on the one hand and efficiency on the other. Generality makes it
possible for the same program to solve many related problems. Modularity

makes it easier to debug, maintain and update the program to satisfy changing requirements, and to replace program parts by equivalent but more efficient versions, a change that can dramatically improve a program's *large-scale* efficiency. On the other hand, a highly modular program often spends a significant amount of time sending data across the intermodular interface, changing representation, *etc,* which can be quite damaging to *small-scale* efficiency. Further, a very general algorithm is all too often very inefficient, as for example in the Earley's parser discussed above.

It is obviously not satisfactory to replace a single general, clear, modular program by a large collection of special-purpose, efficient handwritten programs, one reason being the administrative work necessary to preserve consistensy among the different versions (especially in the face of changing external specifications!).

The parsing example suggests one escape between the horns of this dilemma: write a *program generator,* which transforms a clear, general and understandable problem description into an efficient program that solves the problem. (One example is the YACC parser generator, which transforms certain context-free grammars into efficient specialized parsers.) The only difficulty with this approach is that it takes much time and effort to design and write the program generator.

There is a different way to escape the dilemma: use a program specializer to transform a single general-purpose program into a multitude of more efficient special-purpose programs *by machine.* Consistency is ensured since all are derived from the same ancestor (assuming, of course, correctness of the program specializer!). If external requirements change, it is only necessary to revise the master program, and then regenerate by computer a new version of each specialized program. Further, it will be seen that a program specializer can also *generate a program generator* automatically from the given general-purpose program.

A major goal is to construct systems that treat programs as data objects, to be executed, processed, specialized, improved, *etc.* with little or no human intervention. Partial evaluators and other program specializers should thus be considered more as tools for generating program generators than for use as general purpose compilers. This goal seems to necessitate some form of *self-application* of a program transformation algorithm.

2. Generating program generators by specializing the specializer

Specialization as described above transforms the pair of values:

(a program "P", a stage 1 specification "st1")

into a program P_{st1} that is equivalent to P on all input data described by the stage 1 specification st1. Suppose now that the specialization process itself can be programmed, so there is a program *Spec* which transforms any input pair (P, st1) into P_{st1}. Now suppose the first argument of *Spec* is "frozen", so P will always be the same fixed program (call it Q), regardless of the value of st1. In other words the specializer will now be used only to produce specialized versions of the same program Q. The effect of *specializing the specializer* may be described by:

Program:	the specializer program *Spec* itself
Stage 1:	a program Q
Stage 2:	a stage 1 specification for Q (*e.g.* st1)
Program $Spec_Q$:	a *generator of specialized programs*

Program $Spec_Q$ thus transforms a stage 1 specification st1 for Q into Q_{st1}. Diagrammatically:

$$\begin{array}{ccc} \text{Stage 1} & & \text{Specialized} \\ \text{specification} \Rightarrow & \boxed{Spec_Q} \Rightarrow & \text{program} \\ \text{"st1" for Q} & & "Q_{st1}" \end{array}$$

Some interesting special cases

1. Parser generation

Q	=	General parser, *e.g.* Earley's
st1	=	Context-free grammar G
Q_G	=	Parser for L(G)
$Spec_Q$	=	Parser generator

2. Compiling and compiler generation

Q	=	*Int* (interpreter for language S)
st1	=	An S-program *s*
Int_s	=	Target program for *s*
$Spec_{Int}$	=	Compiler for language S interpreted by *Int*

3.   *Generation of a compiler generator*

Q	$=$	The specializer program *Spec*
stl	$=$	An interpreter *Int* for some language S
$Spec_{Int}$	$=$	Compiler for the language S interpreted by *Int*
$Spec_{Spec}$	$=$	Compiler generator, that transforms interpreters into compilers

4.   *Transforming problem specifications into solutions:*

Q	$=$	Interpretive implementation of a specification language Σ with two inputs: A problem specification σ and its parameters
stl	$=$	A problem specification σ expressed in Σ
Q_{σ}	$=$	A program satisfying σ
$Spec_Q$	$=$	A system transforming specifications into solutions in program form

3. Machine generation of automatic program transformers

Suppose *Int* is an interpreter for language S, and is written in language L. Assume that *Spec* accepts programs written in L and produces as output specialized programs in the same language. Then $Spec_{Int}$ will be a compiler from S to L, and will itself be expressed in L. Diagrammatically:

$$Int \quad \in \quad \boxed{\begin{array}{c} \text{S} \\ \text{L} \end{array}} \quad \textbf{implies} \quad Spec_{Int} \quad \in \quad \boxed{\begin{array}{c} \text{S} \rightarrow \text{L} \\ \text{L} \end{array}}$$

Suppose $Spec_{Int}$ is given as input an S-program p_{in} , and yields an L-program p_{out} as output. Then p_{out} computes exactly the same input-output function as p_{in}.

    If S is identical to L, then $Spec_{Int}$ is a (machine-generated) *program transformer*. The transformed programs will be functionally equivalent to their originals, but may differ in their structure or even in how they work (the relation between p_{in} and p_{out} is determined rather implicitly, entirely by the way that the self-interpreter *Int* is written). Following are several applications of this simple observation.

Language extension
to implement stronger languages with existing processors

Language contraction
for example to compile into more machine-near dialects of the implementation language

Automatic program instrumentation
including *debugging aids* and *source program annotations*, to control the way programs are executed.

4. Metaprogramming without order-of-magnitude loss of efficiency

It is becoming increasingly popular to solve a wide-spectrum problem not by writing a collection of special purpose programs, but rather by revising a *problem-oriented language* in which the user can interactively express a wide variety of computational requests. An example is the current broad interest in *expert systems,* widely hailed as a solution to bridging the gap between the computer and users who are not professional computer scientists.

Such a problem-oriented language needs a processor, and these processors are usually written interpretively, alternating between reading and deciphering the user's requests, and consulting databases and doing problem-related computing. For some sophisticated problem-oriented languages, the system spends a considerable amount of time interpreting as compared to computing or searching, and here automatic optimization of systems programs could yield substantial benefits.

Further, expert and other programming systems are being constructed more and more with the use of a *hierarchy of metalanguages,* each used to control the sequence and choice of operations at the next lower level of abstraction. For instance, there has been much discussion of the need for and benefits of metalevel control of program transformations and is also currently a very high level of interest in metaprogramming in the Prolog community.

In this context the efficiency problem becomes more serious and the benefits of automatic program optimization are correspondingly greater, since widespread use of metaprogramming can easily lead to multiple layers of interpretation, each multiplying the total computation time by a nontrivial factor. On the other hand, program specialization can (and has been shown to) eliminate an entire level of interpretation, so that metaprogramming may be used without order-of-magnitude loss of efficiency.

Partial Evaluation and Mixed Computation
D. Bjørner, A.P. Ershov and N.D. Jones (Editors)
Elsevier Science Publishers B.V. (North-Holland)
© IFIP, 1988

OPENING KEY-NOTE SPEECH

Andrei P. Ershov

Computing Center
USSR Ac. Sci. Siberian Division
Novosibirsk 630090, USSR

Scientific Council for
Cybernetics, USSR Ac. Sci.
Moscow 117333, USSR

1 INTRODUCTION

Dear friends and colleagues:

When Professor Dines Bjørner invited me to address to the audience with a Historical Review and Survey I found myself in difficulty. Obviously, it was tempting to take an opportunity to offer a kind of last word of what has happened in this field in the last decade and, thus, to open a new, not yet written page of development. On the other hand, I still felt myself too warmed up, too close to the events to make the story really objective, distant and authoritative.

When I shared my pain with Dines he gave me a substantial relief advising not to fight my subjectivity but, quite contrarily, to put in into the center, offering a personal account of what I consider to be most interesting and memorable. Moreover, he easily assured me that such a personal story could trigger other people, too, and, since the history of partial evaluation and mixed computation is especially rich by independent discoveries and striking insights, we might hope during this week to collect a series of priceless personal evidences about main events in the passed decade of development and its no less remarkable "prehistorical" period.

For me, the last decade was the most turbulent, painful but rewarding and productive period of my scientific activity. But, of these ten years, the first year covering the period, roughly, from June 1976 to June 1977 was most remarkable and instructive. This period had resulted in two publications: short note "On the Partial Computation Principle" published in "Information Processing Letters" and "Doklady Akademii Nauk SSSR", and a more extended paper "On the Essence of Compilation" delivered in August 1977 to the IFIP Working Conference "Formalization of Programming Concepts" held in Canada, Saint John just prior the IFIP 77 Congress and published in the Soviet Union in the "Programmmirovanie" journal.

Now it is not just my opinion that these two publications attracted general attention and made the main ideas and notions of PE&MS general commodity.

So, that is why I have chosen the story of findings behind these papers the subject of my talk this morning.

2   THE LONG WAY

The previous 22 years — from 1955 to 1976 — I was highly preoccupied with compilers and other program processors; both, theoretical and engineering aspects were involved: a programming program for the BESM computer (1955-1957); the PPS compiler for the Strela computer (1957-1959); an Algol 58 extension later modified into the Input (ALPHA) Language (1958-1960) and its subsequent implementation for the M-20 computer (ALPHA-system) (1960-1964); a programming system for systems programming, so-called Epsilon System (1965-1968); an experimental macroprocessing SYGMA system (1966-1969...1985); BESM-6 implementations of the ALPHA language the ALHYBR (1966-1968) and ALPHA-6 (1970-1974) systems; the huge and ambitious multilanguage BETA-project (1970-1985).

In parallel, some theoretical work on program schemata was conducted: a graph-schema model for imperative programs (so-called operator algorithms) (1956-1960); the theory of Yanov schemata with the so-called labelling concept: (1963-1966); a graph-schemata theory for memory economy (1961-1966-1972); all this concluded by an invited talk to the IFIP 74 Congress at Lyublyana, Yugoslaviya.

The sheer nomenclature of the study, however, says not so much, more important was the general direction and style of the research and development. To this end it is appropriate to mention a very intensive character of work (it was, equally, good and bad feature), tight connection of theoretical, experimental and engineering aspects (very good feature!), constant interest to optimization and general efficiency of program processors, general inclination to transformational approach to programming (as one American colleague said: "We don't write, we rewrite our programs!"). As a consequence of the engineering approach I was always interested in compiler organization (compilation schemas, relation between interpretation and compilation, number of passes, etc.)

The first source of driving force for thoughts that finally led to the mixed computation concept was the experience gained in the ALPHA-project. The ALPHA-compiler was a formidable 24-passes program optimizer forging an efficient object code through a narrow hole of just 4K words of memory.

The rich variety of optimizations implemented in the ALPHA-compiler constitutes three classes of optimizing algorithms:

- mixed strategy of compilation, or casing;

- combinatorial optimization by equivalent transformations;

- compile time expression evaluation or constant propagation.

Casing means that a universal algorithm of compilation of a composite language construct is supplemented by a family of specialized compilation algorithms each of which corresponds to one or another restricted use of the construct under consideration. The choise of a most appropriate compilation algorithm is performed by case analysis of a particular occurrence of the language construct in the program text. The ALPHA-compiler distinguishes, for example, 11 cases of procedure parameter passing implementation and more than 40 cases of multiplication operation due to the variety of operand types.

The experience gained during the design and development of the ALPHA-compiler formed a source of many-years long thoughts about essence of compilation and unifying concepts of optimization. A still vague but finally productive observation was that an efficient compiler gives a plenty of room for an interpreter type activity during compilation, such as constant propagation or type analysis in casing. Another informal but important observation was that a good compiler has to be sensible to specific features of the source program; one of the forms of such a sensibility is that an optimization should be somehow directed by the source program structure. Such a directness is the only means to prevent a combinatorial explosion of "blind" optimizing transformations. To this end, interpreter's behaviour is ideal since from all the variety of computation incorporated in the language it selects just a single one according to the given combination of source program and data.

A further contribution into the "computational" aspects of compilation came from so-called "big" programming languages, especially PL/I and Algol 68. PL/I programs provided enormous material for casing and the "compile time facilities" were a not very successful attempt to make selective compilation user-controlled. Algol 68 brought on the stage such issues as type evaluation and many other things merged later in "static semantics" concept.

Many years we considered casing, schematic conversions and constant propagation as quite different kinds of program processing. A more integrated view gradually emerged in the course of conducting the BETA-project.

An important breakthrough (though never implemented) was a discovery that casing can be implemented on the level of the "flattened", decomposed program as a series of schematic conversions and compile-time reductions. This had been exemplified by selective compilation of procedure calls. This observation contained seeds of the transformational approach to program processing.

Another general observation of the early 1970-ies was a stratification of program according to levels of relative frequency of code execution. Since some variables from a less frequent code level serve as bound parameters for a more frequent level, the program stratification is subordinated to the levels of variable binding. An idea emerged to look at compilation as a maximal unloading of interpreter's work from a more frequent (than compilation) loop of source program interpretation. In its turn, unloading itself could be considered as a sequence of code motions and constant propagations.

This idea of a systematic transformation of a language interpreter into a compiled code was reported in 1976 to the Soviet-American Seminar on Very-High Level Languages and delivered in my lectures during a BCS tour through the United Kingdom and published later in my British Lectures. During the mentioned seminar, Fran Allen of IBM/Yorktown Heights made me acquainted with a similar study of her colleague W. Harrison.

It was, indeed, an exciting and powerful idea but, methodologically, it lacked generality and, technically, it lacked a direction that could properly arrange all the variety of optimizing transformations leading from the interpreter program to the object code. I understand these theoretical deficiencies of the method and, thus, continued to think of the problem of semantics directed compilation.

To finish my account of the prehistory, it only remains to note that while thinking on the problem I have been constantly oscillating between a very concrete view of a program as a specific text in a specific language taken in the strict context of the compilation problem and a rather abstract view of a program as just a set of linear compulational histories (traces). The second view was very helpful but the first one was both stimulating and restrictive. It made me blind and ignorant of several principal findings by other authors. Most of them were read, perhaps briefly, and easily forgotten and thus, did not serve the purpose of my study. Sometimes, this was natural, partially due to a camouflage of basic ideas under the secondary technicalities. Sometimes, it was an unforgivable ignorance which happens, however, more often we would like to admit.

3   THE MAIN FINDINGS

The main insight was a complete departure from the compilation/interpretation problem. I found that there exists a universal process as general and directed as computation itself. It also deals with a single trace of the program's execution but, instead of complete execution, it sorts the trace into executed and suspended parts, thus, combining, mixing ordinary data processing steps with stepwise formation of a residual program as a collection of suspended operations. That is how the mixed computation concept did emerge in the form of a $(P \times D) \to (P \times D)$ mapping, satisfying the obvious condition: if

$$(P', D') = mixcomp(P, D)$$

then *Val(P,D) = Val(P',D')* where *Val* is the ordinary semantics of the language of programs *P* and data *D*.

The most exciting feeling was a clear vision that mixed computation explains and integrates everything: code generation, compilation and compiler construction, variety of compilation schemes, many ad hoc optimizations: constant propagation, procedure integration, loop unrolling, dead code elimination, loop unloading, not speaking of casing, compile time facilities, etc. Outside of compilation field mixed computation embraces all issues of program specialization and adaptation, deriving ad hoc algorithms from universal ones, modular systems simplication, fighting overheads and redundancy wherever they appear.

I would wish that everybody in the audience could experience, let it be once a life, such an overwhelming feeling when one day of thinking provides you with a work plan for many years. It is worth now to note that it was not just a speculation: some immediate technical results had followed. I could account for:

- introducing the mixed computation concept as a mapping $M : (p, d) \to (p', d')$ where $V(p, d) = V(p', d')$;

- giving a name to p': "residual program";

- parametrizing a mixed computation process by various kinds of suspension, most important of which was due to data unavailability;

- finding the first Futamura projection;

- finding the generating extension as a general concept and expressing compiler in its terms; however, I overlooked the generating extension as the second Futamura projection, and I had no idea of F3 at all;

- offering a strict mixed computation processor for a simple imperative language.

All this was described briefly in letters sent at the end of 1976 and at the beginning of 1977 to "Doklady Akademii Nauk SSSR" and "Information Processing Letters", respectively.

4   INTEGRATION

In December 1976 I came to Moscow to share my finding with colleagues. For many reasons it was a kind of sentimental journey. My first talk was in the S.A. Lebedev Institute of Computing Machinery where I started my programmer's career in 1953. The talk was well received and I rushed to repeat it at the famous Institute of Applied Mathematics. I had very tight and long connections with systems programmers from that institute. Many of them graduated from the Moscow University together with me in 1954 and all the time were both my friends, colleagues and rivals in the field of compiler development.

The talk in the Institute of Applied Mathematics was especially memorable. First, it was marked by Academician Mstislav V. Keldysh's attendance. At that time he became the past-President of the Academy of Sciences and, courageously fighting his serious illness, concentrated his activity in scientific matters of the Institute he directed. For me, it was a symbolic closing bracket of a long period opened in 1955 by another seminar chaired by M.V. Keldysh at the same Institute. It was the first in the USSR public discussion of several automatic programming projects conducted at that time. At least three groups were present there: L.V. Kantorovich's group form Leningrad University, M.R. Shura-Bura's team from Keldysh's Institute and our PP BESM group from Lebedev's Institute. Now I was happy to inform the academician that 22 years were not wasted.

No less important was that the IPM seminar was attended by Sergei Romanenko, now one of the delegates to our workshop. He was one of closest assistant to Dr. Valentin Turchin in his Refal project. After my talk Sergei approached me and said that they (Turchin's group) possess a similar knowledge on mixed computation and its relation to compilation. Next day we met in my hotel room with Turchin and Romanenko and went into a rather intensive discusssion. We have established that Turchin's "прогонка", or driving, combined with some generalizing steps is a transformational version of one of the mixed computation instances, what was known as partial evaluation. Refal was for Turchin's team an established metalanguage for writing various program processors so it was natural for him to realize that driving the interpreter as applied to a source program yields an object code at that program. Moreover, he showed me that my generating extension is a selfapplication of the mixed computation processor. The idea of selfapplication was new to me but the resonance was immediate and in few minutes we closed the issue by formulating all three Futamura projections.

I had remembered that in 1972 at a seminar in Alushta, Crimea I listened Turchin's talk where he at the first time presented his concept of driving and showed its usefulness as a powerful means of program transformation. At that time I was unimpressed being unable to distill fundamental properties of driving from the very specific Refal clothes.

For the Refal group this meeting in a hotel room was a fresh stimulus to intensify their work with the selfapplicable driving processor — a formidable task! — and for me it was a strong warning to dig into the literature.

But again, most striking confirmations came from personal contacts. In the spring 1977 an international symposium on Artificial Intelligence was held at Repino near Leningrad. John McCarthy and Erik Sandewall were among participants. I made a presentation on mixed computation at the symposium. In the concluding discussion Erik Sandewall said that what he heard on mixed computation was most interesting to him at the symposium. I appreciated this but what was more important was his information that partial evaluation is an established direction of experimental programming in the LISP environment in his group rooted in an old Lombardi's work of mid-sixties. Sandewall further told me that they had implemented a LISP partial evaluator as a REDFUN function in their LISP library but did not experience with its selfapplication concentrating more on program enhancement through their automated specialization. However, they had heared something similar vaguely described by a Japaneze, certain Futamura, in an obscure technical journal. He promised to send me references and some material.

Coming back home I went to my own library and found all pioneering Lionello Lombardi's works partially brought by me during my 1965 visit to the USA and partially sent later by colleagues from Stanford and Cambridge, MIT. I found the philosophy of incremental computation with incomplete information where the idea of suspended computation forming a residual program was clearly expressed and a brief description of a partial LISP evaluator (in collaboration with B. Rafael) published in the well-known 1964 collection of papers on LISP and its applications. All this had been read and forgotten for more than 20 years.

But the flow of ideas did not die. A few months later I have received from Linköping a xerox copy of Futamura's paper. The journal was really obscure and hardly read more than by a dozen of readers but the paper was clear, original and honest. Referring to Lombardi's work, it contained an explicit formulation of partial evaluator selfapplication in order to obtain object code, compiler and compiler-compiler. It contained also some important ideas on polyvariant partial evaluation. The author admitted, however, that he was unable to offer a closed and coherent description of partial evaluation facing a number of technical difficulties.

The more I read the more I observed that I am far from to be alone in this emerging world of partial evaluation and mixed computation. Mentally, I was conducting a really first workshop on the subject. Reading Futamura, Turchin, Lombardi, Beckman, Haraldsson, coming back up to Uspensky, Kleene, Church and, perhaps finally, Schönfinkel I realized that most of my technical findings were in one or another form found and expressed by somebody else. But, frankly, I was not too much dissappointed. I was loosing the priority but was gaining an intellectual control over all the field. And more! There were so much to do next. With all that rich resource I started to write the paper "On the Essence of Compilation" and a year later my reflections on everything I learned during this unforgottable 1977: "Mixed Computation: Potential Applications and Problems for Study".

Nevertheless, once I was really frustrated. It happened when I reread a paper published by Babish, Shternberg and Yuganova in "Programmirovanie", No. 4, 1976, a bimonthly journal. It was a major work, one of practical applications of a partial evaluator in a language especially designed for programming computations over incomplete information. The study had been done in Lombardi's lines. I subscribe to this journal and scan every issue. I looked through the paper not earlier than few weeks before my insight into mixed computation but was absolutely untouched by its most pertinent contempt. Until now I have to rational explanation for such a strange ignorance.

5   CONCLUSION

The integration of knowledge and vision of partial evaluation and mixed computation triggered an almost explosive development. The number of studied topics is considerable: theoretical models, implementation of partial evaluators for major programming languages, systems of program transformations and reductions, hardware implementation, applications to compilation theory, discussion of similar phenomena in logic proofs, applications to parallel computation, automatic design of efficient ad hoc algorithms, adaptation and generation of application packages — all this and more can be found in the impressive list of literatur prepared by Sestoft and Zamulin.

I was happy to realize that my work was useful, intensively referred and cited. But very recently I found several publications in which PE&MC was taken for granted without any references to sources. We all are only humans and, having painfully overcome my own ignorance, I jealously felt myself obsolete and died, my ash gradually dissolving in the quiet waters of the Ganges. But few minutes later, a saving thought came to my mind that there is no higher award for a scientist if a person's notion became an anonymous general commodity. I cannot inhibit this thought and only insist that it should be shared by all the pioneers and prophets of partial evaluation and mixed computation.

This workshop could not be better timed, thanks to Dines Bjørner and to everybody who has come.

Thank you for your attention.

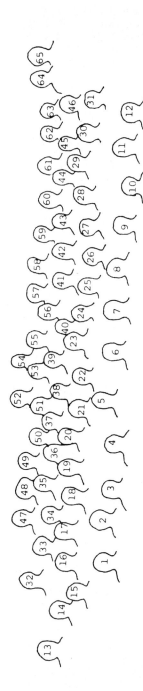

1. A. Haraldsson
2. J. Hughes
3. J. McCarthy
4. V.F. Turchin
5. N.D. Jones
6. A.P. Ershov
7. Y. Futamura
8. D. Bjørner
9. W. Scherlis
10. S.A. Romanenko
11. N. Nepejvoda
12. P. Sestoft

13. J. Maluszynski
14. P. Lucas
15. H. Pull
16. L. Hascöet
17. U. Nilsson
18. H. Fujita
19. D. Fuller
20. E. Tribble
21. A. Norman
22. K. Furukawa
23. G. Levi
24. M. Bonacina
25. A. Rasmussen
26. L. Beckman
27. B. Ostrovski
28. M. Guzowski
29. N.C.K. Holst
30. J. Young
31. A.V. Zamulin

32. H. Christiansen
33. A. De Niel
34. A. Waern
35. P.G. Harrison
36. C. Bjørner
37. H.R. Nielson
38. C. Talcott
39. M. Ryčko
40. A. Lakhotia
41. A. Takeuchi
42. C. Sakama
43. K. Nori
44. E. Berglund
45. P. Mosses
46. G. Howells

47. T. Sjöland
48. H. Barendregt
49. T. Mogensen
50. J. Darlington
51. F. Nielson
52. O. Danvy
53. U. Jørring
54. C. Consel
55. A. Bondorf
56. M. Rosendahl
57. P. Kursawe
58. S. Owen
59. J. Launchbury
60. S.S. Lavrov
61. J.M. Barzdin
62. D.A. Schmidt
63. A. Pettorossi
64. M. Codish
65. J. Gallagher

Partial Evaluation and Mixed Computation
D. Bjørner, A.P. Ershov and N.D. Jones (Editors)
Elsevier Science Publishers B.V. (North-Holland)
© IFIP, 1988

CHALLENGING PROBLEMS IN PARTIAL EVALUATION AND MIXED COMPUTATION

Assembled by Neil D. JONES

DIKU, University of Copenhagen
Universitetsparken 1, DK-2100 Copenhagen Ø, Denmark
(e-mail: uucp: ... ! mcvax ! diku ! neil)

This paper collects together a variety of problems in partial evaluation and mixed computation that appear to be worth solving but as yet lack solutions or (in some cases) precise formulations. The problems come largely from discussions with and notes by participants in the 1987 workshop on Partial Evaluation and Mixed Computation.

Keywords: Partial evaluation, mixed computation, program specialisation; challenging problems, open problems; automation, automatic programming, semantics based program manipulation; self applicable programs, programming tools, program composition, program decomposition.

1. Introduction and Sources

This paper collects together a variety of problems in partial evaluation and mixed computation that appear to be worth solving but as yet lack solutions or (in some cases) precise formulations. The discussion, presentation and organisation of the problems are of my own devising, but the problems themselves come largely from discussions with and notes by participants in the workshop. Sources include the following (with apologies to anyone whose name was inadvertently omitted):

Henk Barendregt	Nijmegen
M. A. Bulyonkov	Akademgorodok, USSR
the DIKU group	Copenhagen
(Bondorf, Danvy, Holst, Jones, Mogensen, Sestoft)	
Andrei P. Ershov	Akademgorodok, USSR
Koichi Furukawa	ICOT, Tokyo
Yoshihiko Futamura	Hitachi, Japan
John Gallagher	Weizmann, Israel
Anders Haraldsson	Linköping, Sweden
John Hughes	Glasgow
Peter Kursawe	Karlsruhe
John Launchbury	Glasgow
S. S. Lavrov	Leningrad
John McCarthy	Stanford

Sergei Romanenko   Moscow
Mads Rosendahl   Cambridge University
Marek Rycko   Warsaw
Bill Scherlis   Carnegie-Mellon University
David Schmidt   Kansas State University
Akikazu Takeuchi   Mitsubishi, Japan
Carolyn Talcott   Stanford
Valentin Turchin   City Univ. of New York

The field of partial evaluation and mixed computation is currently undergoing a rapid expansion in many parts of the world with continued development of new techniques, new applications and fundamental new insights. Essentially similar concepts are being understood independently in diverse parts of the world - one sign that a significant body of ideas is emerging.

Our field is still very young, though, and clearly lacking in focus.

The aim of this paper is to bring some of the many research directions in partial evaluation and mixed computation into sharper focus by listing a set of important problems, some near solution and some not. Ideally, criteria for selection of a problem include:

- it should be simply and precisely stated

- it should be useful and not just an intellectual curiosity: solutions should lead to insights that can be used on other problems and lead to further investigations

- it should seem potentially solvable

Our common field of endeavour has an enormous potential: the fully automatic treatment of programs as data objects, to be adapted, transformed, optimized and otherwise manipulated by machine without the need for human intervention. If successful it could lead to lifting programming above its current state: a handcraft that requires enormous amounts of human work to write, to maintain and to adapt programs. This labour intensive practice was aptly described at the 1986 IFIP Congress as "high technology basket weaving" by Bill Wulf, a world leader in software development.

A worthwhile goal, and one to which our field seems especially able to contribute, is to raise program development to a highly automated, near-industrial process where human creativity and even human comprehension of individual programs is required only occasionally: when high level computational decisions are to be taken.

On the other hand it is often hard to see from published works on partial evaluation and mixed computation just what problem really has been solved, let alone how the solution can be extended or adapted to other languages, program transformations or application areas. In spite of rapid progress and impressive new results there is still a large gap between the state the art of our current research and its potential significance. For this reason I begin by detailing several criticisms of the state of our art, and only afterwards begin to discuss specific challenging problems.

Ameliorating remarks: our situation is not all unusual within programming language research or even within Computer Science as a whole; and the criticisms of the next section can be just as well applied to many if not most Computer Science fields. Reasons include the enormous concrete expectations, financial support and external demands from industry, engineering, business and education that have been placed on Computer Science ever since its birth. These demands are perhaps historically unique for so young a field; and they have in several ways made it harder to achieve academic maturity.

A last remark: these critical comments are in no way based on individual articles in the current proceedings, but rather sum up the opinions I had about the state of our field before the workshop was begun.

2. Challenging Metaproblems

2.1 Overview

We still lack an international intellectual community analogous to those known from atomic physics, mathematical logic, numerical analysis or complexity theory (just to name a few). Such communities have a well established set of fundamental concepts, agreement as to where major problem areas lie, and both an ability and a tradition to see beyond small methodological and terminological differences to find the essential contribution of a new piece of work.

It is of course unrealistic to expect such an intellectual community to develop at once in partial evaluation and mixed computation, but it is *very worth while* to anticipate it and as much as possible to help its development along.

Mature intellectual communities usually have a consensus on what the "state of the art" is in various well-defined subareas, very often expressed via a widely known collection of *important open problems* whose solution would advance that state. Such a collection is not easy to develop since its formulation and its general acceptance require a broad consensus. But once developed it can be an invaluable inspiration for further work and contribute significantly to the further maturing of the field.

A well known example is found in complexity theory, whose open questions include "is P = NP?" and "does context free language recognition require superlinear time?", and as well many other problems whose solution (positive or negative) would have widespread consequences. A more classical example: Hilbert's famous list of problems from the Mathematical Congress of 1900 has greatly stimulated several branches of mathematics including in particular recursive function theory and our understanding the fundamental limitations of formal mathematical systems.

A disclaimer: the problems in the following sections are not in any way claimed to be definitive and far reaching as are the known open problems from complexity and logic. Their purpose is to encourage researchers in our field to clarify and understand their goals, to state them precisely, and thereby to move towards the much broader and deeper understanding that will be necessary to prepare a truly definitive list some time in the future (maybe by the year 2000?).

2.2   Towards Greater Scientific Maturity

There are, alas, many signs that our field (and most current work in the whole programming languages area as well) is far from scientifically mature. One important problem: there is all too little *research* in the classical meaning of the term, meaning to search systematically through the existing literature for ideas and results relavent to one's current goals, even though perhaps expressed in a quite different language or framework. The inevitable result is that many works "reinvent the wheel" and omit highly relevant references to others' work.

A closely related problem: many papers emphasize small and often trivial differences between their works and others. Why is it necessary that every researcher invent his/her own special terminology, when there almost always already exists a well-known and well-tried out terminology for essentially the same concepts? Here we have *much to learn* from the better established scientific disciplines.

Another important problem: very few papers discuss at all the *limitations* of their results and methods, so the reader is left to puzzle over which part of that which was *not* said can be routinely filled in, and which part is completely beyond the reach of the methods presented.

All of these problems hinder formation of a scientific community. It would be far more helpful for the reader and the community for each new scientific contribution to emphasize the deep commonality that usually exists between it and its predecessors rather than superficial differences, to use a consistent notation and terminology (innovating only where essential), and to clarify both the powers and limitations of the new results.

One can speculate over reasons for these phenomena. One common explanation is the "information explosion" - but libraries are on the whole well stocked, and there exist several good periodical collections of reviews of scientific papers. A new source: the bibliography in the workshop proceedings.

Another reason is the "publish or perish" pressure, traditionally most seen in Anglo-saxon countries but now increasingly felt many other places as well. This can make it difficult for take the time necessary for a proper literature search; and it places a premium on factors that superficially differentiate a new paper from earlier works in the same field, even when the differences are conceptually insignificant.

In any case, reasons are not excuses - the lacks and problems discussed above *must* be dealt with if we are to develop a true intellectual community.

2.2.1   Context Dependence in Problem Statements and Their Solutions

Computer Science is to a significant extent an engineering discipline. We take great pride in our ability to build complex systems that work, and many papers in partial evaluation and mixed computation describe automatic program transformation systems the authors have constructed. For an individual to demonstrate his abilities and accomplishments, it is sufficient to describe the technical details of a particular program or system he has constructed. But for the good of the community as a whole, it is essential that a scientific article do more.

It is vital that the *principles* used in a new program or system be described in terms as free as possible from the situational context in which it was created, or in other words: abstractly. Details to be abstracted away when possible can include a particular programming language (complete with its special jargon, set of tricks and ways of looking at problems); a particular user community; or a particular set of possible application areas.

If new results are presented abstractly, there is a chance that others can adapt the ideas to novel applications, new languages, *etc.* If not, the only benefit others can gain is by copying and running the described programming system.

2.2.2 Precision in Problem Definition and Criteria for Solution Evaluation

What should we do next in the field of partial evaluation and mixed computation? There are at least two different categories of answer. The first and by far the easiest answer is to *expand horizons*: to solve new problems, to build new systems with greater efficiency, handling more powerful languages or able to handle new applications. Such improvements are clearly desirable in the long run, but there is a danger as pointed out in the previous section of getting more and larger programs, but of failing to gain new insights usable by others.

A blunt statement: we cannot claim to have solved an open problem if it was not precisely stated before we began, or if we have no clear criteria for what it means to have solved the problem.

A second answer to what we should do next: to understand in precise terms just what it is that our methods and our programs accomplish, to evaluate them, and to find out what their inbuilt limitations are. Such an understanding is essential for two very practical reasons:

- to be able to communicate our results so they can be re-used and adapted to solve related problems

- to achieve greater automation in program handling (ideally our program transformation tools should be anonymous parts of a program management system, as invisible to the user as gears or transistors - and this requires a precise knowledge of their characteristics)

The point is to *understand what it is that we are doing*, in advance and in objective, communicable and evaluable terms. Three essential components are precision in:

Definition: what exactly is the problem to be solved?

Abstraction: defining the problem's essence without irrelevant and perhaps misleading details

Judgement criteria: methods for ascertaining whether or not an alleged problem solution in fact is a correct solution

Following is a list of problems concerning possible applications, theory and understanding of the nature of partial evaluation or mixed computation. There are several different types of problems; some are concrete, some are more general, and others are dreams and directions for future work.

They do not satisfy all the criteria given above but can, we hope, serve as a basis for better understanding of what is worth doing, and for better lists to come.

3. How Much can be Achieved by our Techniques?

In the first Futamura projection

$$\text{target} = \text{L mix <interpreter, source>}$$

the target program is a residual of the interpreter, built as a mixture of pieces of the interpreter and pieces of the source program. Natural questions arise concerning just how the target, interpreter and source programs are or can be related:

Control
3.1   Can the residual program have essential loops or recursions that were not present in the source program?

3.2   Can the source program have loops not present in the target program?

Data
3.3   How can suspension of parts of composite, structured data be achieved? Can PE be adapted to cope with data which is partially dynamic and partially static?

3.4   Can the residual program have composite values that were not composite in the source? Can PE be used to generate new specialized data types, in a way analogous to generating specialized functions?

3.5   Can arbitrary residual programs be produced? This seems to conflict with the idea every residual function and data value is a specialized version of the interpreters' functions and data.

Relation to Traditional Program Architectures
Can mix-produced compilers and target programs achieve the efficiency of traditional architectures? These architectures are efficient, well-developed and well-tested; and they seem at some abstract level both *necessary* and *minimal*.

3.6   Can a traditional run-time architecture be derived automatically from the interpreter text? For example, can residual programs using techniques resembling Pascal's stack of activation records, be automatically generated from an interpreter?

3.7   Can traditional compiler techniques such as symbol tables, multiple passes, constant folding, *etc.* be derived automatically from mix and the interpreter by partial evaluation?

Strength and Nontriviality

3.8   A partial evaluator should be "strong enough" in the following sense. Partial evaluation of a self-interpreter for the subject language with respect to a program should be able to yield essentially the same program as output:

$$P \equiv L \, mix < \text{self-interpreter}, P >$$

This property is nontrivial since it ensures that PE can completely remove all book-keeping associated with one "layer of interpretation".

3.9   What does it mean for a partial evaluator to be *nontrivial?* For example, the traditional construction used in proof of recursive function theory's S-m-n theorem is clearly trivial? The property of the previous point seems to illustrate a form of nontriviality, but it could be achieved by cheating: write mix so it just returns its second argument in case the first argument is the particular self-interpreter referred to above.

4. Getting Nearer the Host Machine

4.1   PE techniques typically yield target programs written in the interpreter's language. Can PE yield efficient low level machine code?

4.2   Can this be done by writing a metacircular interpreter, whose text uses only a machine-like subset of its source language? (The rationale is that the target program is a residual form of the interpreter and so inherits many of its characteristics.)

5. Correctness, Termination and Efficiency

5.1   What is the source of the often large gains in efficiency yielded by even a very straightforward partial evaluation?

In the field of program transformation superlinear speedups are usually thought to require an understanding in principle of the subject algorithm. Examples include
- replacing depth-first search by breadth-first search,
- balancing subproblem size in divide and conquer algorithms and
- removing potential recomputation of values (memo-izing)

5.2 Can one automatically achieve more than linear speedups? (That is, can a residual program run faster than the subject program by more than a linear function of the size of the residual data?)

6. Automation

Our common goal is automatic program manipulation with no need for humans to read the programs produced by partial evaluation (*e.g.* who ever reads a YACC-produced parser?). Human guidance may be useful when developing a program from a problem specification, but is practically impossible when dealing with machine produced programs. Another extreme example: the second Futamura projection - compiler = L mix <mix, interpreter>, where the user would have to give advice on mix, a program he never wrote.

A program is a tool for achieving a purpose. As we know from daily life, to ols suitable for hand work (pliers, hammers, drills) are quite different from machine tools suitable for assembly line production (spot welders, lathes, robots). Analogously it is very likely that we will want to redesign our programming languages for mechanical usage (a homely example: LISP is far easier to manipulate by machine than Ada). This leads to:

6.1 *What types of languages are suitable for partial evaluation?*
What characterizes a language which is expressive and efficient for human usage and where PE is simple, natural and efficient? A minimal requirement: replacement of a function or procedure call by the function or procedure's definition should yield a legal program.

7. Self Application and Automatic Tools for Program Generation

Parser generators provide a classical transformation of a nonprocedural problem specification into an algorithmic solution.

Partial evaluation was first studied for program optimization, but its ability to yield algorithm generators by the second Futamura Projection may be even more significant, since it raises the possibility of automatically transforming wider classes of nonprocedural problem specifications into algorithmic solutions.

One application is indeed parser generation, exemplified by Ostrowski's article in the workshop proceedings. More generally, suppose there is a computable function *solve(problem_specification, parameters)* which outputs solutions when given acceptable problem specifications from a well-defined class, each with certain parameters. Then

$$\text{finder} \quad = \quad \text{L mix} <\text{solve\_program, problem\_specification}>$$

is a *solution finder* that given a parameter value yields a solution (example: finder is a specialized parser mapping input strings into parse trees). Further

$$\text{transformer} = \quad \text{L mix} <\text{mix, solve\_program}>$$

transforms problem specifications into solution finders (*e.g.* transforms a general parser into a parser generator).

7.1   How far can this approach be carried in practice? Some examples:

problem specification	*solution finder*	*transformer*
context free grammar	parser	parser generator
set of Horn clauses	Prolog system	Prolog compiler
interpreter	target program	compiler
first order logic formula	specialized theorem prover	prover generator
second order λ calculus	*all*	*not*
constructive type theory	*nearing*	*yet*
higher order logic	*executability*	*automated*

8. Program Composition and Decomposition

Partial evaluation decomposes a program P into an *executable part* and an *ejectable part*. The first can be executed during partial evaluation, while the second is the residual program. (For interpreters, the executable part consists of all compile time actions and the rejectable part is the target program.)

Each part has its own semantics and so there should be syntactic and semantic *program composition operators* ⊕, ⊕̲ such that

$$P \quad = \text{executable part} \oplus \text{ejectable part}$$
$$\text{semantics(P)} \quad = \quad \text{semantics(executable part)} \; \underline{\oplus} \; \text{semantics(ejectable part)}$$

Other program composition operators have been well studied, for example serial composition (homomorphisms, derivors, attribute coupled grammars) and parallel composition as well (the basis for divide and conquer algorithms). The problem is thus:

8.1   Study program composition and decomposition operators suitable for use in describing and implementing partial evaluation.

9. A Common Technical Problem: Generalization, or Value Division into Static and Dynamic

The following problem appears to be the root of the termination problems that have plagued nearly all work in partial evaluation. We describe it concretely and hope the reader can see the analogy in his own partial evaluation algorithm.

Most partial evaluators work by constructing a set of *configurations*, each of which represents a set of run time computational states (or parts of them) that are reachable in computations on run time input data satisfying the given input restrictions. For instance a configuration could contain the values of some but not all subject program variables. The known values we can call *static* and the others, *dynamic*.

There is a difficult balance to achieve, since configurations must be enumerated in enough detail to exploit what is known about the input, for thereby as much computation as possible can be done at PE time; but if too much detail is recorded there is a strong chance that the configuration set will be infinite and so lead to a PE-time "infinite loop".

Call one configuration a *generalization* of another if it represents a larger set of run time computational states. The problem is thus to develop a good generalization strategy, marking enough of each new configuration as dynamic to guarantee finiteness but keeping enough static to get an efficient residual program.

9.1   Devise good strategies for generalizing configurations.

There are two major alternatives: to generalize *on-line*, during program specialization, or to do it *off-line*, deciding in a preprocessing phase how and when configurations are going to be generalized during the actual partial evaluation. To this writer's knowledge, the only efficient self applicable partial evaluators have used off-line generalization.

10. More Powerful Languages

Functional languages
10.1   With higher order functions (one way to compile from denotational semantics).
10.2   With lazy evaluation.

Prolog
10.3   Efficient compilation of Prolog by PE (and not just production of efficient target programs).

Imperative languages
10.4   Handle assignment in the presence of
   •   recursive procedures
   •   references to variables not declared in the current block/procedure
   •   structured data, *eg* with pointers
10.5   Object-oriented languages.

10.6   *Machine, assembly or other low-level language (for example: C)*

Term rewriting systems
10.7   A self-applicable partial evaluator.
10.8   Aid the efficient implementation of equational specifications (*e.g* . to aid the Knuth-Bendix algorithm).

10.9   *Partial evaluation of nondeterministic and/or parallel languages*
Can the semantics be preserved? What does this mean?

11. Specific Problems with Broader Implications

11.1.   Extend existing languages, *e.g.* with automatic insertion of debugging code, profiling or other instrumentation.

Type checking
11.2   Achieve type security and yet do as few run time type tests as possible.

11.3   Determine from an interpreter whether the language it interprets is strongly typed; and exploit this information to generate highly efficient residual programs.

11.4   Derive from an interpreter an algorithm to do static type checking on the interpreted programs (as much as possible, and by automatic methods).

Program transformations and metacompiling

11.5   Apply partial evaluation to a self-interpreter in order to generate an automatic program transformer, for example:
- from recursive form to tail recursive form
- from lazy evaluation to eager evaluation
- by automatically introducing memo functions

11.6   Implement a truly user-extensible language with acceptable efficiency.

11.7   Semantics directed compiler generation by PE. For example, begin with a meta-interpreter "mint" such that

$$\text{L mint} < \begin{matrix}\text{language}\\\text{specification,}\end{matrix} \quad \text{program,} \quad \begin{matrix}\text{input}\\\text{data}\end{matrix} > = \begin{matrix}\text{output of}\\\text{program}\end{matrix}$$

and proceed as follows:

A.   interpreter = L mix $<$mint, $\begin{matrix}\text{language}\\\text{specification}\end{matrix}>$

B.   compiler = L cogen interpreter

12.   More Distant Horizons

12.1.   Use partial evaluation to make practical use of the "Second Recursion Theorem" from recursive function theory (Kleene, Ju. L. Ershov).

12.2.   Develop a system which will observe program runs and adaptively specialize a program when it is seen to be spending much time on a restricted class of input data. Applications:
- automatically compiling a frequently run program;
- automatically generating a compiler from a frequently run interpreter;
- implementing closures in a high-level language by partial evaluation

12.4.   Automatically construct a program to estimate a subject program's running time.

12.5.   Apply the latter to a "divide and conquer" algorithm to equalize the sizes of subproblems for distribution over a network of parallel processors.

12.6   *Study relationships between learning and partial evaluation.*

In many situations a subject learning a new task begina by using a general problem-solving method for solving the problem, at first inefficiently and with many trials and errors. After some repetitions, the task is mastered and can be performed quickly without error. The analogy with partial evaluation is clear: some "learning"behaviour amounts to specializing a general-purpose trial and error algorithm to a restricted domain of applications.

Another example: suppose one is given a maze, a start point and a goal point. If the maze and start point are fixed, then a specialized version of any familiar maze-searching algorithm is simply an efficient set of directions giving a direct route to every goal point. Is it reasonable to say that this particular maze has been "learned" by partial evaluation? And if not, then how can this type of learning be differentiated from a more "creative", "intelligent" or "insightful" form?

Worse yet: any algorithm whatever may be obtained by partially evaluating, say, a universal Turing Machine with respect to its first input. Does this mean that any procedure at all is learnable, provided the subject is as intelligent as a universal Turing machine and is given the proper input data?

Partial Evaluation and Mixed Computation
D. Bjørner, A.P. Ershov and N.D. Jones (Editors)
Elsevier Science Publishers B.V. (North-Holland)
© IFIP, 1988

MIXED COMPUTATION AND COMPILER BASIS

Guntis J. BARZDIN

Computing Centre
Latvian State University
Riga, USSR

The purpose of the paper is to describe in detail a method
of obtaining a good compiler from an interpreter. The method is the result of developing such methods of the mixed
computation (partial evaluation). It is proposed to transform interpreter into compiler in two phases. In the first
phase an intermediate product called compiler basis is
obtained from the interpreter by mixed computation methods.
In the second phase the required compiler is obtained from
the compiler basis by the original method of global analysis. The structure of the compilers obtained by the new
method approximates that of hand written compilers better
than compilers obtained by mixed computation methods only.

1. AN EXAMPLE AND INITIAL CONCEPTS

The method described will be illustrated by obtaining a compiler
from the Post machine (with a finite tape) interpreter. The Post
machine language commands are WRITE, MOVE, GOTO, IFGO and Stop
with integer parameters. An example of Post machine program is:

```
1. IFGO    4; -- if current cell on the tape contains 1
                 then branch to the command 4.
2. MOVE   -1; -- move head one cell to the left.
3. GOTO    1; -- jump to the command 1.
4. WRITE   0; -- write 0 into the current cell.
5. STOP    0; -- stop (parameter fictitious).
```

Fig.1 and Fig.2 show the interpreter and compiler of the Post
machine language which are written in a graphic Pascal-like language for more visual explanation. There are detailed mainly the
code generation phase of the compiler and the execution phase of
the interpreter, because of these phases are changed most of all,
when an interpreter is converted into a compiler. The input for
the interpreter and compiler is the Post machine program represented by an array of records P containing fields C (command) and
I (parameter). The built-in function Length(P) returns the number
of elements in array P. Record D contains the input data for the
Post machine program where array L represents the tape and field
H contains the number of the head's current position on the tape.
The statements of the compiler program, which generate the object
program statements, are denoted by circles (we will call them
"circled-statements"). Such a circled-statement adds its content
to the generated object program and marks free branches with labels
for the purpose of assembling the generated statements to make a
whole program. When a circled-statement is executed, the underlined expressions are evaluated and substituted by their values.
Other parts of the circled statement are simply copied in the

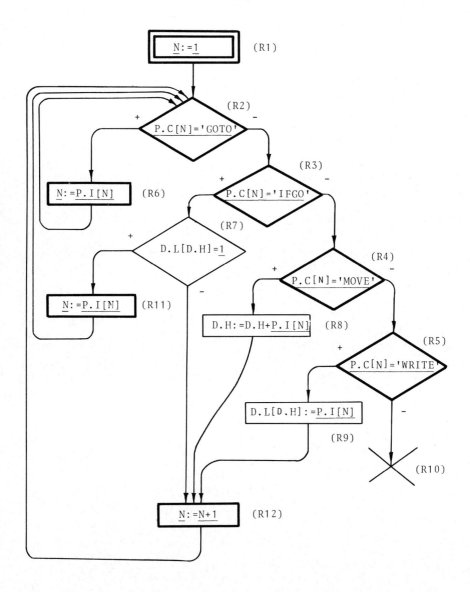

Fig.1. The Post machine interpreter INT(P,D)

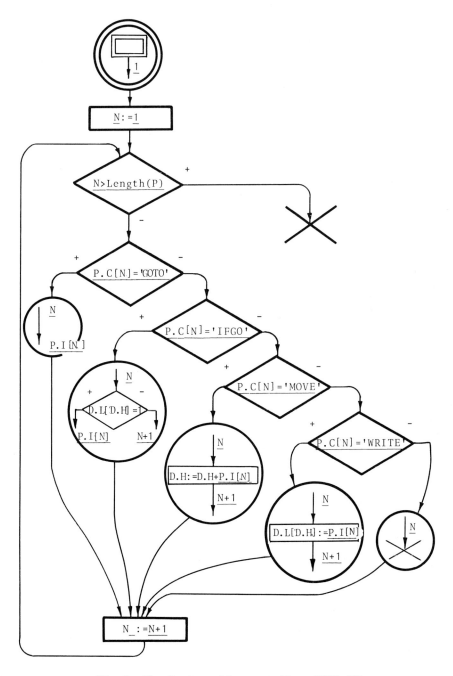

Fig.2. The Post machine compiler COMP (P)

generated object program. The underlined expressions contain compiler variables and constants only.
An example of an object program generated by compiler (Fig.2)
from the above Post machine program is shown in Fig.3. The object
program is obtained in the same Pascal-like graphic language;
translation into low level language is not considered there.

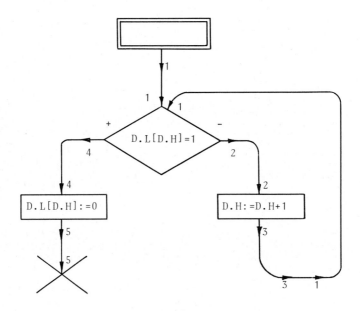

Fig.3. Example of generated object
program OBJ(D) with labels

The main purpose of this paper is to demonstrate a general method
to convert an interpreter to a compiler with as simple structure
as possible. For the interpreter in Fig.1 such a method must produce a compiler similar to that in Fig.2, which can be considered
to be a hand-written "classic" compiler. It should be noted that
the structure of compilers generated from interpreters by mixed
computation (partial evaluation) methods only [2,5,7] do not coincide fully with the structure of "classic" compilers (for more
details see Sect.4).

Definition 1.
A circled-statement in a compiler program is called an annotated
one if it generates a label at entry in the form (A,B), where A is
the number of the current circled-statement and B is the vector of
the current values of all compiler variables; labels generated at
exits (there can be several of them if a branching statement is
generated) must be in the form (A',B'), where A' is the number of
the circled-statement generating the continuation of the branch
and B' is the vector of the values of all compiler variables,

when A' will be executed.

Let us introduce the concept of annotated compiler - it is a compiler in which all circled-statements are annotated.

Actually not a "classic" compiler itself, but a corresponding annotated compiler will be obtained from an interpreter program by methods described below. Let us explain the conversion of an ordinary compiler into an annotated one and backwards by an example of a Post machine compiler. Transformation of an annotated compiler into an ordinary one can be considered to be optimization and will not be gone into in the paper. An annotated compiler corresponding to "classic" compiler in Fig.2 is shown in Fig.5 (for labels see Fig.4). To convert an ordinary compiler into an annotated one, it is necessary to supplement the label-generating parts in the circled-statements by attributes required by the definition (the number of the circled statement and the vector of all compiler variables) and, if it is necessary, by some circled-statements with empty function for matching the new labels (in the annotated compiler in Fig.5 such are R2, R3, R4, R5, R11, R12).

Note
Labels generated by the annotated compiler can be very long, because they contain the vector of values of all compiler variables. It is possible to make them shorter in the annotated compiler. One way to do it, is to delete from the labels the values of the variables, which are not changed during the run of the compiler (for example, the variable containing a source program). Another way is to replace "long" labels by"shorter" ones by means of one-to-one mapping. For the sake of clarity "long" labels will be used in the present paper.

Definition 2.
A program is called syntactically complete if it contains exactly one initial statement and there are no non-completed branches accessible from the initial statement (in the sense of a program graph).

Let us introduce a concept of the complete compiler - it is a compiler which generates only syntactically complete object programs and by the initial statement of such a compiler the initial statement of object program is generated.

This definition allows presence in the object program of statements which are not accessible from the initial statement (they never be performed). The requirement for the first statement of the compiler to generate an initial statement of the object program will be necessary in proving the theorem in next Section. Let us define the equality of compilers as the equality of the object programs they generate on the same input. Equality of object programs will be understood as their functional equality.

2.   COMPILER BASIS CONCEPT

Definition 3.
Let any set of circled-statements be called the basis.

Definition 4.
Let a set of all circled-statements contained in a given compiler be called the compiler basis.

Definition 5.
A basis is called complete if it is basis of some complete and
annotated compiler.
For example, the compiler basis in Fig.4 corresponds to the compiler in Fig.5. It is complete basis because compiler in Fig.5 is
complete and annotated.
A compiler basis does not fully describe the compiler which it
corresponds to. Moreover, there may be an identical basis for different compilers. But a complete basis (i.e. basis of some complete and annotated compiler) has special properties defined by the
following theorem.

Theorem 1.
If the bases of several complete and annotated compilers are identical, then these compilers are equal.

This theorem will not be proved in the present paper, but its correctness follows from the property of the syntactically complete
compiler to generate an initial object program's statement by the
initial statement of the compiler (compile basis contains this
statement) and from the property of the annotated compiler to
label all branches in the generated object program by the "full"
information about the compiler's state when this branch will be
continued (values of compiler variables and the number of circled-
statement are enclosed in the label). Because of the labeling by
"full" information, only identical continuations of branches
accessible from the initial statement can be generated.

Implementation of theorem 1.
Complete basis is the form of full specification of the language.

The importance of theorem 1 and its implementation lies in the
possibility to generate a compiler from a complete basis. So, if
we have to obtain a compiler from an interpreter, we can generate
a complete basis from an interpreter first and then construct the
compiler from the complete basis. Such a method will be described
in Sect.3 and 4 and will be illustrated by the Post machine
example.

3.   OBTAINING A COMPLETE BASIS FROM AN INTERPRETER

The technique of mixed computation (partial evaluation) [1,3,4]
in the form close to compiler-compiler [7] will be used to perform
such a transformation. Let us divide all interpreter variables
into two groups. One group will be called 'compiler variables' and
it must satisfy the following conditions:
1) a 'compiler variable' is that parameter of the interpreter,
which represents the source program and is not the parameter which
represents the data for the source program,
2) there are no such assignment statements in the interpreter
program which assign a value to the 'compiler variable' but operate
on 'non-compiler variables'.

Such a division is not possible for any interpreter program, but it
is possible for many of them. In the case of the Post machine interpreter in Fig.1 such a division is possible and produces a group
of 'compiler variables' containing P (source program) and N (number
of current executed statement). The expressions over 'compiler
variables' and the constants are underlined in Fig.1.
Let the interpreter statements which operates on 'compiler variables'

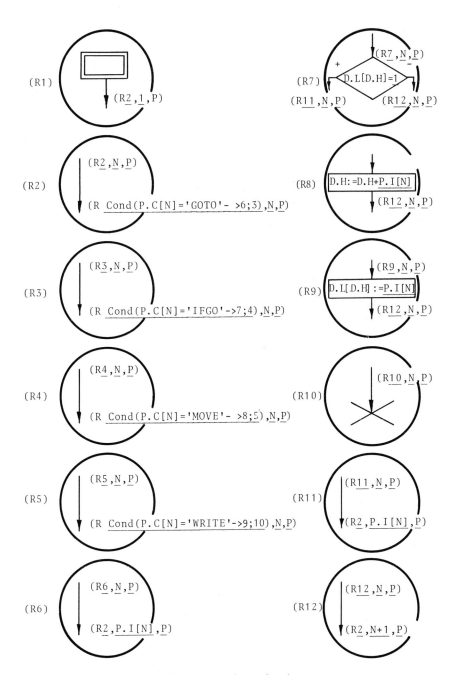

Fig.4. Compiler basis

only be called 'compile time' statements; all other interpreter
statements will be called 'run time' statements. In the case of
the Post machine interpreter 'compile time' statements are R1, R2,
R3, R4, R5, R11, R12 (in Fig.1 they are bold framed).
Let S be the basis to be obtained from the interpreter program.
All interpreter statements will be associated with exactly one
statement in basis S; so enumeration of statements in basis S will
remain the same as in the interpreter. The compiler variables used
in basis S will be those of the 'compiler variables' group from
the interpreter program; so the underlined expressions in the interpreter program must remain underlined in basis S.

Obtaining of basis S:
1) for any 'run time' statement in the interpreter program a circled-statement in basis S containing this 'run time' statement is
associated. The label created at its input branch contains the
number of this statement and a vector with all 'compiler variables';
labels created at output branches contain the number of the next
interpreter statement on a given branch and a vector with all
'compiler variables'.
2) for any 'compile time' statement in the interpreter program a
circled-statement with empty function (GOTO statement) is associated. The label created at the input branch is like that in the 'run
time' statements; the label created at the output branch have a
special form. Because the 'compile time' statements operate on the
compiler variables only (if this is assignment statement) or perform branching which depends on compiler variables only (if this
is conditional branching statement), it is possible to execute
them during compiling. So, in this case the label created at the
output branch contains the calculated number of the following
interpreter statement and the calculated values of the compiler
variables.

Fig.4 shows basis S obtained from the Post machine interpreter in
Fig.1. (Function Cond(A->X;Y) equals X if A and Y if not A).

The properties of the basis S obtained by the above method are
characterized by the next theorem.

Theorem 2.
Basis S generated from an interpreter program by the above method
is complete and specifies the semantics of the same language as
that the initial interpreter specifies.

This theorem will not be proved in the present paper, but the idea
underlying the proof is supplied. Generated basis S is the basis
of the compiler generated by the polyvariant compiler-compiler
described in [7] (similar compiler-compilers are described in [2,
5] too, for more detail see Sect.4). The polyvariant compiler-compiler is obtained from a polyvariant mixed computation (partial
evaluation) algorithm, whose correctness is proved in [4]. Compilers
generated by a polyvariant compiler-compiler are complete and annotated, therefore basis S is complete.

4.   OBTAINING A COMPILER FROM A COMPLETE BASIS

It was shown in Sect.2 that a complete basis specifies the semantics
of a language. But a complete basis does not specify the structure
of a compiler with such a basis (such a compiler can compile a
source program from the beginning or from the end or in any other

way). In this Section three methods how to build a compiler from compiler basis will be described. It will be shown that only a most sophisticated third method can produce compilers with a structure and effectivity similar to hand written ones.

The first method (it is universal, but the compilers obtained are not efficient) for constructing a compiler from a given complete basis follows from the above-mentioned polyvariant compiler-compiler algorithm [2,5,7]. Such a compiler contains in some form a special interpreter, which interprets basis statements beginning from the initial in such a sequence and so long, while a syntactically complete object program is obtained. Such an interpretation requires checking of all the branches in the generated object program to find at any moment the branch which has no continuation yet (this is why the 'polyvarian-' method is not efficient - such checking is very expensive). When a non-continued branch in the object program is found, then from the label of this branch ("long' labels are expected) the current values of the compiler variables are set like they are in the vector of compiler variables values in the label and the basis statement, whose number is taken from the label, is executed. By repeating such steps an object program is constructed by the polyvariant compiler.

The idea of the next two methods is to move the branches continuation checking in the object program from the compiler to the compiler generator by using global analysis methods. Such global analysis requires expressing the domains of all the compiler variables as functions depending on constants and the compiler parameter only. If this is possible, these two methods are usable (in the case with the Post machine basis (Fig.4) it is possible. Let us have a look how both compiler variables P and N are used in the basis statements: compiler variable P is a parameter and is not changed by any statement from the basis, but variable N is used only as an index in array P that causes the domain of variable N [1..Length(P)]). Ways of finding such functions will not be described in this paper, but more sophisticated techniques can be used when more complicated interpreters are transformed, which take into account such things as a correct source program syntaxis, the context conditions, etc. It should be noted that such analysis of variables domains is often done by the programmer who writes the compiler by hand, so it is natural to require such analysis in order to obtain a compiler with a structure similar to that of a hand-written one.

The second method is the following. If domains are expressed then a complete compiler can be obtained by making a loop which executes all the basis statements over all the values of the compiler variables from their domains. This method provides complete compilers, because all basis statements are executed on all the possible compiler variables values, but such a compiler is not efficient because many never-to-be-performed object program statements are generated in this way.

The third method is an optimized variant of the second method described. The idea is to avoid appearance in the object program of many never-to-be-performed object program statements (which are not connected with the initial statement). Let us describe this method in more detail for only one changing compiler variable the way it is in Post machine compiler basis where only N changes. See Fig.5 for an example. (To extend the method to many changing compiler variables, it is necessary to avoid in some way the 'combinatorial

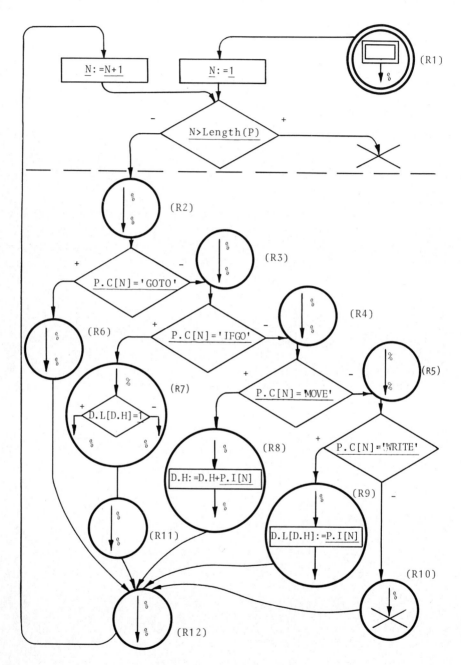

Fig.5. Annotated Post machine compiler
(labels % see Fig.4)

explosion' of variants of compiler variable values. It can be done by more detailed analysis of reasonable combinations of compiler variable values).

Method:
1) the initial statement in the compiler is the one in the compiler basis which is generating the initial statement in the object program.
2) the generated compiler consists of two parts (separated by the dashed line in Fig.5): the loop heading and the loop body. The loop heading is like that of the second method and executes the loop body for all the compile-time values from their domains. The loop body contains all the basis statements (except the initial one) which are chained by the conditional and unconditional branches.
3) compiler basis statements inside the loop body are connected according to the labels they generate in object program. There are two types of exit labels in the compiler basis: in which the vector of the compiler variable values is the same as in the entry label (R2, R3, R4, R5, both in R7, R8, R9), and in which these vectors are different (R6, R11, R12). According to this division, basis statements are chained inside the loop body. If the basis statement number RX appears in the exit label of some statement of the second type or in exit label of initial statement, then RX must be executed always. If the basis statement number RX appears only in the exit labels of the basis statements RA, RB, RC... of the first type, then RX must be executed only if RA or RB or RC or... are executed. If the next statement number is chosen according to some condition (R2, R3, R4, R5) then the conditional branching is used inside the loop body. If some basis statements have more than one exit label (R7), all corresponding continuations are added (R11 and R12). The connection of basis statements inside the loop body, satisfying these conditions, guarantees the completeness of the compiler obtained.

Fig.5 shows a compiler, which can be obtained by the described method from the basis shown in Fig.4. A "classic" compiler as in Fig.2 can be obtained from the compiler of Fig.5 by optimization (labels and circled-statements can be reduced), because the structure of both compilers is identical.

5. CONCLUSION

The compiler generation method described in this paper considers mainly the code generation part of the compiler which is most important when a compiler is obtained from an interpreter. The underlying ideas involved can be summarized as follows:

1) the complete basis (basis of a complete and annotated compiler) fully specifies the language semantics in a denotational way and this specification is always executable by a polyvariant method (the first one in Sect.4).

2) by means of the sophisticated methods (the third one in Sect.4) and optimization it is possible to obtain a "classic" compiler from the basis.

3) a complete basis can be described naturally by an interpreter program in which the 'compiler variables' are underlined and 'compile time' statements are bold framed (Sect.3).

The complete basis conception is applicable in other transformations as well. For example, it can be used to derive a "classic" interpreter from a "classic" compiler. For such a transformation a "classic" compiler must be converted into an annotated one, a basis must be chosen, and an interpreter from such a basis can be easily obtained.

REFERENCES

[1] Y.Futamura. Partial Evaluation of Computation Process - An approach to a Compiler-Compiler. Systems, Computers, Controls, 2(5):45-50, 1971.
[2] M.A.Bulyonkov and A.P.Ershov. How Do Ad-Hoc Compiler Constructs Appear in Universal Mixed Computation Processes? In Applied Logic, Computation Systems, Vol.116, Institute of Mathematics, Novosibirsk, USSR, 1986. (in Russian).
[3] A.P.Ershov. On the Essence of Compilation. Programmirovanie, (5):21-39, 1977. (in Russian).
[4] M.A.Bulyonkov. Polyvariant Mixed Computation for Analyzer Programs. Acta Informatica, 21:473-484, 1984.
[5] N.D.Jones, P.Sestoft and H.Sondergaard. An Experiment in Partial Evaluation: The Generation of a Compiler Generator. In J.P.Jounnaud, editor, Rewriting Techniques and Applications, pages 124-140, Lecture Notes in Computer Science, Vol.202, Springer-Verlag, 1985.
[6] N.D.Jones. Towards Automating the Transformation of Programming Language Specifications into Implementations. 1987. Part I:55 pages.
[7] G.J.Barzdin. Experiments with Mixed Computation. Programmirovanie, (1):30-43, 1987. (in Russian).

Partial Evaluation and Mixed Computation
D. Bjørner, A.P. Ershov and N.D. Jones (Editors)
Elsevier Science Publishers B.V. (North-Holland)
© IFIP, 1988

Towards a Self-applicable Partial Evaluator
for Term Rewriting Systems

Anders BONDORF

DIKU, University of Copenhagen,
Universitetsparken 1, DK-2100 København Ø, DENMARK.
uucp: ...!mcvax!diku!anders

This paper describes a practical experiment in partial evaluation of programs written in the language *Terse*. Partial evaluation is done in two phases, a *binding time analysis* phase and a *function specialization* phase. *Call unfolding* is completely automated; a simple method based on local information is used. The partial evaluator *T-mix* handles *partially static* data; the user does not have to "split" variables into static (known) and dynamic (unknown) parts. Handling partially static data is essential when *higher order functions* are expressed by closures. A LISP implementation of T-mix has given promising results, although there still has to be done a good deal of work in order to achieve self-applicability.

The functional language Terse is a restricted form of a general T̲e̲r̲m̲ r̲ewriting s̲y̲s̲t̲e̲m̲ formalism. It is a very "neutral" language, not aiming at particular applications. Higher order functions are indirectly expressible in it by the use of explicit closures. Terse has a very simple control structure based on *pattern matching*. For this reason, call unfolding is simple to handle in T-mix.

A prototype implementation of Terse (not described in this paper) has shown that the pattern matching can be implemented in a way that gives very good run time properties (matching without backtracking). The compile times are small.

Keywords: Binding time analysis, call unfolding, compiler generation, functional languages, higher order functions, partial evaluation, partially static structures, pattern matching, program specialization, self-application, term rewriting systems.

1. Introduction

The potential use of self-application of a partial evaluator as a method for doing compilation, compiler generation and compiler generator generation has been known since the early seventies. The first partial evaluator having actually been successfully self-applied was *mix*, developed at DIKU, University of Copenhagen, by Neil Jones, Peter Sestoft and Harald Søndergaard during 1984 ([Mix85], [Sestoft85]). Though mix uses a rather primitive base language (a first order subset of statically scoped LISP), it was shown that efficient stand-alone compilers as well as a compiler generator were really obtainable by the use of partial evaluation. The quality of the compilers as well as of the target programs produced by them was good.

It is, however, clear that although mix has given good results, there are several weak points. A stronger and more automated system is clearly desirable. A partial evaluator can be classified in relation to a set of "degrees of freedom" (the set is probably not complete):

1) Does it use automatic call unfolding? (yes/no)
2) Does it handle partially static data? (yes/no)
3) Does the base language allow varying signatures? (yes/no)

A *signature* describes the functionalities of the operators in a program. When varying signatures are allowed, each program has its own set of operators.

The original mix is of type (no, no, no). In [Mix87], a (yes, no, no) system is presented; in [Mogensen87], a (no, yes, no) system is presented. These three systems are all based on first order dialects of LISP.

In this project, a partial evaluator *T-mix* of type (yes, yes, yes) has been developed (but not completely implemented). It is based on the language *Terse*, a restricted form of a general *term rewriting system* formalism (with much inspiration from *REFAL*, see [Turchin86]). Terse is centered around *pattern matching* as the basic control structure. *Tests* are performed implicitly by *function calls* in Terse. This reduces the *call unfolding* problem (degree of freedom 1) to a matter of testing values of arguments in function calls (purely local information). Handling *partially static data* (degree of freedom 2) is integrated completely in T-mix. Higher order functions are indirectly expressible in Terse by the use of *explicit closures*; an abstraction is transformed into a closure ([Reynolds72]). Each abstraction has its own closure forming *operator* with its own functionality (Terse allows varying signatures, degree of freedom 3).

Outline of this paper: we begin (section 2) by describing mix briefly and by pointing out its weak points. In section 3, the language Terse is described. The partial evaluator T-mix is then described in section 4. Some parts of T-mix have been implemented, and the preliminary results achieved by running the implemented parts are given and discussed in section 5. Finally, section 6 contains a conclusion. The paper is based on a Master's thesis ([Bondorf87]); the implementation of Terse is described there and a more comprehensive treatment of partial evaluation, in particular T-mix, is given.

Notation and formalisms: programs and program pieces are written in a special typeface, "helvetica". It looks like this. Descriptions of syntax are given in BNF. Terminal symbols are written in helvetica, non-terminal symbols are written in the same typeface as the text (like this). We do not use brackets ("<" ... ">") around non-terminals.

This project aims at a *fully automated* self-applicable partial evaluator. It should be emphasized that this reports an <u>experiment</u> in partial evaluation of restricted term rewriting systems; the purpose has not been to produce a "production version", but rather to gain understanding and insight. Some arbitrary decisions have had to be made and some could in hindsight have been made better.

2. The first mix system

In the first mix system ([Mix85], [Sestoft85]), a statically scoped first order subset of LISP is used as the base language. The central idea in mix is to perform as many operations (car, cdr, cons etc., and function calls) as possible at partial evaluation time. To give a small example, regard a program for appending two lists (this example was used already in [Futamura71]). The "goal" (main) function is named f; a syntax with prefix operators is used:

```
f(x, y)        = append(x, y)

append(x, y)  = if null(x) then y
                else cons(car(x), append(cdr(x), y))
```

This program is now going to be partially evaluated. If it is specified that x has a fixed, or *static* (this has been referred to as *known* in earlier articles), value (e.g. the list (1 2)), and that y is non-fixed, or *dynamic* (in earlier articles: *unknown*), the program may be simplified considerably by partial evaluation. The car, cdr and if operations may all be performed, and the calls to append may be *unfolded* (replaced by the function body). The specialized program thus becomes (the new goal function is named f*):

```
f*(y) = cons(1, cons(2, y))
```

f* takes only one input, y.

Now suppose that x is dynamic and y static. The car, cdr and if operations now cannot be performed, and the recursive append call should <u>not</u> be unfolded since this would give an infinite unfolding sequence:

```
f(x, y) = if null(x) then y
          else cons(car(x), if null(cdr(x)) then y
                  else cons(car(cdr(x)), if null(cdr(cdr(x))) then ...))
```

It has already been mentioned that there are some problems with mix:

1) The <u>user</u> has to decide — by hand — whether a call should be unfolded or not. All calls are "annotated" as being either *always* unfoldable or *never* unfoldable <u>in advance</u>, i.e. before the actual partial evaluation.
2) mix only operates on values which are either *completely* static or *completely* dynamic. In order to get good results, the user has to program in such a way that static and dynamic data are separated in different variables. For instance, an *environment* in an interpreter typically is a list of name/value-pairs, the names being static, the values dynamic. Such lists have to be split into two lists, a name list and a value list. Otherwise, the names will appear in the specialized (i.e. target) programs.
3) The language is only first order and thus excludes higher order functions.

A new mix, in which the first problem has been solved, is presented in [Mix87] (see also [Sestoft87]). It uses a rather complicated so-called *call graph analysis* in order to decide automatically upon unfoldability of function calls. The second problem has been solved in another mix system described in [Mogensen87]. These new partial evaluators still suffer from the second and the first problem respectively, but there is in principle (according to Torben Mogensen) no hindrance to combine the two new mix'es. This will, on the other hand, require some rather complicated methods involving various heuristics.

3. The language Terse

Term rewriting systems have been studied for several years, especially as a tool for automatic reasoning about equational axiomatic systems (see e.g. [HuetOppen80], [Dershowitz85]). This is, however, of little concern to us (relevant here: [Jones86]).

The main reason for choosing restricted term rewriting systems as the base language for a new mix is due to their very simple semantics. The control structure is "flat" (there are no nested control structures like if-then-else) and is based on *pattern matching*. Term rewriting systems have in principle no built-in functions (like car, cdr, if etc. of LISP). Some functions may be implemented for practical reasons, e.g. functions for doing arithmetic, but in principle such functions can always be user defined.

This section gives a rather detailed description of the language Terse. The main points to notice when comparing Terse with general term rewriting systems are that Terse is first order (operations on higher order functions can be expressed as operations on closures) and uses call-by-value, that the rules are unordered and non-overlapping, that we do not allow repeated variable occurrences in left-hand sides (linearity), and finally that operators are divided into constructors and defined operators (function symbols). Every operator has a fixed functionality given by a signature; the signature may be implicit or explicit.

3.1 Basic data structures in Terse

The fundamental data structure used in Terse is the *term*. Terms play the same role in Terse as S-expressions do in LISP. A term is defined recursively by a tree grammar:

$$\text{term} ::= \text{operator(term, ..., term)} \mid \text{variable}$$

Notes: 1) "term, ..., term" means "a list of zero or more terms";
2) the tree grammar generates <u>tree structures</u>, not strings as in a context free grammar.

We only consider *finite* terms (in [Baren. et al. 87], a *tree* is defined to be the generalization of terms that includes infiniteness). Recursive data structures (see e.g. [Hoare75]) are not expressible in the term formalism.

The set of operators is defined by a (user definable) *signature* Σ. Σ describes the arities and sorts of all operators. Each operator thus has a *fixed* arity and sort. A 0-ary operator — one without arguments — is called a *constant*. We use $T_\Sigma(V)$ to denote the set of terms generated by a signature Σ and a set of variables V. A variable is syntactically identified as a symbol beginning with a capital letter (an idea taken from Prolog); other symbols are operators.

An example of a term is the following:

$$\text{a(2(), 37(), b26(This-is-a-variable))}$$

Terms of the form "operator()" will be abbreviated to simply "operator". So the term above will actually be written a(2, 37, b26(This-is-a-variable))

The leftmost operator is called the *root* of the term. In the term above, the root is the operator a, and b26 is the root of the *subterm* b26(This-is-a-variable). We say that b26(This-is-a-variable) is *rooted by* b26.

Since we require that all operators have a fixed number of arguments given by the signature, a term like a(a(f), b) is illegal; the operator a cannot have one and two arguments at the same time. This gives a primitive, but very useful type concept.

Notice that Terse operators are more expressible than the unnamed binary cons of LISP. Terse operators are named and may have any arity.

3.2 Definitions and program evaluation

We now give some definitions. A Terse *program* is an unordered collection of *rewrite rules*. A rewrite rule consists of two terms: a *left-hand side* (abbreviation: lhs) and a *right-hand side* (abbreviation: rhs). A variable must occur <u>at most once</u> in a left-hand side. A term without variables is called a *variable free* term. A *redex* is a variable free term that *matches* the left-hand side of a program rule. For simplicity, we also say that the redex matches the rule (as a whole). A term without redexes is said to be on *normalized form*.

Matching is a simple form of unification (cf. Prolog) in which only the program rule contains variables. Matching is thus "one way". When a redex is matched successfully against a rule (we say that the match has been *resolved*), a *substitution* containing bindings for the variables is built (this corresponds to the "most general unifier" in Prolog).

Program evaluation now goes like this (informally described): the program is applied to a variable free term called an *input term*. The input term is searched for redexes. When a redex and a successful match has been found, a substitution for the variables of the matched rule is found. The redex is then replaced by a revised version of the right-hand side of the rule in which the substitution has been applied to all variables.

This is the process of *rewriting*; we say that a *rewrite step* has occurred and that the rule has been *applied* to the redex. The process is then repeated for the rewritten input term etc.. Evaluation stops when the term contains no more redexes. The term, which is the result (output) of the run, is then by definition on normalized form.

3.3 Restrictions

In general term rewriting systems there is no difference between operators for constructing terms and operators that are roots in redexes. In Terse, operators are divided into two types: *constructors* and *defined operators*. Constructors are used for building data structures, defined operators are used for defining functions.

Left-hand sides are restricted to be of a form defined by the following grammar:

        lhs   ::= defined-operator(pattern, ..., pattern)
        pattern ::= constructor(pattern, ..., pattern) | variable

The outermost operator must be a defined operator, but inside *patterns* only constructors are allowed. A set of rules having the same defined operator as the root of the left-hand side define a *function*.

Right-hand sides are not restricted:

        rhs ::= constructor(rhs, ..., rhs) | defined-operator(rhs, ..., rhs) | variable

Since left-hand sides are now restricted, redexes will always be right-hand side subterms rooted by defined operators. It is thus possible to identify potential redexes *syntactically*; this is not possible in general term rewriting systems. Due to the similarity between potential redexes and *calls* in LISP-like languages, we will also refer to the former as such.

If a call does not match any rule, we choose to stop evaluation by an *abnormal* stop. A *matching error* occurs (this is a run time error). So if it turns out that a potential redex (a call) is not a redex, an error occurs. This is a design choice which has proved to be a very practical one: program errors usually appear as matching errors.

When evaluation terminates normally (i.e. not because of a matching error), the normalized term contains no more defined operators. Since a normalized term is also variable free, the term only contains constructors. We call such a term a *ground term*:

ground-term ::= constructor(ground-term, ..., ground-term)

As mentioned, a matching error occurs if no rules are applicable to a redex. In order to make Terse deterministic, we also require that *at most one rule* is applicable. The rules must thus be *non-overlapping*. It is possible at *compile time* to determine whether rules are overlapping. If this is the case, the program will be rejected as being erroneous. For coverage of this subject, see [Bondorf87].

3.4 Program example
Consider a program for appending two lists. A list is here defined by the grammar

$$\text{List} ::= \text{nil} \mid \text{Element} : \text{List}$$

(an element may be any term). Infix syntax has been used for the constructor : in order to improve readability. The program is as follows:

Signature:

Syntactic domain:	List ::=	nil | Element : List

Constructors:	::	Element × List → List
	nil:	→ List

Defined operators:	append:	List × List → List

Rewrite rules:

rule 0:	append(nil, Ys)	—> Ys
rule 1:	append(X : Xs, Ys)	—> X : append(Xs, Ys)

3.5 Predefined operators
As mentioned earlier, there are in principle no predefined functions in Terse. It is, however, in practice very inconvenient not to have some available basic functions, at least a function for determining equality. Such a function <u>could</u> be defined by the user by "simply" adding some rules for each operator in use. If, for instance, the signature specifies that only two operators, a 0-ary a and a unary b, are used, then the function equal is definable by the rules

```
equal(a, a)          —> true
equal(b(X), b(Y))  —> equal(X, Y)
equal(a, b(X))      —> false
equal(b(X), a)      —> false
```

Needless to say, this is not a very practical method.

Therefore some *predefined operators* are introduced. The equal function and functions for doing arithmetic are the most important.

3.6 Evaluation strategies
Like in any other language, different *evaluation strategies* may be used when evaluating a Terse program. Two well-known strategies are pure *call-by-value* (or *inside-out*) and pure *call-by-name* (or *outside-in*, also referred to as *normal order* evaluation). Other strategies like *call-by-need* also exist. In Terse, we use <u>call-by-value</u> (left most innermost evaluation). It is the simplest strategy to deal with for two reasons:

1) redexes never contain *nested* calls; this simplifies the process of partial evaluation;
2) Terse can relatively easy be implemented by compilation into LISP.

3.7 Syntax of Terse
The complete (abstract) syntax of Terse is as follows:

$$\begin{array}{lll} \text{program} & ::= & \text{rule}^+ \\ \text{rule} & ::= & \text{lhs} \longrightarrow \text{rhs} \end{array}$$

$$\begin{array}{lll} \text{lhs} & ::= & \text{defined-operator(pattern, ..., pattern)} \\ \text{pattern} & ::= & \text{constructor(pattern, ..., pattern)} \mid \text{variable} \end{array}$$

$$\begin{array}{lll} \text{rhs} & ::= & \text{constructor(rhs, ..., rhs)} \mid \text{defined-operator(rhs, ..., rhs)} \mid \text{variable} \end{array}$$

defined-operator: symbol beginning with a character different from a capital letter; a defined operator is a predefined operator or an operator that is the root of at least one left-hand side of the program;

constructor: same syntax as defined operators;

variable: symbol starting with a capital letter;

The *goal function* is the function having the first rule of the program among its defining rules (this means that although the rules in a program are unordered, the first rule plays a special role). The input term is a call to the goal function with ground terms as arguments.

In the current implementation of Terse, no explicit signature is given (so a program consists only of the rewrite rules). As the reader may have noticed, the signature was not present in the syntax above either. A primitive form of type checking that does not need the explicit signature consists in checking that an operator (in the program as well as in all input terms) always takes the same number of arguments. The Terse semantics below as well as the partial evaluator T-mix expect that programs are correct according to this type condition. It could be interesting to work with a stronger typed Terse, e.g. one in which variables have types, in the future.

3.8 Terse semantics

Here we give a formal near-denotational semantics of Terse (compositionality is violated in the functions "run" and "eval"). The program is evaluated by the main function called "run". Comments begin with a "#" and continue to the end of the line.

Domains and elements:

$\gamma:\ \Gamma$ # the set of constructors

$\delta:\ \Delta$ # the set of defined operators, including predefined operators

$v:\ V$ # the set of variables

$$\begin{array}{llll} \text{pa:} & \text{Pa} & = \Gamma \times \text{Pa}^* + V & = T_\Gamma(V) & \text{\# patterns in left-hand sides} \\ \text{l:} & \text{L} & = \Delta \times \text{Pa}^* & = \Delta \times T_\Gamma(V)^* & \text{\# left-hand sides} \\ \text{r:} & \text{R} & = \Gamma \times R^* + \Delta \times R^* + V & = T_{\Gamma+\Delta}(V) & \text{\# right-hand sides} \\ \text{p:} & \text{Pro} & = \underline{\text{set of}}\ (L \times R) & & \text{\# program} \end{array}$$

$$\begin{array}{llll} & C & = \Delta \times \text{Gnd}^* & = \Delta \times T_\Gamma^* & \text{\# calls} \\ \text{gnd:} & \text{Gnd} & = \Gamma \times \text{Gnd}^* & = T_\Gamma & \text{\# ground terms} \\ \theta: & \text{Subst} & = V \rightharpoonup \text{Gnd} & & \text{\# substitutions} \end{array}$$

Main function:

run: $\text{Pro} \rightharpoonup \text{Gnd}^* \rightharpoonup (\text{Gnd} + \{\ \textbf{match-error}\ \})$

$\text{run}[\![p]\!]\ (\text{gnd}_1, ..., \text{gnd}_n) =$

    $\underline{\text{let}}\ \delta$ be the operator defining the goal function in p $\underline{\text{in}}$ # $\delta(\text{gnd}_1, ..., \text{gnd}_n)$ is the input term

      $\text{eval}[\![\delta(\text{gnd}_1, ..., \text{gnd}_n)]\!]\ (\lambda v.\textbf{undefined})\ p$

eval: R → Subst → Pro → Gnd

This function evaluates the right-hand side of a rule.

eval$\llbracket v \rrbracket \theta$ p = θv

eval$\llbracket \gamma(r_1, ..., r_n) \rrbracket \theta$ p = γ(eval$\llbracket r_1 \rrbracket \theta$ p, ..., eval$\llbracket r_n \rrbracket \theta$ p)

eval$\llbracket \delta(r_1, ..., r_n) \rrbracket \theta$ p =

  <u>let</u> gnd$_k$ = eval$\llbracket r_k \rrbracket \theta$ p <u>for</u> k = 1, ..., n <u>in</u>

    <u>if</u> $\exists$(l, r)$\in$p: success?$\llbracket l \rrbracket$ δ(gnd$_1$, ..., gnd$_n$) <u>then</u> eval$\llbracket r \rrbracket$ (U$\llbracket l \rrbracket$ δ(gnd$_1$, ..., gnd$_n$)) p

    <u>else</u> **match-error**   # some escape mechanism must be used

eval$\llbracket \delta$-predefined$(r_1, ..., r_n) \rrbracket \theta$ p =

  <u>let</u> gnd$_k$ = eval$\llbracket r_k \rrbracket \theta$ p <u>for</u> k = 1, ..., n <u>in</u> evaluate(δ-predefined(gnd$_1$, ..., gnd$_n$))

---

success?: L → C → Boolean

This function is used to see whether a match is successful.

success?$\llbracket \delta$-l$(pa_1, ..., pa_n) \rrbracket$ δ-r$(gnd_1, ..., gnd_m)$ =

  <u>if</u> δ-l $\neq$ δ-r <u>then</u> false

  <u>else</u> success1?$\llbracket pa_1 \rrbracket$ gnd$_1$ $\wedge$ ... $\wedge$ success1?$\llbracket pa_n \rrbracket$ gnd$_n$ # n = m due to the fixed arities
                                                                       # of operators (type correctness)

success1?: Pa → Gnd → Boolean

success1?$\llbracket v \rrbracket$ gnd = true

success1?$\llbracket \gamma$-l$(pa_1, ..., pa_n) \rrbracket$ γ-r$(gnd_1, ..., gnd_m)$ =

  <u>if</u> γ-l $\neq$ γ-r <u>then</u> false

  <u>else</u> success1?$\llbracket pa_1 \rrbracket$ gnd$_1$ $\wedge$ ... $\wedge$ success1?$\llbracket pa_n \rrbracket$ gnd$_n$ # n = m

---

U: L → C → Subst

This function returns a substitution containing bindings for the variables in the lhs. The function is only called if the match is successful.

U$\llbracket \delta(pa_1, ..., pa_n) \rrbracket$ δ(gnd$_1$, ..., gnd$_n$) =

  U1$\llbracket pa_n \rrbracket$ gnd$_n$ (... (U1$\llbracket pa_1 \rrbracket$ gnd$_1$ (λv.**undefined**)) ...)

U1: Pa → Gnd → Subst → Subst

U1$\llbracket v \rrbracket$ gnd θ = [v $\mapsto$ gnd]θ

U1$\llbracket \gamma(pa_1, ..., pa_n) \rrbracket$ γ(gnd$_1$, ..., gnd$_n$) θ = U1$\llbracket pa_n \rrbracket$ gnd$_n$ (... (U1$\llbracket pa_1 \rrbracket$ gnd$_1$ θ) ...)

3.9 Higher order functions

    Terse is basically first order, but higher order functions may be used by converting abstractions into explicit *closures* and applications into calls to an *application function* (the idea comes from [Reynolds72]; see also [Johnsson85] in which similar ideas are implemented). It should be noted that explicit closures are also expressible in languages with fixed signature (e.g. LISP), but not as elegantly as here.

<u>Abstraction handling</u>

An abstraction *a* is used in a rule:

    ... —> ... (λ*variable. body*) ...

where *body* contains free and bound variables. The rule is converted into

> ... —> ... cl-a(free variables in λ*variable.body*) ...

and an application rule is added (where app is the application function):

> app(cl-a(free variables in λ*variable.body*), *variable*) —> *body*

Each abstraction gets its own closure forming operator (like cl-a above), and one application rule must be added for each closure operator.

Application handling
An application is used in a rule:

> ... —> ... (*func arg*) ...

(so *func* will evaluate to a functional object, i.e. a closure). The rule is simply converted into

> ... —> ... app(*func, arg*) ...

Example
To give an example, consider a program containing a rule with abstractions and applications:

> ...   —> ... (λX. (λF. F(F X)) (λY. 2+Y)) V ...

The three abstractions will be referred to as abstraction *1*, *2* and *3*:

> *1*: λF. ...   *2*: λY. ...   *3*: λX. ...

By converting abstraction *1*, we replace the original rule with a new one and add an app rule:

> ...   —> ... (λX. cl-1(X) (λY. 2+Y)) V ...
> app(cl-1(X), F) —> app(F, app(F, X))

After conversion of abstraction 2 and 3, we get:

> ...   —> ... app(cl-3, V) ...
> app(cl-1(X), F) —> app(F, app(F, X))
> app(cl-2   Y) —> 2+Y
> app(cl-3,   X) —> app(cl-1(X), cl-2)

The resulting program is first order.

  If a program like the one above is going to be partially evaluated, it is crucial that the partial evaluator can handle partially static data. Otherwise, if just one subpart of a closure structure is dynamic, the whole closure is treated as a dynamic structure — including the closure operator itself. So all information is lost.

4. The partial evaluator T-mix

  We begin by giving some small partial evaluation examples (to give the "flavor" of T-mix). Using these examples as background material, a "naive" partial evaluator is described.

  This naive partial evaluator works fine on many (also non-trivial) examples. It turns out, however, that when it comes to doing self-application (specializing the partial evaluator itself), the naive partial evaluator will produce correct, but very large and inefficient, specialized programs. This observation originates from [Mix85]. By dividing the partial evaluation process into two phases, the inefficiency problem can be solved. The two phases will be called *binding time analysis* and *function specialization*; these terms come from [Mix85].

  The input to the partial evaluator T-mix consists of

1) a Terse program to be specialized;
2) values of the static input to the Terse program; in the T-mix case this will be an input term containing *variables* representing the dynamic input. We call such variables *stage 2 variables* in order to distinguish them from the *stage 1 variables*, variables of the input program to be specialized.

T-mix works as a kind of Terse interpreter. Starting out with the input term, it evaluates calls in a similar way to what we saw in section 3. But the presence of dynamic values means that it cannot rewrite all calls: sometimes T-mix does not know which rule to apply. We call the evaluation performed by T-mix *symbolic evaluation*.

4.1 First example

Consider the append program with an extra goal rule added:

rule 0:   f(List1, List2)   —>   append(List1, List2)
rule 1:   append(nil, Ys)   —>   Ys
rule 2:   append(X : Xs, Ys) —>   X : append(Xs, Ys)

Let the first argument in the input term be static, e.g. the list 1:nil (say), and let the second argument be dynamic. It will be represented by a stage 2 variable named D. The input term thus is f(1:nil, D). The symbolic evaluation sequence in this case is simple since the D has no influence on the flow of control:

redex		result of rewriting	comment
f(1:nil, D)	$\Rightarrow$	append(1:nil, D)	f(1:nil, D) rewritten by rule 0
append(1:nil, D)	$\Rightarrow$	1 : append(nil, D)	append(1:nil, D) rewritten by rule 2
append(nil, D)	$\Rightarrow$	D	append(nil, D) rewritten by rule 1

We have used the symbol "$\Rightarrow$" to denote a rewriting. Notice that the program (stage 1) variables List2 and Ys are bound to the (stage 2) *variable* D during the rewritings; when performing total evaluation, variables can only be bound to ground terms.

If the three rewrite *steps* are seen as rewrite *rules* instead, we already have a first version of the specialized program:

rule 0:   f(1:nil, D)   —>   append(1:nil, D)
rule 1:   append(1:nil, D) —>   1 : append(nil, D)
rule 2:   append(nil, D)   —>   D

This is a correct specialization of the original program since it will always return the same result when D's value is supplied as the original one would do when run on all the input. It is easy to see that the program may be optimized; the append call in rule 0 of the new program always matches rule 1 (and only rule 1), so the call may be *unfolded*: instead of the call in rule 0, the rhs of rule 1, with a proper variable substitution (here [D ↦ D]), is inserted. This process is similar to the call unfolding in the LISP append example in section 2. The append call in rule 1 also always matches a single rule, namely rule 2, so it may unfolded as well. We then get a simplified specialized program:

rule 0:   f(1:nil, D) —>   1 : D

The fixed static argument need not be present in the left-hand side of the goal function of the specialized program; the specialized program only expects the dynamic input. After removal of 1:nil we get the final specialized program:

rule 0:   f*(D) —>   1 : D

The goal function f* has only one argument. This reflects the fact that the input term f(1:nil, D) contained only one dynamic term, D. Since the new goal function has another arity than the original one, it has been called f* instead of just f.

4.2 Second example

In this example, the treatment of *non-unfoldable* calls is illustrated. Suppose that the first argument to the append program is dynamic and the second *partially static*, e.g. by letting the input term be f(D1, 7:D2). There are two dynamic parts represented by the variables D1 and D2. The rewrite steps encountered during symbolic evaluation are:

redex	result of rewriting	comment
f(D1, 7:D2)	⇒ append(D1, 7:D2)	f(D1, 7:D2) rewritten by rule 0
append(nil, 7:D2)	⇒ 7 : D2	append(D1, 7:D2) rewritten by rule 1
append(X:Xs, 7:D2)	⇒ X : append(Xs, 7:D2)	append(D1, 7:D2) rewritten by rule 2
append(nil, 7:D2)	⇒ 7 : D2	append(Xs, 7:D2) rewritten by rule 1
append(X:Xs, 7:D2)	⇒ X : append(Xs, 7:D2)	append(Xs, 7:D2) rewritten by rule 2

The simulation has now stabilized since all possible calls have been symbolically evaluated. The append call resulting from the first rewrite step may match as well rule 1 as rule 2. The value of the dynamic D1 is the deciding factor. We see that the last two rewrite steps do not differ from the two previous ones, and thus are redundant. The reason is that <u>names</u> of variables have no significance in Terse programs. So there is no difference between symbolic evaluation of append(D1, 7:D2) and append(Xs, 7:D2).

If we regard the rewrite steps as rewrite rules, we get the first version of the specialized program:

```
rule 0:    f(D1, 7:D2)          —>  append(D1, 7:D2)
rule 1:    append(nil, 7:D2)    —>  7 : D2
rule 2:    append(X:Xs, 7:D2) —>  X : append(Xs, 7:D2)
```

Note: Here X and Xs are stage 2 variables.

None of the append calls may be unfolded since rule 1 as well as rule 2 is applicable. A dynamic value is needed to decide which of the rules to apply. The calls are thus *suspended*, which simply means that they are not unfolded and thus will be present in the specialized program.

As in the first example, the static parts of the arguments to f should be removed. So 7 as well as : are removed. Notice also that the append function is always called with 7:D2 as its second argument. This means that 7 and : are redundant and thus removable. The final specialized program then becomes

```
rule 0:    f*(D1, D2)           —>  append*(D1, D2)
rule 1:    append*(nil, D2)     —>  7 : D2
rule 2:    append*(X:Xs, D2) —>  X : append*(Xs, D2)
```

There are two arguments to f* since there were two dynamic subterms in the input term.

4.3 Third example

The third example illustrates the treatment of *nested calls*. Since the symbolic evaluation must simulate the possible rewrite sequences when the dynamic data is supplied, the evaluation order of course has to be the same as in total evaluation. So T-mix handles nested calls inside-out left-to-right.

Consider the following example including nested calls:

```
rule 0:    f(X, Y)        —>  g(h(X), h(Y))
rule 1:    g(one, one) —>  cake
rule 2:    g(one, two) —>  hamburger
rule 3:    g(two, X)    —>  steak(X)
rule 4:    h(1)           —>  one
rule 5:    h(2)           —>  two
```

Let the input term be f(1, D). The call h(X) is then unfoldable (X = 1) and will always evaluate to one. The h(D) call is not unfoldable — we need the value of D in order to see whether to apply rule 4 or rule 5. When the g call is handled, the presence of the suspended h(D) call means that as well rule 1 as rule 2 (but not rule 3) may be matched when dynamic values are supplied. So the g call is also non-unfoldable:

redex	result of rewriting	comment
f(1, D)	$\Rightarrow$ g(h(1), h(D))	h(1) is unfoldable
	$\Rightarrow$ g(one, h(D))	— and is replaced by one
h(1)	$\Rightarrow$ one	h(D) rewritten by rule 4
h(2)	$\Rightarrow$ two	h(D) rewritten by rule 5
g(one, one)	$\Rightarrow$ cake	g(one, h(D)) rewritten by rule 1
g(one, two)	$\Rightarrow$ hamburger	g(one, h(D)) rewritten by rule 2

The specialized program then becomes (after removal of the first of g's arguments):

rule 0:	f*(D)	—>	g*(h(D))
rule 1:	h(1)	—>	one
rule 2:	h(2)	—>	two
rule 3:	g*(one)	—>	cake
rule 4:	g*(two)	—>	hamburger

4.4 Fourth example

This example illustrates how one function in the input program may be found in many *specialized versions* in the specialized program. The following program will be used as input:

rule 0:	f(X, Y)	—>	g(X, Y) : g(X, Y:Y)
rule 1:	g(a, Z)	—>	1 : Z
rule 2:	g(b, Z)	—>	2 : Z

Let the input term be f(D, 3). After simulating the rewrite steps, the first version of the specialized program becomes

rule 0:	f(D, 3)	—>	g(D, 3) : g(D, 3:3)
rule 1:	g(a, 3)	—>	1 : 3
rule 2:	g(b, 3)	—>	2 : 3
rule 3:	g(a, 3:3)	—>	1 : (3 : 3)
rule 4:	g(b, 3:3)	—>	2 : (3 : 3)

None of the g calls may be unfolded since the value of D is needed in order to resolve the matches.
Now notice that g is defined and called with two different static terms as the second argument. But the second argument is still redundant: it will never be matched against anything dynamic. In this case two versions of g appear after removal of the redundant arguments:

rule 0:	f*(D)	—>	g[3](D) : g[3:3](D)
rule 1:	g[3](a)	—>	1 : 3
rule 2:	g[3](b)	—>	2 : 3
rule 3:	g[3:3](a)	—>	1 : (3 : 3)
rule 4:	g[3:3](b)	—>	2 : (3 : 3)

g[3] and g[3:3] are here used as new defined operators (so g[3] is one symbol, just as f* in the previous examples) in order to make the identification clear.

4.5 A naive partial evaluator

Using the examples, we now describe the naive partial evaluator (i.e. the partial evaluator without binding time analysis).

4.5.1 Call unfolding

The unfolding principle used in the introductory examples was the following: if dynamic values are needed in order to determine which rule a call matches, it cannot be unfolded — we do not know which rule to apply.

So let us focus on the calls that only match one rule, independently of the possible values of the dynamic data in the call. All such calls could be unfolded since we always know which rule to apply. An infinite unfolding loop will only be entered if static values cause it; and in that case the program to be specialized will loop anyway (if the looping part is executed). So it seems to be a good idea to unfold all calls that, independently of the values of dynamic data, may match only one rule.

In T-mix we are, however, a little bit more conservative. There are two kinds of calls that we do not unfold, even though it could be done. The first kind is illustrated by the following example. Consider a program containing only one rule defining f: $f(X1:X2) \longrightarrow ....$ Suppose that we meet a call $f(D)$ during symbolic evaluation. Since the stage 2 variable D must be *decomposed* (or *instantiated*, a kind of "backwards unification") in order to succeed the match, we do not unfold. If anything is needed to be assumed about the values of dynamic data inside a call (including the value of a suspended nested call), we do not unfold. This design choice is a technical one: T-mix would turn out to be much more complicated otherwise.

A practical consequence of the design choice is that we do not have to test explicitly whether a call matches more than one rule: if the call matches a left-hand side (no matter what the dynamic values are), it means that there are no other left-hand sides that can be matched successfully. If this were the case, the program would be non-deterministic (a term must never match two rules); it would violate the semantics of Terse.

There is also a second kind of calls that we do not unfold due to the risk of *call duplication*. Consider the following program operating on unary numbers (0, succ(0), succ(succ(0)), ...). The example is a Terse version of one from [Mix85]:

$$
\begin{aligned}
f(0) &\longrightarrow 1 \\
f(succ(X)) &\longrightarrow g(f(X)) \\
g(X) &\longrightarrow X : X
\end{aligned}
$$

Let the input term be $f(D)$. If the call to g is unfolded during symbolic evaluation, we get the specialized program

$$
\begin{aligned}
f(0) &\longrightarrow 1 \\
f(succ(X)) &\longrightarrow f(X) : f(X)
\end{aligned}
$$

The original program runs in *linear* time, whereas the specialized program runs in *exponential* time — and that is certainly <u>not</u> the purpose of doing partial evaluation.

To summarize, a call will be unfolded by T-mix if

1) nothing is assumed about the values of dynamic data (inside arguments to the call) in order to determine whether a match will be successful <u>and</u>
2) the unfolding does not lead to call duplication.

4.5.2 Symbolic evaluation

We now give a sketch of the symbolic evaluation (or partial evaluation) algorithm. You should forget everything about removal of static parts when reading this section. We only consider the specialized program <u>before</u> static parts are removed. The set of stage 1 variables will be denoted by V, the set of stage 2 variables by V2. We use Δ to denote the set of defined operators (typical element: δ) and Γ to denote the set of constructors (typical element: γ), cf. the formalism used in the Terse semantics given earlier.

The <u>input</u> to the symbolic evaluation algorithm is a Terse program p:

$$
p = \{ \, l_i \longrightarrow r_i \mid i \in \{1, ..., n\}, l_i \in \Delta \times T_\Gamma(V)^*, r_i \in T_{\Gamma+\Delta}(V) \, \}
$$

and an input term, a call to the goal function that has $l_1 \longrightarrow r_1$ among its defining rules. There may be stage 2 variables in the input term, whereas the variables in p are stage 1 variables.

A *specializing substitution* is defined to be a function binding stage 1 variables to terms containing constructors and stage 2 variables:

$$
\theta\text{-spec: Spec-subst} = V \rightarrow T_\Gamma(V2)
$$

The <u>output</u> from the symbolic evaluation algorithm is a specialized program p2:

$$
p2 = \{ \, \theta\text{-spec } l_i \longrightarrow r2_i \mid i \in \{1, ..., n\}, \theta\text{-spec} \in \text{Spec-subst}, r2_i \in T_{\Gamma+\Delta}(V2) \, \}
$$

for various choices of specializing substitutions θ-spec. The variables in p2 are stage 2 variables. Some notation: when we write θl_i we mean "l_i with all variables replaced by the values given by the substitution θ".

The <u>algorithm</u> for producing the specialized program is as follows:

<u>begin</u>

   p2 := { }; suspend the input term $\delta_1(...)$;

   <u>repeat</u>

      <u>choose</u> one of:

         1: unfold a left most innermost unfoldable call $\delta_j(...)$ in a rule

$$\delta_k(...) \longrightarrow ... \delta_j(...) ...$$

            of p2;

         2: suspend a non-unfoldable call $\delta_j(...)$ (containing no nested unfoldable calls which
            have not been unfolded) in a rule

$$\delta_k(...) \longrightarrow ... \delta_j(...) ...$$

            of p2;

      <u>until</u> no more calls can be unfolded

         <u>and</u> the execution of the suspension procedure will not enlarge p2

<u>end</u>;

<u>unfolding of a call $\delta_j(...)$</u>:

   replace $\delta_j(...)$ by θr_i

   <u>where</u> p contains $l_i \longrightarrow r_i$ and $\delta_j(...)$ will match l_i no matter which values are supplied for the
      dynamic data in $\delta_j(...)$

   <u>and where</u> $\theta: V \to T_{\Gamma+\Delta}(V2)$ is the substitution found by matching $\delta_j(...)$ against l_i;

<u>suspension of a call $\delta_j(...)$</u>:

   <u>for</u> every rule $l_i \longrightarrow r_i$ in p that $\delta_j(...)$ may match when dynamic values in $\delta_j(...)$ are supplied <u>do</u>
      <u>choose</u> a specializing substitution θ-spec: Spec-subst $= V \to T_\Gamma(V2)$ such that for any
         specific set of values of dynamic data in $\delta_j(...)$:

$$\delta_j(...) \text{ matches } l_i \Rightarrow \delta_j(...) \text{ matches } \theta\text{-spec } l_i;$$

      p2 := p2 $\cup$ { θ-spec $l_i \longrightarrow \theta$-spec r_i };

The algorithm contains many unclear points and involves non-determinism. This has been done on purpose in order to distinguish clearly between <u>what</u> T-mix does and <u>how</u> it does it. Later, a formal and much more operational algorithm is given.

4.5.3 Substitutions in the unfolding case

   The use of a substitution θ in the unfolding case can be illustrated by one of the examples seen earlier. In, for instance, the first append example, we unfolded the call append(1:nil, D) . The call matches the rule append(X:Xs, Ys) —> ... and the following substitution is built: [X $\mapsto$ 1, Xs $\mapsto$ nil, Ys $\mapsto$ D].

   We now give an overview of how a substitution is built when an unfolded call C (possibly containing stage 2 variables and suspended nested calls) is matched against a left-hand side *lhs* (possibly containing stage 1 variables) during symbolic evaluation. We only consider the cases in which we have found out that the match will be successful, i.e. that the constructors in C match the constructors in *lhs*.

   The matching process is described imperatively by a small action table below. The substitution θ is initially [] or "empty" (i.e. the function $\lambda v.\textbf{undefined}$) and is updated according to the table during matching.

Substitutions built when a call is unfolded:

subpattern of *lhs*	subterm of *C*	action
(stage 1) variable v	any term	add a binding [v ↦ subterm of *C*] to θ
γ(a tuple of subpatterns)	γ(a tuple of subterms)	add the bindings found by matching the subterms against the subpatterns

Notice that the case in which the subterm of *lhs* is γ(a tuple of subpatterns), and where the subterm of *C* is a (stage 2) variable or a suspended nested call, is not considered: *C* would not be unfoldable in that case due to the testing of a dynamic value, and so the case is irrelevant here.

4.5.4 Specializing substitutions in the suspension case

Consider a non-unfoldable call f(D1, a, g(D2)) where g(D2) is a suspended nested call. Let p contain the rule f(X1:X2, X3, X4) —> ... . Clearly, the call may match the rule when the dynamic values D1 and D2 are supplied. A specialized rule

$$f(D3:D4, a, D5) \longrightarrow ...$$

is built by T-mix. The specializing substitution used here is:

θ-spec = [X1 ↦ D3, X2 ↦ D4, X3 ↦ a, X4 ↦ D5]

How the specializing substitution θ-spec is chosen depends on the *strategy* of the partial evaluator. For instance, in the example above we chose to bind X3 to the constant a resulting in a specialized rule with a fixed second argument (the constant a). One could also have chosen to bind X3 to a (stage 2) variable; this would have given a "less specialized" program. A partial evaluator using that strategy would not do much more than unfolding.

On the other hand, we could not have chosen to bind e.g. X1 to the constant b (say) and X2 to D3. This would produce a "too specialized" rule: it is possible to find a value for D1 that matches X1:X2, but does not match b:D3. This is trivial to see: for instance, take the value c:d. We would thus violate the condition saying that for any specific set of values for the dynamic data for which the call δ(...) matches l_i, it must also match θ-spec l_i.

Also, we could not have chosen to bind X4 to the call g(D2) since the specialized program in that case would contain a nested defined operator in the left-hand side of the specialized rule. So X4 has been bound to a stage 2 variable D5.

The complete strategy for finding specializing substitutions used in T-mix will be summarized in an action table similar to the one above. We only consider the cases with successful matches. The specializing substitution θ-spec is initially empty (λv.**undefined**). In the resulting specializing substitution, all stage 2 variables are (must be) distinct.

Specializing substitutions built when a call is suspended:

subpattern of *lhs*	subterm of *C*	action
(stage 1) variable v	any term	add a binding [v ↦ a revised version of the subterm of *C* in which all (stage 2) variables and all (suspended nested) calls have been replaced by *distinct* stage 2 variables] to θ-spec
γ(a tuple of subpatterns)	γ(a tuple of subterms)	add the bindings found by matching the subterms against the subpatterns
γ(a tuple of subpatterns)	(stage 2) variable or (suspended nested) call	add bindings for all (stage 1) variables in the subpatterns of *lhs*, where each binding is of the form [(st. 1) variable ↦ (st. 2) variable], all stage 2 variables being *distinct*

It should be emphasized that the process of finding substitutions is <u>not</u> a Prolog-like unification, neither in the unfolding nor in the suspension case. The stage 2 variables in the call C are never instantiated; only the stage 1 variables in *lhs* are. Rather than being full unification, the process is an extension of simple pattern matching. In the extended pattern matching, the variables in the matched rule may be bound to terms that do not only contain constructors, but also variables and (in the unfolding case) calls.

4.5.5 Termination problems caused by unlimited structures

Due to the way the specializing substitutions are chosen, <u>all</u> rhs constructors *inside arguments to calls* will also be present in the corresponding specialized left-hand side matched by the call. In the introductory examples we have seen, this has worked fine; but this is not always the case. To see this, let us consider a simple example. The following program reverses a list:

rule 0:	reverse(L)	$\longrightarrow$	f(L, nil)
rule 1:	f(nil, Ys)	$\longrightarrow$	Ys
rule 2:	f(X:Xs, Ys)	$\longrightarrow$	f(Xs, X:Ys)

Let the input term be reverse(D) (so the input is completely dynamic). The symbolic evaluation rewrite sequence is

redex		result of rewriting	comment
reverse(D)	$\Rightarrow$	f(D, nil)	reverse(D) rewritten by rule 0
f(nil, nil)	$\Rightarrow$	nil	f(D, nil) rewritten by rule 1
f(X0:Xs0, nil)	$\Rightarrow$	f(Xs0, X0:nil)	f(D, nil) rewritten by rule 2
f(nil, X0:nil)	$\Rightarrow$	X0:nil	f(Xs0, X0:nil) rewritten by rule 1
f(X1:Xs1, X0:nil)	$\Rightarrow$	f(Xs1, X1:X0:nil)	f(Xs0, X0:nil) rewritten by rule 2
f(nil, X1:X0:nil)	$\Rightarrow$	X1:X0:nil	f(Xs1, X1:X0:nil) rewritten by rule 1
f(X2:Xs2, X1:X0:nil)	$\Rightarrow$	f(Xs2, X2:X1:X0:nil)	f(Xs1, X1:X0:nil) rewritten by rule 2

$$\vdots \qquad \qquad \vdots$$

The sequence is infinite.

The problem is that the rhs constructor : of rule 2 is reused an infinite number of times during symbolic evaluation. During <u>total</u> evaluation, the program always terminates: the first argument of f definitely decreases for each recursive call. After a finite number of recursive calls, rule 2 of the reverse program will not be applicable and the loop stops. But during <u>partial</u> evaluation, the first argument is dynamic for which reason rule 1 as well as rule 2 may <u>always</u> give successful matches — and so both branches have to be traced.

What happens is in other words that a finite, but *unlimited*, structure having a size determined by the value of <u>dynamic</u> data is attempted being built on the basis of <u>static</u> data only. And this attempt causes non-termination.

To overcome this problem, we (rather ad hoc) introduce a *preprocessing phase*. In this phase we once and for all mark "dangerous" constructor occurrences (like the rhs occurrence of : in rule 2) as being roots of *dynamic rhs terms*. How the dynamic constructors are found will be discussed later. Terms rooted by such dynamic constructors are then handled in a different way during the symbolic evaluation than other terms. The difference is that when a call is <u>suspended</u>, dynamic rhs terms inside arguments to the call are <u>not</u> copied into the specializing substitutions, but are reflected by (stage 2) variables. Thus dynamic rhs terms are handled in the very same way that (stage 2) variables and suspended nested calls are. The treatment of dynamic rhs terms corresponds closely to the *generalization* used in supercompilation ([Turchin86]). See also [Jones87] and [Launchbury87]. The action table describing how a specializing substitution is built of course has to be modified accordingly.

The rewrite sequence for the reverse example now becomes (the rhs : in rule 2 is assumed to be dynamic and therefore marked with a d subscript):

redex		result of rewriting	comment
reverse(D)	$\Rightarrow$	f(D, nil)	reverse(D) rewritten by rule 0
f(nil, nil)	$\Rightarrow$	nil	f(D, nil) rewritten by rule 1
f(X:Xs, nil)	$\Rightarrow$	f(Xs, X:$_d$nil)	f(D, nil) rewritten by rule 2
f(nil, D1)	$\Rightarrow$	D1	f(Xs, X:$_d$nil) rewritten by rule 1
f(X:Xs, D1)	$\Rightarrow$	f(Xs, X:$_d$D1)	f(Xs, X:$_d$nil) rewritten by rule 2

Notice how $X:_d$nil gave rise to the variable D1. $f(Xs, X:_dD1)$ produces the same rewrite steps as $f(Xs, X:_d$nil), so the sequence has stabilized. When the static parts of arguments to calls are removed, we get the simplified specialized program below. The specialized versions of f have been named $f[(D, nil)]$ and $f[(D, D)]$; the postscripts represent the forms of the patterns that specialize the defined operator f, a D indicates a dynamic subpattern/subterm:

$$
\begin{array}{lcl}
\text{reverse(D)} & \longrightarrow & f[(D, nil)](D) \\
f[(D, nil)](\text{nil}) & \longrightarrow & \text{nil} \\
f[(D, nil)](X:Xs) & \longrightarrow & f[(D, D)](Xs, X:nil) \\
f[(D, D)](\text{nil, D1}) & \longrightarrow & D1 \\
f[(D, D)](X:Xs, D1) & \longrightarrow & f[(D, D)](Xs, X:D1)
\end{array}
$$

It might have been a good idea also to mark the nil in the right-hand side of rule 0 of the reverse program as dynamic. In that case, the $f[(D, nil)]$ function would not have been produced and the specialized program would be identical to the original reverse program (except for the variable names).

The preprocessing phase is not yet worked out; at present, the d marks are added by hand. It has turned out to be a rather complicated problem to automate (see [Jones87]). What is needed is a *global flow analysis* of the input program, including at least an analysis of the possible values variables may be bound to during symbolic evaluation (expressed in terms of the relations between the variables and constructors in the program) and an analysis of which parts of the flow of control that are determined by dynamic data.

4.5.6 Removal of static parts in arguments to calls

Redundant static parts are removed in order to compact the specialized programs. When realistic programs are specialized, the static parts may be very large data structures. For instance, if an interpreter is specialized with respect to a static program, the complete program will be found in many places in the specialized interpreter. So it clearly is desirable to remove everything that can be removed.

Recall the second and the fourth of the introductory examples. In the second example (the second append example), a part of the second argument to append was removed from the specialized program since the value never changed (the removed constructors were 7 and :). However, nothing was removed in the first argument since that clearly would destroy the program. In the fourth example (specialization of the program with two functions f and g), the second argument to g was removed resulting in two specialized versions of g (g[3] and g[3:3]). Also here the first argument had to stay untouched.

If we regard the left-hand sides of the specialized rules, the non-removable constructors are those that anything dynamic — a stage 2 variable, a suspended nested call or a term rooted by a dynamic constructor — can possibly "risk" to be matched against.

In the right-hand sides, the non-removable parts are those that were not copied into the specializing substitutions, but generalized to variables: (stage 2) variables, suspended nested calls and terms rooted by a dynamic constructor. The removable parts are the constructors inside calls, but outside terms rooted by a dynamic constructor.

4.5.7 Marking of removable lhs patterns

In T-mix, the non-removable lhs patterns are marked during the symbolic evaluation. A constructor being the root of an non-removable subpattern is identified by marking it with a d subscript. The table below summarizes how these constructors are found and marked when a non-unfoldable call C is matched against a left-hand side *lhs* during symbolic evaluation. The table describes the marking process applicatively; the result of a match (the value) is the marked version of (the subpatterns of the) *lhs*.

subpattern of *lhs*	subterm of *C*	value
(stage 1) variable	any term	the (stage 1) variable
γ(a tuple of subpatterns)	γ(a tuple of subterms)	γ(the marked versions of the *lhs* subpatterns found by matching against the subterms of *C*)
γ(a tuple of subpatterns)	(stage 2) variable <u>or</u> (suspended nested) call <u>or</u> dynamic rhs term	γ_d(the tuple of subpatterns)

One should be aware that even though the d marks in left-hand sides and in right-hand sides appear to be very similar, they are produced and used in very different ways. The lhs d marks are produced <u>during</u> symbolic evaluation in order to pass information to the phase in which static parts are removed. The rhs d marks are produced in <u>preprocessing</u> prior to and independently from the symbolic evaluation phase. They have strong influence on how the symbolic evaluation develop. However, when static parts are removed, the d's mean the same in left- and right-hand sides: patterns/terms rooted by a d constructor are non-removable.

This ends the description of the naive partial evaluator. To summarize, three passes are used in it:

— preprocessing (marking of dynamic rhs constructors);
— symbolic evaluation;
— removal of static parts of arguments to calls.

4.6 Self-application

It was described in [Mix85] that in order to perform efficient self-application, it is necessary to split partial evaluation into two phases: a *binding time analysis* (bta) phase and a *function specialization* (fsp) phase. The argumentation given in [Mix85] is also applicable to T-mix. The function calls will therefore be *annotated* as being either <u>always</u> unfoldable or <u>never</u> unfoldable <u>before</u> the actual partial evaluation. Since we do not have operators (in the LISP sense, e.g. car, cdr etc.) in Terse, there is no equivalent to the operator annotation performed in [Mix85].

When binding time analysis is performed, the specific *values* of the static input to the program to be specialized are not present. Only information about *which* values that are static/dynamic is available. The binding time analyser is not going to be self-applied, so it should be as powerful as possible. A simple principle to be followed is the following:

<u>move as much work as possible from the fsp phase to the bta phase</u>

Everything that can possibly be done without knowledge of the particular values of the static input thus should be done in the bta phase.

This suggests moving the "ad hoc" preprocessing, in which dynamic rhs constructors are marked, from the fsp to the bta phase. So an annotated program should contain call annotations as well as rhs constructor annotations. The preprocessing was only briefly discussed earlier; it is still subject to further research ([Jones87]). It does, however, seem to be the case that the <u>values</u> of static input have no influence on the constructor annotations, implying that the preprocessing certainly can be done in the bta phase. One of the key points in the preprocessing is to point out the places where dynamic data determine the control — but this is exactly what the call annotations are all about (when a dynamic value is tested, the call is not unfoldable), and they are producible at bta time. Furthermore, the nature of the problem with unlimited structures comes up from infinite repeated use of the constructors from the <u>program</u>; it has nothing to do with the static input values.

4.7 The binding time analyser

Here is a small example of how call annotations are produced. Consider the program

```
f(X, Y)          —>   g(X, Y)
g(X, Y)          —>   append(X, Y)
append(nil, Ys)  —>   Ys
append(X:Xs, Ys) —>   X : append(Xs, Ys)
```

If the argument X (of f) is completely dynamic and Y is completely static, it is easily seen that all

X's and Xs's in the program will always be completely dynamic, and that all Y's and Ys's will be completely static. The g call does not require testing of a dynamic value (and there are no nested calls and thus no risk of call duplication), so it is unfoldable. Both of the append calls do however require a dynamic test, so they are not unfoldable.

Binding time analysis is, unfortunately, significantly more complicated when "real" cases are handled. It is necessary to be able to express <u>partially</u> static structures as well as infinite structures. This is possible by using *grammars* ([Jones86], [Mogensen87]). For instance, consider an interpreter using some variable Env holding an *environment* in the form of a list of name/value-pairs, the names being static and the values dynamic:

$$\text{Env} ::= \text{nil} \mid (\text{name} : \text{value}) : \text{Env}$$

The binding time analyser must detect this and could internally describe Env by

$$\text{Env} ::= \text{nil} \mid (S : D) : \text{Env}$$

where S means that the value will be static at fsp time, D that it will be dynamic. Typical environment operations could be done by a call f(Env, ...), where the interpreter contains rules

```
f(nil, ...)                    —>  ...
f((Name:Value):Rest, ...)  —>  ...
```

A call f(Env, ...) is always unfoldable and should be annotated so. The grammar method has been used successfully for a LISP-like language in [Mogensen87].

4.8 A formal description of the function specializer

Here we give a formal description of the function specializer. We use a near-denotational style similar to the one used in section 3 in which the semantics of Terse was described. The following comments apply to the formal description that follows shortly.

<u>Input</u> to the function specializer: dynamic rhs constructor occurrences are subscripted (annotated) with a d. Defined operators are d annotated if the call is non-unfoldable; if the call is unfoldable, the defined operator has no subscript. The set of all stage 1 variables is called V. The program is a set of (lhs, rhs)-pairs with a special goal function.

<u>Output</u> from the function specializer: dynamic constructors in left- and right-hand sides are subscripted with a d (this information is used in the removal of static parts phase). Defined operators are never subscripted. The set of all stage 2 variables is called V2. The specialized program is a set of (lhs, rhs)-pairs.

Comments to the <u>domains and elements</u>: a substitution is a function binding stage 1 variables to terms possibly containing stage 2 variables and defined operators (used when calls are unfolded), whereas a specializing substitution binds stage 1 variables to terms (possibly containing stage 2 variables) without defined operators (used in the non-unfolding case).

A variable named "pending" is used to remember the suspended calls that have not yet been processed. It is done by storing the rules (where the dynamic lhs constructors have been d marked) for which matches are successful. For each stored rule, the proper specializing substitution is also saved.

Comments to the <u>algorithm</u>: the main function is given in an imperative Pascal-like way (this turns out to be the most convenient). First, the output program is set empty. The pending variable is then initialized to contain the rules that the input term may match when dynamic values are supplied.

The algorithm then proceeds by picking an element from pending and processing it. It is tested if the element has not been processed before and if so, it is processed. This may cause addition of new elements to pending. The algorithm stops when pending is empty.

E is the "evaluation" (reduction) function. (Stage 1) variables are replaced by their values, unfoldable calls are unfolded, and unfoldable calls to predefined functions are evaluated. The binding time analyser must ensure that <u>predefined</u> operators are annotated as unfoldable only if <u>all</u> arguments are completely static (predefined operators are assumed to be strict).

P works on the specialized forms output by E. P produces a "small" pending set containing the rules (with specializing substitutions) needed by the suspended calls in the expression. Predefined operators never give rise to new elements in pending. A predefined operator is either completely evaluated (the unfolding case) or not; specialized versions of predefined operators are never produced.

In **E** as well as in **P**, the function "success?" is used. It returns the boolean value "true" if the match may be successful when dynamic values are supplied, otherwise it returns "false". The function is not included here; it is not very different from the success? function used in the semantics for Terse (section 3). Three other functions (also not included) are used: "Us", "Ud "and "mark-l". "Us" returns a substitution; it is used when a call is unfolded. It follows the table presented earlier for non-unfoldable calls. "Ud" returns a specializing substitution; it is used when a call is suspended and is based on the table for non-unfoldable calls. The "mark-l" function marks (annotates) the dynamic lhs constructor occurrences according to the "marking" table given earlier (in order to pass information to the removal of static parts phase).

Some notation: when a substitution θ is applied to a complete left- or right-hand side, we simply write θl and θr as done before.

Domains and elements:

γ:	Γ	# the set of constructors
γ_d:	Γ_d	# dynamic constructors
γ°:	$\Gamma^\circ = \Gamma + \Gamma_d$	# annotated constructors

δ:	Δ	# the set of defined operators (including predefined operators)
δ_d:	Δ_d	# dynamic (non-unfoldable) operators
γ°:	$\Delta^\circ = \Delta + \Delta_d$	# annotated defined operators

v:	V	# the set of stage 1 variables, variables in the <u>input</u> program
$v2$:	$V2$	# the set of stage 2 variables, variables in <u>output</u> program

Input program: rhs constructors and rhs defined operators may be dynamic.

pa:	Pa	$= \Gamma \times Pa^* + V$		$= T_\Gamma(V)$
l:	L	$= \Delta \times Pa^*$		$= \Delta \times T_\Gamma(V)^*$
r°:	R°	$= \Gamma^\circ \times R^{\circ *} + \Delta^\circ \times R^{\circ *} + V$		$= T_{\Gamma^\circ + \Delta^\circ}(V)$
p°:	Pro°	$= \underline{set\ of}\ (L \times R^\circ)$		

Specialized program: lhs and rhs constructors may be dynamic.

	$Pa2^\circ$	$= \Gamma^\circ \times Pa2^{\circ *} + V2$		$= T_{\Gamma^\circ}(V2)$
$l2^\circ$:	$L2^\circ$	$= \Delta \times Pa2^{\circ *}$		$= \Delta \times T_{\Gamma^\circ}(V2)^*$
$r2^\circ$:	$R2^\circ$	$= \Gamma^\circ \times R2^{\circ *} + \Delta \times R2^{\circ *} + V2$	$= T_{\Gamma^\circ + \Delta}(V2)$
$p2^\circ$:	$Pro2^\circ$	$= \underline{set\ of}\ (L2^\circ \times R2^\circ)$		

	Pa°	$= \Gamma^\circ \times Pa^{\circ *} + V$		$= T_{\Gamma^\circ}(V)$
l°:	L°	$= \Delta \times Pa^{\circ *}$		$= \Delta \times T_{\Gamma^\circ}(V)^*$
θ:	$Subst$	$= V \to R2^\circ$		$= V \to T_{\Gamma^\circ + \Delta}(V2)$
θ-spec:	$Spec\text{-}subst$	$= V \to T_\Gamma(V2)$		
pending:	$Pending$	$= set\ of\ (L^\circ \times R^\circ \times Spec\text{-}subst)$		

Main function:

fsp: Pro° → Pa2* → Pro2°

fsp⟦p°⟧ (pa2$_1$, ..., pa2$_n$) = p2° computed by the following algorithm:

begin

    p2° := ∅; pending := **P** δ(pa2$_1$, ..., pa2$_n$) p° where δ defines the goal function;

    while pending ≠ ∅ do

        remove an element, (l°, r°, θ-spec), from pending;

        if ¬(∃(l2°, r2°)∈p2°: l2° = θ-spec l°) then

            r2° := **E**⟦r°⟧θ-spec p°;   # θ-spec is implicitly type converted (Spec-subst to Subst)

            p2° := p2° ∪ {(θ-spec l°, r2°)};

            pending := pending ∪ (**P** r2° p°)

        endif

    endwhile

end

E: R° → Subst → Pro° → R2°

This function reduces an R° term to an R2° term by performing symbolic evaluation (whereby unfoldable calls are unfolded).

E⟦v⟧θ p° = θv

E⟦γ°(r$_1$°, ..., r$_n$°)⟧θ p° = γ°(**E**⟦r$_1$°⟧θ p°, ..., **E**⟦r$_n$°⟧θ p°)

E⟦δ(r$_1$°, ..., r$_n$°)⟧θ p° =

    let r2$_k$° = **E**⟦r$_k$°⟧θ p° for k = 1, ..., n in

        let (l, r°)∈p°: success?⟦1⟧ δ(r2$_1$°, ..., r2$_n$°) in **E**⟦r°⟧ (Us⟦1⟧ δ(r2$_1$°, ..., r2$_n$°)) p°

E⟦δ$_d$(r$_1$°, ..., r$_n$°)⟧θ p° = let r2$_k$° = **E**⟦r$_k$°⟧θ p° for k = 1, ..., n in δ(r2$_1$°, ..., r2$_n$°)

E⟦δ-predefined(r$_1$°, ..., r$_n$°)⟧θ p° =   # must be true: ∀k∈{1, ..., n}: r$_k$° is completely static

    let r2$_k$° = **E**⟦r$_k$°⟧θ p° for k = 1, ..., n in evaluate(δ-predefined(r2$_1$°, ..., r2$_n$°))

E⟦δ-predefined$_d$(r$_1$°, ..., r$_n$°)⟧θ p° =

    let r2$_k$° = **E**⟦r$_k$°⟧θ p° for k = 1, ..., n in δ-predefined(r2$_1$°, ..., r2$_n$°)

P: R2° → Pro° → Pending

This function computes the set of specialized functions needed by an R2° rhs.

P v p° = ∅

P γ°(r2$_1$°, ..., r2$_n$°) p° = (**P** r2$_1$° p°) ∪ ... ∪ (**P** r2$_n$° p°)

P δ(r2$_1$°, ..., r2$_n$°) p° =

    ∪$_{(l,r°)∈p°}$({ (mark-l⟦1⟧ δ(r2$_1$°, ..., r2$_n$°), r°, Ud⟦1⟧ δ(r2$_1$°, ..., r2$_n$°))

        | success?⟦1⟧ δ(r2$_1$°, ..., r2$_n$°)})

    ∪ (**P** r2$_1$° p°) ∪ ... ∪ (**P** r2$_n$° p°)

P δ-predefined(r2$_1$°, ..., r2$_n$°) p° = (**P** r2$_1$° p°) ∪ ... ∪ (**P** r2$_n$° p°)

5. Preliminary results

The function specializer and the removal of static parts have been implemented in Franz LISP (compiled LISP) on a VAX 785. Binding time analysis has been done by hand in these experiments. The input to the function specializer thus is a hand-annotated program in which the calls are annotated as being unfoldable/non-unfoldable and in which some constructors in right-hand sides are annotated as being dynamic.

The first experiment has been to run the small introductory examples from section 4. These runs were all performed in less than 300 milliseconds (plus garbage collection time, from 0 to 540 milliseconds). This figure is the time used for function specialization and removal of static parts.

5.1 Lambda interpreter example

An interpreter (written in Terse) for a small call-by-value based functional language including lambda abstraction, application and a "letrec" construction (cf. [Reynolds72]) has been specialized with respect to a source program in the lambda language. By doing this, the lambda program is transformed into an equivalent Terse program (compilation from the lambda language into Terse). The lambda interpreter will not be presented here. It contains 21 rewrite rules (just to give an idea of its size). A typical lambda program is the popular one for computing the factorial function. In the lambda language, it looks like this (the lambda language variable in is always bound to the input to the lambda program):

```
letrec( f,
        lambda( x,
                if( =(var(x), number(0)),
                    number(1),
                    *(var(x), apply(var(f), -(var(x), number(1))))))),
        apply(var(f), var(in)))
```

In a conventional lambda calculus style, this program would be written as something like

$$\lambda input.(\underline{letrec}\ f = \lambda x.(\underline{if}\ x = 0\ \underline{then}\ 1\ \underline{else}\ x*f(x-1))\ \underline{in}\ f(input))$$

By letting T-mix specialize the lambda interpreter with respect to the factorial program above, we get a specialized interpreter. It looks like this (infix syntax has been used for the predefined operators =, * and -):

```
run-1(V)        —> app-2(V)
app-2(V)        —> cond-3(V = 0, V)
cond-3(true, V) —> 1
cond-3(false, V) —> V * app-2(V - 1))
```

An efficient and nice Terse program for computing the factorial function has been achieved. The time used to specialize the lambda interpreter was 1400 milliseconds (plus 620 milliseconds for garbage collection).

5.2 Self-interpreter example

A self-interpreter is an interpreter written in the same language as it interprets. By specializing a Terse self-interpreter with respect to a Terse program, one "compiles" from Terse into Terse.

Experience from the first mix project has shown that successful specialization of a self-interpreter is a central step towards successful self-application of a partial evaluator. To speak concretely of the T-mix case, the reason for this is that the T-mix function specializer has some central control structures in common with a Terse self-interpreter (the function specializer is a special "smart" kind of interpreter), although T-mix is significantly more complex. To put it in another way, if T-mix cannot specialize a self-interpreter successfully, then the chances of specializing T-mix itself successfully are very small.

When a Terse program is going to be used as input to another Terse program (the self-interpreter), it must be in the form of a ground term. Furthermore, since the self-interpreter has its own signature, the programs and the input data to them must be brought into a form based on that signature. It is thus necessary to *encode* programs and data. This increases the size of the interpreted program and its input, but only in a linear way.

The self-interpreter contains 38 rules. By specializing the self-interpreter with respect to the well-known append program, we get a Terse program equivalent to the append program (although the new program works on data in coded form). We unfortunately get a program containing no less than 68 (!) rules — this should be compared with the 3 rules (a goal rule and two append rules) of the original append program. The specialized program was produced in 5580 ms (plus garbage collection, 4020 ms).

An examination however shows that significant simplification of the 68-rule program is possible: a lot of calls only match one rule, but since a dynamic value is tested, the calls have not been unfolded. The problem can be overcome either by performing some "extra" unfolding in postprocessing, or by changing the function specializer in such a way that it will be able to unfold such a call.

The reduced version of the 68-rule program, produced by doing postprocessing (by hand), contains only 11 rules, so the reduction certainly is important. The 11-rule program still is not satisfactory when compared to the original append program. The left-hand side patterns in the append program appear in the 11-rule program as right-hand side calls to a predefined equal function; these calls are inherited from the self-interpreter which uses the equal function to implement the pattern matching. Each constructor appearing in a left-hand side of the append program is reflected by one equal call.

The conclusion is that T-mix is too weak to handle the self-interpreter. The unfolding methods (the transformation done during an unfolding) as well as the unfolding strategy (the decision of when to unfold) are too conservative. The implementation of the pattern matching needed in a Terse self-interpreter cannot be handled properly.

5.3 New results

In recent work (December 1987), specialization of a self-interpreter with respect to a program p has given the desired result: a program identical to p (except for variable names). The language used in these experiments differs from Terse in several ways and is rather close to REFAL ([Turchin86]):

1) it uses a fixed signature with one cons operator and atoms (LISP-like data structures) thus avoiding the need for encoding programs and data input to the self-interpreter;
2) rules are ordered and overlapping is allowed; this kind of language has been referred to as a *priority rewrite system* language in [Baeten et al. 87]; our language is restricted when comparing to [Baeten et al. 87]: as in Terse, function calls are explicit so redexes can be identified syntactically;
3) repeated variables are allowed in left-hand sides (the language is not linear).

The points 2) and 3) imply that no predefined equal function is needed.

The unfolding methods used in the new partial evaluator are significantly more complicated than the ones used in T-mix. They are similar to the *driving* used in supercompilation ([Turchin86]) and involve a full Prolog-like unification. Stage 2 variables are instantiated during unfolding, thus introducing "backwards unification" in the partial evaluator.

6. Conclusion

This project has been a practical experiment in partial evaluation, aiming at the eventual goal: a fully automated self-applicable partial evaluator for restricted term rewriting systems.

What has been learned?

The methods used in T-mix have been shown to work in practice on non-trivial examples (cf. the lambda interpreter example). Partially static data can be handled; a simple scheme is used for deciding upon unfoldability (and could easily be automated).

The language Terse seems to be a reasonable choice of a base language: it is strong and simple at the same time. The pattern matching based control structure gives a very simple and clean semantics. There are, however, some questionable points: the use of varying signatures, the disallowance of overlapping left-hand sides and the linearity (see section 5.3 for recent results).

The prototype implementation of Terse (not described in this paper) shows that the pattern matching can be implemented in a way that gives very good run time properties (matching without backtracking). The compile times are also small.

What remains to be done?

In order to achieve a self-applicable T-mix, the following has to be done:

1) the function specializer has to be written in Terse;
2) less conservative unfolding methods and strategy have to be implemented (this has recently been done for the language briefly described in section 5.3);
3) the binding time analyser must be implemented; the methods for marking "dangerous" dynamic right-hand side constructors have to be developed and implemented.

None of these problems seem impossible to solve, although it certainly will require a good deal of work to achieve the goal.

Acknowledgements

Several people have contributed to this work, but I want to thank especially three persons: Olivier Danvy and I have had many fruitful discussions. Also, Olivier's considerable LISP experience has been of great help to me. Torben Mogensen has given many suggestions about partial evaluation and implementation methods. My supervisor Neil D. Jones has come up with many of the "underlying" ideas. He has been very engaged in the project, and we have had numerous discussions.

I also want to thank: Peter Sestoft for answering numerous questions, Nils Andersen for teaching me how to use the Macintosh, the people sitting on the floor for having nice tea parties, and finally Elsbeth Teichert who patiently has been competing with partial evaluation for a long time!

References

[Baeten et al. 87]: J. C. M. Baeten, J. A. Bergstra and J. W. Klop:
"Term Rewriting Systems with Priorities",
Rewriting Techniques and Applications (ed. Pierre Lescanne),
Lecture Notes in Computer Science **256**, Springer-Verlag 1987, 83-94.

[Baren. et al. 87]: H. P. Barendregt, M. C. J. D. van Eekelen, J. R. W. Glauert, J. R. Kennaway, M. J. Plasmeijer and M. R. Sleep:
"Term Graph Rewriting",
Conference on Parallel Architectures and Languages, Europe, Eindhoven,
Lecture Notes in Computer Science **259**, Springer-Verlag 1987.

[Bondorf87]: Anders Bondorf:
"Towards a Self-applicable Partial Evaluator for Term Rewriting Systems",
Master's thesis, DIKU student report 87-6-9, Copenhagen, July 1987.

[Dershowitz85]: Nachum Dershowitz:
"Computing with Rewrite Systems", pp. 122-157 in
Information and Control **65**, 1985.

[Futamura71]: Yoshihiko Futamura:
"Partial Evaluation of Computing Process" — an Approach to a Compiler-Compiler",
Systems, Computers, Controls **2**, 5 (1971) 45-50.

[Hoare75]: C. A. R. Hoare:
"Recursive Data Structures",
International Journal of Computer and Information Sciences, **4**, No. 2, 1975.

[HuetOppen80]: Gérard Huet and Derek C. Oppen:
"Equations and Rewrite Rules, A Survey", pp. 349-405 in
Formal Language Theory, Perspectives and Open Problems
(ed. Ronald V. Book), Academic Press, 1980.

[Johnsson85]: Thomas Johnsson:
"Lambda Lifting: Transforming Programs to Recursive Equations",
pp. 165-180 in
Proceedings of the Workshop on Implementation of Functional Languages
(eds. Lennart Augustsson, John Hughes, Thomas Johnsson and Kent
Karlsson), Report 17, Göteborg, February 1985.

[Jones86]: Neil D. Jones:
"Flow Analysis of Lazy Higher Order Functional Programs",
DIKU report 86/15, University of Copenhagen, Denmark 1986.

[Jones87]: Neil D. Jones:
"Automatic Program Specialization: a Re-examination from Basic Principles",
in the North-Holland Publ. proceedings of the
Workshop on Partial and Mixed Computation, Denmark 1987.

[Launchbury87]: John Launchbury:
"Projections for Specialisation",
in the North-Holland Publ. proceedings of the
Workshop on Partial and Mixed Computation, Denmark 1987.

[Mix85]: Neil D. Jones, Peter Sestoft, Harald Søndergaard:
"An experiment in partial evaluation: The generation of a compiler generator."
Rewriting Techniques and Applications (ed. J.-P. Jouannaud),
Lecture Notes in Computer Science **202**, Springer-Verlag 1985, 124-140.

[Mix87]: Neil D. Jones, Peter Sestoft, Harald Søndergaard:
"Mix: A Self-applicable Partial Evaluator for Experiments in Compiler
Generation",
DIKU report 87/8, University of Copenhagen 1987,
to appear in the International Journal,
LISP AND SYMBOLIC COMPUTATION, Kluwer Academic Publishers.

[Mogensen87]: Torben Mogensen:
"Partially Known Structures in a Self-applicable Partial Evaluator",
in the North-Holland Publ. proceedings of the
Workshop on Partial and Mixed Computation, Denmark 1987.

[Reynolds72]: John C. Reynolds:
"Definitional Interpreters for Higher-Order Programming Languages",
ACM Annual Conference 1972, 717-740.

[Sestoft85]: Peter Sestoft:
"The structure of a self-applicable partial evaluator", pp. 236-256 in
Programs as Data Objects, Lecture Notes in Computer Science **217**,
Springer-Verlag 1986 (eds. Neil D. Jones and H. Ganzinger).

[Sestoft87]: Peter Sestoft:
"Automatic Call Unfolding in a Partial Evaluator",
in the North-Holland Publ. proceedings of the
Workshop on Partial and Mixed Computation, Denmark 1987.

[Turchin86]: Valentin F. Turchin:
"The concept of a supercompiler", pp. 292-325 in
ACM Transactions on Programming Languages and Systems, **8**, 3, July 1986.

Partial Evaluation and Mixed Computation
D. Bjørner, A.P. Ershov and N.D. Jones (Editors)
Elsevier Science Publishers B.V. (North-Holland)
IFIP, 1988

A THEORETICAL APPROACH TO POLYVARIANT MIXED COMPUTATION

Mikhail A. Bulyonkov

Computing Center
Siberian Division of the Academy of Sciences
Novosibirsk, USSR

A theoretical foundation of polyvariant mixed computation
is investigated. Four approaches to polyvariancy are
presented and their equivalence is proved.

1. INTRODUCTION

This paper deals with polyvariant mixed computation. Here we
consider mixed computation as partial evaluation, that is in a
more narrow sence than in [1]; and according to Futamura [2] we
define partial evaluation in its most general form - as a process
of adapting a program to its partially defined external
environment in order to obtain a more efficient program.
Efficiency in turn is considered in terms of execution time.

Our main goal is to give a formal ground and account of some
well-known models of polyvariant mixed computation and to compare
them rather than to invent a new method of mixed computation. The
fact is that the concept of polyvariancy was explicitly or
implicitly employed by many authors, whose polyvariant schemes
were rather different or not even explicit. We shall dwell on the
following methods of polyvariant mixed computation:
- *expansion method*, where the residual program is obtained by
  folding a potentially infinite tree of program protocols.
- *iterative method*, based on transitive closure principle. It
  maintains and updates a set of growth points which is a
  source of enlargement of the residual program.
- *transformational method*, where the original program is
  transformed into the residual program by a series of
  transformations.
- *preliminary analysis method*, where a global analysis of the
  original program is made first and the residual program is
  then generated on the basis of collected information.

The next principal constraint is that we restrict ourselves to
deterministic imperative programs, that is the programs, whose
execution process is uniquely defined by a sequence of changing
memory states. Nevertheless, our account is quite abstract, so we
hope that it is possible to expand the results on further classes
of programs.

The term "polyvariancy" was introduced by V.E.Itkin [3]. In his
definition of the deepest partial evaluation algorithm, Futamura
used a concept of a process tree. This approach was formalized by
A.P.Ershov and investigated later by T.A.Shaposhnikova. The
author's investigations dealt with the problems of correct mixed
computation for the class of programs with strict memory partition
into accessible and frozen parts and with finite set of accessible

memory states. Some elements of transformational approach can be found in B.N.Ostrovsky's work [6], which deals with algol-like programs; polyvariancy appears there mainly as a result of processing of conditionals with frozen conditions.

2. COMPUTATIONAL MODEL

First we need to define a computational model that on one hand would be powerful enough to present adequatly all the methods described above, and on the other hand - simple enough not to overload our treatment with redundant details and special cases.

Let $S=\{s\}$ be a set of *memory states*. We shall leave aside the definition of a memory state, as well as the question of existence of structure values and so on.

A *program* p is a quadruple $< V, v_0, f, l >$, where
 - V is an arbitrary (denumerable) set called a program *carrier*; its elements are called *nodes*.
 - v_0 is the *initial node* of p.
 - f : V -> (S -> S) is a function of memory transformation or simply a *transformer*.
 - l : V -> (S -> V) is a *succession function*.

For a program node v and the initial state s we define a *partial protocol*
$$prot(p,v,s) = <v^0,s^0>,<v^1,s^1>,\ldots,<v^i,s^i>,\ldots,$$
where
$$v^0 \equiv v, \quad s^0 = s$$
$$v^{i+1} = l(v^i)(s^i), \quad s^{i+1} = f(v^i)(s^i).$$

Let us define $Sprot(p,v,s) = s^0,s^1,\ldots$

Then for the initial state s we define a *computational protocol*
$$protocol(p,s) = prot(p,v_0,s)$$
 and $\quad Sprotocol(p,s) = Sprot(p,v_0,s).$

Two programs $p=<V,v_0,f,l>$ and $p'=<V',v_0',f',l'>$ are said to be equivalent ($p \sim p'$), if for any $s \in S$
$$Sprotocol(p,s) = Sprotocol(p',s).$$

The program nodes v_1 and v_2 are said to be p-equivalent ($v_1 \overset{p}{\approx} v_2$), if for any $s \in S$
$$Sprot(p,v_1,s) = Sprot(p,v_2,s).$$

Note that we simplified our treatment by not considering a predicate that defines programs termination. However, we can assume that appropriate indication is a part of the memory state an in case it has been set the transformers are considered equal. It doesn't matter much, especially as we consider rather strong equivalence defined by coincidence of *all* intermediate memory states from infinite protocol.

Two programs $p=<V,v_0,f,l>$ and $p'=<V',v_0',f',l'>$ are said to be *isomorphic* if there exists a one-to-one mapping I : V -> V' such that
$$I(v_0) = v_0',$$
$$f = f' \circ I,$$
$$I \circ l = l' \circ I.$$
(o means composition)

It is evident that isomorphic programs are equivalent.

3. ENVIRONMENTS

We shall not define concretely the concept of environment but shall rather fix the demands it has to meet. For example, a partial definition of variables as well as a system of inequalities, etc. can be considered as an environment. Let us use E for the set af all environments and e (maybe indexed) for environments themselves. The essential knowledge is correspondence between the concept of environment and the concept of memory state, that is our ability to answer efficiently whether a given memory state s is *acceptible* by given environment e

$$s \in e,$$

and how an environment is transformed while being transferred through program nodes. Thus we assume that the functions

$$f_E : V \rightarrow (E \rightarrow E) ,$$
$$l_E : V \rightarrow (E \rightarrow 2^V),$$

are defined and for any $v \in V$, $e \in E$, $s \in e$

$$f(v)(s) \in f_E(v)(e) ,$$
$$l(v)(s) \in l_E(v)(e) .$$

We should notice two significant points. The first one is that succession function returns a *set* of program nodes which is one of the sources of polyvariancy. The second one is that f_E and l_E are specified so that it is sufficient for these functions to *cover* the range of actual values of f and l. The more precisely we define these functions the higher quality of the result of polyvariant computation we obtain.

We suppose that there exists an efficiently decidable equivalence on environments (==), such that $e_1 == e_2$ if and only if the set of all states acceptible for e_1 and e_2 coincides.

The way of obtaining transformers f_e and succession functions l_e which are reductions on e of original transformers and functions is also considered known, and for any $s \in e$

$$f_e(v)(s) = f(v)(s),$$
$$l_e(v)(s) = f(v)(s).$$

This point reflects the hierarchial structure of mixed computation, since we assume that the solution of the initial problem is already known for lower level functions.

In the set of environments we shall distinguish the greatest and the least elements ($\perp$ and $\top$ respectively), such that for any $s \in S$

$$\neg(s \in \perp) , \qquad s \in \top$$

and for any v

$$f_E(v)(\perp) = \perp , \qquad l_E(v)(\perp) = \emptyset .$$

4. EXPANSIONS AND SOME OF THEIR PROPERTIES

Our further treatment requires some additional notations. Let V^* stand for a set of sequences of elements of V;

$$\alpha X = \{ \alpha\delta \mid \delta \in X\}, \quad \text{where} \quad \alpha \in V^*, \ X \subseteq V^* ;$$
$$[\alpha] : V \rightarrow V^* \text{ is such that } \forall v \in V \ [\alpha](v) = \alpha v$$

Definition. An *expansion* of a program $p = \langle V, v_0, f, l \rangle$ is a program $\bar{p} = \langle \bar{V}, v_0, \bar{f}, \bar{l} \rangle$, where

$\bar{V} = \bar{v}_0 V^*$ is a set of program node sequences which start with v_0, $\bar{v}_0$ is a one-element sequence v_0, an for any $v \in V$, $\alpha \in V^*$ such that $\alpha v \in \bar{V}$

$\bar{f}(\alpha v) = f(v)$

$\bar{l}(\alpha v) = [\alpha v] \circ l(v)$.

Statement 1. Expansion of a program p is equivalent to p.

Proof.
The proof is done by induction on protocol length.
Let for some s

$protocol(p,s) = \ldots, <v^i, s^i>, \ldots$

$protocol(\bar{p},s) = \ldots, <\alpha^i, \bar{s}^i>, \ldots$

Let us show that

$\alpha^i = \beta^i v^i$ for some β^i,

$\bar{s}^i = s^i$.

Induction base. From the definition of expansion it follows immediately that $\beta^0 = \varepsilon$ (the empty sequence) and from the definition of protocol - that $\bar{s}^0 = s^0 = s$.

Induction step.

$\begin{aligned}
\bar{s}^{i+1} &= \bar{f}(\alpha^i)(\bar{s}^i) && \text{- def. of protocol} \\
&= \bar{f}(\beta^i v^i)(\bar{s}^i) && \text{- induction hyp.} \\
&= f(v^i)(s^i) && \text{- def. of expansion} \\
&= s^{i+1} && \text{- def. of protocol.}
\end{aligned}$

Similarly

$\begin{aligned}
\alpha^{i+1} &= \bar{l}(\alpha^i)(\bar{s}^i) && \text{- def. of protocol} \\
&= \bar{l}(\beta^i v^i)(\bar{s}^i) && \text{- induction step} \\
&= \beta^i v^i l(v^i)(s^i) && \text{- def. of expansion} \\
&= \beta^i v^i v^{i+1} && \text{- def. of protocol.}
\end{aligned}$

So $\beta^{i+1} = \beta^i v^i$.

□

Lemma 1. Let $\bar{p}$ be an expansion of a program p with the carrier V. Then

$$\forall \alpha_1, \alpha_2 \in V^* \quad \forall v \in V \qquad \alpha_1 v \overset{\bar{p}}{\ell} \alpha_2 v.$$

Proof. The proof is done by induction on partial protocol length.
Let for some $s \in S$

$prot(\bar{p}, \alpha_1 v, s) = \ldots, <\alpha_1^i, s_1^i>, \ldots$

$prot(\bar{p}, \alpha_2 v, s) = \ldots, <\alpha_2^i, s_2^i>, \ldots$

Let us show that

$$s_1^i = s_2^i$$

and if $\alpha_1^i = \beta_1^i v^i$ then there exists β_2^i, such that

$$\alpha_2^i = \beta_2^i v^i$$

Induction base. From lemma's condition we have that $\beta_2^0 = \alpha_2$ and by definition of protocol $s_1^0 = s_2^0 = s$.

Induction step. Let $\alpha_1^i = \beta_1^i v^i$. Then

$$
\begin{aligned}
s_1^{i+1} &= \bar{f}(\alpha^i)(\bar{s}_1^i) && - \text{def. of protocol} \\
&= \bar{f}(\beta_1^i v^i)(s_2^i) && - \text{induction hyp.} \\
&= f(v^i)(s_2^i) && - \text{def. of expansion} \\
&= \bar{f}(\beta_2^i v^i)(s_2^i) && - \text{induction hyp.} \\
&= s_1^{i+1} && - \text{def. of protocol} \\
\alpha_1^{i+1} &= \bar{l}(\alpha^i)(\bar{s}_1^i) && - \text{def. of protocol} \\
&= \bar{l}(\beta_1^i v^i)(s_2^i) && - \text{induction hyp.} \\
&= \beta_1^i \, v^i \, l(v^i)(s_2^i) && - \text{def. of expansion}
\end{aligned}
$$

Similarly,

$$\alpha_2^{i+1} = \beta_2^i \, v^i \, l(v^i)(s_2^i),$$

So $v^{i+1} = l(v^i)(s_1^i)$ and $\beta_2^{i+1} = \beta_2^i v^i$.

$\square$

5. MERGE

For $v_1, v_2 \in V$ let $[v_1/v_2]$ be a function such that
$[v_1/v_2](v) = v$ whenever $v \neq v_1$,
$[v_1/v_2](v) = v_2$ when $v = v_1$.

Definition. For a program $p = \langle V, v_0, f, l \rangle$ and two of its nodes $v_1, v_2 \in V$ such that $v_1 \neq v_0$, a *merge* of v_1 and v_2 is a program
$\text{merge}(p, v_1, v_2) = \langle V, v_0, f, [v_1/v_2] \circ l \rangle$,
where succession function of p is replaced by its composition with $[v_1/v_2]$. As a result all transitions to v_1 turn out to be replaced by transitions to v_2; so v_1 becomes unaccessible.

Statement 2. For any program p and a pair of its p-equivalent nodes v_1, v_2
$\text{merge}(p, v_1, v_2) \sim p$.

Proof. Let $\tilde{p} = \text{merge}(p, v_1, v_2)$ and for some $s \in S$
$\text{protocol}(p, s) = \ldots \langle v^i, s^i \rangle, \ldots$
$\text{protocol}(\tilde{p}, s) = \ldots \langle \tilde{v}^i, \tilde{s}^i \rangle, \ldots$

Let us show by induction upon i that
$\tilde{v}^i \underset{p}{\approx} v^i$,
$\tilde{s}^i = s^i$.

Induction base is trivial since $\tilde{v}^0 = v^0 = v_0$ and $\tilde{s}^0 = s^0 = s$.

Induction step. By definition of protocol

$$\tilde{v}^{i+1} = [v_1/v_2] \ o \ l(\tilde{v}^i) \ (s^i)$$
$$v^{i+1} = l(v^i) \ (s^i)$$

So if $v^{i+1} = v_1$ then

$$\tilde{v}^{i+1} = v_2 \qquad \text{- by def. of } [v_1/v_2])$$

and

$$\tilde{v}^{i+1} \ \underset{\sim}{\rho} \ v^{i+1} \qquad \text{- by statement condition.}$$

But if $v^{i+1} \neq v_1$ then by definition of protocol

$$\tilde{v}^{i+1} \ \underset{\sim}{\rho} \ v^{i+1} .$$

Now the required equality $\tilde{s}^{i+1} = s^{i+1}$ follows immediately from the equivalence of $\tilde{v}^i$ и v^i.

$\square$

6. EXPANSION LABELLING

Let e_0 be a given initial environment of a program $p = \langle V, v_0, f, l \rangle$ and expansion $\bar{p} = \langle \bar{V}, \bar{v}_0, \bar{f}, \bar{l} \rangle$ is known.

Let's define a *labelling* M of $\bar{p}$'s nodes with environments as a function

$$M : \bar{V} \rightarrow E$$

such that

$$M(\bar{v}_0) = e_0 ,$$
$$\forall \alpha v v' \in \bar{V} ,$$
$$M(\alpha v v') = \begin{cases} f_E(v)(M(\alpha v)), & \text{if } v' \in l_E(v)(M(\alpha v)), \\ \bot, & \text{, otherwise.} \end{cases}$$

Statement 3. For any $e_0 \in E$, $s_0 \in e_0$, if M is a labelling of p's expansion for the initial environment e_0 and

$$protocol(p, s_0) = \ldots, \langle \alpha^i, s^i \rangle, \ldots$$

then

$$s^i \in M(\alpha^i) .$$

Proof: By induction on protocol length
Induction base. $s_0 \in e_0 = M(v_0) = M(\alpha^0)$

Induction step. Let $\alpha^i = \beta^i v^i$ for some β^i. Then

$$\alpha^{i+1} = \bar{l}(\alpha^i v^i)(s^i) \qquad \text{- by def. of protocol}$$
$$= \beta^i v^i l(v^i)(s^i)_i \qquad \text{- by def of expansion.}$$

By induction hypothesis $s^i \in M(\alpha^i)$ and by l_E properties

$$l(v^i)(s^i) \in l_E(v^i)(M(\alpha^i)) .$$

Therefore

$$s^{i+1} = \bar{f}(\beta^i v^i)(s^i) \qquad \text{- by def. of protocol}$$
$$= f(v^i)(s^i) \qquad \text{- by def. of expansion}$$
$$\in f_E(v^i)(M(\alpha^i)) \qquad \text{- by induction hyp. and def. of } f_E$$
$$= M(\alpha^{i+1}_{i+1}) \qquad \text{- by def. of expansion.}$$

$\square$

This statement shows correctness of definition of an expansion, that is for any execution of a program expansion the memory state in each point corresponds to this point's label.

Corollary. If $M(\alpha) = \bot$ and $s_0 \in e_0$, then α is inaccessible.

Let us introduce an equivalence relation $\underset{\tilde{M}}{\sim}$ among expansion nodes:

$$\alpha_1 \ \underset{\tilde{M}}{\sim} \ \alpha_2 \ \langle = \rangle \ \exists \beta_1, \beta_2 \in V', \ \exists v \in V$$

$$\alpha_1 = \beta_1 v \ \& \ \alpha_2 = \beta_2 v$$
$$\& \ M(\alpha_1^1) == M(\alpha_2^2)^2.$$

7. TRUNCATIONS

Definition. Let $\bar{p} = \langle \bar{V}, \bar{v}_0, \bar{f}, \bar{l} \rangle$ be an expansion of a program p. A truncation of $\bar{p}$ is a finite set $W \subset \bar{V}$ such that a set
$$\underline{W} = \{ \ \alpha \in \bar{V} \ | \ \forall \beta \in W \ \neg (\beta \leqslant \alpha) \}$$
is also finite. $\underline{W}$ is called a *base* of W.

Lemma 2. Let W be a truncation and $\alpha \in \underline{W}$. Then there exists $\delta \in V^*$ such that $\alpha \delta \in W$.

Proof. On the contrary, suppose that
$$\forall \delta \in V^* \quad \forall \beta \in W \quad \alpha \delta \neq \beta .$$
Since W is finite, and so is the set of prefixes of elements of W, then $\{ \ \alpha \delta \ | \ \delta \in V^* \ \}$ contains an infinite number of elements which are <u>not</u> prefixes of elements of W. Therefore W is not a truncation, and it's a contradiction.

□

Thus, informally, truncation "cuts" all infinite sequences, and its base consists of all prefixes of all its elements.

Example. Let
$$W_n = \{ \ \alpha \in \bar{V} \ | \ |\alpha| = n \ \} .$$
It is clear that W_n is a truncation and
$$\underline{W}_n = \{ \ \alpha \in \bar{V} \ | \ |\alpha| < n \ \} .$$

Given a set af all truncations one can naturally define a partial order on it induced by inclusion relation among truncation bases. It is obvious that in this ordering every descending chain is finite and therefore has the least element.

Definition. Let $\sim$ be an equivalence relation on a program p carrier. A truncation W is said to be *closed* if
$$\forall \alpha \in W \quad \exists \beta \in \underline{W} \quad : \ \alpha \sim \beta .$$

Theorem 1. If $\sim$ is an equivalence relation on $\bar{p}$'s carrier that splits $\bar{V}$ into finite set of equivalence classes $V_1, \ldots, V_n$, then there exists a truncation W closed under $\sim$ relation.

Proof. Let
$$m = \max_{i \leqslant n} \ \min_{\alpha \in V_i} \ |\alpha| .$$
Then the required truncation is W_{m+1}.

□

Note that the theorem gives only sufficient condition of closed truncation existence. Really, a truncation can be such that it "cuts off" an infinite set of equivalence classes, leaving in its base only a finite one.

8. EXPANSION METHOD

Now we are ready to describe a method of obtaining a residual program from an original program's expansion.

Let a program $p=<V,v_0,f,l>$ and an environment e_0 be given. Then the residual program is obtained as follows

Step 1. An expansion $\bar{p}=<\bar{V},\bar{v}_0,\bar{f},\bar{l}>$ (equivalent to original program by statement 1) is being obtained.

Step 2. Labelling M of $\bar{p}$ for the initial environment e_0 is being constructed.

Step 3. Minimum truncation W closed over $\underset{\widetilde{M}}{\sim}$ relation is being found.

Step 4. Merge($\bar{p},\alpha,\alpha'$) is being accomplished for all $\alpha \in W$ where $\alpha' \in \underline{W}$ and $\alpha \underset{\widetilde{M}}{\sim} \alpha'$. A program p' thus obtained is equivalent to the expansion by statement 2 and by definition of $\underset{\widetilde{M}}{\sim}$.

Step 5. For all $\alpha v \in \underline{W}$
$$f'(\alpha v) = f_{M(\alpha v)}(v),$$
$$l'(\alpha v) = [\alpha v]^v \circ l_{M(\alpha v)}(v),$$
are being defined. Validity of this step is ensured by statment 3 and by instantiation properties.

Step 6. All inaccessible nodes are being eliminated (that is nodes with $\perp$ label and the nodes that have prefixes from W). If a set thus obtained is denoted by V', then a residual program is declared to be
$$p' = <V',v_0,f',l'>.$$

Sufficient conditions of the finite residual program existence are given by theorem 1.

Minimality condition on step 3 is optional and is intended only to diminish the residual program's size. What is more, minimality of truncation, on the whole, doesn't ensure minimality of the residual program's size. Thus all the residual programs nondeterministically obtained by expansion method are equivalent but not necessarily isomorphic. A more extensive treatment of this problem will be given below.

Expansion method is interesting for it distinguishes contensive actions performed for program protocols represented in the expansion:

    (1) evaluation on environments (step 2)
    (2) forming a structure of the residual program (step 3,4)
    (3) instantiation of transformers and succession functions (step 5)
    (4) elimination of anaccessible branches (step 6)

It's important to note that each step is performed for the whole program. However, this method is hardly useful in practical application, since it deals with an infinite object - a program's expansion, but is rather a standard for comparison and justification of other methods.

9. ITERATIVE METHOD

Constructing a more practical algorithm one should naturally try to minimize the residual program's size by elimination of equivalent nodes. The following theorem shows the way of such elimination.

Theorem 2. It is possible to transform any truncation W closed under $\underset{\widetilde{M}}{\sim}$ into a closed truncation W' such that for any $\alpha_1,\alpha_2 \in \underline{W}'$
    $\neg(\alpha_1 \underset{\widetilde{M}}{\sim} \alpha_2)$.

Proof (a sketch). Let $\alpha_1,\alpha_2 \in \underline{W}$ be such that $\alpha_1 \underset{\widetilde{M}}{\sim} \alpha_2$. Without loss of generality we can assume that $\neg(\alpha_1 < \alpha_2)$. Let

$$W_{\alpha_1} = \{ \ \delta \in V^* \ | \ \alpha_1 \delta \in W \ \} \ ,$$
$$\Delta_{\alpha_1} = \{ \ \delta \in V^* \ | \ \alpha_1 \delta \in \underline{W} \ \} \ .$$

Consider a set

$$W' = (W \setminus \alpha_1 W_{\alpha_1}) \cup \alpha_2 W_{\alpha_1} \cup \{\alpha_1\} \ .$$

It is necessary to prove that W' is a closed truncation. It is easy to show that

$$\underline{W}' = (\underline{W} \setminus \alpha_1 \Delta_{\alpha_1}) \cup \alpha_2 \Delta_{\alpha_1} \ ,$$

from which it follows immediately that $\underline{W}' \subset \underline{W}$. Therefore $\underline{W}'$ is finite. The fact that W is closed follows from the fact that for any δ

$$\alpha_2 \delta \underset{M}{\sim} \alpha_1 \delta .$$

Thus we transformed a truncation reducing the power of its base by eliminating at least one of the equivalent nodes. This transformation can be repeated as long as there remains a pair of equivalent nodes.

$\square$

The fact of existence of a truncation with a base free of M-equivalent nodes leads to the idea of using a subset of a Cartesian product VxE as a residual program's carrier.

The essence of the algorithm given below is in iterative monotonic replentishment of a residual program's carrier along with simultaneous definition of memory state transformer and succession function for each new node. On each iteration a transformer and a succession function of some node are defined. So all successors of this node should be activated to mark that their attributes are to be defined on some further iteration. Initially the set of all active nodes contains the only element $\langle v_0, e_0 \rangle$. The iterative algorithm is

$$A = \{\langle v_0, e_0 \rangle\}, \quad P = \emptyset$$
$\underline{while} \ \underline{not} \ \underline{empty} \ A$
$\underline{do}$

$\qquad \underline{let} \ \langle v, e \rangle \in A$
$\qquad \underline{delete} \ \{\langle v, e \rangle\} \ \underline{from} \ A$
$\qquad \underline{if} \ \langle v, e \rangle \notin P$
$\qquad \underline{then}$

$\qquad\qquad \underline{add} \ \{\langle v, e \rangle\} \ \underline{to} \ P$
$\qquad\qquad e_1 = f_E(v)(e)$
$\qquad\qquad \underline{define}$

$\qquad\qquad\qquad f'(\langle v, e \rangle) = f_e(v)$
$\qquad\qquad\qquad l'(\langle v, e \rangle) = e_1^+ \circ l_e(v)$

$\qquad\qquad \underline{add} \ l_E(v)(e) \times \{e_1\} \ \underline{to} \ A$
$\qquad \underline{fi}$
$\underline{od}$
$\underline{result} \ \langle P, \langle v_0, e_0 \rangle, f', l' \rangle$

where for any $e \in E$ $e^+(v) = \langle v, e \rangle$.

The proof of correctness of this algorithm is based on the isomorphism I between its residual program and the result of the expansion method. To construct such an isomorphism we instill in the program of the iterative algorithm some actions, that do not alter its data flow, and then establish some invariant relations between original and instilled variables.

```
A = {<v₀,e₀>},    AA = {v̄₀}, define M(v̄₀) = e₀
P = ø,            PP = ø,  SS = ø
while not empty A
do
        let <v,e>∈A,
        Δ = { δv∈AA | M(δv)=e }
        delete {<v,e>} from A
        delete Δ from AA
        add Δ to SS
        if <v,e>∉P
        then
                let αv∈Δ
                define I(<v,e>) = αv
                add {<v,e>} to P
                add {αv} to PP
                e₁ = f_E(v)(e)
                define
                        f'(<v,e>) = f_e(v)
                        f"(αv)    = f_e+(v)
                        l'(<v,e>) = e₁ o l_e(v)
                        l"(αv)    = [αv] o l_e(v)
                add l_E(v)(e) x {e₁} to A
                delete {αv} from SS
                add {αvv'| v'∈l_E(v)(e)} to AA
                add {αvv'| v'∉l_E(v)(e)} to SS
                for all v'∈V define
                        M(αvv') = if v'∈l_E(v)(e)
                                  then e₁
                                  else ⊥ fi
        fi
od
result <P,<v₀,e₀>,f',l'>
```

It is easy to see that the definition of M coincides with the definition of expansion labelling, while the definition of transformers and succession functions coincides with their definition in the expansion method.

Let us prove validity of the loop invariant represented as the conjunction of the following assertions:

I.   ∃ <v,e>∈A <=> ∃ αv∈AA : M(αv) = e
II. ∃ <v,e>∈P <=> ∃ αv∈PP : M(αv) = e
III. AA ⊔ SS is a truncation
IV. ∀ α∈SS M(α)≠⊥ => ∃ β∈PP : α$\underset{M}{\sim}$β

These assertions are evidently the loop preconditions. Validity of assertions I and II follows from the fact that in then-clause each re-evaluation of A corresponds to re-evaluation of AA (P and PP respectively). Assertion III is based on a trivial lemma

Lemma 3. If W is a truncation and α∈W then
        (W \ {α}) ⊔ {αv | v∈V}
is also a truncation.

Since an element with a non-⊥ label is added to SS only if it is already in P (and, therefore, by assertion II, in PP) assertion IV is also valid.

A postcondition of the loop implies that A is an empty set, and so is AA (by assertion I), while SS is a truncation (by assertion III). Assertion IV ensures that each element of SS with non-$\perp$ label has a M-equivalent node in <u>SS</u>. The elements with $\perp$ label are unaccessible and are eleminated by the expansion method.

The required coreeespondence between state transformers and sucession functions obtained by the two methods follows naturally from their definition.

Thus the difference between the iterative and the expansion methods is that the program obtained by the iterative method does not contain equivalent nodes (since it processes a Cartesian product) and that the iterative method cuts off the unaccessible branches at once.

10. TRANSFORMATIONAL METHOD

A distinctive feature of the iterative method is that the residual program becomes completely defined only at the moment of the algorithm's termination. The reason is that it is impossible to define a succession function of a newly added element, because it may not have its successors yet.

Transformational method allows to obtain the residual program from the original one by a series of local transformations; at each step the program remains completely defined and is equivalent to the original program to within the environment. Thus the transformational method treats a program not as an argument of the algorithm but rather as a "workpiece" for obtaining the result.

In our description of the transformational algorithm we shall use a simple trick which allows to give a transformational interpretation of the iterative method.

Let a program $p = <V, v_0, f, l>$ and an initial environment e_0 be given. We shall substitute the original program by the isomorphic one by attaching to each node a $\top$ sign, that stands for the environment that accepts any memory state. So the program will be
$$<V', v_0', l', f'>,$$
where
$$V' = V \times \{\top\},$$
$$v_0' = <v_0, \top>$$
and for any $v \in V$
$$l'(<v, \top>) = \top^+ \ o \ l(v),$$
$$f'(<v, \top>) = f(v).$$

A canonical form of the transformational algorithm is

```
        A = {<v_0,e_0>}    P = ∅
        while not empty A
        do
                let <v,e>∈A
                delete {<v,e>} from A
                if <v,e>∉P
                then
                        add {<v,e>} to P
                        add {<v,e>} to V'
                        e_1 = f_E(v)(e)
```

$$\underline{\text{define}}$$
$$f'(<v,e>) = f_e(v)$$
$$l'(<v,e>) = e_1^+ \circ l_e(v)$$
$$\underline{\text{add}}\ l_E(v)(e) \times \{e_1\}\ \underline{\text{to}}\ A$$
$$\underline{\text{add}}\ l_E(v)(e) \times \{e_1\}\ \underline{\text{to}}\ V'$$
$$\underline{\text{for all}}\ v' \in (l_E(v)(e) \times \{e_1\}) \setminus P$$
$$\underline{\text{define}}$$
$$f'(<v,e_1>) = f_{e_1}(v)$$
$$l'(<v,e_1>) = \top^{+1} \circ l_{e_1}(v)$$

$$\underline{\text{fi}}$$
$$\underline{\text{od}}$$
$$\underline{\text{result}}\ <V',<v_0,e_0>,f',l'>$$

A residual program thus obtained is equivalent to the residual program obtained by the iterative method, though it possibly contains some inaccessible nodes. This assertion is based on the fact that P is always a subset of V'. It also permits to conclude that inaccessible are exactly the nodes of the form $<v,\top>$, which never get into P.

It is easy to check that on each iteration a program remains completly defined, since transformers and succession functions of the new nodes added to V' are being defined all at once. Therefore, a loop body can be considered as definition of a transformation which adds a new node to a program. Such a treatment makes it possible to get rid of an algorithm's functionality. Really, a test for the emptiness of a set of active nodes becomes optional for the algorithm termination. Generally speaking, any transitional state can be declared as a residual program. Besides it becomes possible to vary the choice of the next active node and the depth of mixed computation. For example, if it is known that processing of some node leads to excessive growth of the residual program, then the node is simply removed from the set of active nodes and original program nodes become its successors.

11. PRELIMINARY ANALYSIS METHOD

In contrast to the expansion method the iterative and the transformational methods have one thing in common, namely, that for each node of the residual program all actions are made at once. But the alternative approach, when at first some preliminary analysis of the original program is made (that corresponds to step 2 of the expansion method) and then a program is transformed on the basis of collected information, is also interesting.

The preliminary analysis objective is definition of the set of all possible environments for every program node, i.e. to construct for a program $p=<V,v_0,f,l>$ and an environment e_0 a labelling
$$Poss : V \to 2^E,$$
such that
$$e_0 \in Poss(v_0),$$
$$\forall v \in V\quad e \in Poss(v) \Rightarrow \forall v' \in l_E(v)(e)\quad f_E(v)(e) \in Poss(v').$$

The next statement establishes the correspondence between this problem with construction of the expansion labelling.

Statement 5. If M is the labelling of the expansion of a program $p=<\bar{V},v_0,\bar{f},\bar{l}>$ for the initial environment e_0, then *Poss* function can be defined as follows

$$Poss(v) = \{ e \mid \exists \; \alpha v \in \bar{V} : M(\alpha v)=e \}$$

Proof. $M(v_0)=e_0$ by definition, so $e_0 \in Poss(v_0)$. Now let $e \in Poss(v)$. Then by definition of *Poss*

$$\exists \; \alpha v \in V : M(\alpha v) = e.$$

Therefore by definition of M

$$\forall v' \in l_E(v)(e) \quad M(\alpha v v') = f_E(v)(e)$$

and $\quad \forall v' \in l_E(v)(e) \quad f_E(v)(e) \in Poss(v').$

$\square$

Solution of the preliminary analysis problem is given by the following algorithm, which in fact is an algorithm of a global analysis problem [7].

$$A = \{<v_0,e_0>\}$$
<u>while not empty</u> A
<u>do</u>
   <u>let</u> $<v,e> \in A$
   <u>delete</u> $\{<v,e>\}$ <u>from</u> A
   <u>if</u> $e \notin Poss(v)$
   <u>then</u>
     <u>add</u> $\{e\}$ <u>to</u> $Poss(v)$
     <u>add</u> $l_E(v)(e) \times \{f_E(v)(e)\}$ <u>to</u> A
   <u>fi</u>
 <u>od</u>

Correctness of this algorithm is proved in the same way as for the iterative method.

Statement 5 makes it possible to describe the residual program carrier more precisely

$$\bigcup_{v \in V} \{ <v,e> \mid e \in Poss(v) \}.$$

Transformers and succession function are defined in the same way as in the iterative algorithm.

12. CONCLUSIONS

In this paper we described several different approaches to the concept of polyvariant evaluation. The reason for polyvariancy to be a basic component of mixed computation is that a partially defined external environment of a program accepts a number of initial memory states, thus generating a set of computational protocols. Therefore we made an attempt to extract a "pure" polyvariancy by splitting a mixed computation process in two stages: (1) bringing accessible information into program by transforming its structure, an (2) program's subsequent optimization, which by this time has nothing to do with the *external* environment. The range of possible optimizations can be wide and include optimizations specific for mixed computation, classical optimizations and the ones defined by particular sphere of application of mixed computation.

ACKNOWLEDGEMENTS

I am grateful to A.P.Ershov for formulating the problem discussed
in the paper. I also thank Guntis Barzdin for stimulating
discussions. Finally, I owe a great deal to my wife Ann for help
in translating the paper into English.

REFERENCES

[1] **Ershov A. P.** On essence of compilation. In: E.J.Neuhold (ed.),
     Formal description of programming concepts, North-Holland,
     Amsterdam - New York - Oxford, 1977, pp.391-420.

[2] **Futamura Y.** Partial evaluation of programs // RIMS Symposia on
     Software Science and Engineering. Kyoto 1982 proceedings. E
     Goto et al. Lect. Notes in Comp. Sci., 1983. - Vol.147. -
     P.1-35.

[3] **Itkin V. E.** On partial and mixed computation. In: Program
     optimization and transformation. A.P.Ershov (ed.). Part I,
     pp.17-30. Novosibirsk: Computing Center of the Sibirian
     Division of the Academy of Sciences 1983 (in Russian).

[4] **Futamura Y.** Partial evaluation of computation process - an
     approach to a compiler-compiler // Systems - Computers -
     Controls, 1971.- Vol.2. - N.5. - P.45-50.

[5] **Bulyonkov M. A.** Polyvariant mixed computation for analyzer
     programs. - Acta Informatica, 1984, vol.21, Fasc.5, p.473-484.

[6] **Ostrovsky B. N.** Obtaining language-oriented parsers
     systematically by mixed computation. In: Translation and
     program models. I.V.Pottosin (ed.), pp.69-80. Novosibirsk:
     Computing Center of the Sibirian Division of the Academy of
     Sciences 1980 (in Russian).

[7] **Kam J. B., Ullman J. D.** Monotone data flow analysis frameworks
     // Acta Informatica, 1977. - Vol.7, Fasc.3. - P.305-318.

Partial Evaluation and Mixed Computation
D. Bjørner, A.P. Ershov and N.D. Jones (Editors)
Elsevier Science Publishers B.V. (North-Holland)
IFIP, 1988

HOW DO AD-HOC COMPILER CONSTRUCTS APPEAR IN UNIVERSAL
MIXED COMPUTATION PROCESSES?

Mikhail A. BULYONKOV, Andrei P. ERSHOV

Computing Center
Novosibirsk 630090
USSR

An autoprojector of a simple imperative language is
described. The autoprojector is powerfull enough to
produce formally a compiler generator. The essence of
specific compilation constructs such as symbol table,
control stack, code generation patterns and so on is
investigated. A correlation between program decomposition and mixed computation is shown.

1. INTRODUCTION

The fundamental relation between compilation and mixed computation is expressed by the Futamura projections [1]. Let $mix(F,X,Y)$
be a mixed computation processor for an implementation language L
programmed in the same language (autoprojector) where P is a
program in L, X and Y are bound and free arguments of P, respectively. The result of application of mix to its arguments

$$mix(p,x,Y)=p_x(Y),$$

where $p_x(Y)$ is a program in L with the argument Y, is called a
residual program or a projection of p onto x. It satisfies the
identity

$$p_x(y)=p(x,y).$$

Let, further, $C=(SEM,P,D)$ be a class of source languages where
$SEM=\{sem\}$ is the set of language semantics described by interpreters programmed in L, $P=\{p\}$ is the set of programs in a specific
source language sem and $D=\{d\}$ is the set of data of a specific
source program p.

The general formulation of the compilation problem for the class
C is this: to describe a method (compiler compiler) cocom(SEM,
P,D) which allows for every language sem to develop systematically a compiler comp(P,D) which for every program p generates
its object code ob(p) in some object subset of the implementation language L.

Then, the following relations hold:

$$ob(D)=mix(sem,p,D)=sem_p(D) \tag{F1}$$

$$comp(P,D)=mix(mix,sem,(P,D))=mix_{sem}(P,D) \tag{F2}$$

$$cocom(SEM,P,D)=mix(mix,mix,(SEM,P,D))=mix_{mix}(SEM,P,D) \tag{F3}$$

or, verbally:

˙the object code is the interpreter   projection onto the source
 program;

˙the compiler is the autoprojector projection onto the language
 interpreter;

˙the compiler compiler is the autoprojector projection onto
 itself.

These relations found by Futamura [2], Ershov [3] and Turchin [4]
became a common commodity after their discussion in the 1977 IFIP
Working Conference [5]. Though the problem of systematic development of a compiler from a formal language description has a
rather extensive literature and the compiler compiler notion was
coined even in the early 1960-ies [6] the mixed computation concept has given a new thrust to this important systems programming
problem.

The great attractiveness of Futamura projections is in their
fundamentality, regularity and automatism.

On the other hand, direct application of the strict mixed computation schemes gives nothing interesting: because of excessive
suspensions, residual programs appear to be almost identical to
initial ones. Mixed computation does not make the compilation
problem trivial, it just suggests new directions to its solution
and, especially, to its correctness proof.

The first model example of obtaining a translational semantics
from an interpretive one by means of mixed computation was presented in [5]. The F3 projection was not used; its equivalent
referred to as "generating extension" was introduced informally,
ad hoc, and some subtle points dealing with procedure expansions
and name globalization have not been properly treated.

The work [5] stimulated a broader study of generating extension
as a method of compiler development from its operational semantics. This study has resulted in a PhD thesis [7] and a subsequent publication [8]. The Vienna definition language (VDL) was
used as an implementation language. The generating extension
procedure contains many ad hoc restrictions, the source language
interpreter requires a preliminary marking of executed and suspended actions, there is no indication of implementation of the
generating extension processor.

A promising experiment on obtaining a compiler from an interpreter using F3 and F2 is described in [9]. An applicative subset
of Lisp and a simple imperative language are taken as implementation and source languages, respectively. The projected program
also requires a preliminary marking. The experience shows a
considerable speed-up of the object code and compiler performance as compared with that of pure interpretation. The authors
of the report make a remark that, in their opinion, it is difficult task to implement F3 and F2 projections for an imperative
implementation language.

In all works we comment on, an integrative approach prevails,
aimed to establish a mere fact of autoprojector implementability
and its applicability to compilation. In our study, we are trying

to make a step a bit further.

We describe a new autoprojector scheme that implements mixed computation for a class of programs in which the accessible memory domain becomes finitely defined after partial argument binding and the partition of memory onto accessible and suspended parts does not change during computation [10]. In the limits of this class of so called analyzer programs we may resolve the fundamental contradiction between depth and finiteness of mixed computation, not imposing restrictions which are necessary in the strict mixed computation scheme or in various variants of specialized mixed computation.

Our particular interest is in the question how on the way of transforming by means of a universal mechanism of mixed computation an interpreter into a compiler the latter possesses structures which are specific for the compilation technique.

Let us explain our goal in more details. The compiler is one of the most elaborated components of system programming. Its fundamentality is constantly accompanied by a family of special methods and techniques found each in its time and aimed at raising the compilation efficiency. None of universal compiler development schemes can compete with a tailored compiler production if it will not generate in its womb those structures which characterize a well developed and efficient compilation scheme and this is so far a heel of Achilles of every compiler compiler.

That is why there are many questions which can be asked by every compiler designer of a mixed computation advocate. Not pretending to be complete we shall list some of them. All these questions are about a compiler obtained by means of an autoprojector.

1. How do compilation phases appear in a compiler and, in particular, parsing and generation phases?

2. Is the single pass compilation primary or secondary?

3. If the single pass scheme is fundamental, where does it get from special techniques that make single pass processing possible (in particular, indirect addressing of labels and variables)?

4. How do object code templates appear in the generation phase?

5. How does the symbol table appear in the compiler?

6. How does the stack appear in the compiler?

7. Is it possible to obtain a reasonable compiler from a denotational or transformational semantics of the source language by means of mixed computation?

8. Where does the compiler take its operationality: from the mixed computation processor or the interpreter? If the compiler takes it from both then in what extent from each?

9. Is it possible to get an identical object code from compilers corresponding to two different interpreters: recursive and one-loop?

10. In other words: what is the real invariant of various types of semantics which is maintained by the compiler?

In order to achieve a necessary purity in answering these questions we adopt the following methodological principle. An author of the source language semantics has the right to know that he writes it to be used in mixed computation. A compiler designer has the right to know that an autoprojector will be used to obtain the compiler. However, no author of an autoprojector have the right to know what is the compilation technique. All the structures implemented in an autoprojector has to be inherent for the mixed computation concept.

2. THE AUTOPROJECTOR

Let us describe an implementation language (IL) for which and in which the autoprojector will be written. The language will be underdefined but this does not preclude the necessary concretization all key points of the presentation.

The IL program is a sequence of compulsorily labelled instructions with a singled out entry label. The textual order of instructions is unimportant since every instruction appoints a successor explicitly yielding its label. Each instruction consists of two parts: the action and the designator:

$\langle$instruction$\rangle$::=$\langle$action$\rangle$ **goto** $\langle$designator$\rangle$

where

$\langle$action$\rangle$::=$\langle$assignment$\rangle$|$\langle$call$\rangle$|$\langle$print$\rangle$|**stop**|$\langle$empty$\rangle$.

The designator is an expression, either conditional or unconditional, whose values are program labels. The **stop** instruction has the undefined designator ω.

All details of data structuring are hidden in access functions so it is sufficient to admit that all data are called by their names. All the data names occuring in a program constitute its memory.

Mixed computation in IL is defined for a class of so-called analyzer programs with the following postulated properties:

1) a partition of the program memory into bound, accessible and suspended (inaccessible) memories is given before the computation;

2) the bound memory is loaded before the computation and not changed during the computation;

3) the set of names forming the accessible memory does not change during the computation;

4) for every load of the bound memory the set of accessible memory states is finite;

5) every access function for the bound memory is completely and uniquely defined by an accessible memory state.

REMARK. The real restrictions are postulates 3) and 4). The
third postulate emphasizes that the accessible memory is used
mainly for processing information from the bound memory; the
influence of suspended variables on the accessible memory is
restricted. In universal strict mixed computation schemes the
accessible memory is usually narrowed (see, e.g. [11]) during
computation. The fourth postulate is usually valid for various
program processors: if a processed program is given then the
domains of working variables of the processor are confined by
subsets of the general set of program elements. The fifth postulate restricts the influence of suspended variables on acces-
sibility of the bound memory.

In [9] a mixed computation algorithm for analyzer program is described which is based on a theoretical unwinding construction.
Unwinding a processed program means its copying in a number of
copies equal to the cardinality of the set of accessible memory
states. The meaning of this unwinding is that every program copy
is executed for its own single memory state. If the action of an
instruction C is an assignment transforming the i-th accessible
memory state into the j-th state then the designated successor of
the instruction C is taken from the j-th copy of the program.
After all possible reductions, the unwinded program is reduced
to a residual program which contains only the operations with
suspended variables.

The real organization of mixed computation of analyzer programs
is much more economical. Let us relate to a given program a
graph whose vertices are accessible memory states. If a memory
state j can be computed from a state i then the graph contains
an (i,j)-arc. For a given bound memory load, the set of computable memory states is then found as the transitive closure of the
accessible memory initial state. It is the transitive closure
procedure on which the mixed computation processor for analyzer
IL programs is based.

We shall make explanatory comments to the IL autoprojector (i.e.
an IL program of the mixed computation processor for IL) shown
at Fig.1. A program which is the autoprojector input is called
a processed program. The processed program is a vector subscrip-
ted by processed program labels. Vector components are program
instructions represented by a three-field structure: the action
(performed by the instruction), the source (if the action is an
assignment) and the designator (a designating expression which
appoints the successor). A syntactic predicate <u>newst</u> (new state)
is defined for each instruction which distinguishes assignments
to accessible memory elements (i.e. points of state transition)
from other instructions.

Every iterative algorithm of transitive closure type maintains
two sets of corresponding graph vertices: a set A of active
vertices and a set P of passed vertices. The set P is empty at
the beginning and only grows. The set A contains the initial
vertices at the beginning and, at each processing step, returns
the processed vertex to the set P and receives direct successors
of the processed vertex. In the IL autoprojector, these sets
are subsets of the direct product of the program label set by
the set of accessible memory states. An element of the direct
product corresponds to an instruction labelled by the given label
and performed on the given memory state.

```
0: A:={(Πentry,ω)}; P:=∅ goto 1
1: STEP(A,P,a)goto 2
2: goto if a=empty then B else 3
3: ST:=st of a; print(a":")goto 4
4: LAB:=lab of a goto 5
5: goto if newst(LAB)then 6 else 8
6: print("goto" RED(ST,designator of Π[LAB])
              RED(ST,source of Π[LAB]))goto 7
7: S:=POSS(ST,source of Π[LAB])goto A
8: print(REDIN(ST,action of Π[LAB])"goto"
        RED(ST,designator of Π[LAB])ST)goto 9
9: S:={ST}goto A
A: A:=AUPOSSLAB(ST,designator of Π[LAB])×S goto 1
B: stop goto ω
comment: actions in 0 and 3 are combined for the sake of brevity
```

FIGURE 1
The IL autoprojector

The further explanation will be given as comments to autoprojector instructions numbered hexadecimally.

Arguments of the IL autoprojector are a vector Π[M] of the processed program where M is the set of its labels and a variable
Πentry which is equal to the entry label. The processed program
is loaded before the autoprojector starts. The partition of
the processed program memory into bound, accessible and suspended
parts is specified as a tuning of hidden syntactical predicates
defined over program variable names and distinguishing these
sorts of the memory.

Instruction 0. Initialization. The set of active states is a
singleton corresponding the undefined accessible memory state at
the program start.

Instruction 1. Call to an auxiliary procedure STEP dealing with
the sets A and P and a variable a whose values are elements of
the set A and a special symbol empty. If A is empty then a gets
empty as its value. While A is nonempty, its elements are
deleted from it until an element which does not belong to P is
found. This element is assigned to a as a result and is added
to P as well.

Instruction 2. It completes the autoprojector work when the
active state set is exhausted.

Instruction 3. The variable ST (state) contains a current accessible memory state. According the general method, the residual
program is obtained from the initial program multiplied N times
where N is the number of accessible memory states. If the processed program instructions are listed columnwise then the
unwinded program is an (M×N)-matrix in which a column corresponds

to a certain accessible memory state. Each instruction (matrix element) of the unwinded program is labelled by the concatenation of the corresponding element coordinates (processed program label, accessible memory state) that is exactly a textual representation of the processed (current) element of the active element set (the variable a value). The processing of the current active state results in construction of the corresponding residual program instruction. The instruction is formed as concatenation of the text yielded by the <u>print</u> instruction. The argument of a <u>print</u> instruction is a concatenation of concrete literal constants (quoted) and values of literal variables and expressions used as the instruction's parameters. The concatenation operation has no explicit sign and is shown by juxtaposition. The <u>print</u> action in Instruction 3 prints a textual representation of the value of a followed by a colon (i.e. the label of the instruction to be formed).

Instruction 4. The variable LAB (label) takes as value the label of the current processed program instruction.

Instruction 5. The syntactic predicate <u>newst</u> distinguishes two variants of the residual program instruction formation: the case when the corresponding processed program instruction computes a new accessible memory state (Instructions 6 and 7) and the case when the instruction preserves the memory state (Instructions 8 and 9).

Instruction 6. The residual program instruction has the empty action because the processed program action is performed during mixed computation so only designator formation is needed. Since residual program label is a pair (processed program label, accessible memory state), the designator id formed as a concatenation of two expressions: the first one yields a processed program label and the second one yields the new accessible memory state. Both expressions are reductions of those from the processed program. Reduction is performed by an auxiliary operation RED(C,E) which reduces an expression E on a accessible memory state C. The first member of the concatenation reduces the designator of the processed program instruction and the second one reduces the expression which evaluates the new accessible memory state.

Instruction 7. This instruction uses another auxiliary operation POSS(C,E) which yields the set of all possible accessible memory states which might appear as values of an expression E on an accessible memory state C. The operation POSS yields a set rather than one state because, due to suspended variables, E may be irreducible to a constant. On the other hand, the analyzer program properties postulate that in such a case the extent in which the expression remains undefined is restricted by a finite known set evaluated by POSS(C,E).

Instruction 8. This instruction forms a residual program instruction which preserves the accessible memory state. The reduced action of the processed program instruction goes to print. Reduction of constituent expressions of the action is performed by an auxiliary operation REDIN (reduction of instruction). The reduced action is followed by a designator which is the concatenation of the reduced designator of the processed program instruction with the current accessible memory state.

Instruction 9. This instruction loads the variable S by the current accessible memory state.

Instruction A. This instruction concludes the processing of the current active state replenishing the set A of active states by the labels of all possible successors of the constructed residual program instruction. This replenishment is found as the direct product of the set of possible values of the processed program instruction designator evaluated on the current accessible memory state (yielded by an auxiliary operation POSSLAB (possible labels) by the set of possible new accessible memory states (given by the variable S).

3. THE GENERATING EXTENSION PROCESSOR

The IL autoprojector, looking quite simple, has a high "resolving power" as noted in [9]. We shall discuss its capabilities with respect to compilation in the next section but note at the moment that a crucial test of an autoprojector's efficiency is evaluation of its projection onto itself (projection F3). The bound memory for the IL autoprojector is the processed program Π and its entry label Πentry. The only accessible variable is LAB. If Π is loaded by the autoprojector program text then the set of accessible memory states will be labels $\{0,1,\ldots,9,A,B\}$. Thus, the residual program will form a (12×13)-matrix.

For those who would wish to reproduce the projection F3, we shall hint on some specific properties of the REDIN and RED reductions (using RED(S,E) as example):

a) RED advances if S bound and E contains variables occuring in S. In this case such variables are substituted for their values taken from the state S;

b) RED is suspended if S is suspended and E contains variables from the bound memory or those occuring in S;

c) RED is applied and yields either a reduced E if it contains constant terms or non-reduced E if the latter has no information links with variables from S.

It is known from [5] that the projection of an autoprojector onto itself, when applied to a program P(X,Y), works as a generating extension processor G which constructs for P its generating extension GP satisfying the following equality

$$GP(a,Y)=P_a(Y)$$

In the same paper [5] an example of the generating extension of a power function program ($y=x^N$) has been given (for x suspended and N bound). In IL notation the program is this:

```
bound memory N,
accessible memory n,
suspended memory x,y,

start:  n:=N goto init
 init:  y:=1 goto loop
 loop:  goto if n>0 then body else basta
```

```
   body:   goto if odd(n) then yx else xx
     yx:   y:=y×x goto substr
  substr:   n:=n-1 goto xx
     xx:   x:=x×x goto divn
   divn:   n:=n/2 goto loop
  basta:   stop goto ω
```

The generating extension of the program according to [5] has the following form (edited according to IL rules):

```
      start:   n:=N goto start-lab
  start-lab:   LAB:="m0" goto init
       init:   print(LAB":y:=1 goto" next(LAB)) goto next-init
  next-init:   LAB:=next(LAB) goto loop
       loop:   goto if n>0 then body else basta
       body:   goto odd(n) then yx else xx
         yx:   print(LAB":y:=y×x goto" next(LAB)) goto next-yx
    next-yx:   LAB:=next(LAB) goto substr
     substr:   n:=n-1 goto xx
         xx:   print(LAB":x:=x×x goto" next(LAB)) goto next-xx
    next-xx:   LAB:=next(LAB) goto divn
       divn:   n:=n/2 goto loop
      basta:   print(LAB":stop goto ω") goto next-basta
 next-basta:   stop goto ω
```

Here LAB is a literal variable storing a current label of the residual program instruction to be generated, next(LAB) is a next label generator.

The generating extension of the power function program obtained by means of the generating extension processor and some further trivial optimization, such as deletion of transit goto's and merging of equivalent instructions is shown at Fig.2.

Both generating extensions for N=5 produce identical (except for choice of names) residual programs.

According to [5]

According to this paper
(transit goto's with empty
action are deleted)

```
m0:   y:=1 goto m1                 init5:   y:=1 goto yx5
m1:   y:=y×x goto m2                 yx5:   y:=y×x goto xx4
m2:   x:=x×x goto m3                 xx4:   x:=x×x goto xx2
m3:   x:=x×x goto m4                 xx2:   x:=x×x goto yx1
m4:   y:=y×x goto m5                 yx1:   y:=y×x goto xx0
m5:   x:=x×x goto m6                 xx0:   x:=x×x goto basta 0
m6:   stop goto ω                 basta0:   stop goto ω
```

```
0ω:        A:={(start,ω)}, P:=∅ goto 1ω
1ω:        STEP(A,P,a) goto 2ω
2ω:        goto if a=empty then Bω else 3ω
3ω:        ST:=st of a; print(a":") goto 4ω
4ω:        goto 5 lab of a
5start:    print("goto init" RED(ST,"N"))
           S:=POSS(ST,"N")
           A:=AU{init} × S goto 1ω
5init:     print("y:=1 goto loop" ST)
           S:={ST}
           A:=AU{body} × S goto 1ω
5loop:     print("goto" if ST>0 then "body" else "basta" ST)
           S:={ST}
           A:=AU{if ST>0 then body else basta } × S goto 1ω
5body:     print("goto" if odd(ST) then "yx" else "xx" ST)
           S:={ST}
           A:=AU{if odd(ST) then yx else xx } × S goto 1ω
5yx:       print("y:=y*x goto substr" ST)
           S:={ST}
           A:=AU{substr} × S goto 1ω
5substr:   print("goto xx" (ST-1))
           S:={(ST-1)}
           A:=AU{xx}×S goto 1ω
5xx:       print("x:=x*x goto divn" ST)
           S:={ST}
           A:=AU{divn}×S goto 1ω
5divn:     print("goto loop" (ST/2))
           S:={(ST/2)}
           A:=AU{loop}×S goto 1ω
5xx:       print("stop goto ω" ST)
           S:={ST}
           A:=AU∅×S goto 1ω
Bω:        stop goto ω ω
```

FIGURE 2
Generating extension for $y=x^n$

We shall make a few comparative remarks to both generating extension processors (calling them according to the year of invention G-77 anf G-86).

The processors have different mechanisms of residual program label generation. In G-77 label generation is synchronized by the printing of residual program instructions and it forms a linear sequence of labels. In G-86 a residual program label is "computed" on an accessible memory state and the label "syntax" reflects the matrix structure of the residual program.

In G-77 the control of the processed program execution is completely transferred into its generating extension. If the processed program goes into an infinite loop on the bound memory then the same will do its generating extension. In G-86 the generating extension <u>always</u> terminates (if only the domain of the accessible memory is <u>really</u> finite). The expences are high: the generating extension retains in its structure the transitive closure mechanism maintaining the sets A and P. The program indeterminism (arbitrary choice in A) can be reduced, however, by arranging elements of A in a structured memory (stack, queue) with some deterministic access function.

4. ANALYSIS

Below, we shall discuss briefly the ten questions put in the introduction. Some questions are answered according general considerations or other studies but essentially our analysis is based on various experiments made with the autoprojector and the generating extension processor (compiler compiler) described in Sections 2 and 3.

1°. ON COMPILATION PHASES

The basic idea is simple. Let a program P to be projected have a factorized data domain in the form of three independent variables $P=P(X_1,X_2,X_3)$. Then the processing of such a program by a mixed computation processor M is naturally factorized onto three phases:

$$M(P,x_1) \qquad M(P_{x_1},x) \qquad V(P_{x_1,x_2},x)$$
$$P(X_1\big|_{x_1},X_2,X_3) \to P_{x_1}(X_2\big|_{x_2},X_3) \to P_{x_1,x_2}(X_3\big|_{x_3}) \to P_{x_1,x_2}(x_3)$$

Such a phasing, however, does not correspond to an intuitive idea of a compiler decomposition into successively executed blocks. In the case of mixed computation the program is decomposed simultaneously with processing concrete values of the variables X_1,X_2 and X_3 and the decomposition is expressed by the formula

$$P(x_1,x_2,x_3) \to M(M(P,x_1),x_2)(x_3).$$

As for us, we would like to have a decomposition in the form

$$F: P(X_1,X_2,X_3) \to P_3(X_3,P_2(X_2,P_1(X_1)))$$

which satisfies the following condition

$$P(x_1,x_2,x_3)=P_3(x_3,P_2(x_2,P_1(x_1))).$$

It is still an open question whether the operator F is expressible via the mixed computation operator or its derivatives.

Some hints to the direction of search are suggested by the following model examples.

EXAMPLE 1.1. Let the program P have the form

$$z := \frac{aX_1 + bX_2 + cX_3}{X_1^2 + X_2^2 + X_3^2}$$

The intuitive concept of phasing suggests the following view of the components P_1, P_2 and P_3:

P_1: $s_1 := aX_1$; $s_2 := X_1^2$

P_2: $r_1 := s_1 + bX_2$; $r_2 := s_2 + X_1^2$

P : $z := \dfrac{r_1 + cX_3}{r_2 + X_3^2}$

The operator providing such a transformation is well known in systems programming under the name "sequential decomposition operator". Its expression requires, seemingly, a universal procedure which could be called a symmetrized generating extension processor. Ordinary generating extension processor splits the program text into two parts: an executable part and an "ejectable" part which is printed out as a residual program during generating extension execution. Of these two parts, the ejectable part is literalized, i.e. quoted and brought into print instructions as their operand.

A symmetrized generating extension processor has to arrange both, ejectable (second phase) and executable (first phase) parts in the form of integrated program text with provision of necessary information channels and control transfer between phases.

EXAMPLE 1.2. Let us introduce an intermediate Boolean variable a into the power function program. Its value is true if the current value of n is odd and false otherwise. The successive values of a arranged from right to left compose the binary expansion of N (the power).

start:	n:=N goto init
init:	y:=1 goto loop
loop:	goto if n>0 then body else basta
body:	a:=odd(n) goto odd
odd:	goto if a then yx else xx
yx:	y:=y×x goto substr
substr:	n:=n-1 goto xx
xx:	x:=x×x goto divn
divn:	n:=n/2 goto loop
basta:	stop goto ω

Now we want to split the program into two phases: (1) obtaining the binary expansion of the power and (2) use of the expansion obtained. The following phasing seems to be natural:

PHASE1:   n:=N <u>goto</u> init

init: m:=0 <u>goto</u> loop

loop: <u>goto</u> <u>if</u> n>0 <u>then</u> body <u>else</u> PHASE2

body: m:=m+1 <u>goto</u> body1

body1:   a[m]:=<u>odd</u>(n) <u>goto</u> odd

odd: <u>goto</u> <u>if</u> a[m]<u>then</u> substr <u>else</u> divn

substr: n:=n-1 <u>goto</u> divn

divn: n:=n/2 <u>goto</u> loop

PHASE2:   y:=1 <u>goto</u> begin

begin: k:=0 <u>goto</u> control

control: <u>if</u> m>k <u>then</u> work <u>else</u> basta

work: k:=k+1 <u>goto</u> check

check: <u>goto</u> <u>if</u> a[k]<u>then</u> yx <u>else</u> xx

yx: y:=y×x <u>goto</u> xx

xx: x:=x×x <u>goto</u> control

basta: <u>stop</u> <u>goto</u> ω

This example is similar to the problem of compiler decomposition
into parsing and a subsequent generation (if to relate N and its
binary expansion a[1:m] to a source program and its parsing, respectively). The example exposes one more problem, namely, vectorization of a sequence of the intermediate results. At the first
glance, the problem has to be treated quite informally. There
are, however, some indications to a possibility to solve it systematically, at least for analyzer programs where vectorization
emerges naturally due to the necessity to consider the set of
accessible memory states as an actual set.

2°. FUNDAMENTALITY OF THE SINGLE PASS SCHEME

The analysis of the 1st question leads us to the conclusion that
a compiler obtained as the generating extension of an interpreter
is formally single-pass processor since its phasing requires
additional mechanisms.

3°. SINGLE-PASS SCHEME MECHANISMS

The single-pass scheme in its classical form requires a single
linear scanning of the input string and the generation of the
object code. Fulfillment of these requirements leads to some
specific mechanisms of instruction and variable addressing. For
example, the label in a <u>goto</u> instruction quite often can not be
directly replaced by an address since the labelled instruction
has not yet been read and its address in unknown.

A question arises: what is a mixed computation equivalent of
these specific mechanisms.

The analysis shows that there is no single answer to this question and the addressing mechanism used in a compiler obtained via mixed computation is subjected to several factors.

Firstly, the concept of pass is modified. In classical single-pass schemes all the work is synchronized by the strictly linear source string scanning. The pass in mixed computation is a scanning of interpreter instructions with the attempt to execute these instructions using source string fragments as their operands. Such a modification of the pass concept removes some problems but also poses new ones since the source string in mixed computation may require a direct access mode of operation.

Secondly, some seemingly specific compilation techniques actually have their roots in the interpreter's features and are only transmitted into the compiler by means of mixed computation.

Thirdly, and most importantly, the specific problem of source object addressing for analyzer programs is solved "automatically" due to the mechanism of program unwinding.

Let us demonstrate this mechanism using as example the label translation problem.

Let the source string contain the following fragments

goto L... goto M... goto L...   ... $L:I_1...M:I_2$

It is naturally to assume that the interpreter has a variable, say, CURRENT INSTRUCTION storing an information about position of the current instruction in the source string, i.e. its label. Then the processing of the first fragment (goto L) consists of assignment of L to CURRENT INSTRUCTION and control transfer to the interpreter's loop of the current instruction processing labelled by a label NEXT.

The variable CURRENT INSTRUCTION belongs to the accessible memory so the mixed computation processor will put the pair (NEXT,L) to the active state set (all other accessible variables can be forgotten for a moment). Similarly, when processing the second fragment goto M, the pair (NEXT,M) will be added to the active state set. Since the jumps goto L and goto M are assumingly controlled by the source program data their processing (i.e. execution) will be suspended and these jumps will be transferred into the residual program but in the form goto(NEXT,L)   and goto(NEXT,M), respectively.

When the member (NEXT,L) will be selected from the active state set it will activate the interpreter instruction NEXT on the accessible memory state L. This activity will result in a projection of the interpreter's main loop onto the source program instruction K_1 labelled by L. It means that, in the residual program, the label (NEXT,L) will be followed by that projection, i.e. object code $ob(K_1)$ of the instruction K_1. Similarly, the same will happen during the processing of the fragment $M:K_2$. Finally, the residual program will contain the following translations of the corresponding source fragments:

goto(NEXT,L)...goto(NEXT,M)... ... $(NEXT,L):ob(K_1)...(NEXT,M):ob(K_2)$

4°. ON OBJECT CODE TEMPLATES

An object code template is a prefabricated object code construct which is used as an assembly detail during object code generation. Such templates contain numbered empty places, a kind of formal parameters, which are replaced by object program variable names.

In a compiler obtained via mixed computation the role of templates is played by irreducible remnants of the interpreter ejected into the residual program by <u>print</u> instructions. Literal variables embedded in these instructions are used as parameters whose values yield variable names or objects brought to them in a correspondence by the interpreter (e.g. location addresses).

5°. ON THE SYMBOL TABLE

The level of abstraction of mixed computation chosen in this paper is too high to indicate exactly the place of the symbol table. It may come from the interpreter, for example, as a device that maintains correspondence between variable names and location addresses or from the mixed computation processor as an implementation of accessible memory state sets.

6°. ON THE STACK

We have studied what happens with a stack built in an interpreter. Mixed computation performs completely all stack manipulations which are usually considered as belonging to the compile-time period, thus leaving to the residual program only run-time actions. No less interesting study would be incorporating the stack into the mixed computation processor in order to maintain the active state set. This, seemingly, will rise the universality of stack manipulation in compilers.

7° and 9°. OBTAINING COMPILER FROM DENOTATIONAL SEMANTICS

For the MILAN language [5], we have written in IL two variants of executable semantics: a pure operational one-loop interpreter and a denotational semantics imitation in the form of a system of recursive definitions. For that purpose, a stack mechanism for recursive procedures has been implemented in IL. These two rather different interpreters, to our great satisfaction, have produced an identical object code (not regarding notational differences).

There has been no similar study for transformational semantics. On the other hand, the known similarity in the descriptional style of denotational and transformational semantics as mappings $DS:(P \times D \to D)$ and $TS:(P \times D \to P \times D)$, respectively (where P is a program set and D is a data set), suggests a usability of transformational semantics.

8°. THE SOURCES OF COMPILER OPERATIONALITY

This question is rather important methodologically since it suggests the point of investment for the technological capital:

whether the mixed computation processor or the source language interpreter.

The question is better analyzed when the compiler is viewed as a generating extension of the interpreter. There are the following components of a generating extension:

- executed part of the processed program,

- ejected part of the processed program (in the form of literal arguments of print instructions),

- print instructions (generation instructions),

- reduction instructions (which provide, in particular, information connectives between executed and ejected parts),

- general organization instructions (maintenance of active and passed element sets).

The first component is a direct contribution of the interpreter into the compiler (first of all, lexical scan and parsing). On the other hand, introduction of intermediate names during the decomposition depends essentially on reduction procedures (a mixed computation contribution).

The second component is marginal for compiler operationality though it is a focus of the art of interpreter writing and the "resolution power" of the mixed computation processor.

All the other components are a direct contribution of the mixed computation processor.

10°. ON SEMANTICAL INVARIANTS OF THE SOURCE LANGUAGE

It is premature to try to answer this question. We believe that systematic development of a compiler by means of mixed computation will guarantee the compiler correctness with respect to the given language semantics or, contrarily, to check correctness of a newly written semantics, requiring identical object code for compared semantics. Thus, we take object code identity as a semantical invariant of the source language.

This is, however, only a part of the problem. A well developed compiler has a variety of optimization means. Many kinds of optimization   (especially of a reductional character) are covered by mixed computation. On the other hand, combinatorial optimization forms an independent dimension in program processing. It deals with the implementation language semantics rather then with that of the source language. Here we have other, schematic program invariants.

The integration of these two aspects of the compiled program semantics is a matter of future.

5. CONCLUSION

The analysis made is rather preliminary. However, even superficial observations confirm a fruitfulness of studying the compilation problem by means of mixed computation. Moreover, mixed computation on the class of analyzer programs allows us not only to solve the compilation problem in principle but to work in the direction of obtaining compilation schemas competing with ad hoc compilers. This direction, however, still requires of extensive experiments and solution of many technological problems.

REFERENCES

[1] Ershov, A.P., On Mixed Computation: Informal Account of the Strict and Polyvariant Computational Schemes, in: Broy, M. (ed.), Control Flow and Data Flow: Concepts of Distributed Programming (Springer Verlag, Berlin, 1985) pp. 107-120.

[2] Futamura, Y., Partial Evaluation of Computational Process - an Approach to a Compiler-Compiler, Systems-Computers-Controls, v.2, n.5 (1971) pp. 45-50.

[3] Ershov, A.P., On the Partial Computation Principle, Information Processing Letters, v.6, n.2 (1977) pp. 38-41.

[4] Turchin, V.F., A Supercompiler System Based on the Language REFAL, SIGPLAN Notices, v.14, n.2 (1979) pp. 46-54.

[5] Ershov, A.P., On the Essence of Compilation, in: Neuhold, E.J. (ed.), Formal Description of Programming Concepts (North-Holland, Amsterdam, 1977) pp. 391-420.

[6] Brooker, R.A., MacCallum, I.R., Morris, D., Rohl, J.S., The Compiler Compiler, Annual Review in Automatic Programming, v.3 (Pergamon, London, 1963).

[7] Mazaher, S., An Approach to Compiler Correctness, Ph.D. Dissertation, Computer Science Department, University of California in Los Angeles (1981).

[8] Mazaher, S., Berry, D.M., Deriving a Compiler from an Operational semantics written in VDL, Computer Languages, v.10, n.2 (1985) pp. 147-164.

[9] Jones, N.D., Sestoft, P., Sondergaard, H., An Experiment in Partial Evaluation: The Generation of a Compiler Generator, Lecture Notes in Computer Science, v.202 (Springer Verlag, Berlin, 1985) pp. 124-140.

[10] Bulyonkov, M.A., Polyvariant Mixed Computation for Analyzer Programs, Acta Informatica, v.21 (1984) pp. 473-484.

[11] Ershov, A.P., Itkin, V.E., Correctness of the Mixed Computation in Algol-Like Programs, in: Mathematical Foundation of Computer Science, Gruska, J. (ed.), Lecture Notes in Computer Science, v.53 (Springer Verlag, Berlin, 1977) pp.59-77.

Partial Evaluation and Mixed Computation
D. Bjørner, A.P. Ershov and N.D. Jones (Editors)
Elsevier Science Publishers B.V. (North-Holland)
© IFIP, 1988

Across the Bridge between Reflection and Partial Evaluation

Olivier DANVY [1]

DIKU – University of Copenhagen
Universitetsparken 1, DK-2100 Copenhagen Ø, DENMARK
uucp: danvy@diku.dk

Abstract

This article attempts to relate reflection and partial evaluation on the basis that they both involve a program and the interpreter which runs it: reflective procedures in a program reify internal structures in the interpreter (reflection); the interpreter is specialized with respect to a program (partial evaluation). The key points presented here are: partial evaluation collapses levels in a tower of interpreters; specializing a function relies on the environment of the interpreter above it in the tower; partial evaluation of reflective programs generates partially known structures that are instant snapshots of the internal structures which have been reified.

The first part of the paper introduces partial evaluation and reflection and argues why it is worth to build a common understanding of them. It is shown that partial evaluation transforms and reflection evaluates, which is the reason why they had not been mixed so far: a partial evaluator is not situated in the tower but operates on it. Part two describes the impact of a partial evaluator on a tower of interpreters and the effect of its self-application. An interpretive architecture is proposed there: it is shaped in such a way that displaying a functional object gives an intensional view of a tower of interpreters illustrating both reflection and partial evaluation. The third part introduces reflective capabilities in the tower of interpreters, with reflective procedures. They are shown to generate partially known structures. Finally we initiate a discussion on partial evaluation of programs with an arbitrary degree of introspection: either this leads to iterating partial evaluation to get rid of reflection; or to defining the specialization of several levels of interpretations; or it requires building a reflective partial evaluator, that is a partial evaluator which enriches itself at each occurrence of a reflective procedure.

Keywords

Reflection, evaluation, partial evaluation, program transformation, self-application, auto-projection, MIX, function specialization, tower of interpreters, reflective towers, reification.

---

[1] French address: LITP – Université de Paris VI (couloir 45–55, 2e étage), 4 place Jussieu, 75252 Paris Cedex 05, FRANCE (uucp: od@litp.fr).

1 Introduction

Reflection [Smith 82] and partial evaluation [Futamura 71] [Ershov 77] have the common property that they relate a program and the interpreter which runs it: reflective procedures in a program have access to internal structures in the interpreter (reflection); the interpreter is specialized with respect to a program (partial evaluation).

This article believes to be the first investigation of reflection and partial evaluation based on the identities of the interpreters at each level of a reflective tower and of the subject language and the base language in a partial evaluator [Sestoft & Zamulin 88]. These identities are essential: it is because the levels of the tower are all alike that simple and reflective procedures are expressed in the same language (the simple one being performed at the current level and the reflective one at the level above[2]); and it is because a partial evaluator is written in the language it partially evaluates that it can be self-applied and thus generate compilers and compiler generators rather than merely perform a compilation. Without these identities one would miss these issues: defining reflection as the way to mirror a simulation (meta-interpretation) into a direct execution reduces it to an interpretation; and defining partial evaluation as the way to transform an expression which would be meta-interpreted into another which is directly executable reduces it to compilation.

In this article we attempt to relate reflection and partial evaluation on the basis that they both involve a program and the interpreter which runs it. Let us first define them in simple terms and tell how this paper is structured. We have tried to make it self-contained by spreading the key references, to avoid any special pre-requisite.

It can take some time to grasp what partial evaluation means, and this is due to the fact that the term "evaluation" is used in a different way in the LISP programming language [McCarthy 60]. Let us retrace two successive pitfalls in the course of understanding partial evaluation. They are (1) the belief that every Lisp expression can both be evaluated and partially evaluated and (2) the intuition that partial evaluation is related to evaluation in the same way that evalquote [McCarthy *et al.* 62] is related to eval. It makes sense to retrace them, as they originate in [Lombardi & Raphael 64] where the term "partial evaluation" was coined and defined as a special sort of evaluation.

These misunderstandings arise because at first glance, it is not offending to think that a program (typically: a Lisp program) can be evaluated, nor to think that it can be partially evaluated, if some data are missing. Some of its parts will be evaluated according to the available data. The first pitfall originates here, because one considers any Lisp expression as being a program. However, with the picture of LISP 1.5's evalquote in mind[3] it is possible to figure it out and this leads to the second pitfall: to think that

---

[2]In a reflective tower, a level implements the level below it and thus an interpreter is on top of the program it interprets. This is the opposite of the usual picture. The idea is that a designator is *above* the things it designates – see in particular footnotes 3 and 5 in [des Rivières & Smith 84].

[3]In Lisp 1.5, the toplevel loop does not read an expression and eval-uate it, but rather reads two expressions. The first is a function and the second is the list of its arguments. The idea is to apply the function to these arguments. For example, to obtain (a b), one would type with an evalquote toplevel: list (a b), and

partial evaluation is to evaluation what `evalquote` is to `eval`. Since it is familiar to see the (known) datum as a program, or rather the program as a datum (after all, it is Lisp), this seems accurate when one starts to consider an interpreter to be partially evaluated with respect to a program. But with that in mind, one is not at all ready to realize that the result here is a program and not a result in the evaluation sense.

The confusion in the first pitfall is that one thinks a Lisp expression can be both evaluated and partially evaluated. This only holds when that expression is the application of a function to some of its arguments: the function value is the program and the idea is that even if not all of its arguments are known, one can evaluate some parts of its body [Heering 86] and leave the rest as result, that is: to specialize that function with respect to those arguments which are known.

The confusion in the second pitfall is to think that partial evaluation is related to evaluation as `evalquote` is related to `eval`. Actually `evalquote` is not analogous to `eval` but to `apply`[4].

The point here is that an evaluation as well as the Lisp `eval` has the type:

$$Expression \rightarrow Expressible\text{-}Value$$

(forgetting any environment or continuation) while an application as well as the Lisp `apply`[5] has the type:

$$Function\text{-}Value \times Expressible\text{-}Value \rightarrow Expressible\text{-}Value$$

contrary to partial evaluation which has the type:

$$Function\text{-}Value \times Expressible\text{-}Value \rightarrow Function\text{-}Value$$

Partial evaluation is thus better expressed as program transformation[6].

Experience shows that this very didactic presentation does help someone accustomed to Lisp thinking: partial evaluation is not evaluation but program transformation. In the particular case where an interpreter is specialized with respect to a program, it is not that program which matters but its interpreter. The architecture of the resulting (residual) program often mirrors that of the interpreter. It is in fact a specialized form of the interpreter program. For example, we can deduce from the residual programs in [Futamura 71] that his interpreter uses deep binding with an A-list for representing environments. This information is not explicitly mentioned in the article, but is witnessed by the residual programs given in example.

---

with a classical toplevel loop something like (`list 'a 'b`) or rather, to emphasize the `quote` in "evalquote", one could type: (`apply 'list '(a b)`). The footnote {evalquote} p 55 of [Steele & Sussman 78] develops on viewing `eval` or `apply` as the universal symbolic function of Lisp.

[4]Indeed: `evalquote` in Lisp 1.5 replaces the `apply` operator of Lisp 1 [McCarthy *et al.* 60] in the top level loop.

[5]The functionality of `evalquote` being: *Function* × *List-of-Values* → *Value*

[6]In the case where all the arguments are known, an (impartial) evaluation would give an expressible value whereas a (total) partial evaluation produces a "constant" program.

As a consequence, the residual program is expressed in the language in which the interpreter was programmed. Once we understand that, the rest follows much more easily and it becomes a logic game to figure it out how the Futamura projections[7] [Futamura 71] hold: interpreting a program together with some data gives a value[8]; partially evaluating an interpreter with respect to a program gives an object program[9]; partially evaluating the partial evaluator with respect to an interpreter gives a compiler[10] because when it is applied to a program it will compile it; partially evaluating the partial evaluator with respect to itself gives a compiler generator[11] because when it is applied to an interpreter it will produce a compiler. And then a sort of fixpoint is reached: further self-application leads to the same result.

What is remarkable is that we are here very far away from any tower of interpreters interpreting each other meta-circularly [Reynolds 72] or heterogeneously – and thus further away from reflection, since we consider Brian Smith's reflective model[12]. Still, there is this coincidence between the three meaningful self-applications and the three implemented levels that are necessary for a meta-level architecture [Batali 83] [Batali 86]. It is interesting to wonder why these connections appear so elusive.

The point is that in a tower of interpreters:

$$\ldots Int_n \ldots Int_1 \; Int_0 \; Pgm$$

all the interpreters until the program are running, and so is the program. Further, it is a familiar picture to consider only the inner-most part, that is, the program, to be active[13]. This view does not apply to partial evaluation, where the result is a program, not the result of the inner-most program. In particular, when self-application is performed, only the outermost MIX is running: there is no tower of partial evaluators. There is one specialization at a time, and this contrasts definitely with embedded interpretations.

Extensionally, MIX manifests the results of the Futamura projections, and as a mathematical system, it does not run [Smith 84]. Intensionally, there is no tower of self-applicable partial evaluators because only the outer-most one runs.

---

[7]Also known as "MIX equations" [Jones *et al.* 85], where mix is the program and *MIX* is the function it computes:

[8]INT pgm data $\equiv$ value

[9]MIX int pgm $\equiv$ object

[10]MIX mix int $\equiv$ compiler

[11]MIX mix mix $\equiv$ compiler-generator

or rather, MIX mix mix $\equiv$ an intentional version of the Curry function.

[12]A reflective tower is a model of *procedural reflection* [Smith 82]. It supports self-referential behaviour in procedural languages. The point is that a program can reflect upon its procedural state. The idea is to extend a meta-circular interpreter to a reflective tower with the ability to handle procedures that have access to the context of their computation; and with the ability to install new values as contexts. Footnote 6 in [Smith 84] develops on why these causal connections make the interpreters of a reflective tower non meta-circular. This access is renamed *procedural introspection* in later work [Smith 86].

[13]As long as we tend to think to a program in terms of what it does (*i.e.*, extensionally), rather than in terms of how it is performed (*i.e.*, intensionally). A so-called portable program is not intended to run specifically on one particular processor.

This guides us to structure this article in two parts. The first one develops the relations between a tower of interpreters and partial evaluation, especially the impact of a partial evaluator on such a tower and the effect of its self-application. The second part introduces reflective capabilities in the tower of interpreters: they are reflective procedures (reifiers) which reify the current state of the computation (expression to be interpreted, environment and continuation) and whose bodies are to be performed one level higher than the level of their application.

A simple example using reflection is to define the designator `quote` in the reflective language Brown [Friedman & Wand 84] [Wand & Friedman 86a] [Wand & Friedman 86b]: it uses the operator *make-reifier*, which, when applied to a ternary function, returns a reifier. When that reifier is later applied, its arguments, the current environment and the current continuation are reified and passed to the ternary function. The body of that function is evaluated at the level above, instead of the expression that created the level of the application. Applying the reified continuation resumes the computation back down at the calling level. `quote`-ing is thus straightforward: the continuation is just applied to the reified expression without doing any further[14]:

$$make\text{-}reifier(\lambda(e, \, r, \, k) \, . \, k(car(e)))$$
$$make\text{-}reifier: \, Brown\text{-}Function \rightarrow Brown\text{-}Function$$

The type of a Brown function is:

$$List\text{-}of\text{-}Expressions \rightarrow Environment \rightarrow Continuation \rightarrow Meta\text{-}Continuation \rightarrow Answer$$

In the environment of the interpreter, at the level above, the expression, environment and continuation are three common accessible values. In Brown, the meta-continuation represents the tower of interpreters.

What is remarkable here is that a tower of interpreters deals with evaluation[15] whereas partial evaluation deals with program transformation. This explains why a partial evaluator (hence an autoprojector [Ershov 82] such as MIX) cannot be situated in that tower. It would have been beautiful to express the three MIX equations as three snapshots of a same shift in the tower, viewed from three different levels of the same tower. But this cannot be done because partial evaluation transforms and reflection evaluates.

The closest common instance of reflection and partial evaluation appears to be *reification* [Friedman & Wand 84]: a reifier generates a future shift up in the tower, reifying the expression to be evaluated, the environment in which to evaluate it, and the continuation to apply to the result of that evaluation. It is the nearest common instance and it is a trivial one: basically nothing happens in terms of program specialization. *make-reifier* acts as a trivial compiler:

---

[14]Because the reifier can be applied to any number of arguments they are reified in a list. Here that list has one element and the function *car* extracts it.

[15][Smith 82] uses *normalization* which is a semantically rationalized version of evaluation.

- it translates a function from one level to a higher level; the result will be applied at one level and performed (*i.e.*, the body of the function will be evaluated) at the level above;

- that translation is trivial since these levels are identical: the running level is a similar interpreter.

In other words *make-reifier* takes a function and returns a reifier. That reifier is a first-class applicable value, to be used at the current level, and the function contained in it is to be applied at the level above, where the actual parameter list, the environment and the continuation are available values. These values are passed to the function.

The situation can be summarized in:

$$\mathcal{E}_n[\![int_n]\!]\rho_n\kappa_n \simeq \mathcal{E}_{n-1}$$

which expresses that the meaning of what is happening at level $n-1$ is specified by an interpreter int_n run at the level n [Danvy & Malmkjær 88].

This has made us wonder about the possibility of an interpreter suitable for both reflection and partial evaluation. This is the main example of this article: an interpretive architecture where the preliminaries of an application and the actual application are conceptually separated. The reason why is that there are many functions which have the same generic behaviour when they are to be applied and only differ when they are actually applied. For example, the functions *car* and *cdr* are primitive and unary, they evaluate their argument (which must be a pair) and extract its head and tail, respectively. The idea is to define the domain of functions as a direct sum of other domains, *e.g.* of primitive and user-defined functions, of functions that are variadic or anadic [Strachey 67], monadic, dyadic or polyadic, arithmetic or symbolic, and so on. A functional object is thus composed with an injection tag and a functional value:

<*functional-tag, functional-value*>

The functional tag will direct the interpreter to perform the preliminary actions, according to whether the function is primitive, simple or reflective, how many arguments it takes and how many it has, whether they are evaluated or not, and what type they should have. The functional value will perform the action. The essential point of the architecture is this: applying the functional value of a primitive function gives control to the interpreter at the level above, for performing the operation (ultimately in machine code).

The functions *car* and *cdr* have the same functional tag. It directs the interpreter to do the preliminaries for applying the functional value (one argument which is evaluated and must be a pair). Then the first or second projection is performed by their functional value. The essence of this interpreter is presented in the first section and a specification in Scheme [Sussman & Steele 75] appears in the appendix. An initial environment maps the names of the primitive functions to the primitive functional objects. A program is a series of function definitions and is stored in the environment. A function definition binds a name to a functional object (presently: a λ-abstraction).

This interpretive architecture is particularly well-suited to our purposes because both reflection and partial evaluation can be expressed in a way we have found illuminating:

1.1 Tower of interpreters

Any primitive function (such as *car*, *cdr*, *cons*, *etc.*) provides an intensional view of the tower. Indeed, if τ is the functional tag of the function *car* and if v is its functional value, the name `car` is bound in the initial environment to the functional object:

$$< \tau, v >$$

τ is the injection tag in the direct sum of function domains and, confusing expressible and denotable values, v has the type:

$$Denotable\text{-}Value_{n+1} \rightarrow Denotable\text{-}Value_{n+1}$$

v is a function of level $n + 1$. The result of its application is passed to the continuation, which is also a function at level $n + 1$. In contrast, *car* is a function of level n, and its type is:

$$Denotable\text{-}Value_n \rightarrow Denotable\text{-}Value_n$$

These aspects are developed further in [Danvy & Malmkjær 88]. Since we are in a tower, v is in turn a functional object in the environment of the running interpreter. If we suppose that interpreter to have the same architecture, v has the same functional tag and a functional value v':

$$< \tau, v'>$$

and with the same assumption v' is the functional object:

$$< \tau, v''>$$

Now reconsidering the first functional object and substituting the functional values gives the intensional view of the tower that was announced:

$$< \tau, < \tau, < \tau, < \tau, \ldots >>>>$$

The number of functional tags indicates the height of the tower. The final functional value would be the *car* function itself (in practice, the microcode to compute it)[16]. That view is intensional because the injection tags are an intensional property of a direct sum. It is obtained by displaying a functional value with the local (Lisp) `print` function. Assuming the tower to be infinite, the functional values are identical at all the levels.

---

[16]One may note that the function *cdr* is identically shaped, and differs only with its final functional value.

1.2   Partial evaluation

We concentrate here on *function specialization*, which is a central phase in MIX [Jones *et al.* 85] [Sestoft 85] [Jones *et al.* 87] [Bondorf 87]. The aim is to specialize a function call: either it is eliminated (performed statically) or kept residual (to be performed at run-time)[17].

Our model enlights (1) that eliminating the call corresponds to applying its functional value statically, and (2) that making it residual corresponds to selecting a name of that functional value in [the initial environment of] the subject language.

In other words, specializing the expression (`car thing`) leads to replace it by a constant equalling the head of `thing`, if `thing` is a list with a known head, or to replace it with the symbolic expression (`head thing`) if `head` is the name of the base language's equivalent of the function *car*. One corresponds to selecting a value and the other a name in the environment of the subject interpreter.

Similarly, when a call to a user function is to be specialized, either it is unfolded and in that case its functional value is symbolically applied; or it is kept residual (possibly under a specialized form). In the latter case its name is conserved (or created) together with its definition in the residual program. Because a function definition binds a name to a functional object, it will figure in the environment of the subject interpreter. To synthetize: making a call (to a user function) residual propagates the definition of the called function in the residual program, and specializing a call creates the definition of a new functional object in the residual program.

We distinguish between eliminating a call, making it residual and specializing it to handle uniformly primitive and user-defined functions. The point is that a call to a primitive function is eliminated if all of its arguments are known, and kept residual otherwise, where a user-defined function would be specialized. This enlights why making a call residual is not only a trivial specialization, since it is not even specialized with respect to some known argument. Usually primitive functions are not specialized.

To summarize:

- eliminating a call is realized by applying the called function symbolically – either by unfolding it in the case of a user function or by performing the associated operation in the case of a primitive function;

- making a call (to a functional object) residual corresponds to selecting a name for the associated functional value in the environment of the subject language. If it is a call to a primitive function, that binding exists in the initial environment of the subject language. If it is a call to a user function, that binding is created by propagating the function definition in the residual program. And:

- specializing a call (to a user-defined functional object) corresponds to creating a new function definition in the residual program. That function is a specialized version of

---

[17]In contrast, the *binding time analysis* aims to classify a call as eliminable or as residual. During the function specialization, the call is actually eliminated or kept residual.

the functional object.

1.3 Reification

Reification is provided by the transformation (*"reifier"* being the functional tag of a reifier):

$$make\text{-}reifier(functional\text{-}object) = <\text{``reifier''}, functional\text{-}object>$$

which explicitly shifts the functional object. So its application will be performed at the level above. This is more clearly expressed in the unfolded form:

$$make\text{-}reifier(<\tau, v>) = <\text{``reifier''}, <\tau, v>>$$

1.4 Reflection

Reflection occurs by explicitly spawning a new interpreter (by calling the function *meaning* in Brown). This leads to a new environment where all the current functional objects are wrapped with functional tags and become functional values in the new functional objects. In the new environment, these new functional objects are bound to the names of their functional value, in the current environment (where they are functional objects, remembering that a functional object pairs a functional tag and a functional value).

This leaves one wondering which functional tags are to be assigned to the functional objects: for example they could all be declared primitive, being defined at the level above (in such a case there would not be any continuity in the successive functional tags of a functional object[18]). On the other hand, the kernel expressions [des Rivières & Smith 84] could be flagged somehow, to be performed directly (for efficiency). Anyway such an architecture offers a very large latitude for any representation.

1.5 Outline

Our bridge building strategy is to begin from both banks at once and work towards the center. Section 2 concerns an application of partial evaluation to a non-reflective tower of interpreters, that is a tower of interpreters without reflective procedures. It shows that the impact of partial evaluation on that tower is to collapse levels. Function specialization is expressed as selecting either a functional object or its name at the level above. Section 3 considers a reflective tower, that is a tower of interpreters with reflective procedures. Control structures and higher-order functions are recalled to be elementary instances of reflective procedures[19]. The effect of partial evaluation is again to collapse levels but its side effect is to generate partially known structures[20] [Mogensen 87]. The next step is to

---

[18]A primitive at one level could be a closure at the level above: this is a step towards having different interpreters at each level of the tower, as in the *Platypus* system [Sturdy 87] [Sturdy 88].

[19]As `quote` could be, designating an expression: a control structure acts upon the continuation, altering it, and a higher-order function acts upon the environment, enclosing it. And for completeness: dumping a core would reify the store.

[20]For example some reified parts of the environment where the names are known but not yet the values.

consider programs with an arbitrary degree of introspection[21] [des Rivières & Smith 84], rather than a bounded one. This leads to a choice:

- either to specialize all the involved interpreters with respect to the reflective program (supposing it has a finite degree of introspection), to produce a residual program with many partially known structures and no (or less) reflection; the strategy would be to iterate partial evaluation while there are still some reflective procedures in the residual program, using the appropriate projections [Launchbury 87] to separate static and dynamic parts;

- or to build a reflective partial evaluator, that is, a partial evaluator which extends itself at each occurrence of a reflective procedure, either in space or in time, according to that procedure.

That choice makes us believe that there has been a progression in the present article: as partial evaluation transforms and reflection evaluates, which was the reason why they had not been mixed, the choice in realizing their combination is either to iterate partial evaluation to get rid of reflection or to enrich the partial evaluator reflectively.

2 The impact of partial evaluation on a tower of interpreters

This second section analyzes the relations between partial evaluation and a non-reflective tower of interpreters. First the effect of partial evaluation is described. Not surprisingly it is to collapse two levels. Then the essence of our interpretive model is described, in order to focus on the essential part of function specialization next. As the introduction has been large and general these sections will be short and more precise.

2.1 Partial evaluation collapses two levels

2.1.1 Mix Int Pgm

Here is the graphical effect of partially evaluating (say, with Mix) the meta-circular L-interpreter *L-Int-L* for the language L with respect to the L-program L-Pgm[22]:

```
+-------+
|   L   |    ---->    L-Pgm'
|       |
|   L   |
+-------+
  L-Pgm
```

---

[21]That is, the number of levels which perform non-kernel expressions. A normal (non-reflective) program has a degree 1.

[22]Contrary to the Bratman diagrams [Bratman 61], the interpreted language is lowest on the boxes: this is needed to match the structure of the reflective tower. Consistently with earlier, L-Int-L is the program and *L-INT-L* is the function it computes.

The result of specializing *L-Int-L* with respect to L-Pgm is a L-program L-Pgm' because *L-Int-L* is written in L. L-Pgm' is functionally equivalent with L-Pgm but needs not be identical to it. Using the notation of [Jones *et al.* 85], this would be expressed by:

$$\text{L-Pgm'} = L \ MIX \ <\text{L-Int-L, L-Pgm}>$$

The possibility that *L-Int-L* is interpreted by another instance of *L-Int-L* (that is interpreted by another one, *etc.*) can be similarly described by:

$Result \equiv L \ L\text{-}PGM \ \text{data}$
$\quad\quad\ \equiv L \ L\text{-}INT\text{-}L \ <\text{L-Pgm, data}>$
$\quad\quad\ \equiv L \ L\text{-}INT\text{-}L \ <\text{L-Int-L}, \ <\text{L-Pgm, data}>>$
$\quad\quad\ \equiv L \ L\text{-}INT\text{-}L \ <\text{L-Int-L}, \ <\text{L-Int-L}, \ <\text{L-Pgm, data}>>>$
$\quad\quad\ \equiv L \ L\text{-}INT\text{-}L \ <\text{L-Int-L}, \ <\text{L-Int-L}, \ <\text{L-Int-L}, \ <\text{L-Pgm, data}>>>>$
$\quad\quad\ \equiv L \ L\text{-}INT\text{-}L \ <\text{L-Int-L}, \ <\text{L-Int-L}, \ <\text{L-Int-L}, \ <\text{L-Int-L}, \ <\text{L-Pgm, data}>>>>>$
$\quad\quad\ \ \dots$

This can be illustrated on a 3-level tower of interpreters:

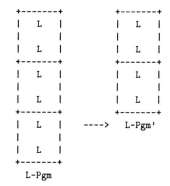

The effect of partially evaluating the lowest interpreter L-Int-L with respect to the program L-Pgm has been to collapse two levels of the tower: the ones where L-Int-L and L-pgm stood are reduced to one where a L-program L-Pgm' stands. In other words:

$Result \equiv L \ L\text{-}INT\text{-}L \ <\text{L-Int-L}, \ <\text{L-Int-L}, \ <\text{L-Pgm, data}>>>$
$\quad\quad\ \equiv L \ L\text{-}INT\text{-}L \ <\text{L-Int-L}, \ <\text{L-Pgm', data}>>$

What happens is straightforward: Mix does not live in the tower, but operates on it.

In order to be complete, here is the effect of an autoprojector on the tower:

2.1.2   Mix Mix Int

Self-applying Mix to Mix with respect to `L-Int-L` will produce a compiler, here better thought of as a collapser: a residual program written in the same language as Mix: the language L. When that collapser is applied to an L-program in the tower it will collapse into a single residual program the level where that program stands and the level above where its L-interpreter stands. The result stands at one level: it is a specialized L-program. This is consistent because Mix is an autoprojector: it is written in its own subject language L.

The point here is that a collapser throws away one level, because `L-Int-L` has been absorbed:

$$Collapser = MIX \text{ mix } \texttt{L-Int-L}$$
$$\texttt{L-Pgm'} = L \; Collapser \; \texttt{L-Pgm}$$

The collapser transforms the level above. It has one argument because the other has already been absorbed.

2.1.3   Mix Mix Mix

Similarly, self-applying Mix to Mix with respect to Mix produces a collapser generator.

2.2   An interpretive architecture

A suitable interpreter for both reflection and partial evaluation was mentioned in the introduction. Its specification in Scheme appears in an appendix and this section focuses on the bootstrap of an initial environment and on the application of a functional object. The essential choice here is to represent the pair <*functional-tag, functional-value*> as a Scheme pair, built up by *cons* and accessed by *car* and *cdr*.

2.2.1   Initialization

As presented in the introduction, to set up a primitive function one just has to wrap it with its functional tag. For example the name of a primitive function *foo* is bound to a cons-cell pairing *foo*'s functional tag and functional value:

$$cons(car(foo), \; foo)$$

foo was already a functional object, pairing a functional tag and a functional value. The point is here that a functional object at one level is a functional value at the level below.

Additionally, to initialize a user function, one needs to determine how to implement recursion: either with a fixed point operator or with circular structures. We choose the latter: a function is bound to a closure whose environment is the extended environment of definition.

For example we can adopt the frame organization of [Steele & Sussman 78][23], that is paired lists of names and values. Initializing the environment then reduces to making a list of names and a list of values.

2.2.2 Application

Now evaluating an application requires evaluating the object in function position and checking that it is indeed a functional object. Then according to its functional tag, say "*car-like*", it is checked whether there is only one argument. That argument is evaluated, and it is checked that it is a pair. Then the functional value is applied. In short:

```
(define _apply_car-like
    (lambda (v l r k)
        (if (= (length l) 1)
            (_eval (car l)
                r
                (lambda (a)
                    (if (pair? a)
                        (k (v a))
                        (_wrong '_apply_car-like "not a pair" a))))
            (_wrong 'apply_car-like "wrong number of arguments" l))))
```

_apply_car-like: *(Pair → Den-Val)* × *List-of-Exp* × *Env* × *Con* → *Ans*

In contrast, treating unary structural primitives which do not evaluate their argument (quote belongs to them) would be simpler:

```
(define _apply_quote-like
    (lambda (v l r k)
        (if (= (length l) 1)
            (k (v (car l)))
            (_wrong '_apply_quote-like "wrong number of arguments" l))))
```

_apply_quote-like: *(Exp → Den-Val)* × *List-of-Exp* × *Env* × *Con* → *Ans*

Worthy of notice: the connection between two levels of the tower is located in a single expression:

$$\textit{Continuation(Functional-Value(Value))}$$

One may note two possible definitions of quote: either as a reflective procedure (as earlier) or as a meta-structural primitive at the level above:

$$\textit{cons(``quote-like'', } \lambda x . \ x)$$

---

[23]{This ain't A-lists}

2.3 Function Specialization

Function specialization plays a central role in a partial evaluator: either it eliminates function calls by unfolding them, or it keeps them residual, possibly specializing the corresponding function. The point here is to underline the relation between that activity and the environment of the interpreter above.

2.3.1 Primitive Functions

When a call to primitive function such as *car* or *cons* is eliminated, for example because the arguments are statically known, its functional value is symbolically performed. It is found in the initial environment of the interpreter to be specialized.

When a call to a primitive function is kept residual, for example because its arguments are classified as dynamic, it is the <u>name</u> of its functional value which remains. It is to be found in the environment of the interpreter above, bound to a functional object which is the present functional value.

2.3.2 User Functions

Unfolding a call to a user function corresponds to eliminating it. This is done using its definition, found in the environment of the interpreter to be specialized.

Creating a residual call requires the definition in the residual program of a specialized instance of the called function. (If the call is completely residual, the instance is identical to the called function.) This correspond to define a new entry in the environment of the interpreter at the next level.

3 The impact of partial evaluation on a reflective tower

This third section analyzes the natural relations in principle between partial evaluation and a reflective tower of interpreters. Later work will describe computational experiments. First it is shown how reflective procedures have the effect of crossing levels of interpretation explicitly rather than implicitly and recursively (when applying a functional value). Control structures and higher-order functions are then recalled to be two common instances of reflection. Partially evaluating a program with higher-order functions is shown to produce partially known structures: reified parts of closure environments. Finally, generalizing to programs with a higher degree of introspection than 1, some solutions are proposed to get rid of multiple levels of reflection.

3.1 Reflective procedures

Reflective procedures are procedures whose bodies are to be executed one level above their application. One view is that each reflective procedure extends the text of the interpreter: these "semantic extensions" form an logical counterpart to the syntactic extensions of [Kohlbecker 86].

Levels are crossed at the application of primitive functions, such as *car*, *cdr*, *etc.*. Each time a primitive operator is applied, machinery is run at the level above to perform the operation. In particular some primitive operators are applied at that level above, leading to activity yet one level higher. As the application of a primitive function provokes the application of several others at the level above, we propose here to turn the picture of a reflective tower ([Smith 84] p 31) upside down[24]:

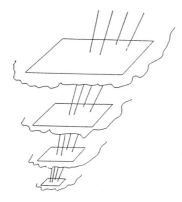

The program point [Landin 65] of a conventional program moves in a completely hierarchic way, between its interpreter and the machine code of that interpreter. Reflective procedures offer larger possibilities than simple ones, because their application makes the program point migrate non-hierarchically in the tower.

Control structures and higher-order functions (abstractions) are classically [Smith 84] expressed as reflective procedures:

- a control structure reifies the continuation and acts upon it (conditional, *etc.*); here is a definition of if as a reifier in Brown, with the usual extensional ef evaluating all its arguments:

```
(make-reifier
  (lambda (e r k)
     (meaning (car e) r (lambda (p)
                       (meaning (ef p (cadr e) (caddr e)) r k)))))
```

$$\text{if}: \textit{List-of-3-Exp} \rightarrow \textit{Env} \rightarrow \textit{Cont} \rightarrow \textit{Meta-Cont} \rightarrow \textit{Ans}$$

This should be compared with some denotational specification *à la* [Schmidt 86]:

$$\mathcal{E} \, [\![(\text{if P T E})]\!] \, \rho \, \kappa = \mathcal{E} \, [\![\text{P}]\!] \, \rho \, \lambda p . ((p \rightarrow \mathcal{E} \, [\![\text{T}]\!] \, [\![\mathcal{E} \, [\![\text{E}]\!]) \, \rho \, \kappa)$$

---

[24]This mirrors the remarks in [Smith 84], footnote 8, and the tiling game in [des Rivières & Smith 84].

- a higher-order function reifies the environment and encloses it:

```
(make-reifier
   (lambda (ed rd kd)
      (kd (cons "closure"
               (make-reifier
                  (lambda (ea ra ka)
                     (meaning (fetch-body ed)
                              (extend-env (fetch-par ed) ea rd)
                              ka)))))))
```

lambda: *Formals-and-Body* $\to$ *Env* $\to$ *Cont* $\to$ *Meta-Cont* $\to$ *Ans*

This should be compared with a denotational specification such as:

$$\mathcal{E} [\![(\text{lambda (x) B})]\!] \, \rho \, \kappa = \kappa(inAbstractions(\lambda v \, . \, \lambda k \, . \, \mathcal{E} [\![B]\!] \, ([x \mapsto v] \rho) \, k))$$

Specialization of control structures leads either to a static execution which eliminates them (sequence, branch, call, conditional) or to a residual control structure (conditional with dynamic test).

Specialization of a higher-order interpreter leads to partially known structures, which are incomplete parts of the environment that have been closed.

3.2   Partial evaluation of reflective programs

In the previous section we have seen that a reflective program can break the hierarchy in the tower of interpreters. This is an uncontrollable situation for partial evaluation: how can a partial evaluator collapse two levels, that is, compress two embedded program points, if the inner one reflectively migrates outside the scope to reappear later in an other instance of the same level? It cannot.

More precisely: it cannot, as it is. What it needs is to have power over the continuation and the meta-continuation [Wand & Friedman 86a]. Then it could lie in wait for the activity locus to arrive at this level of the tower to collapse it without mercy. This is of course very speculative.

Still, here are several possible solutions:

- either one could collapse iteratively (currying) all the levels that are involved, with respect to the successive residual programs; this supposes that the initial reflective program has a finite degree of introspection, but that hypothesis seems reasonable [des Rivières & Smith 84] [Smith & des Rivières 84][25];

---

[25] In this connection, a properly tail-reflective implementation starts to make sense: reflectively inactive levels would not be activated so that a program progressing and reflecting forward, infinitely, would be properly performed. Symmetrically, a program regressing and reifying backwards, infinitely, would be properly

- or collapse them all at once (cartesian product); this would make Mix operate on a larger scale, partially evaluating a series (a tower) of interpreters with respect to a reflective program;

- or enrich the partial evaluator reflectively: each time a reflective procedure is encountered, Mix could enrich itself in order to handle it; only finitely many enrichments would occur for a reflective program that terminates.

4 Comparison with related work

4.1 Reflection

[Smith 82] introduces procedural reflection. The model is a reflective tower and an illustration is 3-Lisp [Smith & des Rivières 84]. [Friedman & Wand 84] [Wand & Friedman 86a] [Wand & Friedman 86b] develop the reflective language Brown, which is not semantically rationalized as 3-Lisp is, but gives a non-reflective account of the reflective tower. A meta-continuation represents the tower. In essence, it stacks all the continuations of the levels above [des Rivières 86]. When reification or reflection occur, the current continuation is popped from or pushed on the meta-continuation. This solves elegantly the problem of having an efficient implementation of a procedurally reflective language: there is one direct level of execution, at any time.

Brown clearly separates reification, which goes up in the tower from reflection, which goes down, and 3-Lisp does not. The reason essentially is to make visible the reification of internal structures in the interpreter, when a reifier is applied. It is distinguished from the creation of a new level down in the tower, when a new level of interpretation is spawned.

3-Lisp and Brown are both concerned with normalization and evaluation (resp.) rather than transformation or program transformation. In this article we propose an interpretive architecture where displaying a primitive functional object gives an intensional view of the tower.

Computational reflection as addressed here concerns procedure-based languages. Logic-based and object-based [Maes 87] reflective architectures exist as well. But to our knowledge, there is still no intended partial evaluator for object-oriented programming, whereas partial evaluation is developed in the area of logic programming [Sestoft & Zamulin 88].

---

performed too. A concrete example of a tail-reflective program is the procedurally reflective definition of **if** both in 3-Lisp and in Brown: two new levels are created for evaluating both the test part and one alternative. The situation is exactly comparable to a call followed by a return in assembly language, the only difference being that the last thing done at one level is to create a new one. In essence: a proper tail-recursion requires a constant continuation; a proper tail-reflection requires a constant meta-continuation.

4.2   Partial evaluation

4.2.1   The origins

[Lombardi & Raphael 64] is the seminal paper that coined the term "partial evaluation". The idea was to extend the "execution" of commands to the "evaluation" of expressions, and to make that "evaluation" total as well as partial: the LISP program given in appendix handles omitted and indefinite arguments, with threshold conditions. It seems to be the first computer-implemented partial evaluator in existence and ever published.

It does not address partial evaluation and simplification of conditional expressions. Partial evaluation is essentially viewed as an extended evaluation. What is remarkable is that the authors do not refer to Kleene's S-m-n theorem [Kleene 52], nor do they mention currying, although Alonzo Church is quoted as the justification of λ-notation in Lisp. This article is completely typical of that time: great ideas addressing indiscriminately syntactic and semantic issues.

The program of [Lombardi & Raphael 64], when transcribed in Scheme (say), gives the results that could be expected: when possible, the evaluation is total; otherwise, one gets a residual program that could be symbolically simplified.

4.2.2   The classics

[Futamura 71], [Futamura 82], [Beckman *et al.* 76] and [Ershov 77], [Ershov 78], [Ershov 82] have pioneered the self-application of partial evaluators. The first concerns Lisp-like functional languages and the latter concern more conventional imperative languages.

We have tried here to relate the necessary identity of the base language and the subject language of such autoprojectors with the phenomenon of reflection. The point was that a reflective tower also requires the identity of the languages at each level.

4.2.3   The moderns

MIX is the first actual self-applicable partial evaluator [Jones *et al.* 85]. The subject language is Mixwell [Jones *et al.* 87]. It is untyped, unsorted, applicative and first order. It provides a pattern matching facility with the `let` construction. It is not procedurally reflective although semantically flat: normal forms are designated by `quoted` expressions.

Making Mixwell procedurally reflective would make it higher-order. It should then be possible to partially evaluate programs written in continuation-passing style or even in continuation-noting style [Talcott 85], that is using, for example, the Scheme operator `call-with-current-continuation` [Rees & Clinger 86].

SCHISM [Consel 88] is a self-applicable partial evaluator for a first-order subset of Scheme: Schismer. Schismer is semantically non-flat, in the sense that the integers, boolean values and null object are implicitly recognized as constants. The interesting point is that both Brown and Schismer get freed from the systematic handles [Smith 82] of 3-Lisp and Mixwell, that is, of the `quotes` overrunning programs.

4.3 Related bridges

According to [Sestoft & Zamulin 88] there is no published bridge between reflection and partial evaluation. The only reference pairing the two terms is [Coscia *et al.* 86] where "to reflect" is taken in the sense "to mirror". The point is to mirror a meta-interpretation (meta-level) into a direct execution (object-level) [Takeuchi 86].

[Talcott & Weyhrauch 87] pairs partial evaluation and reflection principles in a very general way, raising some challenging problems. However it does not address further the self-application of a partial evaluator, referring to it as a "bootstrapping" method.

[Guzowski 87] describes a partial evaluator for Scheme, which is intended to be integrated in a compiler. It is not designed for self-application.

4.4 Interpretive architectures

Functional tags have been introduced empirically in InterLisp [Teitelman 75], to break down any `apply` bottleneck (the explicit tests on the function to apply – see for example the meta-circular definition of [McCarthy 81] p 712). They were named "functional types".

In VLisp [Greussay 77] [Chailloux 80] and Le_Lisp [Chailloux *et al.* 84], the number of functional types is increased to speed up interpretation. In these systems, a Lisp symbol has two special fields for holding a functional type and a functional value if it is defined as a named function.

In Méta-VLisp [Saint-James 87] [Danvy *et al.* 87], functional types are multiplied (about 50 currently) to handle more closely the number and types of arguments to functions and the number and types of intermediary results. The goal is generality and efficiency. Functions are represented with a cons-cell pairing their functional type and value. They are first-class. Functional values are functions in the underlying virtual Lisp machine. By choice they are interpreted as numbers, since these functions are translated to binary code.

KLisp [Danvy 87] is a Scheme-clone which implements the architecture presented here.

5 Conclusion, assessments and issues

A partial evaluator and a reflective tower share the interesting property of keeping their meta-language and their processing language identical. This is necessary to perform the self-application of a partial evaluator and to express simple and reflective procedures in the same language. This article attempts to build a bridge between reflection and partial evaluation on that basis.

It has been discovered that they cannot be directly related as partial evaluation transforms and reflection evaluates. However the impact of partial evaluation on a tower of interpreters has been shown to be collapsing levels. Self-application of a partial evaluator has been shown to generate collapsers and collapser generators. Making the tower reflective with reflective procedures, it has appeared that partially evaluating reflective programs produces partially known structures. Handling reflective programs with a higher degree of introspection than 1 requires collapsing all the involved levels. It leads to a choice: either to iterate partial evaluation to get rid of reflection; or to define the partial evaluation of several successive self-interpreters; or to define a partial evaluator which would enrich itself, reflectively, at each occurrence of a reflective procedure.

What makes reflection valuable is that it offers a greater expressive power. Partial evaluation proposes a semantically sound transformation of powerful and lucid reflective programs into less clear but more conventional versions for the architectures of today[26].

Work remains to be done to achieve the bridge between reflection and partial evaluation. This article has explored the intriguing similarities of procedural reflection and the self-application of partial evaluation. There appears to be ground for further work, both in the theoretical relations of the two fields and in a more practical application of one to the other. Typically, developing

$$3\text{-}MIX \text{ int int pgm}$$

that is a partial evaluator operating on two levels of interpretation, would allow to specialize programs with higher-order functions, which still is an open problem, and control structures as well, since both have been shown to be reflective procedures with a degree of introspection 1.

Acknowledgements

Interacting with Karoline Malmkjær, Torben Mogensen, Mads Rosendahl, Peter Sestoft, Kristoffer Høgsbro Holm, Anders Bondorf, Charles Consel, Bruce F. Duba, John Sturdy and Neil D. Jones has definitely influenced the development of this work. It is a pleasure to thank them here.

6   Appendix: an Interpretive Architecture

This appendix presents a Scheme implementation of the interpretive architecture referred to in this article. It is structured in four parts: the core, the initial environment, the structural and meta-structural primitives (that is, primitive functions and control structures) and the auxiliary functions. The core specifies what is the operator in an expression. The initial environment specifies how operations are performed.

The language defined here is basically Scheme: an expression language, dynamically typed, lexically scoped, properly tail-recursive, applicative and higher order. The central idea of this description is to recognize semantic objects rather than syntactic conditions. This makes it having no "special form" and being easily extensible to support reification and reflection, as described earlier. Finally, the specification is compositional.

Expressible values and denotable values are confused since any result can be bound in the environment. Their domain is noted *Den-Val*. Syntactic expressions, environments, continuations and answers are respectively noted *Exp, Env, Cont, Ans*. The domains of identifiers, numbers and of booleans are noted *Ide, Num* and *Bool*.

---

[26]In a way similar to Prolog [Sterling & Shapiro 86] which expresses concisely goal-directed programs.

The specification language is Scheme. The names of our Scheme functions are prefixed with an underscore. Making the specification meta-circular allows to run it and to actually display the intensional view introduced here. This will conclude the present appendix.

6.1   The Core

The core of the interpreter is the set of functions which are directly involved in evaluating an expression. The central function is _eval. The domain of functional objects is defined as the disjoint sum of the domains of particular functional objects: primitive functions, meta-structural operators and λ-abstractions. The function _apply merely disassembles members of that direct sum, according to their functional tag. The remaining specifies how functions are applied.

An expression is either a constant, an identifier or a combination. A constant denotes itself: it is already in normal form. The *handles* of [Smith 82] would intervene here. An identifier is looked up in the current environment. The functional part of a combination is evaluated and a functional object is expected to be applied later on.

```
(define _eval
    (lambda (e r k)
        (cond
            ((_constant? e)
                (k e))
            ((_identifier? e)
                (_lookup e r k))
            ((pair? e)
                (_eval (car e)
                        r
                        (lambda (f)
                            (_apply f (cdr e) r k)))
            (else
                (_wrong '_eval "unknown form" e)))))
```

$$\texttt{\_eval: } Exp \times Env \times Cont \rightarrow Ans$$

A functional object is represented as a pair, whose first projection is a functional tag and whose second projection is a functional value. The function _apply disassembles it.

```
(define _apply
    (lambda (fo l r k)
        (if (atom? fo)
            (_wrong '_apply "not a functional object" fo)
            (case (car fo)
                ((subr)
                    (_apply_subr (cdr fo) l r k))
                ((fsubr)
                    (_apply_fsubr (cdr fo) l r k))
```

```
((closure)
     (_apply_closure (cdr fo) l r k))
(else
     (_wrong '_apply "unknown functional tag" (car fo)))))))
```

_apply: *(Tag × Functional-Value) × List-of-Exp × Env × Cont → Ans*

The domain of primitive functions is defined as a direct sum of functions, according to their arity. Once again, it is represented with a pair. Applying a primitive function thus reduces to check its arity, to evaluate the arguments, to apply the functional value and pass the result to the continuation.

```
(define _apply_subr
    (lambda (fv l r k)
        (if (= (length l) (car fv))
            (case (car fv)
                ((0)
                    (k ((cdr fv))))
                ((1)
                    (_apply_subr_1 (cdr fv) (car l) r k))
                ((2)
                    (_apply_subr_2 (cdr fv) (car l) (cadr l) r k))
                ((3)
                    (_apply_subr_3 (cdr fv) (car l) (cadr l) (caddr l) r k))
                (else
                    (_wrong '_apply_subr "arity" fv)))
            (_wrong '_apply_subr "wrong number of arguments" l))))
```

_apply_subr: *(Num × (Den-Val* → Den-Val)) × List-of-Exp × Env × Cont → Ans*

For example, the actual application of a binary primitive function looks like:

```
(define _apply_subr_2
    (lambda (s x1 x2 r k)
        (_eval x1 r (lambda (a1)
                    (_eval x2 r (lambda (a2)
                                (k (s a1 a2)))))))))
```

_apply_subr_2: *(Den-Val × Den-Val → Den-Val) × Exp × Exp × Env × Cont → Ans*

Similarly, the domain of meta-structural primitives is defined as a direct sum of polyadic primitives. Applying a meta-structural primitive thus reduces to check its arity and pass the arguments (still unevaluated) to the functional value.

```
(define _apply_fsubr
    (lambda (fv l r k)
        (if (zero? (car fv))       ; arbitrary number of arguments
```

```
((cdr fv) 1 r k)
(if (= (length 1) (car fv))
    (case (car fv)
       ((1)
          ((cdr fv) (car 1) r k))
       ((2)
          ((cdr fv) (car 1) (cadr 1) r k))
       ((3)
          ((cdr fv) (car 1) (cadr 1) (caddr 1) r k))
       (else
          (_wrong '_apply_fsubr "arity" fv)))
    (_wrong '_apply_fsubr "wrong number of arguments" 1)))))
```

_apply_fsubr: *(Num × (Exp* × Env × Cont → Ans)) × List-of-Exp × Env × Cont → Ans*

The domain of abstractions is a direct sum of abstractions, according to their arity. The list of actual parameters must match the list of formal parameters. The arguments are evaluated. The body of the closure is evaluated in its lexical environment, extended with the binding of its parameters.

```
(define _apply_closure
    (lambda (c 1 r k)
       (if (= (length 1) (car c))
           (_evlis 1 r (lambda (lv) ((cdr c) lv k)))
           (wrong '_apply_closure "wrong number of arguments" 1))))
```

_apply_closure: *(Num × (List-of-Den-Val × Cont → Ans)) × List-of-Exp × Env × Cont → Ans*

The function _evlis evaluates all the elements of a list and stores the results in a list.

```
(define _evlis
    (lambda (1 r k)
       (if (null? 1)
           (k '())
           (_eval (car 1)
                  r
                  (lambda (a)
                     (_evlis (cdr 1)
                             r
                             (lambda (lv)
                                (k (cons a lv)))))))))
```

_evlis: *List-of-Exp × Env × Cont → Ans*

The function _lookup maps an identifier to its value in an environment. If the identifier is not in the lexical extension of the environment, it is looked up in the global environment with the function _lookup_global. An environment is either a list of lexical extensions or the global environment. A lexical extension pairs a list of identifiers and a list of values.

```
(define _lookup
    (lambda (i r k)
        (if (null? r)
            (_lookup_global i k)
            (let ((pos (_index i (caar r))))
                (if (number? pos)
                    (k (_access (_nth pos (cdar r))))
                    (_lookup i (cdr r) k))))))
```

_lookup: *Identifier* × *Env* × *Cont* → *Ans*

The global environment pairs a list of names and a list of values:

```
(define _lookup_global
    (lambda (i k)
        (let ((pos (_index i table-global-names)))
            (if (number? pos)
                (k (_access (_nth pos table-global-values)))
                (_wrong '_lookup_global "unbound identifier" i)))))
```

_lookup_global: *Identifier* × *Cont* → *Ans*

NB: as the scope of a variable is lexical, an identifier could be directly coded with its access in the environment. This would be done statically (at compile time) and would provide a direct access to bindings.

6.2   The Initial Environment

The initial environment consists of a list of names and a list of values. The structural and meta-structural promitives are defined there. They are the usual functions operating on elementary data structures and the "special forms" quote, lambda and if. The meta-structural primitive **define** is used to extend the global environment.

(define table-global-names '(	(define table-global-values (list
nil	'()
#t	'#t
#f	'#f
car	(cons 'subr (cons 1 car))
cdr	(cons 'subr (cons 1 cdr))
cons	(cons 'subr (cons 2 cons))
null?	(cons 'subr (cons 1 null?))
atom?	(cons 'subr (cons 1 atom?))
pair?	(cons 'subr (cons 1 pair?))
equal?	(cons 'subr (cons 2 equal?))
quote	(cons 'fsubr (cons 1 _quote))
lambda	(cons 'fsubr (cons 2 _lambda))
if	(cons 'fsubr (cons 3 _if))
define	(cons 'fsubr (cons 2 _define))
list	(cons 'fsubr (cons 0 _evlis))
zero?	(cons 'subr (cons 1 zero?))
add1	(cons 'subr (cons 1 add1))
sub1	(cons 'subr (cons 1 sub1))
))	))

NB: keeping the global environment as a global data structure makes it straightforward to implement recursion.

6.3 The Structural and Meta-Structural Primitives

The functional value of quote realizes the designation: the continuation is applied to its unevaluated arguments.

```
(define _quote
    (lambda (x r k)
        (k x)))
```

_quote: $Exp \times Env \times Cont \to Ans$

The functional value of lambda merely builds closures with appropriate functional tags. They are the operational values of abstractions.

```
(define _lambda
    (lambda (lp b rd kd)
        (kd (cons 'closure
                  (cons (length lp)
                        (lambda (lv ka)
                            (_eval b (_extend_env lp lv rd) ka)))))))
```

_lambda: $List\text{-}of\text{-}Identifiers \times Exp \times Env \times Cont \to Ans$

NB: this specification may look unconvincing, as a closure is implemented using an abstraction. [Reynolds 72] develops on using data structures to represent closures, instead. However, the present specification does not break the denotational assumption: in all equations, what is evaluated on the right part is a proper sub-expression of what appears in the left part. Nonetheless, it is properly tail-recursive.

The functional value of `if` evaluates the "test" argument and, conditionally, the "then" or "else" argument.

```
(define _if
    (lambda (p at af r k)
        (_eval p r (lambda (a) (_eval (if a at af) r k)))))
```

$$\_if:\ Exp \times Exp \times Exp \times Env \times Cont \to Ans$$

The functional value of `define` modifies or extends the global environment.

```
(define _define
    (lambda (i d r k)
        (if (_identifier? i)
            (_eval d r (lambda (a)
                        (let ((pos (_index i table-global-names)))
                            (if (number? pos)
                                (begin
                                    (_update (_nth pos table-global-values) a)
                                    (k i))
                                (begin
                                    (set! table-global-names
                                        (cons i table-global-names))
                                    (set! table-global-values
                                        (cons a table-global-values))
                                    (k i))))))
            (_wrong '_define "undefinable" i))))
```

$$\_define:\ Identifier \times Exp \times Env \times Cont \to Ans$$

6.4   The Auxiliary functions

The function `_wrong` always being called tail-recursively, can merely return the list of its arguments.

```
(define _wrong list)
```

$$\_wrong:\ Den\text{-}Val^* \to Ans$$

A constant is either the empty list, a number or a string.

```
(define _constant?
    (lambda (x)
        (or (null? x)
            (number? x)
            (string? x))))
```

$\text{\_constant?}: Exp \rightarrow Bool$

An identifier is a Scheme symbol.

```
(define _identifier? symbol?)
```

$\text{\_identifier?}: Exp \rightarrow Bool$

The function _index returns the position of an identifier in a list of identifiers or bottom.

```
(define _index
    (lambda (i l)
        ((rec self (lambda (n l)
                    (if (null? l)
                        'bottom
                        (if (equal? i (car l))
                            n
                            (self (add1 n) (cdr l)))))) 0 l)))
```

$\text{\_index}: Ide \times List\text{-}of\text{-}Ide \rightarrow Num \cup \{\bot\}$

The function _nth returns an element at a given offset of a list.

```
(define _nth
    (lambda (n l)
        (if (zero? n)
            l
            (_nth (sub1 n) (cdr l)))))
```

The functions _access and _update act on the first component of a Scheme pair.

```
(define _access car)
(define _update set-car!)
```

The following function lexically extends an environment by pulling a list of identifiers and a list of values at the top of it.

```
(define _extend_env
    (lambda (par l env)
        (cons (cons par l) env)))
```

6.5   Making the interpreter meta-circular

So far, recursion is straightforwardly handled by the global definitions of
`table-global-names` and `table-global-values`. Local recursive definitions can be
achieved with a circular data structure, as suggested in [Landin 64]:

```
(define _rec
    (lambda (i v r k)
        (let ((r (_extend_env (list i) (list "_undef_") r)))
            (_eval v r (lambda (a)
                        (begin
                            (_update (cdr (car r)) a)
                            (k a)))))))
```

To make _rec available, it is sufficient to add its name and the value

$$cons(\text{``fsubr''}, cons(2, \_rec))$$

in the global environment. Similarly, extending the interpreter with a disjunction such as
orelse in ML is realized by adding the name or and the value

$$cons(\text{``fsubr''}, cons(0, \_or))$$

with the function:

```
(define _or
    (lambda (l r k)
        (if (null? l)
            (k '#f)    ; neutral element
            (_or_loop l r k))))

(define _or_loop
    (lambda (l r k)
        (if (null? (cdr l))
            (_eval (car l) r k)
            (_eval (car l) r (lambda (a)
                            (if a
                                (_or_loop (cdr l) r k)
                                (k a)))))))
```

NB: this specification is properly tail-recursive.

To make this description meta-circular, it is sufficient to define in the initial environment all the functions used here, by transitive closure of the relation "is used". Next
section witnesses the intensional view of building a tower of such interpreters.

6.6   A session

The following scenario consists of running the specification under Scheme 84
[Friedman *et al.* 85] and under the interpreter itself, since it is meta-circular:

```
>>> (load "sint.scm")          ; loads the self-interpreter under Scheme
t
>>> (int)                      ; starts it
hello
==> (load "sint.scm")          ; loads the self-interpreter under itself
loaded
==> (int)                      ; starts it
hello
==> car                        ; the tower has a height 3
(subr 1 subr 1 . <CLOSURE>)
==> (car '(a b c))
a
==> (end)                      ; ends the session
bye
==> car                        ; the tower has a height 2
(subr 1 . <CLOSURE>)
==> (end)                      ; ends the session
bye
>>> car                        ; back to one level of interpretation
<CLOSURE>
>>>
```

The self-interpreter is loaded under Scheme and activated. A banner (`hello`) and a
specific prompter (`==>`) are displayed.

The self-interpreter is loaded again and activated. The same banner and prompter are
displayed.

The identifier `car` is evaluated. It is bound in the initial environment to the primitive
function *car*. Its functional tag is `subr`. Moreover, *car* is unary, and thus exhibits an
injection tag 1. The functional value of *car* is the function *car* at the level above, that is
in the interpreter running the current interpreter. There again, *car* is a unary primitive
function, and has two injection tags `subr` and 1. The functional value is the Scheme
function *car*, and Scheme 84 prints it as `<CLOSURE>`. This illustrates intensionally three
levels of interpretation.

Next interaction illustrates the function *car* in action.

The current session is then ended. Evaluating the variable `car` gives again an intensional view of two levels of interpretation.

The current session is then ended. Back under Scheme, the function *car* is displayed.

This intensional view points out the cost of a meta-interpretation. It justifies the
current efforts in partial evaluation for breaking down the resulting order-of-magnitude
loss of efficiency.

References

[Batali 83] John Batali: *Computational Introspection*, MIT-AIL, AI Memo No 701, Cambridge, Massachusetts (February 1983)

[Batali 86] John Batali: *Reasoning about Control in Software Meta-Level Architectures*, Proceedings of the Workshop on *Meta-Level Architectures and Reflection*, Patti Maes and Daniele Nardi (eds.), North-Holland, Alghero, Sardinia (October 1986)

[Beckman *et al.* 76] Lennart Beckman, Anders Haraldsson, Östen Oskarsson, Erik Sandewall: *A Partial Evaluator, and its Use as a Programming Tool*, Artificial Intelligence, Vol. 7 pp 319-357 (1976)

[Bondorf 87] Anders Bondorf: *Towards a Self-Applicable Partial Evaluator for Term Rewriting Systems*, Proceedings of the Workshop on *Partial Evaluation and Mixed Computation*, D. Bjørner, A. P. Ershov and N. D. Jones (eds.), North-Holland, Gl. Avernæs, Denmark (October 1987) (this volume)

[Bratman 61] H. Bratman: *An Alternate Form of the "Uncol Diagram"*, CACM Vol. 4, No 3 p 142 (1961)

[Chailloux 80] Jérôme Chailloux: *Le Modèle VLISP: Description, Implémentation et Evaluation*, thèse de 3e cycle, Université Paris 6, Technical Report LITP 80–20, Paris, France (April 1980)

[Chailloux *et al.* 84] Jérôme Chailloux, Mathieu Devin and Jean-Marie Hullot: *Le_Lisp, a Portable and Efficient Lisp System*, Conference record of the 1984 ACM Symposium on LISP and Functional Programming pp 113–123, Austin, Texas (August 1984)

[Consel 88] Charles Consel: *New Insights into Partial Evaluation: the SCHISM Experiment*, Proceedings of the European Symposium on Programming ESOP '88, Nancy, France (March 1988)

[Coscia *et al.* 86] Patricia Coscia, Paola Francesci, Giorgio Levi, Giuseppe Sardu, Luigia Torre: *Object Level Reflection of Inference Rules by Partial Evaluation*, Proceedings of the Workshop on *Meta-Level Architectures and Reflection*, Patti Maes and Daniele Nardi (eds.), North-Holland, Alghero, Sardinia (October 1986)

[Danvy 87] Olivier Danvy: *A KLISP Primer*, draft, DIKU, University of Copenhagen, Copenhagen, Denmark (April 1987)

[Danvy *et al.* 87] Olivier Danvy, Marc Gengler, Pierre Jeanjean, Francis Kloss, Gérard Nowak, Emmanuel Saint-James: *Higher-Order Applicative Programming in Méta-VLisp*, Technical Report LITP 87-76, Université Paris 6, Paris, France (October 1987)

[Danvy & Malmkjær 88] Olivier Danvy, Karoline Malmkjær: *Intensions and Extensions in a Reflective Tower*, submitted to publication (January 1988)

[des Rivières & Smith 84] Jim des Rivières and Brian C. Smith: *The Implementation of Procedurally Reflective Languages*, Conference Record of the 1984 ACM Symposium on LISP and Functional Programming pp 331–347, Austin, Texas (August 1984)

[des Rivières 86] Jim des Rivières: *Control-Related Meta-Level Facilities in LISP (Extended Abstract)*, Proceedings of the Workshop on *Meta-Level Architectures and Reflection*, Patti Maes and Daniele Nardi (eds.), North-Holland, Alghero, Sardinia (October 1986)

[Ershov 77] Andrei P. Ershov: *On the Partial Computation Principle*, Information Processing Letters, Vol. 6, No 2 pp 38-41 (April 1977)

[Ershov 78] Andrei P. Ershov: *On the Essence of Compilation*, in *Formal Description of Programming Concepts* pp 391-420, E. J. Neuhold (ed.), North Holland (1978)

[Ershov 82] Andrei P. Ershov: *Mixed Computation: Potential Applications and Problems for Study*, Theoretical Computer Science No 18 pp 41-67 (1982)

[Friedman & Wand 84] Dan P. Friedman, Mitch Wand: *Reification: Reflection without Metaphysics*, Conference Record of the 1984 ACM Symposium on LISP and Functional Programming pp 348–355, Austin, Texas (August 1984)

[Friedman et al. 85] Dan Friedman, Chris Haynes, Eugen H. Kohlbecker, Mitch Wand: *Scheme 84 Interim Reference Manual*, Technical Report No 153, Computer Science Department, Indiana University, Bloomington, Indiana (June 1985)

[Futamura 71] Yoshihiko Futamura: *Partial Evaluation of Computation Process – an Approach to a Compiler-Compiler*, Systems, Computers & Control Vol. 2, No 5 pp 45-50 (1971)

[Futamura 82] Yoshihiko Futamura: *Partial Computation of Programs*, RIMS Symposia on Software Science and Engineering, Eiichi Goto et al. (eds.), Lecture Notes in Computer Science No 147 pp 1-35, Kyoto, Japan (1982)

[Greussay 77] Patrick Greussay: *Contribution à la Définition Interprétative et à l'Implémentation de λ-Langages*, thèse d'état, Université Paris 6, Technical Report LITP 78-2, Paris, France (November 1977)

[Guzowski 87] Mark A. Guzowski: *Towards Developing a Reflexive Partial Evaluator for an Interesting Subset of LISP*, Technical Report 871101, Incremental Systems Corporation, Pittsburgh, Pennsylvania (November 1987)

[Heering 86] J. Heering: *Partial Evaluation and ω-Completeness of Algebraic Specifications*, Theoretical Computer Science, Vol. 43 pp 149-167 (1986)

[Jones *et al.* 85] Neil D. Jones, Peter Sestoft, Harald Søndergaard: *An Experiment in Partial Evaluation: the Generation of a Compiler Generator*, Proceedings of the first International Conference on Rewriting Techniques and Applications, Lecture Notes in Computer Science No 202 pp 124-140, Jean-Pierre Jouannaud (ed.), Dijon, France (June 1985)

[Jones *et al.* 87] Neil D. Jones, Peter Sestoft, Harald Søndergaard: *MIX: a Self-Applicable Partial Evaluator for Experiments in Compiler Generation*, to appear in the journal *LISP and Symbolic Computation*, DIKU Report 87/8, DIKU, University of Copenhagen, Copenhagen, Denmark (June 1987)

[Kleene 52] S. C. Kleene: *Introduction to Metamathematics*, Van Nostrand (1952)

[Kohlbecker 86] Eugene E. Kohlbecker: *Syntactic Extensions in the Programming Language Lisp*, Ph. D. thesis, Technical Report No 199, Computer Science Department, Indiana University, Bloomington, Indiana (August 1986)

[Landin 64] Peter J. Landin: *The Mechanical Evaluation of Expressions*, Computer Journal, Vol. 6, No 4 pp 308-320 (1964)

[Landin 65] Peter J. Landin: *A Correspondance between ALGOL 60 and Church's Lambda Notation*, CACM Vol. 8, No 2 pp 89-101 & No 3 pp 158-165 (February & March 1965)

[Launchbury 87] John Launchbury: *Projections for Specialisations*, Proceedings of the Workshop on *Partial Evaluation and Mixed Computation*, D. Bjørner, A. P. Ershov and N. D. Jones (eds.), North-Holland, Gl. Avernæs, Denmark (October 1987) (this volume)

[Lombardi & Raphael 64] Lionello A. Lombardi, Bertram Raphael: *LISP as the Language for an Incremental Computer*, from *The Programming Language LISP: Its Operation and Applications* pp 204-219, Information International, Inc., The M.I.T. Press (1964)

[Maes 87] Patti Maes: *Computational Reflection*, PH. D. thesis, Technical Report 87-2, Artificial Intelligence Laboratory, Vrije Universiteit Brussel, Brussels, Belgium (January 1987)

[McCarthy 60] John McCarthy: *Recursive Functions of Symbolic Expressions and their Computation by Machine, part I*, CACM, Volume 3, No 3 pp 184-195 (March 1960)

[McCarthy *et al.* 60] J. McCarthy, R. Brayton, D. Edwards, P. Fox, L. Hodes, D. Luckham, K. Maling, D. Park, S. Russell: *LISP 1 Programmer's Manual*, Computation Center and Research Laboratory of Electronics, MIT, Cambridge, Massachusetts (March 1960)

[McCarthy *et al.* 62] John McCarthy, Paul W. Abrahams, Daniel J. Edwards, Timothy P. Hart, Michael I. Levin: *LISP 1.5 Programmer's Manual*, MIT Press, Cambridge, Massachusetts (1962)

[McCarthy 81] John McCarthy: *History of LISP*, from *History of Programming Languages* pp 173-197, Richard L. Wexelblat (ed.), Academic Press (1981)

[Mogensen 87] Torben Mogensen: *Partially Static Structures in a Self-Applicable Partial Evaluator*, Proceedings of the Workshop on *Partial Evaluation and Mixed Computation*, D. Bjørner, A. P. Ershov and N. D. Jones (eds.), North-Holland, Gl. Avernæs, Denmark (October 1987) (this volume)

[Rees & Clinger 86] Jonathan Rees, William Clinger (eds): *Revised³ Report on the Algorithmic Language Scheme*, Sigplan Notices, Vol. 21, No 12 pp 37-79 (December 1986)

[Reynolds 72] John C. Reynolds: *Definitional Interpreters for Higher-Order Programming Languages*, Proceedings of the 25th ACM National Conference pp 717–740, New York (1972)

[Saint-James 87] Emmanuel Saint-James: *De la Méta-Récursivité comme Outil d'Implémentation*, thèse d'état, Université Paris 6, Paris, France (December 1987)

[Schmidt 86] David A. Schmidt: *Denotational Semantics: a Methodology for Language Development*, Allyn and Bacon, Inc. (1986)

[Sestoft 85] Peter Sestoft: *The Structure of a Self-Applicable Partial Evaluator*, DIKU Report 85/11, DIKU, University of Copenhagen, Copenhagen, Denmark (1985)

[Sestoft & Zamulin 88] Peter Sestoft, Alexander V. Zamulin: *Annotated Bibliography on Partial Evaluation and Mixed Computation*, Proceedings of the Workshop on *Partial Evaluation and Mixed Computation*, D. Bjørner, A. P. Ershov and N. D. Jones (eds.), North-Holland, Gl. Avernæs, Denmark (October 1987) (this volume)

[Smith 82] Brian C. Smith: *Reflection and Semantics in a Procedural Language*, Ph. D. thesis, MIT/LCS/TR-272, Cambridge, Massachusetts (January 1982)

[Smith 84] Brian C. Smith: *Reflection and Semantics in Lisp*, Conference Record of the 14th Annual ACM Symposium on Principles of Programming Languages pp 23-35, Salt Lake City, Utah (January 1984)

[Smith & des Rivières 84] Brian C. Smith, Jim des Rivières: *Interim 3-LISP Reference Manual*, Intelligent Systems Laboratory, Xerox PARC, Palo Alto, California (1984)

[Smith 86] Brian C. Smith: *Varieties of Self-Reference*, Proceedings of the 1986 Conference on *Theoretical Aspects of Reasoning about Knowledge* pp 19-43, J. Halpren (ed.), Morgan Kaufman, Los Altos, California (March 1986)

[Steele & Sussman 78] Guy L. Steele Jr., Gerald J. Sussman: *The Art of the Interpreter, or the Modularity Complex (Parts Zero, One, and Two)*, MIT-AIL, AI Memo No 453, Cambridge, Massachusetts (May 1978)

[Sterling & Shapiro 86] Leon Sterling, Ehud Shapiro: *The Art of Prolog, Advanced Programming Techniques*, The MIT Press, Cambridge, Massachusetts (1986)

[Strachey 67] Christopher Strachey: *Fundamental Concepts in Programming Languages*, International Summer School in Computer Programming, Copenhagen, Denmark (August 1967)

[Sturdy 87] John C. G. Sturdy: *Six Months Report*, University of Bath, School of Mathematical Sciences, Bath, England (March 1987)

[Sturdy 88] John C. G. Sturdy: Ph. D. thesis (forthcoming), University of Bath, School of Mathematical Sciences, Bath, England (1988)

[Sussman & Steele 75] Gerald Jay Sussman, Guy L. Steele Jr.: *SCHEME: an Interpreter for Extended λ-Calculus*, MIT-AIL, AI Memo No 349, Cambridge, Massachusetts (December 1975)

[Takeuchi 86] Akikazu Takeuchi: *Affinity between Meta Interpreters and Partial Evaluation*, from *Information Processing 86* pp 279-282, H.-J. Kugler (ed.), North-Holland (1986)

[Talcott 85] Carolyn Talcott: *The Essence of Rum: A Theory of the Intensional and Extensional Aspects of Lisp-type Computation*, Ph. D. thesis, Department of Computer Science, Stanford University, Stanford, California (August 1985)

[Talcott & Weyhrauch 87] Carolyn Talcott, Richard Weyhrauch: *Partial Evaluation, Higher Order Abstractions and Reflection Principles as System Building Tools*, Proceedings of the Workshop on *Partial Evaluation and Mixed Computation*, D. Bjørner, A. P. Ershov and N. D. Jones (eds.), North-Holland, Gl. Avernæs, Denmark (October 1987) (this volume)

[Teitelman 75] Warren Teitelman: *InterLISP Reference Manual*, revised edition, Xerox PARC, Palo Alto, California (1975)

[Wand & Friedman 86a] Mitch Wand, Dan P. Friedman: *The Mystery of the Tower Revealed: a non-Reflective Description of the Reflective Tower*, Conference Record of the 1986 ACM Symposium on LISP and Functional Programming pp 298–307, Cambridge, Massachusetts (August 1986)

[Wand & Friedman 86b] Mitch Wand, Dan P. Friedman: *Getting the Levels Right*, Proceedings of the Workshop on *Meta-Level Architectures and Reflection*, Patti Maes and Daniele Nardi (eds.), North-Holland, Alghero, Sardinia (October 1986)

Partial Evaluation and Mixed Computation
D. Bjørner, A.P. Ershov and N.D. Jones (Editors)
Elsevier Science Publishers B.V. (North-Holland)
© IFIP, 1988

A PROGRAM DEVELOPMENT METHODOLOGY BASED ON A UNIFIED APPROACH TO EXECUTION AND TRANSFORMATION

John Darlington and Helen Pull

Department of Computing
Imperial College
London, Great Britain

We discuss the relationship between execution, symbolic execution and program transformation in the context of a functional programming language. We review the fact that in a language incorporating unification, or narrowing, these, previously separate, activities are instances of the same process and that there are precise containment relationships between them.

Based on this unified view of execution and transformation we present a program development methodology that allows a programmer to develop initial, possibly inefficient, versions of his program, control their execution to improve their efficiency and finally incorporate this improvement into the program via a source to source transformation.

A language of *scripts* is developed that allows both execution and transformation strategies to be expressed. We give examples illustrating how a script developed to control a particular execution can be systematically extended to produce the source transformation of the program that will achieve the same improvement.

A *partial evaluator* that supports this methodology has been designed for the functional language Hope and a prototype has been implemented. We give examples showing its use in controlling executions and performing transformations.

Finally we show how such a partial evaluator can be extended to efficiently support *meta-programming* and thus be incorporated into a programming environment to produce a system that supports a simple, but powerful, software development methodology over the whole life cycle.

1. EXECUTION SYMBOLIC EXECUTION AND TRANSFORMATION

1.1 Language

For this exposition we will use the functional language Hope, Burstall et al. [1980], extended with the *absolute set abstraction* construct introduced in Darlington et al. [1987]. This extended language is supported by the Hope in Hope interpreter developed at Imperial by Helen Pull.

We will not rehearse the syntax of standard Hope or the details of execution in a standard functional language. The following example will be used throughout the paper and illustrates the main features.

```
dec double: list num -> list num;
dec sum    : list num -> num;
```

- - - double [ ] <= [ ];
- - - double (x::l) <= (2*x) :: double l;

- - - sum [ ] <= 0;
- - - sum (x::l) <= x + sum l;

sum (double [1, 2, 3]);

12: num

Thus a program is a set of equations defining functions and execution can be viewed as the rewriting of an expression to a normal form (one that contains no defined functions). Crucially in a standard functional language the expression being reduced, and therefore the answer, is not allowed to contain variables.

This is not the case in logic programming languages such as Prolog, Kowalski [1974]. The observation that the capability of operating on expressions involving non-ground terms gives extra expressive power to the language led to our introduction of absolute set abstraction into Hope.

The absolute set abstraction construct allows sets of values to be defined by conditions (equalities between functional expressions) that they must satisfy. Thus variables are introduced into the language as first class objects as the following examples illustrate.

{ l | double l = [2, 4, 6]};

{ [1, 2, 3] } : set (list num)

dec length: list alpha -> num;

- - - length [ ] <= 0;

- - - length (x::l) <= 1 + length l;

l st (length l = 2);

[u, v] : list alpha

To support this construct, the execution mechanism has to be extended from reduction to narrowing as explained in Darlington et al [1987]. Thus unification is used to derive output substitutions to instantiate the variables in the absolute set abstraction expression.

1.2 Transformation

In parallel with the development of functional languages and their execution models, the idea of manipulating the sources of programs using meaning preserving program transformations was being explored.

The 'unfold/fold' transformation system introduced in Burstall and Darlington [1977] has formed the basis of several transformation exercises. This system consists of six rules allowing the safe manipulation of *program equations* viz.

(i)   *Definition.* Introduce a new recursion equation whose left hand expression is not an instance of the left hand expression of any previous equation.

(ii)   *Instantiation.* Introduce a substitution instance of an existing equation.

(iii)   *Unfolding.* If E<=E' and F<=F' are equations and there is some occurrence in F' of an instance of E, replace it by the corresponding instance of E' obtaining F'', then add the equation F<=F''.

(iv)   *Folding.* If E<=E' and F<=F' are equations and there is some occurrence in F' of an instance of E', replace it by the corresponding instance of E obtaining F'', then add the equation F<=F''.

(v)   *Abstraction.* We may introduce a where clause, by deriving from a previous equation E<=E' a new equation

E<=E' [u1/F1,...,un/Fn]
        where (ul,...,un) == (F1,...,Fn)

(E[E1/E2] means E with all occurrences of subexpressions E2 replaced by E1.)

(vi)   *Laws.* We may transform an equation by using on its right hand expression any laws we have about the primitives (associativity, commutativity, etc.) obtaining a new equation.

Note that the unfold and fold steps involve *pattern matching*. The substitution applies to the bound variables of the equation used, no substitution is applied to the variables in the expression being replaced by the unfold/fold step for the very good reason that no variables are allowed in that expression! This exactly mirrors the situation for normal functional evaluation.

Thus, given the previous equations we can transform an equation such as:

dec g: list num -> num;

- - - g l   <= sum (double l);

Thus

- - - g nil   <= sum (double nil)
                                Instantiation
                <= sum (nil)
                                Unfold
                <= 0
                                Unfold

- - - g (x::l) <= sum (double (x::l))
                                Instantiation

                <= sum ((2*x) :: double l)
                                Unfold

                <= (2*x) + sum (double l)
                                Unfold

                <= (2*x) + g l
                                Fold

Giving a final, slightly more efficient, program.

    dec g: list num-> num

    - - - g nil   <= 0;

    - - - g (x::l)   <= (2*x) + g l;

Program transformation is not an automatic process. Intelligence is needed to produce an appropriate sequence of transformation steps, in particular choosing the correct instantiation and selecting the appropriate expression to unfold. Furthermore, as originally conceived, transformation was a separate activity from program execution. The similarity of transformation, particularly the unfold step, to program execution has often been observed. The critical difference is that transformation operates on whole equations and the expressions in the equations may contain (bound) variables. The term *symbolic execution* has been coined to express this relationship, or more particularly the activity of 'executing' a program with symbolic (non-ground) values.

1.3 Symbolic Evaluation and Transformation

The insight is, of course, that in a language employing unification or narrowing there is no distinction between execution and symbolic execution, variables are first class objects and as we can evaluate programs some of whose arguments are non-ground we can evaluate programs all of whose arguments are non-ground (i.e. symbolicly).

Again this relationship was not lost on the logic programming or partial evaluation communities, Ershov [1982], but its (re)-discovery has proved an exhilarating and eye-opening discovery for ourselves.

Armed with this insight we were able to re-express our previous transformation work. Recall that in transformation we are operating on equations, that is left hand sides as well as right hand sides. This is easily accomplished if for the function in question, f say, we consider the expression

    { (l, lr) | f l = lr }

the variable l will gather instantiations to be applied to the left hand side and lr will represent the right hand side.

Returning to our transformation example.

    --- g l <= sum (double l) ;

We can re-express this by considering the expression

    { (l, lr) | g l = lr }

The Hope in Hope interpreter will evaluate this expression just as any other. It immediately expands it to

    { (l, lr) | sum (double l) = lr }

The next step is to narrow the expression double l. Two equations

    - - - double nil <= nil;

and

    - - - double (x::l) <= (2*x) :: double l;

can be used and we get

$$\{(nil, lr) \mid sum (nil) = lr\} \cup \{(x::l, lr) \mid sum ((2*x) :: double\ l) = lr\}$$

(This is exactly as executed on the interpreter except that we have substituted for some internally generated variables for readability purposes)

Two further reductions and unifications get us to

$$\{ (nil, 0)\} \cup \{(x::l, (2*x) + lr) \mid sum (double\ l) = lr\}$$

Thus in two steps we have almost achieved our transformation by straight forward evaluation. Note critically that the unification has automatically generated sensible instantiations for the bound variable l. Left to itself the interpreter would carry on unwinding indefinitely, we still need a fold step to complete the process. This simply consists of replacing sum (double l) in the above with g l getting

$$\{(nil, 0)\} \cup \{(x::l, (2*x) + lr) \mid g\ l = lr\}$$

Which is equivalent to the pair of equations

$$- - - g\ nil <= 0;$$

$$- - - g\ (x::l) <= (2*x) + g\ l;$$

Two things of importance should be noted. The first is that the introduction of unification into the basic execution mechanism has unified execution and symbolic execution. The second is that the ability of unification to generate sensible output substitutions has combined the instantiation and unfold steps of the previous transformation. The whole process looks more systematic and uniform.

The observations that using unification enables the instantiation and unfold step to be combined into a more directed single operation gives rise to the question, can the same thing be done for the fold step? The answer is that it certainly can, that is we can regard folding as just narrowing against the reversed equation, but as yet we have been unable to generate a (sensible) example where one needs to perform an instantiation to enable a fold to be done. In all cases simple pattern matching is sufficient. This issue is closely related to idea of 'forced folding' discussed in Darlington [1981] but there the manipulations induced to allow folding are more complex than simple instantiation involving auxiliary function definition and synthesis.

The idea is also closely related to the Knuth-Bendix process and further investigation is necessary to compare the two approaches.

2. SCRIPT DRIVEN EVALUATION AND TRANSFORMATION

2.1 Algorithm = Logic + Control

Stealing clothes from the logic programming and partial evaluation communities and finding them comfortable encouraged us to re-examine another idea, that of algorithm = logic + control expounded in Kowalski [1979].

We have therefore augmented our interpreter to allow execution to be controlled by a data structure we call a *script*. Our experience of unifying execution and transformation led us to conceive of the idea of using the same methodology both to control execution and to direct source transformations. We give a brief introduction to these ideas in 2.1.1 below and expand in more detail on the actual structures involved and their implementation in 2.1.2.

2.1.1. Evaluation control

If we return to our example of computing g [1, 2, 3] where g is defined as

  dec g: list num -> num;

  - - - g l <= sum (double l);

we see that their are basically two evaluation strategies. One, corresponding to strict evaluation, builds all of the intermediate list [2, 4, 6] before summing it. The other strategy, lazy evaluation, co-routines between double and sum, never completely building the intermediate data structure. We can use scripts to specify these, and other behaviours. Thus, informally, the scripts

  seq [repeat (unfold double), repeat (unfold sum)]

  repeat (seq [unfold (double), unfold (sum)])

represents the strict and lazy strategies respectively. seq is the script operator that applies a list of scripts sequentially and repeat is the operator that continually re-applies its argument as long as it succeeds, i.e. causes a rewrite to be applied.

The lazy strategy is to be preferred as it avoids building the intermediate data structure. However, implementing it by a controlled evaluation has unnecessary overheads, the transformed version of g produced earlier is more efficient, nevertheless it implements the same evaluation strategy, can we get to it systematically from our script?

We saw earlier that folding was basically used to 'tie up' a potentially infinite symbolic evaluation. Thus if we wish to re-use scripts to control evaluation the systematic step seems to be to replace repeats by folds and then use the script to execute the program totally non-ground. This works very nicely with our example. Thus the script

  fold (seq [unfold (double), unfold (sum)])

applied to the execution of

  {(l, lr) | g l = lr}

produces the equations exactly as before

  { (nil, 0) } ∪ { (x::l, (2*x) + lr) | g l =lr }

We would, therefore, like to develop a methodology that allows a programmer to develop initial, possibly inefficient, program specifications, experiment with alternative evaluation strategies using scripts and then encapsulate the chosen strategy via a source transformation. Again the attraction of unifying execution and transformation is that the programmer is nowhere presented with a discontinuity in the development of his program, the knowledge gained about the program's behaviour can be directly used to produce the appropriate transformation.

2.1.2 The Script Language

Let us now define the simple script language as it is currently implemented.

The script we use is:

data script == narrow (list char) ++ seq (list script) ++ repeat (script) ++ fold (script);

The narrow operator applies equations to expressions allowing the instantiation of variables in the argument where necessary. When no such output substitutions occur, the narrow operator is identical to unfolding. This simply restates our previous observation - that narrowing subsumes unfolding.

For more complex transformations the script operators may require extra information.

The seq and repeat script primitives are as described in a previous section.

As a programming example the following function will be used, front(l, n) returns the initial segment of l of length n.

dec front : list alpha # num -> set (list alpha)

--- front (l, n) <= { l1 | length (l1) = n, append (l1, _) = l };

dec append : list alpha # list alpha -> list alpha
! joins two lists together

--- append(nil, l) <= l;

--- append(x::l1, l2) <= x :: append(l1, l2);

Some sample scripts which could be used for this program are:

Strategy_1:
      repeat (seq ([narrow ("append"), narrow ("length")]))

Strategy_2:
      seq ([repeat (narrow ("append")), repeat (narrow ("length"))])

Strategy_3:
      seq ([repeat (narrow ("length")), repeat (narrow ("append"))])

Notice the relationship between the repeat and seq operators, and the concept of breadthfirst/depthfirst search strategies from logic programming. A script of the form:

      repeat (seq [narrow (f1), narrow (f2)])

is equivalent to a breadthfirst search, where at each node in the search space f1 is evaluated before f2. In other languages this fine level of control could only be achieved by textual alterations to the program text.

By contrast the script:

      seq [repeat (narrow (f1)), repeat (narrow (f2))]

defines a depthfirst search with f1 being evaluated to completion before the evaluation of f2 commences.

2.1.3. Search Trees

The purpose of using a script is to be able to alter, and hopefully improve, a program's execution behaviour. It therefore follows that the programmer needs to be able to observe his program's behaviour. In keeping with an underlying philosophy that all objects of interest should have a concrete, manipulable, and storable representation at the appropriate level in the programming environment, we introduced the data type *search_tree* to represent the evaluation behaviour of a program.

A search tree is currently defined as:

data search_tree == search_node (search_info # list search_tree);

The second parameter to the search_node holds the branches from that node. Alternative branches in the tree represent different paths to an object level result. These results will be elements of a set during standard evaluation of absolute set abstractions or alternative equations during symbolic execution.

The parameter search_info will hold one of the following:

> If the node is a leaf, a Hope expression which is an object level result.

> If the node is an internal node, it will identify which equations were applied at that step in the execution. The order in which equations were applied is then evident from the level in the tree that the equation appears.

With such a data structure available the programmer may now analyse an execution strategy. He may, for example, count the total number of equations applied during the execution. Alternatively, he may be interested in the number of branches in the tree which do not have an object level result at the leaf, representing unsuccessful searches.

This particular definition of a search tree is given by way of example only.It may not provide the data required in all cases. In particular, for the two scripts given above for the sum double example, the number of equations applied is the same regardless of the script used. In this case we would like the search tree to record the size of the data structures generated during the execution. We envisage, therefore, search trees which may hold a variety of types of information.The programmer may specify for any particular execution, exactly which type of search tree is to be built.

3.   META LEVEL PROGRAMMING

So far we have attempted to put execution and transformation on a uniform basis. To implement and make use of transformation we need to be able to write functions that manipulate program representations and to be able to take such representations and use them as normal functions.The term meta programming is usually applied to this activity.

Thus we wish to be able to apply user defined functions to structures which are internal to the programming environment, i.e. those which represent functions. Although a function is accessible to the programmer its representation, normally, is not.

One method of implementing meta programming in a typed language involves making the type of such internal structures visible to the programmer and transferring the arguments of his (meta) function to the object level prior to application.The results of such computations must be transferred back to the meta level before being incorporated into the programming environment. This, obviously, has severe overheads.

Our approach not only eliminates these inefficiencies but also relieves the programmer from the burden of writing such meta level functions, or even of having to be familiar with the types of internal structures.

The script primitives represent a complete set of execution and transformation operations.The programmer is required only to name the operations to be performed via a script. In interpreting the script, the partial evaluator applies the operations at the meta level.

In making the primitives predefined we ensure that only meaning preserving transformations can be applied. No direct access to the program data structure is possible. We apply the same methodology to search trees which, because they can contain program representations, are meta level objects.

So far then, we have discussed various programming styles ranging from the familiar reduction and narrowing through to symbolic evaluation and investigation of execution strategies, and eventually to program transformation. We have claimed that all these activities can be integrated into a single framework and that a programming session may involve any or all of these with no discontinuities between them. In the next section we will give an example of a programming session involving all these activities.

3.1 Classification of Programming Activities

This table attempts to categorise the various operations a programmer may perform:

Level	Mode	
	Evaluation	Program Manipulation
Level I - object level programming, optionally script driven		
Level II - meta level search tree built and visible		
Level III - object level representation of search tree is manipulable		

Modes

The two modes, evaluation and program manipulation or transformation, separate the evaluation of expressions from computations which are applied to programs, i.e. equations. As previously stated, this is a conceptual difference, not an operational one - the same processing engine is used. It should not be assumed that unground terms do not exist in real execution mode, since this mode incorporates the normal use of absolute set abstractions in which such terms often appear. Rather, the mode of a particular computation reflects the programmer's goal. As soon as he starts to operate on equations, with the intention of generating a new, transformed set of equations, he is in transformation mode. The only other difference is that some script primitives are only meaningful during the latter mode

Levels

The activities which the three levels reflect have all already been discussed. They identify the run time structures which are built and the extent to which they are manipulable.

Level I involves normal evaluation. In evaluation mode this will be either according to the default evaluation strategy or script-driven. In transformation mode it will always be script-driven, since there is no concept of program transformation which is not controlled by a script. The latter, on successful termination, will produce equations which may subsequently be added to the program. At the object level the search tree is not built and no meta level objects may be converted to the object level.

At Level II the search tree is built. It remains a meta level object but may be displayed and analysed by predefined functions. The investigation of alternative execution strategies and "trial" transformations takes place at this level. Also under consideration is the possibility of incorporating all the normal debugging facilities at this experimentation level. The tree holds object level results at its leaves. These are accessible and, therefore, any new equations generated may be subsequently added to the program, as at the previous level.

At Level III a representation of the search tree is built at the object level. Hence, the programmer may define and apply functions to analyse the search tree. Representations of 'equations' appear in the tree and these equations may not be added to the program because they exist as a representation of a representation.

This division of the programming activities into levels corresponding to the extent to which the programmer wishes to see and manipulate run time structures achieves our aim of giving him full access to program structures without compromising safety or efficiency.

3.1.1 Predefined Meta Functions

Obviously, some predefined meta functions will be necessary to carry out the activities described above. A minimum set of such functions is defined below:

The first four of these take the same pair of arguments.

Function Name:	**Apply_script**
Arguments:	1. Either a Hope expression or a set of equations defining a function 2. A Script
Action performed:	The script is interpreted and applied to the first argument. The set of object level results is returned
Level(s) of operation:	I

Function Name:	**Trace_search**
Arguments:	1. Either a Hope expression or a set of equations defining a function 2. A Script
Action performed:	The script is interpreted and applied to the first argument. The search tree is built and displayed
Level(s) of operation:	II

Function Name:	**Trace_with_Results**
Arguments:	1. Either a Hope expression or a set of equations defining a function 2. A Script
Action performed:	The script is interpreted and applied to the first argument. The search tree is built and displayed and the set of object level results is returned
Level(s) of operation:	II

Function Name:	**Build_tree**
Arguments:	1. Either a Hope expression or a set of equations defining a function 2. A Script
Action performed:	The script is interpreted and applied to the first argument. An object level representation of the search tree is constructed and returned
Level(s) of operation:	III

Two more meta functions are needed:

Function Name:	**Eqns**

Argument:	The name of function
Action performed:	The equations of the function are returned
Level(s) of operation:	I, II & III

Function Name:	**Extend_program**

Arguments:	1. A function name
	2. A set of equations
Action performed:	The program is extended with the equations defining the function named.
Level(s) of operation:	I & II

4. SAMPLE PROGRAMMING SESSION

In this section, a sample programming session illustrates the categories of activities introduced in the previous session.

We will use the program introduced earlier viz:

dec append : list alpha # list alpha -> list alpha ;

--- append (nil, l) <= l ;

--- append (x::l1, l2) <= x :: append (l1, l2) ;

dec length : list alpha -> num ;

--- length (nil) <= 0 ;

--- length (x::l) <= 1 + length (l) ;

dec front : list alpha # num -> set (list (alpha)) ;

--- front (l, n) <= { l1 | length (l1) = n, append (l1,_) = l }

along with the following scripts:

dec strategy_1, strategy_2, strategy_3 : script ;

--- strategy_1
    <= repeat (seq ([**narrow** ("append"), **narrow** ("length")])) ;

--- strategy_2
    <= seq ([repeat (**narrow** ("append")), repeat (**narrow** ("length"))]) ;

--- strategy_3
    <= seq ([repeat (**narrow** ("length")), repeat (**narrow** ("append"))]) ;

The meta functions introduced in the previous section appear in bold typeface.

Execution

Level I

At this level, the programmer would enter, for example,

  front ([1,2,3], 2);

or

  apply_script (front ([1,2,3], 2), strategy_1);

In either case the response from the system would be:

{ [1,2] } : set (list num)

Level II

Here the programmer is trying to determine the differences between various evaluation strategies.

The command **trace_search** (front ([1,2,3], 2), strategy_1) results in the search tree being displayed:

```
BRANCH
  PATH
    NARROW  append (x::l, 11)
    NARROW  length (x::l)
    BRANCH
      PATH
        NARROW  append (x::l, 11)
        NARROW  length (x::l)
        BRANCH
          PATH
            NARROW        append (x::l, 11)
            FAIL
          PATH
            NARROW  append (nil, l)
            NARROW  length (nil)
            RESULT  [1,2]
      PATH
        NARROW  append (nil, l)
        FAIL
  PATH
    NARROW  append (nil, l)
    FAIL
```

Alternatively **trace_search** (front ([1,2,3], 2), strategy_2) displays:

```
BRANCH
    PATH
            NARROW  append (x::l1, l2)
            BRANCH
                PATH
                        NARROW  append (x::l1, l2)
                        BRANCH
                            PATH
                                    NARROW append (x::l1, l2)
                                    NARROW  append (nil, l)
                                    NARROW  length (x::l)
                                    NARROW  length (x::l)
                                    FAIL
                            PATH
                                    NARROW  append (nil, l)
                                    NARROW  length (x::l)
                                    NARROW  length (x::l)
                                    NARROW  length (nil)
                                    RESULT [1,2]
                PATH
                        NARROW  append (nil, l)
                        NARROW  length (x::l)
                        FAIL
    PATH
            NARROW  append (nil, l)
            FAIL
```

while

trace_search (front ([1,2,3], 2), strategy_3)

also produces the corresponding search tree.

Level III

The simple trees shown above can easily be analysed visually. This might not always be the case and if the system does not provide the analysis functions the programmer requires, he may write his own. Say, for example, he wished to count the total number of rules used in each execution he would define a function, count say, thus:

dec count: search_tree -> num ;

--- count (tree) <= .... ;

Then he could compare the efficiencies of the alternative execution strategies simply by executing the following expressions:

count (**build_tree** (front ([1,2,3], 2), strategy_1));
9 : num

count (**build_tree** (front ([1,2,3], 2), strategy_2)) ;
13 : num

count (**build_tree** (front ([1,2,3], 2), strategy_3)) ;
6 : num

Transformation

Level I

At this point the programmer may be satisfied the a particular script, say strategy_1, satisfies his requirements. Using his expertise, he would know that the next step would be to change the repeats in the script to folds giving:

dec transformation_strategy_1 : script;

--- transformation_strategy_1 <= fold (seq ([narrow ("append"), narrow ("length")])) ;

By issuing the command:

     apply_script (**Eqns** ("front"), transformation_strategy_1) ;

the equations representing the new front function would be generated:

--- front (l, 0) <= nil ;
--- front (x::l, succ (n)) <= x:: front (l, n) ;

These might then be incorporated into the program:

     extend_program("new_front",
                           apply_script(**Eqns** ("front"),transformation_strategy_1)) ;

If strategy_2 had been chosen instead a slightly more complex transformation strategy would produce

--- front (l, n) <= { l1 | (l1,_) in append*(l) : length (l1) = n };

where append*(l) finds all pairs of lists (l1, l2) such that append (l1, l2) = l. This version uses *relative set abstraction* and is therefore totally functional.

Strategy_3, on the other hand, would lead to

--- front (l, n) <= { l1 | l1 in append** (l), l1 in length*(n) };

where append**(l) returns all initial segments of the list l, and length*(n) returns a list of length n.

Level II

In more complex examples, it may will not be sufficient to take a script which defines a satisfactory execution strategy and produce the appropriate transformation script automatically. It is, however, our experience so far that the structure of the execution script very often carries over to the transformation script.

If the script fails to return a suitable set of equations, the search tree will help to uncover the reason:

     trace_search (**Eqns** ("front"), transformation_strategy_1) ;

This tree may also be required by the more confident programmer for developing transformation strategies without previously experimenting with execution strategies.

Level III

As would be expected, the programmer would construct the object level representation of the transformation search tree here, in order to scrutinise it more closely:

dec transf_tree : search_tree ;

--- transf_tree <= **build_tree** (**Eqns** ("front"), transformation_strategy_1) ;

5.   CONCLUSIONS

Unifying execution and transformation reduces the number of concepts to be handled and simplifies matters both for the programmer and system implementor. We propose to develop our prototype partial evaluator and experiment with it to carry out more complex execution modifications and transformations.

ACKNOWLEDGEMENTS

This research is part of the Flagship project, a collaborative project between Imperial College, Manchester University and I.C.L., funded under the U.K Alvey programme. We thank all our colleagues and collaborators for their contributions

REFERENCES

[Burstall 1977]   R.M. Burstall and J. Darlington. A Transformation System for Developing Recursive Programs, *J.ACM, 24* , 1977.

[Burstall 1980]   R.M. Burstall, D.M. MacQueen and D. Sanella. Hope: an Experimental Applicative Language. *Proc LISP and Functional Programming Conference, Stanford,* 1980.

[Darlington 1981]   J. Darlington. An Experimental Program Transformation System. *Artificial Intelligence Journal,* 1981.

[Darlington 1987]   J. Darlington. H. Pull and A.J. Field. The Unification of Functional and Logic Languages. In *G. Lindstrom and D. de Groot,* editors, Logic Programming: Functions, Relations and Equations, Prentice/Hall, 1987.

[Ershov 1982]   A.P. Ershov. Mixed Computation: Potential Apllications and Problems for Study. *Theoretical Computer Science,* (18):41-67,1982.

[Kowalski 1974]   R. A. Kowalski. Predicate Logic as a Programming Language. *Proc IFIP 74, North Holland, Amsterdam,* 1974.

[Kowalski 1979]   R. A. Kowalski. Algorithm = Logic + Control. *CACM,* August 1979.

Partial Evaluation and Mixed Computation
D. Bjørner, A.P. Ershov and N.D. Jones (Editors)
Elsevier Science Publishers B.V. (North-Holland)
© IFIP, 1988

GENERALIZED PARTIAL COMPUTATION

Yoshihiko Futamura and Kenroku Nogi

Advanced Research Laboratory
Hitachi, Ltd.
Kokubunji, Tokyo, Japan

In this paper, a new partial computation method that makes use of a theorem prover when evaluating conditions of conditional expressions is proposed. This method is called "Generalized Partial Computation (GPC)" because it is more powerful than conventional methods that use interpreters when evaluating conditions of conditional expressions (The old method is called "Interpreter Dependent Partial Computation (IDPC)" in this paper).
To show GPC's power, it is applied to a program transformation of an O(m*n) time program to an O(m+n) program. Also shown is that the combination of GPC and recursion removal methods is a very powerful program transformation technique. Finally, two more order changing program transformation examples are given.

1. INTRODUCTION

The practical importance of partial computation in computer science was first recognized around 1970. Partial computation has been considered in the following way with this kind of program transformation [2]:

Let f be a program (function) with two parameters k (a known parameter) and u (an unknown parameter). First, finish all the f computations that can be performed by using only the k value while f computations that cannot be performed without knowing the u value should be left intact. Then we have a new program, f_{k0}, having the property
$$f_{k0}[u] = f[k0;u]$$
where $k0$ stands for the k value.

This formula is similar to Kleene's s-m-n theorem [7] as first pointed out by Ershov [5]. However, f_{k0} of the s-m-n theorem is just a function closure $\lambda[[u];f[k0;u]]$ and it does not improve program efficiency. On the contrary, since computations concerning k have been finished in f_{k0} produced by partial computation, the $f_{k0}[u0]$ may run quicker than $f[k0;u0]$ when a given u value is $u0$.

Let $\alpha[f;k0]$ be the result of partially computing f when $k=k0$, i.e. if α is a partial evaluator, then $\alpha[f;k0]=f_{k0}$. Let I be a programming language interpreter and p be a program. The following relationships are then well known [2, 3, 12]:

$\alpha[I;p]$ is an object program.
$\alpha[\alpha;I]$ is a compiler.
$\alpha[\alpha;\alpha]$ is a compiler-compiler.

By using an interpreter for evaluating conditions of conditional expression, α's have been implemented. This implementation has a limitation that it uses only the k value. The basic idea of α and its limitation will be discussed in Appendix 1.

In this paper, a new partial evaluator using not only the k-value, but also all information on the operating environment of a program is proposed. Let β be a new partial evaluator, e a program and i information on the operating environment. The result of partially computing e on i is described as β [e;i] in full, or $(e)_i$ as an abbreviation.

β uses a theorem prover and information i when it evaluates conditions of a conditional expression. Note that, for notational convenience, program e is a form (function with its parameters) for β while a program is a function for α (see Appendix 1).

Let b be a program, and k and u be free variables in b. If $f = \lambda [[k;u];b]$ then $\alpha [f;k0] = \lambda [[u]; \beta [b; \{k=k0\}]]$ where $\{k=k0\}$ is a predicate (information) denoting that $k0$ is the k-value. This shows that β can be considered to be more general than α. Therefore, β is called a Generalized Partial Computation (GPC) while α is called an Interpreter Dependent Partial Computation (IDPC) (see Appendix 1).

The principle of β is simple and has been used in informal program transformations. It was also implicitly used in Kahn's partial evaluator [6]. This paper extends the principle to a more powerful and systematic partial computation method. First, the basic idea of β and its application to program transformation from a nonlinear pattern matcher to a KMP type linear pattern matcher [8] are shown. This is an example transformation of an O(m*n) time program to an O(m+n) time program. Finally, least fixpoints of recursive programs are produced using a combination of partial computation and recursion removal techniques. These productions are also examples of order changing program transformations.

2. GENERALIZED PARTIAL COMPUTATION PRINCIPLE

Generalized Partial Computation (GPC) has been established by formalizing human informal program transformation processes (getting a fixpoint of a recursive function [9] is an example of the transformation). GPC uses a logic system to evaluate a predicate which is not evaluable for an interpreter . The logic system is consistent with the interpreter and is called underlying logic. Before explaining the basic idea of GPC, definitions will be provided for u-form, u-information and underlying logic. Reader's knowledge about PAD [4] (a graphical representation for structured programs) and LISP M-expression [10] are assumed in the following discourse.

u-form: $\perp$, a constant, variable u, or a form including only u as free variables. The symbol $\perp$ is called bottom and is used to stand for an undefined value.

Example 1: A conditional u-form written in PAD:

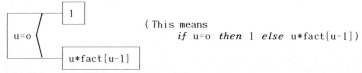

(This means
    if u=o *then* 1 *else* u*fact[u-1])

When a form includes more than one kind of variable, for example x and y, then the variables are treated as a variable-vector such as $u = \langle x, y \rangle$.

value of u-form: Let e be a u-form and *eval* be a fixpoint interpreter of u-forms. Then $eval[e;((u.c))]$ stands for a value of e when the constant c is a value of u. If the value of $eval[e;((u.c))]$ is undefined then $eval[e;((u.c))] = \perp$.

Definition 1: Let a and b be constants or $\perp$. Then $a \subseteq b$ if and only if $a=b$ or $a = \perp$.

u-information: A conjunction of predicates on *u* (Note that this is a u-form too).

Example 2: Examples of u-information:
    ¬null[u]∧(A=car[u])∧null[cdr[u]]
    true (This is represented by ϕ.)

Definition 2: Compatibility with *eval*:
Let *i* and *p* be any u-information such that i ⊢*p, where i ⊢*p means that *p* is provable from *i* based on some logic system. The logic system is compatible with *eval* if and only if eval[p;((u.c))]⊆true for any constant c such that eval[i;((u.c))]⊆true.

When eval[p;((u.c))] is always true or false for any u-form (predicate) *p* and any constant c, then ⊆ is equivalent to =. The compatibility property guarantees the soundness of a logic system with respect to the interpreter *eval*.

Example 3: Let *L0* be a logic system in which i=p if i ⊢*p. Then *L0* is a trivial logic system that is compatible with *eval*.

underlying logic: The logic system is called underlying logic if and only if it is compatible with eval.

Depending on the predicate evaluation power of eval, an underlying logic can be any logic system, for example propositional logic, predicate logic, or informal logic.

generalized partial computation method β and β-L partial evaluator:
Let *L* be an underlying logic, *e* be a u-form and *i* be a u-information. Then any transformation *β* of *e* to a u-form using *L* and *i* is called a generalized partial computation method. The result of the transformation is written as *β*[L;e;i]. The pair *β-L* is called the *β-L* partial evaluator or the *β* -partial evaluator if *L* is not very important. When there is no confusion, *β* can stand for both the partial computation method and the *β* partial evaluator. For example, *β* in *β*[e;i] in the following discourse means a *β-L* partial evaluator, and *β*[e;i]=*β*[L;e;i] for some *L*. When *β* is also clear in the context, (e)ᵢ is used to represent *β*[e;i].

In the following discourse, *β* and *L* stand for a nonspecific partial computation method and its underlying logic, respectively. *β*0,*β*1,*β*2 and *β*3 stand for specific partial computation methods.

Example 4: Let *β0* be a transformation such that *β0*[e;i]=e. Then *β0* is a very trivial partial computation method.

Example 5: Partial computation method *β* 1:
(1) If e is a conditional expression, i.e.

then
    (1.1) If i ⊢*p , then (e)ᵢ=(x)ᵢ
    (1.2) If i ⊢*¬p , then (e)ᵢ=(y)ᵢ
    (1.3) If it is not easy to decide if i ⊢*p or i ⊢*¬p, then

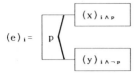

$$(e)_i = p \left\{ \begin{array}{l} (x)_{i \wedge p} \\ \\ (y)_{i \wedge \neg p} \end{array} \right.$$

(2) If e is not a conditional expression, then
    $(e)_i = e$ (i.e. there is no transformation)

Theorem proving and generation of a new predicate have also been conducted in symbolic execution and program verification [11] as in $\beta1$. However, they have never had the function of generating a conditional form described in the (1.3) above.

Example 6: Let $\beta1$ be the $\beta1$-LO partial evaluator for *LO* of Example 3. Then $\beta1[e; \phi] = e$.

Example 7: Partial computation of Ackermann's function when $\beta1$ uses informal logic on natural numbers:
  $a[m;n] =$

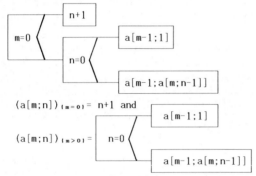

$$(a[m;n])_{\{m=0\}} = n+1 \text{ and}$$

$$(a[m;n])_{\{m>0\}} = \left| n=0 \left\{ \begin{array}{l} a[m-1;1] \\ \\ a[m-1;a[m;n-1]] \end{array} \right. \right.$$

Definition 3: Let d and e be u-forms, and i be u-information. Then $d \subseteq^i e$ if and only if $eval[d;((u.c))] \subseteq eval[e;((u.c))]$ for any constant c such that $eval[i;((u.c))] \subseteq true$.

This means that e is more defined than d for a constant c when c does not make i false. Therefore, $d \subseteq^\phi e$ means that the domain of e is larger than that of d.

Definition 4: Correctness of β partial evaluator:
β partial evaluator is correct if and only if $e \subseteq^i \beta[e;i]$ for any u-form e and any u-information i.

The correctness of $\beta0$ partial evaluator and $\beta1$-LO partial evaluator is trivial. Let f be an undefined function, and e be a u-form described below:

$$e = \left| f[u]=0 \wedge f[u] \neq 0 \left\{ \begin{array}{l} 1 \\ \\ 0 \end{array} \right. \right.$$

Then Definition 4 suggests that $\beta[e;i]$ may be 0 while $eval[e;((u.c))]$ for any c is undefined. Therefore, program transformation by partial evaluators does not always preserve least fixpoints of programs.

Definition 5: Correctness of partial computation method β:
Partial computation method β is correct if and only if β-L partial evaluator is correct for any underlying logic *L*.

It is trivial that partial computation method $\beta0$ is correct. Two correctness theorems will be given in Appendix 2. Proofs can be conducted by induction on the depth of conditional forms contained in a u-form.

Theorem 1: Partial computation method $\beta1$ is correct.

Definition 6: Let d and e be u-forms and i be a u-information. $d \equiv^i e$ if and only if $d \subseteq^i e$ and $e \subseteq^i d$.

$\equiv^i$ stands for a kind of a strong equivalence. $\equiv^*$ stands for a strong equivalence itself. Symbol $\equiv$ will be used as an abbreviation for $\equiv^*$.

Definition 7: Strict correctness of β partial evaluator:
β partial evaluator is strictly correct if and only if $e \equiv^i \beta[e;i]$ for any u-form *e* and any u-information *i*.

If β partial evaluator is strictly correct, then $e \equiv \beta[e;\phi]$. $e \equiv \beta[e;\phi]$ means that $eval[e;((u.c))]=eval[\beta[e;\phi];((u.c))]$ for any constant c . Therefore, the transformation $\beta[e;\phi]$ by a strictly correct β partial evaluator preserves the least fixpoint of *e*.

Theorem 2: If every predicate, say *p*, in underlying logic is total, i.e. $eval[p;((c.u))]$ is defined for any constant c, then $\beta1$ partial evaluator is strictly correct.

Note that u-information is a dynamic part of information on the operating environment of a program. It varies during partial computation depending on program structure. On the contrary, information on functions (for example $car[con\ s[x;y]]=x$) does not vary during partial computation, i.e. it is static. Let $g0$ be static information, *i* be dynamic u-information, *g* be a higher order variable with its domain of predicates, and $\beta'[e;i;g]$ be $\beta[e;i \wedge g]$. Then $\beta'_{g0}[e;i]=(\beta[e;i \wedge g])_{|g=g0}$. Therefore, β'_{g0} is a partial evaluator including $g0$ static information in it. Thus, generality will not be lost if it is thought that static information is included in a partial evaluator.

3. MORE PRACTICAL GPC

As described in the previous section, $\beta0$ partial evaluator is correct for any underlying logic. Therefore, there are an infinite number of correct partial evaluators. However, $\beta0$ partial evaluator has no practical significance because it does not improve program efficiency. $\beta1$ is still far from being practical because it does not perform any transformation for non conditional u-forms. In this section, partial computation method $\beta2$ that performs significant transformation on u-forms is described. $\beta2$ changes u-form e depending on *e* types such as constant, variable, or composite expression. b/g stands for a u-form obtained from *b*, substituting *g* for all the free occurrences of *u* in *b*. For example, if $b=car[u]$ and $g=cdr[u]$ then $b/g=car[cdr[u]]$.

$\beta2$ handles conditional u-forms the same as $\beta1$. The hardest point in implementing $\beta2$ is when *e* is a composite u-form. Let $e=f[g]$ where *f* is a function not including u as a free variable and *g* is a u-form. Furthermore, let $f=\lambda[[u];b]$ for a u-form *b*. To carry out partial computation of *e* with u-information *i* in this case, just replacing $(f[g])_i$ by $(b/g)_i$ is not enough. This is because when *b* includes recursive calls to *f*, the substitution often causes repetition of similar computation. A technique called "partial definition" is introduced below to eliminate the repetition as often as possible.

Before starting partial computation of u-form f[g] with u-information i, let $f_g{}^i$ be a new function name as a result of the partial computation. *f, g* and *i* is called a nonprimitive function, a symbolic argument and partial information, respectively. $f_g{}^i$ is called a partially defined function for $(f[g])_i$. After completing partial computation, $f_g{}^i$ is finally defined. However, the fact that $f_g{}^i$ will be the result of partial computation may be used during the partial computation. This is a sort of indirect addressing.

A program transformation technique using $f_g{}^i$ during partial computation has already been developed [2]. This is a special case of a general program transformation technique called folding [1]. Introducing a partially defined function is nearly equal to adding the rule $f_g{}^i[u] <= \beta 2[f[g];i]$ to a system of recursion equations and then continuing program transformation with unfolding $\beta 2[f[g];i]$. The use of a partially defined function is similar to folding $\beta 2[f[g];i]$ to $f_g{}^i[u]$.

Let *H* be a global set of functions which is empty before starting partial computation. Using *H*, partially defined functions will be defined below:
Definition 8: Partial definition:
Let *i* be u-information and e=f[g] be u-form. Then $(e)_i$ is partially defined if and only if there is u-information *j* such that
$$i \vdash {}^* j/k \text{ and } f_d{}^j[u] \in H$$
where *d* and *k* are u-forms such that g=d/k.

Definition 9: Partially defined function:
Function $f_d{}^j$ in Definition 8 is called a partially defined function for $(e)_i$.

Example 7: Partially defined functions for $(e)_i$ where e=f[g]:
(1) Let j=ϕ, *i* be any u-information, and *d* and *k* be any u-forms such that g=d/k. If $f_d{}^j \in H$, then $f_d{}^j$ is a partially defined function for $(e)_i$ because $i \vdash {}^* \phi$ and $\phi/k=\phi$.
(2) Let g=cdr[u], k=cdr[u], d=u and j2=ϕ. If $f_u{}^\phi \in H$, then $f_u{}^\phi$ is a partially defined function of $(e)_i$ because of (1).
(3) Let g=cdr[u], k=cdr[u], d=u, j3=$\neg$null[cd²r[u]]∧(cadr[u]=A)∧(car[u]=A), i=$\neg$ null[cd³r[u]]∧$\neg$(cad³r[u]=B)∧(cad²r[u]=A)∧(cadr[u]=A)∧(car[u]=A). If $f_d{}^{j3} \in H$, then $f_d{}^{j3}$ is a partially defined function for $(e)_i$ because $i \vdash {}^* j3/cdr[u]$.

Two partially defined functions $f_d{}^{j2}$ and $f_d{}^{j3}$ in the examples above are for $(f[g])_i$ and $j3 \vdash {}^* j2$. In this case *j3* is called to be closer to *i* than *j2*, and *j2* is called to be further from *i* than *j3*. It is clear that ϕ is the furthest from any *i*.

Assume that $f_d{}^j$ is a partially defined function for $(f[g])_i$ and that the underlying logic is substitutive (i.e. if $i \vdash {}^* j$ then $i/k \vdash {}^* j/k$), then $(f[g])_i$ can be replaced by $(f_d{}^j[k])_i$. The very rough explanation for the correctness of this replacement is:
$$(f_d{}^j[k])_i \equiv {}^i ((f[d])_j/k)_i \equiv {}^i ((f[d]/k)_{j/k})_i \equiv {}^i ((f[g])_{j/k})_i \equiv {}^i (f[g])_i.$$

This use of partially defined function $f_g{}^i$ causes introduction of recursive calls to $f_g{}^i$. Therefore, the result of partial computation is a set of recursive functions (for example, pattern matcher h1 and its auxiliary functions h2, h3 and h4 in the next section). This recursion introduction has the following two effects:
(1) It may dramatically increase the effectiveness of partial computation by partially computing the partial result of $f_g{}^i$ (see the example in a later section).
(2) It may terminate an infinite partial computation caused by repetition of a similar computation.

Note that (1) and (2) above are exclusive. When effect (1) is not expected, i.e. when a program will not be improved, the result of partial computation will be too large or partial computation will not terminate. Thus, (2) is expected. Selecting either (1) or (2) is not decidable. However, a practical heuristic automated method for the selection is an interesting future problem. Partial definition and its proper use may be essential to implementing practical partial evaluators.

To implement partially defined functions, $\beta 2$ uses partial definition operator $<=$. Let f be a function name. Then $f[u]<=\beta 2[e;i]$ (or $f[u]<=(e)_i$) means that when f is referred after the execution of $<=$ operator, the body of f is the result of transformation of e by $\beta 2[e;i]$ at the time of f reference. Therefore f is a dynamically changing nonprimitive function.

Example 8: Partial computation method $\beta 2$:
(1) If e is a conditional form then do the same as $\beta 1$.
(2) If e is a constant then $(e)_i=e$.
(3) If e is a variable then $(e)_i=e$.
(4) If e is a composite form such as $e=f[g]$ for a function f,
  (4.1) If f is a primitive function such as LISP SUBR, then $(e)_i=f[(g)_i]$.
  (4.2) If f is a nonprimitive function such as LISP EXPR, then
    let $f=\lambda[[u];b]$ and:
    (4.2.1) *If $(e)_i$ is partially defined*, then let $f_d{}^j=\lambda[[u];m]$ be one of the partially defined functions (if a function with the closest partial information j to i is selected, the partial evaluator can be executed most quickly). Let $g=d/k$ and $i \vdash {}^*j/k$, then $(e)_i=(f_d{}^j[k])_i$.
    (4.2.2) *If $(e)_i$ is not partially defined*, then select one of the following operations (4.2.2.1) or (4.2.2.2) depending on its effectiveness (note that this selection is up to the user of the partial evaluator).
      (4.2.2.1) If it is effective in performing further partial computation, then $(e)_i=f_g{}^i[u]$; $H=H \cup \{f_g{}^i\}$; $f_g{}^i[u]<=(b/g)_i$.
      (4.2.2.2) Otherwise, $(e)_i=e$.

Example 9: Partial computation of append:

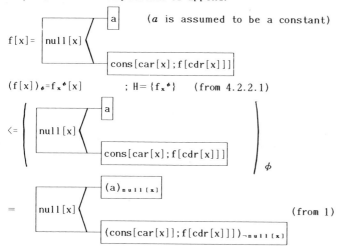

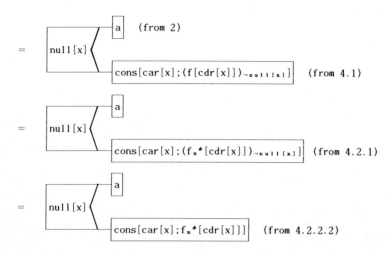

$\beta 2$ terminates when e is a constant or a variable, or when the user of $\beta 2$ decides to terminate. Finding practical methods for automatic termination is an interesting research problem. The correctness of $\beta 2$ will not be discussed in this paper. In the following discussion, $f_x{}'$ may be represented by such a simpler symbol as hn. Furthermore, partial definitions may be omitted when partially defined functions will not be used later.

4. PARTIAL COMPUTATION OF A SIMPLE PATTERN MATCHER

As an example showing the behavior of $\beta 2$, a simple nonlinear pattern matcher m[p;t] is partially evaluated with pattern p=(A A A B) using $\beta 2$ described in the previous section. The definition of m[p;t] is given in Appendix 1. The partial computation result is a KMP [8] type linear pattern matcher. This is an example of order changing program transformation.

For computation convenience, $m_{(A \; A \; A \; B)}[t]$ is first derived by using α instead of directly applying $\beta 2$ to m (see Appendix 1). Partial definitions which are not used later will not be stated explicitly in the following discourse (for example in (1), (3), (5) and (7) below). Note also that m_1 is an abbreviation for $m_{(A \; A \; A \; B)}$ and informal logic on LISP is used as underlying logic.

$h1[t] = (m_1[t])_t{}^{\bullet} \Leftarrow$

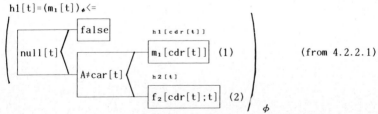

where $h1$ stands for $m_1{}_t{}^{\bullet}$ and forms written in small letters stand for the final result of partial computation with the original forms just beneath them. Numbers such as (1) and (2) written right side of PAD rectangles mean that the partial computation of t-forms contained in the rectangles will be referred later by the numbers.

(1) $i1 = \neg null[t] \wedge (A \neq car[t])$
$(m_1[cdr[t]])_{i1} = h1[cdr[t]]$ (from 4.2.1 and 4.2.2.2)

(2) $i2 = \neg null[t] \wedge (A = car[t])$
$(f_2[cdr[t];t])_{i2} = h2[t] <=$

$$
\left(
\begin{array}{l}
null[cdr[t]]
\left\langle
\begin{array}{l}
\boxed{false} \\[1mm]
A \neq cadr[t]
\left\langle
\begin{array}{l}
\overset{h1[cddr[t]]}{\boxed{m_1[cdr[t]]}} \quad (3) \\[2mm]
\overset{h3[t]}{\boxed{f_3[cddr[t];t]}} \quad (4)
\end{array}
\right.
\end{array}
\right.
\end{array}
\right)_{i2}
$$

(from 4.2.2.1; $h2$ stands for $f_{2\,<cdr[t],t>}{}^{i2}$)

(3) $i3 = i2 \wedge \neg null[cdr[t]] \wedge (A \neq cadr[t])$
$(m_1[cdr[t]])_{i3} =$
$(h1[cdr[t]])_{i3} =$

$$
\left(
\begin{array}{l}
null[cdr[t]]
\left\langle
\begin{array}{l}
\boxed{false} \\[1mm]
A \neq cadr[t]
\left\langle
\begin{array}{l}
\boxed{h1[cddr[t]]} \\[2mm]
\boxed{h2[cdr[t]]}
\end{array}
\right.
\end{array}
\right.
\end{array}
\right)_{i3}
$$

(from 4.2.1 and 4.2.2.1)

$= (h1[cddr[t]])_{i3}$
$= h1[cddr[t]]$ (from 4.2.1 and 4.2.2.2)

(4) $i4 = i2 \wedge \neg null[cdr[t]] \wedge (A = cadr[t])$
$(f_3[cddr[t];t])_{i4} = h3[t] <=$

$$
\left(
\begin{array}{l}
null[cddr[t]]
\left\langle
\begin{array}{l}
\boxed{false} \\[1mm]
A \neq caddr[t]
\left\langle
\begin{array}{l}
\overset{h1[cdddr[t]]}{\boxed{m_1[cdr[t]]}} \quad (5) \\[2mm]
\overset{h4[t]}{\boxed{f_4[cdddr[t];t]}} \quad (6)
\end{array}
\right.
\end{array}
\right.
\end{array}
\right)_{i4}
$$

(from 4.2.2.1)

(5) $i5 = i4 \wedge \neg null[cddr[t]] \wedge (A \neq caddr[t])$
$(m_1[cdr[t]])_{i5} =$

$$
\left(
\begin{array}{l}
null[cdr[t]]
\left\langle
\begin{array}{l}
\boxed{false} \\[1mm]
A \neq cadr[t]
\left\langle
\begin{array}{l}
\boxed{h1[cddr[t]]} \\[2mm]
\boxed{h2[cdr[t]]}
\end{array}
\right.
\end{array}
\right.
\end{array}
\right)_{i5}
$$

(from 4.2.1 and 4.2.2.1)

$= (h2[cdr[t]])_{i5} =$

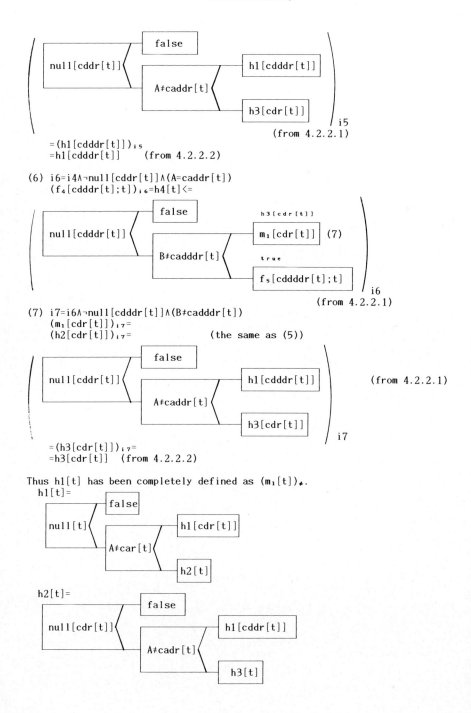

$$= (\text{h1}[\text{cdddr}[t]])_{i5}$$
$$= \text{h1}[\text{cdddr}[t]] \qquad (\text{from } 4.2.2.2)$$

(6) $i6 = i4 \wedge \neg \text{null}[\text{cddr}[t]] \wedge (A = \text{caddr}[t])$
   $(f_4[\text{cdddr}[t]; t])_{i6} = \text{h4}[t] <=$

(7) $i7 = i6 \wedge \neg \text{null}[\text{cdddr}[t]] \wedge (B \neq \text{cadddr}[t])$
   $(\text{m1}[\text{cdr}[t]])_{i7} =$
   $(\text{h2}[\text{cdr}[t]])_{i7} = \qquad (\text{the same as } (5))$

$$= (\text{h3}[\text{cdr}[t]])_{i7} =$$
$$= \text{h3}[\text{cdr}[t]] \qquad (\text{from } 4.2.2.2)$$

Thus h1[t] has been completely defined as $(\text{m1}[t])_\phi$.
   h1[t]=

   h2[t]=

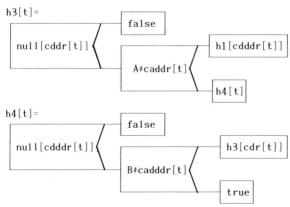

```
h3[t]=
                        ┌─── false
    null[cddr[t]] ──┤                     ┌─── h1[cdddr[t]]
                        └─── A≠caddr[t] ──┤
                                             └─── h4[t]

h4[t]=
                         ┌─── false
    null[cdddr[t]] ──┤                      ┌─── h3[cdr[t]]
                         └─── B≠cadddr[t] ──┤
                                              └─── true
```

Example computation :
  h1[(A A B C A A A B)]=h2[(A A B C A A A B)]=h3[(A A B C A A A B)]=
  h1[(C A A A B)]=h1[(A A A B)]=h2[(A A A B)]=h3[(A A A B)]=h4[(A A A B)]=true

It is clear from the above example that h1[t] runs in almost the same manner
as the KMP pattern matcher. Therefore, if cd"r can be executed in constant
time, h1[t] can run in linear time. Note that the transformation from
$(m_1[cdr[t]])_{17}$ to $(h2[cdr[t]])_{17}$ in (7) is almost the same as that of
$(m_1[cdr[t]])_{15}$ to $(h2[cdr[t]])_{15}$ in (5). This means that $\beta 2$ fails to avoid
repeating the same computation. However, it is not very difficult to correct
$\beta 2$ not repeating this kind of computation.

5. PARTIAL COMPUTATION AND LEAST FIXPOINT

Generalized partial computation is similar to a program transformation technique [9] often used to derive a least fixpoint of a recursive function. Let
β be a strictly correct β partial evaluator, τ [f] be a functional,
$f[u]==\tau$ [f][u] be a recursive program, and $lf\tau$ be a least fixpoint of τ [f].
Then $lf\tau =lub\{\tau$ "$[\Omega]\}$. Let *eval* be a fixpoint interpreter. Then
  $\beta [\tau [f][u];\phi] \equiv \tau [f][u]$ (from strict correctness of β)
  $\tau [f][u]\equiv lf\tau [u]$ (from the definitions of *eval* and $lf\tau$)
Therefore $lf\tau [u]\equiv \beta [\tau [f][u];\phi]$. If the right side does not include a recursive call, $\lambda [[u];\beta [\tau [f][u];\phi]]$ is a fixpoint of $\tau [f]$. Since β often
introduces recursive calls by use of partial definition, it is necessary to
remove recursion from partial computation results to obtain least fixpoints.

To derive a fixpoint of a recursive program, a program transformation rule
called "distribution of a function over a conditional expression" or "merging
of functions" is important. Partial computation method $\beta 3$ described below
incorporates this rule (4.4) and two others (3 and 4.5) with $\beta 2$.

Example 10: Partial computation method $\beta 3$
Execute one of the four operations below depending on its effectiveness:

(1) If e is a conditional form then do the same as $\beta 2$.
(2) $(e)_i=e$.
(3) $(e)_i=(v)_i$ for u-form v such that $i \vdash^{\bullet}\{v=e\}$.
(4) If e is a composite form such as e=f[g] for a function f, then execute
     one of the following five operations depending on its effectiveness:

  (4.1) Partially define $(e)_i$, i.e. $(e)_i=f_{g}{}^i[u]$; $H=H\cup\{f_{g}{}^i\};f_{g}{}^i[u]<=e'$ where e'
         is one of the right side of the transformation rules of $\beta 3$ exept
         (4.1).

(4.2) If $(e)_i$ is partially defined, then let $f_d{}^j=\lambda[[u];m]$ be one of the partially defined functions (if a function with the closest partial information j to i is selected, the partial evaluator can be executed most quickly). Let $g=d/k$ and $i \vdash^{\bullet} j/k$, then $(e)_i=(f_d{}^j[k])_i$.

(4.3) If f is a nonprimitive function such as $f=\lambda[[u];b]$ then $(e)_i=(b/g)_i$.

(4.4) If g is a conditional form:

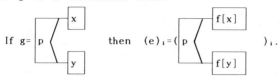

If $g=$ p ⟨ x / y   then $(e)_i=($ p ⟨ f[x] / f[y] $)_i$.

(4.5) $(e)_i=(f[\text{result of } (g)_i])_i$.

By combining $\beta 3$ with some recursion removal rules, least fixpoints of McCarthy's 91-function and Takeuchi's Tarai-function can be derived as follows:

Example 11: McCarthy's 91-function:

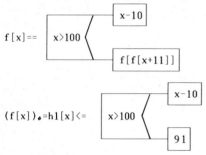

$f[x]==$ x>100 ⟨ x-10 / f[f[x+11]]

$(f[x])_{\bullet}=h1[x]<=$ x>100 ⟨ x-10 / 91

The derivation process is described in Appendix 3 which shows that $\beta 3$ is a highly nondeterministic procedure. To make $\beta 3$ more deterministic is a future research problem.

Example 12: Takeuchi's Tarai-function:

$c[x;y;z]==$

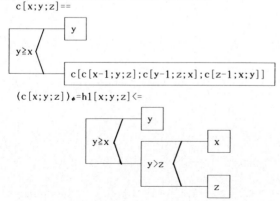

y≥x ⟨ y / c[c[x-1;y;z];c[y-1;z;x];c[z-1;x;y]]

$(c[x;y;z])_{\bullet}=h1[x;y;z]<=$

y≥x ⟨ y / y>z ⟨ x / z

(Derivation process is omitted because of its lengthiness.)

6. CONCLUSION

The Generalized Partial Computation method and its applications to order changing program transformations have been presented in this paper. Proving the correctness of various partial computation procedures and their efficient implementation are future research problems. The idea of GPC came to one of the authors while visiting UPMAIL (Uppsala Programming Methodology and Artificial Intelligence Laboratory) from October, 1985 to September, 1986. The author is grateful to the members of UPMAIL for their fruitful discussion which encouraged him very much. The authors are also grateful to Academician A. P. Ershov for his long time encouraging them to continue partial computation research.

7. REFERENCES

1) Burstall, R.M. and Darlington, J.: A transformation system for developing recursive program, JACM, Vol.24, No.1, 1977, pp.44-67.
2) Futamura, Y.: Partial evaluation of computation process--an approach to a compiler-compiler, Computer, systems, controls 2, No.5, 1971, pp.45-50.
3) Futamura, Y.: Partial computation of programs, In E. Goto[et al](eds.),RIMS Symposia on Software Science and Engineering, Kyoto, Japan, 1982. Lecture Notes in Computer Science 147(1983) 1-35, Springer-Verlag.
4) Futamura, Y., Kawai, T., Tsutsumi, M. and Horikoshi, H.: Development of computer programs by Problem Analysis Diagram (PAD), Proc. of 5ICSE, IEEE Computer Society, New York, 1981.
5) Ershov, A.P.: Mixed computation in the class of recursive program schema, Acta Cybernetica, Tom.4, Fosc.1, Szeged, 1978.
6) Kahn, K. M.: A partial evaluation of Lisp written in Prolog, UPMAIL Report Department of Computing Science, Uppsala University, Uppsala, Sweden, March 11, 1982.
7) Kleene, S. C.: Introduction to Meta-Mathematics. North-Holland Publishing Co., Amsterdam, 1952.
8) Knuth, D. E., Morris, J. H. and Pratt, V. R.: Fast pattern matching in strings, SIAM Journal of Computer, Vol.6, No.2, June 1977, pp.323-350.
9) Manna, Z.: Mathematical Theory of Computation, McGRAW-HILL, 1974.
10) McCarthy, J. et al: LISP 1.5 Programmer's Manual M.I.T. Press Cambridge, Massachusetts, 1962.
11) Nelson, G. and Oppen, D. C.: Simplification by cooperating decision procedures, ACM TOPLAS, Vol.1, No.2, October 1979, pp245-257.
12) Turchin, V. F.: The concept of a supercompiler, ACM TOPLAS, Vol.8, No.3, July 1986, pp.292-325.

APPENDIX 1: DIFFERENCES BETWEEN α AND β

In this section, the basic idea of the conventional partial computation method α and its weakness are discussed. Partial computation of a simple pattern matcher concerning a given pattern is presented as an example. Let $f= \lambda [[k;u];b]$. The basic idea of α can be described by the following two steps (1) and (2) where *eval* is a fixpoint interpreter of recursive programs. α is named as an Interpreter Dependent Partial Computation because it uses an interpreter, *eval*, when it evaluates conditions of a conditional expression.

Interpreter Dependent Partial Computation α :
(1) If b is a conditional expression, i.e.

then

    (1.1) if eval[p;((k.k0))] is true, then $f_{k0}=\alpha$ [λ [[k;u];x];k0].

    (1.2) if eval[p;((k.k0))] is false, then $f_{k0}=\alpha$ [λ [[k;u];y];k0].

    (1.3) if eval[p;((k.k0))] is undefined, then

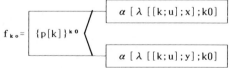

where $\{p[k]\}^{k0}$ is a form obtained by substituting k0 for all free occurrences of k in p.

(2) If b is not conditional, then $f_{k0}=\lambda$ [[u];$\{b[k]\}^{k0}$].

Syntactic differences between α and β are summarized in Table 1.

Table 1: Syntactic differences between α and β

	first argument	second argument	result
α	function f	known value k0 of variable k	f_{k0}
β	u-form e	predicate i on variable u	$(e)_i$

Differences between α and β in the power of partial computation are described below:

(1) β is more powerful than α in selecting one of two branches of a conditional expression. Assume that m>0 is known and and a[m;n] is Ackermann's function. If the value of *m* is unknown, eval[m>0;a] is undefined (where *a* is any environment not including m-value). Therefore, α cannot choose one of the conditional branches. On the contrary, since m>0⊢·m>0, β can choose the m>0 branch.

(2) Even when β cannot choose one of the conditional branches, it utilizes the condition, say *p*, of the branches, say *x* and *y*, in the later phase of partial computation. That is, $(x)_{i \wedge p}$ or $(y)_{i \wedge \neg p}$ will be performed. On the contrary, α does not use *p* in the partial computation of *x* and *y*. Therefore, β is considered more powerful than α.

To show the weakness of an Interpreter Dependent Partial Computation (IDPC), a simple pattern matcher is partially evaluated concerning a given pattern below. Note that the IDPC method being used here is an extension of α [3]. The extension is almost the same as the one used to obtain β 2 from β.

Let *p* and *t* be a pattern and a text, respectively. If *p* is contained in *t*, the value of a pattern matcher m[p;t] is true. If otherwise, the value is false. *m* is defined by using the auxiliary function *f* below. Symbol == is used to represent recursive definition of functions.

    m[p;t]==f[p;t;t]

    f[i;u;t]==

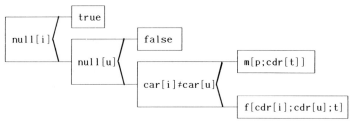

(where *p* is global).

The pattern matcher *m* will be partially evaluated concerning p= (A A A B).
The result is represented as m_1. For notational convenience, lists are represented as follows:

1 for (A A A B)
2 for (A A B)
3 for (A B)
4 for (B)
5 for ()

$m_1[t]==f_1[t;t]==$

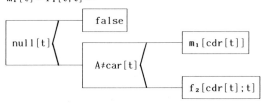

(from null[i]=null[(A A A B)]=false and car[i]=car[(A A A B)]=A)

$f_2[u;t]==$

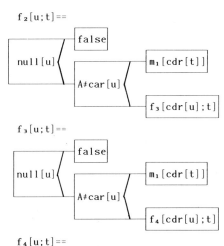

$f_3[u;t]==$

$f_4[u;t]==$

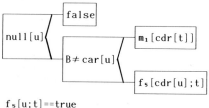

$f_s[u;t]==true$

The $m_1[t]$ is almost four times as large as $m[p;t]$. However, $m_1[t]$ is still an $O(m*n)$ time program where m and n are the lengths of p and t, respectively. On the contrary, $h1[t]$, obtained by using $\beta\,2$ in Section 4, is an $O(m+n)$ program.

APPENDIX 2: CORRECTNESS PROOF OF $\beta\,1$

Two lemmas are given before the proof of Theorem 1.

Lemma 1: Let i be any u-information and e be a conditional u-form such that

$e=$ $\left|\, p \left\langle \begin{array}{c} x \\ \\ y \end{array} \right. \right.$ then (1) if $i \vdash^* p$ then $e \subseteq {}^i x$.
(2) if $i \vdash^* \neg p$ then $e \subseteq {}^i y$.

Proof of Lemma 1: (1) If $i \vdash^* p$ then $eval[p;((u.c))] \subseteq true$ for any c such that $eval[i;((u.c))] \subseteq true$ from the definition of the underlying logic. Therefore, $eval[e;((u.c))]$ is $\perp$ or $eval[x;((u.c))]$. Therefore, $e \subseteq {}^i x$. (2) The same as (1).

Lemma 2: Let e be a conditional u-form the same as above and $e1$ be a conditional u-form described below. Then $e \supseteq {}^i e1$ when $x \supseteq {}^{i\wedge p} x1$ and $y \supseteq {}^{i\wedge \neg p} y1$.

$e\,1=$ $\left|\, p \left\langle \begin{array}{c} x1 \\ \\ y1 \end{array} \right. \right.$

Proof of Lemma 2: Assume that $eval[i;((c.u))] \subseteq true$. If $eval[p;((u.c))]=\perp$ then $eval[e;((u.c))]=eval[e1;((u.c))]=\perp$. If $eval[p;((u.c))]=true$ then $eval[e;\ ((u,c))]=eval[x;((u.c))] \supseteq eval[x1;((u.c))]=eval[e1;((u.c))]$. When $eval[p;((u.c))]=false$, it can be proved that $eval[e;((u.c))] \supseteq eval[e1;((u.c))]$ almost the same as above. Therefore, $e \supseteq {}^i e1$.

Proof of Theorem 1: Let e be a u-form and i be u-information. By using induction on the nesting depth of conditional forms in e, $\beta\,1[e;i] \supseteq {}^i e$ will be proved.
(1) When e is not a conditional form, $\beta\,1[e;i]=e \supseteq {}^i e$.
(2) When e is a conditional form,
    (2.1) Assume that $i \vdash^* p$:
        $\beta\,1[e;i]=\beta\,1[x;i] \supseteq {}^i x$ (from the induction hypothesis)
        $\supseteq {}^i e$ (from Lemma 1).
    (2.2) Assume that $i \vdash^* \neg p$: The same as above.
    (2.3) Assume that neither $i \vdash^* p$ nor $i \vdash^* \neg p$:

$$\beta\, 1[e;i] = \quad p \left\{ \begin{array}{l} \beta\, 1[x;i\wedge p] \\[1em] \beta\, 1[y;i\wedge\neg p] \end{array} \right.$$

and $\beta\, 1[x;i\wedge p] \sqsupseteq^{i\wedge p} x$ and $\beta\, 1[y;i\wedge\neg p] \sqsupseteq^{i\wedge\neg p} y$ from the induction hypothesis. Therefore, from Lemma 2,

$$\beta\, 1[e;i] \sqsupseteq^{i} \quad p \left\{ \begin{array}{l} x \\[1em] y \end{array} \right. \qquad = e \, .$$

(QED)

Proof of Theorem 2: Replace $\sqsupseteq^{i}$ by $\equiv^{i}$ in the proof above.

APPENDIX 3: PARTIAL COMPUTATION OF MCCARTHY'S 91-FUNCTION

To obtain the minimal fixpoint of McCarthy's 91-function, the following two recursion removal rules are used where a, b and c stand for forms not containing x as a free variable:

(1)

$$h[x] = \quad x > b \left\{ \begin{array}{l} a \\[1em] h[x+1] \end{array} \right.$$

and $h[x] = a$ for any x.

(2)

$$h[x] = \quad x > b \left\{ \begin{array}{l} a \\[1em] g[h[x+c]] \end{array} \right.$$

If $c > 0$ and $g[a] = a$ then $h[x] = a$ for any x where g is a function not containing x as a free variable.

The correctness of the rules above is trivial.

$(f[x])_{\bullet} = h1[x]$ (from 4.1)   Note that h1 stands for $f_x^{\bullet}$: The h2 and h3 below are used in a similar way.

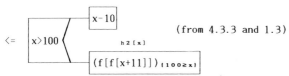

$(f[f[x+11]])_{(100\geq x)} = h2[x]$ (from 4.1)
     $\<= (f[(f[x+11])_{(100\geq x)}])_{(100\geq x)}$ (from 4.5)
     $= (f[(h1[x+11])_{(100\geq x)}])_{(100\geq x)}$ (from 4.2)

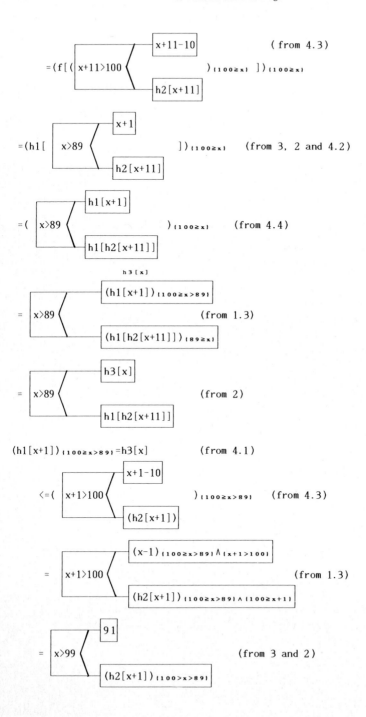

$= (f [(\begin{cases} x+11>100 \begin{cases} x+11-10 \\ h2[x+11] \end{cases} \end{cases})_{\{100 \geq x\}}])_{\{100 \geq x\}}$ (from 4.3)

$= (h1 [\begin{cases} x>89 \begin{cases} x+1 \\ h2[x+11] \end{cases} \end{cases}])_{\{100 \geq x\}}$ (from 3, 2 and 4.2)

$= (\begin{cases} x>89 \begin{cases} h1[x+1] \\ h1[h2[x+11]] \end{cases} \end{cases})_{\{100 \geq x\}}$ (from 4.4)

$h3[x]$

$= \begin{cases} x>89 \begin{cases} (h1[x+1])_{\{100 \geq x>89\}} \\ (h1[h2[x+11]])_{\{89 \geq x\}} \end{cases} \end{cases}$ (from 1.3)

$= \begin{cases} x>89 \begin{cases} h3[x] \\ h1[h2[x+11]] \end{cases} \end{cases}$ (from 2)

$(h1[x+1])_{\{100 \geq x>89\}} = h3[x]$ (from 4.1)

$\leq = (\begin{cases} x+1>100 \begin{cases} x+1-10 \\ (h2[x+1]) \end{cases} \end{cases})_{\{100 \geq x>89\}}$ (from 4.3)

$= \begin{cases} x+1>100 \begin{cases} (x-1)_{\{100 \geq x>89\} \wedge \{x+1>100\}} \\ (h2[x+1])_{\{100 \geq x>89\} \wedge \{100 \geq x+1\}} \end{cases} \end{cases}$ (from 1.3)

$= \begin{cases} x>99 \begin{cases} 91 \\ (h2[x+1])_{\{100>x>89\}} \end{cases} \end{cases}$ (from 3 and 2)

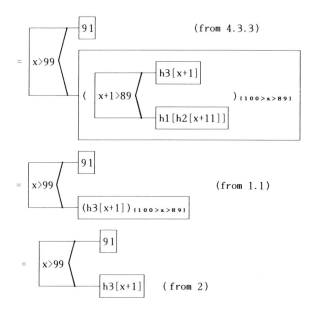

From the rule (1), h3[x]=91. Therefore,

h2[x] =

Since h1[91]=91, h2[x]=91 from the rule (2). Therefore,

h1[x] =

Partial Evaluation and Mixed Computation
D. Bjørner, A.P. Ershov and N.D. Jones (Editors)
Elsevier Science Publishers B.V. (North-Holland)
© IFIP, 1988

Function inversion

P.G. Harrison
Department of Computing
Imperial College
London SW7 2BZ

December 1987

Relations may be used in any mode in logic programming languages, and this feature may be incorporated into functional languages if the *inverses* of the functions corresponding to any one of these modes are available. Moreover, inverse functions also have an important role in other areas, for example in the transformation of abstract data types into more efficient concrete forms. The inversion of a function may always be performed by using unification, as in the logic languages, but the performance of such implementations is typically poor whilst often more efficient recursive inverses are known to exist. We present a method for synthesising recursive inverse function definitions for certain first order recursive functions defined in terms of the construction, composition and conditional combining forms. This synthesis is based upon the successive application of the axioms of a functional algebra, extended to accomodate multiple valued functions since inverses are not in general single valued. We also apply the inversion results to the synthesis of efficient implementations of abstract data types. This function-level approach is mathematically rigorous on the one hand, and has considerable potential for automation on the other. A pilot inversion system has already been implemented, and an extension has been designed to provide all modes of use of relations over and above a function and its simple inverse.

1. Introduction

The benefits of declarative programming languages are becoming increasingly recognised in problem-solving: for both small-scale problems and those facing the engineers of large-scale software. Such languages fall into two classes: *functional* and *logic* languages which have operational semantics based on *reduction* and *resolution* respectively, [RS82, SY84, R86]. Of these, reduction is the more efficient and the easier to implement, but resolution has the greater expressive power, in particular providing multi-mode use of relations. Ideally, therefore, we would like to have a language with features that involve resolution, and to *transform* expressions into forms that can be evaluated using only reduction. Such transformation would then enhance both logic languages and functional languages which are augmented with absolute set abstraction to provide relations as well as functions, for example HOPE+Unification, [DFP85].

Although the incorporation of resolution increases the expressive power of a functional language, its unification-based implementation leads to run-time performance problems. For example, there are problems in managing the search space of possible evaluations and in co-ordinating updates to shared logical variables. Thus we would like to transform the parts of the program that require unification at run-time (e.g. the parts that use variables) into equivalent purely functional form, which can be executed more efficiently using only deterministic computation (i.e. reduction).

Rather than unification per se, it is the multi-mode use of relations which we most want to incorporate into a functional language. This would be facilitated by *function inversion*, for a function together with its inverse constitutes a relation, and in this paper we synthesise recursive inverse functions using symbolic unification and program transformation performed at compile time.

Every transformation system may be regarded as a form of mixed or partial evaluation. For example, the unfold/fold methodology of Darlington and Burstall [BD77] takes a set of functions defined by their application to formal parameters of various patterns and derives new functions which are equivalent (or at least partially so in that strictly we can only say that a transformed function is *weaker* in the approximation ordering of the function space). Moreover, the generality of this methodology is such that most transformation schemes can be expressed in terms of it - even though such an equivalence may be hard to find, and is certainly hard to automate. (The difficulty of mechanisation is the main obstacle to the advancement of transformation systems based on the unfold/fold methodology). Of course, the interpretation of the fold operation as 'evaluation' is a little contentious in that the computation is 'going backwards', but in our variable-free presentation the optimisation proceeds by successive application of the axioms of a functional algebra and theorems derived from them. The folds are essentially encapsulated in the theorems and the transformation is clearly a form of symbolic evaluation and a special form of partial evaluation in which the object data is absent: the transformation is of type Programs→Programs.

Our system converts inverses, which can easily be defined for any given function in terms of unification, into the more efficient reduction-based form by applying axioms which perform 'function level unification' to instantiate function variables, so avoiding the use of object-level unification. In many cases, all such unification can be removed, leaving the inverse in purely recursive form. We illustrate this by synthesising the function 'split' as the inverse of 'append'. The transformation may therefore be viewed as a form of partial evaluation which specialises the general function inversion formula to a particular class of first order functions. In the terminology of this workshop, we have a general inversion function, T : F→F where F is the function space concerned, and stage 1 input data, St1, which is the definition of the class of functions that can be inverted more efficiently - for example as given by the conditions for Theorem 1 in Section 3. The stage 2 input data, St2, specifies a particular function of this class, such as append in our case study. Now, T involves unification, being the general program which inverts *any* function, and the partial evaluation, E, takes T and the specification St1 and specialises T to the range of functions given by St1. The result of this application of E, when applied to the function St2, then synthesises a more efficient inverse, based on reduction semantics, than would be obtained by applying T to St2 directly.

Since functions are not in general 1-1, their inverses are not in general single valued and so we consider functions which map sets of objects to sets of objects. The semantics of such functions is given in terms of a Hoare powerdomain in Section 2, and this is used in Section 3 to provide a formal definition of a function's inverse in general and a recursive definition for a certain class of first-order functions. An axiomatic system for removing unification from functional expressions is also presented and its application is illustrated in its conversion of the inverse of append into recursive form. In Section 4 we consider the transformation of abstract data types into efficient concrete forms. The basis of this is a 'commutative square' of functions comprising horizontally a user-defined function and its corresponding concrete version, and vertically the abstraction functions between the domain- and range-types. Expressions defining the concrete functions are then obtained in the form of compositions involving abstraction functions, their inverses and the user-defined functions; the same axiomatic system developed for the synthesis of inverses is used to simplify them. The paper concludes in Section 5. Throughout the paper we will use the following notation:

T, F	truth values "TRUE" and "FALSE"
$\bot$	the undefined object, "bottom"
$\underline{a}$	constant function, such that $\underline{a}x = a$ for all objects $x \neq \bot$, $\underline{a}\bot = \bot$. (e.g. $\underline{0}, \underline{T}, \underline{1}$ etc.)
$\underline{\bot}$	constant function s.t. $\underline{\bot}x = \bot$ for all objects x
fx	application of the function f to the element x is shown by juxtaposition
∘	function composition, i.e. $(f \circ g)x = f(gx)$ for objects x
[,]	function construction, i.e. $[f,g]x = <fx, gx>$ for objects x
$f = p \rightarrow q; r$	$fx = \underline{if} \ px=T \ \underline{then} \ qx \ \underline{else} \ \underline{if} \ px=F \ \underline{then} \ rx \ \underline{else} \ \bot$ for objects x
succ, pred	primitive functions 'successor' and 'predecessor'
id	the identity function, i.e. id x = x for all objects x.
hd, tl, null, cons, eq, etc.	Standard primitive functions
P	powerdomain construction functor e.g. PD denotes the powerdomain of domain D
$\varnothing$	empty set
2^S	powerset of S
$\subset$	set inclusion

2. Outline of the underlying semantics

Our notation is based on a functional language in which no syntactical distinction is made between functions and inverse functions. We use the FP style because of that language's emphasis on function-level expressions and reasoning, [HK87b, B81], but make a number of extensions to it in order to cater for inverses. In general the inverse, f^{-1}, of a function f will return several values when applied to an argument, x, in the codomain of f; when f is applied to *any* of these values, the result will be x. Thus, to be a complete inverse, f^{-1} must map objects to sets, but we ensure a consistent system by making *all* functions have type "set of values to set of values". Then an inverse function can be freely composed with any function. "Values" also has its own type, e.g. integers, sequences etc, and an undefined object "bottom", denoted by $\perp$, is also included in every type, so that the type can become a domain (under further standard constraints). We therefore consider functions defined on *powerdomains*, as opposed to domains of objects, and for reasons of computability we must consider *continuous* functions.

Given the domain $(D,<)$ with least element $\perp$ (i.e. $\perp<d$ for all $d \in D$), let PD be the *Hoare powerdomain* of D which consists of the non-empty *Scott-closed* members of 2^D, with subset inclusion, $\subset$, for its ordering and least element $\perp_{PD}=\{\perp_D\}$. In fact, we use an equivalent, non-standard definition which excludes $\perp_D$ from all sets in PD, i.e. PD has for its elements *all* the Scott-closed sets of $2^{D\setminus\{\perp\}}$ with $\perp_{PD}=\varnothing$, the empty set, for its least element. This definition conforms closely with intuition when the domain D is flat. We also assume that D includes sequences, $\langle d_1,...d_n \rangle$ for $d_i \in D$, $1 \leq i \leq n$, where $\langle d_1,...d_n \rangle < \langle e_1,...e_m \rangle$ iff n=m and $d_i < e_i$ for $1 \leq i \leq n$.

Given any continuous function (in the basic language, e.g. FP), $f': D \rightarrow E$, where D and E are domains, we define the corresponding function f: PD $\rightarrow$ PE, where PD, PE are the respective powerdomains of D, E, by

$$f X = \{ f' x \mid x \in X \}^* \in P(E) \quad \text{for } X \in PD$$

(S^* denotes the *Scott closure* of the set S, i.e. if $s \in S$ and $x<s$ then $x \in S^*$, and S^* also contains the limits of all increasing sequences in S). We refer to f' as the *sister* function for f. With this definition, f is continuous and union-preserving, i.e.

$$f(A \cup B) = fA \cup fB.$$

We denote the domain of continuous functions: $D \rightarrow E$ for domains D, E by $[D \rightarrow E]$.

There is now no distinction between "ordinary" and inverse functions, but our extensions have a number of implications on the language syntax. For example, an application, f x, should be replaced by f{x}. We will also find considerable repercussions on the axioms for the functional algebra of [B78].

3. Synthesis of inverse functions and their transformation

Since we will be considering first-order functions and give all functional expressions in variable-free form, a language based on first-order categorical combinatory logic augmented to facilitate the definition of inverse functions is suitable, and certainly provides the required composition operator. We therefore adopt a suitably augmented variant of an FP-like language,

[B78]. All the primitive functions of FP are assumed to be available, together with their corresponding inverses, but the selector primitives of FP, 1,2,... are represented by n_m, where $1 \leq n \leq m$. The primitive n_m reads as "select the nth element of a sequence of m elements". Similar dialects of FP have been used in other transformation systems, e.g. [KS81], since these selectors convey some typing information, namely the size of the sequences to which they can be applied.

We also introduce *function variables* which represent (unknown) functions, and appear in the function-level expressions for the inverses of selector functions and of constructions of functions. Function variables are denoted by the infinite set of primitives ?1, ?2, ... and are bound to ground function-values by the application of our axioms below which essentially perform function-level unification. Examples of expressions with occurrences of inverse-functions and variables are:

$$\text{hd}^{-1}\text{of} = \text{cons}\circ[f,?1] \qquad \text{tl}^{-1}\text{of} = \text{cons}\circ[?1,f] \qquad 5_9{}^{-1}\text{of} = [?1,?2,?3,?4,f,?5...8]$$

In these examples we have used the inverses of certain primitive functions, and the equations are certainly consistent with intuition, but we need a formal definition for the inverse of any given function. This is considered in the next section. Having introduced this new feature into the language syntax, it is also important to define rigorously the semantics of function variables. This may be found in [HK87a].

3.1 Definition of inverses

For f: $D \rightarrow E$, we might try defining the inverse f^{-1}: $E \rightarrow D$ by $f^{-1}e = \{d \mid fd = e\}$, but this is "badly typed" because $f^{-1}e$ would not be in D. We therefore give the following:

DEFINITION 1

The inverse, f^{-1}:PE $\rightarrow$ PD, of a function f: PD $\rightarrow$ PE is given by

$$f^{-1}X = \bigcup \{Y \mid Y \in PD, \ fY \subset X\} \quad \text{for } X \in PE, \text{ where D, E are domains.}$$

For a *continuous* function f, it is easily shown that $f^{-1}X = \{y \in D \mid y \neq \perp, f\{y\}^* \subset X\}$ (which is Scott-closed). Thus we find that for flat domains D, E and continuous function f with sister f´,

$$f^{-1}\{x\} = \{y \mid f\{y\} \subset \{x\}\} \quad \text{since } \{x\} = \{x\}^* \quad \text{for all } x \in E, D$$
$$= \{y \mid f´y = x\} \cup \{y \mid f´y = \perp_E\}$$

which corresponds with our intuition above, exactly so if f is total.

As an example, we give the inverse of a *constant* function. For $A \in PD$,
$$\underline{A}^{-1}X = \bigcup \{Y \mid \underline{A}Y < X\} = \bigcup \{Y \mid A \subset X\} = D \quad \text{if } A \subset X$$
$$\varnothing \qquad \text{otherwise}$$

In particular, $\underline{\perp}^{-1} = \underline{D}$, the *top* element of PD, since $\perp_{PD} = \varnothing \subset X$ for all $X \in PD$.

3.2 Extended definitions of the primitive functionals

The program forming operations of FP, abbreviated to PFOs, must be generalised to operate on powerdomains so that they can be applied to set-valued functions and so accomodate inverse functions which are not single-valued. Although the definition of composition need not be changed, the generalisations needed for the construction and conditional PFOs are non-trivial. The extended construction-PFO is defined by

$$[f_1,...,f_n]X = \{ <y_1,...y_n> \mid y_i \in f_i\{x\}^*, 1 \le i \le n, x \in X \}$$

for functions $f_1,...,f_n$ and set X of objects. Thus for single valued sister functions $f_1',...,f_n'$ and flat domain D, $[f_1,...,f_n] X = \{<f_1'x,...,f_n'x> \mid x \in X\}$ as required.

Extension of the conditional PFO is less obvious, and we define

$$(p \to q; r)X = \bigcup\{q\{x\}^* \mid T \in p\{x\}^*, x \in X\} \cup \bigcup\{r\{x\}^* \mid F \in p\{x\}^*, x \in X\}.$$

It is shown in [HK87a] that the extended PFOs composition, construction and condition all preserve continuity and the union-preserving property.

We also define the new PFO 'unify-at-function-level', denoted by $\ll , \gg$ which is used for the inversion of *constructions* of functions. $\ll , \gg$ takes two or more functions as arguments and returns a new function as its result. This PFO is essentially *first-order* unification, as can be seen by inspecting the axioms given in the next section, function-expressions being the objects of the unification. In general a 'failed unification' merely means that a compile-time optimisation cannot be performed since no axiom can be applied. The precise semantics of $\ll , \gg$, however, is defined in [HK87a] in terms of set intersections and substitutions for the function variables involved in the arguments:

$$\mathcal{S}[\ll E_1,E_2 \gg] X = \bigcup\{(\mathcal{S}[\sigma E_1] \{x\}) \cap (\mathcal{S}[\sigma E_2] \{x\}) \mid \sigma \in \Sigma, x \in X\} \qquad (X \in PD)$$
$$(\mathcal{S}[\ll E_1,...,E_n \gg] \text{ is given by the equation } \ll E_1,...,E_n \gg = \ll \ll E_1,...E_{n-1} \gg, E_n \gg)$$

In this semantic equation, $\mathcal{S}$ is the semantic function, E_i is a syntactic expression and Σ is the set of possible substitutions for the variables contained in the E_i, viz $\Sigma = \{ \Pi_{i \ge 1}[\{\underline{x}_i\}/?i] \mid x_i \in D \}$ where $[X/?i]$ denotes the substitution of X for the variable $?i$ and $\Pi_{i \ge 1}$ denotes the composition of substitutions for every variable $(i=1,...,n)$. As with unification, $\ll , \gg$ is associative and commutative, and it is also shown that $\ll , \gg$ preserves continuity and union-preservation.

3.3 Axioms

Since we have introduced set-valued functions and correspondingly generalised some of the definitions of the PFOs, as noted in the previous section, some of the FP axioms of [B78] no longer hold as they stand. For example, it may no longer be that $[f,g]{\circ}h = [f{\circ}h, g{\circ}h]$ for all functions f, g, h, although it does remain the case that $n_m{\circ}[f_1,...,f_m] = f_n$ for $1 \leq n \leq m$. The FP axioms are included in our system in appropriately modified form, and we also introduce additional axioms which involve the extensions that we have made, most notably the PFO $\ll\gg$ and the inverses of primitive functions. We can then use the axioms to simplify functional expressions, and in particular reduce the dependence on run-time unification by removing occurrences of $\ll\gg$ through compile-time, 'function-level' first order unification.

For any functional expression f, we define the axioms:

(A0) $?i{\circ}f = ?i$ $\quad\quad$ (i≥1)

(A1) $\ll ?1, f \gg \ = f$ $\quad\quad$ (including $\ll f \gg = f$)

(and thus $\ll ?1,...,?i,f,?(i+1),...,?k \gg = f$ for $1 < i \leq k$ by associativity and commutativity).

(A2) For the inverse selector function i_j^{-1} $(0 \leq i \leq j)$ $\quad i_j^{-1}{\circ}f \ = \ [?1...i\text{-}1,f,?i+1...j]$

(A3) $\ll [a1_1,...,a1_n],[a2_1,...,a2_n],...,[am_1,...,am_n] \gg$
$= [\ll a1_1,a2_1,...,am_1 \gg, \ll a1_2,a2_2,...,am_2 \gg,..., \ll a1_n,a2_n,...,am_n \gg]$ $\quad$ (m,n≥1)

(A4) $hd^{-1}{\circ}f \ = \ cons{\circ}[f,?1]$

(A5) $tl^{-1}{\circ}f \ = \ cons{\circ}[?1,f]$

(A6) $cons^{-1} \ = \ [hd,tl]$

(A7) $h{\circ}\ll f,g \gg = \ll h{\circ}f, h{\circ}g \gg$ and $\quad \ll f,g \gg {\circ}j = \ll f{\circ}j, g{\circ}j \gg$ $\quad$ where h, j have single valued sister functions and h is 1-1

(A8) $\ll f{\circ}h, g{\circ}k \gg = \ll f{\circ}1_2, g{\circ}2_2 \gg {\circ}[h,k]$

(A9a) $\ll p \rightarrow q; r, p' \rightarrow q'; r' \gg$
$= p \rightarrow (p' \rightarrow \ll q,q' \gg; \ll q,r' \gg); (p' \rightarrow \ll r,q' \gg; \ll r,r' \gg)$

(A9b) if p implies p' $\ll p \rightarrow q; r, p' \rightarrow q'; r' \gg = p \rightarrow \ll q,q' \gg; (p' \rightarrow \ll r,q' \gg; \ll r,r' \gg)$

Note that these axioms are *consequences* of object-level unification semantic properties, abstracted to the function-level (i.e. the variables have been abstracted). In particular, it is easy to show that the expressions given by Definition 1 for the inverses of the primitive functions used are consistent with the axioms concerned. It will also be noticed that Axioms (A7) and (A8) are non-trivial consequences of the preceding theory, the detailed justification being available in [HK87a]. Two 'theorems' that derive from these axioms, and which we will find important for removing unification from the definitions of inverses are:

(T1) $\ll 1_n^{-1} \circ a_1, ..., n_n^{-1} \circ a_n \gg = [a_1, ..., a_n]$

which follows by repeated application of (A2), and then (A3) and (A1)

(T2) $\ll hd^{-1} \circ f, tl^{-1} \circ g \gg = cons \circ [f, g]$

which follows by application of (A4), (A5), (A7) and then (A3)

3.4   Function inversion

We now summarise the main results for constructing the inverses of various fixed and recursively defined functions. First, the inverses of the *composition, construction* and *conditional* of continuous functions are given by

(I1) $(f \circ g)^{-1}$ $=$ $g^{-1} \circ f^{-1}$

(I2) $[f_1, ..., f_n]^{-1}$ $=$ $\ll f_1^{-1} \circ 1_n, ..., f_n^{-1} \circ n_n \gg$

(I3) $(p \to f; g)^{-1}$ $=$ $((p \to id; \perp) \circ f^{-1}) \cup ((p \to \perp; id) \circ g^{-1}) \cup (p^{-1} \circ \perp)$

The proofs of these results can be found in [HK87a], and the use of (I1) and (I2) will be illustrated in examples. (I3) is used in the proof of our main theorem below.

Now consider the function f defined recursively by the equation $f = p \to q; E$ for fixed functions p, q and expression E having the following syntax

E ::= f | a | E$\circ$E | [E,E,...,E]

where the syntactic type a denotes fixed functions and f is the function variable. (The further syntactic type, $a \to E$; E may also be added if we include the result for the inverse of a conditional. However, we will not find this necessary here). We may now write down an expression for E^{-1} by hierarchical decomposition into the syntactic types corresponding to composition and construction. For example, if $E = E_1 \circ E_2$, then $E^{-1} = E_2^{-1} \circ E_1^{-1}$. If $E_1 = [E_3, E_4]$ and $E_2 = add1$, then $E_1^{-1} = \ll E_3^{-1} \circ 1_2, E_4^{-1} \circ 2_2 \gg$ and $E_2^{-1} = sub1$ (a primitive type) and so on. Moreover, again by a case analysis of the syntactic types, we can see that for any such expression E, E^{-1} may be written $H'f^{-1}$ for some fixed functional H'. The rigorous proofs are very easy inductions on the types. Given E with this syntax, a functional H defined by $Hf = E$ is called *composite*.

The main result on the inversion of recursively defined functions is the following, the proof again appearing in [HK87a].

THEOREM 1

Let f be defined by $f = p \rightarrow q$; Hf for composite functional H and continuous functions p, q. If p is total (i.e. $pY=\varnothing \Rightarrow Y=\varnothing$) and has sister function p' which is single-valued, then

(i)   For $X \in PD$, f^{-1} satisfies the equation
$$f^{-1}X = \{y \mid y \in q^{-1}X, T \in p\{y\}^*\}^* \cup \{y \mid y \in (Hf)^{-1}X, F \in p\{y\}^*\}^*$$

(ii) f^{-1} is the greatest fixed point of the equation
$$g = \cup \circ [(p \rightarrow id; \perp) \circ q^{-1}, (p \rightarrow \perp; id) \circ H'g]$$
where H' is defined by $H'f^{-1} = (Hf)^{-1}$ for function variable f.

If in addition to the conditions of the theorem we have for all $X \in PD$, $p \circ r^{-1}X \subset \{F\}$, then the following corollary is satisfied:

(i)   For $X \in PD$, f^{-1} satisfies the equation
$$f^{-1}X = \{y \mid y \in q^{-1}X, T \in p\{y\}^*\}^* \cup (Hf)^{-1}X$$

(ii) f^{-1} is the greatest fixed point of the equation
$$g = \cup \circ [(p \rightarrow id; \perp) \circ q^{-1}, H'g]$$

3.5   An example: append^{-1} (split)

For the sake of greater clarity, we now use the notation f:x for the application of function f to object $x \in D$, and we will also further abuse our notation by writing x to denote $\{x\} \in PD$ when the meaning is clear, e.g. $succ^{-1}:3 = pred:3 = 2$ rather than $succ^{-1}:\{3\} = pred:\{3\} = \{2\}$.

The function that appends two lists may be defined by the equation
$$app = null \circ 1_2 \rightarrow 2_2; \; al \circ [hd \circ 1_2, app \circ [tl \circ 1_2, 2_2]]$$

or $app = null \circ 1_2 \rightarrow 2_2; Happ$ for appropriately defined composite functional H:

$$(Happ)^{-1} = ([hd \circ 1_2, app \circ [tl \circ 1_2, 2_2]])^{-1} \circ al^{-1}$$
$$= \langle\!\langle (hd \circ 1_2)^{-1} \circ 1_2, (app \circ [tl \circ 1_2, 2_2]])^{-1} \circ 2_2 \rangle\!\rangle \circ al^{-1}$$
$$= \langle\!\langle 1_2^{-1} \circ hd^{-1} \circ 1_2, ([tl \circ 1_2, 2_2]])^{-1} \circ app^{-1} \circ 2_2 \rangle\!\rangle \circ al^{-1}$$
$$= \langle\!\langle 1_2^{-1} \circ hd^{-1} \circ 1_2, \langle\!\langle (tl \circ 1_2)^{-1} \circ 1_2, 2_2^{-1} \circ 2_2 \rangle\!\rangle \circ app^{-1} \circ 2_2 \rangle\!\rangle \circ al^{-1}$$
$$= \langle\!\langle 1_2^{-1} \circ hd^{-1} \circ 1_2, \langle\!\langle 1_2^{-1} \circ tl^{-1} \circ 1_2, 2_2^{-1} \circ 2_2 \rangle\!\rangle \circ app^{-1} \circ 2_2 \rangle\!\rangle \circ al^{-1}$$
$$= \langle\!\langle 1_2^{-1} \circ hd^{-1} \circ 1_2, [tl^{-1} \circ 1_2, 2_2] \circ app^{-1} \circ 2_2 \rangle\!\rangle \circ al^{-1} \qquad \text{by (T1)}$$
$$= \langle\!\langle 1_2^{-1} \circ hd^{-1} \circ 1_2, [al \circ [?1, 1_2], 2_2] \circ app^{-1} \circ 2_2 \rangle\!\rangle \circ al^{-1} \qquad \text{by axiom (A5)}$$

$$= \ll 1_2^{-1} \circ \text{al} \circ [1_2,?2],[\text{al} \circ [?1,1_2],2_2] \circ \text{app}^{-1} \circ 2_2 \gg \circ \text{al}^{-1} \qquad \text{by axiom (A4)}$$

$$= \ll [\text{al} \circ [1_2,?2],?3],[\text{al} \circ [?1,1_2],2_2] \circ \text{app}^{-1} \circ 2_2 \gg \circ \text{al}^{-1} \qquad \text{by axiom (A2)}$$

$$= \ll [\text{al} \circ [1_2,?2],?3] \circ 1_2,[\text{al} \circ [?1,1_2],2_2] \circ 2_2 \gg \circ [\text{id},\text{app}^{-1} \circ 2_2] \circ \text{al}^{-1} \quad \text{by axiom (A8)}$$

$$= \ll [\text{al} \circ [1_2 \circ 1_2,?2 \circ 1_2],?3 \circ 1_2],[\text{al} \circ [?1 \circ 2_2,1_2 \circ 2_2],2_2 \circ 2_2] \gg \circ [\text{id},\text{app}^{-1} \circ 2_2] \circ \text{al}^{-1}$$

$$\text{by FP axiom since selector functions are single-valued}$$

$$= [\text{al} \circ [1_2 \circ 1_2,1_2 \circ 2_2],2_2 \circ 2_2] \circ [\text{id},\text{app}^{-1} \circ 2_2] \circ \text{al}^{-1} \quad \text{by axioms (A3,A1,A0,A7)}$$

Checking the condition of the theorem we see that p (i.e. $\text{null} \circ 1_2$) is total as long as append is applied to pairs of sequences. Checking the extra condition of the corollary to the theorem we have,

$$p \circ (\text{Happ})^{-1} = \text{null} \circ 1_2 \circ [\text{al} \circ [1_2 \circ 1_2,1_2 \circ 2_2],2_2 \circ 2_2] \circ [\text{id},\text{app}^{-1} \circ 2_2] \circ \text{al}^{-1}$$

$$= \text{null} \circ \text{al} \circ [1_2 \circ 1_2,1_2 \circ 2_2] \circ [\text{id},\text{app}^{-1} \circ 2_2] \circ \text{al}^{-1}$$

Thus $p \circ (\text{Happ})^{-1} X \subset \{F\}$ since for all functions a, $(\text{null} \circ \text{al} \circ a) X \subset \{F\}$.

Thus we have:

$$\text{app}^{-1} : x = \cup : < \{y \mid y \in q^{-1} : x, \ T \in p : \{y\}^* \}^*, (\text{Happ})^{-1} : x >$$

$$= \cup : < \{y \mid y \in 2_2^{-1} : x, \ T \in \text{null} \circ 1_2 : \{y\}^* \}^*, (\text{Happ})^{-1} : x >$$

Finally, the base case $[[],\text{id}]$ is synthesised by straightforward, non-recursive, compile time unification, so that the function definition generated for app^{-1} is

$$\text{app}^{-1} = \cup \circ [\ [[],\text{id}], \ [\text{al} \circ [1_2 \circ 1_2,1_2 \circ 2_2],2_2 \circ 2_2] \circ [\text{id},\text{app}^{-1} \circ 2_2] \circ \text{al}^{-1} \ ]$$

i.e. the normal recursive definition for "split" that does not require unification when executed.

4. Mechanical transformation of data types

Consider now the pair of abstract data-types α, β, and the corresponding pair α', β' which we take to be *concrete* types that provide realisations of α, β respectively. Then, given the function $f: \alpha \to \beta$, it is required to synthesise a corresponding function, say $f': \alpha' \to \beta'$, which performs operations on objects of type α' which are isomorphic in some sense to the operations performed by f on corresponding objects of type α. The function f' might then be the "implementation function" of f, which can be executed more efficiently than f and, together with the types α' and β', removes from the run-time system the need to represent the abstract types at all. Let the *abstraction function* for abstract type σ be $\text{abs}_\sigma : \sigma' \to \sigma$ where σ' is the concrete, implementation type corresponding to σ. The concrete function f' must therefore form a *commutative square* in the following diagram:

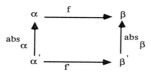

In other words, $f \circ abs_\alpha = abs_\beta \circ f'$, or $f' = abs_\beta^{-1} \circ f \circ abs_\alpha$, assuming that the inverse function, abs_β^{-1}, exists. If the range-types are the same, i.e. $\beta = \beta'$, we obtain a triangle, and the result $f' = f \circ abs_\alpha$, and similarly for the domain types. Here, for simplicity, we assume abstraction functions are *single-valued* although this is not necessary.

In general, therefore, we wish to find $f' = abs_\beta^{-1} \circ f \circ abs_\alpha$, expressed purely in terms of the types α', β'. For a primitive function, a say, we attempt to find a' by simplifying the right hand side of the above expression with f=a and abs_α, abs_β^{-1} expanded. Given the definitions for the primitive functions, it is easy to see (by induction on the type structure of expressions) that the concrete version, E', of any first-order applicative expression, E, mapping the abstract types, is that expression obtained by replacing in E every function name f by its concrete version, f'. This translation includes recursion equations since f may either be a primitive function or the name of a user defined function.

It is then possible to construct a transformation system which operates by successively rewriting the expressions defining the functions conc and f' defined above, in terms of abs and f, using the set of axioms given in the previous section, together with additional axioms arising from the user-supplied definitions of the abstract data types. As an example, consider the following Hope style data definition for the type 'tree' which we wish to use as a representation for lists:

> data tree α == empty ++ node(tree $\alpha \times \alpha \times$ tree α)

and that we have the abstraction function 'abs' defined by

> dec abs : tree $\alpha \rightarrow$ list α
>
> abs(empty) = nil
>
> abs(node(t1, n, t2)) = abs(t1) <> n :: abs(t2)

(:: is the infix form of 'cons' and <> is the infix form of 'append').

Suppose we wish to find, in terms of these types and functions, a concrete version of rev, 'revtree', that maps trees to trees. Now, the function abs can be expressed in variable-free form as follows:

> abs = empty $\rightarrow$ <u>nil</u>; append$\circ$[abs$\circ$1,cons$\circ$[2,abs$\circ$3]]

By mechanically applying our inversion axioms and standard FP laws, we synthesise the inverse function of abs, i.e. conc, to get

> conc = abs^{-1} = null $\rightarrow$ empty; [conc$\circ1_2$,hd$\circ2_2$,conc$\circ$tl$\circ2_2$]$\circ$append^{-1}

Although append^{-1} is not single valued, any pair of lists it returns in its result will yield a valid representation, there being in general more than one tree representing a given list. Certainly, we may replace append^{-1}∘append by the identity function, id, to obtain *one* representation of revtree below.

Now from the commutative diagram, we have revtree = conc∘rev∘abs and using the single additional axiom that rev(x ◇ y :: z) = rev(z) ◇ y :: rev(x) for all lists y, z and objects y, together with the FP axioms we obtain

> revtree = empty → empty; [revtree∘3,2,revtree∘1]

In other words we have synthesised revtree that corresponds to the following definition:

> revtree(empty) = empty
> revtree(node(t1, n, t2)) = node(revtree(t2) , n , revtreee(t1))

The execution time of reverse(x) is of order the length of x, whereas revtree(conc(x)) can theoretically execute in time of order log_2 of the length of x on parallel processors. The additional axiom is clearly a valid *definition* of rev (excluding the case of the null list) but the problem is how can we *deduce* that this is the axiom we require rather than, say, the simpler rev(x◇y) = rev(y) ◇ rev(x). (In fact the latter choice does give a correct representation of rev between trees, but it constructs extremely imbalanced trees and does not exclude the abstract type entirely from its definition). However, up to the introduction of the reverse-axiom, this transformation is mechanical and many other transformations may be similarly automated. In particular, the method does generate automatically the definitions, where-abstractions and folds needed by the unfold/fold style. These arise naturally in the inversions of selectors and of constructions of functions, such as [2,abs∘3]$^{-1}$ in the example.

7 Conclusion

We have developed a method that will automatically generate inverses for a substantial class of functions. By performing unification where possible and applying an extended set of function-level axioms at compile-time, expressions for many inverses may be transformed so that no unification is required at run-time. This makes the cost of their execution comparable with that of reduction-based semantics, i.e. with ordinary recursive functions.

An important role was identified for the inverse function theory in the transformation of data types which, to the author's best knowledge, has not been mechanised hitherto to any significant extent. We observed, however, that our axiom set required extension by further axioms representing operations on the particular data types in question, and in the examples these were not necessarily expressed in a form that would normally be given by the programmer. This is certainly the area of the work which is the least mechanised, and some interface between the programming of data types and this type of transformation system should be investigated. A much more substantial generalisation would use *many-valued* abstraction and concretisation functions - the work described here involved a simplified set of axioms and rules because of the fact that all functions were singled valued, so that the FP axioms held unchanged for example. Using many-valued functions, it becomes possible to represent sets by lists in which no element is duplicated, and to synthesise given set operations as corresponding (concrete) functions on lists.

Another significant area of interest is the synthesis of *partially-grounded* inverses. Given a function f of n arguments we may wish to generate a recursive function which returns sets of m valid arguments (m<n) when applied to values corresponding to the other (n-m) arguments of f and some result in the range of f. For example, given the definition f (a , b) = c we may like to generate the function which, given the values for c and a, returns the set of all possible values for b. Although this problem can be solved in general using unification at run-time, a recursively-defined solution is preferable, again for reasons of efficiency. Our algebraic approach is currently enjoying some success in this area, and K.Sephton in our research group has recently shown how to synthesise a recursive form for the function that finds the 'difference' between two lists from the append function.

References

[B78]   J W Backus; 'Can Programming be Liberated from the von Neumann Style? A Functional Style and its Algebra of Programs', CACM 21,8, pp. 613-641, (1978)

[B81]   J W Backus; 'The Algebra of functional programs: Function level reasoning, linear equations and extended definitions', In Lecture Notes in Computer Science, Vol 107: Formalization of Programming Concepts, Springer-Verlag, New York, pp. 1-43, (1981)

[BD77]   R M Burstall, J Darlington; 'A Transformation System for Developing Recursive Programs', JACM 24, 1, pp. 44-67 (1977)

[BG77]   R M Burstall, J A Goguen; 'Putting Theories Together to Make Specifications', Proc. 5th IJCAI, Boston, pp. 1045-1058 (1977)

[DFP86]   J Darlington, A J Field, H Pull; 'The Unification of Functional and Logic Languages', D DeGroot, G Lindstrom (editors), "Functional and Logic Programming", Prentice-Hall (1986)

[G77]   J V Guttag; 'Abstract Data Types and the Development of Data Structures', CACM Vol. 20, pp. 397-404 (1977)

[HK87a]   P G Harrison, H Khoshnevisan; 'On the synthesis of inverse functions', Research Report, Department of Computing, Imperial College, London (1987)

[HK87b]   P G Harrison, H Khoshnevisan; 'A Functional Algebra and its Application to Program Transformation', S Eisenbach, C Sadler (editors), "Functional Programming: Languages, Tools and Architectures", Ellis-Horwood (1987)

[KS81]   R B Kieburtz, J Shultis;   'Transformations of FP Program Schemes', In Proceedings of ACM Conference on Functional Languages and Computer Architecture, Portsmouth, New Hampshire (1981)

[R86]   U S Reddy; 'On the Relationship Between Logic and Functional Languages', D DeGroot, G Lindstrom (editors), "Functional and Logic Programming", Prentice-Hall (1986)

[R65]   J A Robinson; 'A Machine-Oriented Logic Based on the Resolution Principle', Journal of the Association for Computing Machinery, Vol. 12, No. 1 pp. 23-41, (January 1965)

[RS82]   J A Robinson, E E Sibert; 'LOGLISP: Motivation, Design and Implementation', In "Logic Programing", K L Clark, Academic Press, pp. 299-314, (1982)

[SY84]   P A Subrahmanyam, J H You; 'FUNLOG = Functions + Logic: a Computational Model Integrating Functional and Logical Programming', International Symposium on Logic Programming, IEEE, pp. 144-153, (1984)

Partial Evaluation and Mixed Computation
D. Bjørner, A.P. Ershov and N.D. Jones (Editors)
Elsevier Science Publishers B.V. (North-Holland)
© IFIP, 1988

Language Triplets: The AMIX Approach

N.Carsten Kehler Holst

DIKU : Institute of Datalogy,

University of Copenhagen.

Universitetsparken 1,

DK-2100, Copenhagen Ø

DENMARK - uucp ..!mcvax!diku!kehler

Abstract: This paper presents a new concept: Language Triplets. Language triplets have shown to be useful in describing compiler generator systems and partial evaluators. First we define a language triplet and prove some rather strong and surprising propositions about these. Secondly it is shown how the partial evaluator MIX and the compiler generator system CERES can be described as instances of language triplets. Finally we describe the AMIX system: a compiler generator system using partial evaluation. The AMIX is capable of deriving compilers from interpreters written in a high-level language. These compilers themselves written in a near assembly-level language produces target programs written in the same low-level language.

Keywords: Partial evaluation, compiler generation, language definitions, language triplets, self-application, program transformation.

Introduction.

This article is built upon the work done in the area of partial evaluation by [Futamura71,Ershov82,Jones et al85] therefore some knowledge about the contents of these papers are needed.

A lot of work is currently being done in the areas of partial evaluation and compiler generator construction. The general idea is that a compiler generator derives a compiler from a language definition and a partial evaluator specializes a program with respect to some partial known input. This paper presents a unifying concept: the language triplet. Language triplets can be viewed as a generalization of the concept of compiler generation as well as the concept of partial evaluation. Apart from the presentation of language triplets a compiler generator/partial evaluator system AMIX built from the concept of language triplets is presented.

This article is divided into three parts. First a theoretical part in which the definitions and notations used in the rest of the artical are introduced and some interesting properties about language triplets are shown. Secondly a very short description of the compiler generator system CERES [Christiansen,Jones83, Tofte84] and of the partial evaluator system MIX [Jones et al85,Sestoft86] are given, the emphasis being on the connection with language triplets. Thirdly a new partial evaluation / compiler generator system AMIX is introduced. AMIX though highly based upon the MIX system takes some ideas from the CERES system.

1. The theory of Language Triplets.

The main part of the notation in this section is borrowed from [Jones,Tofte85] which has shown to be very useful.

In the following section A will denote a suitable data domain e.g. LISP-lists or strings. First we give the definitions of language, interpreter and compiler.

Definition 1: A language is a partial function $L : A \to (A \to A)$. The domain of L is the programs written in L: Dom(L) = L-programs. If $l \in$ L-programs then L l is the input output function denoted by l when viewed as an L-program. Now let $a \in A$. Then (L l a) is the result of running the L-program l on input a.

Definition 2: $n \in$ N-programs is said to be a L-interpreter written in N if the following holds:
$$N n < l, a > \approx L l a$$
for each $l \in$ L-programs and for each $a \in A$. We write the set of all L-interpreters written in N as L:N.

The notation <l,a> means the tupel with elements a and l.

One should be aware of the very general flavour of these definitions. Take an arbitrary N-program n.. Then we can define an language N^n in such a way that n is an N^n-interpreter. Obviously the opposite is not allways possible.

Whenever we write something of the form $f \approx g$ the intended meaning is: f and g are both defined and equal or f and g are both undefined.

Definition 3: $n \in$ N-programs is said to be a L to M compiler written in N if the following holds

$$M (N n \, l) \approx L \, l$$

for each $l \in$ L-programs. The set of all L to M compilers written in N is written L-M:N.

Definition 4: A language triplet (L, S, L^S) is a relation between three languages fullfilling the following requirements

$$L \, l < a, b > \approx S \, (L^S \, l \, a \,) \, b \quad \forall \, l \in \text{L-programs} \, , a, b \in A^*.$$

and

$$L \quad : A \to (A \times A \to A).$$
$$L^S \quad : A \to (A^* \to A).$$
$$S \quad : A \to (A^* \to A).$$
$$\text{Dom}(L) = \text{Dom}(L^S) = \text{L-programs} = L^S\text{-programs}$$

In other words an L-program l taking two arguments can be viewed as an L^S-program taking one argument giving as result an S-program which given the second argument yields the final answer.

It is worth noticing that a language triplet describes the presence of a special relation between three languages. It does not describe any language nor does it denote a certain set of programs as does L-S:T which is the set of L to S compilers written in T. The important point about a language triplet is that it constitutes a duality between two languages in the language triplet. In the notation above L's dual language is L^S and as proposition 1 states: the dual to an interpreter in L is a compiler in L^S.

Proposition 1: If (L, S, L^S) is a language triplet the following holds for every language M

$$i \in \text{M:L} \quad \Leftrightarrow \quad i \in \text{M-S:}L^S$$

Proof: Let $i \in$ M:L then definition 2 gives

(1) $L\, i < m, a > \, \approx M\, m\,\, a$ $\forall\, m \in$ M-programs , $a \in A^*$

Now definition 6 of a language triplet gives

(2) $L\, i < m, a > \, \approx S\, (\, L^S\, i\,\, m\,\,)\,\, a$

(1) and (2) put together gives

$S\, (\, L^S\, i\,\, m\,\,)\,\, a\,\, \approx M\, m\,\, a$

and this is the definition of i being an M to S compiler written in L^S or $i \in$ M-S:L^S

$\square$

Definition 5: A definitional language $D : A \rightarrow (A \rightarrow (A \rightarrow A))$ is a function from Dom(D) = D-definitions into Ran(D) which is the set of languages one can define in D. Let $d_L \in$ D-definitions, now if $D\, d_L \approx L$ then d_L is called a D-definition of L. The set of D-definitions defining L is written $D^{-1}(L)$.

Ex. A denotational definition for a programming language can be thought of as written in a definitional language.

Definition 6: We will define n $\in$ N-programs as a compiler generator with definitional language D. This compiler generator produces compilers written in M, these compilers again producing T-programs as target code.

$T\,(\,M\,(\,N\,n\,\, d_L\,\,)\,\, 1\,\,)\,\, \approx\,\, D\, d_L\, 1$ $\forall\, d_L \in D^{-1}(\,L\,)$

$\forall\, 1 \in$ L-programs

Proposition 2: Let (L, S, L^S) be a language triplet. Then an interpreter $c \in L^S$:L is a compiler generator written in L^S producing compilers written in S. The definitional language for c is D where Dom(D) = L-programs and D fulfills that $D^{-1}(M) =$ M:L. i.e. a D-definition of the language M is an M interpreter written in L.

Proof:

$c \in L^S$:L

$\Leftrightarrow$ $c \in L^S$-S:L^S (Proposition 1)

and $d_M \in$ M:L   ($= D^{-1}(\,M\,)$)

$\Leftrightarrow$ $d_M \in$ M-S:L^S (Proposition 1)

Using definition 3 we get

$S\,(\,L^S\, c\,\, d_M\,\,)\,\, m\,\, \approx\,\, L^S\, d_M\,\, m$ $\forall\, m \in$ M-programs

And using definition 3 once more

$$S(L^S d_M \ m \ ) \ \approx \ M \ m \qquad\qquad \forall \ m \in \text{M-programs}$$

combining these two we get

$$S(S(L^S c \ d_M \ ) \ m \ ) \ \approx \ M \ m \qquad\qquad \forall \ m \in \text{M-programs}$$

and this is the definition of c being a compiler generator and d_M being a definition of M

□

Definition 7: $pe \in$ M-programs is a partial evaluator for L if

$$L \ (\ M \ pe < l, a >) \ b \ \approx \ L \ l < a, b > \quad \forall \ l \in \text{L-programs}$$

if M = L the partial evaluator is called self applicable or an autoprojector.

Proposition 3: Given language triplet (L, L, L^L), $pe \in L^L$:L is a self applicable partial evaluator.

Proof: we have $\quad L \ (\ L^L l \ a \ ) \ b \ \approx \ L \ l < a, b >$ (def 4)

$\qquad\qquad$ and $\quad L \ (\ L \ pe < l, a >) \ b \ \approx \ L \ (\ L^L l \ a \ ) \ b$ (def 2)

$\quad$ which gives $\quad L \ (\ L \ pe < l, a >) \ b \ \approx \ L \ l < a, b >$

which concludes our proof $\qquad\qquad\qquad\qquad\qquad\qquad\qquad\qquad$ □

Corollary 1: Given language triplet (L, A, L^A) and $\delta \in L^A$:L, the result of

$$L \ \delta < \delta, \delta > \ = \text{cocom} \in L^A\text{-A:A}, \quad \text{and A cocom} = L^A \ \delta$$

cocom is a compiler generator with definitional language D. D-definitions = L-programs and $D^{-1}(\ M \ ) = $ M:L.

Proof: $\delta \in L^A$:L $\Leftrightarrow \delta \in L^A$-A:$L^A$ (proposition 1)

we have $\qquad L \ \delta < \delta, \delta >$

$\qquad \approx \qquad L^A \ \delta \ \delta \qquad\qquad$ (def 2, $\delta \in L^A$:L)

$\qquad = \qquad \text{cocom} \in L^A\text{-A:A} \qquad$ (def 3, $\delta \in L^A$-A:L^A)

and

$\qquad\qquad A \ \text{cocom}$

$\qquad \approx \qquad A \ (\ L \ \delta < \delta, \delta >)\qquad$ (thats the way we made it)

$\qquad \approx \qquad A \ (\ L^A \ \delta \ \delta \ )\qquad\qquad$ (def 2, $\delta \in L^A$:L)

$\qquad \approx \qquad L^A \ \delta \qquad\qquad\qquad$ (def 3, $\delta \in L^A$-A:L^A)

if $d_M \in$ M:L we have

A cocom $d_M \approx L^A \ \delta \ d_M \approx \text{com}_M \in$ M-A:A (def 3, $\delta \in L^A$-A:L^A) □

Both CERES, MIX and AMIX use the technique from corollary 1 to generate compiler generators. In AMIX and in MIX this is done automatically in CERES by hand.

2. CERES & MIX.

This section will not attempt a detailed description of the MIX and the CERES systems. Instead it will be shown how the theory of language triplets gives a natural description of the two systems. Both systems are interesting, if for no other reason, then because they were the first two self generating compiler generating systems.

MIX was made by [Jones et al85] and has been described in [Sestoft86]. The MIX system was the first system which had a self applicable partial evaluator and therefore was able to make compilers and compiler generators. Partial evaluation is the process of specializing programs with respect to a partially known input. Given a program taking two parameters and the value of the first parameter, partial evaluation of the program with respect to the first parameter will yield a specialized program of one parameter, which when applied to the value of the second parameter yields the final result. This can be described by the language triplet

$$(L, L, L^L).$$

Proposition 3 tells us that mix $\in L^L$:L is a self applicable partial evaluator, and corollary 1 tells us that it is possible to generate a compiler generator by running

$$L \text{ mix} < \text{mix}, \text{mix} > = \text{cocom} \in L^L\text{-L:L}$$

where cocom has definitional language D, D-definitions = L-programs and $D^{-1}(M) = M$:L. These are indeed the propeties of mix in the MIX system.

One of the things that makes the MIX system unique is the annotation of programs. The language L above is a first order lexically scoped subset of LISP with annotated operators. Every operator/subexpression are annotated with an "R" or an "E". The latter is used when the value of the subexpression depends only on the first parameter of the L program. The effect is that the subexpression can be evaluated to its value when the program is considered as an L^L program. If the annotation is "R" we can not deduce the value of the subexpression from the value of the first parameter alone. Thus in evaluating the program as an L^L program we have to generate code (or a residual L expression) which given the value of the second parameter will yield the final result. This annotation or binding time analysis is determined as the result of an abstract interpretation over the abstract domain {Known, Unknown} ordered as a lattice.

$$\text{Unknown} \atop | \atop \text{Known}$$

where Known means that the value can be deduced from the value of the first parameter. This means that the MIX system should be considered an instance of the language triplet (L-ann, L, L-ann^L) where L-ann is the annotated L language. There is a great technical difference between this language triplet and the language triplet above but no real theoretical difference, because one could use the language triplet (L-ann, L-ann, L-ann$^{L\text{-ann}}$) as well. This just means that all the operators in the residual program would be annotated with an "E".

This does not describe the internal structure of the MIX system. But viewing the mix program as an interpreter for L^L written in L as well as a compiler from L^L to L written in L^L has shown to be valuable since AMIX arose from this idea.

CERES first made by [Jones,Christiansen83] and later refined by [Tofte84] is a compiler generator system. The system makes it possible to write a denotational like definition of a language and translate it into a compiler for this language. The compiler produces code in a fixed target language. Defining the semantics of a language one would have to write a definition which is a specification of a tree to tree transformation, transforming the abstract syntax tree of the language being defined into an abstract syntax tree of a fixed semantic language. Diffrent semantic languages have been used both the lambda calculus and a low level set of combinators [Tofte84], e.g. the definition is a compiler from the language being defined to a fixed semantic language. Call the language we are defining L, the fixed semantic language S, and the target language T. Then the definition of L is an L to S compiler and the result is a L to T compiler written in T.

In the context of language triplets we would say that we have two language triplets

$$(D, S, D^S)\quad \text{and} \quad (D, T, D^T)\quad \text{where}$$

S - is the fixed semantic language used to define the meaning of the language being defined.

D - is the language in which the definition of L would be thought of as an L interpreter.

D^S - is the definition language. Describes tree to tree transformations.

T - the target language.

D^T - the language in which the definition af L is an L to T compiler.

A definition of L is an L to S compiler written in D^S. Call it $d_L \in$ L-S:D^S. Using the theory of language triplets we get

$$d_L \in \text{L-S:}D^S$$

$$\Leftrightarrow \quad d_L \in \text{L:D}$$

$$\Leftrightarrow \quad d_L \in \text{L-T:}D^T.$$

To create a compiler generator cocom according to corollary 1 one should run

$$D \text{ cc} < \text{cc, cc} > = \text{cocom} \quad \text{where cc} \in D^T\text{:D} = D^T\text{-S:}D^S$$

This is actually not the way it is done in CERES, because CERES has not got a D interpreter. Instead one does the following (by hand).

$$S \, (\, D^S \text{ cc cc }) \text{ cc} \qquad = \text{cocom,} \quad \text{(this is not as hard as it looks)}$$

To get an idea of what these languages look like, consider the following example which is a part of a CERES definition.

Example:

| D [+(e1, e2)   ] | => | add(D[e1], D[e2]) |
| D [*.id   ] | => | get-value-of(*.id) |

It should be clear how this can be viewed both as an interpreter and as an compiler. In the semantic language S we have instructions like add(...) and get-value-of(...) which operate on basic values and environment. In the language D^T add(...) and get-value-of(...) would be code generating instructions instead. Notice how the annotation from the MIX system is built into the language. The pattern matching on the left sides correspond to the expressions annotated with an E while the right sides correspond to the ones annotated with R. [end example]

This finishes our very superficial description of the CERES system. The essence has been revealed but one thing which in my opinion makes the CERES system unique has been left untouched. The composabillity of the definitions. The idea in CERES can be summarised as: Given language triplets (D, S, D^S) and (D, T, D^T) a definition of L is an L to S compiler written in D^S . This compiler is then viewed as an L to T compiler written in D^T and translated into T thereby obtaining the desired L to T compiler written in T.

3. The system AMIX.

In this section we will describe the first actual result obtained using the concept of language triplets: The AMIX system. The AMIX system has been developed from the MIX system plus some ideas from the CERES system. The AMIX system allows one to derive compilers automaticaly from interpreters written in high-level language, the compilers producing target code in low level assembly language. We give a high-level description of the AMIX system using language triplets.

In the AMIX system we use the language triplet

$$(L, T, L^T) \text{ where}$$

T   is a low-level assembly language, actually a stack assembly for a virtual lisp machine.

L   is the same L language as in the MIX system extended with some arithmetic operations.

L^T looks very much like the L^L language of MIX but produces T programs instead of L programs.

Again the theory of language triplets tells us that amix $\in L^T$:L is a compiler generator written in L^T and that we are able to generate a compiler generator written in T by

$$L \text{ amix} < \text{amix, amix} > = \text{cocom}_A \in L^T\text{-T:T}$$

the definitional language of cocom$_A$ being D where D-definitions = L-programs and $D^{-1}(M) = M$:L. One can summerise the difference between AMIX and MIX as: In MIX one writes an interpreter for M in L and gets a M to L compiler written in L. ie. if one wants a compiler which produce low level code one has to develop a MIX system with a low level L-language and write an M-interpreter in this low level language with all the problems that raises. In AMIX as in CERES one writes definitions [interpreters or compilers] in a high level language and obtains compilers and target code in low level language.

4. The implementation of AMIX.

The overall description of the AMIX system has been given in the previous section. In this section we are going to describe the semantics of the three languages in the language triplet (L, T, L^T) which is the basis for the AMIX system. Apart from this a very small example is given and some results are figured.

First let us look at the syntax of L-programs and L^T-programs (afterwards only called L-programs). An L-program consists of a set of recursive functions. We recall that in order to be a language triplet the L-programs should take two arguments. We call the data to the first argument the primary data and the data to the second argument the secondary data. Each function in an L-program has two arguments lists, the first one holding the parameters which we call Known and the other holding the Unknown. The value of the Known parameters is known from the primary data alone (no information is needed in the secondary data). The first function (the goal function) has exactly one Known parameter and one Unknown parameter.

SYNTAX OF L AND L^T PROGRAMS

Program	::=	(Equation *)
Equation	::=	(Name (Parameter-list) (Parameter-list) = ExpR) [1]
ExpR	::=	(VarR Name) [2]
	|	(IfR ExpR ExpR ExpR)
	|	(IfE ExpE ExpR ExpR)
	|	(EquelR ExpR ExpR)
	|	(ConsR ExpR ExpR)
	|	(CarR ExpR)
	|	(CdrR ExpR)
	|	(OpR ExpR ExpR) [3]
	|	(CallR Name ExpE* ExpR*)
	|	(Call Name ExpE* ExpR*)
	|	ExpE
ExpE	::=	(Quote S-expression)
	|	(VarE Name) [2]
	|	(IfE ExpE ExpE ExpE)
	|	(EquelE ExpE ExpE)
	|	(ConsE ExpE ExpE)
	|	(CarE ExpE)
	|	(CdrE ExpE)
	|	(OpE ExpE ExpE) [3]
	|	(Call Name ExpE* ())

1) The first parameterlist contains the parameters wich is known the second the unknown.Known and Unknown with respect to the first parameter of the program. In the body of the equation you must only reference to the parameters of the equation.

2) VarR is a variable from the second parameterlist and VarE one from the first.

3) Op is Add, Sub and the other normal arithmetic operations postfixed with R or E

L-programs have the standard LISP semantics if you ignore the E's and R's. Before we describe the semantics of L^T we will look at T. Rember that the result of running an L^T program is a T program.

The target language T is a stack assembly language. A T-program consists of a sequence of instructions and labels. The instructions operate on three stacks called Stack, Dump and Environment. the syntax and semantics of T is given below as a set of state to state transformations in the traditional SECD style. At the moment the T instructions are implemented as a set of LISP macros.

THE SYNTAX AND SEMANTICS OF T

The state is described as a quadruple $< Code,Stack,Dump,Env>$.
Initially the state is $<C,(),(()()()),x_0 ... x_n >$ where $x_0 ... x_n$
is the input values.At the end of execution the state is $<(), (r),(),()>$
r being the result of the computation.

$$< (var\ n).C, S, D, x_0...x_n..> \Rightarrow \quad < C, x_n.S, D, x_0 ... x_n...>$$

$$< (q\ e).C, S, D, E > \quad \Rightarrow \quad < C, e.S, D, E >$$

$$< (fst).C, (a.b).S, D, E > \quad \Rightarrow \quad < C, a.S, D, E>$$

$$< (lst).C, (a.b).S, D, E > \quad \Rightarrow \quad < C, b.S, D, E>$$

$$< (at?).C, a.S, D, E > \quad \Rightarrow \quad < C, (atom\ a).S, D, E>$$

$$< (pair).C, a\ b\ .S, D, E > \quad \Rightarrow \quad < C, (a.b).S, D, E >$$

$$< (eq?).C, a\ b\ .S, D, E > \quad \Rightarrow \quad < C, (a = b).S, D, E >$$

$$< (op).C, a\ b.S, D, E > \quad \Rightarrow \quad < C, (a\ op\ b).S , D, E > \quad *)$$

$$< (jfalse\ lb).C, b.S, E > \quad \Rightarrow \quad < C', S, D, E >$$

where C' = if b then C else the code following label lb

$$< (jmp\ lb).C, S, D, E > \quad \Rightarrow \quad < C', S, D, E >$$

where C' is the code following lb

$$< (new\text{-}frame).C, S, D, E > \Rightarrow \quad < C, (), S.D, E >$$

< (call fn).C, S, D, E >   ⇒   < C_{fn}, (), C E.D, S >

< (ret).C, x.S, c e s.D, E >   ⇒   < c, x.s, D, e >

*) again op is add sub mul div and eq

The only thing left is to describe the semantics of L^T. The L^T language of AMIX is very much like the L^L language of MIX. Instead of reducing the residual expressions as in MIX one translate them to T code.

THE SEMANTICS OF L^T

When the program is run as an M^T program it is called with one argument and the main equation (the first) has one known and one unknown parameter.

The semantics of L^T will be given in a rather operational style.
The semantic functions are P, R and E. The environment for the Known variables is named ε the environment for the Unknown are named ρ. In all the semantic schemes the T-instructions has been written in **bold** and are concatenated with ";"
(ex. (**q add**) ; **var** 0 ; **pair**)

The types of the semantic functions

P   : M-program → Initial-value → T-program
R   : Expression → Env → T-code+
E   : Expression → Env → Value

The translation scheme **P** are used to denote the value of the whole program.

We use the following datastructures :
pcalls   a set of possible calls. A possible call being recorded as the function name and the value of the Known parameters. There will be built a specialized function for each possible call.
out   used to collect the T-program being generated.
initially pcall and out are empty.

$\mathbf{P}[\![\ ((f_1\ (x)\ (y) = e\ )\ ...)\ ]\!]\ iv = \text{add-to-pcalls}(\ f_1, iv\ )$

$\qquad\qquad\qquad$ while pcalls not empty

$\qquad\qquad\qquad\qquad$ extract-from-pcalls(f_i, v^*)

$\qquad\qquad\qquad\qquad$ if (f_i, v^*) has not allready been specialised

$\qquad\qquad\qquad\qquad\qquad$ add-to-out(f_i: $\mathbf{R}[\![\ \text{body}\ ]\!]\ \rho\ \varepsilon$; $\mathbf{ret}$)

where "the entire program" $= (...(f_i\ (k_1\ ...\ k_n)\ (u_1\ ...\ u_m) = \text{body}\ )...)$

$\qquad\qquad\qquad v^* \qquad\qquad = (v_1\ ...\ v_n\ )$

$\qquad\qquad\qquad \rho \qquad\qquad = [u_1 \mapsto \mathbf{var}\ m\text{-}1, ... , u_m \mapsto \mathbf{var}\ 0]$

$\qquad\qquad\qquad \varepsilon \qquad\qquad = [k_1 \mapsto v_1, ... , k_n \mapsto v_n]$

add-to-pcalls and extract-from-pcalls are defined in the obvious way.

it is possible that there will be added more "possible calls" to pcalls under the evaluation of $\mathbf{R}[\![\ \text{body}\ ]\!]\ \rho\ \varepsilon$. Some renameing is performed under the specialisation in order to distinguish two different instances of a specialised function for each other.

The scheme **E**. The E scheme is used to denote the value of a subexpression whose value is known to be known from the annotation.

$\mathbf{E}[\![\ (\text{quote}\ s)]\!]\ \varepsilon \qquad\qquad = s$

$\mathbf{E}[\![\ (\text{varE}\ v)]\!]\ \varepsilon \qquad\qquad = \varepsilon\ (\ v\ )$

$\mathbf{E}[\![\ (\text{atomE}\ e)]\!]\ \varepsilon \qquad\quad = \text{atom}(\ \mathbf{E}[\![\ e\ ]\!]\ \varepsilon\ )$

$\mathbf{E}[\![\ (\text{equalE}\ e_1\ e_2)]\!]\ \varepsilon \qquad = \text{equal}(\ \mathbf{E}[\![\ e_1\ ]\!]\ \varepsilon, \mathbf{E}[\![\ e_2]\!]\ \varepsilon)$

$\mathbf{E}[\![\ (\text{ifE}\ e_1\ e_2\ e_3)]\!]\ \varepsilon \qquad = \text{if}\ \ \mathbf{E}[\![\ e_1]\!]\ \varepsilon\ \text{then}\ \mathbf{E}[\![\ e_2]\!]\ \varepsilon\ \text{else}\ \ \mathbf{E}[\![\ e_3]\!]\ \varepsilon$

$\mathbf{E}[\![\ (\text{consE}\ e_1\ e_2)]\!]\ \varepsilon \qquad = \text{cons}(\ \mathbf{E}[\![\ e_1]\!]\ \varepsilon, \mathbf{E}[\![\ e_2]\!]\ \varepsilon)$

$\mathbf{E}[\![\ (\text{carE}\ e)]\!]\ \varepsilon \qquad\quad = \text{car}(\ \mathbf{E}[\![\ e\ ]\!]\ \varepsilon\ )$

$\mathbf{E}[\![\ (\text{cdrE}\ e)]\!]\ \varepsilon \qquad\quad = \text{cdr}(\ \mathbf{E}[\![\ e\ ]\!]\ \varepsilon\ )$

$\mathbf{E}[\![\ (\text{call}\ f_n\ e_1^*\ ())]\!]\ \varepsilon \qquad = \mathbf{E}[\![\ e'\ ]\!]\ \varepsilon'$

$\qquad$ where "the entire program" $= (\ ...\ (\ f_n\ (v_1\ ...\ v_n)\ () = e'\ )\ ...\ )$

$\qquad\qquad$ and $\qquad\qquad e_1^* = (e_1\ ...\ e_n\ )$

$\qquad\qquad$ and $\qquad\qquad \varepsilon'\quad = [\ v_1 \mapsto \mathbf{E}[\![\ e_1\ ]\!]\ \varepsilon, ... , v_n \mapsto \mathbf{E}[\![\ e_n\ ]\!]\ \varepsilon\ ]$

The **R** scheme : the R scheme is used to denote the value of an subexpression of which the value is not Known from the primary data alone. The value of such a subexpression is a piece of T-code which will leave the final value on top of the stack when the secondary data are availeble to the T-program. The environment ρ gives for each Unknown variable a piece of code which will compute the value of this variable.

$\mathbf{R}[\![$ (quote s)$]\!]\,\rho\,\varepsilon$ $\qquad$ = code-constant(s)

$\mathbf{R}[\![$ (varR v)$]\!]\,\rho\,\varepsilon$ $\qquad$ $= \rho(\,v\,)$

$\mathbf{R}[\![$ (atomR e)$]\!]\,\rho\,\varepsilon$ $\qquad$ $= \mathbf{R}[\![\,e\,]\!]\,\rho\,\varepsilon\,;\,$**at?**

$\mathbf{R}[\![$ (equalR e_1 e_2)$]\!]\,\rho\,\varepsilon$ $\qquad$ $= \mathbf{R}[\![\,e_1\,]\!]\,\rho\,\varepsilon\,;\,\mathbf{R}[\![\,e_2\,]\!]\,\rho\,\varepsilon\,;\,$**eq?**

$\mathbf{R}[\![$ (ifR e_1 e_2 e_3)$]\!]\,\rho\,\varepsilon$ $\qquad$ $= \mathbf{R}[\![\,e_1\,]\!]\,\rho\,\varepsilon\,;\,$**jfalse** $\mathbf{lb_1}\,;\,\mathbf{R}[\![\,e_2\,]\!]\,\rho\,\varepsilon\,;\,$**jmp** $\mathbf{lb_2}\,;$
$\qquad\qquad\qquad\qquad\qquad\qquad \mathbf{lb_1}:\;\mathbf{R}[\![\,e_3\,]\!]\,\rho\,\varepsilon\,;\,\mathbf{lb_2}:$

$\qquad$ where $\mathbf{lb_1}$ and $\mathbf{lb_2}$ are unique labels.

$\mathbf{R}[\![$ (consR e_1 e_2)$]\!]\,\rho\,\varepsilon$ $\qquad$ $= \mathbf{R}[\![\,e_1\,]\!]\,\rho\,\varepsilon\,;\,\mathbf{R}[\![\,e_2\,]\!]\,\rho\,\varepsilon\,;\,$**pair**

$\mathbf{R}[\![$ (carR e)$]\!]\,\rho\,\varepsilon$ $\qquad$ $= \mathbf{R}[\![\,e\,]\!]\,\rho\,\varepsilon\,;\,$**fst**

$\mathbf{R}[\![$ (cdrE e)$]\!]\,\rho\,\varepsilon$ $\qquad$ $= \mathbf{R}[\![\,e\,]\!]\,\rho\,\varepsilon\,;\,$**lst**

$\mathbf{R}[\![$ (call f_n e_1* e_2*)$]\!]\,\rho\,\varepsilon$ $\qquad$ $= \mathbf{R}[\![\,e'\,]\!]\,\rho'\,\varepsilon'$

$\qquad$ where "the entire program" $= (\,\dots\,(\,f_n\,(v_1\,..\,v_n)\,(u_1\,..\,u_m) = e'\,)\,\dots\,)$

$\qquad\qquad$ and $\qquad e_1$* $= (e_1\,\dots\,e_n\,)$

$\qquad\qquad$ and $\qquad \varepsilon'\quad = [\,v_1 \mapsto \mathbf{E}[\![\,e_1\,]\!]\,\varepsilon,\,\dots\,,\,v_n \mapsto \mathbf{E}[\![\,e_n\,]\!]\,\varepsilon\,]$

$\qquad\qquad$ and $\qquad e_2$* $= (\,ue_1\,\dots\,ue_m\,)$

$\qquad\qquad$ and $\qquad \rho'\quad = [\,u_1 \mapsto \mathbf{R}[\![\,ue_1\,]\!]\,\rho\,\varepsilon,\,\dots\,,\,u_m \mapsto \mathbf{R}[\![\,ue_n\,]\!]\,\rho\,\varepsilon\,]$

$\mathbf{R}[\![$ (callR f_n e_1* e_2*)$]\!]\,\rho\,\varepsilon$ $= $ **new-frame** $;$
$\qquad\qquad\qquad\qquad\qquad \mathbf{R}[\![\,ue_1\,]\!]\,\rho\,\varepsilon\,;\,\dots\,;\,\mathbf{R}[\![\,ue_m\,]\!]\,\rho\,\varepsilon\,;\,$**call** f_n

$\qquad$ where "the entire program" $= (\,\dots\,(\,f_n\,(v_1\,..\,v_n)\,(u_1\,..\,u_m) = e'\,)\,\dots\,)$

$\qquad\qquad$ and $\qquad e_1$* $= (e_1\,\dots\,e_n\,)$

$\qquad\qquad$ and $\qquad e_2$* $= (\,ue_1\,\dots\,ue_m\,)$

The fact that we will have to specialise fn with respect to the values of the known parameters at this call are recorded by adding the possible call to the list of possible calls.

add-to-pcalls(fn , $\mathbf{E}[\![\,e_1\,]\!]\,\varepsilon,\,..,\,\mathbf{E}[\![\,e_n\,]\!]\,\varepsilon$)

This call will then be specialised later.

$\mathbf{R}[\![\,e\,]\!]\,\rho\,\varepsilon$ $\qquad$ = code-constant($\mathbf{E}[\![\,e\,]\!]\,\varepsilon$)

$\qquad$ if e does not match one of the expressions above.

The auxillary function code-constant are defined as

code-constant(a) $\qquad$ $= (\mathbf{q}\ a)\qquad$, if a is an atom.

code-constant(x : xs) $\qquad$ = code-constant(x) ; code-constant(xs) ; **pair** , otherwise

---

This concludes our semiformal description of AMIX. We will give a very small example before we look at some results obtained with the system.

A small example

We have the following program which implements the function append

---

```
( ( Append (x) (y) =
(ifE      (varE x)   (varR y)
          (consR (carE (varE x)) (call Append ((cdrE (varE x))) (varR y)) ) )
) )
```

Now let us run this as an L^T program on the partial data (3 4) e.g. the list with the elements 3 and 4.

---

using the abrivations

body = (ifE (varE x)(varR y)(consR (carE (varE x)) (call Append ((cdrE (varE x))) (varR y))))

call = (call Append ((cdrE (varE x))) ((varR y))))

we get

P⟦ ((Append (x)(y) = ...)) ⟧ (3 4)

=   **Append: R⟦** *body* **⟧** ρ[y↦**var** 0] ε[x↦(3 4)] **; ret**

=   **Append: (q 3) ; R⟦** *call* **⟧** ρ ε **; pair ; ret** *,because E⟦ x ⟧ε[x↦(3 4)] = (3 4)*

=   **Append: (q 3) ; R⟦** *body* **⟧** ρ[y↦**var** 0] ε[x↦(4)] **; pair ; ret**

=   **Append: (q 3) ; (q 4) ; R⟦** *call* **⟧** ρ ε **; pair; pair ; ret**

=   **Append: (q 3) ; (q 4) ; R⟦** *body* **⟧** ρ[y↦**var** 0] ε[x↦()] **; pair ; pair ; ret**

=   **Append: (q 3) ; (q 4) ; R⟦** y **⟧** ρ ε **; pair; pair ; ret**

=   **Append: (q 3) ; (q 4) ; var** 0 **; pair ; pair ; ret**

Results.

The AMIX system has proved to be self applicable just like the MIX system. It has been possible to generate compilers and a compiler generator with the technichs described in the theoretical section. The AMIX systems runs at the same speed as the MIX system and it would run even faster if the T-code was compiled into real machine language instead of beeing interpreted. The speedups is about 10 to 20 as in the MIX system.

In the following we will use the following programs.

amix	the amix program a L^T interpreter written in L.
si	a self interpreter for L written in L
mp	an interpreter for a little imperative language M with LISP datastructures writte in L.
rev	an implementation of the function reverse written in M
$target_1$	the reverse program after it has been translated to T.
$target_2$	the si program after it has been translated to T.
mcom	the result of L amix <amix,mp>, an M compiler written in T
scom	the result of L amix <amix,si>, an L compiler written in T
cocom	the result of L amix <amix,amix>, a compiler generator written in T

Size: the table below shows the size of the various programs in number of lines after the programs have been pretty printed with the LISP pretty printer.

amix	529	si	135
mp	160	rev	12
mcom	1488	scom	1559
cocom	5086	$target_1$	57
$target_2$	842		

Runtimes: The following runtimes are cpu milliseconds.

L amix <mp,rev>	260	ms.
T mcom <rev>	20	ms.
L amix <si,si>	2.020	ms.
T scom <si>	180	ms.
L amix <amix,mp>	3.140	ms.
T cocom <mp>	260	ms.
L amix <amix,si>	2.520	ms.
T cocom <si>	100	ms.
L amix <amix,amix>	5.600	ms.
T cocom <amix>	740	ms.

Perspectives

Because the AMIX system is strongly related to in the MIX system it is not surprising that the AMIX system benefits from a large part of the improvements of the MIX system. As for now I see three roads along which the AMIX system can be improved.

Safe semantics: In the current version of the MIX and AMIX system it is not true that

$$L (L \text{ mix} <p,a>) b \approx L p <a,b> \text{ or } T (L \text{ amix} <p,a>) b \approx L p <a,b>.$$

Instead we have

$L (L \text{ mix} <p,a>) b \subset L p <a,b>$	for some programs.
$L(L \text{ mix} <p, a>) b \supset L p <a,b>$	for other programs.

Where "$\subset$· means less defined ie. the mix program goes into an infinite loop even if the program p is defined on input <a,b>, and "$\supset$" means more defined in the standard way.

In the AMIX system though it is always the case that

$$T(L \text{ amix} <p,a>) b \subseteq L p <a,b> \qquad \forall p \in L\text{-programs}.$$

But the difference is only technical. The AMIX system always uses a call by value strategy and the MIX system uses a mixed call by text and call by value strategy. Currently work is being done which should solve this problem. An other important project in this category is the removal of the need to annotate the programs for call unfolding by hand. This has been obtained in [Sestoft87] in which it is shown how to annotate programs for call unfolding automatically.

Apart from making the abstract interpretation of the programs "safe" it is desirable to raise the information level of the results from the abstract interpretation. This has been obtained by the use of a richer domain than {Known, Unknow} in the abstract interpretation thereby gaining knowledge about the datastructures in the program. A way of doing this is described in [Mogensen87]. There are two reasons why this is important. First it allows the definitional interpreters to use more complex datastructures. A typical example is the assoc list which in the MIX and AMIX system has to be divided into a namelist and a value list in order to make the namelist Known. Second it makes it possible to use a much more efficient memory allocation scheme in the residual programs. This was obtained in the old version of the MIX system by annotating the programs by hand with information about the structures of the variables and was called variable splitting [Sestoft86].

In the AMIX system the code generation is rather naive and it is indeed improvable. One very interesting improvement will be the detection of tailrecursiveness in the interpreters defining a language. Also other improvements of the memory allocation scheme are possible. At the moment the generated code uses most of its time packing and unpacking data.

An other interesting possibility is to use some of the results obtained in the AMIX system and in other partial evaluation based systems in a compiler generator system as CERES. Thereby one automatically obtaines the same results obtained by the use of <u>quote</u> and <u>antiquote</u> in CERES85 [Christensen84, Storm85] <u>quote</u> and <u>antiquote</u> resembling backquote and comma in LISP.

Acknowlegments.

I would like to thank the MIX group at DIKU, special thanks goes to Olivier Danvy for having read several sketches for this artical and to Peter Sestoft for encouranging me to make this paper about language triplets.

Conclusion.

It has been shown that the concept of Language Triplets is a useful tool in describing and developing compiler generator systems. Language Triplets introduces a duality between compilers and interpreters and compilers for the same language producing different target code.

AMIX: A compiler generator system using techniques from partial evaluation has been presented. AMIX being a "partial evaluator" specializing programs written in high level language while producing residual programs in low level language.

The principles in AMIX have proved to be good while the implementation still is fairly slow.

References.

[Christensen84]   A.Christensen, *Development of a Semantic Language for the proposed CERES-85 Compiler Generator.* (cand. scient. thesis), Institute of Datalogy, Copenhagen University, Denmark 1984.

[Ershov82]   A.P.Ershov, Mixed Computation: Potential Applications and Problems for Study, *Theor. Comp. Sci.* **18** (1982) pp. 41-67

[Futamura71]   Y.Futamura, Partial Evaluation of Computation Processes - an Approach to a Compiler-compiler, *Systems, Computers, Controls* **2,5** (1971) pp. 721-728

[Christiansen,Jones83] H.Christiansen,N.D.Jones, Control flow treatment in a simple semantics-directed compiler generator, in *Proc. IFIP W.G. 2.2: Formal Description of Programming Concepts II*, (D.Bjørner (ed)) North-Holland 1983.

[Jones,Tofte85]   N.D.Jones, M.Tofte, Towards a theory of compiler generation, *Proc. Workshop on Formal Software Development Methods*, (D.Bjørner (ed)), North-Holland, 1985.

[Jones et al85]   N.D.Jones, P.Sestoft, H. Søndergaard, An Experiment in Partial Evaluation: The Generation of a Compiler Generator, Springer *Lecture Notes on Computer Science* **202** (1985) pp. 124-140

[Mogensen87]   T.Mogensen, Handling Partial known Structures in a Self-applicable Partial Evaluator, Submittet to the workshop on mixed and partial evaluation autum 87

[Sestoft86]   P.Sestoft, The Structure of an Self-applicable Partial Evaluator, *Springer Lecture Notes on Computer Science* **217** (1986) pp. 237-256

[Sestoft87]   P.Sestoft, Automatic Call Unfolding in a Partial Evaluator, submitted to the workshop on mixed and partal computation autum 87.

[Storm85]   K.F.Storm, *Design and Implementation of the Compiler Generator CERES-85*, (cand. scient. thesis) Institute of Datalogy, Copenhagen University, Denmark, 1985.

[Tofte84]   M.Tofte, *Compiler generators - What they can do, what they might do and what they will probably never do*, 224 pp. (cand. scient. thesis) tecnical report, Institute of Datalogy, Copenhagen University, Denmark 1984.

Partial Evaluation and Mixed Computation
D. Bjørner, A.P. Ershov and N.D. Jones (Editors)
Elsevier Science Publishers B.V. (North-Holland)
© IFIP, 1988

Backwards Analysis of Functional Programs

John Hughes
University of Glasgow

1. Introduction

Analysis techniques for functional programs are becoming increasingly important as good optimising compilers are developed [Fairbairn85] [Fairbairn86] [Hudak84]. So far, the most widely studied analysis problem is *strictness analysis*, which identifies strict functions and allows the expensive call-by-need mechanism to be replaced by call-by-value. Analysis methods are equally important for partial evaluation. The most important seems to be "known/unknown" or "binding-time" analysis [Jones87].

Many analysis methods are based on *abstract interpretation*, which essentially consists of running the program with "abstract data", and extracting desired information from the abstract results. The first successful strictness analysis technique worked in this way [Mycroft80], and so do recent extensions to higher-order functions [Burn et.al.85] and lazy data-structures [Wadler87a]. However, a number of techniques have appeared that work "backwards" rather than forwards — from information about a large expression to information about its subexpressions, the opposite of an abstract execution. Examples include Wray's strictness analyser for Ponder [Wray85] [Wray86], and various strictness analysers that aim to cope well with lazy data structures [Dybjer87] [Hall87] [Hughes85] [Hughes87] [Karlsson87] [Wadler87b].

In this paper we introduce a framework for backward analysis, and argue that it can be more efficient than forward analysis. We show that backward analysis can be extended to derive information about data-structures and higher-order functions (in typed languages), and we illustrate the techniques by applying them to strictness analysis and other problems. Finally we suggest a way to extend the techniques in this paper to polymorphic languages.

2. Abstract Interpretation, or Forward Analysis

2.1 Introduction

We begin with a summary of the main ideas behind abstract interpretation. Many of the same ideas emerge in backward analysis.

Consider a first-order functional language, manipulating values in the domain D. An abstract interpretation is based on a domain of abstract values A, and a function abs from D to A. An abstract function f# is associated with every function f in the language. f# is intended to approximate f, in the sense that
$$\text{abs } (f\ v1\ ...\ vn) \leq f\#\ (\text{abs } v1)\ ...\ (\text{abs } vn)$$
This condition is known as *safety*: it states that f# safely approximates f.

Given safe approximations to the primitive functions of the language, safe approximations to other functions can be derived by taking their definitions and replacing every use of a primitive by its approximation, and every constant by its abstract value. For example, if
$$f\ x\ y = x\ ^*\ y + 1$$
then since
$$\text{abs } (f\ x\ y) = \text{abs } (x^*\ y + 1)$$
$$\leq \text{abs } (x^*y) +\# \text{ abs } 1$$
$$\leq \text{abs } x\ ^*\#\ \text{abs } y +\# \text{ abs } 1$$
it is certainly safe to define
$$f\#\ a\ b = a\ ^*\#\ b +\# \text{ abs } 1$$
When this is done, we end up, in general, with recursive definitions of approximations to

user-defined functions. Thus these abstract functions are the fixed points of higher-order operators. It is well known that we can express the fixed point of an operator P as the limit of an infinite iteration.

$$\text{fix } P = \bigcup_{i=0}^{\infty} P^i \perp$$

However, if the fixed point lies in a *finite* domain then the limit is certain to be reached after a finite number of steps and can therefore be calculated by iteration. Provided the abstract domain A is finite, then all first-order function domains (A->A, A->A->A, etc.) are also finite, and so these fixed points can be found by iteration. The result is a tabular definition of each abstract function, which can be used to calculate it even in cases where the concrete function would fail to terminate.

2.2 Extension to Higher-Order Languages

Abstract interpretation cannot be applied to higher-order languages in general, because the domain of higher-order functions over a base domain A is infinite, even if A is finite.

$$HOFS(A) = A + (HOFS(A) \rightarrow HOFS(A))$$

However, Burn, Hankin and Abramsky have shown that it can be applied to typed higher-order languages. An abstract domain A_T is associated with each type T, by associating a finite domain with objects of order zero, and then defining

$$A_{T->T'} = A_T \rightarrow A_{T'}$$

for all types T and T'. Each of these abstract domains is finite, although the domain of all values

$$A = A_{T1} + A_{T2} + A_{T3} + ...$$

is infinite. Any particular fixed point iteration can therefore be carried out in a finite domain.

The idea breaks down in polymorphic languages, because the type-checker cannot assign a unique type to each expression. To overcome this Abramsky has defined the notion of "polymorphic invariance" [Abramsky85]. An analysis is a polymorphic invariant if it gives the same results for every instance of a polymorphic object. If this is the case, then the analysis can be applied to the simplest instance, and the result re-used for all instances. Abramsky has shown that their strictness analysis, at least, is a polymorphic invariant.

2.3 Example: Mycroft Strictness Analysis

We can illustrate some of the strengths and weaknesses of abstract interpretation using Mycroft's strictness analysis method [Mycroft80]. Mycroft used a two point abstract domain $\{0 \leq 1\}$, with 0 corresponding only to $\perp$, and 1 corresponding to all other values. So

$$\text{abs } \perp = 0$$
$$\text{abs } x = 1 \qquad \text{if } x \neq \perp$$

If an abstract function is strict in one of its arguments (maps 0 to 0), the corresponding concrete function must also be. For example, if

$$f\# \ 1 \ 0 \ 1 = 0$$

then

$$\text{abs } (f \ x \perp z) \leq f\# \ (\text{abs } x) \ 0 \ (\text{abs } z) \leq f\# \ 1 \ 0 \ 1 = 0$$

so abs $(f \ x \perp z) = 0$, and $f \ x \perp z = \perp$. Thus once abstract functions have been tabulated by iteration, they can be applied to various trial arguments to discover whether the corresponding concrete function is strict.

One strength of abstract interpretation is that it captures dependencies between function arguments. For example, we may find that

$$f\# \ 1 \ 0 \ 1 = 1$$
$$f\# \ 1 \ 1 \ 0 = 1$$

but

$$f\# \ 1 \ 0 \ 0 = 0$$

In this case f is not strict in either of its second or third arguments, but it is strict in them "jointly" — intuitively, it is certain to evaluate one of them, but we don't know which. Mycroft's method makes use of such dependency information; indeed, the conditional function if has the behaviour illustrated. Its abstract function is

$$\text{if\# a b c} = a \wedge (b \vee c)$$

where $\wedge$ and $\vee$ are the normal boolean operators on the domain $\{0,1\}$.

2.4. Problems with Abstract Interpretation

In a sense, this strength is also a weakness. If we are not really interested in dependency information then it is wasteful to calculate it. Let us estimate the cost of an abstract interpretation. To find an abstract function with n arguments, it is necessary to calculate a fixed point in the domain $A^n \text{->} A$. If the number of elements of A is a, then the height of this domain is roughly a^n. In principle, the fixed point iteration may therefore require a^n steps, and so abstract interpretation may take exponential time in the size of the program. The larger and more sophisticated the abstract domain, the more severe this problem becomes. (It is aggravated when functions have a large number of parameters. Note that compile-time transformations such as lambda-lifting [Johnsson85], super-combinator abstraction [Hughes82] and serial combinator abstraction [Hudak85] tend to generate such functions). Even if the worst case rarely arises, we believe that abstract interpretation is likely to be expensive in practice.

Another objection is that abstract interpretation is usually a two-stage process. As in the example of strictness analysis, the abstract functions themselves do not explicitly provide the desired information. It is necessary to apply them to sample arguments in order to extract information about strictness. Thus we first compute the abstract functions, at considerable expense, and then throw away some of the information they contain. Computing strictness (or other) information directly would in many ways be more natural. This is the motivation for studying backward analysis.

3. Backward Analysis of First-Order Languages

3.1 Contexts

Backward analysis calculates information about the context of an expression that can be used to compile it more efficiently. Thus the flow of information is inwards, from enclosing expressions to enclosed sub-expressions, rather than outwards as is the case in an abstract interpretation. The kind of information we are interested in is statements such as

    ¤   this expression is certain to be evaluated
    ¤   this expression will certainly not be needed
    ¤   this expression must be stored on the heap
    ¤   if this expression is ever evaluated then the program will
        certainly crash

We will use the word *context* as a technical term for the information that a backward analysis calculates. In this section we state some general properties that all contexts should satisfy.

We will restrict our attention to domains of contexts, so that we can use least fixed points to analyse recursive programs. We also assume that the use made of calculated contexts is monotonic: so if α gives the correct result (is *safe*), so will any context $\beta \geq \alpha$. We say that β *safely approximates* α in this case. The normal intuitive interpretation of the domain ordering is therefore reversed in a context domain: if $\alpha \leq \beta$ then α gives <u>more</u> specific information than β. As a result the <u>least</u> fixed point of any context function is the <u>most</u> informative one.

Often it is impossible for a compiler to find the best context exactly. For example, we may know that either α or β is a safe context for a particular expression, but not know which one it is. In such a case we can use the least upper bound, $\alpha \cup \beta$, provided it exists since it safely approximates both. We can think of $\cup$ as expressing uncertainty, and read it as "or". This motivates the following definition:

Definition A *proto-context domain* is a complete lattice.

Any proto-context domain has a maximal element, which we interpret as "no information". It is always safe. We interpret the minimal element $\perp$ as "contradictory requirements": it could arise, for example, if a value is used in a context requiring an integer, and also in a context requiring a boolean. If evaluation ever reaches an expression standing in the context $\perp$, then the program will inevitably crash. Notice that, since $\alpha \cup \perp = \alpha$, and we use $\cup$ to express uncertainty, cases that lead inevitably to a crash are ignored by a backward analyser. As a result, although the behaviour of correct programs is preserved, a faulty program may crash with a different error as a result of backward analysis.

Whatever domain of contexts we use, we need an element which represents "no context" or "unused" — for example, if a variable x does not occur in the expression E, then its context in that expression is this element. This is different from both "conflicting requirements" and "no information" (that something is unused is quite definite information). We call the element ABSENT, and require that every context domain have one.

Definition A *context domain* is a domain of the form $\{ABSENT\}_\perp \times P$, where P is a proto-context domain.

We will write ABSENT for $\langle ABSENT, \perp \rangle$ and $\alpha \in P$ for $\langle \perp, \alpha \rangle$, so we consider the elements of a context domain to be $\perp$, ABSENT, α and ABSENT$\cup \alpha$, where $\alpha \in P$. Elements such as ABSENT$\cup \alpha$ denote uncertainty whether or not an expression is used, but knowledge that if it <u>is</u> used, it will be in context α. We refer to elements of P as the *strict* contexts (by analogy with strictness analysis, because the expression is certainly used). The projection function into P takes the *strict part* of a context; we name it STRICT.

3.2. Context Functions

We expect functions between context domains to respect the intuitions above. Every context function should preserve uncertainty, contradiction, and absence.

Definition A context function f : D -> E is a function satisfying
$$f(\alpha \cup \beta) = f\alpha \cup f\beta$$
$$f\perp = \perp$$
$$f\,ABSENT = ABSENT$$

It follows that $f(ABSENT \cup \alpha) = ABSENT \cup f\alpha$.

It is convenient to define an operator to help define context functions by guaranteeing the preservation of contradiction and absence. The notation is $\alpha \text{->} \beta$, reminiscent of a conditional expression, which returns β, modified to preserve any contradiction or absence in α.

Definition $\alpha \text{->} \beta$ is defined as follows:

$\perp \text{->} \beta = \perp$	
$ABSENT \text{->} \beta = ABSENT$	
$\alpha \text{->} \beta = ABSENT \cup \beta$	if ABSENT$<\alpha$
$\alpha \text{->} \beta = \beta$	otherwise

If f preserves uncertainty, then $\lambda \alpha.\alpha \text{->} f\alpha$ is a context function. If f is a context function, then
$$f(\alpha \text{->} \beta) = \alpha \text{->} f\beta$$
$$f\alpha = \alpha \text{->} f(STRICT\ \alpha)$$

3.3. Propagating Contexts in a First-Order Functional Language

Given an expression E and its context, α, we wish to propagate information inwards to find a resulting context for each subexpression. We define a function **C** such that, if x is a free variable of E, then $Cx [E] \alpha$ is the context propagated from E to x. The language we analyse is first-order recursion equations with conditional expressions.

Two clauses of the definition of **C** are clear already:
$$Cx [x] \alpha = \alpha$$
$$Cx [E] \alpha = \text{ABSENT} \qquad \text{if x does not occur free in E}$$

Now consider the context propagated to a function argument. If E is (f E1 ... En) then each of the Ei is in a context depending on α and on the function f. We capture this dependence by associating n context functions with f, denoted by f#1...f#n, such that the context of each Ei is f#i α.

Context functions play the rôle that abstract functions play in an abstract interpretation, but note that in a backwards analysis f#1 maps from the context of the <u>result</u> to the context of the <u>argument</u>. Note also that backward analysis inherently treats function arguments independently, in constrast to abstract interpretation. As a notational convenience we will write f# instead of f#1 when f takes only one argument.

The context propagated from each Ei to x is therefore $Cx [Ei] (f\#i \ \alpha)$, but the context propagated from E to x is a combination of these. We introduce a binary operator & which gives the *net context* when two different contexts are propagated to the same variable, and define
$$Cx [f \ E1 \ ... \ En] \ \alpha = Cx [E1] (f\#1 \ \alpha) \ \& \ ... \ \& \ Cx [En] (f\#n \ \alpha)$$
When a backward analysis is defined, & must be given a definition which reflects the meaning of the particular contexts used. However, we always require that ABSENT be an identity of &, so that if x only occurs in some of the Ei, then nothing is propagated to it from the others. We also require & to preserve uncertainty and contradiction.

Let us now define **C** for conditional expressions. If the expression
if E1 **then** E2 **else** E3
is in the context α, then one of the the expressions E2 or E3 is also in this context, but we cannot know which. We remarked above that $\cup$ can be used to express uncertainty, so we define
$$Cx [\textbf{if} \ E1 \ \textbf{then} \ E2 \ \textbf{else} \ E3] \ \alpha =$$
$$Cx [E1] (\textbf{if\#} \ \alpha) \ \& \ (Cx [E2] \ \alpha \cup Cx [E3] \ \alpha)$$
The context of E1 will vary from analysis to analysis, and must be defined by giving an appropriate interpretation to **if#**. Compare this definition to the abstract function if# used in Mycroft's strictness analysis:
$$\textbf{if\#} \ a \ b \ c = a \wedge (b \vee c)$$
Where abstract interpretation captures the dependency between the two branches in an abstract function, our backward analysis captures it by treating conditionals as a special case.

Using **C** we can derive context functions from the definitions of concrete functions. If f is defined by
$$f \ x1 \ ... \ xn = E$$
then we define
$$f\#i \ \alpha = \alpha \ \text{->} \ Cxi \ [E] \ \alpha$$

The framework constructed so far is quite general. To define a particular backward analysis we choose a context domain, define &, and give the context functions associated with language primitives. We then have a set of recursive equations for the context functions which can be solved by a fixed point iteration, just as in an abstract interpretation (provided the context domain is finite). Once the context functions have been found, the context of any expression can be derived by straightforward calculation.

Presentation of a scheme such as that above naturally raises the question of correctness. This scheme has not been proved correct. The reason is that any program analysis method must be proved correct relative to a semantics for programs which is detailed enough to discuss the properties being analysed. In the case of strictness analysis a standard denotational semantics is sufficient; backward analysis has been proved correct for this case by Wadler and Hughes [Wadler87b] [Hughes87]. Most of the other analyses considered require more detail - either a non-standard denotational semantics such as Bloss and Hudak use [Bloss86] [Hudak87] or an operational semantics. To prove backward analysis correct in general, we would need to establish what class of semantics can be used, and what properties can be so derived. This has not yet been done.

3.4. The Cost of Backward Analysis

It might appear that backward analysis is as expensive as forward analysis, as it also involves the solution of a set of recursive equations by iteration in a finite domain. However, there is an important difference. Every context function has only *one* argument. If C is the domain of contexts, then every context function is in the domain C->C. This domain is of a fixed (small) size, so the iterations are certain to terminate quickly. Consider a user-defined function with n arguments: a forward analysis must perform an iteration in the domain A^n->A, whose size is doubly exponential in n, whereas a backward analysis need only perform n iterations in C->C. It is easy to show that at most O(program size) iterations are required to find all context functions, and since each iteration can be completed in time O(program size) the total time for a backward analysis is proportional to the square of the program size in the worst case. As with forward analysis, we expect the worst case to arise rarely. There are therefore grounds for believing that backward analysis will be considerably more efficient than forward analysis. Wray's backward strictness analyser, used in the Ponder compiler, has indeed proved satisfyingly fast.

However, it should be noted that the distinction between forwards and backwards analysis is not absolutely clear. In fact, backwards analysis can be expressed as an abstract interpretation in which the abstract values of expressions are *environments* - functions from the variables in them to contexts. Bloss and Hudak use a similar idea to define their *path semantics*, which can be used to answer detailed questions about evaluation order [Bloss86]. Moreover, even when forwards and backwards analysis can be used to solve the same problem, they are not necessarily of equal power. There are programs for which forwards strictness analysis produces a better result than backwards strictness analysis, and the converse is also true. There are also problems which yield naturally to one approach but not the other. Thus the relative efficiency of the two techniques is only one factor of many to consider.

3.5. Abstractions of Context Domains

It is often the case that a context domain makes more distinctions than necessary for the desired analysis. In these circumstances we can often use an abstract interpretation of contexts instead. We choose a subdomain of the true context domain that contains enough points to make all the distinctions we need, and define an abstraction function abs which maps each context to the least point in the subdomain that safely approximates it. Every context function f can be promoted to a function on the subdomain by composing abs with it. We can then perform the analysis entirely within the subdomain. We call such a subdomain an abstract context domain.

Definition
- ¤   An *abstract context domain* A is (a domain isomorphic to) a subset of a context domain C closed under lub and glb of finite and infinite sets, including the top element but not necessarily $\perp$. A has a bottom element of course, but this need not necessarily be that of C.
- ¤   The *abstraction map* abs : C -> A maps each context to the most informative abstract context that safely approximates it.
      $$\text{abs } \gamma = \bigcap \{\alpha \in A \mid \alpha \geq \gamma\}$$
      We will write ABSENT for abs ABSENT.
- ¤   The *abstraction* of any function f : D -> C is abs∘f : D -> A. Any function from C to C can be promoted to a function from A to A in this way.
- ¤   An *abstract context function* is the abstraction of a context function.

Notice that the abstract interpretation above is characterised completely by the chosen subset. An important application is when the most natural context domain for an analysis is infinite: we can choose any finite subset satisfying the condition to derive a practical analysis technique. Of course, in general using an abstract context domain loses precision.

Abstract context domains do not necessarily satisfy all the properties of context domains. ABSENT may not be distinguished from other elements. Abstract context functions may not preserve contradiction, although they do preserve uncertainty and also absence, in the sense that any element safely approximating ABSENT is mapped to another element safely approximating ABSENT. In our experience, abstract context domains usually suffice. We will be sloppy and use "context domain" from time to time when we mean abstract context domain; we will say *concrete context domain* to emphasize the distinction.

4. Examples of Backward Analysis

4.1. Strictness Analysis

Johnsson discovered a simple backward strictness analysis using an abstract context domain with just two elements — S (for strict) and L (for lazy) [Johnsson81]. An expression in the context S is certain to be evaluated; nothing is known about an expression in the context L. The ordering on this domain is therefore

$$\begin{array}{c} L \\ | \\ S \end{array}$$

In this case the abstraction identifies ABSENT with L and $\bot$ with S. As a result $\alpha\text{->}f\ \alpha$ is always equal to f α, so -> need not appear explicitly. Because of the meaning of the domain elements, & is the greatest lower bound operator.

Strict primitive functions (such as +, -, *, **if#** etc.) have $\lambda x.x$ as their associated context functions. Non-strict primitives have $\lambda x.L$. These are the only possible context functions, as they are the only functions that preserve absence.

Analysis is particularly simple using this domain, because every context function is characterised completely by one value — its result when applied to S. Taking an example due to Mycroft,

$$f\ x\ y = \textbf{if}\ x{=}0\ \textbf{then}\ y\ \textbf{else}\ f\ (x{-}1)\ y$$

we find

$$f\#1\ S = S\ \&\ (L \cup f\#1\ S)$$
$$f\#2\ S = L\ \&\ (S \cup f\#2\ S)$$

We can solve these equations by a fixed point iteration. The first approximation to each is S, the bottom of the domain. The second approximation is

$$f\#1\ S = S\ \&\ (L \cup S) = S$$
$$f\#2\ S = L\ \&\ (S \cup S) = S$$

which is the same as the first, so the iteration terminates. The function is strict in both arguments.

The example is interesting because Mycroft proposed it as a difficult case. Of course, abstract interpretation finds the correct result here, but a naive analysis that assumes everything is lazy until shown to be strict fails to discover that f is strict in y. Such an analysis corresponds to doing our fixed point iteration, but starting from the top of the domain (L) rather than the bottom. The result is the greatest fixed point, which is safe, of course, in that it is above the least fixed point, but in general is less precise.

This very simple domain does not even distinguish ABSENT from lazy contexts. Yet knowing that something is in the context ABSENT is useful in itself: a compiler need not generate code for such an expression, for example, since it would certainly never be executed. We can discover absence as well as strictness using the concrete context domain that {S,L} is an abstraction of:

```
        L
       / \
      A   S
       \ /
        ⊥
```

where A denotes ABSENT. A new definition (shown below) must be given for &, since the greatest lower bound operator does not have ABSENT as an identity.

```
&  |  ⊥   A   S   L
⊥  |  ⊥   ⊥   ⊥   ⊥
A  |  ⊥   A   S   L
S  |  ⊥   S   S   S
L  |  ⊥   L   S   L
```

Primitive context functions such as +#1, +#2, and if# are λx.x in this domain also. Lazy functions such as cons have λx.x->A∪x as their associated strictness functions, so that for example cons#1 A = A, but cons#1 S = L. Also, the arrow operator can no longer be ignored.

Now consider a function such as
$$f \ x \ y = \textbf{if } x{=}0 \textbf{ then } x \textbf{ else } f \ (x{-}1) \ y$$
Its second context function is
$$f\#2 \ \alpha = \alpha\text{->}A \ \& \ (A \cup f\#2 \ \alpha)$$
which we can calculate by the fixed point iteration shown in the table below.

```
f#2  |   1st   2nd   3rd
⊥    |   ⊥     ⊥     ⊥
A    |   ⊥     A     A
S    |   ⊥     A     A
L    |   ⊥     A     A
```

As we expect, the analysis discovers that y will never be used. (Note that contradiction is preserved, so f#2 ⊥ is ⊥, not A).

Wray has implemented a strictness analysis algorithm based on this context domain [Wray85,Wray86]. His analyser is particularly interesting because he has extended it analyse second-order functions in addition to first-order ones. His work forms the basis for our own extension of backward analysis to higher-order functions.

In the last example we discovered that a parameter was certain not to be needed. Choosing a different abstract context domain {A,L} gives an analysis which discovers only expressions that are certainly not needed. We may refer to this as needed/unneeded analysis, and rename A as U and L as N. The domain then looks like

```
      N
      |
      U
```

In a sense this analysis is dual to known/unknown analysis and has applications to partial evaluation. The MIX partial evaluator [Jones87] omits "known" parameters from residual functions. It could also omit unneeded parameters, thus producing a more efficient residual program. While it is presumably rare for a programmer to write functions with unneeded parameters, partial evaluation may well remove uses of an argument thus making unneeded parameters more common in residual programs.

4.2. Optimising Call-by-Need to Call-by-Name

As another example, we can construct an analysis to estimate the number of times that an expression would be evaluated by a call-by-name (normal order) interpreter. This is closely related to strictness analysis: an expression known to be evaluated one or more times is in a strict context.

Strictness analysis is used to optimise call-by-need to call-by-value, which saves the cost of constructing a closure, overwriting it later when its value is known, and testing at each use to see whether the closure has yet been evaluated. The analysis in this section can be used to optimise call-by-need to call-by-name: an argument which is known to be evaluated only zero or once can be passed as a cheaper sort of closure which is not overwritten after its value is known. This saves the cost of the overwrite, and also the cost of testing to see whether or not the overwrite has been performed. While this is a less significant improvement, it is still worthwhile. (Fairbairn and Wray estimate that "sharing analysis", as they call it, is worth 10% in their new abstract machine [Fairbairn87]).

We will only distinguish evaluation zero, one, and many times; we therefore define a context to be a subset of $\{0,1,M\}$, with the meaning that an expression in a context C may be evaluated n times for any n in C. The context domain is ordered by set inclusion, so $\varnothing$ is the least element and $\cup$ is set union. The following equivalences hold between certain "strictness analysis" contexts and these:

$$\bot = \varnothing \qquad\qquad S = \{1,M\}$$
$$A = \{0\} \qquad\qquad L = \{0,1,M\}$$

Intuitively, & represents evaluation in both operand contexts, so we define
$$\alpha \,\&\, \beta = \{a+b \mid a \in \alpha, b \in \beta\}$$
(where + is the abstract version of natural number plus on the set $\{0,1,M\}$). Once again, strict operators have $\lambda x.x$ as their associated context function. Lazy operators such as cons have
$$\lambda\alpha. \{b \mid \exists a \in \alpha.\ b \le a\}$$
so, for example, cons#1 $\{M\} = \{0,1,M\}$ and cons#1 $\{1\} = \{0,1\}$.

Let us analyse Mycroft's example again:
$$f\ x\ y = \textbf{if}\ x{=}0\ \textbf{then}\ y\ \textbf{else}\ f\ (x{-}1)\ y$$
The context functions are
$$f\#1\ \alpha = \alpha \to \alpha \,\&\, (\{0\} \cup f\#1\ \alpha)$$
$$f\#2\ \alpha = \alpha \to \{0\} \,\&\, (\alpha \cup f\#2\ \alpha)$$
Now suppose a call of f x y is evaluated once; that is, stands in the context $\{1\}$. We can calculate f#1 $\{1\}$ and f#2 $\{1\}$ by iteration as usual.

	1st	2nd	3rd	4th
f#1 $\{1\}$	$\varnothing$	$\{1\}$	$\{1,M\}$	$\{1,M\}$
f#2 $\{1\}$	$\varnothing$	$\{1\}$	$\{1\}$	$\{1\}$

The function is strict in both arguments, but will only evaluate its second argument once.

An advantage of this method is that it also discovers simple strictness. A separate strictness analysis phase is therefore unnecessary.

The method in this section was discovered in collaboration with Stuart Wray.

4.3. Determining the Life-time of Data

Consider the function
$$f\ x = g\ (h\ x)$$
Often in a case such as this, the result of h is an intermediate value which is used solely by g and then discarded. Yet if the result returned by h is a data-structure, then (in most functional language implementations) it is allocated on the heap and must be de-allocated by the garbage collector, which is expensive. If a compiler could detect that the result is short-lived, it could compile code to create it in a short-term store, and discard all the contents of the short-term store when the function f returns. In this section we describe an analysis to detect this.

We ignore two potential problems. Firstly, in a lazy language h's result could be used only by g, but might have a long life-time because a closure referring to it is not evaluated until long after f returns. In this case the use of short-term storage would be inappropriate. We assume either that strictness analysis has been performed, or that the analysis is used in a compiler for a strict language. Secondly, implementation of multiple short-term stores of different sizes and life-times may present formidable problems. We will not address these, except to remark that a store of known size can simply be allocated on the run-time stack.

We will again use a two point abstract context domain:

$$H$$
$$|$$
$$S$$

where H means that the corresponding expression must be stored on the heap, and S means that it can be stored in a short-term store. S, ABSENT and $\perp$ are identified; the -> operator can therefore be ignored, and STRICT is the identity function. In this domain the & operator is least upper bound (in contrast to the previous examples), since an object required to be on the heap by one of its occurrences must certainly be placed there.

Every function which uses and discards its argument has $\lambda x.S$ as its associated context function, including in particular +#i, -#i, =#i, and **if#**. Considering Mycroft's example once more,

$$f \; x \; y = \textbf{if} \; x=0 \; \textbf{then} \; y \; \textbf{else} \; f(x-1)y$$

we find that the context functions are

$$f\#1 \; \alpha = S \; \& \; (S \cup S)$$
$$f\#2 \; \alpha = S \; \& \; (\alpha \cup f\#2 \; \alpha)$$

and, by fixed point iteration, f#1 H = S and f#2 H = H. Therefore f's first argument can be created in short-term store, but the second must be placed on the heap.

5. Backwards Analysis of Data-Structures

Very simple context domains such as those introduced above can be used to analyse programs that manipulate data-structures, provided context functions for the primitive operations are given. However, they do not yield good results. Ideally, an analyser should distinguish between the context of a data-structure as a whole, and the context of each component within it. For example, the length function needs its (list) argument, but does not need any of its components. Small context domains are not capable of such fine distinctions.

Fortunately it is possible to develop richer context domains that provide very good information about data-structures. Indeed, this has often been the motivation for using backward analysis. In this section we will describe a way of constructing richer domains from the simple ones we have seen so far.

Since there are infinitely many different data-types, the domain of all data-structures with components in a given domain is infinite. However, it is possible to define a useful finite context domain for each data-type. We use the type-system of the object language to decide on a particular finite domain for each context. The type-system we use is that of the simple typed λ-calculus; we will discuss an extension to Hindley-Milner polymorphism. This idea is the same one that Burn, Hankin and Abramsky used to extend abstract interpretation to higher-order functions.

5.1. Contexts for Data-Structures

Call the context domain taken as a starting point C_A, the domain of atomic contexts, where A is the type of atomic values. We assume that C_A is a concrete context domain, so

$$C_A = \{ABSENT\}_\perp \times P_A$$

and P_A is the proto-context domain of strict contexts. We will show how to construct a suitable domain of strict contexts P_T for any type T; C_T is then defined by

$$C_T = \{ABSENT\}_\perp \times P_T$$

A context for a sum type T1+T2 must contain a context for use if the value is in the first summand, and a context for use if the value is in the second. We therefore define

$$P_{T1+T2} = P_{T1} \times P_{T2}$$

As usual, we write α for $<\alpha,\perp>$ and β for $<\perp,\beta>$, so that elements of this domain will be written $\alpha \cup \beta$.

A context for a product type T1×T2 must also contain a context for each component, and also a context referring to the value as a whole. (For example, a pair may be short-lived even though both its componenets are long-lived). However, if any of these contexts is contradictory then the whole context must be contradictory. We therefore use the smash product and define

$$P_{T1 \times T2} = P_A \otimes C_{T1} \otimes C_{T2}$$

It is natural to construct a context for a data-structure from an atomic context (for the whole structure) and component contexts. Let us define a (polymorphic) operator

$$- \Delta - : C_A \to D \to (\{ABSENT\}_\perp \times (P_A \otimes D))$$

to do so, as follows

$$<\alpha,\beta> \Delta \ \delta = <\alpha,<\beta,\delta>>$$

The inner pair on the right hand side is, of course, a strict one. As a result

$$\perp \Delta \ \beta = \perp$$
$$\alpha \ \Delta \perp = \perp \qquad \qquad \text{if } \alpha \text{ is a strict context}$$
$$ABSENT \ \Delta \ \beta = ABSENT$$
$$(ABSENT \cup \alpha) \ \Delta \ \beta = ABSENT \cup (\alpha \ \Delta \ \beta)$$

We will usually write elements of such a domain in the form $\alpha \ \Delta \ \beta$.

Now let us define contexts for lists in the same style.

$$P_{List(T)} = P_A \otimes (\{NIL\}_\perp \times (C_T \otimes C_{List(T)}))$$

Note that the same context applies to the structure as a whole whether the value is a NIL or a CONS. We write elements of the domain $C_T \otimes C_{List(T)}$ in the form CONS $\alpha \ \beta$, and use our usual convention to embed NIL and CONS contexts in the product domain.

The intuitive meaning of a context such as $\alpha \ \Delta$ CONS $\beta \ \gamma$ is that the associated expression must be a cons, that the cons-cell itself is in the context α, and that the components are in the contexts β and γ. The intuitive meaning of $\alpha \ \Delta$ NIL is that the expression must evaluate to nil, and the meaning of $\alpha \ \Delta$ NIL $\cup$ CONS $\beta \ \gamma$ is that it may evaluate to nil or a cons-cell, but if it is a cons-cell then the contexts β and γ propagate to the components.

This domain has infinite elements. Far from being pathological, they are among the most interesting and useful. For example, the context

$$\alpha \bullet \beta = \beta \ \Delta \ NIL \cup CONS \ \alpha \ \alpha \bullet \beta$$

requires a list of any length, each of whose elements is in the context α, with each cons-cell in the context β. There is no requirement for the list itself to be infinite, because a NIL is allowed at any stage. Thus infinite contexts can be useful even if all data-structures are finite.

& is extended pointwise to the larger domain; of course, different constructors are contradictory:

$$NIL \ \& \ CONS \ \alpha \ \beta = \perp$$

We extend the object language with a **case** statement, which can be used to define head, tail and null. The only primitive function operating on data-structures is therefore cons. Consider an expression cons b c in the context $\alpha \ \Delta$ CONS $\beta \ \gamma$. The context of b is β and the context of c is γ. Using **C** we find that the context of b is cons#1 ($\alpha \ \Delta$ CONS $\beta \ \gamma$), and the context of c is cons#2 ($\alpha \ \Delta$ CONS $\beta \ \gamma$), so we must have

$$cons\#1 \ (\alpha \ \Delta \ CONS \ \beta \ \gamma) = \beta$$
$$cons\#2 \ (\alpha \ \Delta \ CONS \ \beta \ \gamma) = \gamma$$

Similarly we see that cons#i ($\alpha \ \Delta$ NIL) = $\perp$. Together with the requirement that cons#1 and cons#2 preserve uncertainty, absence, and contradiction, these conditions are a sufficient definition.

Now consider the **case** expression

case E1 **in** nil => E2; cons y z => E3

If α propagates to this expression, it also propagates to one of E2 and E3, but we don't know which. As a result contexts **Cy** [E3] α and **Cz** [E3] α propagate to y and z, and then to the components of E1 if it is a cons. A context

$$\beta \ \Delta \ (NIL \cup CONS \ (Cy \ [E3] \ \alpha) \ (Cz \ [E3] \ \alpha))$$

for some β therefore propagates to E1 from the branches of the **case** (if one of the cases is omitted, so is the corresponding context). β may depend only on α, so we write it as **case#** α and define

$$Cx \, [\textbf{case} \, E1 \, \textbf{in} \, nil => E2; \, cons \, y \, z => E3] \, \alpha =$$
$$\alpha \rightarrow Cx \, [E1] \, ((\textbf{case\#} \, \alpha') \, \Delta$$
$$(NIL \cup CONS \, (Cy \, [E3] \, \alpha') \, (Cz \, [E3] \, \alpha')))$$
$$\& \, (Cx \, [E2] \, \alpha' \cup Cx \, [E3] \, \alpha')$$
$$\text{where } \alpha' = STRICT \, \alpha$$

case# must be defined along with the other primitive context functions for any particular analysis.

As an example, head and null are defined by
$$head \, xs = \textbf{case} \, xs \, \textbf{in} \, cons \, x \, xs' => x$$
$$null \, xs = \textbf{case} \, xs \, \textbf{in} \, nil => true; \, cons \, x \, xs' => false$$
and so their context functions are
$$head\# \, \alpha = \alpha \rightarrow (\textbf{case\#} \, \alpha') \, \Delta \, (CONS \, (STRICT \, \alpha) \, ABSENT)$$
$$null\# \, \alpha = \alpha \rightarrow (\textbf{case\#} \, \alpha') \, \Delta \, (NIL \cup CONS \, ABSENT \, ABSENT)$$
Because of the use of STRICT, if β is strict
$$head\# \, (ABSENT \cup \beta) = ABSENT \cup$$
$$(\textbf{case\#} \, \beta \, \Delta \, (CONS \, \beta \, ABSENT))$$
The uncertainty over whether or not the value is used is expressed at the top-level of this equation; it is unnecessary to express it again for each component. Intuitively, this equation states that the argument of head may not be needed, but if it is then its first component certainly will be.

5.2. A Finite Abstract Context Domain for Lists

The context domain introduced in the previous section is very expressive — it can, for example, represent a different context for every element of an infinite list. However, it is unsuited to practical use because it is infinite. In this section we choose a finite subdomain which is suitable for use in practice.

We construct a finite subdomain for lists by limiting ourselves to contexts which do not distinguish between the different elements of a list. We define
$$\alpha \bullet \beta = NIL \cup CONS \, \alpha \, (\beta \, \Delta \, \alpha \bullet \beta)$$
Note that
$$\bot \bullet \beta = NIL = \alpha \bullet \bot$$
$$\alpha \bullet ABSENT = NIL \cup CONS \, \alpha \, ABSENT$$
List contexts which do not distinguish between list elements take the general form
$$\gamma \, \Delta \, \alpha \bullet \beta.$$

We choose a (concrete) domain isomorphic to just these contexts.
$$C_{List(T)} = \{ABSENT\}_\bot \times (P_A \otimes C_T \otimes C_A)$$

The abstractions of the context functions CONS and cons#i to these domains are easily calculated:
$$CONS \, \alpha \, (\beta \, \Delta \, \gamma \bullet \delta) = (\alpha \cup \gamma) \bullet (\beta \cup \delta)$$
$$cons\#1 \, (\alpha \, \Delta \, \beta \bullet \gamma) = \beta$$
$$cons\#2 \, (\alpha \, \Delta \, \beta \bullet \gamma) = \gamma \, \Delta \, \beta \bullet \gamma$$

5.3. Starting from an Abstract Context Domain

The construction described in the last two sections is appropriate if the domain of atomic contexts is concrete. More often C_A will be abstract, in which case we wish the constructed domains to be similarly abstract. Suppose C_A is an abstraction of $\{ABSENT\}_\bot \times P_A$, and abs_A is the abstraction map. Then we can define an abstraction map (and hence an abstract context domain) for each type T in the style
$$abs_{T1+T2} \, <\alpha,\beta> = <abs_{T1}\alpha, \, abs_{T2}\beta>$$
$$abs_{T1 \times T2} \, (\alpha \, \Delta \, <\beta,\gamma>) = abs_A\alpha \, \Delta \, <abs_{T1}\beta, \, abs_{T2}\gamma>$$
$$abs_{List(T)} \, (\alpha \, \Delta \, \beta \bullet \gamma) = abs_A \, \alpha \, \Delta \, (abs_T \, \beta \bullet abs_A \, \gamma)$$
In fact, we do not need to know what concrete context domain C_A is an abstraction of, if we just wish to construct further abstract context domains from it; it is sufficient to know which element is abs_A ABSENT and whether or not $abs_A \bot$ is $\bot$. If $abs_A \bot$ is $\bot$ then, since $\alpha \bullet \bot$ is NIL, identified with $\bot$
$$abs_{List(T)} \, ABSENT = ABSENT$$

that is, ABSENT is present in the list context domain. If $\text{abs}_A \perp$ is not $\perp$ or ABSENT then
$$\text{abs}_A \perp \Delta\ \beta\bullet\gamma$$
is a one-to-one function of $\beta\bullet\gamma$, and satisfies
$$\text{abs}_A\ \alpha\ \Delta\ \beta\bullet\gamma = (\text{abs}_A\ \alpha) \cup (\text{abs}_A \perp) \Delta\ \beta\bullet\gamma$$
so in this (common) case we can regard $\beta\bullet\gamma$ as an element of $C_{\text{List}(T)}$ and CONS as a function of type $C_T\text{->}C_{\text{List}(T)}\text{->}C_{\text{List}(T)}$. This simplifies our notation since Δ need not appear.

5.4. Example: Strictness Analysis of Lazy Lists

We will apply the construction in the previous section to Johnsson's two point domain for strictness analysis. The result is the eight point domain for strictness analysis of lazy lists that appears in [Wadler87b]. Its elements are S•S, L•S, S•L and L•L, together with L∪ each of these. (Since S is the bottom element of Johnsson's domain, S∪ may be dropped). For brevity, we will write SS for S•S etc. Note that each of these is a *strict* context, requiring a list whose components may or may not be evaluated. The interpretation of these contexts is as follows:

SS   evaluates every element of the corresponding list, which could be constructed with a strict version of cons. This is sometimes called hyper-strictness.

LS   evaluates the spine of the corresponding list, but may or may not evaluate any particular element. The list could be constructed with a version of cons strict in its second argument, so this is often called tail-strictness.

SL   evaluates the corresponding list lazily: however, the head of every evaluated list cell is also certain to be evaluated. The list could be constructed with a version of cons strict in its first argument, so this is often called head-strictness. This is the context in which the input and output of a functional program usually appears.

LL   might only evaluate the corresponding list to one level. A completely lazy cons must be used to construct the list. This is the least informative list context, and gives no more information than Johnsson's original context S.

We can display the relationship between these four contexts as follows:

```
        LL
       /  \
     SL    LS
       \  /
        SS
```

The whole domain contains another copy of this diamond, and looks like a cube balanced on one corner.

Calculation shows that the & operator behaves as follows:

&	SS	LS	SL	LL
SS	SS	SS	SS	SS
LS	SS	LS	LS	LS
SL	SS	LS	SL	LL
LL	SS	LS	LL	LL

The most interesting point in this table is that LS&SL is LS, not SS. If a list is used once in a head-strict context, and once in a tail-strict context, this does not imply that the net context is completely strict. It could be that the head-strict context in fact never uses more than one element of the list.

For reference, we also tabulate the functions CONS, cons#1, and cons#2.

CONS	SS	LS	SL	LL	L∪SS	L∪LS	L∪SL	L∪LL
S	SS	LS	SL	LL	SL	LL	SL	LL
L	LS	LS	LL	LL	LL	LL	LL	LL

	SS	LS	SL	LL
cons#1	S	L	S	L
cons#2	SS	LS	(L∪SL)	(L∪LL)

We have to define **case#**: it is just $\lambda\alpha.\alpha$->SS (because SS is the bottom element of the domain).

Now let us analyse the strictness of some list-processing functions. We take the functions append and reverse as examples.

app xs ys = **case** xs **in** nil => ys; cons x xs' => cons x (app xs' ys)

rev xs = **case** xs **in** nil => nil; cons x xs' => app (rev xs') (cons x nil)

The context functions associated with them are

app#1 α = α -> NIL $\cup$ CONS (cons#1 α') (app#1 (cons#2 α'))

app#2 α = α -> α' $\cup$ app#2 (cons#2 α')

rev# α = α -> NIL $\cup$ CONS (cons#1 (app#2 α')) (rev# (app#1 α'))

where α' is again used as a shorthand for STRICT α. Rather than perform the complete fixed point iteration to tabulate the three context functions, we will look at a few examples.

First consider a call of append in the completely strict context SS. We can find the context of the first argument of append by calculating app#1 SS. But

app#1 SS = SS -> SS $\cup$ CONS (cons#1 SS) (app#1 (cons#2 SS))

= CONS S (app#1 SS)

and the least solution of this equation can be found by iteration: the first approximation is SS naturally, and the second is CONS S SS which is equal to SS. So in this case the iteration terminates after one step, and we know the first argument of append is also in the completely strict context SS. To find the context of the second argument we calculate app#2 SS:

app#2 SS = SS -> SS $\cup$ app#2 (cons#2 SS)

= app#2 SS

and the least solution of this equation is also SS, showing that every component of the second argument will also be evaluated.

Now consider a call of append in the head-strict context SL. In the same way, we find

app#1 SL = SL -> SS $\cup$ CONS (cons#1 SL) (app#1 (cons#2 SL))

= CONS S (app#1 (L$\cup$SL))

= CONS S (L $\cup$ app#1 SL)

Iterating to find the solution, the first approximation is SS, the second is CONS S (L $\cup$ SS) = SL, and the third is CONS S (L $\cup$ SL) = SL. The iteration is complete, and we conclude that the first argument of append is in a head-strict context. Going on to the second argument,

app#2 SL = SL -> SL $\cup$ app#2 (cons#2 SL)

= SL $\cup$ app#2 (L $\cup$ SL)

= SL $\cup$ L $\cup$ app#2 SL

Iterating in the same way, the approximations are SS, SL $\cup$ L $\cup$ SS which equals L$\cup$SL, and SL $\cup$ L $\cup$ SL which equals L$\cup$SL. This is therefore the result: the second argument of append may or may not be evaluated, but if it is it will be in a head-strict context. It is interesting that it appears to be impossible to detect head-strictness by abstract interpretation [Wadler85].

Finally, consider a call of reverse in the least informative strict context, LL. We do not know whether any components of the result will be required; we know only that the result will be evaluated to one level. We can even get some useful information out of this.

rev# LL = LL -> SS $\cup$ CONS (cons#1 (app#2 LL)) (rev# (app#1 LL))

= CONS (cons#1 (app#2 LL)) (rev# (app#1 LL))

We will use without proof the results that

app#1 LL = LL

app#2 LL = L $\cup$ LL

which allow us to simplify this equation to

rev# LL = CONS L (rev# LL)

We can now use iteration, the successive approximations being SS, CONS L SS which equals LS, and CONS L LS which equals LS. We have reached the fixed point, which reveals that, even in this weak context, reverse evaluates the spine of its argument.

5.5. Life-time Analysis of Lists

In this section we apply the list context construction to the {S,H} domain for life-time analysis. Some of the resulting contexts are meaningless, because of the constraint that no pointer may point from the heap to the short-term store. The components of every data-structure which resides on the heap must also be on the heap. We cannot use contexts such as H∪SS (allowing part of a list to be in short-term store while requiring the top-level node to be on the heap). We therefore use a further abstraction of the context domain in which all contexts of the form H∪α are identified with H, as are SH and HH. The result is a three point domain, shown below.

$$H$$
$$|$$
$$HS$$
$$|$$
$$SS$$

The interpretation of these contexts is as follows:

H	a list in this context must be stored on the heap
HS	the spine of a list in this context may be stored in the short-term store, but the elements must be stored on the heap
SS	the spine and elements of a list in this context can be kept in short-term storage

This is the domain $C_{List(A)}$; repeating the construction would give
$$C_{List(List(A))} = \{SSS, HSS, HS, H\}$$
$$C_{List(List(List(A)))} = \{SSSS, HSSS, HSS, HS, H\}$$
and so on.

The definitions of CONS, cons#1 and cons#2 are easily derived:

CONS	SS	HS	H			SS	HS	H
S	SS	HS	H	cons#1		S	H	H
H	HS	HS	H	cons#2		SS	HS	H

The **case#** function is $\lambda\alpha.SS$.

As an example, here is the definition of append again:
$$app\ xs\ ys = \textbf{case}\ xs\ \textbf{in}\ nil => ys;\ cons\ x\ xs' => cons\ x\ (app\ xs'\ ys)$$
and here are the associated context functions:
$$app\#1\ \alpha = CONS\ (cons\#1\ \alpha)\ (app\#1\ (cons\#2\ \alpha))$$
$$app\#2\ \alpha = \alpha \cup app\#2\ (cons\#2\ \alpha)$$
Let us calculate app#1 H, to discover how much of the first argument of append can be held in short-term storage.
$$app\#1\ H = CONS\ (cons\#1\ H)\ (app\#1\ (cons\#2\ H))$$
$$= CONS\ H\ (app\#1\ H)$$
The successive approximations to this fixed point are SS, HS and HS, which tells us that the spine of the list can be held in short-term storage, but the elements must reside on the heap.

As another example, consider reverse. Need the argument of reverse be stored on the heap? From the definition
$$rev\ xs = \textbf{case}\ xs\ \textbf{in}\ nil => nil;\ cons\ x\ xs' => app\ (rev\ xs')\ (cons\ x\ nil)$$
we obtain the context function
$$rev\#\ \alpha = CONS\ (cons\#1\ (app\#2\ \alpha))\ (rev\#\ (app\#1\ \alpha))$$
Using the facts that app#1 H is HS and app#2 H is H we find
$$rev\#\ H = CONS\ H\ (rev\#\ HS)$$
and similarly
$$rev\#\ HS = CONS\ H\ (rev\#\ HS) = rev\#\ H$$
Now a fixed point iteration gives the successive approximations SS, HS and HS, so the spine of the argument of reverse is a candidate for the short-term store.

5.6. Needed/Unneeded Analysis of Lists

In this section we apply the same technique to the {U,N} domain for needed/unneeded analysis. As in the last section, some contexts are senseless, because components of unneeded lists cannot be needed. We choose to use the domain

$$NN$$
$$|$$
$$UN$$
$$|$$
$$U$$

with the interpretations

NN	all of a list in this context may be needed
UN	the elements of a list in this context are not needed
U	a list in this context is not needed at all

Here are the definitions of CONS, cons#1 and cons#2:

CONS	U	UN	NN
U	U	UN	NN
N	NN	NN	NN

	U	UN	NN
cons#1	U	U	N
cons#2	U	UN	NN

The abstraction of NIL is UN, and of ABSENT is U; the **case#** function is $\lambda\alpha.\alpha\text{->}UN$; & is least upper bound.

As an example, let us analyse length.

length xs = **case** xs **in** nil => 0; cons x xs' => 1 + length xs'

The associated context function is (after simplification)

length# $\alpha = \alpha$ -> UN $\cup$ CONS U (length# α)

Solving for length# N gives UN — so the length function does not need the elements of its arguments.

Launchbury's projection-based known/unknown analysis [Launchbury87] is capable of discovering, for example, that the spine but not the elements of an argument to a particular call of length is known. However, the argument to such a call would still be classified as residual, because it contains unknown components. Needed/unneeded analysis of lists could be used to classify the whole argument as eliminable, since all the unknown components are unneeded.

6. Backward Analysis of Higher-Order Functions

6.1. Why it's Difficult

Applications of higher-order functions cannot usefully be analysed backwards. To see why, consider an expression such as

apply f x

where apply just calls its first argument with its second as the parameter. Suppose the context of this expression is so restrictive that we know the value of the expression must be zero. What do we then know about x, independent of the value of f? The only property we know x satisfies is that there is some function f mapping it to zero, but this is true of all values and so no information propagates at all. The information propagating to f is only slightly better — we know only that it is a function that can, in some circumstances, return zero. But f could be the constant zero function, or it could be the increment function and x could be -1, or it could be head and x could be cons 0 nil — the possibilities are endless. No useful analysis can be performed without taking into account the dependency between f and x.

In this section we show how backward analysis can be extended to higher-order functions by blending it with abstract interpretation.

6.2. Parameterised Context Functions

Consider another higher-order function, compose.

compose f g x = f (g x)

What is the context of x in compose? If we blindly apply the rules, we find

compose#3 α = g# (f# α)

but of course this is no use, since f and g are parameters rather than globally known function names. However, if we parameterise the context function with respect to f# and g# then we can define

compose#3 f# g# α = g# (f# α)

and the problem is solved. This leads to the idea that the functions associated with higher-order functions should themselves be higher-order, taking a package of context functions for each function argument of the original higher-order function. This is the basis of Wray's second order strictness analyser [Wray85,86]. Functions such as compose#3 are still members of finite domains, and so fixed points can be found iteratively as usual.

If we take strictness analysis as an example, then the only context functions are $\lambda x.x$ and $\lambda x.L$, and we find

compose#3 ($\lambda x.x$) ($\lambda x.x$) S = S
compose#3 ($\lambda x.x$) ($\lambda x.L$) S = L
compose#3 ($\lambda x.L$) ($\lambda x.x$) S = L
compose#3 ($\lambda x.L$) ($\lambda x.L$) S = L

which shows that compose is strict in its third argument only if f and g are both strict.

As an example of combining higher-order functions with lazy lists, let us analyse the strictness of map.

map f xs = **case** xs **in** nil => nil; cons x xs' => cons (f x) (map f xs')

Its second context function is

map#2 f# α = α -> CONS (f# (cons#1 α')) (map#2 f# (cons#2 α'))
where α' = STRICT α

Suppose map is called in the hyper-strict context SS, but f is non-strict. The context of map's second argument is then

map#2 ($\lambda x.L$) SS = CONS L (map#2 ($\lambda x.L$) SS)

The least solution is LS, showing that map is tail-strict in these circumstances. On the other hand, suppose map is called in a head-strict context with a strict function argument; the context of xs is then

map#2 ($\lambda x.x$) SL = CONS (cons#1 SL) (map#2 ($\lambda x.x$) (L $\cup$ SL))
= CONS S (L $\cup$ map#2 ($\lambda x.x$) SL)

The least solution of this recursion is SL, showing that in these circumstances map is head-strict.

What of the contexts of arguments which are functions? We assume that an atom context (member of C_A) is appropriate for a function, and introduce a new primitive **fun#** which maps the context of a call into the context of the function. Now

compose#1 f# g# α = **Cf** [f (g x)] α
= **fun#** α
compose#2 f# g# α = **fun#** (f# α)

fun# must project from any C_T into C_A. For strictness analysis, we take it to be

fun# α = α -> S

Returning to the example,

compose#1 f# g# S = S
compose#2 f# g# S = f# S

so compose is always strict in its first argument, and strict in its second if f is strict. If we apply the same exercise to map, on the other hand, we find

map#1 f# α = α -> L $\cup$ map#1 f# (cons#2 (STRICT α))

Iteration shows that map#1 f# α is L for all α — in other words, map is never strict in its function argument (because it is not used if the list argument is nil).

6.3. First-Class Functions

The technique just developed is fine as far as it goes, but it is really only applicable to "first and a little bit" order languages. It relies on knowing a package of context functions for each function argument, and so restricts function arguments to be globally known functions. The method is out of its depth as soon as we start constructing new functions by partial application, and is completely unable to cope with functions extracted from lists and the like. What is needed is a generalisation that treats functions as first class values.

We can no longer rely on knowing which function is passed as an argument in any call of a higher-order function. We must therefore find another way of discovering the function's package of context functions. We will introduce an abstract interpretation to do this, such that the abstract value of a first-order function is a package of context functions. We introduce a domain of abstract values A_T for each type T. Since we intend to analyse ground types (zeroth order) using backward analysis, we define A_G to be $\mathbf{1}$ for any ground type G ($\mathbf{1}$ is the one point domain $\{\bot\}$). We will give a definition of A_T for all types T, and we expect to find at least that

$$A_{G1\text{-}>G2} \cong C_{G2} \to C_{G1}$$

We will define the abstract value of a list of functions (or indeed any list) to be the least upper bound of the abstract values of the elements, so

$$A_{List(T)} = A_T$$

Context functions will be parameterised with respect to the abstract values of all (non-ground) parameters.

Before we define abstract values for higher types, let us look at an example of the kind of analysis we plan to do. Consider the function

composeall fs x = **case** fs **in** nil => x; cons f fs' => f (composeall fs' x)

Its context functions are parameterised with respect to the abstract value of fs, which is just a first-order context function.

composeall#1 fs# α = α -> CONS (**fun**# α)
                                        (composeall#1 fs# (fs# α'))
composeall#2 fs# α = α -> α' $\cup$ composeall#2 fs# (fs# α')
        where α' = STRICT α

If all the functions in the list are strict, then fs# is $\lambda x.x$, and iteration gives

composeall#1 $(\lambda x.x)$ S = SS
composeall#2 $(\lambda x.x)$ S = S

so as we would expect, composeall uses every function in the list and is strict in its second argument.

What if one or more of the functions in the list is lazy? Then the least upper bound of their context functions is $\lambda x.L$. Of course we find composeall is now non-strict in its second argument, but its strictness in its first argument is surprising.

composeall#1 $(\lambda x.L)$ S = CONS S (composeall#1 $(\lambda x.L)$ L)
                            = CONS S (L $\cup$ composeall#1 $(\lambda x.L)$ S)

and iteration yields SL as the fixed point. Thus composeall is head-strict in its first argument — it may not use all the functions in the list, but it does use any function in a cons cell it evaluates. Why isn't composeall tail-strict? The answer is because, if the first function (say) is non-strict, then none of the others is used.

Now let us return to our abstract interpretation. What should the abstract value of a function be? For abstract interpretation to be possible, we need to find the abstract value of a function call from the abstract values of the function and argument. Thus $A_{T1\text{-}>T2}$ must contain a function in $A_{T1}\text{-}>A_{T2}$ at least. Also, in order that backwards analysis be possible, we need a function from the context of the result to the context of the argument - which may also depend on the abstract value of the argument. We therefore define

$$A_{T1\text{-}>T2} = (A_{T1} \times C_{T2} \to C_{T1}) \times (A_{T1} \to A_{T2})$$

Since A_G is $\mathbf{1}$, and $\mathbf{1} \times D \cong D \cong \mathbf{1} \to D$, we find as a consequence that

$$A_{G\text{-}>G} \cong C_G \to C_G$$

as expected.

Now consider the abstract value of a binary function:

$$A_{T1\text{-}>T2\text{-}>T3} = (A_{T1} \times C_{T2\text{-}>T3} \to C_{T1}) \times$$
$$(A_{T1} \to (A_{T2} \times C_{T3} \to C_{T2}) \times (A_{T2} \to A_{T3}))$$
$$\cong (A_{T1} \times C_{T2\text{-}>T3} \to C_{T1}) \times$$
$$(A_{T1} \times A_{T2} \times C_{T3} \to C_{T2}) \times$$
$$(A_{T1} \to A_{T2} \to A_{T3})$$

Let us examine the three components of this product to see if they are as expected. The third component can be used to find the abstract value of the call from the abstract values of the arguments — so abstract interpretation is possible. The second component can be used to find the context of the second argument from the abstract values of the first and second, and the context of the call — just as expected. We therefore expect to use the first component to find the context of the first argument from the abstract values of both and the context of the call, but where we would expect to see $A_{T2} \times C_{T3}$ we have $C_{T2\text{-}>T3}$ instead. Fortunately we have not yet defined $C_{T1\text{-}>T2}$ so

we can achieve the expected result just by defining
$$C_{T1->T2} = A_{T1} \times C_{T2}$$

This definition is perfectly reasonable: it states that a context for a function consists of the abstract value of the argument it is called with, and the context of the call. We will write such contexts as APPLY u α. Of course we must extend & to this domain, as follows
$$\text{APPLY u } \alpha \text{ \& APPLY v } \beta = \text{APPLY } (u \cup v) (\alpha \text{ \& } \beta)$$
In fact we must add a little more to function contexts — a context referring to the function value itself. For example, a function might need to reside on the heap even though none of its results do. We therefore extend this definition to
$$P_{T1->T2} = P_A \otimes (A_{T1} \times C_{T2})$$
As with data-structures, we will write elements of $C_{T1->T2}$ in the form $\alpha \, \Delta \, <v,\beta>$.

Now we can redefine **C** and introduce another function **A** which finds the abstract value of an expression. Both functions now require an environment ρ giving the abstract values of names in scope. The following clauses are trivial:
$$\textbf{C}x \, [x] \, \rho \, \alpha = \alpha$$
$$\textbf{A} \, [x] \, \rho = \rho \, x$$

$$\textbf{C}x \, [E] \, \rho \, \alpha = \text{ABSENT} \qquad\qquad \text{if x does not occur in E}$$
$$\textbf{A} \, [E] \, \rho = \bot \qquad\qquad\qquad\quad \text{if E has a ground type}$$
The definition of **C** for **if** and **case** expressions is unchanged, except for the introduction of the environment. The definition of **A** is
$$\textbf{A} \, [\text{if E1 then E2 else E3}] \, \rho = \textbf{A} \, [E2] \, \rho \cup \textbf{A} \, [E3] \, \rho$$
$$\textbf{A} \, [\text{case E1 in nil => E2; cons y z => E3}] \, \rho =$$
$$\qquad \textbf{A} \, [E2] \, \rho \cup \textbf{A} \, [E3] \, (\rho[a/y,a/z]) \qquad\qquad \text{where a} = \textbf{A} \, [E1] \, \rho$$

The hard part is the definition of **C** and **A** for functions and applications. Fortunately it is sufficient to consider functions of one argument, since we are now working in a higher-order language. The abstract value of an application is found by applying the second component of the abstract function value to the abstract argument:
$$\textbf{A} \, [f \, e] \, \rho = \text{snd}(\textbf{A} \, [f] \, \rho) \, (\textbf{A} \, [e] \, \rho)$$
To find the context propagated to x from a function application (f e) in a context α we reason as follows: the context propagated to f is **fun#** $\alpha \, \Delta$ APPLY (**A** [e] ρ) α. The context propagated to e can be derived by applying the second component of f's abstract value to the abstract value of e and α, and so the net context propagated to x is
$$\textbf{C}x \, [f \, e] \, \rho \, \alpha = \textbf{C}x \, [f] \, \rho \, (\textbf{fun\#} \, \alpha \, \Delta \text{ APPLY } (\textbf{A} \, [e] \, \rho) \, \alpha) \text{ \& }$$
$$\qquad\qquad\qquad\qquad \textbf{C}x \, [e] \, \rho \, (\text{fst}(\textbf{A} \, [f] \, \rho) <\textbf{A} \, [e] \, \rho, \alpha>)$$

To match these definitions the abstract value of a lambda expression must be
$$\textbf{A} \, [\lambda x.e] \, \rho = <\lambda(\text{APPLY v } \alpha). \, \alpha \text{ -> } \textbf{C}x \, [e] \, \rho[v/x] \, \alpha, \, \lambda v. \, \textbf{A} \, [e] \, \rho[v/x]>$$
The context propagated to a variable in a lambda-expression includes the context propagated from the calls, and potentially also a context propagated from the function value itself. To capture this, we define
$$\textbf{C}x \, [\lambda y.e] \, \rho \, (\alpha \, \Delta \text{ APPLY v } \beta) = \textbf{C}x \, [e] \, \rho[v/y] \, \beta \text{ \& } \textbf{L}x \, [\lambda y.e] \, \rho \, \alpha$$
where **L** must be defined for each analysis. For example, in a strictness analysis
$$\textbf{L}x \, [\lambda y.e] \, \rho \, \alpha = L$$
since a lambda expression has no evaluable components, but in a life-time analysis
$$\textbf{L}x \, [\lambda y.e] \, \rho \, \alpha = \alpha \qquad\qquad\qquad \text{if x is free in e}$$
$$\qquad\qquad\qquad\quad = S \qquad\qquad\qquad\quad \text{otherwise}$$
which expresses the fact that a free variable must be stored on the heap if the function is on the heap.

Using these definitions we can derive recursive equations for the abstract version of each function and solve them by fixed point iteration in the usual way. Since ground objects have trivial abstract values, first-order parts of the program are analysed exactly as before. The more costly method only comes into effect when analysing higher-order functions.

We remarked above that the new context domains are isomorphic to our old ones. However, they are <u>not</u> the same, and as a result the definitions of **C** and **A** just given are inconvenient to use by hand. This is why we have not included a more formal example of a higher-order analysis. Of course, this is not a problem when the analysis is done by machine.

6.4. Generalisations

In the preceding section we showed how a backward analysis could be combined with an abstract interpretation trivial for zero-order values. In the same way we could start with a non-trivial abstract interpretation for ground values and combine it with a trivial ground backward analysis to give other useful analyses. For example, if we define

$$C_G = 1$$
$$A_G = \{K,U\} \quad \text{(the abstract domain for known/unknown analysis)}$$

then, for example,

$$C_{G->G} \cong A_G$$

A function context is just the lub of all the arguments it is called with. Now the techniques of the previous section can be used to discover whether a function is always called with a known argument. An analysis of this kind is performed by the MIX partial evaluator [Jones87].

Alternatively we could define

$$A_G = \wp V$$

where V is the domain of values. Now the context of a function is the set of values it could be called with, which is related to the minimal function graph [Jones86].

7. Polymorphism

Throughout much of the development above, we assumed that the language being analysed was monomorphically typed. Yet strongly typed functional languages generally use a polymorphic type system. We could treat a polymorphic function by analysing it separately for every type of argument that it is actually passed, but this would be unpleasantly expensive. Fortunately it seems to be unnecessary. Abramsky has shown that, in the case of strictness analysis by abstract interpretation, it is only necessary to analyse a polymorphic function at its simplest possible instance. The result is then applicable to every instance [Abramsky85].

It seems likely that an analogous result holds for backward analysis: that the context functions associated with arbitrary instances of a polymorphic function can be derived systematically from those associated with its simplest possible instance. We conjecture that if a function is polymorphic then so is its context function, in a corresponding way. Thus since the type of append is

$$\text{append} : \text{List}(*) \to \text{List}(*) \to \text{List}(*)$$

the type of its context functions must be

$$\text{app\#1, app\#2} : C_{\text{List}(*)} \to C_{\text{List}(*)}$$

This is a powerful constraint. For example, knowing that

app#1 SS = SS	app#2 SS = SS
app#1 SL = SL	app#2 SL = L $\cup$ SL

we can conclude that

app#1 αS = αS	app#2 αS = αS
app#1 αL = αL	app#2 αL = L $\cup$ αL

for all contexts α, because the functions above are the only polymorphic ones that satisfy the given constraint.

Conclusions

Some properties of programs are naturally viewed as propagating inwards from expressions to sub-expressions. Such properties are suited to calculation by backward analysis. We have presented a framework for backward analysis, and applied it to four analysis problems: strictness analysis, call-by-need to call-by-name optimisation, life-time analysis, and needed/unneeded analysis. We offered some evidence that backward analysis is an efficient analysis method.

We showed how a backward analysis suited to first-order programs operating on atomic values can be extended to a mixed analysis capable of analysing monomorphic higher-order programs operating on structured data, and suggested that the extension to polymorphic languages is not difficult.

Acknowledgements

This paper owes a great deal to other people. I have had particularly helpful discussions with Phil Wadler, Stuart Wray and Peter Dybjer. Thomas Johnsson and Kent Karlsson have also influenced the ideas, and the paper would have been far harder to understand had Jon Fairbairn and John Launchbury not criticised an earlier draft so carefully. Several referees for the Partial Evaluation and Mixed Computation workshop also made very useful comments.

References

[Abramsky85]   Samson Abramsky, *Strictness Analysis and Polymorphic Invariance*, in Proc. Workshop on Programs as Data Objects, Copenhagen, eds. H. Ganzinger and N. Jones, Springer-Verlag Lecture Notes in Computer Science Vol 217, 1985.

[Bloss86]   Adrienne Bloss and Paul Hudak, *Variations on Strictness Analysis*, Proc. ACM Conference on Lisp and Functional Programming, 1986.

[Burn et.al.85]   G. Burn, C. Hankin, S. Abramsky, *The Theory of Strictness Analysis for Higher-Order Functions*, in Proc. Workshop on Programs as Data Objects, Copenhagen, eds. H. Ganzinger and N. Jones, Springer-Verlag Lecture Notes in Computer Science Vol 217, 1985.

[Dybjer87]   P. Dybjer, *Computing Inverse Images*, Proc. Int. Comp. on Automata, Languages and Programming, 1987.

[Fairbairn85]   J. Fairbairn, *Design and Implementation of a Simple, Typed Language Based on the λ-calculus*, University of Cambridge Computer Laboratory Technical Report 75, 1985.

[Fairbairn86]   J. Fairbairn, S. C. Wray, *Code Generation Techniques for Functional Languages*, ACM Conference on Lisp and Functional Programming pp95-104, 1986.

[Fairbairn87]   J. Fairbairn, S. C. Wray, *Tim: A Simple, Lazy Abstract Machine to Execute Super-combinators*, Proc. IFIP Symposium on Functional Programming Languages and Computer Architecture, Portland, Oregon, September 1987.

[Hall87]   C. Hall and D. S. Wise, *Compiling Strictness into Streams*, ACM Conference on Principles of Programming Languages, Hamburg, 1987.

[Hudak84]   P. Hudak and D. Kranz, *A Combinator-based Compiler for a Functional Language*, Proc. ACM Symposium on Principles of Programming Languages, Salt Lake City, 1984.

[Hudak85]   P. Hudak and B. Goldberg, *Serial Combinators: Optimal Grains of Parallelism*, in Proc. IFIP Conference on Functional Programming and Computer Architecture, Nancy, ed. J-P. Jouannaud, Springer-Verlag Lecture Notes in Computer Science Vol. 201, 1985.

[Hudak87]   P. Hudak, *A Semantic Model of Reference Counting and its Abstraction*, in Abstract Interpretation, eds. Abramsky and Hankin, Ellis-Horwood, 1987.

[Hughes82]   J. Hughes, *Super-combinators: A New Implementation Method for Applicative Languages*, Proc. ACM Symposium on Lisp and Functional Programming, Pittsburgh, 1982.

[Hughes85]   J. Hughes, *Strictness Detection in Non-Flat Domains*, in Proc. Workshop on Programs as Data Objects, Copenhagen, eds. H. Ganzinger and N. Jones, Springer-Verlag Lecture Notes in Computer Science Vol 217, 1985.

[Hughes87]   J. Hughes, *Analysing Strictness by Abstract Interpretation of Continuations*, in Abstract Interpretation, eds. Abramsky and Hankin, Ellis-Horwood, 1987.

[Johnsson85]   T. Johnsson, *Lambda-lifting: Transforming Programs to Recursive Equations*, in Proc. IFIP Conference on Functional Programming and

Computer Architecture, Nancy, ed. J-P. Jouannaud, Springer-Verlag
Lecture Notes in Computer Science Vol. 201, 1985.

[Johnsson81]   T. Johnsson, *Detecting when Call-by-Value can be used instead of Call-by-Need*, Programming Methodology Group Memo PMG-14, Institutionen för Informationsbehandling, Chalmers Tekniska Högskola, Göteborg, 1981.

[Jones86]   Neil D. Jones and Alan Mycroft, *Data Flow Analysis of Applicative Programs using Minimal Function Graphs*, Proc. 13th ACM Principles of Programming Languages, 1986.

[Jones87]   Neil D. Jones, Peter Sestoft, Harald Søndergaard, *MIX: a Self-Applicable Partial Evaluator for Experiments in Compiler Generation*, to appear in Journal of LISP and Symbolic Computation.

[Karlsson87]   K. Karlsson, *Access and Demand Analysis of Functional Programs*, Programming Methodology Group Memo, Institutionen för Informationsbehandling, Chalmers Tekniska Högskola, Göteborg, 1987.

[Launchbury87] J. Launchbury, *Projections for Specialisation*, Proc. IFIP Workshop on Partial Evaluation and Mixed Computation, Gammel Avernaes, Denmark, October 1987.

[Mycroft80]   A. Mycroft, *The Theory and Practice of Transforming Call-by-Need into Call-by-Value*, Proc. International Symposium on Programming, Springer-Verlag Lecture Notes in Computer Science Vol. 83, 1980.

[Wadler87a]   P. Wadler, *Strictness Analysis on Non-Flat Domains*, in Abstract Interpretation, eds. Abramsky and Hankin, Ellis-Horwood, 1987.

[Wadler87b]   P. Wadler and J. Hughes, *Projections for Strictness Analysis*, Proc. IFIP Symposium on Functional Programming Languages and Computer Architecture, Portland, Oregon, September 1987.

[Wray85]   S. C. Wray, *A New Strictness Detection Algorithm*, Proc. Workshop on Implementations of Functional Languages, Aspenäs, eds. Augustsson et.al., Programming Methodology Group Report 17, Institutionen för Informationsbehandling, Chalmers Tekniska Högskola, Göteborg, 1985.

[Wray86]   S. C. Wray, *Implementation and Programming Techniques for Functional Languages*, PhD thesis, University of Cambridge Computer Laboratory, 1986.

Partial Evaluation and Mixed Computation
D. Bjørner, A.P. Ershov and N.D. Jones (Editors)
Elsevier Science Publishers B.V. (North-Holland)
IFIP, 1988

AN ALGEBRA AND AXIOMATIZATION SYSTEM OF MIXED COMPUTATION

Vladimir E. ITKIN

Department of Informatics, Computing Center
Sibirian Division of the Academy of Sciences
Novosibirsk, 630090, USSR

An algebraic and axiomatic tools for Mixed Computation are
presented. Some axioms for program functions, inputs and
outputs are introduced. These axioms are sufficient for
the correct Mixed Computation of some basic forms of
program composition.

1. INTRODUCTION

1.1. The historical information

The concept of Mixed Computation [1] is conceived for a partial
execution of programs where a result has two components: an
intermediate memory state $\underline{and}$ a residual program. In [2] three
algorithms mix, mix^o, and $\overline{mix}$ of Mixed Computation were developed.
The mix algorithm is very natural but in general it is not
correct. In [4] the correctness of mix was achieved by algebraic
tools. The algebra [4] is realization of a transformational
approach [3] to Mixed Computation.

1.2. DMS-algebra

The algebra from [4] is a deterministic memory state one. Let R be
a set of $memory\ locations$ and C be a set of $constants$, then the
partial function s from R to C is a deterministic memory state.
The DMS-$algebra\ constructed\ on$ (R, C) is defined as the frame

$$(2^R,\ \cup,\ \cap,\ \backslash;\ S,\ 0,\ +,\ *,\ \Delta),$$

where S is the set of all memory states; $0 \in S$, $0(r)$ is undefined
for any $r \in R$; $+: S \times S \to S$; $*, \Delta: S \times 2^R \to S$; for any $s, s_1, s_2 \in S$, $Y \subseteq R$:

$$graf(s) = \{ (r, c) \mid s(r) = c \},$$
$$d(s) = \{ r \mid s(r) \text{ is defined} \},$$
$$d(s_1 + s_2) = d(s_1) \cup d(s_2),$$
$$(s_1 + s_2)(r) = \begin{cases} s_1(r), & \text{if } r \in d(s_1) \\ s_2(r), & \text{if } r \notin d(s_1) \text{ and } r \in d(s_2) \end{cases}$$
$$d(s * Y) = d(s) \cap Y, \quad graf(s * Y) \subseteq graf(s),$$
$$d(s \Delta Y) = d(s) \backslash Y, \quad graf(s \Delta Y) \subseteq graf(s).$$

1.3. Operators

A notion of a program is modeled by an abstract "operator". An
$operator$ is defined as a frame

$$(p, \bar{p}, in(p), out(p), yes(p)) \,,$$

where p is the *name*, $\bar{p}$ is the *function* (the partial function from S to S), $in(p) \subseteq R$ is the *input*, $out(p) \subseteq R$ is the *complete output*, $yes(p) \subseteq R$ is the *obligatory output* of the operator. Here we are speaking that p is the operator and

$$p = (\bar{p}, in(p), out(p), yes(p)) \,.$$

The notion of the obligatory output was introduced in [11]. If *prog* is an Algol-like program then $yes(prog)$ is the set of locations which get some value on any path of the program from <u>begin</u> to <u>end</u>.

The operator p is said to be *fundamental* iff it satisfy the following conditions (axioms):

$$\forall s_1 \forall s_2 \ (\bar{p}(s_1) \text{ is defined} => \bar{p}(s_1 + s_2) = \bar{p}(s_1) + s_2) \,,$$
$$\forall s \ (\bar{p}(s) \text{ is defined} => \bar{p}(s * in(p)) \text{ is defined}) \,,$$
$$\forall s \ (\bar{p}(s) \text{ is defined} => \bar{p}(s) = \bar{p}(s) * out(p) + s) \,,$$
$$\forall s \ (\bar{p}(s) \text{ is defined} => yes(p) \subseteq d(\bar{p}(s))) \,.$$

A fundamental operator may be regarded as a closed information module.

1.4. Explicators

For any $s \in S$ the operator $[s]$ is defined as

$$\overline{[s]}(s_1) = s + s_1 \text{ for any } s_1 \in S,$$
$$in([s]) = \emptyset,$$
$$out([s]) = yes([s]) = d(s).$$

Let us call operator $[s]$ the *explicator* of s.

For example, if

$$s = \{r_1 = 4, r_2 = 8\}$$

then

$$[s] = \{r_1 := 4, r_2 := 8\}.$$

The operator $[s]$ is fundamental for any $s \in S$.

1.5. Superposition of operators

Let $p_1 \cdot p_2$ is the name of such operator that

$$\forall s \ (\overline{p_1 \cdot p_2}(s) = \overline{p_2}(\overline{p_1}(s))) \,,$$
$$in(p_1 \cdot p_2) = in(p_1) \cup (in(p_2) \setminus yes(p_1)),$$
$$out(p_1 \cdot p_2) = out(p_1) \cup out(p_2) \,,$$
$$yes(p_1 \cdot p_2) = yes(p_1) \cup yes(p_2) \,.$$

The operation "." is associative. If p_1 and p_2 are fundamental then $p_1 \cdot p_2$ is fundamental too.

1.6. Mixed Computation

Mixed Computer is defined [4] as a multivalue mapping M from $P \times S$ to $P \times S$, where P is the set of all operators. If (p', s') is one value of $M(p, s)$, then p' is the *residual program*, s' is the *intermediate memory state*.

The transformation

$$(p, s) \rightarrow (p', s')$$

may be represented as

$$[s].p \rightarrow [s'].p' \ .$$

If $p' = p'' \cdot [s'']$, then s'' is the *partial result* of $M(p, s)$ and for any $s_0 \in S$

$$\bar{p}(s + s_0) = s'' + \overline{p''}(s' + s_0) \ .$$

An abstract example of computation process of $M(p_1 \cdot p_2 \cdot p_3, s)$:

$$[s].p_1 \cdot p_2 \cdot p_3 \rightarrow$$
$$[s_1].p_1 \cdot [s_2].p_2 \cdot p_3 \rightarrow$$
$$[s_1].p_1 \cdot [\overline{p_2}(s_2)] \cdot p_3 \rightarrow$$
$$[s_1].p_1 \cdot [s_3].p_3 \cdot [s_4] \ .$$

Here s_4 is the partial result, s_1 is the intermediate memory state.

In this process two sorts of transformations are used:

$$\text{if } \bar{p}(s) \text{ is defined} \quad \text{then } [s].p \rightarrow [\bar{p}(s)] \ , \qquad (\text{TRANS}_1)$$

$$[s].p \rightarrow [s'].p.[s''] \ , \qquad\qquad\qquad (\text{TRANS}_2)$$

where these expressions are considered on a metasyntactic level. The transformation TRANS_2 is important for Mixed Computation. If p is fundamental and

$$s' = s * (in(p) \cup (out(p) \setminus yes(p))) \ ,$$
$$s'' = s \ \Delta \ out(p) \ ,$$

then

$$\overline{[s].p} = \overline{[s'].p.[s'']} \ .$$

There are some possibilities for *merging* of operators together and for *parallel* execution of transformations.

1.7. Non deterministic memory states and information elements

In [8,9] all previous notions are translated into a language of *nondetermenistic* memory states and further into a language of abstract *information elements*.

In a simple case a nondeterministic memory state is defined as $s \subseteq R \times C$. It is deterministic one iff from $(r, c_1) \in s$ and $(r, c_2) \in s$ follows that $c_1 = c_2$ for any r, c_1, c_2. Thus, one may use the nondeterministic memory state $R_1 \times C$ instead of R_1, where $R_1 \subseteq R$; operations $\cup$, $\cap$, $\setminus$ submerge into +, *, Δ respectively.

If $p(x) = y$, where the *information* elements x and y are the sets of *statements*, then one may regard p as the *inference operator*.

2.AXIOMATIZATION OF DMS-ALGEBRA

2.1. Algebra of nondeterministic memory states

A *basis* (*of memory*) is a triple (R, C, T), where R is a set of *memory locations*, C is a set of *constants*, $T \subseteq R \times C$ is a set of *permissible pairs*.

The NDMS-*algebra constructed on the basis* (R, C, T) is the frame

$$(S, 0, +, *, \Delta),$$

where $S = 2^T$ is the set of *memory states* (T is the *total* memory state); $0 \in S$ is the empty subset of T (*empty memory state*); +, *, $\Delta: S \times S \to S$; for any $s, s_1, s_2 \in S$, $r \in R$:

$$s(r) = \{ c \in C \mid (r, c) \in s \},$$
$$d(s) = \{ r \in R \mid s(r) \neq \emptyset \},$$
$$D(s) = \{ (r, c) \in T \mid r \in d(s), \ c \in C \},$$
$$s_1 + s_2 = s_1 \cup (s_2 \setminus D(s_1)),$$
$$s_1 * s_2 = s_1 \cap D(s_2),$$
$$s_1 \Delta s_2 = s_1 \setminus D(s_2) .$$

For any $s_1, s_2 \in S$, $r \in R$:

$$(s_1 + s_2)(r) = \begin{cases} s_1(r), & \text{if } r \in d(s_1) \\ \\ s_2(r), & \text{if } r \notin d(s_1) \end{cases} \tag{1}$$

$$(s_1 * s_2)(r) = \begin{cases} s_1(r), & \text{if } r \in d(s_2) \\ \\ \emptyset, & \text{if } r \notin d(s_2) \end{cases} \tag{2}$$

$$(s_1 \Delta s_2)(r) = \begin{cases} \emptyset, & \text{if } r \in d(s_2) \\ \\ s_1(r), & \text{if } r \notin d(s_2) \end{cases} \tag{3}$$

If *generalization*$(Y) = \{ (r, c) \in T \mid r \in Y, c \in C \}$ for any $Y \subseteq R$, then

$$D(s) = generalization(d(s)). \tag{4}$$

For any $s, s_1, s_2 \in S$:

$$D(D(s)) = D(s), \tag{5}$$
$$D(s_1 \cup s_2) = D(s_1) \cup D(s_2) = D(s_1 + s_2) = D(s_1) + D(s_2), \tag{6}$$
$$D(s_1 \cap D(s_2)) = D(s_1) \cap D(s_2) = D(s_1 * s_2) = D(s_1) * D(s_2), \tag{7}$$
$$D(s_1 \setminus D(s_2)) = D(s_1) \setminus D(s_2) = D(s_1 \Delta s_2) = D(s_1) \Delta D(s_2) \quad . \tag{8}$$

For any $s_1, s_2 \in S$:

$$\exists s(s_2 = s_1 + s) \iff s_2 * s_1 = s_1 \iff s_1 + s_2 = s_2 , \tag{9}$$
$$D(s_1) \subseteq D(s_2) \iff s_1 \subseteq D(s_2) \iff s_1 * s_2 = s_1 \quad . \tag{10}$$

For any $s \in S$:

$$D(s) = T * s \quad . \tag{11}$$

Let $\text{NOT}(s) = T \setminus D(s)$. Then for any $s_1, s_2 \in S$

$$s_1 \Delta s_2 = s_1 * \text{NOT}(s_2) \quad . \tag{12}$$

2.2. Quasi-Boolean algebra

A frame

$$(X, 0, +, *, \Delta)$$

(now the symbols $0, +, *, \Delta$ have new meaning) is the *quasi-Boolean algebra* iff
    (i) X is a nonempty set (of *information elements*);
    (ii) $0 \in X$;
    (iii) $+, *, \Delta : X \times X \to X$; these operations satisfy the following conditions (axioms): for any $x, y, z \in X$:

(A1) $(x + y) + z = x + (y + z)$,

(A2) $(x * y) * z = x * (y * z)$,

(A3) $x * (y * z) = x * (z * y)$,

(A4) $(x + y) * z = x * z + y * z$,

(A5) $z * (x + y) = z * x + z * y$,

(A6) $x * 0 = 0$,

(A7) $0 * x = 0$,

(A8) $x * x = x$,

(A9) $x + y * x = x$,

(A10) $x \Delta x = 0$,

(A11) $x * y + x \Delta y = x$,

(A12) $x * y + z \Delta y = z \Delta y + x * y$,

(A13) $(x + y) \Delta z = x \Delta z + y \Delta z$,

(A14) $x \Delta (y + z) = (x \Delta y) \Delta z$,

(A15) $(x * y) \Delta z = x * (y \Delta z)$,

(A16) $(x * y) \Delta z = (x \Delta z) * y$.

Theorem 1. For any basis of memory, NDMS-algebra constructed on the basis is the quasi-Boolean algebra.

It is true that the A1-A16 axiom system is the complete axiomatization of equality in any NDMS-algebra (for any basis of memory) [10].

Further through the text we suppose some quasi-Boolean algebra $(X,0,+,*,\Delta)$ *to be fixed.*

Let, by definition, for any $x,y \in X$

$$x \leqslant y \quad <=> \quad \exists z(y = x + z) \quad .$$

For any $x, x_0, y, y_0, z, z_1, z_2 \in X$:

$$x + x = x \ , \tag{13}$$

$$x * y + x = x \ , \tag{14}$$

$$x \leqslant y <=> y * x = x <=> x + y = y \ , \tag{15}$$

$$x \leqslant x \ , \tag{16}$$

$$x \leqslant y \text{ and } y \leqslant z => x \leqslant z \ , \tag{17}$$

$$x \leqslant y \text{ and } y \leqslant x => x = y \ , \tag{18}$$

$$x + x * y = x \ , \tag{19}$$

$$x \leqslant y => y + x = y \ , \tag{20}$$

$$x * y = 0 => z_1 * x + z_2 * y = z_2 * y + z_1 * x \ , \tag{21}$$

$$x + x \Delta y = x \Delta y + x \ , \tag{22}$$

$$x * y \leqslant x \ , \tag{23}$$

$$x \leqslant y => x * z \leqslant y * z \ , \tag{24}$$

$$x \leqslant y => z + x \leqslant z + y \ , \tag{25}$$

$$y \leqslant z => x * x_0 + y * x_0 \leqslant x + z * x_0 \ , \tag{26}$$

$$x * y = 0 => z * y \leqslant z \Delta x \ , \tag{27}$$

$$x * y + y * x = x * y \ , \tag{28}$$

$$x * y + z \Delta x = z \Delta x + x * y \ , \tag{29}$$

$$x \Delta y + y \Delta x = y \Delta x + x \Delta y \ , \tag{30}$$

$$x + y + x = x + y \ , \tag{31}$$

$$x + y = x + y \Delta x \ , \tag{32}$$

$$x * z + y * z + x = x + y * z \ , \tag{33}$$

$$x + y + x * z = x + y \ , \tag{34}$$

$$x + y + z * x = x * y \ , \tag{35}$$

$$x + (x + y) * z = (x + y) * z + x \ , \tag{36}$$

$$y \leqslant x \Delta z => y * z = 0 \ , \tag{37}$$

$$x \leqslant y => x + (y + y_0) * z = (y + y_0) * z + x \ , \tag{38}$$

$$x * (y + z) = x * (z + y) \ , \tag{39}$$

$$(x \Delta y) * (x \Delta z) = (x \Delta z) * (x \Delta y) \ , \tag{40}$$

$$x \Delta y + x \Delta z = x \Delta z + x \Delta y \ , \tag{41}$$

$$(x \Delta y) \Delta z = (x \Delta z) \Delta y \ , \tag{42}$$

$$x \Delta (y * z) = x \Delta (z * y) , \tag{43}$$

$$x\Delta(\ y^{*}z\ ) \ = \ x\Delta y + x\Delta z \ , \tag{44}$$

$$(\ x\Delta y)\Delta(\ y\Delta z) \ = \ x\Delta y \ , \tag{45}$$

$$x\Delta(\ y\Delta x) \ = \ x \ , \tag{46}$$

$$(\ x^{*}z)\Delta(\ y\Delta z) \ = \ x^{*}z \ , \tag{47}$$

$$(\ y^{*}z)^{*}(\ y\Delta z) \ = \ 0 \ , \tag{48}$$

$$(\ y^{*}z)\Delta(\ y\Delta z) \ = \ y^{*}z \ , \tag{49}$$

$$x\Delta(\ y\Delta z) \ = \ x^{*}y^{*}z + x\Delta y \ , \tag{50}$$

$$x\Delta(\ y\Delta z) \ = \ x^{*}z + x\Delta y \ , \tag{51}$$

$$x^{*}y \ = \ 0 \ <=> \ y^{*}x \ = \ 0 \ . \tag{52}$$

3. FUNDAMENTAL OPERATORS AND RECOGNIZERS

3.1. Fundamental operators

Let for any partial functions f, f_1, f_2 from X to X , for any $x, y \in X$:

$$\square(\ f, x) \ <=> \ f(x) \ \text{is defined};$$
$$f_1(x) \ == \ f_2(y) \ <=> \ (\square(\ f_1, x) \ <=> \ \square(\ f_2, y)) \ \&$$
$$\& \ (\square(\ f_1, x) \ => \ f_1(x) = f_2(y))) \ .$$

An *operator* is a frame

$$(\ f, x, y, z) \ ,$$

where f is a partial function from X to X; $x, y, z \in X$.

If the operator (f, x, y, z) is marked by p, then f, x, y, z marked by

$$\bar{p}, \ in(p), \ out(p), \ yes(p)$$

respectively.

We state for any operators p_1, p_2:
$$p_1 \ = \ p_2 \ <=> \ \overline{p_1} \ = \ \overline{p_2} \ \&$$
$$\& \ in(p_1) \ = \ in(p_2) \ \&$$
$$\& \ out(p_1) \ = \ out(p_2) \ \&$$
$$\& \ yes(p_1) \ = \ yes(p_2) \ .$$

An operator p is *fundamental* iff the following properties hold:

(F0) $\forall x \forall y(\square(\ \bar{p}, x) \ => \ \bar{p}(x+y) \ = \ p(x) \ + \ y)$,

(F1) $\forall x(\square(\ \bar{p}, x) \ => \ \square(\ \bar{p}, x^{*}in(p)))$,

(F2) $\forall x(\square(\ \bar{p}, x) \ => \ \bar{p}(x) \ = \ \bar{p}(x)^{*}out(p) \ + \ x)$,

(F3) $\forall x(\square(\ \bar{p}, x) \ => \ yes(p)^{*}\bar{p}(x) \ = \ yes(p))$.

For any operator p:

$$F0(p) \ => \ \forall x(\square(\ \bar{p}, x) \ => \ \bar{p}(x) \ = \ x), \tag{53}$$

$$F0(p) \ => \ \forall x \forall y(\square(\ \bar{p}, x) \& x \leqslant y \ => \ \square(\ \bar{p}, y) \& \bar{p}(x) \leqslant \bar{p}(y)) \ . \tag{54}$$

For any operator p:

$$F3(p) \ <=> \ \forall x \forall y(\square(\ \bar{p}, x) \ => \ \bar{p}(x) \ = \ \bar{p}(x) \ + \ y^{*}yes(p)) \ .$$

For any fundamental operator p, for any $x, y, z \in X$: the operator

$$(\bar{p}, in(p)+x, out(p)+y, yes(p)+z)$$

is fundamental.

An operator p is *directed* iff $out(p) = yes(p)$ and for any x from $\Box(\bar{p}, x)$ follows

$$in(p)*x = in(p) \ \& \ out(p)*\bar{p}(x) = out(p) \ \& \ \bar{p}(x)*out(p) = \bar{p}(x).$$

For example, an assigment operator is directed.

We state for any operator p: $|p|$ is such operator that

$$\forall x(\overline{|p|}(x) == \bar{p}(x*in(p)) + x),$$

$$in(|p|) = in(p),$$

$$out(|p|) = out(p),$$

$$yes(|p|) = yes(p).$$

For any directed operator p : the operator $|p|$ is fundamental.

3.2. Fundamental recognizers

A *recognizer* is a frame

$$(v, x) \ ,$$

where v is a partial predicate from X to $\{$**TRUE**,**FALSE**$\}$, $x \in X$.

If the recognizer (v, x) is marked by u, then v, x are marked by

$$\bar{u}, \ in(u)$$

respectively.

A recognizer u is *fundamental* iff two properties hold:

(F0) $\forall x \forall y(\Box(\bar{u}, x) \Rightarrow \bar{u}(x+y) = \bar{u}(x))$,

(F1) $\forall x(\Box(\bar{u}, x) \Rightarrow \Box(\bar{u}, x*in(u)))$.

4. COMPOSITION OF OPERATORS AND RECOGNIZERS

4.1. Superposition of operators

Let for any operators p_1, p_2: $p_1 \cdot p_2$ be such operator for wich

$$\forall x(\overline{p_1 \cdot p_2}(x) == \bar{p}_2(\bar{p}_1(x))),$$

where $\Box(\overline{p_1 \cdot p_2}, x)$ iff $\Box(\bar{p}_1, x)$ and $\Box(\bar{p}_2, \bar{p}_1(x))$,

$$in(p_1 \cdot p_2) = in(p_1) + in(p_2) \Delta yes(p_1) \ ,$$

$$out(p_1 \cdot p_2) = out(p_2) + out(p_1) \ ,$$

$$yes(p_1 \cdot p_2) = yes(p_2) + yes(p_1) \ .$$

The operation "." is associative.

Theorem 2. For any fundamental operators p, q the operator $p.q$ is fundamental.

Proof of F1($p.q$). We have to prove $\Box(\overline{p.q}, x*in(p.q))$, i.e.

$$\Box(\bar{p}, x*in(p.q)) \ \& \ \Box(\bar{q}, \bar{p}(x*in(p.q))) \ .$$

$\square(\bar{p}, x)$ and $F1(p)$ imply

$\qquad \square(\bar{p}, x^* in(p)));$

$in(p) \leqslant in(p.q)$ and (54) imply

$\qquad \square(\bar{p}, x^* in(p.q))).$

Now we have to prove

$\qquad \square(\bar{q}, \bar{p}(x^* in(p.q)))).$

$\square(\bar{q}, \bar{p}(x))$ and $F1(q)$ imply

$\qquad \square(\bar{q}, \bar{p}(x)^* in(q)));$

(54) for q and

$\qquad \bar{p}(x)^* in(q) \leqslant \bar{p}(x^* in(p.q))) \qquad\qquad (55)$

imply

$\qquad \square(\bar{q}, \bar{p}(x^* in(p.q)))).$

Now we have to prove (55). $\square(\bar{p}, x)$ and $F1(p)$ imply

$\qquad \square(\bar{p}, x^* in(p)));$

$F0(p)$ implies

$\qquad \bar{p}(x) = \bar{p}(x^* in(p)) + x\Delta in(p)$.

We have

$\qquad \bar{p}(x)^* in(q) = \bar{p}(x^* in(p))^* in(q) + (x\Delta in(p))^* in(q)$. $\qquad (56)$

The equality

$\qquad \bar{p}(x^* in(p.q)) = \bar{p}(x^* in(p)) + x^* in(q) \qquad\qquad (57)$

is true since

$\qquad \bar{p}(x^* in(p.q)) = /F0(p)/$

$= \bar{p}(x^* in(p)) + x^*(in(q)\Delta yes(p)) = /F3(p)/$

$= \bar{p}(x^* in(p)) + (x^* in(q))^* yes(p) + (x^* in(q))\Delta yes(p) =$

$= \bar{p}(x^* in(p)) + x^* in(q)$.

The relation (55) is equivalent to the relation $\leqslant$ between right parts of (56) and (57). This relation follows from the relation (26) by some substitutions.

Proof of F2$(p.q)$. Let $\square(\overline{p.q}, x)$. Then

$\qquad \overline{p.q}(x) = \bar{q}(\bar{p}(x)) = /F2(q)/$

$= \bar{q}(\bar{p}(x))^* out(q) + \bar{p}(x) \overset{1}{=}$

$= \bar{q}(\bar{p}(x))^* out(q) + \bar{q}(\bar{p}(x))^* out(p) + \bar{p}(x) \overset{2}{=}$

$= \bar{q}(\bar{p}(x))^* out(q) + \bar{q}(\bar{p}(x))^* out(p) + x =$

$= \bar{q}(\bar{p}(x))^*(out(q) + out(p)) + x$.

Let us denote $\bar{q}(\bar{p}(x))$ by y.

$\qquad$ Proof of $\overset{1}{=}$:

$\qquad y^* out(q) + y^* out(p) + \bar{p}(x) = /F2(q)/$

$= y^* out(q) + (y^* out(q) + \bar{p}(x))^* out(p) + \bar{p}(x) = /F2(p)/$

$= y^* out(q) + \bar{p}(x)$.

$\qquad$ Proof of $\overset{2}{=}$:

$$y^{\ast}out(p) \; + \; \bar{p}(x) \; = \; /\mathrm{F}2(p)/$$
$$= \quad y^{\ast}out(p) \; + \; \bar{p}(x)^{\ast}out(p) \; + \; x \; =$$
$$= \quad (y \; + \; \bar{p}(x))^{\ast}out(p) \; + \; x \; = \; /(53) \; \text{for} \; q/$$
$$= \quad y^{\ast}out(p) \; + \; x \; .$$

4.2. Filtration of input and output of operator

Let for any operator p and any $x_1, x_2 \in X$:

$$(x_1 : p : x_2)$$

be the operator such that

$$\forall x(\overline{(x_1:p:x_2)}(x) \; == \; (\bar{p}(x^{\ast}x_1))^{\ast}x_2 \; + \; x) \; ,$$
$$in((x_1:p:x_2)) \; = \; in(p)^{\ast}x_1 \; ,$$
$$out((x_1:p:x_2)) \; = \; out(p)^{\ast}x_2 \; ,$$
$$yes((x_1:p:x_2)) \; = \; yes(p)^{\ast}x_2 \; .$$

Theorem 3. For any fundamental operator p, for any $x_1, x_2 \in X$: operator $(x_1:p:x_2)$ is fundamental.

4.3. If-then-else

Let for any operators p_1, p_2 and for any recognizer u:

$$(u \mid p_1 \mid p_2)$$

be the operator such that

$$in((u \mid p_1 \mid p_2)) \; = \; in(u) \; + \; in(p_1) \; + \; in(p_2) \; ,$$
$$out((u \mid p_1 \mid p_2)) \; = \; out(p_1) \; + \; out(p_2) \; ,$$
$$yes((u \mid p_1 \mid p_2)) \; = \; yes(p_1)^{\ast}yes(p_2) \; ,$$

for any $x \in X$:

$$\overline{(u \mid p_1 \mid p_2)}(x) \; == \; \begin{cases} p_1(x), \; \text{if} \; u(x) \; = \; \mathbf{TRUE} \\[2mm] p_2(x), \; \text{if} \; u(x) \; = \; \mathbf{FALSE} \end{cases}$$

if $\bar{u}(x)$ is undefined then $\overline{(u \mid p_1 \mid p_2)}(x)$ is undefined.

Theorem 4. For any fundamental operators p_1, p_2 and any fundamental recognizer u: operator $(u \mid p_1 \mid p_2)$ is fundamental.

4.4. While-do

Let for any operator p and recognizer u:

$$(u \; \# \; p)$$

be the operator such that

$$in((u \; \# \; p)) \; = \; in(u) \; + \; in(p) \; ,$$
$$out((u \; \# \; p)) \; = \; out(p) \; ,$$
$$yes((u \; \# \; p)) \; = \; 0 \; ,$$

for any $x \in X$:

if $\bar{u}(x) \; = \; \mathbf{FALSE}$, then $\overline{(u \# p)}(x) \; = \; x,$

for any $n > 0,$

$$\text{if } \bar{u}(\overline{p^0}(x)) = \ldots = \bar{u}(\overline{p^n}(x)) = \text{TRUE } \&$$

$$\& \ \bar{u}(\overline{p^{n+1}}(x)) = \text{FALSE},$$

$$\text{then } \overline{(u\#p)}(x) = \overline{p^{n+1}}(x),$$

otherwise $\overline{(u\#p)}(x)$ is undefined ,

where $\overline{p^0}(x) = x, \ p^1 = p, \ p^2 = p.p, \ \ldots$.

Theorem 5. For any fundamental operator p and any fundamental recognizer u : operator $(u \# p)$ is fundamental.

4.5. Superposition of operator and recognizer

Let for any operator p and recognizer u:

$$p.u$$

is the recognizer such that

$$\forall x(\overline{p.u}(x) == \bar{u}(\bar{p}(x)))),$$

$$in(p.u) = in(p) + in(u).$$

Theorem 6. For any fundamental operator p and any fundamental recognizer u: recognizer $p.u$ is fundamental.

5. INFORMATION CONNECTIONS BETWEEN OPERATORS

5.1. Definition

For any operators p and q: if

$$out(p)*in(q) \neq 0 \quad ,$$

then we state that there is an *information connection from p to q*.

The relations

$$out(p)*in(q) = 0, \ out(p)*out(q) = 0$$

are denoted by

$$pNIq, \ pNOq$$

respectively.

5.2. Some results

For any fundamental operator p, for any $x \in X$:

$$\square(\bar{p}, x) \iff \square(\bar{p}, x*in(p)) \ , \tag{58}$$

$$\bar{p}(x) == \bar{p}(x*in(p)) + x \ , \tag{59}$$

$$\square(\bar{p}, x) \implies \bar{p}(x)\Delta out(p) = x\Delta out(p) \ . \tag{60}$$

For any fundamental operators p and q, for any $x \in X$: if $pNIq$ then

$$\square(\bar{p}, x) \implies x*in(q) = \bar{p}(x)*in(q) \ , \tag{61}$$

$$\square(\bar{p}, x) \implies \bar{p}(x)*in(q) < x\Delta out(p) \ , \tag{62}$$

$$\overline{p \cdot q}(x) \;==\; \overline{q}(x*in(q)) \;+\; \overline{p}(x) \;, \tag{63}$$

$$\overline{p \cdot q}(x) \;==\; \overline{q}(x\Delta out(p)) \;+\; \overline{p}(x) \;, \tag{64}$$

$$\overline{p \cdot q}(x) \;==\; (\overline{q}(x*in(q)))*out(q) \;+$$
$$+\; (\overline{p}(x*in(p)))*out(p) \;+\; x \;, \tag{65}$$

$$out(q) = yes(q) \;=>\; \overline{p \cdot q}(x) \;==\; \overline{q}(x)*out(p) \;+\; \overline{p}(x) \;, \tag{66}$$

$$qNI\,p \;\&\; pNO\,q \;=>\; \overline{p \cdot q}(x) \;==\; \overline{q \cdot p}(x) \;. \tag{67}$$

The relations (63)-(66) may be used for parallel computation of $\overline{p_2}(\overline{p_1}(x))$.

6. MIXED COMPUTATION

6.1. Explicators

For any $x \in X$ we define the operator $[x]$ as follows:

$$\forall y(\overline{[x]}(y) = x+y) \;,$$
$$in([x]) = 0, \; out([x]) = yes([x]) = x \;.$$

The operator $[x]$ is called the explicator of x.

Note. It would be natural to state $out([s]) = yes([s]) = D(s)$ in NDMS-algebra. But s plays the role of $D(s)$ when s is used as the right argument of operation $*$.

The operator $[x]$ is fundamental for any $x \in X$.
For any $x, y \in X$:

$$[x] \; NI \; [y] \;,$$
$$[x] \; . \; [y] = [y+x]$$

6.2. Principal clause

Theorem 7. For any fundamental operator p, for any $x \in X$:

$$\overline{[x] \cdot p} = \overline{[x'] \cdot p \cdot [x'']} \;, \tag{68}$$

$$in([x] \cdot p) = in([x'] \cdot p \cdot [x'']) \;, \tag{69}$$

$$out([x] \cdot p) = out([x'] \cdot p \cdot [x'']) \;, \tag{70}$$

where

$$x' = x*(in(p) + out(p)\Delta yes(p)),$$
$$x'' = x\Delta out(p) \;.$$

Proof of (68). We denote $in(p) + out(p)\Delta yes(p)$ by z. For any $y \in X$:

$$\overline{[x'] \cdot p \cdot [x'']}(y) \;==$$
$$==\; \overline{p \cdot [x'']}(x'*z+y) \;==/(58),(59)/$$
$$==\; \overline{p \cdot [x'']}((x*z+y)*in(p)) \;+\; x*z \;+\; y \overset{1}{==}$$
$$==\; \overline{p \cdot [x'']}((x+y)*in(p)) \;+x*z \;+\; y \;==$$
$$==\; x\Delta out(p) \;+\; \overline{p}((x+y)*in(p)) \;+\; x*z \;+\; y \overset{2}{==}$$
$$==\; \overline{p}((x+y)*in(p)) \;+\; x\Delta out(p) \;+\; x*z \;+\; y \;==\; /F3(p)/$$
$$==\; \overline{p}((x+y)*in(p)) \;+\; (x*out(p))*yes(p) \;+$$
$$+\; x\Delta out(p) \;+\; x*z \;+\; y \overset{3}{==}$$

$$== \bar{p}((x+y)*in(p)) + (x+y) == /(58),(59)/$$

$$== \bar{p}(x+y) == \bar{p}([\bar{x}](y)) == [\bar{x}].\bar{p}(y) \quad .$$

Proof of $\overset{1}{==}$:

$$(x*z+y)*in(p) =$$

$$= (x*(in(p) + out(p)\Delta yes(p)) + y)*in(p) =$$

$$= (x + x*(out(p)\Delta yes(p)))*in(p) + y*in(p) =$$

$$= x*in(p) +y*in(p) = (x + y)*in(p) \quad .$$

Proof of $\overset{2}{==}$. Let denote $(x+y)*in(p)$ by w . Then

$$x\Delta out(p) + \bar{p}(w) ==$$

$$== x\Delta out(p) + \bar{p}(w)*out(p) + \bar{p}(w)\Delta out(p) == /(60)/$$

$$== \bar{p}(w)*out(p) + x\Delta out(p) + w\Delta out(p) ==$$

$$== \bar{p}(w)*out(p) + (x+w)\Delta out(p) == /(36)/$$

$$== \bar{p}(w)*out(p) + (w+x)\Delta out(p) == /(60)/$$

$$== \bar{p}(w)*out(p) + \bar{p}(w)\Delta out(p) + x\Delta out(p) ==$$

$$== \bar{p}(w) + x\Delta out(p) \quad .$$

Proof of $\overset{3}{==}$:

$$(x*out(p))*yes(p) + x\Delta out(p) + x*in(p) +$$
$$+ x*(out(p)\Delta yes(p)) =$$

$$= x*in(p) + x\Delta out(p) + (x*out(p))*yes(p) +$$
$$+ (x*out(p))\Delta yes(p) =$$

$$= x*in(p) + x\Delta out(p) + x*out(p) =$$

$$= x*in(p) + x = x.$$

We denote $[x].p$, $[x'].p.[x'']$ by p_1, p_2 respectively.

Proof of (69):

$$in(p_2) = in(p)\Delta(x*(in(p) + out(p)\Delta yes(p))) =$$

$$= (in(p)\Delta(x*in(p)))\Delta(x*(out(p)\Delta yes(p))) =$$

$$= (in(p)\Delta x)\Delta(x*(out(p)\Delta yes(p))) =$$

$$= in(p)\Delta(x + x*(out(p)\Delta yes(p))) = in(p)\Delta x = in(p_1).$$

Proof of (70):

$$out(p_2) = x\Delta out(p) + out(p) + x*in(p) +$$
$$+ x*(out(p)\Delta yes(p)) =$$

$$= out(p) + x + x*in(p) + x*(out(p)\Delta yes(p)) =$$

$$= out(p) + x = out(p_1) \quad .$$

6.3. Some others results

We state that for any operators p and q:

$$p =_{in} q <=> \bar{p}=\bar{q} \& in(p)=in(q) \quad ,$$

$$p =_{in,out} q <=> \bar{p}=\bar{q} \& in(p)=in(q) \& out(p)=out(q) \quad .$$

For any fundamental operator p , any operator q, any $x, y \in X$:

$$y < x\Delta out(p) => [x].p =_{in,out} [x].p.[y] \quad , \tag{71}$$

$$pNI q => [x].p.q =_{in} [x].p.[x*in(q)].q \tag{72}$$

The relation (63) may be represented by transformations

$$[x].p.q \rightarrow /(72)/$$
$$\rightarrow [x].p.[x^* in(q)].q \rightarrow /\Box(\bar{p},x), \Box(\bar{q},x^* in(q))/$$
$$\rightarrow [\bar{p}(x)].[\bar{q}(x^* in(q))] \rightarrow$$
$$\rightarrow [\bar{q}(x^* in(q)) + \bar{p}(x)] .$$

6.4. Polyvariant Mixed Computation

Note. In [6] a notion of polyvariant Mixed Computation was introduced. It was specified in [7] by following transformations:

$$[s].(u|p_1|p_2) \rightarrow ([s].u|[s].p_1|[s].p_2) ,$$
$$(u|p_1.[s_1]|p_2.[s_2]) \rightarrow (u|p_1.[s_1]|p_2.[s_2]).[s_1 \hat{\ } s_2] ,$$

where $\hat{\ }: S{\times}S{\rightarrow}S$, $graf(s_1 \hat{\ } s_2) = graf(s_1) \cap graf(s_2)$.

Let us introduce an operation $\hat{\ }: X{\times}X{\rightarrow}X$, for which the following axioms hold:

(INT1) $(x \hat{\ } y) + x = x$,

(INT2) $(x \hat{\ } y) + y = y$.

For any x,y:

$$x \hat{\ } y \leqslant x^* y , \qquad\qquad\qquad\qquad\qquad (73)$$
$$x \hat{\ } y \leqslant x , \qquad\qquad\qquad\qquad\qquad (74)$$
$$x \hat{\ } y \leqslant y , \qquad\qquad\qquad\qquad\qquad (75)$$
$$x + y + z\Delta(x \hat{\ } z) = x + y + z . \qquad\qquad (76)$$

Theorem 8. For any operators p_1,p_2, any recognizer u and any $x,x_1,x_2 {\in} X$:

$$[x].(u|p_1|p_2) =_{in} (\lfloor x \rfloor.u|\lfloor x \rfloor.p_1|\lfloor x \rfloor.p_2) ,$$
$$(u|p_1.[x_1]|p_2.[x_2]) =$$
$$= (u|p_1.[x_1]|p_2.[x_2]).[x_1 \hat{\ } x_2 \rfloor =$$
$$= (u|p_1.[x_1\Delta(x_1 \hat{\ } x_2)]|p_2.[x_2\Delta(x_1 \hat{\ } x_2)]).[x_1 \hat{\ } x_2 \rfloor$$

7. PROBLEMS

Note some problems for further investigations.

* Specification of programs by Mixed Computation algebras.

* Expanding of NDMS and quasi-Boolean algebras by introducing D, T and NOT.

* Introducing arrays as information elements.

* Representation of explicators systems.

* Design of transformational semantics of program languages which would allow to use the reserves of partial and parallel computation.

ACKNOWLEDGEMENT

The author would like to thank Academician A. Ershov for his insights and helpful discussions, referees of an earlier version who have provided useful guidance resulting in a greatly improved presentation, and M.Bulyonkov for great help in preparing the text.

REFERENCES

[1] Ershov A.P. On the partial computation principle. Information Processing Letters, April 1977, v.6, N 2, p. 38-41.

[2] Ershov A.P.,Itkin V.E. Correctness of mixed computation in Algol-like programs. - Lecture Notes in Comp. Sci., v.53, 1977, p.59-77.

[3] Ershov A.P. Mixed computation: potential applications and problems for study. Theoretical Computer Science, 1982, v.18, p.41-67.

[4] Itkin V.E. An algebra of mixed computation. - Reports of Academy of Sciences of the USSR, 1984, v.275, N 6,p. 1332-1336. (in Russian)

[5] Itkin V.E. Dynamic desequencing of programs by mixed computation method. - In: Theoretical Problems of Parallel Programming and Multiprocessing Computers. Novosibirsk, 1983, p. 110-126. (in Russian)

[6] Itkin V.E. On partial and mixed computation of programs. - In: Optimization and Transformations of Programs. Part 1. Novosibirsk, 1983, p. 17-30. (in Russian)

[7] Itkin V.E. An algebra of program desequencing. - In: Theoretical and Applied Problems of Parallel Information Processing. Novosibirsk, 1984, p. 3-24. (in Russian)

[8] Itkin V.E. An algebra and logic sequencing of functions superposition. In: Theoretical Problems of Information Processing. Novosibirsk, 1986, p. 18-33. (in Russian)

[9] Itkin   V.E.   An   axiomatization   of   inputs   and   outputs   of
    functions.   -   In: Methods   of   Programs   Translation   and
    Construction. Novosibirsk, 1986, p. 23-28. (in Russian)

[10] Itkin V.E. An axiomatization of the equality in an algebra of
     nondeterministic memory states. - In: Parallel and theoretical
     programming methods. Novosibirsk, 1987, p. 5-19. (in Russian)

[11] Kasyanov   V.N.   Towards   grounds   of   large-block   program
     transformation algorithms. Programmirovanie,   1981,   N   3,   p.
     16-25. (in Russian)

Partial Evaluation and Mixed Computation
D. Bjørner, A.P. Ershov and N.D. Jones (Editors)
Elsevier Science Publishers B.V. (North-Holland)
© IFIP, 1988

AUTOMATIC PROGRAM SPECIALIZATION:
A RE-EXAMINATION FROM BASIC PRINCIPLES

Neil D. JONES

DIKU, University of Copenhagen
Universitetsparken 1, DK-2100 Copenhagen Ø, Denmark
(e-mail: uucp: ... ! mcvax ! diku ! neil)

This paper describes in abstract terms the principles underlying one method for compiler generation by partial evaluation, the goal being to isolate fundamental concepts of automatic program transformation. The possibility in principle of generating compilers by partial evaluation was known in Japan and Russia as long ago as 1971, but the first realization of the idea in computational practice seems to have been the Copenhagen MIX project (in 1984, using first order pure LISP). Our early papers reported successful application of partial evaluation to compiling, compiler generation and compiler generator generation, given as input data an interpretive definition of a programming language; and naturally emphasized the particular techniques used in our system.

In the current paper we abstract those techniques to make them easier to apply to other languages or to adapt to other requirements. For the sake of notational and conceptual simplicity we limit the discussion to simple flow chart programs, but the ideas and algorithms have natural extensions to functional or logic programs. Special attention is paid to the phase called "binding time analysis": its exact mathematical nature, and its role in producing finite and efficient specialized programs.

The problem of *termination* has plagued most if not all work in this field and seems always to have been solved by *ad hoc* methods. The paper ends by outlining a new method for binding time analysis. This yields a specializer that is guaranteed to terminate provided the program being specialized has no infinite loops depending only on data available at specialization time. In particular, the compiler generated from a well-written interpreter will always terminate.

Keywords: Partial evaluation, program specialization, compiler generation, binding time analysis, data division, program point division, call unfolding, self application, partially static data structures.

1. Introduction and Preliminaries

The partial evaluation (or more generally: program specialization) project reported in [Jones, Sestoft, Søndergaard 85, 88]) was an attempt to see whether it was possible in practice to build a nontrivial program, here called "mix", satisfying the following three equations. As foreseen in [Futamura 71] and brought to western attention in [Ershov 77], their practical significance is to describe a way to use a partial evaluator such as mix and an interpreter defining a programming language as tools to compile, to generate compilers and even to generate a compiler generator:

target	=	L mix <interpreter, source program>
compiler	=	L mix <mix, interpreter>
cogen	=	L mix <mix, mix>

Review of notation: L program data = the result, if any, of running L-program "program" on input "data", and $<d_1, d_2>$ is a data value in the form of a pair. L-program "mix" is one which performs program specialization; it must satisfy

$$L \: l \: <d_1, d_2> \: \equiv \: L \: (\: L \: mix \: <l, d_1>) \: d_2$$

for any L-program l and data d_1, d_2, where $\equiv$ is equality of partial values.

The main goal of the MIX project was nontrivially to achieve the self application used in constructing compiler and cogen by applying the "Futamura projections" above, and it seems to have been the first successful such attempt. While the automatic program specialization techniques used there work reasonably well in practice, a number of more or less *ad hoc* design decisions were taken under way, many motivated by the need to repair observed inadequacies of the then current version of mix.

The sequence of papers [Jones, Sestoft, Søndergaard 85], [Sestoft 86], [Sestoft 88] and [Jones, Sestoft, Søndergaard 88] reveals a progressively better understanding of the problem area, and contains detailed descriptions of the techniques used by successive versions of mix. They naturally emphasize concrete and detailed system descriptions, since the purpose was to document the first successful experiments in compiler generation by partial evaluation.

Apparently vital decisions were to use *binding time analysis*, a prepass that classifies and marks function variables and program operations as "known" or "unknown" (later "static" or "dynamic"); and to mark each function call as "to be unfolded" or "to be suspended" (initially by hand). With time it became possible to automate this often tricky hand work, eventually yielding a completely automatic version of mix nontrivially satisfying the equations above, using methods described in [Sestoft 88] in this volume.

1.1 Goals of the Paper

After the initial pragmatic success the time has come to re-examine basic assumptions, and to answer the question: what *basic principles* are sufficient to construct a nontrivial and self applicable partial evaluator? This is desirable to make it easier for others to build analogous systems with differing languages, other basic assumptions or better worst case behavior. (or more generally: specialization of a program to a subset of all possible input data)

A main goal of this paper is thus to describe the principles underlying the MIX system in rather abstract terms, to isolate fundamental concepts rather than just giving the reader programs to copy or algorithms to code. On the other hand it is essential to describe the techniques concretely enough so they may be applied to other programming languages or adapted to meet other requirements.

Instead of "partial evaluation" we will use the term "program specialization", meaning the construction from a program $\mathfrak{L}$ and a given subset of all possible input data of a *residual program* $\mathfrak{L}'$ equivalent to $\mathfrak{L}$ when run on input from the subset. Program specialization is more general, since freezing one component of an argument pair to a constant value as in the Futamura projections is just one way of selecting an input subset. Further, the new term leaves open the possibility for more general program transformations than the straightforward symbolic execution implied by partial evaluation.

It is clearly important that our presentation be as independent as possible of specific details of programming language syntax and even semantics. It may seem strange that the discussion below is limited to simple flow chart programs, but this is done for the sake of notational and conceptual simplicity, so the ideas may be seen in their simplest manifestations. (We have recently seen that the ideas and algorithms have natural extensions to functional, logic, and term rewriting programs as well; some hints on how to do this will be given along the way.)

In the following *one* approach to program specialization is presented, essentially "polyvariant mixed computation" as reported in [Bulyonkov 84]. Successive concepts and techniques will as much as possible be brought in only on the basis of need. The reason is to distinguish necessary from arbitrary design decisions and so to avoid the problems of complexity that inevitably occur when documenting an existing system.

Our discussion is neither intended to cover all partial evaluation, program specialization and program transformation methods, nor all programming languages; for example some of Turchin's methods ([Turchin 80], [Turchin 86]) seem to use techniques essentially stronger than polyvariant specialization. A central aim is to identify fundamental concepts and terminology in order better to understand other systems for automatic program transformation, for example [Turchin 86], [Romanenko 88] or [Fuller, Abramsky 88]. In particular we precisely formulate concepts usually treated informally, including termination problems, the problem of "generalization" of computational configurations and the semantic foundations of binding time analysis.

Two fundamental assumptions dominate this paper, and differentiate it from much other work in program transformation. The first is that we are only interested in methods that are *completely automatic,* with no need at all for online user advice. The second is that our methods must be strong enough to compile by specializing an interpreter to a fixed source program (target = L mix <interpreter, source>).

Remarks: user advice is clearly undesirable during compiling, and quite impractical during compiler generation since it requires giving advice about mix itself, a program not written by the user.

A practical test of the adequacy of a mix program for a new language L is whether: ℓ = L mix <L-interpreter, ℓ> can be achieved, where "L-interpreter" is a metacircular interpreter for L (written in L) and ℓ is a nontrivial L-program. This signifies that mix has completely eliminated the computational overhead associated with the "interpretation loop". It is in our experience one of the most important hurdles in constructing a satisfactory mix program for a new language.

A more ambitious goal is to generate compilers by self application (as seen above: compiler = L mix <mix, interpreter>). The special problems caused by self application will be addressed in a forthcoming paper.

We pay special attention to "binding time analysis": its exact nature and its role in producing finite and satisfactorily efficient specialized programs. The paper ends by describing some new and improved algorithms for binding time analysis, and application of binding time analysis to the unfolding problem.

1.2 Prerequisites, Style, Thesis and Outline

We assume the reader to be generally knowledgeable about programming languages and to understand the elements of semantics (*e.g.* by [Gordon 79] or [Schmidt 86]), but will not assume specific knowledge about domains (set theory will be enough). Familiarity with partial evaluation (*e.g.* [Jones, Sestoft, Søndergaard 85 or 87] or [Ershov 82 or 77]) would be helpful but is not essential.

Higher order functions will be used for descriptive purposes but not in our languages. We write $X \to Y$ to denote the set of all total functions from X to Y, and $X - \to Y$ for the partial functions. A function type expression $X \to Y \to Z$ is parenthesized as $X \to (Y \to Z)$, and a double function application f x y is parenthesized (f x) y, so f, x, and y have types f: $X \to Y \to Z$, x: X, y: Y for some X,

Y, and Z. Parentheses will only be used when necessary to disambiguate expressions.

Style

Our aim throughout is to define concepts and algorithms as precisely as possible, partly in order to counter the vague operational discussions all too prevalent in this field. Definitions are consequently written with a certain amount of mathematical terminology and in the form "**Definition** ... □ ", where □ indicates the definition's end. Intuitive explanations are typically given afterwards, so the reader may be advised to read the definitions and ensuing discussions in parallel. We have also tried to formulate the various ideas as abstractly as possible, so the results and ideas can (we hope) be applied to a wide variety of special instances including ones not yet thought of. A Turing machine intepreter is used as a concrete example to make the formal definitions easier to read and interpret.

Thesis

Our main thesis is that partial evaluation can be done by three steps, all essentially independent of the particular programming language being transformed. The underlying ideas are not new, having been seen implicitly in several earlier works including [Beckman *et al* 76], [Ershov 77], [Turchin 80, 86] and even [Lombardi 67], and more explicitly in [Bulyonkov 84].

We consider only deterministic languages, and suppose that any program has a set of *program points* which include the "current control point" at any instant during program execution. Examples include labels in a flow chart language, function names in a functional language, or procedure names in a logic programming language. The essence can be briefly stated:

- Given a specified subset of input data, obtain a description of all states reachable in computations on inputs from the subset

- Redefine the program's control by incorporating parts of the data state into the control state, yielding several specialized versions of each of the program's control points (0, 1 or more); hence the term *polyvariant* specialization

- The resulting program usually contains many trivial transitions. Optimize it by traditional techniques, yielding the specialized (or *residual*) program.

Outline

The paper is organized as follows. In this section we define program, program specialization, *etc.*, introduce a simple flow chart language and give an example of an program written in it (an interpreter for Turing machine programs).

Section 2 develops a formal framework that abstracts principles and optimizing techniques used in most existing partial evaluators, in particular the division of data values (*e.g.* the store) into *static* and *dynamic* components. Using this framework, section 3 describes the principle of polyvariant specialization in abstract terms, independent of command or expression syntax.

Section 4 contains asyntax-independent abstract program specialization algorithm, together with an analysis of the problems involved for implementation practice. It ends with a more concrete algorithm for programs with assignments and goto's. In section 5 the problems involved in generating code for the residual program are discussed, and a complete program specialization algorithm with code generation is given.

Section 6 outlines some algorithms to obtain a program division such that specialization always terminates if the input program has no infinite loops depending only on data available at program specialization time.

Section 7 discusses rather less formally the question of whether the data divisions should be done by an *a priori* preprocessing step as in the Copenhagen "mix", or on-line as in most other partial evaluators. It concludes that program preprocessing is a great aid to solving termination and efficiency problems.

1.3   Programming Languages

We identify a programming language with its semantic function on whole programs (assumed to be computable). We assume the existence of a fixed "universal" data set V, capable of expressing both data and program texts in a variety of languages. (This is done in order to treat programs as data, as in the Futamura projections. If necessary, "type tags" could be used to distinguish among different sorts of objects.) A suitable V would be the set of all LISP lists.

Definition A *programming language* L is a function L: V − → V − → V. The *input-output function* computed by l is (L l): V − → V (which is partial since l may loop). The *well-formed* L-programs are those to which L assigns a meaning:

$$L\text{-programs} = domain\ (L).$$

□

1.4   Imperative Programming Languages

We consider languages with deterministic and purely linear control flow in order to express the essence of our ideas in the simplest possible framework, hoping the reader will be convinced that they may be generalized to other language types.

1.4.1 Intensional and Extensional

A program's "extension" has come to refer to its net effect (*what* it does - often computing an input-output function), while its "intension" refers to its text or appearance (a specification of *how* it does it).

The semantics of an entire program is thus its extension (alternate terms: denotation or meaning). A compiler must be semantics-preserving on whole programs to be correct, but in operation it is mainly concerned with intensional aspects, in particular how to translate syntactic phrases from the source program into target language fragments.

A compositional semantics links the two: it requires that every syntactic subphrase of the program has a denotation, and that these must satisfy the *denotational assumption:* the denotation of any composite syntactic phrase is a mathematical combination of the denotations of its subphrase.

This is the starting point of semantics-directed compiler generation: to derive target language code fragments from source program phrases, so that any target fragment's meaning correctly represents the denotation of the source program phrases from which it was compiled.

Most extensionally and abstractly, an imperative language consists of a set C whose elements we call *states*, together with a *transition function.* $nx : C \to C$ transforming the current program state into the next one. More formally: a *transition system* is a pair $\mathcal{l} = (C, nx : C \to C)$. For notational convenience we can define *transition relations* on C by:

$\mathcal{l} \vdash c_1 \to c_2$ if and only if $c_2 = nx(c_1)$

$\mathcal{l} \vdash c_0 \to^* c_n$ if and only if $\mathcal{l} \vdash c_i \to c_{i+1}$ for $i = 0,1,...,n-1$

$\mathcal{l} \vdash c_0 \to^+ c_n$ if and only if $\mathcal{l} \vdash c_i \to c_{i+1}$ for $i = 0,1,...,n-1$ and $n \geq 1$.   □

Termination may be identified with entering a trivial loop.

1.4.2 Program Points

For practical usage we would also need a finite way to describe states and the next state function, and a way to compute the latter. A first step towards finite represention is to regard each state as bipartite, with a *control* part ranging over a fixed and usually finite set of possibilities for any one program; and a *data* part, with infinitely many possible values. We make no assumptions as yet about program syntax or the exact nature of either the program points or the store.

Definition

1.   A *program* is a triple $\ell = (P, V, nx)$ where $nx : C \to C$ for some $C \subseteq P \times V$. P is called the set of *program points* and V, the set of *values* or *stores*.

2.   An *interface* for program ℓ is a pair of functions (in, out : $V \to V$). The *function computed by* ℓ with this interface is $L \ell : V - \to V$ defined by

$$L \ell v = \begin{array}{ll} out(v') & \text{if } \ell \vdash (p_0, in(v)) \to^* (p, v') \text{ and } \ell \vdash (p, v') \to (p, v') \\ \bot & \text{otherwise} \end{array}$$

3. $\text{Reach}(p_0, \ell) = \{ (p, v) \mid \ell \vdash (p_0, in(v_0)) \to^* (p, v) \text{ for some } v_0 \in V \}$ □

"In" maps program input into the initial store, and "out" maps its final store (if any) into the program output. Execution begins in state $(p_0, in(v))$ where v is the input, and it terminates by entering a "one instruction loop", in which case out(v') is the output value, given final store v'. Output is undefined ($\bot$) if the program does not terminate.

Reach$(p_0, \ell) \subseteq C$ is the set of all states reachable from initial program point p_0. Clearly C could be restricted to equal Reach(p_0, ℓ) without changing the program's input-output behavior.

"In" and "out" have been included for completeness, but in order to reduce the notational overhead we will assume in(v) = out(v) = v in the rest of the paper.

1.4.3   Intensional Imperative Programming Languages

In reality a program does not contain an abstract transition function, but rather each program point p is bound to a piece of "code" that defines the state transition when control reaches p. The definition below abstracts away from specific details of form and interpretation of code, since these vary greatly from one concrete imperative language to another.

In the following, sets $\mathcal{P}$, $\mathcal{V}$ are "universal sets" containing all possible program points and stores (resp.). The semantic function $[\![\_]\!]$ determines the connection between program text in Code and the state transition it specifies.

Definition

- An *intensional inperative programming language* consists of sets $\mathcal{P}$, Υ and Code, and a function $[\![\ \_\ ]\!] : \text{Code} \to \Upsilon \to \mathcal{P} \times \Upsilon$.

- An *intensional inperative program* is a triple $\mathit{l}_{code} = (P, V, code : P \to \text{Code})$ with $P \subseteq \mathcal{P}$ and $V \subseteq \Upsilon$.

- The *program defined by* l_{code} is $\mathit{l} = (P, V, nx)$ where for any p, v:

$$nx(p, v) = [\![code(p)]\!]\, v$$

□

1.5 Concrete Imperative Languages

For the reader's intuition we briefly mention some concrete imperative languages. The following has very familiar components and will be used in several examples.

1.5.1 A Language of Assignments and Goto's

Let $X_1, X_2, \ldots$ be *program variables* with values from a value set A and let the store be $V = A^*$, so $v = (x_1, x_2, \ldots) \in V$ contains the values of $X_1, X_2, \ldots$. Assume each program point p labels a *command*, with syntax given by:

<command>	::=	X_i := <expression> ; <command>
	|	**goto** <program point>
	|	**if** <expression> **then** <command> **else** <command>
<expression>	::=	X_i (i = 1, 2, ...)
	|	B(<expression>,..., <expression>)

Here expressions are constructed from basic functions $B : A^* - \to A$ and program variables $X_1, X_2, \ldots$ The effect of a command is to perform a series of tests and assignments, followed by a **goto**. A concrete program specifies an abstract program $\mathit{l} = <P, V, nx>$ where the next state nx(p, v) is obtained by executing the command at program point p in the obvious way .

1.5.2 Other Imperative Languages

Other quite different ways to use concrete syntax to specify "nx" could well be imagined. For an essentially equivalent example, consider first-order *tail recursive* functional programs of the form

$$f_1(X_1, X_2,...) = \text{expression}_1$$
$$\ldots$$
$$f_n(X_1, X_2,...) = \text{expression}_n$$

where each expression$_i$ has syntax:

<expression>	::=	f_i(<simple_exp>,...., <simple_exp>) (i = 1, 2, ...)
	|	**if** <simple_exp> **then** <expression> **else** <expression>
<simple_exp>	::=	X_1 | X_2 |...
	|	B(<simple_exp>,...., <simple_exp>)

In this case the store V will for each f_i contain sequences of length equal to the number of its arguments.

Further examples correspond to building the runtime structures (stacks, heaps, *etc.*) of traditional implementation methods into the store. For instance a target language for non tail recursive first order functional programs could use a "store" which is a single stack containing: argument values, temporary results and program points ("return addresses").

Another example: consider an environment-based intermediate language for evaluating lambda expressions, for instance the CAM or SECD machine. Let a "value" be either an atomic value or a "closure" of form ($\lambda x.\text{expression}$, environment), where an environment has form   [Variable$_1 \mapsto$ value$_1$, ..., Variable$_n \mapsto$ value$_n$]. In this case a "program point" would naturally be a subexpression of the initial lambda expression, and the "store" could consist of an environment together with a stack of pending values waiting to be evaluated. Representing such an evaluator in the form $\ell = < P, V, nx >$ is straightforward.

Similar considerations could be applied to programs in the form of term rewriting systems with a fixed deterministic evaluation order. Here a "program point" could be the skeleton of a term, in which defined function names are prerserved but atomic values are replaced by variables.

1.6   Example: An Interpreter for Turing Programs

The following concrete program will be used to illustrate several points later in the article. It interprets programs for a Turing machine (Post's variant) with tape alphabet A = {0, 1, B}, where B stands for "blank". A program Q is a list $I_0\ I_1\ ...\ I_n$

of instructions each of form: *right, left, write a* or *if a goto I*, where I is the number of the successor instruction in Q.

A computational state consists of a current instruction I_i, about to be executed and an infinite tape

$$... a_{-2} \, a_{-1} \, a_0 \, a_1 \, a_2 ...$$

Only finitely many of whose squares contain symbols a_i not equal to B, and one of which is the *scanned square* a_0.

Instruction effects: *write a* changes a_0 to a, *right* and *left* change the scanning point, and *if a goto i* causes the next control point to be I_i in case $a_0 = a$; in all other cases the next control point is the following instruction (if any).

The input to program Q is $a_0 a_1 ... a_n \in \{0, 1\}^*$, and the initial tape contains B in positions $a_{n+1}, a_{n+2}, ..., a_{-1}, a_{-2}, ...$ Program output is the final value of $a_0 \, a_1 ...$ (up to and including the last nonblank symbol) and is produced when there is no next instruction to be executed.

Example: Program Q is: *1: if 0 goto 4 2: right 3: goto 1 4: write 1,* a program that finds the first 0 in T and converts it to 1 (and goes into an infinite loop if none is found). If the input to Q is 110101, the output will be 1101.

The interpreter has a variable Q for the whole Turing program, and the control point is represented via a suffix Qtail of Q (the instructions remaining to be executed). The tape is represented by variables Left, Right with values in A*, where Right equals $a_0 \, a_1 \, a_2 ...$ (up to and including the last nonblank symbol) and Left similarly represents $a_{-1} \, a_{-2} \, a_{-3} ...$ (note that the order is reversed). The corresponding abstract imperative program has

- program points P = {Run, Cont, Hop, Test}

- store set V = (Program × A*) ∪ A* ∪ (Program × Program × A* × A*)
  (respectively interpreter inputs; outputs; and other states with current values of Q, Qtail, Left and Right)

- interface
in(Q, Right)	=	(Q, Q, emptytape, Right)
out(Q, Qtail, Left, Right)	=	Right

Interpreter in intensional form:

Run: **if** Qtail = empty **then goto** Run **else**
      if *"right"* = head(Qtail)
          then   Left := cons(head(Right), Left);
                         Right := tail(Right);   **goto** Cont **else**
      if *"left "* = head(Qtail)
          then   Right:= cons(head(Left), Right);
                         Left := tail(Left);   **goto** Cont **else**
      if *"write a"*= head(Qtail)
          then   Right := cons(Symbol(Qtail), tail(Right)); **goto** Cont **else**
      if *"goto I"* = head(Qtail)   **then**   **goto** Hop **else**
      if *"if a goto I"* = head(Qtail)   **then**   **goto** Test **else**
          Right := cons(Right, Right); **goto** Run;   { abort }

Cont: Qtail := tail(Qtail); **goto** Run;
Hop: Qtail := nth(Q, successor(head(Qtail))); **goto** Run;
Test: **if** head(Right) = symbol(Qtail) **then**   **goto** Hop **else goto** Cont;

Various base functions are used: symbol(*"if a goto I"*...) = symbol(*"write a"*...) = a
and successor(*goto I*) = successor(*if a goto I*) = I; nth(Q, I) yields the I'th
instruction in program Q; and string manipulating functions: head($a_0 a_1 ... a_n$) = a_0
and head(empty) = B, tail($a_0 a_1 ... a_n$) = $a_1 ... a_n$ and tail(empty) = B, and cons(a,
$a_0 a_1 ... a_n$) = a $a_0 a_1 ... a_n$.

2.   Program Specialization

The term "program specialization" implies that a *source program* is to be
specialized with respect to known information about its input data (this part we call
static), while the remainder will be supplied to the *residual program* resulting from
specialization (this part we call dynamic).

An important class of specialization algorithms work by "polyvariant"
specialization as described in [Bulyonkov 84]). The method is based on dividing the
possible run time values associated with each program point into static and dynamic
parts. A residual program point consists of a source program point, *specialized* to a
value of static data that can occur at that point in some computation on the given set
of input data. The residual program may contain zero, one or more specialized
versions of the same source point.

2.1 Data Divisions and Specialized Programs

The following formalization of the idea of dividing data is simply a product decomposition of value set V, as seen in recursive functions or category theory. A domain-based approach to program specialization can be found in [Launchbury 88].

Definition A tuple div = (stat: $V \to V_s$, dyn: $V \to V_d$, pair: $V_s \times V_d \to V$) which for any $v \in V$, $v_s \in V_s$, $v_d \in V_d$ satisfies the following is called a *division*:

$$\begin{aligned}
\text{pair (stat v, dyn v)} &= v \\
\text{stat (pair}(v_s, v_d)) &= v_s \\
\text{dyn (pair}(v_s, v_d)) &= v_d
\end{aligned}$$
□

Values in V_s will be called *static values* with typical element v_s (possibly decorated, for example v'_s, v''_s, v_{1s}, *etc.*), while those in V_d (typical element v_d) will be called *dynamic*. The intention is that static value v_s is the part of the state of program l which will be known at program specialization time.

Definition Let div = (stat, dyn, pair) be a division of V. Program l_{vs} is a *residual program for* l *(or specialization of* l *to* v_s *)* if and only if for any $v_d \in V_d$,

$$L\, l_{vs}\ v_d \equiv l\ \text{pair}(v_s, v_d)$$

where $v \equiv v'$ is equality of partial values (true if v and v' are defined and equal, or both undefined). □

The static input v_s is known at specialization time, and the dynamic input v_d is known at run time.

2.2 An Example of Program Specialization

Let l be the Turing machine interpreter from section 1.6. The input to the interpreter is a Turing machine program and the nonblank portion of its initial tape: a pair (Q, Right) $\in$ V = Programs $\times$ A*. Compiling can be done by specializing l to a fixed Turing program Q, yielding an equivalent flow chart program l_Q. A suitable input data division is div = (stat, dyn, pair) where stat(Q, Right) = Q, dyn(Q, Right) = Right and pair(Q, Right) = (Q, Right).

Now let Q be

$$Q = 1\text{: } if\,0\ goto\ 4\quad 2\text{: } right\quad 3\text{: } goto\ 1\quad 4\text{: } write\ 1,$$

a program that finds the first 0 in T and converts it to 1 (and goes into an infinite loop if none is found). The following is the result of specializing interpreter ℓ to Q by the methods of the next section. The net effect has been to compile Q from "Turing code" into equivalent flow chart code by specializing the interpreter to Q.

Run_1:   **if** first(Right) = 0 **then** **goto** Run_4 **else**   **goto** Run_2;
Run_2:   Left := cons(head(Right), Left); Right := tail(Right); **goto** Run_1;
Run_4:   Right := cons(1, tail(Right));   **goto** Run_5;
Run_5:   **goto** Run_5;

2.3 Examples of Divisions

In section 2.1 a "division" was simply a device used to define program specialization. It has, however, a much wider significance: polyvariant specialization algorithms including [Jones, Sestoft, Søndergaard 85, 88] construct ℓ_{vs} from ℓ and v_s by a state division step followed by an optimization step. The first step divides into static and dynamic parts the program's computational states, *e.g.* the stores, environments, control points, *etc.* traditionally used by interpreters or denotational semantics, and then incorporates part of the data values into the control. (In computational practice the two steps are usually intermingled.)

As defined earlier, a division div = (stat, dyn, pair) is essentially a product decomposition of V with projection functions stat, dyn and pairing function pair. The following examples are particularly relevant to program specialization. We begin with two extreme cases, where • stands for "not present".

A.   <u>The minimal division</u> div = (stat : $V \rightarrow \{\bullet\}$, dyn : $V \rightarrow V$, pair: $\{\bullet\} \times V \rightarrow V$) where:

$$
\begin{array}{lcl}
stat\ (v) & = & \bullet \\
dyn\ (v) & = & v \\
pair\ (\bullet, v) & = & v
\end{array}
$$

In this case no information at all is static. Clearly ℓ_{vs} must compute the same input-output function as ℓ.

B.   <u>The maximal division</u> div = (stat: $V \rightarrow V$, dyn: $V \rightarrow \{\bullet\}$, pair: $V \times \{\bullet\} \rightarrow V$) where:

$$
\begin{array}{lcl}
stat\ (v) & = & v \\
dyn\ (v) & = & \bullet \\
pair\ (v, \bullet) & = & v
\end{array}
$$

In this case all input information is static. Clearly residual program ℓ_{vs} can be of the form **"write** answer" if L ℓ v_s is defined, or **"loop forever"** if undefined.

C.   Projection onto first and second components with
$div = (stat: A \times A \to A, dyn: A \times A \to A, pair: A \times A \to A \times A)$ defined by:

$$stat(v_1, v_2) = v_1$$
$$dyn(v_1, v_2) = v_2$$
$$pair(v_1, v_2) = (v_1, v_2)$$

This was implicitly used in the Futamura projections cited in the introduction.

D.   A generalization: selection of tuple components

Let $V = A*$ where $A*$ is the set of sequences $a_1...a_n$ $(n \geq 0)$ of elements from A. We write $\underline{a}$ for a typical element of A, and let $\underline{a} \downarrow i = a_i$ if $\underline{a} = a_1...a_n$ and $1 \leq i \leq n$ (undefined otherwise).
Let S, D be two symbols, which we will interpret as signifying "static" and "dynamic", respectively, and let $\underline{b} \in \{S, D\}*$. The idea is that $\underline{b}$ contains S's to indicate which components of an input tuple $a_1...a_n$ are to be included in v_s, and D's to indicate those included in v_d. For example $\underline{b} = SD$ is appropriate to the Futamura projections of the introduction.
    More formally, let $\underline{a}$ **selectS** $\underline{b}$ be (for $\underline{a} \in V = A*$ and $\underline{b} \in \{S, D\}*$) the subsequence of components $\underline{a} \downarrow i$ from $\underline{a}$ such that $\underline{b} \downarrow i$ equals S, and let $\underline{a}$ **selectD** $\underline{b}$ be analogous for D. We now consider divisions $div_{\underline{b}} = (stat_{\underline{b}}, dyn_{\underline{b}}, pair_{\underline{b}})$ where $stat_{\underline{b}}, dyn_{\underline{b}}, pair_{\underline{b}} : A* \times A* \to A*$ and

$$stat_{\underline{b}} (\underline{a}) = \underline{a} \text{ selectS } \underline{b}$$
$$dyn_{\underline{b}} (\underline{a}) = \underline{a} \text{ selectD } \underline{b}$$
$$pair_{\underline{b}} (v_s, v_d) = \text{ - straightforward but a trifle messy and so omitted -}$$

E.   Term decomposition

Let Σ be a many-sorted signature (*e.g.* as in [ADJ 78]), and let $Z = \{Z_1, Z_2,...\}$ be a countable set of sorted *term variables* (not to be confused with program variables). Define T_Σ and $T_\Sigma(Z)$ to be the sets of well-formed terms over Σ (respectively without and with variables).
    We give a single example, natural for the environment structures typically used in interpreters; a more general formulation is easily defined but requires a more complex notation. In this case Σ can be described by

sorts   Name, Value, Environment
variables $Z_1, Z_2, ...$: Value
operators
constants: john, mary,... : Name
                 0, 1, 2,...   : Value
                 "nil"   : Environment
nonconstant: bind   : Name × Value × Environment → Environment

Now let div = (stat: $V \to V_s$, dyn: $V \to V_d$, pair : $V_s \times V_d \to V$) as below, where the n_i and v_i are constants of sort Name and Value, respectively:

$$
\begin{aligned}
V &= \quad \{ \, t \in T_\Sigma \mid t \text{ has sort Environment}) \\
V_s &= \quad \{ \, \text{bind}(n_1, Z_1, \text{bind}(..., \text{bind}(n_m, Z_m, \text{nil})...))) \mid m \geq 0 \} \\
V_d &= \quad \{ \, \theta : \text{Subst} = Z \to T_\Sigma \, \}
\end{aligned}
$$

stat(bind(n_1, v_1, bind(..., bind(n_m, v_m, nil)...)))) =   { value v_i is replaced
      bind(n_1, Z_1, bind(..., bind(n_m, Z_m, nil)...))   by placeholder Z_i}

dyn(bind(n_1, v_1, bind(..., bind(n_m, v_m, nil)...)))) = [$Z_1 \mapsto v_1$, ..., $Z_m \mapsto v_m$]
                                               { gives the values of the placeholders }
pair(v_s, θ) = $\theta(v_s)$

Informally: input data is a list of name - value pairs of variable length. At program specialization time one specifies the names but not their corresponding values, and the values are filled in at run time.

3. Polyvariant Specialization of Imperative Programs

To begin with we consider programs only extensionally, without considering program syntax at all aside from program points. Surprisingly, this meager framework is enough to describe the essence of polyvariant program specialization, which we divide into three phases for conceptual clarity (in practice they will be combined into a single, more complex phase, described in later sections).

Suppose the given program ℓ has initial program point p_0 and that it is to be specialized with respect to static value v_{0s}. Then residual program ℓ_{v0s} can be built as follows:

I.   Construct a first residual program by shifting static data from store into control.

II. Restrict the residual program to contain only program points reachable from (p_0, v_{0s}).

III. Eliminate trivial computational steps by compressing transitions.

3.1 Transition Compression and Restriction to Reachable Program Points

We describe several ways in which one program can realize or simulate another, beginning with II and III since they are simpler. Intuitively: If ℓ' is obtained from ℓ by removing all pairs (p, v) not reachable from initial program point p_0, then $p_0 : \ell$ **reach** ℓ'. And if ℓ' is obtained from ℓ by replacing some multiple-step transitions by single steps, then $\ell \rightsquigarrow \ell'$.

Definition $p_0 : \ell$ **reach** ℓ' if $\ell = (P, V, nx: C \rightarrow C)$, $\ell' = (P, V, nx': C' \rightarrow C')$ where $C' = \text{Reach}(p_0, \ell)$ and nx' is the restriction of nx to C'. $\square$

Definition If $\ell = (P, V, nx:C \rightarrow C)$, $\ell' = (P', V, nx':C' \rightarrow C')$ and $C' \subseteq C \subseteq P \times V$ then $\ell \rightsquigarrow \ell'$ if

1. $\ell' \vdash (p_1, v_1) \rightarrow (p_2, v_2)$ implies $\ell \vdash (p_1, v_1) \rightarrow^+ (p_2, v_2)$, and

2. $\ell \vdash (p_1, v_1) \rightarrow (p_2, v_2)$ implies there are (p_0, v_0), (p_3, v_3) such that $\ell \vdash (p_0, v_0) \rightarrow^* (p_1, v_1) \rightarrow (p_2, v_2) \rightarrow^* (p_3, v_3)$ and $\ell' \vdash (p_0, v_0) \rightarrow (p_3, v_3)$
$\square$

Condition 1 requires every transition by ℓ' to correspond to one or more transitions by ℓ, while condition 2 requires that all transitions by ℓ are represented in ℓ'. Note that $\ell \rightsquigarrow \ell'$ does not determine ℓ' uniquely from ℓ.

3.2 Shifting the Boundary between Data and Control

Definition A *program division* of P, V is a triple

$$d = (\sigma : P \rightarrow V \rightarrow V_s, \ \delta : P \rightarrow V \rightarrow V_d, \ \pi : P \rightarrow V_s \times V_d \rightarrow V)$$

such that for every program point p, $(\sigma p, \delta p, \pi p)$ is a division of V. $\square$

To aid readability, we often write $(\sigma_p, \delta_p, \pi_p)$ instead of $(\sigma p, \delta p, \pi p)$.

A state in program l is a pair (p, v) where p is the control and v the store. Let d be a program division of P, V. We will construct $\mathit{l} \setminus d$, a specialized (residual) version of l, by splitting each program point's store into static and dynamic parts, and incorporating the static parts into the program points of the specialized program. The correspondence is:

$$(p, v) = (p, \pi_p(\sigma_p v, \delta_p v)) \text{ in } \mathit{l} \quad \Leftrightarrow \quad ((p, \sigma_p v), \delta_p v) \text{ in } \mathit{l} \setminus d$$

or, writing   div = (stat, dyn, pair) for $(\sigma_p, \delta_p, \pi_p)$:

$$(p, v) = (p, \text{pair(stat } v, \text{dyn } v)) \text{ in } \mathit{l} \quad \Leftrightarrow \quad ((p, \text{stat } v), \text{dyn } v) \text{ in } \mathit{l} \setminus d$$

In words, program specialization is a kind of "reassociation" with respect to the store division at each program point p, where the pair $(p, \text{stat } v)$ is a specialized version of program point p, regarded as a single program point in $\mathit{l} \setminus d$. (*Remark:* we use symbol "$\setminus$" since the splitting involved in constructing $\mathit{l} \setminus d$ seems dual to factoring a set into equivalence classes $A / \equiv$ by an equivalence relation $\equiv$ as is done in abstract algebra.)

Transitions by $\mathit{l} \setminus d$ are in a one to one correspondence with those of l:

$$\mathit{l} \vdash (p, v) \rightarrow (p', v') \quad \Leftrightarrow \quad \mathit{l} \setminus d \vdash ((p, \sigma_p v), \delta_p v) \rightarrow ((p', \sigma_{p'} v'), \delta_{p'} v')$$

The question could be raised: why does every program point p have its own division $(\sigma_p, \delta_p, \pi_p)$ - wouldn't it be simpler to use the same store at all program points and so just one division? One reason is that the store division into static and dynamic might vary. For example if X is static and Y is dynamic then the assignment $X := Y; Y := 1$ would reverse their status. Another reason is the application to functional programs, whose program points are names of defined functions and whose "stores" are environments binding formal parameters to their values. Different functions have different parameters, so it is entirely natural that they have different divisions.

We now proceed to define "reassociation" formally and a bit more generally. One way a program can realize or simulate another is a quite classical "behavior preserving function": the homomorphism of abstract algebra:

Definition h: $\mathfrak{l}$ **hom** $\mathfrak{l}'$ if $\mathfrak{l} = (C, nx)$ to $\mathfrak{l}' = (C', nx')$ and $h : C \rightarrow C'$ is a function such that for all $c \in C$, $h(nx(c)) = nx'(h(c))$. If so, h is called a *homomorphism* from $\mathfrak{l}$ to $\mathfrak{l}'$. Further, $h : \mathfrak{l}$ **hom** $\mathfrak{l}'$ is said to be *onto* if h is an onto function, *i.e.* $C' = \{h(c) \mid c \in C\}$. □

We now describe shifting the boundary between p and v, for example by incorporating the static part of the store into the control or *vice versa*. In the following, f(p,v) is the control point in transformed program $\mathfrak{l}'$ and g(p,v) is the store.

Definition

1. f, g : $\mathfrak{l}$ **shift** $\mathfrak{l}'$ if $\mathfrak{l} = (P, V, nx)$, $\mathfrak{l}' = (P', V', nx')$ and f: $P \times V \rightarrow P'$, g: $P \times V \rightarrow V'$ are functions such that h: $\mathfrak{l}$ **hom** $\mathfrak{l}'$ is onto, where h is defined by

$$h(p,v) = (f(p,v), g(p,v))$$

2. Let $d = (\sigma, \delta, \pi)$ be a program division of P, V. Then $d : \mathfrak{l}$ **DCshift** $\mathfrak{l}'$, read as: $\mathfrak{l}$ is obtained from $\mathfrak{l}'$ by a *data to control shift* , if $\mathfrak{l} = (P, V, nx)$, $\mathfrak{l}' = ((P \times V_s), V_d, nx')$ and h: $\mathfrak{l}$ **hom** $\mathfrak{l}'$ is onto, where for any p, v

$$h(p, v) = ((p, \sigma_p v), \delta_p v)$$

The transition function of $\mathfrak{l}'$ may be defined by

$$nx'((p, v_s), v_d) = ((p', \sigma_{p'} v'), \delta_{p'} v') \text{ where } (p', v') = nx(p, \pi_p(v_s, v_d))$$

□

Clearly a data to control shift is a shift. Analogously, one could define a *control to data shift* using $\mathfrak{l} = ((P \times V_s), V_d, nx)$, $\mathfrak{l}' = (P, V, nx')$ and

$$h((p, v_s), v_d) = (p, \pi_p(v_s, v_d))$$

3.3 State Division as a General Method for Program Specialization

The three step approach to polyvariant specialization described in the beginning of this section can now be stated more concisely. The term "polyvariant" comes from "polyvariant mixed computation" as used by [Bulyonkov 84] and others, and alludes to the fact that the same p may be specialized to several values of v_s (*e.g.* "Run" in the example).

Definition $v_{0s} : \mathfrak{l}$ **polyspec** $\mathfrak{l}_{v0s}$ if $\mathfrak{l}$ is a program with initial program point p_0 and there is a program division d and programs $\mathfrak{l}_1, \mathfrak{l} \setminus d$ such that the following hold:

I. $d : \mathfrak{l}$ **DCshift** $\mathfrak{l}_1$,

II. $(p_0, v_{0s}) : \mathfrak{l}_1$ **reach** $(\mathfrak{l} \setminus d)$ and

III. $(\mathfrak{l} \setminus d) \rightsquigarrow \mathfrak{l}_{v0s}$ □

In practice $\mathfrak{l}_1$ will often be infinite, so steps I and II are combined: $\mathfrak{l} \setminus d$ is computed directly from $\mathfrak{l}$, generating only those specialized control points (p, v_s) reachable from (p_0, v_{0s}).

Depending on the choice of program division d, residual program $\mathfrak{l} \setminus d$ (and so $\mathfrak{l}_{v0s}$) may or may not be finite. This is so important for practical purposes that we elevate it to a definition: d is *finite* if every possible $\mathfrak{l} \setminus d$ (and so $\mathfrak{l}_{v0s}$) is finite:

Definition   Let $d = (\sigma, \delta, \pi)$ be a program division, let $\mathfrak{l} = (P, V, nx)$ be a program with initial program point p_0. We say d is *finite* for if for every $v_{0s} \in V_s$, the following set is finite:

$$\{ (p, \sigma_p v) \mid (p, v) \in \text{Reach}((p_0, v_{0s}), \mathfrak{l}_1) \}$$

□

Finiteness of d requires that for all static inputs v_{0s}, there are only finitely many static parts among all states reachable from inputs of form $\text{pair}(v_{0s}, v_d)$, and so only finitely many specialized program points in $\mathfrak{l} \setminus d$ as constructed above.

3.4 Discussion and the Example Revisited

We now show how the residual program of section 2.2 can be derived from the interpreter of section 1.5. Recall the interpreter $\mathfrak{l}$ with program text:

```
Run:  if  Qtail = empty then goto Run  else
          if "right" = head(Qtail)
              then    Left := cons(head(Right), Left); Right := tail(Right);  goto Cont  else
          if "left" = head(Qtail)
              then    Right:= cons(head(Left), Right); Left := tail(Left);    goto Cont  else
          if "write a" = head(Qtail)
              then    Right := cons(symbol(Qtail), tail(Right));              goto Cont  else
          if "goto I"= head(Qtail)       then goto Hop   else
          if "if a goto I" = head(Qtail) then goto Test  else
              Right := cons(Right, Right); goto Run;                         { abort }
Cont: Qtail := tail(Qtail); goto Run;
Hop:  Qtail := nth(Q, successor(head(Qtail)));          goto Run;
Test: if head(Right) = symbol(Qtail) then                goto Hop else goto Cont;
```

Note that static input Q is unchanged, and Qtail is always a suffix of Q, so we choose a division making Q and Qtail static in all stores. On the other hand Right is initially a dynamic input, and Left can be built up dynamically, so we choose to make them dynamic. Thus as program division we choose $d = (\sigma, \delta, \pi)$ where for all program points p,

$$\sigma_p(Q, Qtail, Left, Right) = (Q, Qtail)$$
$$\delta_p(Q, Qtail, Left, Right) = (Left, Right)$$
$$\pi_p((Q, Qtail), (Left, Right)) = (Q, Qtail, Left, Right)$$

This determines the form of ℓ_1 and $\ell \setminus d$, whose labels have form (p, (Q, Qtail)) for $p \in$ {Run, Cont, Hop, Test}. For readability we write this as p_{QQtail}. The Turing machine program of section 2.2 was:

$$Q = 1: if\, 0\, goto\, 4 \quad 2: right \quad 3: goto\, 1 \quad 4: write\, 1$$

Reachable states will be of form (p_{QQtail}, (Left, Right)) where Qtail is one of Q's five suffixes, which we dub Q1 (= Q), Q2, Q3, Q4 and Q5 (= empty). There are thus in all 20 possible residual labels.

Note that much of the commands' computations depend only on the static data Q and Qtail: all at Cont and Hop, and the tests on the Turing command type at Run. This means that those commands assigning values to Qtail will not be performed at all in the residual program, and others can be much simplified. The resulting program $\ell \setminus d$, is thus (before transition compression):

```
Run_QQ:    goto Test_QQ;
Test_QQ:   if head(Right) = 0 then goto Hop_QQ else goto Cont_QQ;
Hop_QQ:    goto Run_QQ4;
Cont_QQ:   goto Run_QQ2;
Run_QQ2:   Right:= cons(head(Left), Right);  Left := tail(Left); goto Cont_QQ2;
Cont_QQ2:  goto Run_QQ3;
Run_QQ3:   goto Hop_QQ3;
Hop_QQ3:   goto Run_QQ;
Run_QQ4:   Right := cons(1, tail(Right));   goto Cont_QQ4;
Cont_QQ4:  goto Run_QQ5;
Run_QQ5:   goto Run_QQ5;
```

If all transitions into Cont, Hop, Test and Run_{QQ3} are removed by compression, the result is isomorphic with that of section 2.2:

```
Run_QQ:    if head(Right) = 0 then goto Run_QQ4 else goto Run_QQ2;
Run_QQ2:   Right:= cons(head(Left), Right); Left := tail(Left); goto Run_QQ;
Run_QQ4:   Right := cons(1, tail(Right));   goto Run_QQ5;
Run_QQ5:   goto Run_QQ5;
```

4.   Algorithms for Program Specialization

In section 3 we argued that the essence of polyvariant program specialization is a reassociation to shift the boundary between control and data, followed by simple optimizations. In this section we give computational procedures for specializing, again in as abstract terms as possible. The essence of the problem and the main emphasis of this section is to collect the set of specialized program points (p, v_s) of the residual program. The next section treats code generation.

4.1   Overview

Given L-program ℓ, program division $d = (\sigma, \delta, \pi)$ and initial static information $v_{0s} \in V_s$, program specialization to ℓ_{v0s} with $v_{0s} : \ell$ **polyspec** ℓ_{v0s} can in principle be done as in section 3.3:

    1.   Given ℓ, select a program division d, thus determining the ℓ_1 satisfying
        $d : \ell$ **DCshift** ℓ_1
    2.   Given v_{0s}, construct $\ell \setminus d$ such that $(p_0, v_{0s}) : \ell_1$ **reach** $(\ell \setminus d)$
    3.   Obtain residual program ℓ_{v0s} with $(\ell \setminus d) \rightsquigarrow \ell_{v0s}$ by compressing
        transition chains

Step 1 determines how program points are to be specialized - how large a part of a store v at any program point p is to be regarded as static, and how much is to be dynamic and so present in the residual program. An additional input to step 2 is v_{0s}, the static part of ℓ's input. This step obtains $\ell \setminus d$ by restricting the program points of ℓ_1 to those $(p, \sigma_p v)$ where state (p, v) is reachable in a computation from initial program point p_0 on static input v_{0s}. Step 3 optimizes by compressing transition chains. The total effect is to do as much of ℓ's computation as possible on the basis of the known static parts $\sigma_p v$ appearing in the specialized program points $(p, \sigma_p v)$.

An optimized ℓ_{v0s} can be faster than ℓ for two reasons:

1.   Computations involving only the static part of the store are not performed at run time - they are done during program specialization.

2.   Transitions of ℓ that do not change the dynamic part of the store can be compressed in ℓ_{v0s}, since they simply go from one residual program point to another without changing the store.

Many existing partial evaluators work in essentially this way, although the three steps above are usually more or less intermingled. A practical reason: we cannot build ℓ_1 with $(p_0,v_{0s}) : \ell_1$ **reach** $(\ell \setminus d)$ by constructing ℓ_1 first, since it is nearly always infinite. In most published accounts, d is not built in advance. The static part of data is often selected *on-line*, and $\ell \setminus d$ is optimized during construction rather than afterwards.

We argue in section 7 that an efficient and reliably terminating program specializers cannot be based on a program division d computed on-line during program specialization, but requires a separate preprocessing phase such as the "binding time analysis" used in the Copenhagen MIX. Discussion of another reason for preprocessing: to make self-application possible and acceptably efficient, will appear in [Bondorf, Jones, Mogensen, Sestoft 88].

4.2 On the Choice of Program Division

The choice of d is obviously of vital importance. To gain a more efficient $\ell_{v_{0s}}$, we want each static projection function σ_p chosen so that $\sigma_p v$ describes as *large* a part of v as possible, so there will be much statically computable data, and long static transition chains may be compressed away at specialization time, as was seen in the example of section 3.4.

On the other hand, in practice it is of course essential that $\ell_{v_{0s}}$ be finite, which argues that the static projections should be chosen so that $\sigma_p v$ does not describe *too large* a part of v. In section 6 we discuss binding time analysis: how to obtain a d satisfying these contradictory demands.

4.3 An Abstract Algorithm

The construction of program $\ell \setminus d$ in section 3.3 is described in a nonalgorithmic way. Further, it *cannot* be made totally algorithmic, since its program points are the reachable pairs in $P \times V_s$:

$$\{ (p, \sigma_p v) \mid \ell \vdash (p_0, \text{pair}(v_{0s}, v_d)) \rightarrow^* (p, v) \text{ for some } v_d \in V_d \} = P'$$

where pair is the input pairing function π_{p0}. Constructing these requires in principle anticipating all runtime stores possible during computations with static input v_{0s}, which is of course unrealistic in practice and undecidable in theory as well.

4.3.1 Collecting Specialized Program Points

We get around this difficulty by two means. The first is to define a superset of P', defined exclusively in terms of *the information available at program specialization time* (static values and program points). Using specialized program point sets larger than P' above may yield a larger ℓ_{v0s} than that of section 3.3, but there is clearly no danger of obtaining an incorrect specialized program.

To see how to construct the superset, define a binary relation $\looparrowright_0$ on $P \times V_s$ by:

$$\ell \vdash (p, v_s) \looparrowright_0 (p', v'_s) \quad \text{iff } \ell \vdash (p_0, v_0) \to^* (p, v) \to (p', v')$$
$$\text{for } v_0, v, v' \in V \text{ such that } v_s = \sigma_p v \text{ and } v'_s = \sigma_{p'} v'.$$

It is easy to see that $P' = \{ (p, v_s) \mid \ell \vdash (p_0, v_{0s}) \looparrowright_0^* (p', v'_s)\}$, but this as mentioned depends on data not available at program specialization time. Weakening the relation as follows will give a larger but more tractable program point set:

$$\ell \vdash (p, v_s) \looparrowright_1 (p', v'_s) \quad \text{iff } \ell \vdash (p, v) \to (p', v')$$
$$\text{for some } v, v' \in V \text{ such that } v_s = \sigma_p v \text{ and } v'_s = \sigma_{p'} v'.$$

Clearly $P'' = \{ (p, v_s) \mid \ell \vdash (p_0, v_{0s}) \looparrowright_1^* (p', v'_s)\}$ is a superset of P', possibly a proper superset containing some unreachable pairs (p, v_s). However it is still not clear whether this superset is computable from program ℓ and v_{0s} (even if finite).

To solve this in algorithmic practice we construct *computable safe approximations* to the uncomputable parts, *i.e.* find a computable binary relation $\looparrowright$ on $P \times V_s$ so $\ell \mid (p, v_s) \looparrowright_1 (p', v'_s)$ implies $\ell \vdash (p, v_s) \looparrowright (p', v'_s)$.

The term "safe" is used in the same sense as in program flow analysis, and amounts to seeing that a $\{ (p, v_s) \mid \ell \vdash (p_0, v_{0s}) \looparrowright^* (p', v'_s)\}$ is a superset of P'' (see *e.g.* [Muchnick, Jones 81] .) Section 4.5.2 contains a concrete example.

4.3.2 The Specialization Algorithm

In the following "poly" is a set of pairs (p, v_s) where $p \in P$ and $v_s \in V_s$. The following program, given ℓ and v_{0s}, finds a set poly large enough to include P' as defined before, but containing only those pairs (p, v_s) necessary according to $\looparrowright$. Thus ℓ' in the following approximates $\ell \setminus d$ (from above, since it may have more program points than $\ell \setminus d$).

procedure Specialize(ℓ, v_{0s}, d);
begin
    { Step 1: find poly specialized to v_{0s} by transitive closure}

poly :=   the smallest subset of $P \times V_s$ such that
        • $(p_0, v_{0s}) \in$ poly, and for any $p \in P$, $v_s \in V_s$:
        • $(p, v_s) \in$ poly and $\ell \vdash (p, v_s) \rightsquigarrow (p', v'_s)$ implies $(p', v'_s) \in$ poly;

    { Step 2: construct a specialized program (extensional form) }

ℓ' :=   (poly, V, nx') where
$$nx'((p, v_s), v_d) = \textbf{let} \ (p', v') = nx(p, \pi_p(v_s, v_d))$$
$$\textbf{in} \ ((p', \sigma_p'v'), \ \delta_p'v') \ ;$$

    { Step 3: optimize the result }
ℓ_{v0s} := ℓ', after optimizing by compressing transitions.

end of Specialize;

4.3.3 Critique of the Abstract Algorithm

Nontermination:
    the algorithm could attempt to add infinitely many elements to poly.

Incompleteness:
    the algorithm is based on a *deus ex machina:* the program division d is assumed
    given in advance.

Compression:
    no criteria are given for how much compressing to do in the optimization step.

Code generation:
    no scheme is given to generate a concrete residual program.

Generality:
    it does not cover some program specialization schemes seen in the literature.

On Termination
This important problem is closely connected with the choice of d. For example, taking the minimal division for every program point p beyond the initial one ensures termination but no improvement in program performance; and use of the maximal division will nearly always give infinitely many specialized program points. Section 6 concerns the choice of d.

On Incompleteness
There is no explanation above of how a safe division $d = (\sigma, \delta, \pi)$ is to be chosen. There are two possibilities: either d can be obtained in advance, by preprocessing of the program; or the algorithm above can be extended somehow to classify the variables at the various program points as static or dynamic during program specialization, that is *on-line*. In section 7 we consider the latter possibility, since it on the surface appears simpler and more direct, and then point out its weaknesses.

On Code Generation
This is a tactical problem, depending closely on the concrete details of the programming language, and is discussed in the next section. The essential issue is to what extent the language allows symbolic specialization of individual computation steps on the basis of static data, and to what extent transitions can be symbolically composed.

On Generality
The set poly is a safe approximation to (a superset of) $\{ \sigma_p v \mid (p, v) \in R(v_{0s}) \}$ where

$$R(v_{0s}) = \{ (p, v) \mid \ell \vdash (p_0, pair(v_{0s}, v_d)) \rightarrow^* (p, v) \text{ for some } v_d \in V_d \}$$

and, at least conceptually, obtains static data by applying projection function σ_p to the store, incorporating it into the current program point and simplifying the resulting program.

Other representations of $R(v_{0s})$ can be imagined and have been used in the literature, for example "configurations", each of which represents a set of computational states. A configuration can be a term containing free variables, as is done for REFAL in [Turchin 80, 86] and for Prolog in [Fuller, Abramsky 88], [Kursawe 87] and others. These references generalize the technique above in at least two other dimensions. First, different configurations may represent *overlapping* sets of computational states, allowing greater freedom in the choice of residual program. Second, if the language allows more than one evaluation order (which flow charts do not), the order chosen at program specialization time need not precisely reflect the order of run time evaluation. This concept is seen clearly in the "supercompilation" of [Turchin 86] and "listless" and "treeless" transformations of [Wadler 84, 85, 88].

We do not handle these generalizations here for several reasons: a unifying framework in which to express them has not been developed; termination problems appear even more difficult to deal with than in our simpler framework; and the more powerful methods just mentioned have not yet been able to handle the self application involved in the second and third Futamura projections (to the knowledge of this writer).

On the other hand it must certainly be admitted that such schemes can give stronger efficiency improvements than ours, for example transforming multipass algorithms into singe pass equivalents. Similarly, classical program transformation techniques (*e.g.* [Burstall, Darlington 77]) are still less fully automated but can yield yet more dramatic efficiency improvements.

4.4 A More Concrete Algorithm for the Language of Assignments and Goto's

We now develop a more detailed and efficient specialization algorithm for the concrete language of section 1.5.

4.4.1 Collecting Specialized Program Points

Suppose each program variable is separately classified as static or dynamic as in section 2.3D. A suitable relation $\ell \vdash (p, v_s) \looparrowright (p', v'_s)$ for the abstract algorithm can be described concretely by giving function Successors: $P \times v_s \to \wp(P \times V_s)$ with

$$\text{Successors}(p, v_s) = \{ (p', v'_s) \mid \ell \vdash (p, v_s) \looparrowright (p', v'_s)\}$$

Below "booleval" does approximate boolean expression evaluation on the basis of the known static data, and returns the appropriate element of {true, false, don't know}. (Examples: if X_1, X_2 are respectively as static and dynamic, and V_s is the integers (values for X_1), then booleval($X_1 > 0$, 5) = true and booleval($X_1 > X_2$, 5) = don't know). "Update" yields the static part of the new store, given an assignment and the static part of the current one. It should be obvious how both can be defined, if one is given a concrete set of base functions (they also depend on the program division and current program point, but these are omitted to aid simplicity).

Keywords of the subject program have been italicized to avoid confusion with those of Successors itself.

Successors(p, v_s) = Succ(**the** <command> **at program point** p, v_s);

Succ("X_i := expression; <command>", v_s) =
    Succ(<command>, v_{s1}) **where** v_{s1} = update("X_i .= expression", v_s);

Succ("***goto*** p", v_s) = {(p, v_s)}

Succ("***if*** expression ***then*** <command$_1$> ***else*** <command$_2$>", v_s) =
    if booleval(expression, v_s) = true **then** Succ(<command$_1$>, v_s) **else**
    if booleval(expression, v_s) = false **then** Succ(<command$_2$>, v_s) **else**
        Succ(<command$_1$>, v_s) $\cup$ Succ(<command$_2$>, v_s)

4.4.2 On-line Chain Compression Using Goto Annotations

The abstract algorithm involves first collecting the full set "poly" of program point variants, then building a preliminary residual program, and at last optimizing it by removing trivial transitions. While this method works in principle for any finite program division d, in practice it seems wasteful first to build a large preliminary residual program and then to cut it down (in the example of section 3.4, 12 transitions were cut down to 5). It seems more economical to do the transition chain compression *on-line,* while collecting "poly".

Given a finite program division d, one may before program specialization recognize definitely "static" commands and tests - those independent of the dynamic component $\delta_p v$ of store v at program point p. Following the lines of [Jones, Sestoft, Søndergaard 85], we suggest that this information be used to *annotate* l by replacing certain comands "**goto** p" by "**residualgoto** p". The annotations will be used on-line during program specialization to decide which transitions to compress: a pair will (p, v_s) be added to "poly" *only* if it is accessed by a **residualgoto** (or is the start point). All other transitions will be compressed on-line, thus avoiding the need for a separate compression step.
    We assume the annotations are such that no infinite chains of transition compression can occur. Exactly how annotation can be done will be discussed in section 6 after a more thorough discussion of binding time analysis; for now we just assume it has been done. *Remark:* one could go even one step further, and generate the residual program along the way while building poly.

For example in the Turing interpreter, the tests on "head(Qtail)" in Run are static, as are the entire commands following Cont and Hop; all other tests and commands will appear in some form in the residual program. Specialized versions of the the test on head(Right) and the commands updating Left and Right must therefore appear in the specialized program ℓ_{v0s}. Here is a suitably annotated version of that interpreter:

```
Run:  if  Qtail = empty then residualgoto Run else
        if "right" = head(Qtail)
            then   Left := cons(head(Right), Left);  Right := tail(Right);  goto Cont else
        if "left" = head(Qtail)
            then   Right:= cons(head(Left), Right);  Left := tail(Left);    goto Cont else
        if "write a" = head(Qtail)
            then   Right := cons(symbol(Qtail), tail(Right));               goto Cont else
        if "goto I"= head(Qtail)       then goto Hop  else
        if "if a goto I" = head(Qtail) then goto Test  else
            Right := cons(Right, Right);  residualgoto goto Run;        { abort }
Cont: Qtail := tail(Qtail);                          goto Run;
Hop:  Qtail := nth(Q, successor(head(Qtail)));       residualgoto Run;
Test: if head(Right) = symbol(Qtail) then            goto Hop else goto Cont;
```

Note that every nontrivial transition sequence from Run to Run either Qtail becomes smaller or there is a residual **goto**. Thus chain compression during specialization cannot lead to infinite loops.

4.4.3 A More Concrete Algorithm

The two ideas above may be combined to yield a more concrete and efficient version of the specialization algorithm given earlier. We assume program ℓ has **goto**s annotated as in the previous section. The set "poly" contains only residual specialized program points, and has been split into two disjoint parts: "out", containing those whose successors according to $\multimap$ have already been collected; and "pending" containing the remainder. Further, function "Successors" has been modified to continue searching as long as nonresidual **goto**s are encountered.

The reader may verify that this algorithm, if applied to the annotated interpreter of the previous section and $v_{0s} = 1: if 0 goto 4 2: right 3: goto 1 4: write 1$ will yield the same residual program as in section 3.4.

procedure Specialize(ℓ, v_{0s}, d);
begin
       {   Find poly (= pending $\cup$ out) specialized to v_{0s} by transitive closure,
           optimizing by chain compression along the way.}
      pending := { (p_0, v_{0s}) }; out := {};

while pending $\neq$ {} **do begin**
    Pick $(p, v) \in$ pending;   next := Successors(p, v);
    pending   :=   (pending $\cup$ next) $\setminus \{(p, v)\}$;
    out   :=   out $\cup \{(p, v)\}$
end;

    { Step 2: construct a specialized program (extensional form)}
ℓ' :=   (out, V, nx') **where**
               $nx'((p, v_s), v_d) =$ **let** $(p', v') = nx(p, \pi_p(v_s, v_d))$
                                    in $((p', \sigma_p'v'), \delta_p'v')$
end of Specialize;

function Successors$(p, v_s) =$ Succ(**the** <command> **at program point** p, v_s);

function Succ(Cmd, v_s) =
case form of Cmd **of**

"$X_i :=$ expression; Cmd_1":   Succ(Cmd_1, v_{s1})
                               where $v_{s1} =$ update("$X_i :=$ expression", v_s);

"*goto* p":   Successors(p, v_s);

"*residualgoto* p":   **if** $(p, v_s) \in$ pending $\cup$ out **then** {} **else** $\{(p, v_s)\}$;

"*if* E *then* Cmd_1 *else* Cmd_2":
    if booleval(expression, v_s) = true   **then** Succ(Cmd_1, v_s) **else**
    if booleval(expression, v_s) = false   **then** Succ(Cmd_2, v_s) **else**
        Succ(Cmd_1, v_s) $\cup$ Succ(Cmd_2, v_s)};
end;

5. Intensional Considerations: the Question of Code Generation

As defined in section 3.3, $\ell \setminus d$ may in principle be constructed for any program ℓ and division d at all, and has transition function nx' : $C \to C$ for $C \subseteq (P \times V_s) \times V_d$ defined as in Step 3 above by

$$nx'((p, v_s), v_d) = ((p', \sigma_p'v'), \delta_p'v') \; where \; (p', v') = nx(p, \pi_p(v_s, v_d))$$

This definition is purely extensional and takes no account of how the commands in the residual program are to be built. In a real programming language the question of code generation arises: how can one generate the necessary code to specify transition functions for ℓ_1 and $\ell \setminus d$?

5.1 Code Generation: Discussion in Principle

We will adhere to the following *principle of congruence:*

Given a source program text ℓ, the residual code for specialized program point (p, v_s) should be a specialized version of the source code for p.

In the following sections we will see that the congruence principle imposes some subtle extra conditions on the program division. After their formulation we give in the last section our most concrete program specialization algorithm.

Remark: we require congruence for simplicity and generality of code generation. It is not, however, essential for program specialization and stronger program transformations can sometimes be done by violating it. Examples include the "filter promotion" of [Burstall, Darlington 77] and "driving" of [Turchin 86].

5.1.1 Transition Compression and Restriction to Reachable Program Points

The relation $p_0 : \ell$ **reach** ℓ' gives no problems in principle, since if each program point of ℓ is labelled with a command, then ℓ' is just the same program, but with inaccessible program points and their labels deleted. Further, suppose

$$\ell = ... p_1: ... ; \ \textbf{goto } p_2 \quad ... ; \quad p_2 : <command_2>; ...$$

as in section 1.5. Then an ℓ' satisfying $\ell \rightsquigarrow \ell'$ is easily obtained by collapsing the transition from p_1 to p_2:

$$\ell = ... p_1: ... ; \ <command_2> ... ; \quad p_2 : <command_2>; .... $$

For the concrete language, the result may be improved by local optimizations using standard methods such asdeletion of trivial statements and test simplification. Similar compression techniquess could be used for languages with different code forms, as long as they have natural properties of syntactic composibility.

5.1.2   Shifting the Boundary between Data and Control

Now suppose d : ℓ **DCshift** ℓ' as above where d = (σ, δ, π) and a transition in ℓ is realized in ℓ' by:

$$\ell \vdash (p, v) \to (p', v') \quad \Leftrightarrow \quad \ell \setminus d \vdash ((p, \sigma_p v), \delta_p v) \to ((p', \sigma_{p'} v'), \delta_{p'} v')$$

Suppose further that ℓ is given intensionally, so its transitions from p are specified by syntactic "code", for example a <command> as defined in section 1.5.1.   In practice we need to construct a corresponding residual <command> specifying the transitions from specialized program point (p, $\sigma_p v$) in ℓ_{v0s} .

Generating code to construct the new store $\delta_{p'}$ v' is straightforward for most programming languages (an example method appears at the end of this section). On the other hand, determining to which specialized program point control should be transferred can be a bit tricky.   One needs additional restrictions on program division d, whose exact formulation requires some care.

5.1.3   The Store in the Specialized Program

At specialization time $v_s = \sigma_p v$ will be known, while $v_d = \delta_p v$ will not. The code to be generated for specialized program point (p, v_s) transforms the specialized store v_d at p into v'_d:

$$v_d \Rightarrow v'_d \qquad [\ v'_d = \delta_{p'}\ v'\ where\ (p', v') = nx(p, \pi_p(v_s, v_d))\ ]$$

In essence all that is required is that this transformation be expressible, in other words programmable in the language's syntax.   (In languages with poor expressiveness an external function call might be required.)   In practice, optimizations would of course be applied to exploit the known information v_s to generate more efficient code.

In functional or logic programming languages: the "store" v is a tuple of function or predicate parameters (without or with free variables, resp.), so the new v' is straightforwardly obtainable by partially evaluating the argument expressions on those parameters on the basis of the known data v_s.

The specialized store is also easily constructed for the concrete language with assignments, tests and **gotos**. Suppose variables are classified separately as static or dynamic as in section 2.3D, so v_s gives the values of some but not all variables X_i. The problem is one of partial evaluation or specializing at the command level. The "dag method" of [Aho, Sethi, Ullman 86] is an efficient algorithm realizing both "constant folding" and the elimination of common subexpressions.

If for instance p labels an assignment statement "X_i := expression; **goto** p_1" and v_s gives the current values of some variables X_j, these may be substituted into the right side, and the resulting expression simplified. It may even be eliminated completely in case the expression contains only static variables. Similarly, tests may be simplified or eliminated on the basis of known values. A simple algorithm will be seen in section 5.3.

5.1.4 Control in the Specialized Program: Congruence

Consider residual transition $((p, \sigma_p v), \delta_p v) \to ((p', \sigma_{p'} v'), \delta_{p'} v')$ above. The destination program point p' may of course depend on $\delta_p v$ (the dynamic part of v) since the command at p may be a test.

Given that point p' has been selected, it seems unreasonable in the transition above for the *static* part $\sigma_{p'} v'$ of the new state to depend on the dynamic part of v. Why? Because if it could, then the dynamic data could determine *which one* of the possible destinations (p', $\sigma_{p'} v'$) control will be transferred to in the residual program.

But the dynamic data is not available during program specialization time. Thus code generation requires the residual program $\ell \setminus d$ to contain tests on dynamic data not corresponding to tests seen in the source program commands, which violates the congruence principle stated above. A program division which does not violate the principle we call *congruent,* and our current task is to find a good definition for this term.

Some examples for imperative languages illustrate the problems in formulating this subtle concept (exactly analogous problems arise for other language types). We assume every program variable is separately classified as static or dynamic as in section 2.3D and range over value set A.

Suppose X_1 is static and X_2 is dynamic at every program point. Consider

$$p_1 : \quad X_1 := X_2; \textbf{ goto } p_2;$$

Control in $\ell \setminus d$ would pass from $((p_1, 1), x_2)$ to $((p_1, x_2), x_2)$ for any $x_2 \in A$, so the new destination depends on a runtime value and thus requires a test in the residual program - even though the source program had no corresponding test. So d is not congruent at this p_1.

On the other hand, we cannot require that the pair (p', $\sigma_{p'} v'$) be completely determined by (p, $\sigma_p v$), since this rules out all dynamic tests, *e.g.*

p_1 :   **if** $X_2 = 1$ **then goto** p_2 **else goto** p_3; .

Another try at defining congruence: perhaps $\sigma_{p'} v'$ should be functionally determined by $\sigma_p v$ *whenever control goes from p to p'*. But this also fails, as evidenced by:

p_1 : **if** $X_2 = 1$ **then** $(X_1 := 1;$ **goto** $p_2)$ **else** $(X_1 := 2;$ **goto** $p_2)$;

The proper residual command is easily generated:

(p_1, x_1) : **if** $X_2 = 1$ **then goto** $(p_2, 1)$ **else goto** $(p_2, 2)$;

but the new condition fails at p_1: the choice between (p', 1) and (p', 2) is independent of $\sigma_p v = x_1$, since X_1 is overwritten. The problem is that the new trial condition does not differentiate between control transfers - and p_1's command has two essentially different transitions to the same point p_2.

5.1.5   Control Structures

Performing a command in an imperative language, a function call in a functional language, or a pattern match or a Prolog procedure call can all be thought of as applying a set of tests (perhaps empty) to the current value, the outcome of which determines both where control will be transferred and how the value v will be updated. We now express the idea of how control transfers work in abstract terms, without reference to any particular concrete syntax.

Definition Let $\mathscr{l} = (P, V, nx)$ be a program. Then

1.   A *control transfer* $p -f_i \to p_i$ consists of program points p, p_i and a function $f_i : V_i \to V$ where $V_i \subseteq V$, such that $nx(p, v) = (p_i, f_i v)$ for all $v \in V_i$.

2.   A *control structure* on a program $\mathscr{l} = (P, V, nx)$ associates with each program point p a finite set of control transfers $p -f_i \to p_i$ $(f_i : V_i \to V$ for i = 1,2,...,m), such that $V = V_1 \cup ... \cup V_m$ is a partition of V into disjoint subsets, and for all $v \in V_i$, $nx(p, v) = (p_i, f_i v)$.
              □

In the concrete imperative language below the most natural control structure for a given <command> defines V_i to be the set of stores causing the i-th **goto** in

<command> to be executed, p_i to be the **goto**'s destination and f_i to be the store transformation realized by executing the sequence of assignments leading to that **goto**. For example the command

$$p: \quad \textbf{if } X_2 = 5 \textbf{ then } (X_1 := 1; \textbf{ goto } p') \textbf{ else } (X_1 := 2; \textbf{ goto } p'');$$

would naturally have control transfers $p -f_1 \rightarrow p'$ with $f_1(v_1,v_2) = (1,v_2)$ for all values $(v_1,5)$, and $p -f_2 \rightarrow p'$ with $f_2(v_1,v_2) = (2,v_2)$ for (v_1,v_2) with $v_2 \neq 5$.

A control structure allows differentiation among transitions with the same source and destination points. For example the command

$$p: \quad \textbf{if } X_2 = 5 \textbf{ then } (X_1 := 1; \textbf{ goto } p') \textbf{ else } (X_1 := 2; \textbf{ goto } p');$$

would naturally have two control transfers to p', with different store transformations f_1, f_2.

Analogies should be clear for other languages. For instance such a set of control transfers is determined by evaluating conditionals to select a function call in LISP, or the pattern matching or unification done in a term rewriting language or in a deterministic version of Prolog (*e.g.* guarded Horn clauses).

5.2 An Extensional Definition of Congruence

We are at last ready to define the concept of a "congruent program division". Assuming that the given control structure faithfully reflects source program tests, we use the definition above to require all residual program tests to be images of source program tests.

Definition Division $d = (\sigma, \delta, \pi)$ is *congruent at p* for the given control structure on $\mathcal{l} = (P, V, nx)$ provided for any control transfer $p -f_i \rightarrow p_i$, $\sigma_p v_1 = \sigma_p v_2$ implies $\sigma_{pi}(f_i v_1) = \sigma_{pi}(f_i v_2)$ for any $v_1, v_2 \in \text{domain}(f_i)$. It is *congruent* if it is congruent at every program point p.
□

By this definition, the division making X_1 static and X_2 dynamic is congruent at p_1 for the natural control structure and the last example command above.

A good choice of program division is essential as it determines:
- whether or not the residual program is finite
- its efficiency after compressing transitions

-      whether or not code generation may be accomplished in a natural way (the congruence condition).

5.3   An Intensional Definition of Congruence

Proof of a simple sufficient condition for congruence in the concrete language is easy.   A different concrete language would most likely require a different version of intensional congruence.

Suppose d is a program division which classifies each variable X_j at p as static or dynamic as in section 2.3D.   For any program point p_i, there is $\underline{b}_i \in \{S, D\}*$ such that

$$dp_i = (stat_{\underline{b}i}, dyn_{\underline{b}i}, pair_{\underline{b}i}).$$

Definition

•   A *position* is a pair (X_j, p) where X_j is a variable and p is a program point.

•   Position (X_k, p') *depends on* position (X_j, p) if there is a path from p to p' containing a series of assignments defining X_k at p' in terms of X_j at p (and possibly on other values as well).

                                                                                    □

Remark: this is not the strongest possible definition of dependence.   For example, it does not capture the indirect dependence of (X_k, p') on (X_j, p) in the following:

p :   **if** $X_j = 0$ **then** $X_k := 0$; **goto** p' **else**
          if $X_j = 1$ **then** $X_k := 1$; **goto** p' **else goto** p"

For the formally inclined reader, "depends on" may be defined more precisely with the aid of an auxiliary relation $X_j = Command \Rightarrow (X_k, p')$ as follows.   Intuitively, this means: "the value of X_k at p' can depend on the value X_j had before executing Command".

a. $X_j =$"**goto** p"$\Rightarrow (X_j, p)$
b. $X_j =$"$X_\ell := E; Cmd$"$\Rightarrow (X_k, p')$ if E contains X_j and $X_\ell = Cmd \Rightarrow (X_k, p')$
c. $X_j =$"**if** E **then** C_1**else** C_2"$\Rightarrow (X_k, p')$ if $X_j = C_1 \Rightarrow (X_k, p')$
                                                                                    or $X_j = C_2 \Rightarrow (X_k, p')$
d. (X_k, p') depends on (X_j, p) if $X_j = Com \Rightarrow (X_k, p')$ where Com is the command at p
e.   transitive closure: (X_k, p') depends on (X_j, p) if (X_k, p') depends on $(X_\ell, p")$

and (X_ℓ, p'') depends on (X_j, p).

The following condition says intuitively that any variable at p' must be assigned D if it depends on some variable assigned D at p. The reason is that violation could allow the corresponding static variable at p' to depend on values dynamic at p.

Definition Let d assign to program points p and p' tuples $\underline{b}_1, \underline{b}_2 \in \{S, D\}^*$ describing their store variables. If $\underline{b}1{\downarrow}j = D$ implies $\underline{b}2{\downarrow}k = D$ whenever (X_k, p') depends on (X_j, p), then d is *intensionally congruent*. □

Lemma Any intensionally congruent program division is also extensionally congruent.

The lemma is easily verified. Expressed concisely this is the

Dependency principle: any variable that depends on a dynamic value must itself be classified as dynamic.

5.3 Code Generation for the Concrete Language

We now extend the last algorithm of section 4 to generate code, using a function Generate : $P \times V_s \rightarrow$ Programtexts with structure parallel to the last Successors algorithm. In the following ◊ is used to denote concatenation of program text fragments; the reader is left to fill in the details of Residual_expression.

procedure Specialize(ℓ, v_{0s}, d);
begin
    { Find poly (= pending ∪ out) specialized to v_{0s} by transitive closure, optimizing by chain compression along the way.}

pending := { (p_0, v_{0s}) }; out := { }; residual := empty program;

while pending ≠ { } **do begin**
    Pick $(p, v) \in$ pending; next := Successors(p, v);
    pending   :=   (pending ∪ next) \ {(p, v)};
    out   :=   out ∪ {(p, v)};
    residual   :=   residual ◊ Generate(p, v)
end;

end of Specialize;

function Generate(p, v_s) =   "(p, v_s):" ◊ Gen(Cmd, v_s) **where**
                              Cmd =   **the <command> at program point** p;

function Gen(Cmd, v_s)   =
     case form of Cmd **of**

"X_i := expression; Cmd_1":
     let v_{s1} = update("X_i:= expression", v_s) **in**
     if X_i is a static variable **then** Gen(Cmd_1, v_{s1})
     else "X_i:=" ◊ Residual_expression(expression) ◊ ";" ◊ Gen(Cmd_1, v_{s1});

"*goto* p":   Gen(Cmd, v_s) **where**
                                   Cmd = the <command> **at program point** p;
"*residualgoto* p":   "*goto*(p, v_s)";

"*if* E *then* Cmd_1 *else* Cmd_2":
     if   booleval(expression, v_s) = true   **then** Gen(Cmd_1, v_s) **else**
     if   booleval(expression, v_s) = false   **then** Gen(Cmd_2, v_s)
     else
              ("*if*"   ◊   Residual_expression(v_s, expression)   ◊
              "*then*"   ◊   Gen(Cmd_1, v_s)   ◊
              "*else*"   ◊   Gen(Cmd_2, v_s));
end;

Using the same program division as before, we obtain from Turing machine program

$$Q = 1: if\ 0\ goto\ 4\quad 2: right\quad 3: goto\ 1\quad 4: write\ 1$$

the same residual program as before:

        (Run, QQ):   **if** head(Right) = 0 **then goto** (Run, QQ4) **else goto** (Run, QQ2);
        (Run, QQ2):   Right:= cons(head(Left), Right); Left := tail(Left); **goto** (Run, QQ);
        (Run, QQ4):   Right := cons(1, tail(Right));   **goto** (Run, QQ5);
        (Run, QQ5):   **goto** (Run, QQ5);

6 Binding Time Analysis: How to Choose a Program Division

The binding time analysis problem is:

Given	A program ℓ and an initial division div_0 of input values
To construct	A program division d = (σ, δ, π) of values at all program points

The choice of d is obviously vital since it determines the size and efficiency of the residual program ℓ_{v0s} and the possibility for code generation. (Its representation is also important since the relation $\circ\!\!\rightarrow$ should be computable, but we defer that discussion to a later article.)

To gain a more efficient ℓ_{v0s}, we want each static projection function σ_p chosen so that $\sigma_p v$ describes as *large* a part of v as possible, so there will be much statically computable data, and long static transition chains may be compressed away at specialization time, as was seen in the example of section 3.4.

On the other hand, in practice it is of course essential that ℓ_{v0s} be finite, which argues that the static projections should be chosen so that $\sigma_p v$ describes *not too large* a part of v. In the remainder we discuss how to obtain a d satisfying these contradictory demands, using the concrete language with assignments and **goto**s, and divisions as in section 2.3D with variables separately classified as static or dynamic and set of stores $V = A^k$ for some $k \geq 0$.

More precisely, d must be both *finite* as in section 3.3 and *intensionally congruent* as in 5.3 (called just "congruent" in the rest of this section). Our strategy is first to see how to obtain a congruent division that is "as static as possible" but sometimes infinite (sections 6.1, 6.2). We then outline a more sophisticated algorithm yielding congruence and finiteness as well, as long as infinite purely static computations cannot occur (sections 6.3-6.6). In effect this algorithm gives a static method to do "generalization" as described in [Turchin 86, 88].

6.1 Congruent Divisions in the Concrete Imperative Language

Recall from section 5.3 the sufficient condition for congruence: any value depending on a value classified as dynamic by d must itself be classified as dynamic. The following can be described informally as: find that division of variables into static and dynamic which makes as many variables as possible static, but still is congruent and is compatible with the program's input division.

A review from 2.3D. Let $\underline{a}$ **selectS** $\underline{b}$ be (for $\underline{a} \in V = A^*$ and $\underline{b} \in \{S, D\}^*$ of the same length) the subsequence of components $\underline{a}{\downarrow}i$ from $\underline{a}$ such that $\underline{b}{\downarrow}i$ equals S, and let $\underline{a}$ **selectD** $\underline{b}$ be analogous for D. We now consider divisions $div_{\underline{b}} = (stat_{\underline{b}}, dyn_{\underline{b}}, pair_{\underline{b}})$ where $stat_{\underline{b}} : A^* \to A^*$, $dyn_{\underline{b}} : A^* \to A^*$, $pair_{\underline{b}} : A^* \times A^* \to A^*$ and

$$
\begin{array}{lll}
stat_{\underline{b}} (\underline{a}) & = & \underline{a} \text{ selectS } b \\
dyn_{\underline{b}} (\underline{a}) & = & \underline{a} \text{ selectD } b \\
pair_{\underline{b}} (v_s, v_d) & = & \text{- still omitted -}
\end{array}
$$

Definition A function $\beta : P \to \{S, D\}^k$ is called a *binding time assignment*, and its *associated division* is $d\beta = (\sigma, \delta, \pi)$ with $(\sigma_p, \delta_p, \pi_p) = (stat_{\beta p}, dyn_{\beta p}, pair_{\beta p})$ for all $p \in P$. Such a binding time assignment β is called *congruent* if $d\beta$ is congruent and *finite* if $d\beta$ is finite.   □

The concept "as static as possible" can be formalized as "β is as small as possible in the following partial order on $P \to \{S, D\}^{k}$":

Definition Let $\{S, D\}$ be partially ordered by: $S \sqsubset D$, and define $\underline{b} \sqsubseteq \underline{b}'$ for $\underline{b}, \underline{b}'$ in $\{S, D\}^*$ iff $length(\underline{b}) = length(\underline{b}')$ and $\underline{b}{\downarrow}i \sqsubseteq \underline{b}'{\downarrow}i$ for all i. Define $\beta \sqsubseteq \beta'$ iff $\beta p \sqsubseteq \beta'p$ for every program point p.   □

For example $SSSD \sqsubseteq SDSD$, and the least $\underline{b}$ of length n is S^n. Note that the least upper bound $\underline{b} \sqcup \underline{b}'$ and greatest lower bound $\underline{b} \sqcap \underline{b}'$ exist for any $\underline{b}, \underline{b}'$ in $\{S, D\}^*$.

6.2 An Algorithm to Obtain a Congruent Binding Time Assignment

The following is essentially the least fixed point algorithm used in [Jones, Sestoft, Søndergaard 85, 88]. It yields an analysis which is always congruent, but often infinite. We assume given a program *input data division* $div_0 \in \{S, D\}^*$ describing the initial state at p_0.

β may be obtained by beginning with $\beta p_0 = div_0$ and $\beta p = SS...S$ for all other program points p, and iterating by the rules of section 5.3 to make β larger as long as necessary. β increases monotonically and has only finitely many possible values, so the algorithm terminates.

procedure Find_Congruent_BTA(p, div_0);
begin
    $\beta p_0 := div_0$; $\beta p := SS...S$ for all $p \neq p_0$;
    repeat
        for each $p \in P$ **do** Updateβ(**the command at** p, βp);
    until β is unchanged;

procedure Updateβ(Cmd, div);　　　{ As in section 5.3 }

begin case Cmd **of**
goto p　　　: βp := βp ⊔ div;

X_i := E; Cmd_1 : b := **if** E contains a variable X_j with div $\downarrow$j = D **then** D **else** S;
　　　　　　Updateβ(Cmd_1, div [X_i ↦ b]);

if E*then* Cmd_1 *else* Cmd_2:
　　　　　　Updateβ(Cmd_1, div); Updateβ(Cmd_2, div);
end

For example consider the Turing interpreter from section 1.6, with variables (Q, Qtail, Left, Right) = (X_1,...,X_4). Initially div_0 = SSSD and β = [Run ↦ SSSD, Hop ↦ SSSS, Cont ↦ SSSS, Test ↦ SSSS]. The first iteration recognizes that Left can depend on Right (by a right shift), yielding

β = [Run ↦ SSDD, Hop ↦ SSDD, Cont ↦ SSDD, Test ↦ SSDD]

which is stable and so the desired congruent division.

6.3　　The Finiteness Problem: Discussion and Examples

Congruence alone is not enough to achieve our goal: generation of target programs by specializing interpreters to source programs. Finiteness is of course also essential, and in this section we give examples to point out some of the problems. In the following sections we develop more sophisticated analyses that appear sufficient to reach that goal for interpreters as one sees them in practice. Later work will report implementation details and practical evaluation.

The problem is to decide whether variable X_i at program point p should be classified as static or dynamic. We use "position (X_i, p)" and " (X_i, p) depends on (X_j, p')" as in section 5.3. The start point of the algorithm below will be the program division computed as in the previous section. At each iteration there will be a current program division (always congruent), and certain positions (X_i, p) will be reclassified from static to dynamic in order to achieve finiteness.

First, a simple example of nonfiniteness. Consider the following program with variables X_1, X_2 and div_1 = DS (initially (X_1, p_0) is dynamic and (X_2, p_0) is static).

p_0 : $X_2 := 0$;   **goto** p_1;
p_1 :   **if** $X_1 = 0$ **then**   **goto** p_1
                    else $X_1 := X_1 - 1$; $X_2 := X_2 + 1$;   **goto** p_1;

Initially $\beta = [p_0 \mapsto DS, p_1 \mapsto SS]$ which stabilizes to $\beta = [p_0 \mapsto DS, p_1 \mapsto DS]$ after one iteration. This value of β is certainly congruent but yields an infinite residual program with specialized program points $(p_1, 0)$, $(p_1, 1)$, $(p_1, 2)$, ..., one for each possible value of X_2.

The problem is that while (X_2, p_1) is not directly computed from (X_1, p_1), it is in fact *indirectly* dependent on (X_1, p_1), since the number of times 1 is added to (X_2, p_1) is determined by the value of (X_1, p_1). This problem manifests itself in the fact that division DS leads to an infinite "poly" whereas the choice of DD would yield a finite specialized program. Exactly the same problem arises with the NORMA interpreter from [Jones, Sestoft, Søndergaard 85].

The choice to classify (X_2, p_1) as static in spite of the fact that X_2's value can be computed at specialization time is an example of Turchin's *generalization* operation, an essential key to obtaining finite residual programs in both his and our work. The main difference is that binding time analysis in effect decides how to generalize before program specialization begins, while Turchin's generalization is done on-line [Turchin 86, 88].

6.3.1   A sufficient condition for finiteness

A sufficient condition for finiteness of a program division is that for any static position (X_i, p):

*   no value of (X_i, p) may depend on the value of any dynamic program input; and

*   any value of (X_i, p) must be less than or equal to some static program input (according to a given well-founded order).

For example in the Turing interpreter, (Q, p) always equals the static input Q and $(Qtail, p)$ is always a suffix of it, so they can only account for finitely many specialized program points. Many arguments of interpreters for traditional programming languages satisfy this condition since they (mostly but not exclusively) work by the principle of *recursive descent*. On the other hand the condition is very restrictive since it classifies as dynamic *all* variables which can ever become larger, even if built up noniteratively, or if built exclusively from constants and static program inputs under static control.

6.3.2   Recognizing Recursive Descent

For a natural example where the analysis just described is too conservative, consider

$$E \quad \equiv \quad if\, X = 0\; then\; (let\, Z = X\text{-}Y\; in\; X*Z)\; else\; ...$$

in a functional language with lexical scoping. An interpreter for this language might have an evaluation function eval(Expression, Names, Values) where the environment is represented for example by name list *(X, Y)* and value list (3, 2) when evaluating E. Expression is certainly static since it is always a subexpression of the program being interpreted.

One would naturally expect the name list to be static so specialized programs would contain functions of form: $eval_{E,Names}(Values) = ...$, with the list of variables' values as run-time formal parameter, but no run-time names. The variables' values, however, are certainly dynamic. The environment when evaluating E1 = *(let Z = X-Y in X*Z)* has name list *(X, Y, Z)*, since naturally

eval(E, *(X, Y)* , (3, 2)) calls eval(E1, *(X, Y, Z)* , (3, 2, 1))

Thus Names has grown in size, so the analysis above will classify it as dynamic. However this growth in size cannot possibly lead to an infinite "poly", since the interpreter has, while building Names up, at the same time descended from the definitely static E to its proper substructure E1; a series of such descents must eventually "bottom out".

On the other hand achieving finiteness can involve some subtle problems, as illustrated by:

p: **if** $X_1 < X_3$ **then**
      if $test1(X_2, X_3)$ **then** $X_1 := X_1 + 1$; $X_2 := X_2 - 1$ **goto p else**
      if $test2(X_2, X_3)$ **then** $X_1 := X_1 - 1$; $X_2 := X_2 + 2$ **goto p end else**
      goto p'

with $v_s = 1\ 2$ (the values of X_1, X_2), and X_3 dynamic. Here each loop repetition causes *either* X_1 or X_2 to become smaller, but if the tests alternately evaluate to "true", then X_2 will grow unboundedly. Clearly both X_1 and X_2 should be classified as dynamic, else poly becomes infinite.

6.4   Towards a More Sophisticated Binding Time Analysis Algorithm

An improved binding time assignment β can be constructed by a nested iterative algorithm, using in the outermost loop *three* variable descriptions: S (definitely classified as static), D (definitely classified as dynamic) or ? (status not yet determined).   We also assume given as above a well-founded order on A, the set of variable values.

Our motivation is to get a finite program division, and our methods nearly always yield this.   The only exception is that programs containing infinite computations depending only on static data can yield an infinite set of program point variants.   This could be avoided by a more conservative strategy but seems not unreasonable to accept, using the rationale that infinite computations without tests on dynamic data indicate poor interpreter design and so are not the proper responsibility of the program specializer.

Definition
1.   A function β : program points $\rightarrow$ {D, S, ?}* is called an *extended binding time assignment*.

2.   The binding time assignments up(β) and down(β) are defined by:

$$up(\beta)p{\downarrow}i \quad = \quad \text{if } \beta p{\downarrow}i = ? \text{ then D else } \beta p{\downarrow}i$$
$$down(\beta)p{\downarrow}i \quad = \quad \text{if } \beta p{\downarrow}i = ? \text{ then S else } \beta p{\downarrow}i \qquad \qquad \square$$

The algorithm starts with β_0 (incorporating the input data division div_0 and assigning ? to all other positions) as the current binding time assignment and iteratively improves it by reclassifying ? positions as S or D.   Positions classified as S or D are never changed and so are called "definitely static" or "definitely dynamic".   At the end, any remaining ? positions are reclassified as D.

For technical reasons we assume there are no transitions to p_0 (this is easy to ensure).   Three subprocedures are used:

Dynamic_dependencies closely resembles the inner loop of the algorithm of section 6.2: any position classified as ? by β but dependent on a definitely dynamic position is itself reclassified as D.

Statically_dominated reclassifies remaining ? positions as S if never larger than some definitely static positions or program constants, thus yielding a more static binding time assignment.

Suppose position (X_i, p) is classified as ? after the two previous steps. Then X_i at p must be independent of dynamic variables but constructed from constants, definitely static positions or ? positions in a way that is not necessarily decreasing.

Dynamic_constructor_analysis reclassifies such ? positions as D in case they may grow due to being built from static positions under dynamic control, and as S if they can only be built from constants and definitely static positions under static control.

The overall structure of the algorithm (annotated with invariants) is as follows, where $div_0 \in \{D, S\}*$ describes the program input:

procedure Find_Congruent_and_Finite_BTA(p, div_0);
begin

$\beta := \beta_0 = [p_0 \mapsto div_0, \ p \mapsto ??...?$ for all $p \neq p_0]$;   {Initialize β}

    repeat

                 { up(β) is a congruent program division }
    Dynamic_dependencies(β);
                 { up(β) and down(β) are congruent program divisions }
    Statically_dominated(β);
                 { up(β) and down(β) are congruent program divisions }
    Dynamic_constructor_analysis(β);
    until
               β is unchanged;
    $\beta := $ up(β);
end

Our goal is to find a binding time assignment between up(β_0) and down(β_0) that has as many static variables as possible but still yields a finite and congruent program division. Taking the final down(β) as the final besult of binding time analysis will yield the most reduced program, while up(β) is more likely to be finite. By the loop invariant above both are congruent at termination, since β is unchanged in the last iteration.

We now examine the alleged invariants. Initially up(β_0) is congruent since there are no transitions into p_0 and all other positions are D in up(β_0).

    "Dynamic_dependencies" leaves up(β) unchanged since it only changes some ?'s to D's. By congruence of up(β) no S position in β can depend on a D position, so if down(β) is not congruent after the call it must be because some ? position was changed to S and is dependent on a D position in β. But then that position would have been changed to D by "Dynamic_dependencies". Consequently down(β) is congruent after the call.

"Statically_dominated" leaves down(β) unchanged. That up(β) is congruent before the call implies no ? position can depend on any dynamic position, so any of these may safely be changed to S without violating congruence of the new up(β).

"Dynamic_constructor_analysis" can change both up(β) and down(β), but we only need to show congruence of the latter. Noncongruence of up(β) after the call would imply some position changed from ? to S depends on a dynamic position in the new β. But by definition of "Dynamic_constructor_analysis" such positions can only depend on S positions in β and these cannot be changed, so up(β) is also congruent after the call.

6.5 Static Domination

Assuming given a well-founded order $\leq$ on static values, this analysis can be realized by a simple abstract interpretation to trace descending chains of values. The following value descriptions can be used in both Statically_dominated and Dynamic_constructor_analysis, and in deciding which **goto**s to mark as residual for on-line transition compression.

Call a position (X_i, p) or a constant appearing in the program a *data source,* and let

ValueDescriptions = { $\perp$, =ds, <ds, #ds, D | ds is a data source }

be partially ordered by: $\perp \sqsubseteq$ =ds $\sqsubseteq$ #ds $\sqsubseteq$ D and $\perp \sqsubseteq$ <ds $\sqsubseteq$ #ds. Value descriptions are interpreted as follows:

$\perp$	no value
=ds	a value equal to some value occurring at ds in some computation
<ds	a value less than some value occurring at ds in some computation
#ds	a value otherwise dependent on some value occurring at ds in some ...
D	a dynamic value

Define

PositionDescriptions = { pd $\subseteq$ ValueDescriptions | pd is downwards closed }

where pd is *downwards closed* if whenever it contains any value description, it also contains all value descriptions that are smaller according to $\sqsubseteq$. It is easy to see that PositionDescriptions is closed under union.

Statically_dominated(β) can be computed by a fixpoint algorithm resembling the others and yielding a function of type

$$\gamma : \text{Program Points} \rightarrow \text{PositionDescriptions*}$$

If $\gamma p = pd_1...pd_n$ then pd_i describes the values assumed by variable X_i at program point p. If $pd_i = \gamma p \downarrow i = \{vd_1, vd_2, ...\}$ then any value assumed by X_i at point p must be correctly described by one or more of the vd_i.

Given the current extended binding time assignment β, the iteration for Statically_dominated(β) begins as follows, where dc(X) is the *downward closure* of X:

$$dc(X) = \{ vd \mid vd \sqsubseteq x \text{ for some } x \in X \}$$

$$\gamma_0 p \downarrow i = \begin{array}{ll} dc(\{D\}) & \text{if } (X_i, p) \text{ is definitely dynamic by } \beta \\ dc(\{=(X_i, p)\}) & \text{if } (X_i, p) \text{ is definitely static by } \beta \\ \{\bot\} & \text{if } (X_i, p) \text{ is ? by } \beta \end{array}$$

The iteration will never change descriptions of positions classified as S or D by β, and will use the interpretation above to find the best (smallest) description of ? positions. Updating of g occurs by abstractly evaluating expressions and executing commands over PositionDescriptions.

We give two examples. First consider the command "p_1: **goto** p_2", and let $\gamma p_1 = pd_1...pd_n$. Then γp_2 is updated by

$$\gamma p_2 := pd'_1...pd'_n \text{ where } pd'_i = \textbf{if } (X_i, p_2) \text{ is ? by } \beta \textbf{ then } pd_i \cup \gamma p_2 \downarrow i \textbf{ else } \gamma p_2 \downarrow i$$

Explanation: the description of a ? variable X_i at p_2 is updated to account for the fact that control can flow directly from p_1 to p_2; other position descriptions are unchanged.

Now consider the command "p_1: X_i := expression; **goto** p_2", and denote the right side of the assignment to γp_2 by $f(pd_1,...,pd_n)$. Then γp_2 is updated by

$$\gamma p_2 := f(pd_1,..., pd_{i-1}, \text{abs\_eval(expression, } p_1, \gamma), pd_{i+1},...,pd_n)$$

In words: abs_eval is used to obtain a new description of X_i's value, and γp_2 is updated using this new value as above. Extension to arbitrary commands is straightforward.

Abs_eval is a straightforward abstract evaluation over PositionDescriptions:

function abs_eval(expression, p, γ) =
case expression of
      constant : dc({=constant})
      X_i : $\gamma p{\downarrow}i$
      else   **if** for all stores value(expression) < variable X_j that occurs in it
                  then dc({<(X_j, p)})
                  else dc({#(X_j, p) | X_j occurs in expression})

For example one would expect: abs_eval(tail(X), p, γ) = dc({<(X, p)}} since
tail(X) < X for all X, and abs_eval(cons(X, Y), p, γ) = dc({#(X, p), #(Y, p) }} since
cons(X, Y) depends on X and Y but is not less than either.

6.6   Construction under Dynamic Control

is can also be done by abstract interpretation techniques, of which we give only the
barest outline.   The analysis just given can recognize positions built by
nondecreasing operations (those containing #(X, p)). Dynamic tests are of course
commands "**if** expression **then** ..." where "expression" contains one or more
dynamic variables, and static tests are those where it contains only static variables.
Note that a test dependent on ? variables may be is not static and might not be
dynamic either.

    The key problem is to recognize value transformations during the traversal of
loops, so a ? position is reclassified as S if in every loop that can change it, only static
values enter into values on which the position is dependent and tests.
Reclassification as D can occur if there is a loop with a dynamic test and the position
is self dependent by nondecreasing operations. Deciding just when to reclassify can
be rather subtle, as indicated by the examples of section 6.3.2.

6.7   Application to Transition Compression during Program
      Specialization.

Suppose now that a finite binding time analysis β : program points $\rightarrow$ {S, D}* of
program ℓ has been constructed that is congruent and, we hope, finite. We will
show how this information can be used to aid in deciding which program points
should appear in the specialized program ℓ_{v0s} and which may be compressed, even
before knowing v_{0s}.

    Given β it is possible before program specialization to recognize "trivial"
program points whose actions will not appear at all in the residual program - those
whose store transformations or tests involve only static variables. For example in
the Turing interpreter both Cont and Hop are trivial.

Annotation can be done by replacing occurrences of **goto** p by **residualgoto** p as follows. Construct the control flow graph of ℓ in the obvious way. Perform a depth first search of the graph, and each time a "back edge" of form p' : ... **goto** p; is encountered, trace the path from the previous traversal of p to the current one.

If no dynamic variable has been tested along that path, then leave the **goto** unchanged, so it will be collapsed during program specialization. Otherwise, if some static variable has at every path transition been either copied or made smaller, and made properly smaller at least once, then leave the **goto** unchanged, otherwise change it to **residualgoto** M. (The "Statically_dominated" abstract interpretation would be useful for gathering this information.)

If applied to the Turing interpreter, it will be found that most back edges involve no dynamic tests. The back edge from Cont satisfies the condition that static Qtail becomes smaller on all cycles, but the back edge from Hop in the path: Run → Test → Hop → Run fails the condition, as does the last comparison in Run; thus both are made residual.

7. Can Program Division be Done On-line?

In this section we consider doing the necessary subdivision of arguments of the various program points into static and dynamic on-line, *during* program specialization, as is done by most publshed partial evaluators. In other words, the program division d will be developed progressively, rather than being assumed given *a priori*.

We finish the paper with several arguments that it is preferable to construct a program division in a separate phase prior to specialization, for example the binding time analysis of section 6. Our conclusion is not that binding time analysis is indispensable, but that it gives better efficiency and more natural algorithms, and seems able to handle a larger class of source programs than purely on-line methods.

This section concerns a class of algorithms which are intuitively defined, and so is of necessity less mathematically precise than its predecessors or successors.

We again use the concrete language with divisions $d = (\sigma, \delta, \pi)$ classifying variables as static or dynamic as in section 2.3D, and function Successors as in section 4.4.1. Since d is to be developed progressively, we choose a representation of v_s that avoids explicit mention of d: a sequence from $V' = (V \cup \{D\})^*$. For instance $v' = 8D9D$ at program point p, could stand for $v_s = 89$ in a division of p's store with $\sigma_p(x_1 x_2 x_3 x_4) = x_1 x_3$.

7.1   On Termination

In the abstract algorithm, nontermination can only arise due to an attempt to construct an infinite poly or due to infinite compression of deterministic chains of **goto**s. Either must of course involve program loops. We will ignore the problem of infinite chains since it can at least in principle be avoided by first building poly and doing all compression thereafter (so compression would not happen at all if poly turns out to be infinite).

An infinite poly can of course arise even though no argument patterns are repeated. For example consider a flow chart for the following, with loop start program point N:

$$p : \textbf{if } X_1 \neq 0 \textbf{ then } X_1 := X_1 + 1; \ X_2 := X_2 - 1; \ \textbf{goto } p$$

with $v_{0s} = 1D$ (initially $X_1 = 1$ and X_2 is unknown). This yields the infinite set

$$poly \supseteq \quad \{ (p, 1D), \ (p, 2D), \ (p, 3D), ...\}$$

This is an example of a static loop, a computation which is infinite even though no dynamic program inputs are ever tested, operated upon or otherwise involved, and corresponds to a trivial infinite loop in $\ell \setminus d$. Deciding whether a division makes poly finite is related to the halting problem, and clearly undecidable.

But then how can we ensure termination of our program specialization algorithm? One strategy would be to equip the abstract algorithm with some form of "loop detector". For example suppose we have a well-founded measure of argument value size. If at a loop re-entry an argument X_i always increases in size, and there is no certainty the loop must terminate, then the position of the current v_s corresponding to X_i could be *reclassified* as dynamic. Applied to the example above we would get $(N, DD) \in poly$.

Such a policy seems likely to be too conservative for practical programs, since it says that stage 1 computations in any loop can *only* involve decreasing values. It is likely to be computationally expensive as well since every recursive loop traversal would require comparing the new v_s with the previous values of v_s for the same function. Conclusion: it seems difficult and inefficient to add "on-line" testing sufficient to ensure termination to the abstract algorithm.

7.2   On Finiteness of Poly and the Choice of d

In the present context the decision in the function "Successors"of which variables are to be called "dynamic" is the key to the program specialization process. Recall its form:

function Successors(p, v_s) = Succ(**the** <command> **at program point** p, v_s);

function Succ(Cmd, v_s) = **case form of** Cmd **of**

"X_i := expression; Cmd$_1$":   Succ(Cmd$_1$, v_{s1})
                                    where v_{s1} = update("X_i:= expression", v_s);

"*goto* p":   **if** ...goto should be unfolded...
                                    then Successors(p, v_s) **else**
                                    if $(p, v_s) \in$ pending $\cup$ out **then** { } **else** {(p, v_s)};

"*if* E *then* Cmd$_1$ *else* Cmd$_2$":
   if booleval(expression, v_s) = true   **then** Succ(Cmd$_1$, v_s) **else**
   if booleval(expression, v_s) = false   **then** Succ(Cmd$_2$, v_s) **else**
        Succ(Cmd$_1$, v_s) $\cup$ Succ(Cmd$_2$, v_s)};
end;

A vital question: how best to choose the v_{s1} in a pair (p_1, v_{s1}) in Successors(p, v_s)? (Recall that d is being developed progressively, so N_1's variables may not yet have been classified as static or dynamic.) At the extremes: finding the best possible v_{s1} is patently uncomputable, and choosing v_{s1} = DD...D would be inefficient since it gives a completely unspecialized p_1, so a better choice method is needed.

Recall that v_s contains the values of some of the components of v, and D for the others. If the expression in assignment "X_i := expression" contains a dynamic variable then its value may not be computable on the basis of the information in v_s. Thus it seems logical to suggest :

function Succ(Cmd, v_s)   =
case form of Cmd **of**

"X_i := expression; Cmd$_1$":   Succ(Cmd$_1$, v_{s1}) **where** v_{s1} = v_s except that
                                    $v_{s1}\downarrow i$ = **if** expression contains one or more dynamic
                                    variables **then** D **else** value of expression;

"*goto* p":   as above;
"*if* E *then* Cmd$_1$ *else* Cmd$_2$":   as above;
end;

One complication with this strategy is that control may come to a program point p_1 from more than one place. If so, it is not clear whether the new description v_{s1} should differ according to each route. If not, it is rather complex to delay and then choose a common v_{s1} for p_1, since global iteration would be needed to maintain information about all program points.

A more serious complication is that the strategy is too liberal, as shown by the program:

p : $X_2 := 0$;
p_1 :   **if** $X_1 \neq 0$ **then** $X_1 := X_1 - 1$; $X_2 := X_2 + 1$; **goto** p_1

with $v_s = D0$ (D describes X_1 and 0 describes X_2), which yields the infinite set

poly $\supseteq$ { (N, D0), (N, D1), (N, D2), ...}

The problem here is that X_2 is built up dynamically even though only from the constants 0 and 1. The right choice was $v_s = DD$. A proper solution seems to require recognizing the fact that X_2 grows, and does so *under the control of dynamic values,* a fact very difficult to recognize on-line since it can depend on nonlocal information.

This kind of problem arises often in our experiences of compiling by specializing interpreters.

7.3 A Conservative Program Specializer

One way out is to require the interpreter to satisfy the conservative finiteness conditions of section 6.3.1. Infinite compression is easy to avoid while processing **goto** commands. The reason is that in a recursive loop all static arguments must be equal to or smaller than their previous values (since all variables violating this will have been reclassified as dynamic). The tactic is thus: compress at a loop reentry if at least one static argument decreases in size.

This technique is clearly extremely limited, although it can in fact handle some metacircular interpreters. It cannot, however, handle many natural interpreters (*e.g.* the growing name lists needed to process a *let* construction). Further, the problems with self-application described in [Jones, Sestoft, Søndergaard 85, 88] and [Sestoft 86] would still arise, and lead to the desirability of an analysis phase prior to the actual program specialization.

7.4 Summary of Problems with On-line Program Specialization

The discussion above centered on two problem types: some decisions seem very hard to take, and some seem computationally expensive. It could be argued that our binding time analysis is also very expensive due to the uses of fixpoint computations. But this cost can be much better tolerated during preprocessing since it is done only once and not every time the program is specialized (*e.g.* at compiler generation time, not at compile time). Further, the costs of preprocessing are independent of the size of the source or residual programs.

Summing up:

0. The version of 6.3.1 is far too conservative for practical use.

1. On-line avoidance of constructing an infinite poly seems to be both computationally expensive and not general enough for practically interesting programs.

2. On-line choice of v_{s1} also seems to be both computationally expensive, and difficult without nonlocal information.

3. Self-application (for example: compiler = L mix <mix, interpreter>) of the program specializer causes special problems even more intricate than those just discussed, but which can also be alleviated by annotating program $\mathfrak{l}$ prior to specialization.

4. On-line tests are also bad for self-application, since they depend on the program being specialized, and so can't be computed at compiler generation time. For a more detailed explanation of this, see [Jones, Sestoft, Søndergaard 85, 88].

5. Program specialization *must be fast* when used for compiling and compiler generation for practical reasons. This argues for a minimum number of on-line tests during specialization.

6. Building poly first and doing loop compression after has in our experiments turned out to be impractical due to space problems.

7. It is hard to avoid infinite loops when doing on-line unfolding.

These remarks all suggest the desirability of finding a program division function d prior to program specialization, to collect information to make the specialization algorithm easier and more efficient.

8. Related Work

In addition to the works discussed earlier, the articles by [Launchbury 88], [Nielson 88] and [Schmidt 88] in this proceedings concern related questions. All three are domain-based, in opposition to our more operational approach. None describe methods that have been implemented in practice.

The papers by Nielson and Schmidt (among other things) develop methods to decorate expressions in the lambda calculus with binding time information, to determine which redexes are static and so could in principle be reduced away at compile time. This could be applied, for example, to compiling from a denotational semantics - the source program is mapped into a lambda expression, whose static subexpressions are reduced to yield a residual lambda expression as target program. The binding time analyses amount to an extension to the typed lambda calculus of our dependency analysis (sections 5.3 and 6.2).

The paper by Launchbury sets up a mathematical framework for projections, a domain-based counterpart of our divisions. He proves their existence for a fairly general class of first order recursively defined domains and concludes with a discussion of some practical issues.

One difference between our work and these papers is that none gives methods for program point specialization or for solving the finiteness question, two problems which we feel are at the heart of program specialization. The lambda calculus is certainly much more expressive than the rather rudimentary languages of this article, but we chose them due to realizing that our finiteness problems for a functional language would be precisely the same in an imperative language, and were easier to formalize and solve [Jones, Sestoft, Søndergaard 85, 88]. There is clearly room and need to do analogous work for stronger languages, and we are curently working on partial evaluation of untyped lambda expressions.

Another difference is that we work with untyped languages and use operational methods rather than domain theory. Work without types was partly motivated by difficulties in earlier work with strongly typed systems, and especially by the question "what is the type of a self interpreter for a strongly typed language"? The value of an interpreter's program argument completely determines the necessary type of its data argument - with all types expressible by programs being possible. We thus have a severe *dependent type* problem, one to this writer's knowledge beyond the scope of existing type systems. The use of universal reflexive domains will not solve this problem unless a way can be found to handle the ubiquitous sum injection tags necessary to implement this approach.

Our emphasis on operational methods stems from difficulties with seeing how to trace data flow through higher order programs when using the traditional reflexive domains as denotations of higher order functions. For example, what is a program point, and how can a complete set of specialized program points be collected?

ACKNOWLEDGEMENTS

Many people have directly or indirectly helped, both during the crystallization of the concepts expressed here and during the actual writing of the paper. Special, thanks are due to Olivier Danvy, Torben Mogensen and Peter Sestoft and as well to: Nils Andersen, Anders Bondorf, Carsten Kehler Holst, John Launchbury and Mads Rosendahl.

BIBLIOGRAPHY

[ADJ 78]
  J. Goguen, J. Thatcher & E. Wagner, An initial Algebra approach to the specification, correctness and implementation of abstract data types, in *Current Trends in Programming Methodology IV* (ed. R. T. Yeh), pp. 80-149, Prentice-Hall, 1978

[Aho, Sethi, Ullman 86]
  Aho, A. V., R. Sethi, & J. D. Ullman, *Compilers: Principles, Techniques and Tools,* Addison Wesley, 1986

[Arbib, Manes 75]
  Arbib, M. & E. Manes, *Arrows, Structures, and Functors The Categorical Imperative,* 185 pp., Academic Press, 1975

[Beckman *et al* 76]
  Beckman, L., A. Haraldson, O. Oskarsson & E. Sandewall, A partial evaluator and its use as a programming tool, *Artificial Intelligence Journal,* Vol. 7, No. 4, pp. 319-357, 1976

[Bird 76]
  Bird, R., *Programs and Machines,* 214 pp., Wiley, 1976

[Bondorf, Jones, Mogensen, Sestoft 88]
  Bondorf, A. & N. D. Jones, T. Mogensen, P. Sestoft, Self application and binding time analysis, *in preparation*

[Bulyonkov 84]
  Bulyonkov, M. A., Polyvariant mixed computation for analyzer programs, *Acta Informatica* 21, pp. 473-484, 1984

[Ershov 77]
    Ershov, A. P., On the partial computation principle, *Inf. Proc. Letters* 6, 2, pp. 38-41, 1977

[Ershov 82]
    Ershov, A. P., Mixed computation: potential applications and problems for future study, *Theoretical Computer Science*, No. 18, pp. 41-67, 1982

[Fuller, Abramsky 88]
    Fuller, D. & S. Abramsky, Mixed computation of Prolog programs, *this volume*, 1988

[Futamura 71]   *l*
    Futamura, Y., Partial evaluation of computation process - an approach to a compiler-compiler, *Systems, Computers, Controls* 2,5, pp. 45-50, 1971

[Futamura 83]
    Futamura, Y., Partial computation of programs, *in* LNCS 147: *Proc RIMS Symp. Software Science and Engineering*, Kyoto, Japan, pp. 1-35, Springer-Verlag, 1983

[Ganzinger, Jones 86]
    Ganzinger, Harald & N. D. Jones (eds.), *Programs as Data Objects*, Lecture Notes in Computer Science 217, Springer -Verlag, 1986

[Gécseg, Steinby 84]
    Gécseg, F. & M. Steinby, *Tree Automata*, Akadémiai Kiadó, Budapest, 235 pp., 1984

[Gordon 79]
    Gordon, M., *The Denotational Description of Programming Languages*, Springer -Verlag, 1979

[Hecht 77]
    Hecht, M. S., *Flow Analysis of Computer Programs*. New York: Elsevier North-Holland, 1977.

[Hopcroft, Ullman 79]
    Hopcroft, J. & J. Ullman, *Introduction to Automata Theory, Languages and Computation*, Addison-Wesley, Reading, Mass., 1979

[Jones 87]
    Jones, N. D., Flow analysis of lazy higher order functional programs, *Abstract Interpretation of Declarative Languages*, S. Abramsky & C. Hankin (eds.), Michael Horwood, Chichester, England, 1987

[Jones, Muchnick 76]
    Jones, Neil D. & Steven S. Muchnick, Automatic optimization of binding times, *Conf. Rec. of Third ACM Symp. on Principles of Programming Languages*, Atlanta, GA., pp. 77-94, 1977

[Jones, Muchnick 81]
    Jones, N. D. & S. S. Muchnick, Flow analysis and optimization of LISP-like structures, in [Muchnick, Jones 81]

[Jones, Sestoft, Søndergaard 85]
    Jones, N. D., P. Sestoft & H. Søndergaard, An Experiment in Partial Evaluation: the Generation of a Compiler Generator, *Proc. Conf. on Rewriting Techniques and Applications, Lecture Notes in Computer Science* 202, pp. 124-140, Springer-Verlag, 1985

[Jones, Sestoft, Søndergaard 87]
Jones, N. D., P. Sestoft & H. Søndergaard, MIX: a self-applicable partial evaluator for experiments in compiler generation, invited paper to appear in *Journal of LISP and Symbolic Computation,* 1988

[Launchbury 88]
Launchbury, J., Projections for specialisation, *this volume,* 1988

[Lombardi 67]
Lombardi, L.A., Incremental computation, *Advances in Computers,* F. Alt & M. Rubinoff (eds.), pp. 247-333, Academic Press, 1967

[McNaughton 82]
McNaughton, R. *Elementary Computability, Formal Languages, and Automata,* Prentice-Hall, Englewood Cliffs, N.J., 1982

[Mogensen 86]
Mogensen, T., *The Application of Partial Evaluation to Ray-tracing,* Master's thesis, Institute of Datalogy, University of Copenhagen, Denmark, 1986

[Mogensen 87]
Mogensen, Torben, Partially static structures in a self-applicable partial evaluator, *this volume.*

[Mosses 79]
Mosses, P. D., *SIS - Semantics Implementation, Reference Manual and User Guide,* DAIMI MD-30, University of Aarhus, Denmark, 1979

[Muchnick, Jones 81]
Muchnick, S. S. & N. D. Jones (eds.), *Program Flow Analysis: Theory and Applications,* Prentice-Hall, Englewood Cliffs, New Jersey, 1981

[Nielson 88]
Nielson, F., A formal type system for compareing partial evaluators, *this volume,* 1988

[Romanenko 88]
Romanenko, S. A., A compiler generator produced by a self-applicable specializer can have a surprisingly natural and understandable structure, *this volume,* 1988

[Salomaa 69]
Salomaa, A., *Theory of Automata,* Oxford: Pergamon Press

[Schmidt 86]
Schmidt, D. A., *Denotational Semantics,* Allyn and Bacon, Boston, 1986

[Schmidt 88]
Schmidt, D. A., Static Properties of Partial Reduction, *this volume,* 1988

[Sestoft 86]
Sestoft, Peter, The structure of a self-applicable partial evaluator, in [Ganzinger, Jones 86]

[Sestoft 87]
Sestoft, Peter, Automatic call unfolding in a partial evaluator, *this volume.*

[Thatcher 73]
Thatcher, J., Tree automata: an informal survey, in *Currents in the Theory of Computing* (ed. A. V. Aho), Prentice-Hall, Englewood Clifs, N. J., pp. 143-172, 1973

[Turchin 80]
Turchin, V., Semantic definitions in REFAL and automatic production of compilers, in Semantics-Directed Compiler Generation, N. D. Jones (ed.), *Lecture Notes in Computer Science* 202, pp. 441-474, Springer-Verlag, 1980

[Turchin 86]
Turchin, V., The concept of a supercompiler, *ACM Transactions on Programming Languages and Systems,* b(3), pp. 292-325, 1986

[Turchin 88]
Turchin, V., The algorithm of generalization in the supercompiler, *this volume,* 1988

[Wadler 84]
Wadler, P., Listlessness is better than laziness: lazy evaluation and garbage collection at compile time, in *ACM Symposium on LISP and Functional Programming,* pp. 45-52, ACM, 1984

[Wadler 85]
Wadler, P., Listlessness is better than laziness II composing listless functions, in [Ganzinger, Jones 85], pp. 282-305, 1985

[Wadler 88]
Wadler, P., Deforestation: transforming programs to eliminate trees, in *European Symposium on Programming, Lecture Notes in Computer Science,* Springer-Verlag, 1988

Partial Evaluation and Mixed Computation
D. Bjørner, A.P. Ershov and N.D. Jones (Editors)
Elsevier Science Publishers B.V. (North-Holland)
    IFIP, 1988

Pure Partial Evaluation and Instantiation[*]

Peter Kursawe

Gesellschaft für Mathematik und Datenverarbeitung
Forschungsstelle an der Universität Karlsruhe
Haid-und-Neu-Str.7, D-7500 Karlsruhe 1, Germany (West)

e-mail: kursawe@karlsruhe.gmd.dbp&de

We give precise definitions for declarative languages and partial evaluation of such languages executing only interpretative steps (*pure* partial evaluation). The definitions are based on a rule oriented view of the languages and relate the problem of implementing a partial evaluator to searching an or-tree. The success of pure partial evaluation is shown to depend on (at least some) known input arguments: these are formalized by instantiations that are instances of language expressions. Considering Horn clause logic and Prolog it is shown that instantiations can be got by pure partial evaluation itself. Formal proofs for a pure partial evaluation procedure for Horn clause logic are given.

1. Introduction

The definition of partial evaluation by a semantic preserving mapping

$$pe : \textbf{Program} \times \textbf{Data} \rightarrow \textbf{Program}$$

is used by many authors to characterize their work. But the realizations of partial evaluation range from a slightly modified interpretation process to using a rather complicated set of transformation rules. So we raise the question: what is the core of partial evaluation?

Because of the large number of execution, transformation, and evaluation rules necessary for imperative languages (e.g. [Ershov 86]) and because of the difficulties arising with the concepts of assignment and memory states (e.g. handled in [Ershov 85]) we restrict our attention to rather simple languages with only some rules describing the execution of programs. Such languages are *declarative* languages and include λ-calculus, term rewriting systems, and logical calculi. These languages have in common a single assignment property, a simple operational semantic, and it is possible to handle incomplete data structures (containing variables). We give a rule based definition for such languages. Then interpretation of a call means searching an or-tree spanned by the call and all applicable rules until an expression is reached which represents a solution. The operational instances of the mentioned languages (pure LISP, equational logic programming languages, pure Prolog) are characterized by searching this or-tree according to a certain strategy.

Because the execution rules are applicable to incomplete data also, we first define *pure* partial evaluation as executing these rules according to *any* strategy to produce a *finite* or-tree. From this tree either a single expression or some new specialized definitions can be extracted.

Pure partial evaluation enables handling of given arguments properly but there are two problems: the first one occurs with too less instantiated calls: either no rule might be applicable (in term rewriting systems when no match is possible), or a reduction is useless (in λ-calculus when a function applies to a variable), or even too much rules can be applied (in Horn clause logic when a predicate is defined by a large set of facts). On the other hand: if some more (parts of

---

[*] This work has been done within a joint project of the GMD and the SFB 314 (artificial intelligence) at the University of Karlsruhe

the) input is known then application of rules is very useful. This leads to the concept of *instantiations* of calls: given a finite set of instances of a call, it is possible to derive a specialized version for each member of the set by pure partial evaluation.

A second problem is a more technical one but also of great importance: can the new definitions extracted from an or-tree *replace* the original definitions or are some solutions lost (because the new definitions are not as general as the old ones)? From an or-tree new definitions are created for instantiated calls in the tree. So this is the same as asking: does an instantiation contain enough calls handling all calls occuring at run time? We handle this problem by imposing the property of *completeness* on instantiations: a finite set of instances of a call has to cover all possible solutions of the call. That is, each solution must be an instance of at least one member of the set.

So our attention is shifted to the problem ,,how to get complete instantiations" for the calls of the program. We study this problem for Horn clause logic. We propose a *user mode* where possible instantiations can be described by Horn clauses itself. Calls can be inserted into a program and pure partial evaluation itself produces the instances. Inserted calls are like assertions and their completeness has to be proved. They do not affect the semantics of a program. As an example types can be used to derive instances for the possible term structures of arguments.

Considering *automatic inference* of instantiations it turns out that for Horn clause logic pure partial evaluation itself yields complete instantiations w.r.t. a special call. This knowledge can be incorporated into a pure partial evaluation algorithm as the strategy for building a finite or-tree. So we give a formal foundation for a (pure) partial evaluator of pure Prolog.

This last result does not hold for term rewriting systems because the "one-way" property of matching prevents variable arguments from getting instantiated. But if matching is replaced by unification the same results as for Horn clause logic can be got.

1.1 Relation to Other Work

Note that for declarative languages partial evaluation and "mixed computation" is the same. The latter differs from the former by resulting in a program *and* some data [Ershov 85]. But in declarative languages data is contained in the program itself (as λ-expressions or terms).

[Ershov 78] essentially defines pure partial evaluation (mixed computation) for recursive program schemata. Using a rule based language definition and stressing the strategy aspect simplifies such presentations. Especially the usage of a set of rewrite rules in term rewriting systems (Horn clauses in Horn clause logic) defining a function (a predicate) makes it easy to add specialized definitions to an existing program.

[Komorowski 82] describes a (pure) Prolog interpreter and partial evaluator in a denotational semantics like style. He defines partial evaluation as pruning (deleting unnecessary clauses), forward, and backward data structure propagation. All these are included in pure partial evaluation but in a simple uniform way. Also we give some considerations about the strategy of applying pure partial evaluation and we do not use an other formalism (like Meta IV as Komorowski does).

[Venken 84] gives an *implementation* which does pure partial evaluation for full Prolog. No formal justification is given: see [O'Keefe 85] for further critics on this work.

In [Ershov, Ostrovski 86] mixed computation is a special case of our finite or-tree construction: the strategy always selects exactly one rule. Mixed computation is defined for a statement oriented language with 10 rules for interpretation. These rules (with some minor modifications), 3 additional rules, and 10 "ad hoc" transformations are used for mixed computation.

[Heering 86] gives a theoretical framework for systems of equations which goes beyond pure partial evaluation: he proves some theorems which allow the usage of nontrivial equations to simplify terms. Up until now analogous work for Horn clause logic (or Prolog) does not exist (to the best of our knowledge).

1.2 Overview

The next chapter 2. defines declarative languages and pure partial evaluation. Some considerations about implementing a pure partial evaluator are given. In chapter 3. we give an example and in 4. we investigate instantiations in the form of *complete pattern sets* for Horn clause logic. In 5. we show how complete pattern sets given by the user can be used and in 6. the strategy for pure partial evaluation is refined to produce a complete pattern set during the pure partial evaluation process itself.

2. Pure Partial Evaluation

In this chapter we give a formal framework for reasoning about the operational semantics of a language. We define pure partial evaluation and apply this definition to Horn clause logic. Problems with a pure partial evaluator for Prolog derived from the formal definition are discussed.

2.1 Declarative Languages

We formalize our notion of a declarative language by the following rule based definition:

DEFINITION 1. Let E be a set of *expressions* and $R[d]$ be a set of *rules* $r : E \rightarrow E$ (possibly depending on a finite set d of *definitions* (of the form **head :: expression**)) which map expressions into expressions. Let $S(e)$ be an unary predicate on E, the *stopping condition*. Then $DL = \langle E, R, S \rangle$ is (the operational part of) a *declarative language*.

Interpretation of an expression e (a *call*) w.r.t. a set of definitions d is done by constructing a *derivation* $e \rightarrow_{r1[d]} e_1 \rightarrow_{r2[d]} e_2 \cdots \rightarrow_{rn[d]} e_n$ where $S(e_n)$ holds. ■

Here we are not concerned with the semantics of declarative languages: the correctness of partial evaluation is proved against the effect of a given program (as described by interpretation) whatever the semantics of this program might be.

Starting with an expression e several derivations may be possible: these can be pictured in an or-tree rooted in e where the nodes are expressions and the branches represent the possible (different) derivations. A declarative language with an arbitrary search strategy for interpretation is called *pure* while the practical instances of declarative languages operate according to a given strategy.

Example 1: pure declarative languages are λ-*calculus* ($E = \lambda$-expressions, $R = \alpha$-, β-, η-reduction, $S = $ „no rule is applicable"), *term rewriting systems* ($E = $ terms, $R = $ term reduction, $S = $ „no rule is applicable", $d = $ a set of rewrite rules), *Horn clause logic* ($E = $ conjunctions of literals (written $L_1, \ldots, L_n$), $R = $ resolution, $S(e) = e$ is the empty clause (denoted by □), $d = $ a set of Horn clauses (written $L_0 :- L_1, \ldots, L_n$)). Practical instances of these languages are pure LISP, „equational programming" [O'Donnell 87], pure Prolog. ■

Note that the definition does not specify „input" or „output". It depends on the special language what the output should be: e.g. the expression where the stopping condition holds (as in λ-calculus and term rewriting systems), or the substitution computed during derivations (as in Horn clause logic).

2.2 Pure Partial Evaluation

To emphasize the aspect of partial evaluation as doing essentially interpretative steps (in contrast to applying other transformations as well) we define *pure* partial evaluation:

DEFINITION 2. Let DL be a declarative language and e an expression of DL. *Pure partial* *evaluation* of **e** is the expansion of **e** to a finite or-tree according to the rules of **DL**. ∎

So pure partial evaluation differs from interpretation only in strategy and the stopping conditions, but not in the applied rules. Because no distinction between programs and data are made, for declarative languages pure partial evaluation is the same as *mixed computation* [Ershov 78].

In practice the result of pure partially evaluating an expression **e** should itself be an expression or definition of the language. Fig. 1 shows schematically an or-tree rooted in a call **c** with expressions e_i at the leafs. It is understood that for all inner nodes of the tree all possible succes-

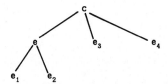

Figure 1. Or-tree for a call **c**.

sors are constructed. There are two ways to map this tree into expressions of the language: either replace the call **c** by e_1 OR e_2 OR e_3 OR e_4 where OR is a construct of the language that allows the derivation of either of it's two arguments according to the language's strategy. The other way is to include new definitions like **c** :: e_i into the corresponding program, thereby shifting the ,,OR'' to the rule selection process.

Example 2: Fig. 2(a) gives a nondeterministic term rewriting system for yielding a member

```
mem([X|_]) -> X
mem([_|R]) -> mem(R)
```

    (a)   (b)

Figure 2. Rewrite rules (a) and an example or-tree (b) for getting elements of a list.

of a list. Pure partial evaluation of **mem([a,b|Rest])** may result in the tree of Figure 2(b). So either **mem([a,b|Rest])** can be replaced by **or(a,or(b,mem(Rest)))** provided the definition of **or** is given by:

```
or(A,B) -> A
or(A,B) -> B
```

or additional rules are included in the rewrite rule program:

```
mem([a,b|Rest]) -> a
mem([a,b|Rest]) -> b
mem([a,b|Rest]) -> mem(Rest)
```

In both cases the normal forms are the same. ∎

Considering a practical implementation of the or-tree expansion, two improvements can be made depending on special properties of the rule system:

- We say: two rule applications r_1, r_2 for the same expression **e** are *commutative* when **e** $\rightarrow_{r1}$ e_1 $\rightarrow_{r2}$ e_2 and **e** $\rightarrow_{r2}$ e_3 $\rightarrow_{r1}$ e_2. Then for **e** only one of the alternatives **r1**, **r2** has to be applied; the or-tree rooted in **e** becomes smaller without loss of results.
- If there are "independent" subexpressions **s1**, **s2** of an expression **e[s1;s2]** then pure partial evaluation of **s1** and **s2** can be done separately (*splitting*). The results **S1** and **S2** can be composed either to **e[S1;S2]** or itself be decomposed into OR-alternatives **s11 OR ... OR s1n** and **s21 OR ... OR s2m** and then be incorporated into **e[s11;s21] OR ... OR e[s1n;s2m]** (**n*m** components) depending on the number of the components.

2.3 Pure partial evaluation for pure Prolog

Pure partial evaluation for pure Prolog is the construction of the or-tree starting with a conjunction of literals at the root and applying resolution where possible. Now we give some practical considerations how to span this tree and how to extract a result from the tree.

In a conjunction **(A,B)** possible resolutions on **A** are commutative with such possible in **B**. So only one part is chosen for the or-tree expansion. Optimal is the selection of a literal with only one solution. Otherwise the first literal has to be processed for keeping the resulting solutions in the same order as before.[1] Instantiations of common variables then diminish the number of solutions for the other calls. Splitting is only possible if two literals have no vari-

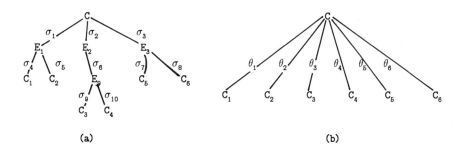

(a)   (b)

Figure 3. or-tree for a Horn clause program and a compacted form of the tree. The substitutions θ_i in (b) are compositions of the corresponding substitutions σ_j in (a).

ables in common.

As mentioned above, there are two ways of extracting a result from an or-tree. Consider the tree in figure 3(a) and it's *compacted* form in 3(b). For a substitution $\theta = \{X_1 \rightarrow t_1, \ldots, X_n \rightarrow t_n\}$ let $|\theta|$ be the conjunction $X_1 = t_1, \ldots, X_n = t_n$. Then there are two procedures for result extraction:

Expression extraction: from figure 3(b) the expression **E** = $(|\theta_1|, C_1); \ldots; (|\theta_n|, C_n)$ can be constructed and **C** and **E** give the same results (= answer substitutions).[2]

Definition extraction: works only if **C** is a single literal. Then for figure 3(b) 6 clauses $\theta_i C$:- C_i can be derived and added to the program. With the new program **C** can be processed faster because it can be derived to a C_i with a single step while it tooks several steps with the origi-

---

1 This is the only difference between pure partial evaluation for pure Prolog and Horn clause logic: for Horn clause logic it does not matter which literal is selected.

2 ; is the Prolog-OR: it reduces to it's first argument and on backtracking to it's second one.

nal program. Definition extraction can also be applied to *parts* of the or-tree: from the tree in figure 4(a) the clauses in 4(b) can be derived. The general (indeterministic) procedure is as follows:

if the tree is only a literal L then the result of pure partial evaluation is the call of L;

if the tree contains a literal L as inner node with leafs $C_1, \ldots, C_n$ reachable from L (and corresponding substitutions θ_i), then create new clauses $\theta_i L$:- C_i and delete the C_i-branches from the tree (so L becomes a leaf);

proceed until the tree is empty.

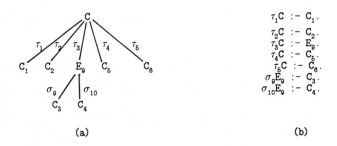

$$\tau_1 C :- C_1.$$
$$\tau_2 C :- C_2.$$
$$\tau_3 C :- E_9.$$
$$\tau_4 C :- C_5.$$
$$\tau_5 C :- C_6.$$
$$\sigma_9 E_9 :- C_3.$$
$$\sigma_{10} E_9 :- C_4.$$

(a)   (b)

Figure 4. Partly compacted or-tree and example of an extracted program (C and E_9 must be literals!).

What are the criteria to prefer expression or definition extraction?

1. The optimized program should contain optimized clauses for all occuring calls: so expression extraction can only be used if no further calls occur at the leafs which there is no optimized version for. General definition extraction provides a tool to handle this aspect. For further problems with definition extraction see below.

2. Which extraction is more efficient? This depends strongly on the actual Prolog implementation: using a (e.g.) CProlog interpreter the ; is implemented by an expensive meta call while in compiler based systems the alternative construct usually is treated in a more efficient way. We are oriented on state-of-the-art compilation techniques for Prolog and normally use definition extraction because compilers provide efficient clause selection mechanisms w.r.t. to the arguments in the head of a clause. But if two alternatives are not different w.r.t. the substitutions $|\theta_i|$ we use the ;-construct.

It is possible to *add* the extracted definitions to the old program and provide a mechanism for first looking if an optimized version exists for a call. But it would be more satisfying if the optimized program can *replace* the old program. This leads to the problem of *completeness*: which clauses have to be extracted from the or-tree so that no solution necessary for running a goal C is lost? The given procedure for extracting clauses is indeterministic. So detailed knowledge of the calls occuring at run time is necessary for a complete extraction. We solve this problem by the *complete pattern sets* defined in chapter 4. But first we will make an extensive example in the next chapter.

Finally note that pure partial evaluation of Prolog is a much harder task to accomplish. The main problem is that the backward propagation of variable bindings might effect the execution of instance dependent predicates. That is, the rules describing Horn clause logic alone can not be used to pure partially evaluate Prolog properly. We are currently working on a formal treatment of the backward unification problem.

3. An Example: Searching in strings

We show the advantages and disadvantages of pure partial evaluation with a partial evaluation based description of the well-known Knuth-Morris-Pratt algorithm [Knuth et al. 77] for searching (constant) patterns in strings. The problem is as follows: Given two strings, a (short) *symbol* and a (long) *text*. Does *symbol* occur as substring in *text*?

We give a Horn clause logic program[1] for this problem. The idea is as follows: the symbol under consideration is splitted into a prefix (initially empty) and a postfix (initially the symbol itself). If the next character in the text matches the next character of the symbol this character is deleted from the postfix and appended to the prefix. Otherwise characters from the prefix are shifted to the postfix such that the new character is accepted correctly (this is done by the last three calls to **append** in the second clause of **new**). **SymbInfo** is the tuple (prefix,postfix).

```
contains(Text,Symbol) :- con(Text,([],Symbol)).

con(_,(_,[])).                 % Symbol found
con([C|Rtext],SymbInfo) :- new(C,SymbInfo,SymbInfoNew),
                           con(Rtext,SymbInfoNew).
new(C,(Prefix,[C|RestPostfix]),(PrefixNew,RestPostfix))
          :- append(Prefix,[D], PrefixNew).
new(C,(Prefix,[D|RestPostfix]),(PrefixNew,PostfixNew))
          :- C\==D, append(Prefix,[C],H), append(_,PrefixNew,H),
                    append(PrefixNew,Rest,Prefix),
                    append(Rest,[D|RestPostfix],PostfixNew).

append([],L,L).
append([X|L1],L2,[X|L3]) :- append(L1,L2,L3).
```

Now let **Symbol** be **[a,a,b]**. Pure partial evaluation of **contains(Text,[a,a,b])** with **Text** being a variable may result in the or-tree of figure 5. From this or-tree by definition extraction the following clauses can be derived:

```
con([a|R],([],[a,a,b])) :- con(R,([a],[a,b])).
con([C|R],([],[a,a,b])) :- C\==a, con(R,([],[a,a,b])).
```

That is, for the call **con(R,([a],[a,b]))** always the nonoptimized version has to be used. Now consider the or-tree in figure 6, which shows a partly compacted version of a bigger or-tree for the same call. According to the two ways of result extraction the result is either the disjunction

```
T=[C|R], (C=a,R=[C1|R1], (C1=a,R1=[C2|R2], (C2=b
                                       ; (C2=a, con(R2,([a,a],[b]))
                                        ;C2=a, con(R2,([a],[a,b]))
                                        ;C2\==b, con(R2,([],[a,a,b])))
                                        )
                           ;C1\==a, con(R1,([],[a,a,b])))
          ;C\==a, con(R,([],[a,a,b]))
          )
```

or clauses like

```
contains(T,[a,a,b]) :- con(T,([],[a,a,b])).

con([a|R],([],[a,a,b])) :- con(R,([a],[a,b])).
con([C|R],([],[a,a,b])) :- C\==a, con(R,([],[a,a,b])).
con([a|R],([a],[a,b]))  :- con(R,([a,a],[b])).
con([C|R],([a],[a,b]))  :- C\==a, con(R,([],[a,a,b])).
```

---

1 The program uses the Prolog built-in \== for syntactical inequality.

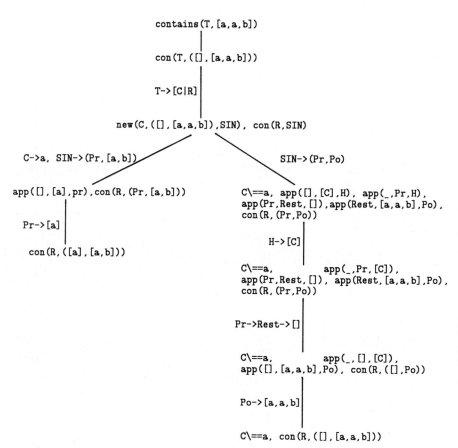

Figure 5. An or-tree for `contains(T, [a,a,b])`. Due to lack of space append is abbreviated to **app**.

```
con([b|R],([a,a],[b])).
con([a|R],([a,a],[b])) :- con(R,([a,a],[b])) ; con(R,([a],[a,b])).
con([C|R],([a,a],[b])) :- C\==b, con(R,([],[a,a,b])).
```

This set of clauses can be used to *replace* the old definition of the **con**-predicate: all calls occurring in the bodies are solved by this set of clauses. A further advantage is the uniform structure of the clause heads. This permits an efficient implementation due to the deterministic clause selection (for calls with instantiated arguments) in connection with the clause selection facilities of state-of-the-art Prolog compilers. Moreover, additional optimizations can easily be applied to that clauses: e.g. replace ($[s_1,\ldots,s_i], [s_{i+1},\ldots,s_n]$) by the number i to reduce unification effort.

The possible forms of the **SymbInfo** correspond to the states of a finite automaton and the **con**-predicate realizes the state transitions of this automaton as described in [Knuth et al. 77].

These advantages mainly come from

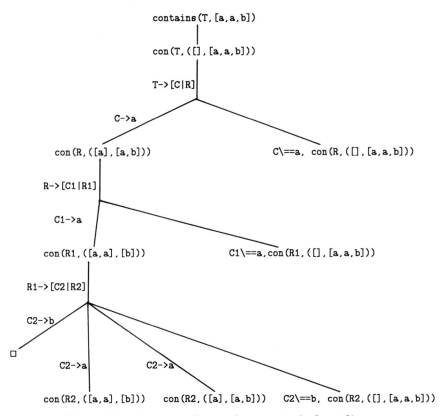

Figure 6. Partly compacted or-tree for contains(T, [a,a,b]).

1. extensively using terms as data representation facility (in contrast to a relational style of programming where data is represented using facts), and from

2. getting a set of instances for a predicate which covers all cases the predicate can be called. In the following we will investigate sets of instances (called pattern sets) more closely and we will find ways how to get them.

This sort of optimization comes with a special program structure; some *control* recurs (perhaps indirectly) on arguments that are not known at partial evaluation time; the control calls *operations* with parts of these unknown arguments and some known arguments: here partial evaluation brings efficiency while partial evaluation of control via expression extraction might complicate things. An important instance of this class of programs is a Prolog interpreter recurring on a conjunction not known at partial evaluation time.

4. Complete Pattern Sets

Now we are going to formalize the idea of complete instantiations for Horn clause logic (we assume some familiarity with the theory of Horn clauses as can be found in [Lloyd 84]).

DEFINITION 3. A finite set of literals with the same predicate symbol p/n is called a *pattern set* for p/n (we write $PS_{p/n}$ but note that there is no unique pattern set for a predicate).

Let $P_{p/n}$ be a finite set of Horn clauses (a *procedure*) with same head predicate p/n and let Ax be a finite set of arbitrary Horn clauses. Let C be a conjunction and consider all possible successful derivations for C to the empty clause w.r.t. Ax. Then $Nec[C]$ is the set of all solved[1] literals in these derivations (*necessary* for the derivation of C). $Nec[C]$ can be divided into classes $Sol_{q/m,C}$ for each m-ary predicate q (the *solutions* of q w.r.t. the goal C).

A *complete pattern set* $CPS_{p/n,C}$ is a pattern set with: for all solved literals $p(t_1, \ldots, t_n) \in Sol_{p/n,C}$ there exists a literal $L \in CPS_{p/n,C}$ such that $p(t_1, \ldots, t_n)$ is an instance of L. For $C = p(X_1, \ldots, X_n)$ we write $CPS_{p/n}$ and $Sol_{p/n}$. The latter is the set of all p-literals L derivable from Ax (usually written $Ax \; |-- \; L$). ∎

A complete pattern set $CPS_{p/n,C}$ comprises all calls occuring while running C as well as taking into account the possible substitutions resulting from successful derivations.

Example 3: A complete pattern set for $con/2$ w.r.t. the call $contains(T, [a, a, b])$ is
$$CPS_{con/2, contains(T, [a, a, b])} = \{ \; con(T, ([], [a, a, b])),$$
$$con(T, ([a], [a, b])),$$
$$con(T, ([a, a], [b])),$$
$$con(T, ([a, a, b], [])) \; \}$$
A trivial one is $\{con(T, S)\}$. Note that all following theorems also hold for this always existing trivial set. ∎

With a complete pattern set $CPS_{p/n,C}$ the following construction is defined:

CONSTRUCTION (*Complete Instantiation*)
for every literal $L \in CPS_{p/n,C}$ get all clauses the head of which is unifiable with L. Instantiate the matching clauses with the respective unifier. This forms a new set of clauses $N_{p/n,C}$.
Then it holds:

THEOREM 1. Let $P_{p/n}$ be a procedure, Ax a set of Horn clauses, C a call, $CPS_{p/n}$ a complete pattern set and $N_{p/n}$ the result of completely instantiating $P_{p/n}$ w.r.t. $CPS_{p/n,C}$. Then: for all instances C' of C it holds: $Ax \cup P_{p/n} \; |-- \; C'$ iff $Ax \cup N_{p/n} \; |-- \; C'$.

Proof: Consider a successful derivation D of C' to the empty clause in $Ax \cup P_{p/n}$. D can be represented in an and-tree which nodes are conjunctions and where each literal of a conjunction corresponds to a successor-conjunction. The leafs are labelled with the empty clause and all computed substitutions are applied. For every literal L and its successor conjunction $Conj$

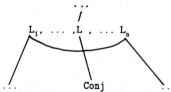

Figure 7. Part of an and-tree ($Conj$ is a conjunction of literals).

it holds (cf. fig. 7), that $Cl = L \; :- \; Conj$ is an instance of a clause $H \; :- \; Body$ from $Ax \cup P_{p/n}$. We show that every Cl is also an instance of a clause from $Ax \cup N_{p/n}$. This is nontrivi-

---
1 These are literals where the corresponding answer substitution [Lloyd 84] is applied.

al only for $L = p(t_1, \ldots, t_n)$. Let $p(t_1, \ldots, t_n) = \theta H$. It holds that $p(t_1, \ldots, t_n) \in$ $\text{Sol}_{p/n,c}$ w.r.t. $\text{Ax} \cup P_{p/n}$. Then (according to the definition of complete pattern sets) there exists a literal $P \in \text{CPS}_{p/n,c}$ and a substitution σ with $\sigma P = p(t_1, \ldots, t_n)$, that is: $\sigma P = \theta H$. So $\sigma \theta$ is a unifier for P and H (variables in P and H are disjunct!). Let τ be their most general unifier. According to the construction of complete instantiaton $N_{p/n}$ contains the clause $\tau(H :- \text{Body})$. Because $\sigma \theta$ is a unifier of P and H there is a $\hat{\tau}$ with $\sigma\theta = \hat{\tau}\tau$ and $L = \hat{\tau}\tau H$. Because **Body** is an instance of θ**Conj** and $\theta = \hat{\tau}\tau$, **Body** is an instance of τ**Conj**, too.

The converse that all derivations in $\text{Ax} \cup N_{p/n}$ can be done in $\text{Ax} \cup P_{p/n}$ is trivial. ∎

Using a pattern set for transforming sets of Horn clauses enables further partial evaluation in the bodies of the resulting clauses. By making them "complete" no solution is lost.

Theorem 1 says that a set of clauses can be replaced by another set if the latter can be obtained from the former by complete instantiation. The question raised in section 2.3 (which clauses extracted from an or-tree can replace the original program?) is answered by this theorem. The clauses resulting from definition extraction correspond to a set of literals in the or-tree used as heads. It remains to decide if this set of literals form a complete pattern set or not. This question is studied in chapter 6.

Problems in constructing suitable complete pattern sets occur in balancing the number of elements in the set against the possible optimization effects. A large pattern set usually contains more instantiated literals, so there might be less calls with unknown arguments in the body of the clauses in $N_{p/n}$. Of course the partial evaluation effort to process all these clauses increases with the number of elements in the pattern set.

Instantiation is not the same as tabulation in [Futamura 82]. The latter collects all *partially evaluated* functions and makes them available for the partial evaluator in an efficient manner. Instantiation on the other hand provides special calls that *should* be partially evaluated.

The two following chapters discuss how to get suitable pattern sets either from the user or automatically.

5. User Given Pattern Sets

Complete pattern sets might be given by the user. Then two problems arise:

1. How to specify a pattern set?
2. How to prove a pattern set to be complete?

Specifying a pattern set means characterizing a finite set of literals with the same predicate symbol: so essentially a set of terms has to be described. *The* tool for describing sets of terms is Horn clause logic itself. So we propose that the user gives some Horn clauses for specifying the arguments of the predicate under consideration such that the characterized terms are a superset of the actually occuring arguments. These predicates can be inserted into the call (or the program) properly and then itself be pure partially evaluated yielding the desired literals for further pure partial evaluation.

Example 4: The complete pattern set for **con/2** in example 3 can be generated by pure partial evaluation from the call **append(Pre,Post,[a,a,b])**, **con(T,(Pre,Post))**. Figure 8 shows the beginning of an or-tree for this call. ∎

The problem of *proving* a pattern set to be complete leads to the problem of proving invariants and assertions of programs. In example 4 **append(Pre,Post,[a,a,b])** can be seen as an assertion "every time **con** is called, **Pre** and **Post** appended together give the symbol **[a,a,b]**". The assertion is formulated in the programming language itself. If the assertion holds, the effect of the program is the same with or without the call to **append**.

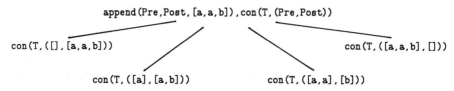

Figure 8. Beginning of an or-tree producing instances of **con**.

We have not developed special methods for proving such invariants. See [Hsiang, Srivas 85] for an environment for reasoning about abstract data types in Prolog programs.

A special case of term characterization is *typing* as described for Prolog in [Mycroft, O'Keefe 84]. Type definitions usually describe an infinite set of terms. They can be used to derive predicates for type checking which in turn can be pure partially evaluated to produce a finite set of terms of the corresponding type. Completeness of the pattern set is ensured if for each argument all not unifiable patterns and all combinations of such patterns at different argument positions are created.

Example 5: From the type definition for lists

```
type list(A) = [] ; [A | list(A)] .
```

the following clauses can be derived:

```
has_type(list(A),[]).
has_type(list(A),[X|L])  :- has_type(X,A), has_type(list(A),L).
```

If a program using lists can be proved well typed [Mycroft, O'Keefe 84] it does not affect semantics if calls to the type check predicates are inserted properly or not. In this case we first add some type check predicates, use them to derive instances of calls, and then delete the remaining checks.

For the example of chapter 3. the following types may be given:

```
type alph = a ; b ; c ; d.
type text = list(alph).
type tuple(T) = (T,T).

pred con( text , tuple(text) )
```

Fig. 9 shows pure partial evaluation of the call **con(T,(Pre,Post))** enriched by type checking predicates. ■

This method does not cover cases where negative knowledge (like $C \neq a$) is necessary. In general pure partial evaluation with such type informations alone is of restricted use because programs with extensive use of compound terms usually contain clauses for each type constructor: so the specialization is done by the programmer in advance.

The general advantage of user given complete pattern sets is that *additional* information not derivable directly from the program can be stated and used within the framework of pure partial evaluation.

6. Inferring Pattern Sets Automatically

Now we investigate the automatic inference of complete pattern sets for a **n**-ary predicate **p** in a program **Ax** w.r.t. a call **C**.

It is possible to use the most general complete pattern set $\{p(X_1, \ldots, X_n)\}$. But complete instantiation of the procedure $P_{p/n}$ leaves the clauses unchanged. Next it is possible to use all

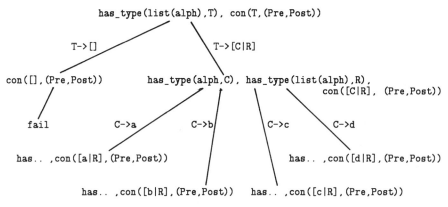

Figure 9. Or-tree with type checking predicates.

calls of **p** occuring in any body of the clauses in the program **Ax** (because all calls occuring at runtime must be instances of these). But in general this brings no advantage because calls in the body often do not contain structures but only variables (look at the bodies of the clauses in chapter 3).

How is it then possible to get calls of a predicate w.r.t. a special goal **C**? We are looking for a method of propagating the given values (in **C**) through the program to the calls of **p**. But this is exactly what pure partial evaluation does! So we are using pure partial evaluation itself to get instances of calls. That is, pure partial evaluation of **C** expands an or-tree containing literals. From this or-tree we extract the **p**-literals which are used as clause heads in the way the complete instantiation does. Pure partial evaluation of these literals then is not necessary: the result can be taken from the or-tree, too.

There remains one problem: how to decide if a set of **p**-literals taken from an or-tree is really a *complete* pattern set? In the following we formulate the property "**p**-completeness" of an or-tree: if an or-tree is **p**-complete then all **p**-literals in the tree form a complete pattern set. In practice this property is used to *construct* the or-tree. From this point of view it is a form of strategy and theorem 2 below together with theorem 1 ensures that the clauses created from an **p**-complete or-tree can replace the original clauses without loss of results.

The following very technical definitions 4 and 5 are used to refine the usual call graph of a Horn clause logic program: *head partitions* decompose a procedure according to the unifiability of heads of clauses in the procedure. If some heads are unifiable they are replaced by their *most common special literal*. Instead of using predicate names in the usual call graph, we use these not unifiable heads (*minimal instances*) and the literals in the bodies as nodes in a *specialized call graph*. The relation P *reaches* L then is defined in an obvious way. The specialized call graph allows more exact propositions about the call structure (cf. to the example in fig. 10).

DEFINITION 4. Let $P_{p/n}$ be a procedure. The *head partition* **Part** $=(S,M)$ of $P_{p/n}$ comprises two sets **S** and **M** of literals with: **S** contains all heads of clauses not unifiable with any other head of a clause in $P_{p/n}$; and **M** contains all clause heads unifiable with at least one other head of a clause in $P_{p/n}$.
A literal **K** is the *most special common literal* of two literals L_1, L_2 iff L_1 and L_2 are instances of **K** and there is no instance L of **K** (with $L \neq K$) which L_1 and L_2 are instances of (write **K** = **mscl**(L_1, L_2)). This definition generalizes in an obvious way to sets of literals. ∎

The definition of a **p**-complete or-tree depends on the call structure of the corresponding pro-

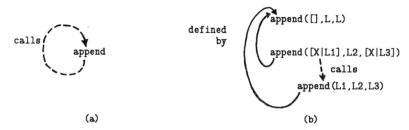

(a)   (b)

Figure 10. Usual (a) and specialized call graph (b) for **append**. A call like **append([],X,Y)** can be recursive according to (a) but not according to (b)!

gram. We refine the usual call graph to contain also certain instances of calls and clause heads in the following way:

DEFINITION 5. Let **Ax** be a program, for each predicate in **Ax** form it's head partition **(S,M)** and for each partition consider **S** ∪ **{mscl(M)}**, the set of *minimal instances.*

The *specialized call graph* for **Ax** is a directed graph with the minimal instances of each predicate in **Ax**, and all literals in the bodies as nodes (distinguish literals in seperate bodies). The edges are defined by two relations:

$p(u_1, \ldots, u_n)$ *calls* $r(s_1, \ldots, s_m)$ for all minimal instances $p(u_1, \ldots, u_n)$ iff there is a clause **Head:-Body** in **Ax** and $p(u_1, \ldots, u_n)$ is unifiable with **Head** and $r(s_1, \ldots, s_m)$ occurs in **Body**.

$r(s_1, \ldots, s_m)$ *defined by* $r(t_1, \ldots, t_m)$ for all calls $r(s_1, \ldots, s_m)$ iff the minimal instance $r(t_1, \ldots, t_m)$ is unifiable with $r(s_1, \ldots, s_m)$.

The transitive closure of *calls* ∪ *defined by* is called *reaches.* ◼

The specialized call graph is used in the following definition:

DEFINITION 6. Let **Ax** be a set of Horn clauses, **p** a **n**-ary predicate with clauses in **Ax** and let **T** be an or-tree rooted in a call **C**. **T** is **p/n**-*complete* iff for all paths in the tree it holds: either the path ends in a call which do not reach a **p**-call in the specialized call graph of **Ax**, or the path contains a **p**-call and then there is a path in **T** containing this same **p**-call twice (modulo renaming of variables). ◼

Now we can state the central theorem:

THEOREM 2. Let **T** be a **p/n**-complete or-tree rooted in a call **C** w.r.t. a program **Ax**. Then all calls $p(t_1, \ldots, t_n)$ in **T** form a complete pattern set $CPS_{p/n,c}$ w.r.t. **Ax**.

Proof: We have to show: for all $P \in Sol_{p/n,c}$ there is a $P' \in CPS_{p/n,c}$ which can be instantiated to P. Consider a successful derivation containing P. If P is in the part of the derivation overlapping with the or-tree then the theorem holds trivially. If not then the beginning of the derivation overlaps with a path **Pa** in the or-tree. There are two cases according to the **p/n**-completeness of **T**:

Pa ends in a call which does not reach a **p**-call in the specialized call graph for **Ax**: this is a contradiction.

Pa contains a **p**-call: then there is a path **Pa1** in the or-tree containing the same call twice. But from the same instance of a **p**-call it is impossible to derive two different sets of other **p**-calls. So the conditions of **p/n**-completeness ensure that all possible different instances were generated by pure partial evaluation. At runtime only instances of these can occur.

◼

The main question with complete pattern sets is: does a **p/n**-complete or-tree always exist?

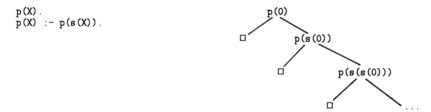

```
p(X) .
p(X)  :- p(s(X)) .
```

Figure 11. No **p/1**-complete or-tree possible.

Fig. 11 shows a program and a call for which no **p/1**-complete or-tree exist. In general the problem is undecidable (termination problems), but two cases can easily be identified:

1. increasing arguments: these might be detectable in special cases, but there are also cases where arguments grow and then shrink again. More investigation is necessary.

2. different but not increasing arguments: cf. to the calls to **con** in the example of chapter 3. These cases can be handled because there are only finitely many terms of the Herbrand universe which are "smaller" than a given term.

7. Conclusion

We defined pure partial evaluation for declarative languages as executing the same inference rules that are used for interpretation but with a special control mechanism to produce a finite OR-tree. We combined pure partial evaluation with the concept of complete instantiation to overcome some problems with getting all interesting calls that can be partially evaluated. For Horn clause logic we studied pure partial evaluation in more detail and gave a user supported and an automatic method for creating complete instantiations.

The advantages of using pure partial evaluation with complete instantiations are:

1. Suitable complete instantiations can be used to enable partial evaluation without the existence of any known arguments - just regarding the possible structure of the arguments (see also [Komorowski 82]).

2. Several phases of partial evaluation can be distinguished by using different complete instantiations. As an example consider two phases: (a) partial evaluation w.r.t. a type structure, and (b) partial evaluation w.r.t. concrete arguments. In phase (b) all partial evaluation steps depending on the *structure* of the arguments have not to be performed, they have been done in (a). This improves the efficiency of step (b) (this view is generalized to arbitrary program transformations in [Jørring, Scherlis 86]).

3. Additional partial evaluation is possible using user given complete instantiations even if automatic inference could not derive all possible calls.

The usage of Horn clause logic - more exactly: of unification - is crucial. For term rewriting systems the same results cannot be got in the same clean way. This comes from the difference between unification and matching: the former is a "two-way" operation that instantiates also unknown arguments while the latter don't. But replacing matching by unification admits to find all results given in this paper for term rewriting systems also. Of course, using unification instead of matching is not "pure" partial evaluation according to our definition. But it clarifies what is necessary for doing partial evaluation: it is some operation that anticipates the possible inputs which are unknown at partial evaluation time. For pure λ-calculus we failed to find such an easy solution - in our opinion progress in this direction will depend on the use of typing, at least for separating data and functions.

This work is closely connected to the derivation of Prolog machines and the construction of practical verifiable compilers for such machines. The gap of how to get the "interpretative enrichment" of [Kursawe 86] can be closed by using a complete pattern set for a Prolog interpreter w.r.t. a given program.

Acknowledgment: The KAP-group (*KA*rlsruhe *P*rolog compiler, environment, ...) provided stimulating discussions on implementiation and optimization issues. I owe special thanks to Roland Dietrich and Igor Varsek for their permanent encouragements.

Literature

[Ershov 78] A.P.Ershov, *Mixed Computation in the Class of Recursive Program Schemata*, Acta cybernetica, 4 (1978) 1, 19-23.

[Ershov 85] A.P.Ershov, *On Mixed Computation: Informal Account of the Strict and Polyvariant Computational Schemes*, in: M.Broy (ed.), *Control Flow and Data Flow Concepts of Distributed Programming*, NATO ASI Series Vol.F14, Springer Berlin, 1985

[Ershov, Ostrovski 86] A.P.Ershov, B.N.Ostrovski, *Controlled Mixed Computation and its Application to Systematic Development of Language-Oriented Parsers*, TC2 Working Conference on Program Specification and Transformation, Bad Tölz, Germany, April 1986.

[Futamura 82] Y.Futamura, *Partial Computation of Programs*, in: E.Goto et al. (eds.), *RIMS Symposia on Software Engineering*, LNCS 147, (1982),1-34.

[Heering 86] J.Heering, *Partial Evaluation and ω-Completeness of Algebraic Specifications*, Theoretical Computer Science 43 (1986) 149-167.

[Hsiang, Srivas 85] J.Hsiang, M.K.Srivas, *A Prolog Environment for Developing and Reasoning About Data Types*, in: H.Ehrig et al. (eds.), *Formal Methods and Software Development*, TAPSOFT 1985, LNCS 186, 276-293.

[Jones, Mycroft 86] N.D.Jones, A.Mycroft, *Data Flow Analysis of Applicative Programs Using Minimal Function Graphs: Abridged Version*, ACM Conference on Principles of Programming Languages, 1986.

[Jørring, Scherlis 86] U.Jørring, W.L.Scherlis, *Compilers and Staging Transformations*, ACM Conference on Principles of Programming Languages, 1986.

[Kahn, Carlsson 84] K.M.Kahn, M.Carlsson, *The Compilation of Prolog Programs Without the use of a Prolog Compiler*, in: *Proc. of the Int. Conf. on Fifth Generation Computer Systems*, Tokyo, Japan, 1984, 348-355.

[Knuth et al. 77] D.E.Knuth, J.H.Morris, V.R.Pratt, *Fast Pattern Matching in Strings*, SIAM J. Comput., 6,2, (1977), 323-350.

[Komorowski 82] H.J.Komorowski, *Partial Evaluation as a Means for Inferencing Data Structures in an Applicative Language: a Theory and Implementation in the Case of Prolog*, ACM Conference on Principles of Programming Languages, 1982.

[Kursawe 86] P.Kursawe, *How to Invent a Prolog Machine*, in: E.Shapiro (ed.), *Proc. of the 3rd International Conference on Logic Programming*, LNCS 225,(1986),134-148.

[Lloyd 84] J.W.Lloyd, *Foundations of Logic Programming*, Springer Berlin, 1984.

[Mycroft, O'Keefe 84] A.Mycroft, R.O'Keefe, *A Polymorphic Type System for Prolog*, Artificial Intelligence 23 (1984),295-307.

[O'Donnell 87] M.J.O'Donnell, *Term Rewriting Implementation of Equational Logic Programming*, in: P.Lescanne (ed.), *Rewriting Techniques and Applications*, LNCS 256 (1987), 1-12.

[O'Keefe 85] R.A.O'Keefe, *On the Treatment of Cuts in Prolog Source-Level Tools*, Symposium on Logic Programming, Boston, 1985, 68-72.

[Venken 84] R.Venken, *A Prolog Meta-Interpreter for Partial Evaluation and its Application to Source to Source Transformation and Query-Optimisation*, ECAI 84.

Partial Evaluation and Mixed Computation
D. Bjørner, A.P. Ershov and N.D. Jones (Editors)
Elsevier Science Publishers B.V. (North-Holland)
© IFIP, 1988

Projections for Specialisation

John Launchbury

Computing Science
Glasgow University
Glasgow
Scotland

email: launchbj@cs.glasgow.ac.uk

Abstract

Experience suggests that static analysis of programs is an important precursor to partial evaluation. In earlier work the parameters of a function were annotated to show which would have set values during partial evaluation and which would not. In this paper we show that domain projections naturally capture this distinction. Furthermore, using such projections it is possible to distinguish between the static and dynamic parts of a single parameter. We prove that this use of projections has a sound mathematical basis. In the rest of the paper we develop a method of constructing finite domains of projections that may be used in practice, discuss some practical issues, and suggest future work.

0. Introduction

Partial evaluation seems to be a promising and powerful technique. It allows a greatly increased level of modularity to be used by the programmer, without incurring a significant run time penalty. For example, programs that interpret explicit data are more modular and more flexible than programs with implicit in-line data. However, the interpreted version will be the slower of the two. Partial evaluation of the first with respect to its explicit data can automatically produce a program in the style of the second. So the programmer is able to write and manipulate the modular version, but run the efficient version. Useful background material on partial evaluation may be found in such references as [Ershov 82], [Futamura 71], and [Turchin 86].

Ph.D. research, funded by the Science and Engineering Research Council of Great Britain.

One approach to partial evaluation requires an assessment of what data will be static (i.e. will never change), and what will be dynamic (may possibly change) when the partial evaluation takes place. This approach was used at DIKU in Copenhagen and is detailed in papers such as [Jones 85] and [Sestoft 86]. It will be assumed that the reader has at least a little knowledge of these. In this paper we show that domain projections naturally capture the distinction between static and dynamic data. A projection is chosen so that when it is applied to a partially known argument, only the static part is selected. This data may then be used to produce a specialised version of the original function. We introduce the notion of a complement to express the dynamic part of the original argument that must be present at run time.

For the purposes of this paper we will assume that a functional language is being used. In section 1 we concentrate on using projections and complements to distinguish between static and dynamic data. In later sections of the paper we show how to obtain finite domains of projections that may be used in practice, and consider how to choose which projections to use. The paper closes with some practical issues, and some suggestions for future work.

1. Projections differentiate between static and dynamic data

Intuition

Typically a program contains functions that are called in many different places with (possibly) different arguments in each. The aim of partial evaluation is this: to replace the many calls of one function with calls of more specialised versions of that function. Because these versions - called residual functions - are less general, they have the potential to be made more efficient than the original.

The key problem that we consider in this paper is this: which of the calls to a function should be represented by the same residual function? We show how projections may be used to do this. A projection may be thought of as a function that discards part of its input and returns the remainder as its result. Suppose f is a function that is called in a number of different places with (possibly) different arguments in each. We apply the projection to each argument. Because the projection may discard parts of its input, two different arguments can have equal images. In this case we would say that the arguments are 'similar', and represent both function calls by the same residual function.

Having identified similar function calls, we need a way of expressing any differences that remain. The simplest way is to pass the original argument in its entirety to the residual function. This is unsatisfactory because much of the information in the argument may already have been used in selecting which residual function to call. To pass it around at run time incurs a needless penalty. To do better we introduce the notion of a complement projection. Between a projection and its complement no information is discarded. Thus any part of an argument that is discarded by a projection will not be discarded by its complement. However the complement is quite at liberty to discard information not discarded by the projection. We show that residual functions can be defined so that the only part of the original argument they require is the part not discarded by the complement. As a result, we can safely subject the original argument to the complement projection and only pass the image. If we choose a complement that discards as much as possible then this represents a significant improvement.

Projections

In this paper we use the word *domain* to refer to Scott domains [e.g. Scott 82] i.e. a c.p.o. with a least element (which is written $\perp$). We now give the standard definition of domain projections.

Definition

A *projection* on a domain $\mathbb{D}$ is a continuous mapping $p : \mathbb{D} \rightarrow \mathbb{D}$ such that

      (1) $p \subseteq ID_{\mathbb{D}}$, and
      (2) $p \circ p = p$

The first condition in the definition means that a projection cannot introduce information into its result that was not already present in its argument. The second says that all of the work of the projection is done immediately, and that nothing more will be discarded if the projection is re-applied. Examples of projections are ID (the identity function), and ABSENT (the constant function with value $\perp$). Later we will meet more interesting examples. Notice that it is a consequence of the definition that ID is the greatest projection, and ABSENT the least. In the rest of the paper we will explicitly subscript projections with their domain when confusion may otherwise result. In cases where no confusion should arise the subscript will be omitted.

Equivalence

Suppose that a program contains calls of a function f. Given a projection p we define an equivalence relation on the arguments that appear in the calls of f. Suppose that one of the calls has argument x, and another has argument y. Then we say that

      x is equivalent to y under p   iff $p\,x = p\,y$.

It is easy to verify that this is indeed an equivalence relation. Using this relation we partition the calls of f into a set of equivalence classes, and for each equivalence class we produce a residual version of f to represent the class. Then each original call to f may be replaced by a call to the particular residual version of f.

Complements

Projections are used to discard part of the argument to a function. This includes the possibilities of either discarding all of the argument or none of it. We use projections to collect similar calls of a function into one class. The role of the complement of a projection is to express the differences that may exist among these similar calls.

Definition

If p and q are projections, and $p \sqcup q = ID$ then q is a *complement* of p (and vice versa).

The definition states what it means for one projection to be *a* complement of another. It is useful to be able to choose one complement in particular and to describe it as *the* complement. For now we will assume that this can be done - this assumption will be justified in section 2. We write the complement of p as p'.

If p and q are complements then $\forall x$. $p\,x \sqcup q\,x = x$. This is a consequence of the way in which $\sqcup$ is defined on functions. Thus, no part of an argument is discarded between a projection and its complement. In practice we choose complements that discard as much as possible consistent with this condition. Examples of complements are:

$$ID' = ABSENT$$
$$ABSENT' = ID$$

The original projections are chosen to express similarities between two function calls. Similar function calls are placed in an equivalence class. We use the complement projection to express the differences between the functions within an equivalence class. Operationally, the complement tells us how much of the original parameters need to be preserved for use at run time. Thus the complement will select the dynamic data and ignore as much of the static (compile time) data as possible.

Residual Functions

Our aim is to show that it is possible to define a single residual function to represent each equivalence class. We do so in two stages. First a lemma to show that, given any projection p, we may define a function equivalent to f but which takes the original argument in two parts - the part in the range of p, and the part in the range of the complement of p. Then a theorem to show that the residual function f_{pa} is suitable for all arguments in the same equivalence class as the element a.

<u>Lemma 1.1</u>
If $f : D \to E$ is a function, and $p : D \to D$ is a projection, then there exists a function f_{p*} such that
$$\forall a \in D . f\,a = f_{p*}\,(p\,a)\,(p'\,a)$$
<u>Proof</u>
Define $f_{p*}\,x\,y = f\,(x \sqcup y)$. Result follows as $p \sqcup p' = ID$.

Suppose that we take a function f, and a projection p, and that we partition the argument domain of f using p. For any $a \in D$, a will be a member of one equivalence class. Treating f_{p*} as a Curried function we can partially apply it and write f_{pa} for $f_{p*}\,(p\,a)$. We claim that f_{pa} is the residual function for the whole equivalence class from which a is taken.

<u>Theorem 1.2</u>
Let f and p be as in lemma 1.1, and $a \in D$ be chosen. If any $b \in D$ is equivalent to a under p then
$$f\,b = f_{pa}\,(p'\,b)$$
<u>Proof</u>

$f\,b$	$= f_{p*}\,(p\,b)\,(p'\,b)$	[lemma 1.1]
	$= f_{p*}\,(p\,a)\,(p'\,b)$	[b equivalent to a under p]
	$= f_{pa}\,(p'\,b)$	[definition of f_{pa}].

Examples

The nature of the residual function depends on the choice of the projection p. Let us consider the extreme cases. Suppose p is the projection ABSENT. Then for all $a \in D$ the value of (p a) is $\bot$. Moreover, as the complement of ABSENT is ID, the value of (p' a) is a. Thus, the function $f_{ABSENT a}$ is effectively no different from f. ABSENT partitions the domain of the argument of f into a single equivalence class, and so the residual function for that class is, naturally, f itself.

At the other extreme, suppose that p is the identity projection. ID partitions the domain into singleton equivalence classes. As the complement of ID is ABSENT, the residual parameter always has the value $\bot$, so in effect, the residual functions have no parameters. Therefore $f_{ID a}$ has the value (f a) itself. So for each possible argument the function will be completely evaluated and the residual function will represent the result.

More interestingly, let us preempt the next section and consider pairs. To select parts of the pair we may use the projections LEFT and RIGHT defined by:

$$\text{LEFT} \ (a, b) = (a, \bot)$$
$$\text{RIGHT} \ (a, b) = (\bot, b).$$

The complement of LEFT is RIGHT and vice versa. If the argument to a function consists of a pair, and if the first argument is known during partial evaluation (and has only finitely many values), then LEFT is the obvious choice of projection. For each possible value of the first argument, a residual function is produced, and the second argument passed as the parameter.

This last example corresponds exactly to the DIKU work. Each function has a fixed number of parameters each of which is either selected for partial evaluation (Known) or left for run-time (Unknown). In the formalism presented here, we represent n parameters by an n-tuple, and the Known/Unknown distinction with generalisations of LEFT and RIGHT. The Known parameters are selected by ID, and the Unknown parameters discarded with ABSENT. The complement does the reverse, of course, in selecting the run-time data.

However, this is not the only possible way for parameters to be selected. It is possible to select parts of a parameter for partial evaluation, and to leave the remainder for run-time. It is even possible to use projections that select particular values, specialise the function to these values, and leave a general function to handle any others. While this last possibility could allow additional optimisation we do not consider it further in this paper because of the highly heuristic nature of analysis that seems to be required.

The mix program

We are now in a position to be able to define precisely the action of the mix program. In order to analyse - and partially evaluate - a function we need to examine the program text that defines it, i.e. we work with a *representation* of the function. The same applies to projections and values. Thus mix is a function that takes representations of a function, a projection, and a value, and produces a representation of the residual function. Suppose that mix is written in a programming language L. Then

$$L \text{ mix } f \ p \ a \ = \ f_{pa}$$

In the DIKU work mix has only two arguments. This is because the projection is given implicitly as annotations within the definition of f.

2. Choosing domains of projections

In the previous section no explicit assumptions were made about the domain from which projections are to be chosen. Almost certainly ID and ABSENT should be present. Beyond this is a matter of choice. An apparently natural choice is to select the domain of *all* projections. However, if this is chosen then not only are there infinitely many projections in general, but there can be non-computable ones also.

Current practice in choosing domains for analysis (strictness etc.) is to choose finite domains [e.g. Hughes 87]. Typically the analysis is cast as finding the least fixed point of some function within a domain. If the domain is finite then the process of finite iteration may be used. This is just a direct application of Kleene's First Recursion Theorem. The least value in the domain is chosen and the function applied to produce a new value. If this differs from the first then the function is reapplied. The process continues until applying the function leaves the value unchanged. Kleene's Theorem states that this is the least fixed point. The process is bound to terminate because the range of the function is finite. When infinite domains are used, algebraic methods must be developed and analysis proceeds by formal manipulation. While this method is far more general, it also seems to be far more difficult. Therefore, in this paper we will follow current practice and choose finite domains of projections.

Typed Languages

We have already referred to the projections ID and ABSENT. Because these projections occur over every domain they may be used in a language without any type discipline, and as we have seen, they correspond directly with the Known/Unknown values used in the DIKU mix program. These are the only projections that may be used in an untyped language. However, in a typed language we know in which domains the arguments to functions lie, and so can use projections particular to those domains.

For the purpose of this paper we will assume a first order monomorphic language. We do not consider function domains beyond noticing that the discussion may be extended to higher order functions in a fairly trivial way by using only ID and ABSENT for such arguments.

In many typed languages (e.g. ML, Miranda, Ponder, Orwell) the user has certain domain constructors available. Typically these are ×, + (separated sum), and recursion. We restrict attention to domains constructed in this way, which, at the very least, shows the style in which other constructions could be handled. We define operations on projections that parallel the domain constructors, and then associate a finite domain of projections with each domain construction.

Before proceeding, however, we must note that the following represents just *one* way of choosing domains of projections. The results of the previous section are independent of the constructions within this section, and hold whatever projections are chosen.

Constructing Projections

We will be constructing projections out of smaller projections. We need to define product and sum operators for projections.

Definition

a.　If $p : D \rightarrow D$ and $q : E \rightarrow E$ are projections, then we define the *product*

$p \times q : D \times E \rightarrow D \times E$ by

$$p \times q \ (d, e) = (p \ d, q \ e)$$

b.　If $p : D \rightarrow D$ and $q : E \rightarrow E$ are projections, then we define the *sum*

$p + q : D + E \rightarrow D + E$ by

$$
\begin{aligned}
(p + q) \ x &= \bot, && \text{if } x = \bot \\
&= p \ x, && \text{if } x \text{ is in } D \\
&= q \ x, && \text{if } x \text{ is in } E
\end{aligned}
$$

The projection product and sum above are continuous operators. A proof is outside the scope of this paper, but we will need this continuity property later.

Both of these definitions may be easily generalised to cope with n-ary sums and products. Notice that the projection ABSENT cannot be expressed in terms of the sum of any two other projections. We will have to add ABSENT as an extra projection when defining the projections over a sum domain.

We can define complements of projections formed from the product or sum of other projections. The complement of $p \times q$ is just $p' \times q'$, and the complement of $(p + q)$ is $(p' + q')$ except that the complement of ID is ABSENT as usual. Note that this exception means that, in general, p'' is not equal to p. For later developments it will be useful to define a variant of + that encapsulates the exception.

Definition

If $p : D \rightarrow D$ and $q : E \rightarrow E$ are projections, then we define the *complement sum*

$p +' q : D + E \rightarrow D + E$ by

$$
\begin{aligned}
p +' q &= \text{ABSENT}_{D+E}, && \text{if } p = \text{ABSENT}_D \text{ and } q = \text{ABSENT}_E \\
&= p + q, && \text{otherwise}
\end{aligned}
$$

Thus the complement of $p + q$ may be written $p' +' q'$. Complement sum is also a continuous operator - this property can be derived quite easily from the continuity of sum.

Domain and Projection Formulae

Domains may be defined in terms of domain formulae (e.g. $F(\mathcal{T}) = 0$, or $F(\mathcal{T}) = \mathcal{D} + \mathcal{T}$ where $\mathcal{D}$ is some given domain) and previously defined domains. In many cases, the 'previously defined domain' is a recursive application of the formula. Suppose that $F(\mathcal{T})$ is a domain formula. The recursive application is written $\mu\mathcal{T}.F(\mathcal{T})$, and represents the least domain fixed by $F(\mathcal{T})$. Construction parallels finding least fixed points within a domain. We start with the smallest domain 0 (the one-point domain), then form $F(0)$, then $F(F(0))$ etc. The chain of constructions has a limit point, given by $\bigsqcup F^n(0)$, which is a fixed point of the formula (technical note: this limit is well defined if we consider all the domains to be embedded in $P\omega$, or if the domains are defined using Information Systems - it is hard to define when using inverse limit constructions).

A domain formula takes a domain as an argument and returns a domain as a result. We use the name 'formula' rather than 'function' to remind us that it is a *constructive* function. In this paper we only consider domain formula with at most one variable, which we will write $\mathcal{T}$. The only reason for this is that it allows us to develop the ideas without becoming bogged down in unnecessary detail. Without becoming unnecessarily formal, we define the set of domain formulae recursively as

1. the sum of two formulae,
2. the product of two formulae,
3. a domain variable $\mathcal{T}$,
4. basic domains - typically just 0 but it can include any flat domain,
5. the least domain fixed by a formula.

We parallel the notion of a domain formula with the notion of a projection formula. Just as $F(\mathcal{T})$ corresponds to a domain when $\mathcal{T}$ has a domain value, so $f(p)$ corresponds to a projection when p is a projection. Restricting domain formulae to a single variable means that projection formulae also have at most one projection variable, which we write as $p_{\mathcal{T}}$.

Domain of Projections

Given a domain formula $F(\mathcal{T})$ we write Proj $F(\mathcal{T})$ to denote a corresponding domain of projections. There are five cases.

$$\text{Proj}\,(\,G(\mathcal{T}) + H(\mathcal{T})\,) = \{\, g\,(p_{\mathcal{T}}) + h\,(p_{\mathcal{T}}) \mid g\,(p_{\mathcal{T}}) \in \text{Proj}\,G(\mathcal{T}),\ h\,(p_{\mathcal{T}}) \in \text{Proj}\,H(\mathcal{T})\,\}$$
$$\cup\ \{\text{ABSENT}\}$$
$$\text{Proj}\,(\,G(\mathcal{T}) \times H(\mathcal{T})\,) = \{\, g\,(p_{\mathcal{T}}) \times h\,(p_{\mathcal{T}}) \mid g\,(p_{\mathcal{T}}) \in \text{Proj}\,G(\mathcal{T}),\ h\,(p_{\mathcal{T}}) \in \text{Proj}\,H(\mathcal{T})\,\}$$

$$\text{Proj}\,\mathcal{T} = \{\, p_{\mathcal{T}}\,\}$$
$$\text{Proj}\,0 = \{\,\text{ID}\,\} \qquad (\text{ note: } \text{ID}_0 = \text{ABSENT}_0\,)$$
$$\text{Proj}\,(\,\mu\mathcal{T}\,.\,F(\mathcal{T})\,) = \{\,\mu p_{\mathcal{T}}\,.\,f\,(p_{\mathcal{T}}) \mid f\,(p_{\mathcal{T}}) \in \text{Proj}\,F(\mathcal{T})\,\}$$

If there are other flat domains present (e.g. the integers) then we only consider their ID and ABSENT projections. To ensure that the definition is well founded we need to prove some theorems.

Theorem 2.1

If $p : D \to D$ is a projection, F a domain formula, and $f(p) \in \text{Proj } F(J)$ then $f(p)$ is a projection on $F(D)$.

Proof

There are four cases: either $F(J)$ is the sum of two formulae, the product of two formulae, or is just 0 or J itself. In the first two cases the result is by a simple induction and in the others the result is trivial.

Corollary

If F is a domain formula, and $f(p) \in \text{Proj } F(J)$, then $\mu J . f(p)$ is a projection on $\mu J . F(J)$.

Proof

According to the definition of the μ operator we have

$$\mu J . F(J) = \bigsqcup F^n (0) , \text{ and}$$
$$\mu p . f(p) = \bigsqcup f^n (\text{ABSENT}).$$

By the theorem, $f^n (\text{ABSENT})$ is a projection on $F^n (0)$ for any n. The result follows by continuity.

The theorem and its corollary state that the elements of the projection domain really are projections over the original domain. It is fairly clear from the definitions that the projection ABSENT is always present, but not so clear that ID is. The following theorem rectifies this.

Theorem 2.2

If F is a domain formula, and $f(p) \in \text{Proj } F(J)$ is a formula containing only ID, p_J, $\times$, and $+$, then $\mu p . f(p)$ is the identity projection on $\mu J . F(J)$.

Proof

The proof is by induction and continuity. As a preliminary, note that a projection constructed out of ID, $\times$, and $+$ only, is the identity projection (over the corresponding domain, of course). For the induction hypothesis we assume that $f^n (\text{ABSENT})$ is the identity function on $F^n (0)$. This holds for the base case when n=0 because $F^0 (0) = 0$ and ABSENT=ID on this one-point domain. For the inductive step we note that

$$F^{n+1} (0) = F (F^n (0))$$

and similarly

$$f^{n+1} (\text{ABSENT}) = f (f^n (\text{ABSENT})).$$

By the induction hypothesis, $f^n (\text{ABSENT}) = \text{ID}_{F^n (0)}$ hence

$$f^{n+1} (\text{ABSENT}) = f (\text{ID}_{F^n (0)}).$$

The projection $f (\text{ID}_{F^n (0)})$ has all occurrences of p_J replaced with the identity function, and so by our initial remark it is itself an identity function. The domain and range of this function is, according to theorem 2.1, just $F^{n+1} (0)$. This completes the inductive part of the proof. Thus we have proved that for all n, $f^n (\text{ABSENT}) = \text{ID}_{F^n (0)}$. But $\mu p . f(p) = \bigsqcup f^n (\text{ABSENT})$ by definition, and so the result follows by continuity.

Examples

Pairs

Earlier we came across the projections LEFT and RIGHT which were defined on pairs. These are actually just convenient names for ID × ABSENT and ABSENT × ID. If the elements a and b are drawn from flat domains then LEFT, RIGHT, ID, and ABSENT are the only projections we can construct with ×. But, if the domains are not flat then there may be projections other than just ID and ABSENT over these domains. Suppose the domains are $\mathcal{A}$ and $\mathcal{B}$, and $p_a: \mathcal{A} \to \mathcal{A}$ and $p_b: \mathcal{B} \to \mathcal{B}$ are projections. Then we can construct the projections $p_a \times p_b$. Notice that

$$ID_{\mathcal{A} \times \mathcal{B}} = ID_{\mathcal{A}} \times ID_{\mathcal{B}}, \text{ and}$$

$$ABSENT_{\mathcal{A} \times \mathcal{B}} = ABSENT_{\mathcal{A}} \times ABSENT_{\mathcal{B}}$$

Lists

As another example, consider the domain of lists of elements drawn from a flat domain. The projections over this domain are ABSENT, STRUCT, and ID, where

$$STRUCT = ID + (ABSENT \times STRUCT)$$

This projection ignores the contents of the list and identifies two lists iff they have the same (possibly partial) length. When specialising programs we will usually only ever apply this projection to subsets of the list domain whose elements have finite non-partial length and so its generality is no problem. Notice how the definition of STRUCT corresponds with the definition of the list domain:

$$list\alpha = O + (\alpha \times (list\alpha))$$

(α is some arbitrary type). If the elements of the list are drawn from a domain that is richer in projections then we generalise STRUCT so that

$$STRUCT(p) = ID + (p \times STRUCT(p))$$

and now the correspondence between the definition of the list type, and the projection STRUCT is almost exact. It is a consequence of the last theorem that STRUCT(ID) = ID, but because the list type is constructed using separated sum the corresponding case for ABSENT does not hold i.e. STRUCT(ABSENT) ≠ ABSENT. STRUCT(ABSENT) is the projection that earlier was just called STRUCT. For those familiar with list functions it may be instructive to note that STRUCT is just the standard function 'map'.

Finding Complements

We fulfil a promise from section 1 to show how to find complements. Suppose we have a projection formula f. We associate with it its complementary formula f '.

Definition

Given a projection formula f we define the projection formula f ' by

1. $f(p_T) = g(p_T) + h(p_T)$ ⟹ $f'(p_T) = g'(p_T) +' h'(p_T)$
2. $f(p_T) = g(p_T) \times h(p_T)$ ⟹ $f'(p_T) = g'(p_T) \times h'(p_T)$
3. $f(p_T) = p_T$ ⟹ $f'(p_T) = p_T$
4. $f(p_T) = ID$ ⟹ $f'(p_T) = ABSENT$
5. $f(p_T) = ABSENT$ ⟹ $f'(p_T) = ID$

It is a consequence of the definition, that if $f(p_T) \in \text{Proj } F(T)$ then $f'(p_T) \in \text{Proj } F(T)$ also. In the next lemma and theorem we prove that the complement of a projection $\mu p_T . f(p_T)$ is the projection $\mu p_T . f'(p_T)$.

Lemma 2.3

Let F be a domain formula. If $p, q : D \to D$ are complementary projections, and $f(p_T) \in \text{Proj } F(T)$, then

$$f(p) \ \sqcup \ f'(q) = \text{ID}_{F(D)}$$

Proof

There are five distinct cases corresponding to the five clauses in the definition above. The first two require an inductive step, and the last three are base cases. The induction is on the size of the formula.

1. $f(p_T) = g(p_T) + h(p_T)$. Then $f(p) \ \sqcup \ f'(q) = g(p) + h(p) \ \sqcup \ g'(q) +' h'(q)$. There are two sub-cases to consider:

   a. First suppose that $g'(q) = \text{ABSENT}$ and $h'(q) = \text{ABSENT}$. Then the complement sum also has the value ABSENT. By the induction it follows that $g(p) = \text{ID}$ and $h(p) = \text{ID}$ also, thus
   $$f(p) \ \sqcup \ f'(q) = \text{ID} + \text{ID} \ \sqcup \ \text{ABSENT} = \text{ID}$$
   as required.

   b. Now suppose that $g'(q) \neq \text{ABSENT}$ or $h'(q) \neq \text{ABSENT}$. Then the complement sum is identical to normal sum. Thus
   $$\begin{aligned}
   f(p) \ \sqcup \ f'(q) &= g(p) + h(p) \ \sqcup \ g'(q) +' h'(q) \\
   &= g(p) + h(p) \ \sqcup \ g'(q) + h'(q) \\
   &= g(p) \ \sqcup \ g'(q) \ + \ h(p) \ \sqcup \ h'(q) \\
   &= \text{ID}_{G(D)} + \text{ID}_{H(D)} \qquad \text{[induction step]} \\
   &= \text{ID}_{F(D)}
   \end{aligned}$$

2. $f(p_T) = g(p_T) \times h(p_T)$. The proof is a simplified version of the proof for case 1.

3. $f(p_T) = p_T$. Then $f(p) \ \sqcup \ f'(q) = p \sqcup q = \text{ID}_{F(D)}$

4. $f(p_T) = \text{ID}_{F(D)}$. Then $f(p) \ \sqcup \ f'(q) = \text{ID}_{F(D)} \ \sqcup \ \text{ABSENT}_{F(D)} = \text{ID}_{F(D)}$

5. $f(p_T) = \text{ABSENT}_{F(D)}$. Then $f(p) \ \sqcup \ f'(q) = \text{ABSENT}_{F(D)} \ \sqcup \ \text{ID}_{F(D)} = \text{ID}_{F(D)}$

Corollary

If F is a domain formula, $p : D \to D$ a projection, and $f(p_T) \in \text{Proj } F(T)$, then the complement of $f(p)$ is $f'(p')$.

Theorem 2.4

If F is a domain formula and $f(p_T) \in \text{Proj } F(T)$, then the complement of $\mu p_T . f(p_T)$ is

$$\mu p_T . f'(p_T)$$

Proof

The proof uses induction and continuity. As an induction hypothesis we will assume that

$$f^n(\text{ABSENT}) \ \sqcup \ f'^n(\text{ABSENT}) = \text{ID}_{F^n(0)}$$

This holds for the base case when n=0 because $F^0(0) = 0$ and ABSENT=ID on this one-point domain. For the inductive step we note that

$$f^{n+1}(\text{ABSENT}) \ \sqcup \ f'^{n+1}(\text{ABSENT}) = f(f^n(\text{ABSENT})) \ \sqcup \ f'(f'^n(\text{ABSENT}))$$

Using the induction hypothesis, the conditions of lemma 2.4 are met, and the result follows.

Environments

We close this section with a practical application of the theory. A promising use for partial evaluation is in specialising interpreters to particular programs. This results in programs that are virtually compiled equivalents of the original. A common data structure within interpreters is an environment.

Typically this is a list of name-value pairs. The names are the names of the variables occurring within the original program, and the values are the run time values of the variables. During partial evaluation the original program is known, and so all the names within the environment are also known. However the data for the program is unknown, and so the value part of the environment is also unknown.

We consider the environment domain to be the domain of lists of pairs of elements taken from a flat domain. Diagram 1 shows the domain of projections constructed for this domain. The projection to pick out the names is STRUCT(LEFT), and its complement (which defines the residual parameter) is STRUCT(RIGHT). A specialiser could identify STRUCT(LEFT) as the projection which selects the data known during partial evaluation, and leave only the image of STRUCT(RIGHT) (i.e. the list of values) to be manipulated at run time.

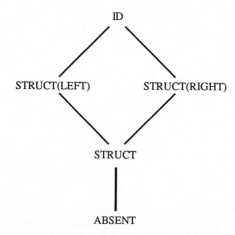

Diagram 1. Projections over a list of pairs

As the original DIKU mix program only uses tuples containing ID and ABSENT (Known and Unknown), the only way that this separation could be achieved was by a different style of programming. Rather than pass the environment as a list of pairs it was necessary to pass two lists - a name list and a value list - so destroying the modularity inherent in the concept of an environment, and potentially forcing the programmer to rewrite the program.

3. Choosing projections

In the previous sections we have done two things. We have shown that projections may be used to get at the static data to use it in the definitions of the residual functions, and we have the machinery to build finite domains of projections that correspond with the function's argument's types. Now suppose that we wish to evaluate a function given a partially known argument. What projection should be chosen in order to distinguish between the separate calls so that as many residual functions as possible may be defined?

The DIKU group noted that the projection should not be bigger than the known information. In the context of this paper this means that if p is the projection and x the argument, then we must be able to fully evaluate the expression (p x) when we perform the partial evaluation. This is reasonable because we need to compare the value of (p x) with the value of (p y) where y is the argument to the function in a different call of the function. If we are unable to evaluate (p x) completely then the comparison becomes very difficult. This gives us an upper bound on the particular choice of projection.

To find this upper bound the DIKU team presented a technique called known/unknown abstract interpretation. Details may be found in [Sestoft 86]. Using this technique the parameters to a function are classed as Known - "surely known for all possible values of the known input" - or Unknown - "possibly unknown for some (or all) values of the known input". As has been noted earlier, Known and Unknown correspond to ID and ABSENT. The technique can easily be extended to handle other projections. The only requirement is that the domain of projections is finite because the interpretation is iterated until a fixed point is found. One minor difference is that in the DIKU formalism, Known is considered weaker than Unknown and the least fixed point of the equations is found. However, as a projection, ID is stronger than ABSENT. As it would be counter-intuitive to think of it in any other way, in the projection version we find the greatest fixed point instead (maximising the known information). This is actually only a minor difference because all the domains of projections we use are lattices.

Finiteness

So far, we have emphasised that a projection must pick out the known part of the arguments to functions. Then whenever any two function calls agree on the known parts we use the same specialisation of the function as the residual function. If we come across a new function that does not agree on the known parts then a new specialised version is produced. Intuitively, one feels that only finitely many specialisations will be produced, because only a finite amount of information may be 'known' during partial evaluation. Unfortunately this is not the case. Consider the function:

$$f\ (x,\ y) = x\,, \qquad\qquad \text{if } y = 0$$
$$= f\ (x+1,\ y-1)\,, \quad \text{otherwise}$$

Suppose we were to specialise f to a given value for x (to the value 9, say), with y remaining unknown. Initially x is completely known and y unknown, so the first approximation in the analysis is:

$$f\,(\text{ID, ABSENT})\,,\quad\text{(f is an abstract version of f defined on projections)}$$

On the next iteration we note that
$$x + 1 \;\rightarrow\; \text{ID} \sqcap \text{ID} \;=\; \text{ID}$$
and that
$$y - 1 \;\rightarrow\; \text{ABSENT} \sqcap \text{ABSENT} \;=\; \text{ABSENT}$$

which means that the recursive call to f is

$$f\;(\text{ID, ABSENT}).$$

We have immediately reached the fixed point. What is more, the result agrees with our intuition: the value of the first parameter is always known, the value of the second never. However, the specialisation may go something like this:

$$
\begin{aligned}
f_0\ y\ &=\ 9\,, && \text{if } y = 0\\
&=\ f_3\ (y - 1)\,, && \text{otherwise}
\end{aligned}
$$

$$
\begin{aligned}
f_1\ y\ &=\ 10\,, && \text{if } y = 0\\
&=\ f_4\ (y - 1)\,, && \text{otherwise}
\end{aligned}
$$

$$
\begin{aligned}
f_2\ y\ &=\ 11\,, && \text{if } y = 0\\
&=\ f_5\ (y - 1)\,, && \text{otherwise}
\end{aligned}
$$

. . . . etc.

The problem is not that the function calls are residual rather than being unfolded. Unfolding would give a single specialised function, but its body would be infinite. Neither is the problem introduced by the added variety of projections. A parallel example gives rise to exactly the same situation with the original Known/Unknown abstract interpretation.

The problem is that the chosen projection differentiates between infinitely many different situations, all reachable from the initial state. For the problem to arise, the projection must give rise to an infinite partition, *and* the transitive closure of function calls must also be infinite. Unfortunately, most of the interesting projections can give rise to infinite partitions - for example, both STRUCT and ID can. Even worse is that calculating the transitive closure exactly is equivalent to the halting problem. Much more work needs to be done in this area in order to produce reasonable solutions.

4. Practical Issues

This section contains discussion about two points of practical relevance. Each is effectively a form of optimisation.

Discarding irrelevant fields

If a parameter to a function was a triple of, say, flat domains, then we may, for example use a specialisation projection as given by the map: (a, b, c) goes to (a, $\perp$, $\perp$). The complement of this is the map: (a, b, c) goes to ($\perp$, b, c). The range of the domain is clearly isomorphic to the domain of objects (b, c). It is a sensible and easy optimisation to implement the residual parameter as a pair, rather than as a triple with a dummy field. Similarly, if only one field remains then the 1-tuple need not be constructed, the value itself can be passed instead. Finally, if all the fields are dummy fields then the parameter may be omitted. Notice that in this case the complement would be the projection ABSENT.

Complement of STRUCT

The complement of STRUCT is ID, which is also the complement of ABSENT. This means that the parameters to a function specialised by STRUCT cannot be reduced in any way. There is therefore no saving in terms of the data that is to be passed at run time. In view of this, we may wonder whether STRUCT is a useful projection.

The information that STRUCT does provide is the length of the list parameter. There may be computations dependent on this value that may be performed during partial evaluation rather than at run time. This could be especially significant since calculating the length of a list takes time proportional to the length.

A more interesting possibility is that the contents of the list may be passed as individual parameters. This applies for all projections expressible as STRUCT(p) (which includes STRUCT itself for STRUCT = STRUCT(ABSENT)). The idea of replacing a list of known length by separate parameters is discussed in [Sestoft 86]. In practice *variable splitting* (as it is known) gives significant performance improvement. In the DIKU work, an extra annotation is introduced and inserted by hand to enable the partial evaluator to perform this optimisation. With the projection approach such an extra annotation is unnecessary.

5. Future Work

Strictness analysis

An idea (suggested by John Hughes) is to generalise the notion of complement, to one of projection difference. Given projections p and q we define q - p to be a projection such that $p \sqcup (q - p) = q$. Just as with complements, we define *one* such projection to be *the* difference. For the definition of difference to make sense we require that $p \subseteq q$. With this definition, the complement of p may be expressed as ID - p. The motivation for the definition may be seen in the following example.

Suppose we define a length function on lists:

$$\text{length xs} = 0 , \qquad\qquad \text{if xs = Nil}$$
$$= 1 + \text{length (tail xs)} , \text{ otherwise}$$

Also suppose that at specialise time we specialise length using the projection STRUCT. The length of the list can be worked out completely and no information needs to be passed at run time. However the complement of STRUCT is ID, and so the whole input list would be passed.

Strictness analysis [Wadler 87] can discover that (length ∘ STRUCT) = length, i.e. the only information that length needs about its argument is its STRUCT. So when length is specialised with respect to some projection p, the only information that needs to be passed at run time is STRUCT - p. When p is itself STRUCT, as in the example above, the run time information is STRUCT - STRUCT which equals ABSENT. Therefore the parameters of specialised versions of length may be omitted. This seems an exciting possibility because it allows analysis techniques developed for other purposes to be applied to partial evaluation.

Least Fixed Point

The projection abstract interpretation requires the greatest fixed point of a set of recursive equations to be found. This contrasts with the more common practice of finding least fixed points. It may be desirable therefore to recast the abstract interpretation into the more usual mode.

6. Conclusion

Differentiating between static and dynamic data is an important analysis for partial evaluation. In this paper we have shown that this distinction is captured naturally using domain projections. The complement relationship between projections was introduced so that a large degree of separation could be achieved. The theorems of the first section showed that specialising functions to the projection images has a sound mathematical basis. In the second section we saw how finite domains of projections may be constructed that relate to the domain definitions. In the remainder of the paper other related issues were seen, and it was also shown that using projections in this way has the potential to combine well with other methods of analysis of functional programs.

Acknowledgements

Thanks are due to the many people who have helped me to reach the stage at which this paper became possible. Notable amongst them are Professor John Hughes, my supervisor, who directed and encouraged me; Gebre Baraki with whom I had many mathematical discussions; Phil Wadler who significantly helped to clarify my thoughts; Dave Schmidt for helping to tighten up the mathematics; and the referees for the workshop on Partial Evaluation and Mixed Computation, Denmark, 1987, for their observations and criticisms. I also thank the Science and Engineering

Research Council of Great Britain for funding my Ph.D. research, and the members of the Glasgow University Computing Science department for providing a stimulating environment.

References

[Ershov 82]   A. P. Ershov. Mixed Computation: Potential Applications and Problems for Study. *Theoretical Computer Science*, (18): 41-67, 1982.

[Futamura 71]   Y. Futamura. Partial Evaluation of Computation Process - An Approach to a Compiler-Compiler. *Systems, Computers, Controls*, 2(5): 45-50, 1971.

[Hughes 87]   R. J. M. Hughes. Backwards Analysis of Functional Programs. In A. P. Ershov and D. Bjørner, editors, *Proc. of Workshop on Partial Evaluation and Mixed Computation, Gl. Avernaes, Denmark, October 1987*, North-Holland, 1988 (to appear)

[Jones 85]   N. D. Jones, P. Sestoft and H. Søndergaard. An Experiment in Partial Evaluation: The Generation of a Compiler Generator. In J. P. Jouannaud, editor, *Rewriting techniques and Applications*, pages 124-140, Lecture Notes in Computer Science, Vol 202, Springer-Verlag, 1985.

[Sestoft 86]   P. Sestoft. The Structure of A Self-Applicable Partial-Evaluator. In H. Ganzinger and N. D. Jones, editors, *Programs as Data Objects, Copenhagen, Denmark, 1985*, pages 236-256, Lecture Notes in Computer Science, Vol 217, Springer-Verlag, 1986.

[Scott 82]   D. S. Scott. Domains for Denotational Semantics. Presented at ICALP 1982, Aarhus, Denmark, July 1982.

[Turchin 86]   V. F. Turchin. The Concept of a Supercompiler. *ACM Transactions on Programming Languages and Systems*, 8(3): 292-325, July 1986.

[Wadler 87]   P. Wadler, R. J. M. Hughes. Projections for Strictness Analysis. Presented at the *Third International Conference on Functional Programming Languages Computer Architecture*, Portland, Oregon, September 1987.

Partial Evaluation and Mixed Computation
D. Bjørner, A.P. Ershov and N.D. Jones (Editors)
Elsevier Science Publishers B.V. (North-Holland)
© IFIP, 1988

ON THE ESSENCE OF MIXED COMPUTATION

Sviatoslav S. LAVROV

Institute for Theoretical Astronomy
USSR Academy of Sciences
Leningrad, USSR

The relationship between the common and partial (mixed) computation
is considered. Examples of computations able to be regarded as
partial ones (in a more general sense than usual) are given. The
Futamura's projections are analysed from both functional and lin-
guistic points of view. The connection between interpretation and
compilation is reconsidered.

1. INTRODUCTION

In human communication the same words may have different meaning and the same
thing may be called differently. Happily or not, one meets the same situation
in mathematics and in any other exact science. Programming makes no exception
from the rule. A text may be considered as just a text, or a program text, or a
language definition (of the input language of the program, cf. S. Lavrov [5]).

A computation process may be viewed as an ordinary computation or as a partial/
mixed one. In a sense it is a matter of taste. The rest of the paper may be
considered as the development of this assertion.

2. COMMON AND MIXED COMPUTATIONS

If one thinks over a little, the usual words "to compute (to evaluate) something" assume a rather hazy sense. Apparently the sense is "to point out the
object which is the result of the computation". If there exists a denotation of
the result all is plain enough: 2+3=5, 2*3=6 - the digits 5 and 6 here are just
as simple, not reducible to anything (in common sense) denotations, as 2 and 3.
What is, however, the result of evaluation of 2*10+3? If we say that it is
equal to 23, then nothing is said, because 23 is a text defining a number as a
result of just the same actions, which have to be performed. This example is a
typical one, it has a series of analogies. Thus 2/3 is a denotation of a number
and of an action leading to the number as well. The situation with the numbers
√2, 2+3i is a similar one. The sum of two classical mathematical constants
π and e has no denotation essentially differing from π+e.

So some numbers (natural numbers from 0 to 9, constants like π etc.) have their
individual names, while others have to be denoted by writing some kind of an
algorithm leading to the required result. This is true for the various classes
of numbers - from the natural numbers to the complex ones and further on.
Therefore any computation consists usually of building a composition of the
algorithms representing the given data, of transforming the composition to the
desired form (by opening brackets, eliminating irrationalities in the denomi-
nator etc.) and - in a very limited extent - of actual evaluation (e.g. the
calculation of decimal digits in numerical coefficients).

Thus the boundary between "common" and "mixed" computation is very vague. The
difference between "numbers" and more general "residual programs" is that the

former have all their arguments explicitly given. The term "mixed computation"
defines no specific class of computation and its use may be justified only by
the desire to emphasize the transformational aspect of the computation – the
fact that while performing it one has to construct and to transform compositions of algorithms. This emphasis, however, has no deep reason. Nearly all
formulas of the calculus may be considered as the rules of algorithms transformation. If one is not inclined to consider the common denotations of series,
integrals etc. as algorithms, he (or she) may agree that such a denotation is a
rather acceptable algorithm specification. A way from the specification to an
algorithm is also an object studied in the calculus. Therefore the word "calculus" used above is more adequate than the more up-to-date term "mathematical
analysis".

3. KINDS OF MIXED COMPUTATIONS

Mixed computation is often mentioned in the following context. Let f be a
function of two arguments. The value a of the first argument being fixed let us
examine the function $f_a = \lambda y.f(a,y)$. If the function f is defined by means of an
algorithm A having input data (x,y) then the problem of transforming A into an
algorithm A_a implementing the function f_a can be stated. But this is only one
aspect of the mixed computation problem and possibly not the most important and
interesting one. As a matter of fact it is reduced to the study of a restriction of the function f to the subset $\{a\} \times Y$ of the set $X \times Y$ – the domain of the
function. It is possible to study properties of a restriction to any other subset of the domain. M.S. Margolin [6] has proposed the concept of an "areal" of
the domain of a function. The set $\{(a,y) : y \in Y\}$ is a possible but not a unique
example of an areal.

With the more general approach there is no sense to divide the arguments of a
function into two groups of the given (a) and frozen (y) arguments.

The areal defined as $\{x : \|x-a\| < c\}$, where $\|\ \|$ is a norm in the space of
arguments of the function f, is rather important from the practical point of
view. It is typical for the consideration of the precision of problem solution,
its stability with respect to the initial perturbation and so on. In such consideration, however, one is less interested in the restriction of f to U itself
than in the range

$$f\uparrow(U) = \{y : \exists x(x \in U \ \& \ y=f(x))\}$$

of the restriction, i.e. in the image of U by the mapping f. The inverse image

$$f\downarrow(V) = \{x : f(x) \in V\}$$

of a subset V of the range of mapping f is of interest too.

In common practice the denotations like $f\uparrow$ and $f\downarrow$ are rarely used. Usually the
correspondence between a set U and its image is denoted with the same letter f.
It means that one considers the function f as able to "evaluate" not only the
images of its domain elements but the images of subsets of the domain as well.
On the same basis the correspondence between a set V and its reverse image is
denoted with the symbol f^{-1}.

Besides the above mentioned applications the induced mappings $f\uparrow$ and $f\downarrow$ are
intensively studied because of their close relation to the denotational
semantics of algorithmic languages.

A program is considered in the semantics as being simultaneously a state
transformer and a predicate transformer. Each predicate may be practically
identified with its characteristic function – a mapping of the set Σ of

program variables states into the set {0,1}. In a Hoare's formula P{S}Q the
logical expressions P and Q form the bodies of such predicate definitions.
If the expression P (all program variables occuring in it considered free)
has value 1 on the starting state 6 then the formula implies that Q has the
same value on the state τ arising from 6 after the execution the statement S.
One may say that Q is the result of partial evaluation of P by the statement.

The predicate transformations allow the generalization that was firstly investigated apparently by S.A.Abramov [1]. He has proposed to consider pairs of
functions (g,h), g,h: Σ→H, where H is an arbitrary set, instead of predicate
pairs. Let G and H be bodies of g and h definitions. Then they are bound in the
same manner: the value of H on τ is equal to the value of G on 6.

Example:

   n {n := n+1} n-1

Such functions are nearly as simple to deal with as predicates. They can,
however, represent the information about states in a more concise manner than
predicates do. In the example the pair of expressions (n,n-1) replaces an infinite family of logical expressions pairs (n=k, n-1=k), k being the parameter
of the family.

A very interesting class of partial evaluation was proposed independently by
A.S. Narinjani [7] and A.M. Stepanov [8,9]. This class has a close relation
with the concept of an abstract data type. The definition of a type consists of
the list of its components and of a set of dependences between the components.
The values of the type have, however, an active behavior. As soon as the value
of a component is changed or restricted the dependences are used to evaluate or
to restrict other components. This approach was successfully applied in constructing knowledge representation (expert) systems.

One more approach to partial computations binds them with symbolic computations
(the former being a partial case of the latter, of course). In the initial
treatment we construct the function f_a by equalizing the value of the argument
x of f to the value a that belongs to the object field D of a natural interpretation of the function f. Instead one can substitute for x a symbolic value
(expression). It may simply be an identifier in which case it is sometimes
possible to simplify the algorithm implementing f.

More interesting though is the case when the value is defined by the more complex expression up to the case when the program (procedure) calculating the
value is given. Such an approach is rather natural in functional programming,
where any program is a function having some value. Nevertheless in common (procedural) programming this approach makes sense too. Let G be a program, x is
the intersection of (the set of variables representing) the results of the
program with the arguments of another program F. One can consider the program
G;F and state the problem of simplifying the part F of the program taking into
account that the value of x is supplied by the program G and is therefore not
an arbitrary one but is bounded to some restrictions. Essentially it is a way
to specify an areal of the value of x (in the above mentioned sense).

Following the analogy with inverse predicate transformers in denotational
semantics the problem of transformation of program G may be stated as well.
This time one has to start from the fact that the results of the program G are
used not in arbitrary way but as the initial values for the program F.

In other words any composition of algorithms naturally leads to the optimization
(mixed evaluation, if you like) problem for the resulting algorithm.

4. MIXED COMPUTATION AND COMPILATION

Let us have another look at the mixed computation theory. Let I be an interpreter for a language L, f - a program written in the language. The program
takes the data x which in turn should be written in some language. The main
property of the interpreter is to compute from a pair (f,x) the value f computes being applied to x:

$$\forall f,x(I(f,x) = f(x)). \qquad\qquad (1)$$

Let M be a mixed evaluator which has to construct a section g_a of a given
function g of two arguments by the given value a of its first argument:

$$M(g,a) = g_a = \lambda u.g(a,u), \qquad\qquad (2)$$

or

$$\forall g,a,u(M(g,a)(u) = g(a,u). \qquad\qquad (3)$$

Such a property of a universal mixed evaluator allows one to write the
equalities:

$$M(I,f)(x) = I(f,x), \qquad\qquad (4)$$
$$M(M,I)(f) = M(I,f), \qquad\qquad (5)$$
$$M(M,M)(I) = M(M,I). \qquad\qquad (6)$$

Resting upon the main property (1) of an interpreter one can transform the
formula (4) into

$$M(I,f)(x) = f(x). \qquad\qquad (7)$$

As the result of applying $M(I,f)$ to data x coincides with the result of f
being applied to the same data, $M(I,f)$ is often said to be an object code for
the function f. Then since $M(I,f)$ arises as a result of application $M(M,I)$
to f, $M(M,I)$ is asserted to be a compiler from the language L to the object
language. Finally, emerging of the compiler $M(M,I)$ as a result of applying
$M(M,M)$ to I gives occasion to call $M(M,M)$ a compilers compiler (Y. Futamura [2]).

The matter is, however, not so simple. In programming a program is not just a
function but an algorithm written in a specific language. Some authors (N.D.
Jones and M. Tofte [4], N.C.K. Holst [3]) prefer to denote a program written in
a language L by f and the function realized in the program by L f. Such elaborate denotations make sense on various occasions, esp. when a text may be
viewed as a description of two or more different functions in different
languages.

Let as look at the formula (2). While performing some parts of computation
prescribed by the program g the mixed evaluator M inserts other fragments of
the program into the residual program g_a. So g_a and g are programs written in
the same language. A mixed evaluator transforms a program but not the language
in which it is written.

For $M(I,f)$ to be an object code, i.e. machine language code, the interpreter
I transformed by the mixed evaluator M into this object code should be also
written in the machine language.

Consider now the formulas (4) and (5). The second argument of the function M in
their left parts is f and I correspondingly. It is quite natural to assume that
the argument should be written in both cases in the same language. We have just
stated, however, that for I it should be the machine language. It follows that

the program f which is given on the input of the mixed evaluator H has to be written in machine language too, i.e. should be an object code of a function from the very beginning.

Thus the mixed evaluator H does not produce an object code for a function f, but only transforms an existing object code into another form, namely $H(I,f)$. This form is functionally equivalent to the given one and is written in the same language. Whether the new program is better or worse according to some criteria than the program f depends on the optimizing abilities of the mixed evaluator.

From the purely functional point of view the functions $H(I,f)$ and f are identical. The formula (5) may be rewritten as

$$H(H,I)(f) = f,$$

i.e. $H(H,I)$ is (functionally) an identical transformation. Consequently $H(H,H)$ is an interpreter tester (though not an effective one since functional equivalence is not recognizable). If an interpreter is given as an input then an identity mapping has to appear on output.

Inversely, let $H(H,H)(I)$ be an identical transformation. Then on account of formula (6)

$$H(H,I)(f) = f,$$

owing to (5)

$$H(I,f)(x) = f(x)$$

and according to (4)

$$I(f,x) = f(x),$$

i.e. I is nothing but an interpreter.

These considerations partially explain the sources of the often mentioned difficulties that one meets while constructing a practical mixed evaluator.

Are there gaps in this reasonning? Apparently the answer is — yes, since the examples of successful practical application of mixed evaluators are known.

First of all a mixed evaluator need not be a universal one. Let us take into account that functions $H(I,f)$ and $H(H,I)$ in the formulas (4) and (5) have essentially different (from a programmer's point of view) classes of arguments. In the former case these are data x and if among the data a program text is encountered then it is treated as any other text. In the latter case the argument may be nothing but a program text f and it has to be treated quite definitely as such a text. So it is but natural to assume that the evaluators H1 and H2 dealing with such different input data must differ themselves. The formulas (4), (7) and (5) get the following forms:

$$H1(I,f)(x) = I(f,x) = f(x), \qquad (4')$$
$$H2(H1,I)(f) = H1(I,f). \qquad (5')$$

For the algorithm $H1(I,f)$ to be an object code and the mixed evaluator H1 to assume its second argument as a program written in the language of a higher level than that of the machine language, H1 should be a compiler from the language into the machine code.

Moreover, H1 has to be a parameterized compiler. It gets on input not only a

program *f* to be compiled but an interpreter *I* as well. The interpreter contains
the rules for the analysis of program texts in the input language and the rules
for the execution of primary fragments of the texts. The execution rules are
usually defined by the explicit inclusion of the machine language texts corresponding to the fragments. The rules of composition of these fragments into an
integral program may be extracted from the interpreter text as well. The evaluator *M*1 supplies as an output the algorithm translated into the object code.
The higher the requirements to the translation quality are, the more knowledge
of the methods of algorithms translation, transformation and optimization we
have to put into the evaluator *M*1.

The mixed evaluator *M*2 has more moderate task. It transforms the pair $(M1,I)$
abstracting from all semantic and pragmatic knowledge implemented in *M*1.
Therefore it is a very general program, rather simple but not very efficient.
It lies nearer to the pure idea of a mixed evaluator than *M*1.

If one accepts a pragmatic approach and does not afford *M*2 to be a universal
mixed evaluator, then the argument *M*1 becomes redundant and the formula (5')
transforms into

$$M2'(I)(f) = M1(I,f).$$

In this case *M*2' may be obtained as the result of applying a mixed evaluator *M*
(or rather *M*3 taking in mind the specific nature of its arguments) to the arguments *M*2 and *M*1. There exists, however, only a very poor reason for creating
the evaluator since it has to be applied only once. It is more practical to
write *M*2' by hand with due regard to all the peculiarities of the omitted first
argument *M*1.

With this modification *M*2' is a universal compiler generator which transforms
an interpreter *I* of a programming language into the compiler *M*2'(*I*) for the
language.

5. INTERPRETERS AND COMPILERS

It is commonly believed that an interpreter is much simpler to write than a
compiler for the same language. On the other side we have seen that the interpreter *I* must contain all the information about the syntax and the semantics
of the input language which is needed for the mixed evaluator *M*1. Is there any
contradiction in it? The answer to this question was actually be given above.
If one does not afford the high quality of translation, if all pieces of program text needed for constructing an object code are mechanically transferred
from the interpreter *I* into residual (i.e. object) program, then we get a compiler not in the least more complex than the interpreter *I*.

Let us consider for the sake of demonstration an informal description of the
syntax and the semantics of a very simple language.

The language uses unsigned integer denotations treated in a usual way. The text
'int *x*' means that a store for an integer value is to be created, the value
being called the current value of the variable *x*. Expessions are constructed
from constant denotations and variable names with the help of + symbols. The
variable name in an expression always stands for its current value. A condition
consists of two expressions connected by a < symbol. Expressions and conditions
are evaluated by the common rules.

A statement of the form '*x*:=*e*', where *e* is an expression, prescribes to replace
the current value of the variable *x* by the value of the expression *e*. The
statement '*S*1;*S*2' prescribes to execute the statements *S*1 and *S*2 in turn.
The loop statement 'while *b* do *S*' is executed as follows. The condition *b* is

checked. If it is not satisfied then the loop execution is finished. If the condition is satisfied then the statement S is executed and all is repeated again.

The question arises whether the structure of an interpreter or that of a compiler was described. The answer is - both were.

If while reading the program text we execute all the actions prescribed (and return back through the text if needed), then we perform the interpretation of the program. If, however, we bound ourselves by remembering all the sequence of actions (including the repeated execution of some parts of the sequence), then the program is compiled. In both cases we have to deal with the pieces of the object code (e.g. with a jump instruction to the point of loop condition check-up). But in the case of interpretation these pieces of the code stored in the text of the interpreter are executed when needed and in the case of compilation they are transferred into the object program text for the future execution.

This approach was taken in a more formal (and, possibly, more confusing) way in the papers by N.D. Jones and M. Tofte [4] and N.C.K. Holst [3]. It is, however, a rather obvious consequence of the widely accepted in the programming milieu view that (the semantics of) a programming language is fully defined by its interpreter. This allows one to consider a program as an interpreter in one language and as a compiler in another language. Surely the execution of the program in the first language means its evaluation while in the second language it means its partial evaluation. If we call it a "program" in both cases why should we not call the process by the single word "evaluation"?

The structure of both interpreter and compiler and their complexity are identical. It is clear, however, that a compiler without any optimization was mentioned. As soon as we want to transform the object program text (while it is constructed or after that) the structure of the compiler gets much more complicated. (Sure enough, the similar assertion is valid with respect to the interpreter, if we want to make the initial program text easier for inter-pretation.)

Looking back at the mixed evaluator $M1$ from the previous section we have to note that its practical value depends directly on the extent to which it is able to create an efficient object code departing from an abstract scheme of program interpretation. Transformation without optimization is rather an ele-mentary task owing to the above mentioned structural identity of an interpreter and a non-optimizing compiler. Such a transformation is restricted to the composition of the object code fragments explicitly given in the interpreter.

REFERENCES

[1] Abramov, S.A., Program Analysis and Binary Relations, Zh. Vychislitel'noj Matematiki i Matematicheskoj Fiziki, 23(2)(1983) 440-452. (In Russian.)
[2] Futamura, Y., Partial Evaluation of Computation Process - An Approach to a Compiler-Compiler, Systems, Computers, Controls, 2(5)(1971) 45-50.
[3] Holst, N.C.K., Language Triplets: the AMIX Approach, this volume.
[4] Jones, N.D. and Tofte, M., Towards a Theory of Compiler Generation, in: Bjørner, D., (ed.), Proc. Workshop on Formal Software Development Methods (North-Holland, Amsterdam, 1985).
[5] Lavrov, S.S., Les Langages de Programmation, in: Actes du Congrès Interna-tional des Mathématiciens 1970, publies sous la direction du Comité d'Orga-nisation de Congrès, Tome 3 (Gautier-Villars, Paris, 1971) pp. 275-279. (In French.)
[6] Margolin, M.S. and Potapenko, T.P., Employment of Incomplete Input Data to Simplify Program, Upravlyajushchie Sistemy i Mashiny (Control Systems and Machines), (6)(1981) 78-81. (In Russian.)

[7] Narinjani, A.S., Subdefinite Sets - a New Data Type for Knowledge Representation, Preprint 232, Computing Center, Novosibirsk, USSR, 1980. (In Russian.)

[8] Stepanov, A.M., Frames and Parallel Mixed Computation, Preprint 297, Computing Center, Novosibirsk, USSR, 1981. (In Russian.)

[9] Stepanov, A.M., Experimental Programming System, Preprint 305, Computing Center, Novosibirsk, USSR, 1981. (In Russian.)

Partial Evaluation and Mixed Computation
D. Bjørner, A.P. Ershov and N.D. Jones (Editors)
Elsevier Science Publishers B.V. (North-Holland)
© IFIP, 1988

Partially Static Structures
in a
Self-Applicable Partial Evaluator

Torben Ægidius MOGENSEN

Institute of Datalogy

University of Copenhagen

Universitetsparken 1, DK-2100 København Ø

Denmark

While partially static structures can be handled in partial evaluation, they cause specific problems when self-application of a partial evaluator is attempted. The reason is that the binding-time analysis that increases in complexity when its domain is non-flat. Binding-time analysis has been found essential for realistic self-application in the first MIX system.

This paper describes a method for binding-time analysis, producing a context-free tree-grammar. This binding-time information is then used to produce an efficient self-applicable partial evaluator. This has been realized in practice and gave satisfactory results.

First the idea of binding-time analysis is discussed, then a method to handle partially static structures by using grammars is presented and finally the actual use in a partial evaluator is detailed. It is also shown that the variable splitting that was done on the basis of user-annotation in the MIX project can be achieved automatically and naturally by using partially static structures.

1. Introduction

This paper presents a partial evaluator which extends the one from [Sestoft 86] to handle partially static structures. We assume some familiarity with the basic concept of partial evaluation (eg. [Jones 85]), at least to the extent of knowing how compilation and compiler generation can be achieved by partial evaluation of interpreters. Some domain theory will be used, so familiarity with this will be beneficial.

The paper starts by showing how partial evaluation of expressions is done in a partial evaluator that operates on completely static / completely dynamic values (like the one in [Jones 85]), and explains binding time analysis in this context. Then a natural extension of the partial evaluation method to partially static values is presented, and through several steps a suitable domain for binding time information is derived. A partial evaluation method using this information is presented and results of an implementation are reported.

The paper can be seen as a presentation of some techniques and a report on a succesful experiment in BTA and partial evaluation. It doesn't attempt to define or proof a formal relation between the semantics of BTA, partial evaluation and normal evaluation.

2. Partial evaluation with completely static / dynamic values

A simple partial evaluator will normally operate on a domain that conceptually is the tagged sum of values and expressions. Thus values that are known at partial evaluation time are represented by their values, while those that are unknown are represented by expressions that will evaluate to the correct values when the remaining input is supplied. These are called *residual expressions*. In this paper the known values are called *static* (at partial evaluation time) and the unknown values are called *dynamic*. These terms correspond well to their usual meanings when partial evaluation is used for compilation.

Examples:

> S(3)   represents the static value 3.
> D(x+y)   represents a dynamic value. "x+y" is the residual expression.

In actual implementations explicit tags like S and D need not be used, since static values can be represented by constant expressions and thus be implicitly tagged. But to facilitate reading all such tags will be made explicit in this paper.

When performing an operation the partial evaluator will test to see if the values of the parameters to the operation are static, and if they are then just perform the operation. If some were dynamic a new residual expression will be constructed from the operator and the residual expressions of the parameters.

Examples:

> **car(** S((a . b)) **)** = S(a)
> **car(** D(cdr(x)) **)** = D(car(cdr(x)))

As can be seen from the examples the result of an operation depends very much on whether or not the arguments are static or dynamic. The Copenhagen group [Jones 85] found that these tests on the staticness of values would remain in compilers and other residual programs that were obtained by self-application of such a partial evaluator. This resulted in large and slow residual programs. To overcome this as many as possible of these tests were tried to be decided at self-application time. It was found that the value of most of these tests depended only on *which* of the programs parameters were static, and *not* their actual values.

Thus a *binding-time analysis* was performed: given a program and information about *which* of the parameters would be static at partial evaluation time, it would return information for all local expressions. It would be determined whether their values would *always* be static (meaning: a function only of the data known at partial evaluation time) or *possibly* dynamic (sometimes dependent on data *not* present at partial evaluation time). This information was then used to decide the tests, marking the operators in the program that had static parameters. Since this information was available at self-application time the tests became decidable at this time, giving smaller and faster residual programs when the partial evaluator was self-applied (for producing compilers *etc*).

The BTA (short for binding-time analysis) used a two-value domain to abstract the values used during partial evaluation:

where S denotes values that are always Static and D values that in some (or all) instances are Dynamic. Note that S and D represent sets of values used in the partial evaluator. S represent the set of all static values (the values tagged by S in the partial evaluator, and D represent the set of *all* values, both static and dynamic. The BTA finds for each local expression in a program the smallest element in the BTA-domain that safely describes (represents a superset of) the set of values that the expression can evaluate to at partial evaluation time.

3. An extension to partially static structures

When using structured data (like the S-expressions of LISP) it is often useful to handle values where some parts are static and other parts dynamic.

A partial evaluator handling partially static structured values in S-expression can use a domain that would have partially static values in addition to the static and dynamic values of the simple partial evaluator described above. These are tagged with a P and have a pair of values, which again can be static, dynamic or partially static.

Examples:

P(S(3),D(cdr(x)))	A pair with a static head and a dynamic tail
P(P(S(x),D(y+z)),S(nil))	A list of (static) length 1, with a static/dynamic pair at the head

In addition to rules for partial evaluation like those before, new rules for the partially static cases would be added:

```
car( P(A , B) ) = A
cons( S(V) , D(E) ) = P(S(V),D(E))
```

A generalization of the BTA described above to such structures would operate on a domain BTA_0 with values like these:

$$P(S,D)$$
$$P(P(S,D),S)$$

for the partially static values above. These are partially ordered so D is the top element in the domain ($x \leq D$ for all x), S is the bottom element ($S \leq x$ for all x) and $P(x,y) \leq P(x',y')$ iff $x \leq x'$ and $y \leq y'$. $P(S,S)$ is equal to S as a pair of two static values still is a static value.

The values in BTA_0 are however too restrictive as one (among other things) can't describe a list where the length is static (but not constant), but the values of the elements are dynamic. To do this *sets* of BTA_0 values must be used, eg.:

$$\{ S , P(D,S) , P(D,P(D,S)) , \cdots \}$$

to describe lists of static length. The meaning of such a set as a description of an expression is that the expression may obtain values at partial evaluation time that at each instance will be of *one* of the forms from the set.

Since we are interested in worst case behaviour of the partial evaluator, any set containing a certain value will also contain all values that are "more static" than this. For this reason the set of *left-closed* subsets of BTA_0 will be used instead of the powerset. This will be called BTA_1. Each element in BTA_1 is thus a left-closed subset of BTA_0 and they will be ordered by set inclusion. A left-closed set is a non-empty set that satisfies the following property:

if an element x is in the set, all elements y such that $y \leq x$ will also be in the set.

For each set of BTA_0 values the *left-closure* of that set is defined by the smallest (by set inclusion) left-closed superset. A left-closed set can be represented by a set which left-closure is that set. Thus the set $\{D\}$ represents the top element in BTA_1 (since its left-closure is the whole of BTA_0), and the set $\{S\}$ is the bottom element.

Note that the set of left-closed subsets is similar to the *Hoare power domain*, which consists of the *Scott-closed* subsets that also require that limits of chains of elements of a set also are in the set. BTA_1 is actually the Hoare power domain of the chain-completion of BTA_0. We do not need to consider limits of chains, so we use the simpler construction.

A set M seen as a BTA_1 element will (by its left-closure) also represent all the BTA_0 values that are smaller than the elements of M by the ordering of BTA_0. Thus the set describing lists of static length shown in the example above will, as an element of BTA_1, also represent lists where some of the elements are static (eg. $P(S,P(D,S))$ and $P(D,P(S,P(D,S)))$).

Sets of BTA_0 elements can clearly be infinite (as the above example is), so a way of finitely describing such sets is needed. But as the number of elements in BTA_1 is uncountable there is no way of describing them all finitely, so we must use approximations of the elements. This can be done by constructing a subdomain BTA_2 of finitely describable elements of BTA_1, where each element in BTA_1 is represented by a finitely describable safe approximation in BTA_2. A safe approximation of an element M in BTA_1 is an element M' in BTA_2, so $M \subseteq M'$ in the ordering of BTA_1.

A way of finitely describing infinite sets of tree-structures is to use *tree-grammars*, and it will be used here.

Tree-grammars are analogous to a context-free grammar and use non-terminals *etc.* in the same way. They just describe sets of tree structures instead of sets of character sequences.

$$x \to S \mid P(D,x)$$

will thus describe the set in the example above. Similarly

$$\begin{aligned} \text{a-list} &\quad\to\quad S \mid P(\text{pair},\text{a-list}) \\ \text{pair} &\quad\to\quad P(S,D) \end{aligned}$$

will describe lists of pairs where the first element of the pairs is static and the second is dynamic.

In this approach we will actually construct an infinite series of BTA_2 domains: BTA_{2_n}, where n is the number of different non-terminals in BTA_{2_n}. Restrictions are made on the forms of the right sides of the productions in the tree-grammar describing a BTA_{2_n}: a right side is either D, or a list of alternatives separated with |'s. The alternatives are S or $P(x,y)$ where x and y are S, D or non-terminals.

The BTA_2 value of a right side is the left-closure of the set of BTA_0 values that the right side produces in the grammar. Thus D as a right side will represent the BTA_{2_n} value {D}. A non-terminal and its right side will denote the same value, so they will be used interchangeably. The requirement that non-terminals must be inside $P(,)$'s makes circular derivations impossible.

If we assume that there are no repeated alternatives in any right side and that the number of different non-terminals used in right sides is a finite number, n, we will have a finite number of possible right sides, and thus a finite BTA_{2_n} domain. However, one may note that two different right sides can very well represent the same BTA_{2_n} value. This is not important in the present application, and it is not difficult to see when two right sides represent the same value.

The least upper bound of two BTA_{2_n} values in a certain grammar will be the smallest BTA_{2_n} value that safely approximates the least upper bound of the values seen as elements in BTA_1, which is the (left-closure of) the union of the sets of

BTA_0 values that represents the BTA_{2_n} values.

A right side representing this can be constructed by adding the alternatives of the right sides representing the two values, unless one of the right sides is D, in which case the least upper bound is just D, as this is the top element.

In binding type analysis the non-terminals will correspond to variables or functions in a program, and the values of them will describe the values that the variable or function can obtain during partial evaluation.

Normally the analysis will start by assigning the value S to all non-terminals except those that represent the parameters to the goal function, and then do a fixed point iteration where at each step the non-terminals will be updated with new values. When a non-terminal changes value all the right sides that refer to it will also change values *etc.*, but as all changes are monotonic in the ordering of BTA_{2_n}, the result will still be a safe approximation, only it is less precise.

Note that the abstract evaluation handles values in the form of right sides to a grammar. The actual values these right sides represents are the left-closures of the sets they derive relative to the grammar.

A tree grammar is equivalent to a set of recursive set-equations, and a method like [Reynolds 69] or [Jones 86] could be used to obtain such descriptions. The method shown below is however simpler in the treatment of selectors (eg. car and cdr).

Part of the difficulty of the BTA presented stems from the fact that the language is untyped: the analysis must do a kind of type inference to find good binding time information. With a typed language a fixed set of possible BT values can be found for each type, making the use of grammars unnecessary. The projections in [Launchbury 88] use this idea.

4. Binding-time analysis

To make a partial evaluator self-applicable, one must be able to find BTA values automatically. In the case of the two-value domain this can be done with a simple abstract interpretation over a two-value domain, but when recursive descriptions are required it is not obvious how it can be done.

The language that is used is called L and is a small functional language similar to that of [Jones 85] with a few additions. Fig. 3.1 below presents the syntax of the language.

The semantics are straight-forward. The program is a list of function definitions where the first is the goal function. The scope of each functions is the whole program, and there are no local function definitions. The calling mechanism is applicative (call-by-value) . The parameters and other variables are statically scoped.

```
┌─────────────────────────────────────────────────────────┐
│         fig. 3.1  The syntax of the language  L.        │
├─────────────────────────────────────────────────────────┤
│                                                         │
│  <program>      →    ( <function>* )                   │
│                                                         │
│  <function>     →    ( <name> ( <name>* ) <exp> )      │
│                                                         │
│  <exp>          →    <name>                            │
│                 |    ( quote <constant> )              │
│                 |    ( car <exp> )                     │
│                 |    ( cdr <exp> )                     │
│                 |    ( atom <exp> )                    │
│                 |    ( null <exp> )                    │
│                 |    ( cons <exp> <exp> )              │
│                 |    ( equal <exp> <exp> )             │
│                 |    ( if <exp> <exp> <exp> )          │
│                 |    ( let ( <binding>* ) <exp> )      │
│                 |    ( call <name> <exp>* )            │
│                                                         │
│  <binding>      →    <name> = <exp>                    │
│                                                         │
└─────────────────────────────────────────────────────────┘
```

An expression is either a name, which is a variable, or a list consisting of an operator followed by one or more arguments. The operators quote, car, cdr, atom, null, cons and equal behave exactly as in LISP. if is an if-then-else operator with the usual semantics. let defines a set of new name/value bindings with a local scope (as in ML or Scheme). call is the function application operator. All parameters to a function must be supplied when it is called, so there will be no building of closures and thus no higher order functions.

The idea is to use names from the program as non-terminals in the BTA descriptions, so the non-terminal corresponding to a variable would describe the set of values that the variable can take, and non-terminals for function names describe the set of possible result values of the function.

Since the right sides of the productions can refer to other non-terminals, this approach requires all variables to have distinct names even if they have disjoint scopes (actually this is not strictly required, as the BTA would still give a safe result: it would only be less precise). Due to the limitations to the right sides involving $P(x,y)$ there are further restrictions. Since the x's and y's can either be S, D or non-terminals, it would help if the parameter expressions of cons were of forms that are always describable by such values. Such forms are constants (describable by S), variables or function calls (describable by non-terminals). This property is easily achieved by adding let-expressions where necessary.

There are thus some small changes in the syntax of the language that is required as input to the BTA (fig. 3.2).

---

fig. 3.2 The changes in syntax for the input to the BTA.

```
<exp>                →    ...
                     |    ( cons <restricted-exp> <restricted-exp> )
                     |    ...

<restricted-exp>     →    <name>
                     |    ( quote <constant> )
                     |    ( call <name> <exp>* )
```

The BTA computes by a fixed-point iteration that starts with a global grammar containing S productions for all non-terminals except those describing the values of the parameters to the the goal-function. Alternatives are added to the productions until a fixed-point is achieved. As the number of non-terminals is a fixed number n, the number of right sides is limited. And since all changes are monotonic in the domain of BTA_{2_n} values, there will be a finite fixed-point grammar which can be obtained in a finite number of steps. Such a fixed-point iteration is well known from flow analysis (eg. [Mycroft 80]).

Each step in the iteration recomputes the values of expressions each time the variables or functions they use change value. This is done by evaluating the expressions in the BTA domain. Instead of checking for each expression if it needs to be recomputed, *all* expressions are recomputed at each iteration step until no changes occur between two such steps.

The abstract evaluation is described in appendix A. The values that are actually computed are right sides of productions, but when alternatives are added to a right side in the global grammar, this changes the meaning of a non-terminal, and thus the right sides that use it. The places in the abstract evaluation where the updating occurs are marked by comments. The updating is done by replacing a right side with the least upper bound of the old value and the new.

As an example, here is a function which constructs an a-list structured environment from a list of names and a list of values.

```
(Make_env (names values)
  (if (null names)
    (quote nil)
    (let
      (hd = (let (hd1 = (car names) tl1 = (car values)) (cons hd1 tl1)))
      (cons hd (call Make_env (cdr names) (cdr values)))
)  )  )
```

Assume that the function Make_env has static first parameter (names → S) and dynamic second parameter (values → D), then the initial environment would be:

names	→	S
values	→	D
hd1	→	S
tl1	→	S
hd	→	S
Make_env	→	S

The first iteration step of the binding-time analysis would yield this environment:

names	→	S
values	→	D
hd1	→	S
tl1	→	D
hd	→	S | P(S,D)
Make_env	→	S | P(hd,S)

After the second iteration step the value of Make_env is S | P(hd,S) | P(hd,Make_env) which is unchanged after the third step, giving this final environment:

names	→	S
values	→	D
hd1	→	S
tl1	→	D
hd	→	S | P(S,D)
Make_env	→	S | P(hd,S) | P(hd,Make_env)

The P(hd,S) alternative in the value of Make_env is redundant since all the values could be obtained from the other two alternatives alone. Such redundancies often occur, but since they do not influence the later use of the description no attempt is made to reduce the environment.

The number of iterations required before a fixed-point is reached depends on the program that is analyzed, but with the optimizations that are included in the actual implementation of the BTA most programs need only four iterations.

5. Annotation

The binding-time information is used for annotation of the program in question. Expressions that operate entirely on static data are marked by putting the tag S in front of them. Other expressions are marked operator by operator. The operators that have some possibly dynamic (D) operands are marked by adding a D to the operator name, so car becomes carD *etc*. The remaining operators are partially (or possibly completely) static and they are marked with a P.

There are some special cases with cons, if-expressions, let-expressions and function calls. cons is not marked as it doesn't have to access the operands (in terms of partial evaluation it is non-strict in both arguments). if-expressions are only marked after the condition (they are strict only in their first argument). In let-expressions each binding is marked if it can be statically determined that the variable will occur at most once in any residual program, in which case it can be safely unfolded at partial evaluation time. If all bindings can be unfolded the let-expression is marked as eliminable by adding an E to the operator. It can be determined from the BTA-values of the formal parameters of a function, whether the actual parameters are static *etc.*, so no extra marking is used there. Function calls are marked to indicate whether they should be unfolded (β-reduction) or left as calls in the residual program. Residual calls are marked by changing the call operator to rcall. At present this is done by hand, but promising experiments combining automatic call marking in a pre-process and unfolding in a post-process are being made ([Sestoft 88]).

Several other annotations are used. In general as many as possible of the tests that the partial evaluator would otherwise make at partial evaluation (dynamic) time are determined by using the binding-time information (at static time). The results of these tests are added to the program as annotation of operators *etc*.

The example program from above would yield the following annotated program:

```
(Make_env (names values)
  (ifS (null names)
    (S (quote nil))
    (letE
      (hd =1 (letE (hd1 =1 (S (car names)) tl1 =1 (carD values))
                (cons (S hd1) tl1)
      )    )
      (cons hd (call Make_env (S (cdr names)) (cdrD values)))
)) )
```

6. Function specialization

The previous phases (BTA and annotation) are done at *metastatic* time, that is only knowing *which* of the parameters of the subject program (the program that is being partially evaluated) are static. When the *values* of these parameters become known (at *static* time) a residual program is constructed by making specialized versions of the functions in the subject program. The residual program can then be given various values of the dynamic parameters (at *dynamic* time) to produce final results.

The functions are specialized with respect to the static parts of their parameters. The parameters to a specialized function correspond to the dynamic parts of the parameters to the original function. The static parts are absorbed into the residual expression that becomes the body of the new function. As each function from the original program is specialized into several variant functions in the residual program, the algorithm is of the class called *polyvariant* [Bulyonkov 84], [Bulyonkov 88].

The algorithm used to perform this is an extension of the algorithm of [Sestoft 86] to include partially static structures.

The static parts of the parameters to the Make_env function above are the contents of the names variable, and the dynamic parts are the contents of the values variable. Assume the value of names is (x y z), then the specialized version would be:

```
(Make_env_1 (values)
  (cons (cons 'x (car values))
  (cons (cons 'y (cadr values))
    (cons (cons 'z (caddr values))
        'nil
)))))
```

where 'x, (cadr values) *etc.* are the usual shorthand for (quote x) , (car (cdr values)) *etc.*

Note that the recursive calls have been unfolded and that the structure of the static variables has been absorbed into the structure of the new function body. Often the value will be completely absorbed, so no part of it can be directly seen in the new body (unlike 'x *etc.*).

If a function call is not unfolded the residual expression will contain a call to a specialized version of the called function. If this has not already been generated it will be. Specialized functions can be uniquely identified by the original function name and the values of the static parts of the parameters. The specialized function above (Make_env_1) is thus identified by the name Make_env and the static value (x y z).

The body of a specialized function is of course an expression, but the result of partially evaluating the original expression is a value in the PE domain (using S D and P), so this value is made into an expression by making the static parts into constant expressions, and making cons expressions for P terms. In the Make_env example above the value

    P(P(S(x),D((car values))),
      P(P(S(y),D((cadr values))),
         P(P(S(z),D((caddr values))), S(nil))
))

was converted to the expression shown in the example as the body to the residual function. If the value was used as a parameter to a residual (not unfolded) call to a function f, the static parts are used to identify the specialized function and the dynamic parts are used as parameters to the function. This would give the residual expression

    (call f_1 (car values) (cadr values) (caddr values))

where f_1 is identified by the original name (f) and the values of the static parts:

    P(P(S(x),D(_))
      P(P(S(y),D(_)),
         P(P(S(z),D(_)), S(nil))
))

As can be seen from the example the static parts are obtained by blanking out the dynamic parts. The static parts thus reflects the structure of the value and it can be seen how many dynamic parts there are. This is important because the number of dynamic parts is needed to find the number of parameters to the specialized function. As the example shows, a single parameter in the original function call can result in several parameters in the residual call, so the definition of the specialized version must reflect this by having the same number of formal parameters. This automatically realizes the *variable splitting* that was done in [Sestoft 86] on the basis of an annotation by hand.

During the partial evaluation the annotations in the program are used. The expressions that are marked as Static are thus just evaluated without testing whether the variables in them have static values (they will have, the BTA ensures that). The operators marked Dynamic are used to construct new expressions even if the arguments by chance are static (remember that D means *possibly* dynamic). This makes the partial evaluator more conservative than a naive partial evaluator (without BTA), but experience has shown that this rarely causes problems and that it often improves the quality of residual programs by avoiding generation of almost identical specialized functions. This can happen when a function uses an accumulating parameter to build the result (like in tail-recursive list-reversal). This parameter will initially be the constant nil which is a static value but later recursions will change this to a dynamic value. The naive partial evaluator will generate a specialized version for the nil case and another for the general (dynamic) case, whereas the BTA will show that the value is actually dynamic and thus only generate a specialized function for the general case. Note that with the naive partial evaluator no residual program can contain function calls with constant parameters as the static parts of the parameters are absorbed. It is generally a good idea to avoid such restrictions on residual programs.

During the function specialization phase lists are kept of descriptions of specialized functions that have been generated and of specialized functions that have been called but not yet generated. The latter list initially contains a description consisting of the name of the goal-function and the values of the static parameters to the program. When it becomes empty all the needed specialized functions are generated and the partial evaluation is finished. There are cases when this will not happen: either a recursive function call is unfolded infinitely, or an infinite number of specialized functions are generated. The first case can be solved by marking the call as *not* unfoldable, but this will in some cases just change the problem to the other type. Infinitely many specialized functions occur when the static parts of the parameters to a function obtain infinitely many different values during the function specialization phase. This is more difficult to solve. It is possible to restrict the number of possible values by forcing some of the static parts of a variable to be dynamic by giving them dynamic initial descriptions for the BTA (so it becomes not only the parameters to the goal-function that should be specified). This will however in some cases give too conservative descriptions for other variables (as a consequence of the BTA). Another solution is to restructure the program so the problem doesn't occur. This can be *very* tricky, and in a few cases one must conclude that for some problems it is not possible (in the present framework) to find programs where the partial evaluation will terminate with a non-trivial solution.

An extended example showing compilation by partially evaluating an interpreter is shown in appendices B to D. Timings are shown in section 6. Appendix B shows an interpreter for a simple imperative language called MP. It is the same language that is used in [Sestoft 86]. Appendix C shows an exponentiation program in MP and Appendix D contains the program that is obtained by partially evaluating the MP interpreter with respect to the exponentiation program. This process translates the exponentiation program from MP to L which is the language the interpreter is written in.

7. Results

The partial evaluator has been implemented and satisfactory results have been obtained. Table 6.1 shows some execution times. The system is implemented using Franz Lisp on a Vax 785. All executions are done using compiled LISP programs. In addition to the total execution time the table shows how much of that is spent doing garbage collection (GC). Where applicable a ratio of execution times for original and residual programs is shown.

The program Btann performs both BTA and annotation, of which the BTA is the major part. Fsp performs function specialization. The notation L program $\langle x_1, \dots, x_n \rangle$ represents execution of the L program program with input $x_1, \dots, x_n$. program$_{ann}$ represents the annotated version of program.

Two interpreters are used for the executions. mp–interp is the MP interpreter from appendix B. self–interp is an interpreter for L. Since the source and object languages for compilations using a self-interpreter is the same, they should ideally be near-identity mappings or at least not yield programs that are markedly less efficient than the originals. For this system such compilations are in fact near-identity mappings. Apart from renaming and permutation of functions and variables and the addition of an extra goal function (that splits the *list* of parameters that the interpreter requires into *separate* parameters when calling the new version of the original goal function) there are virtually no differences between the original program and the new. In addition to comparing execution times for self–interp interpreting a L-program and the compiled L-program table 6.1 also compares the compiled program with the original program (this makes sense as they are in the same language).

The results from this table compares satisfactorily to the results in [Sestoft 86]. Though the time used to partially evaluate programs is longer, especially for the BTA phase, the compiled programs are faster. The ratio between compiling with the partial evaluator and a generated compiler is lower than in [Sestoft 86], mainly because the present partial evaluator does more manipulation on dynamic data (such manipulations are not improved by knowledge of static data). On the other hand the ratio between interpreting a program and executing a compiled program is higher, which is partly due to the extra manipulation of dynamic data and the automatic splitting of parameters.

Table 6.2 shows the sizes of the programs. Three numbers are shown: the number of tokens, the number of functions and a ratio. The number of tokens is measured by adding the number of CONS-cells to the number of non-NIL atoms in the data structures. L-programs are measured *before* the restrictions from fig. 3.2 are applied, as this gives the fairest comparison with residual programs where these restrictions do not apply. The number of functions only apply to L-programs. The ratio is between the number of tokens in an interpreter and the corresponding compiler.

The compiler/interpreter ratio for the small interpreters are fairly large compared to the ratio between cocom and Fsp. This is because the compilers consist of a constant part which is virtually the same in all compilers and a interpreter-dependent part which is roughly linear in the size of the interpreters, so the ratio converges to about 3.3 when the size of the interpreter increases.

The names of the programs are the same as in table 6.1.

Table 6.1 Execution times for the partial evaluator and residual programs.

job	exec. time	GC time	ratio
Fsp$_{ann}$ = L Btann⟨Fsp⟩	196160 ms	56560 ms	
cocom = L Fsp⟨Fsp$_{ann}$, Fsp$_{ann}$⟩	352460 ms	73980 ms	
cocom = L cocom⟨Fsp$_{ann}$⟩	88360 ms	50620 ms	3.9
mp–interp$_{ann}$ = L Btann⟨mp–interp⟩	6560 ms	620 ms	
l–expo = L Fsp⟨mp–interp$_{ann}$, mp–expo⟩	2560 ms	540 ms	
l–expo = L mp–compiler⟨mp–expo⟩	360 ms	0 ms	7.1
output$_1$ = L mp–interp⟨mp–expo, input$_1$⟩	7520 ms	0 ms	
output$_1$ = L l–expo⟨input$_1$⟩	200 ms	0 ms	37
mp–compiler = L Fsp⟨Fsp$_{ann}$, mp–interp$_{ann}$⟩	35760 ms	8720 ms	
mp–compiler = L cocom⟨mp–interp$_{ann}$⟩	5520 ms	2540 ms	6.4
self–interp$_{ann}$ = L Btann⟨self–interp⟩	5100 ms	560 ms	
self–int' = L Fsp⟨self–interp$_{ann}$, self–interp⟩	25920 ms	10560 ms	
self–int' = L self–compiler⟨self–interp⟩	2560 ms	500 ms	10
output$_2$ = L self–interp⟨self–interp, input$_2$⟩	48940 ms	2400 ms	
output$_2$ = L self–int'⟨input$_2$⟩	1100 ms	0 ms	44
output$_2$ = L self–interp⟨input$_2$⟩	1080 ms	0 ms	1.02
self–compiler = L Fsp⟨Fsp$_{ann}$, self–interp$_{ann}$⟩	41700 ms	11600 ms	
self–compiler = L cocom⟨self–interp$_{ann}$⟩	5580 ms	2440 ms	7.4

Table 6.2 Sizes of various programs and residual programs.

program	tokens	functions	ratio of tokens
Fsp	13172	66	
cocom	44545	105	3.4
mp–interp	903	8	
mp–compiler	11282	51	12.5
mp–expo	171		
l–expo	293	4	
self–interp	985	8	
self–compiler	11830	54	12.0
self–int'	1009	9	

8. Conclusion

The main purpose of handling partially static structures in a partial evaluator is to increase the generality of it, that is extend the class of programs that are handled non-trivially. Experience shows that programs using structures that will be partially static/dynamic at partial evaluation time normally can be rewritten so all variables/functions are either totally static or totally dynamic. This however puts extra demands on the user and often decreases the efficiency of the program.

In the sense of extending the class of programs that are handled non-trivially by the partial evaluator the project has been a success. Even so, it is still sometimes necessary to rewrite programs to get good results from the partial evaluator.

In addition to this generalization the method gives a natural and automatic way of achieving the variable-splitting that in [Sestoft 86] is done in an *ad hoc* fashion on the basis of user annotation. Another way of achieving variable-splitting automatically is by doing a kind of type inference on the residual program, and using this to split variables of composite type [Romanenko 88].

The quality of residual programs is very good, in the sense that there is little that obviously can be done to improve the programs obtained by partial evaluation of the MP interpreter and the self-interpreter. The compilers are fairly large and slow compared to those achieved by later versions of the partial evaluators described in [Jones 85] and [Sestoft 86], but this is mostly due to greater complexity of the partial evaluator of which they are residual programs.

As mentioned earlier the call unfolding are still made according to hand-made annotations as in [Jones 85]. Something similar to the combined pre- and post-processing of [Sestoft 88] could be used, though it would require an extension of the static analysis in the pre-process to handle calls to functions with partially static results.

The handling of the partially static structures has given rise to some subtle problems in connection with some language constructions. As an example imagine a let-expression of the form:

(let (*bindings to dynamic variables*) *partially static expression*)

The bindings are needed to define variables in the expressions that form the dynamic parts of the value of the partially static expression, and should thus be a part of the result of the let-expression. But the result of the partially static body must be of a form using P(x,y), where both x and y can contain dynamic parts, so the question is where to put the bindings. A possible way to do this is to copy the let-bindings onto each of the expressions in the partially static value. This would however cause duplication of code and possibly repeated calculations in the residual programs. Another possibility would be to make the value of the let-expression completely dynamic so there would be only one expression to add the bindings to. This is however unsatisfactory due to the loss of static data. The solution that is used is to keep a field in the representation of partially static structures that contain bindings that are *common* to all expressions in the structure. These bindings are copied along when access is made to substructures, and when two structures are concatenated a union of the bindings are made. This requires some rather complex manipulations to ensure that the bindings are kept in the proper order, but it solves the problem satisfactorily.

Such problems seem to arise from certain properties in the language, so it would be a good idea to find a language that does not give rise to such problems. The experiments that are at present being made with term-rewriting systems in seem to point to a possible candidate for such a language [Bondorf 88].

The way tree grammars are used in the BTA can be extended to a framework that is useful for other kinds of abstract interpretation, such as type inference and possibly strictness analysis.

The way BTA is handled in this paper is an operational way; it approximates sets of values in a naive partial evaluator. But a naive partial evaluator, and thus also a partial evaluator using an operational BTA, can build infinite sets of static structures because the things which limit the sets are dynamic. Such values should be regarded as dynamic rather than static, making the term *dynamic* apply to all values that are not limited at static time. Such a *semantic* (as opposed to operational) BTA that is sufficiently liberal (not making too much dynamic) has not yet been achieved, but work is being done in Copenhagen towards this goal.

Appendix A, Abstract evaluation in the BTA domain.

Only the abstract interpretation of expressions is shown. The values are represented by right sides of a grammar. The actual values are the left-closures of the sets the right sides derive relative to the grammar.

Aeval(name) = the right side of name in the global grammar

Aeval((quote constant)) = S

Aeval((car exp)) = Car*(Aeval(exp))

Aeval((cdr exp)) = Cdr*(Aeval(exp))

Aeval((atom exp)) = Aeval((null exp)) =
    let val = Aeval(exp) in
      if val = D then D
      else S

Aeval((cons rexp1 rexp2)) =
    let rval1 = Reval(rexp1) , rval2 = Reval(rexp2) in
      if rval1 = S and rval2 = S then S
      else P(rval1, rval2)

Aeval((equal exp1 exp2)) =
    let val1 = Aeval(exp1) , val2 = Aeval(exp2) in
      if val1 = S and val2 = S then S
        (* val1 = S means that there are only one *)
        (* alternative on the right side, and that is S *)
      else D

Aeval((if exp1 exp2 exp3)) =

```
        let val1 = Aeval( exp1 ),
            val2 = Aeval( exp2 ),
            val3 = Aeval( exp3 ) in
        else if val1 = D then D
        else Least-upper-bound(val2, val3)
```

Aeval((let bindings exp)) =
    Aeval(exp)
        (* Here the non-terminals in the global grammar corresponding to the names of *)
        (* the bindings are updated by the abstract values of the expressions of the bindings. *)

Aeval((call name . actual-params)) =
    the right side of name in the global grammar
        (* Here the non-terminals in the global grammar corresponding to the names *)
        (* of the formal parameters of the function are updated by the *)
        (* abstract values of the actual parameters. *)

        (* Reval evaluates restricted expressions returning restricted values. *)

Reval(name) =
    let val = the right side of name in the global grammar in
    if val = S or val = D then val
    else name   (* non-terminal *)

Reval((quote constant)) = S

Reval((call name . actual-params)) =
    let val = the right side of name in the global grammar in
    if val = S or val = D then val
    else name   (* non-terminal *)
        (* Here the non-terminals in the global grammar corresponding to the names *)
        (* of the formal parameters of the function are updated by the *)
        (* abstract values of the actual parameters. *)

    (* Car* and Cdr* evaluates head and tail of abstract values *)

Car*(D) = D
Car*(S) = S
Car*(P(x,y)) =
    if x = S or x = D then x
    else the right side of x in the global grammar
Car*(a | b) = Least-upper-bound(Car*(a),Car*(b))

Cdr*(D) = D
Cdr*(S) = S
Cdr*(P(x,y)) =
    if y = S or y = D then y
    else the right side of y in the global grammar
Cdr*(a | b) = Least-upper-bound(Cdr*(a),Cdr*(b))

    (* Least-upper-bound evaluates the least upper bound of two abstract values *)

Least-upper-bound(D , x) = D

Least-upper-bound(x , D) = D
Least-upper-bound(S , S) = S
Least-upper-bound(x , y) = x | y
                (* The alternatives from both right sides with duplicate alternatives removed *)

Appendix B, an interpreter for MP

The interpreter is shown in the syntax that is required by the partial evaluator. It was originally written using a syntactically sugared form which was translated into what is shown here. xcall calls an "external" function which is not defined in the program but in the run-time environment.

The language MP is taken from [Sestoft 86]. It is a simple imperative language using while-statements for repetition. The interpreter differs from the one in [Sestoft 86] in using an environment that is a list of name/value pairs instead of using separate name and value lists.

Each MP program declares a list of input variables and a list of other variables. The input variables are initialized with variables from the input list and the others with the value nil. The result of interpreting a MP program is the final values of all variables represented by the final environment.

```
(
 (Mp (program input)
  (let (I4 = (car (cdr program))
       I5 = (car (cdr (cdr program))))
       )
       (rcall Block (car (cdr (cdr (cdr program))))
                    (call Initvars (cdr I4) (cdr I5) input)
 )) )

 (Initvars (parlist varlist input4)
  (if (null parlist)
   (if (null varlist) 'nil
     (let (hd9 = (let (hd8 = (car varlist)) (cons hd8 input4)))
         (cons hd9 (call Initvars parlist (cdr varlist) input4))
   ) )
   (let (hd7 = (let (hd5 = (car parlist) tl6 = (car input4)) (cons hd5 tl6)))
       (cons hd7 (call Initvars (cdr parlist) varlist (cdr input4)))
 )))

 (Block (block env)
  (let (I6 = (car block))
     (if (null block) env
        (if (equal (car I6) ':=)
        (call Block (cdr block)
                    (call Update env
                          (car (cdr I6))
                          (call Exp (car (cdr (cdr I6))) env)
        )          )
        (if (equal (car I6) 'if)
           (if (call Exp (car (cdr I6)) env)
```

```
            (call Block (call Append (car (cdr (cdr I6))) (cdr block)) env)
            (call Block (call Append (car (cdr (cdr (cdr I6)))) (cdr block)) env)
        )
      (if (equal (car I6) 'while) (rcall While block env)
      (xcall writeln 'Unknown_command (car block))
) ) ) ))))

(While (block11 env10)
  (if (call Exp (car (cdr (car block11))) env10)
    (call Block (call Append (car (cdr (cdr (car block11)))) block11) env10)
    (call Block (cdr block11) env10)
) )

(Exp (exp env12)
  (if (atom exp) (call Lookup exp env12)
  (if (equal (car exp) 'quote) (car (cdr exp))
  (if (equal (car exp) 'car) (car (call Exp (car (cdr exp)) env12))
  (if (equal (car exp) 'cdr) (cdr (call Exp (car (cdr exp)) env12))
  (if (equal (car exp) 'atom) (atom (call Exp (car (cdr exp)) env12))
  (if (equal (car exp) 'cons)
    (cons (call Exp (car (cdr exp)) env12) (call Exp (car (cdr (cdr exp))) env12))
  (if (equal (car exp) 'equal)
    (equal (call Exp (car (cdr exp)) env12) (call Exp (car (cdr (cdr exp))) env12))
  (xcall writeln 'Unknown_expression exp)
) )))))))

(Update (env13 var val)
  (if (null env13) (xcall writeln 'Unknown_variable var)
    (if (equal (car (car env13)) var)
      (let (hd15 = (cons var val) tl16 = (cdr env13)) (cons hd15 tl16))
      (let (hd14 = (car env13)) (cons hd14 (call Update (cdr env13) var val)))
) ) )

(Lookup (var18 env17)
  (if (null env17) (xcall wrlteln 'Unknown_variable var18)
    (if (equal (car (car env17)) var18)
      (cdr (car env17))
      (call Lookup var18 (cdr env17))
) ) )

(Append (a b)
  (if (null a) b (let (hd19 = (car a)) (cons hd19 (call Append (cdr a) b))))
)
)
```

Appendix C, Exponentiation program in MP.

This is an exponentiation program in MP. It is taken from [Sestoft 86].

Input: Two lists x and y.

Output: The variable out is a list the length of which is the number of all tuples of length |y| of elements from x, which is |x|^|y|

```
(program (pars x y) (dec out next kn)
((:= kn y)
 (while kn
     ((:= next (cons x next))
      (:= kn   (cdr kn))
      )
  )
 (:= out (cons next out))          ; First combination
                        ; Invariant: |next| + |kn| = |y|
 (while next                  ; while more tuples
    ((if (cdr (car next))          ;   if next(1) can be increased
     ((:= next (cons (cdr (car next)) ; do that
                 (cdr next)) )
      (while kn               ; while |next| < |y| do
        ((:= next (cons x next)) ;   put x in front of next
         (:= kn   (cdr kn))        ;    preserving invariant
         )
       )
      (:= out (cons next out))
      )
                    ; else, backtrack, preserving invariant
     ((:= next (cdr next))
      (:= kn   (cons '1 kn))
      )
    ))
 )
 )
 )
```

Appendix D, Residual exponentiation program.

This program is the residual program obtained by partially evaluating the MP interpreter from appendix B with respect to the exponentiation program from appendix C. It accepts a list of input parameters (of length one) and returns a final binding of variables to values. Note that the environment from the interpreter is split into several parameters to each function (all the names beginning with env), each of which represent a variable from the MP program.

```
((Mp (input-4)
  (call Block-5 (car input-4)
          (car (cdr input-4))
```

```
            (cdr (cdr input-4))
            (cdr (cdr input-4))
            (cdr (cdr input-4))
  ) )

  (Block-5 (env-10 env-9 env-8 env-7 env-6)
   (call While-11 env-10 env-9 env-8 env-7 env-9)
  )

  (While-11 (env10-16 env10-15 env10-14 env10-13 env10-12)
   (if env10-12
      (call While-11 env10-16 env10-15 env10-14 (cons env10-16 env10-13) (cdr env10-12))
      (call While-19 env10-16 env10-15 (cons env10-13 env10-14) env10-13 env10-12)
  ) )

  (While-19 (env10-24 env10-23 env10-22 env10-21 env10-20)
   (if env10-21
     (if (cdr (car env10-21))
       (call While-11 env10-24
               env10-23
               env10-22
               (cons (cdr (car env10-21)) (cdr env10-21))
               env10-20
     )
     (call While-19 env10-24 env10-23 env10-22 (cdr env10-21) (cons '1 env10-20))
     )
     (cons (cons 'x env10-24)
      (cons (cons 'y env10-23)
       (cons (cons 'out env10-22)
        (cons (cons 'next env10-21)
         (cons (cons 'kn env10-20) 'nil)
  )) ) ) ) ) )
```

References

[Bondorf 88]
   A. Bondorf. Towards a Self-Applicable Partial Evaluator for Term Rewriting Systems. In
   D. Bjørner, A.P. Ershov and N.D. Jones, editors, *Workshop on Partial Evaluation and Mixed
   Computation, Gl. Avernæs, Denmark, October 1987, North-Holland* 1988.

[Bulyonkov 84]
   M.A. Bulyonkov. Polyvariant Mixed Computation for Analyzer Programs. *Acta Informatica*, 21:473-484, 1984

[Bulyonkov 88]
   M.A. Bulyonkov. A Theoretical Approach to Polyvariant Computation. In D. Bjørner, A.P.
   Ershov and N.D. Jones, editors, *Workshop on Partial Evaluation and Mixed Computation,
   Gl. Avernæs, Denmark, October 1987, North-Holland* 1988.

[Ershov 82]
A.P. Ershov. Mixed Computation: Potential Applications and Problems for Study. *Theoretical Computer Science,* (18):41-67, 1982.

[Futamura 71]
Y. Futamura. Partial Evaluation of Computation Processes - An Approach to a Compiler-compiler. In *Systems, Computers, Controls,* 2(5)721-728, 1971.

[Jones 85]
N.D. Jones, P. Sestoft, H. Søndergaard. An Experiment in Partial Evaluation: The Generation of a Compiler Generator. In J.-P. Jouannaud, editor, *Rewriting Techniques and Applications,* pages 124-140, Lecture Notes on Computer Science, Vol. 202, Springer-Verlag, 1985.

[Jones 86]
N.D. Jones. Flow Analysis of Lazy Higher Order Functional Programs. In S. Abramsky and C. Hankin, editors, *Abstract Interpretation of Declarative Languages,* Ellis Horwood, London, 1987.

[Mycroft 80]
A. Mycroft. The Theory and Practice of Transforming Call-by-Need into Call-by-Value. Lecture Notes on Computer Science, Vol. 83, Springer-Verlag, 1980.

[Launchbury 88]
J. Launchbury. Projections for specialisation. In D. Bjørner, A.P. Ershov and N.D. Jones, editors, *Workshop on Partial Evaluation and Mixed Computation, Gl. Avernæs, Denmark, October 1987, North-Holland* 1988.

[Reynolds 69]
J.C. Reynolds. Automatic Computation of Data Set Definitions. *Information Processing* (68):456-461, 1969.

[Romanenko 88]
S.A. Romanenko. A Compiler Generator Produced by a Self-Applicable Specializer can have a Surprisingly Natural and Understandable Structure. In D. Bjørner, A.P. Ershov and N.D. Jones, editors, *Workshop on Partial Evaluation and Mixed Computation, Gl. Avernæs, Denmark, October 1987, North-Holland* 1988.

[Sestoft 86]
P. Sestoft. The Structure of an Self-applicable Partial Evaluator. In H. Ganzinger and N.D. Jones, editors, *Programs as Data Objects, Copenhagen, Denmark, 1985,* pages 236-256, Lecture Notes on Computer Science, Vol. 217, Springer-Verlag, 1986.

[Sestoft 88]
P. Sestoft. Automatic Call Unfolding in a Partial Evaluator. In D. Bjørner, A.P. Ershov and N.D. Jones, editors, *Workshop on Partial Evaluation and Mixed Computation, Gl. Avernæs, Denmark, October 1987, North-Holland* 1988.

Partial Evaluation and Mixed Computation
D. Bjørner, A.P. Ershov and N.D. Jones (Editors)
Elsevier Science Publishers B.V. (North-Holland)
© IFIP, 1988

A Formal Type System for Comparing Partial Evaluators

Flemming Nielson

Department of Computer Science
The Technical University of Denmark
Building 344
DK-2800 Lyngby, Denmark

The theory of partial evaluation has been hampered by the absence of *formal* definitions of when one partial evaluator *is better than* another. We consider a monotyped λ-calculus (with products, sums, and recursive types) and *extend* its type system to express the binding times of variables and parameters. For a λ-expression and an extended type we prove the existence of a *best λ-expression* in the extended λ-calculus; this generalizes previous binding time analyses for first-order recursion equation schemes. We then define several *comparison relations* that formally express when one partial evaluator is better than another, and by means of examples we identify one that corresponds to (our) intuition.

1 Motivation

Partial evaluation and mixed computation are useful concepts for improving the efficiency of programs by precomputing those computations that only involve variables whose values will be available earlier than others [3]. In this paper we shall concentrate on partial evaluation as it is the foundation also for mixed computation. The main point of our study is the clarification of how to compare two partial evaluators and deem one better than the other. We believe that this must be expressed formally since a main purpose of partial evaluation and mixed computation is to develop efficient and provably correct implementations of programming languages. However, to the author's knowledge no formal definitions exist and therefore one must rely on *intuitive* (and hence *debatable*) arguments.

To be a bit more concrete, we shall begin by reviewing A. P. Ershov's characterization of partial evaluation [2]. So we consider a program $p \in P$ with data d, $d' \in D$. The *semantics* then is a function

$$Sem : P \times D \to D$$

such that $d' = Sem(p, d)$ is the output resulting from running p with d as input. We shall not specify the structure of D in detail, but we shall assume that it contains pairs of data elements, i.e. $D = \ldots + (D \times D)$. *Partial evaluation* then amounts to a function

$Part : P \times D \to P$

that satisfies

$$Sem(p, (d_1, d_2)) = Sem(Part(p, d_1), d_2)$$

for all $d_1, d_2 \in D$. So $p' = Part(p, d_1)$ is a (residual) program that produces the same output on input d_2 as p does on input (d_1, d_2). This is closely related to the concept of *currying* in functional programming and denotational semantics [13,14] and to the S_{mn} theorem of computability theory.

Many partial evaluators will fit the above description. They will all be *correct*, but not equally useful because some $Part_2(p, d_1)$ may execute much faster on d_2 than some other $Part_1(p, d_1)$. To exemplify this we shall assume that p is an *interpreter* for a simple calculator language, that d_1 is the calculator "program", e.g. a list of operations, and that d_2 is the "data", e.g. a list of values. A good example of $Part_1$ is the *trivial partial evaluator* that transforms

$p = \lambda(v_1, v_2).$ if $v_1 = nil$ then v_2 else

              if $hd(v_1) = mul$ then $p(tl(v_1), MUL(v_2))$ else

              if $hd(v_1) = add$ then $p(tl(v_1), ADD(v_2))$ else

               . . .

$d_1 = [add]$

to

$p' = \lambda v_2.$ if $[add] = nil$ then v_2 else

             if $hd([add]) = mul$ then $p'(tl([add]), MUL(v_2))$ else

             if $hd([add]) = add$ then $p'(tl([add]), ADD(v_2))$ else

              . . .

A good example of $Part_2$ is a *compiler* that transforms

$$\left.\begin{array}{l} p \\ d_1 \end{array}\right\} \text{ as above}$$

to

$p' = \lambda v_2. ADD(v_2)$

We refer to [5] for a more elaborate example.

In this particular example it is "obvious" that $Part_2$ is "better" than $Part_1$. In general this will not be as obvious since both $Part_1(p, d_1)$ and $Part_2(p, d_1)$ may be large programs. One possibility is to compare the running times of $Part_1(p, d_1)$ and $Part_2(p, d_1)$ on input d_2. However, only a few instances of d_1 and d_2 can be tried, and no firm conclusions can be drawn from such an experiment. Another possibility is to compare the lengths of $Part_1(p, d_1)$ and $Part_2(p, d_1)$, but again it is hard to draw any firm conclusions from this. A better possibility is to inspect the residual programs $Part_1(p, d_1)$ and $Part_2(p, d_1)$ and determine to what extent the partial evaluators behave as the "trivial partial evaluator" or a "compiler". However, such a comparison will be based on intuitive considerations, and the conclusions drawn from this are likely to give rise to debate. To overcome this problem we claim it is necessary to give a *formal definition* of when one residual program, $Part_2(p, d_1)$, is better than another, $Part_1(p, d_1)$.

To give such definitions we introduce in Section 2 the language **DML** that is to play the role of P. It is a monotyped λ-calculus with product types, sum types, and recursive types in addition to the function types. This language may be motivated by the current interest in functional programming or the use of denotational semantics in semantics directed compiling. We then extend the λ-calculus so that it explicitly records the fact that some parameters, e.g. d_1, are supplied before others, e.g. d_2. The resulting λ-calculus (called **TML**$_e$) thus makes the different *binding times* explicit. In Section 3 we take the view that the times at which parameters are supplied to an expression of **DML** may be described by a type of **TML**$_e$. We then show how to propagate this information throughout all of the **DML** expression, and this yields an expression in **TML**$_e$. This "binding time analysis" extends previous work [4] from a first-order language of recursion equation schemes to the full typed λ-calculus (although the methods are different). This allows us, in Section 4, to propose three definitions of when one residual program is "better" than another. These definitions build on the ability to rewrite those parts of a **TML**$_e$ expression that are bound early. Based on examples we then adopt one of these definitions as the "intuitive one". Finally, Section 5 contains the conclusions.

2 Two Monotyped λ-Calculi

The programming language **DML** to be studied in this paper is a functional language similar to the denotational metalanguage in [14]. To be more specific, it is a monotyped λ-calculus (or λ-notation) with types given by the abstract syntax

$$dt ::= A_i \mid dt \times dt \mid dt + dt \mid dt \to dt \mid recX_i.dt \mid X_i$$

The A_i are base types where i ranges over some index set I containing *bool*, 1, 2 and 3. We shall think of A_{bool} as the type of booleans and A_1, A_2, A_3 might be the types of integers, reals and characters. We have binary products and sums, but these could easily be generalized to K-ary versions. As in any typed λ-calculus, we have function types, but in addition we have a type $recX_i.dt$ for the solution to the type equation (or "domain equation") $X_i = dt$. In general dt will contain the type variable X_i so that the equation is recursive, and this allows us to model structures like lists and trees. The expressions are given by the abstract syntax

$$de ::= \quad f_i[dt] \mid (de, de) \mid de{\downarrow}i \mid in_i[dt]de \mid is_i\ de \mid out_i\ de \mid \lambda x_i[dt].de$$
$$\mid de \cdot de \mid x_i \mid mkrec[dt]de \mid unrec\ de \mid fix[dt]de \mid de \to de, de$$

where again i ranges over the index set I. For the constants $f_i[dt]$ we assume we have a set D_i of the permissible types dt. (In a purely monotyped λ-calculus it is natural to let the D_i be singletons.) We then have notation for constructing pairs, selecting a component, injecting into a sum, testing the summand, and projecting out of a sum. For functions we have λ-abstraction, application (using an explicit operator $\cdot$ for notational reasons to become clear shortly), and variables. For a recursive type $dt = recX_i.dt'$ we distinguish between the left-hand side and the right-hand side in the type equation $X_i = dt'$, and therefore we have notation for passing from dt' to X_i and for passing from X_i to dt'. Finally we have fixedpoints and conditional.

The types and expressions of **DML** are subject to certain well-formedness criteria. For types we define a well-formedness relation

$$V \vdash dt$$

(where V is a finite subset of $\{X_i \mid i \in I\}$) by requiring that the free type variables of dt are contained in V. We shall mostly be interested in *closed* types which are types dt satisfying $\emptyset \vdash dt$. In particular we shall constrain the types in D_i to be closed. For expressions the well-formedness relation has the form

$$tenv \vdash de : dt$$

where $tenv$ is a type environment, i.e. a partial function from variables (in $\{x_i \mid i \in I\}$) to types such that the domain $dom(tenv)$ is finite. An expression de is *closed* if $\emptyset \vdash de : dt$ for some dt where $\emptyset$ is the empty type environment. The detailed definition is by means of the inference system given in Table 1. Here $dt'[dt/X_i]$ denotes the result of substituting dt for X_i in dt' and $tenv[dt/x_i]$ is the type environment that maps x_j to dt for $i = j$ and otherwise maps x_j to $tenv(x_j)$. For later reference we note that

Fact 2.1 If all $tenv(x_i)$ are closed and $tenv \vdash de : dt$ then dt is closed.   □

Fact 2.2 (Determinacy) If $tenv \vdash de : dt_1$ and $tenv \vdash de : dt_2$ then $dt_1 = dt_2$.   □

The proofs are by induction on the inference of $tenv \vdash de : \ldots$ and the induction step merely amounts to checking that the inference rules preserve the claims.

Syntax of types

$$dt ::= A_i \mid dt \times dt \mid dt + dt \mid dt \to dt \mid recX_i.dt \mid X_i \qquad \text{(for } i \in I)$$

Well-formedness of types

$V \vdash dt$ if the free variables of dt are contained in V

Syntax of expressions

$$de ::= f_i[dt] \mid (de, de) \mid de{\downarrow}i \mid in_i[dt]de \mid is_i\, de \mid out_i\, de \mid \lambda x_i[dt].de$$
$$\mid de \cdot de \mid x_i \mid mkrec[dt]de \mid unrec\, de \mid fix[dt]de \mid de \to de, de$$
$$\text{(for } i \in I)$$

Well-formedness of expressions

$tenv \vdash f_i[dt] : dt$ if $dt \in D_i$, $\emptyset \vdash dt$

$$\frac{tenv \vdash de_1 : dt_1 \quad tenv \vdash de_2 : dt_2}{tenv \vdash (de_1, de_2) : dt_1 \times dt_2}$$

$$\frac{tenv \vdash de : dt_1 \times dt_2}{tenv \vdash de{\downarrow}i : dt_i} \quad \text{if } i \in \{1, 2\}$$

$$\frac{tenv \vdash de : dt_i}{tenv \vdash in_i[dt]de : dt} \quad \text{if } i \in \{1, 2\},\ dt = dt_1 + dt_2,\ \emptyset \vdash dt_{3-i}$$

$$\frac{tenv \vdash de : dt_1 + dt_2}{tenv \vdash is_i\, de : A_{bool}} \quad \text{if } i \in \{1, 2\}$$

$$\frac{tenv \vdash de : dt_1 + dt_2}{tenv \vdash out_i\, de : dt_i} \quad \text{if } i \in \{1, 2\}$$

$$\frac{tenv[dt/x_i] \vdash de : dt'}{tenv \vdash \lambda x_i[dt].de : dt \to dt'} \quad \text{if } \emptyset \vdash dt$$

$$\frac{tenv \vdash de_1 : dt \to dt' \quad tenv \vdash de_2 : dt}{tenv \vdash de_1 \cdot de_2 : dt'}$$

$$tenv \vdash x_i : dt \quad \text{if } x_i \in dom(tenv), \ tenv(x_i) = dt$$

$$\frac{tenv \vdash de : dt'[dt/X_i]}{tenv \vdash mkrec[dt]de : dt} \quad \text{if } dt = recX_i.dt'$$

$$\frac{tenv \vdash de : dt}{tenv \vdash unrec \ de : dt'[dt/X_i]} \quad \text{if } dt = recX_i.dt'$$

$$\frac{tenv \vdash de : dt \to dt}{tenv \vdash fix[dt]de : dt}$$

$$\frac{tenv \vdash de_1 : A_{bool} \quad tenv \vdash de_2 : dt \quad tenv \vdash de_3 : dt}{tenv \vdash de_1 \to de_2, \ de_3 : dt}$$

Table 1: The syntax of **DML**

Example 2.3 The B combinator takes three arguments x, y, and z and yields $x(y\ z)$ as its result. In **DML** we may define it by the expression

$$B \equiv \lambda x_1[A_2 \to A_1].\lambda x_2[A_3 \to A_2].\lambda x_3[A_3].x_1 \cdot (x_2 \cdot x_3)$$

where the parentheses are used to indicate how to parse the applications. It is straight-forward to verify that

$$\emptyset \vdash B : (A_2 \to A_1) \to (A_3 \to A_2) \to A_3 \to A_1$$

so that B is a closed expression of the expected functionality.   □

Turning to partial evaluation we consider a computation $Sem(p, (d_1, d_2))$, and we will supply d_1 before we supply d_2. In the example from the Introduction d_1 is a calculator "program" and d_2 is the "data", so one might say that d_1 is supplied at *compile-time* and that d_2 is supplied at *run-time*. Some of the computation steps in $Sem(p, (d_1, d_2))$ will depend on d_2 and must be left to *run-time* whereas others will only depend on d_1 and therefore may be carried out at *compile-time*. A typical example of this is the decoding of the "program" d_1 as illustrated in the Introduction. To carry out at *compile-time* those computations that do not depend on *run-time* data it is helpful to annotate the operations in p according to whether they are to be carried out at compile-time or at run-time. In our setting, p will be an expression in **DML**, and the annotated version of p will be an expression in another monotyped λ-calculus called $\mathbf{TML}_e$.

The types of $\mathbf{TML}_e$[*] are given by the abstract syntax

$$tt ::= \underline{A_i} \mid \overline{A_i} \mid tt \underline{\times} tt \mid tt \overline{\times} tt \mid tt \underline{+} tt \mid tt \overline{+} tt \mid tt \underline{\rightarrow} tt \mid tt \overline{\rightarrow} tt$$
$$\mid \underline{rec}X_i.tt \mid \overline{rec}X_i.tt \mid X_i$$

where again i ranges over the index set I. Here $tt_1 \underline{\rightarrow} tt_2$ is intended to be the type of a computation to be performed at run-time, whereas $tt_1 \overline{\rightarrow} tt_2$ is intended to be the type of a computation to be performed at compile-time. In general underlining is used to indicate types "living" at run-time, whereas overlining is used to indicate types "living" at compile-time. Similarly the syntax of expressions is given by

$$te ::= f_i[tt] \mid \underline{(te, te)} \mid \overline{(te, te)} \mid te\underline{\downarrow}i \mid te\overline{\downarrow}i \mid \underline{in}_i[tt]te \mid \overline{in}_i[tt]te$$
$$\mid \underline{is}_i\ te \mid \overline{is}_i\ te \mid \underline{out}_i\ te \mid \overline{out}_i\ te \mid \underline{\lambda}x_i[tt].te \mid \overline{\lambda}x_i[tt].te$$
$$\mid te \underline{\cdot} te \mid te \overline{\cdot} te \mid x_i \mid \underline{mkrec}[tt]te \mid \overline{mkrec}[tt]te$$
$$\mid \underline{unrec}\ te \mid \overline{unrec}\ te \mid \underline{fix}[tt]te \mid \overline{fix}[tt]te \mid te \underline{\rightarrow} te, te \mid te \overline{\rightarrow} te, te$$

Again we have used underlining to indicate those computations that must wait until run-time, and we have used overlining to indicate those computations that may be performed at compile-time. Considering once again the interpreter p from the Introduction, the operation tl appearing there would be overlined whereas the operation MUL would be underlined. We shall consider further examples below.

Syntax of types

$$tt ::= \underline{A_i} \mid \overline{A_i} \mid tt \underline{\times} tt \mid tt \overline{\times} tt \mid tt \underline{+} tt \mid tt \overline{+} tt \mid tt \underline{\rightarrow} tt \mid tt \overline{\rightarrow} tt$$
$$\mid \underline{rec}X_i.tt \mid \overline{rec}X_i.tt \mid X_i$$

(for $i \in I$)

---

[*] The syntax of $\mathbf{TML}_e$ is closely related to that of the two-level denotational metalanguages $\mathbf{TML}_m$ and $\mathbf{TML}_s$ for which a theory of code generation and abstract interpretation has been developed in [6,7,8,9,11].

Well-formedness of types

tt	$kenv \vdash tt : c$	$kenv \vdash tt : r$
$\underline{A_i}$	false	true
$\overline{A_i}$	true	false
$tt_1 \underline{\times} tt_2$	false	$kenv \vdash tt_1 : r \ \wedge \ kenv \vdash tt_2 : r$
$tt_1 \overline{\times} tt_2$	$kenv \vdash tt_1 : c \ \wedge \ kenv \vdash tt_2 : c$	false
$tt_1 \underline{+} tt_2$	false	$kenv \vdash tt_1 : r \ \wedge \ kenv \vdash tt_2 : r$
$tt_1 \overline{+} tt_2$	$kenv \vdash tt_1 : c \ \wedge \ kenv \vdash tt_2 : c$	false
$tt_1 \underline{\rightarrow} tt_2$	$\emptyset \vdash tt_1 : r \ \wedge \ \emptyset \vdash tt_2 : r$	$kenv \vdash tt_1 : r \ \wedge \ kenv \vdash tt_2 : r$
$tt_1 \overline{\rightarrow} tt_2$	$kenv \vdash tt_1 : c \ \wedge \ kenv \vdash tt_2 : c$	false
$\underline{rec}X_i.tt_0$	false	$kenv[r/X_i] \vdash tt_0 : r$
$\overline{rec}X_i.tt_0$	$kenv[c/X_i] \vdash tt_0 : c$	false
X_i	$kenv(X_i) = c$	$kenv(X_i) = r$

Syntax of expressions

$$te ::= \ f_i[tt] \mid \underline{(te, te)} \mid \overline{(te, te)} \mid te\underline{\downarrow i} \mid te\overline{\downarrow i} \mid \underline{in}_i[tt]te \mid \overline{in}_i[tt]te$$
$$\mid \ \underline{is}_i \ te \mid \overline{is}_i \ te \mid \underline{out}_i \ te \mid \overline{out}_i \ te \mid \underline{\lambda}x_i[tt].te \mid \overline{\lambda}x_i[tt].te$$
$$\mid \ te \underline{\cdot} te \mid te \overline{\cdot} te \mid x_i \mid \underline{mkrec}[tt]te \mid \overline{mkrec}[tt]te$$
$$\mid \ \underline{unrec} \ te \mid \overline{unrec} \ te \mid \underline{fix}[tt]te \mid \overline{fix}[tt]te \mid te \underline{\rightarrow} te, te \mid te \overline{\rightarrow} te, te$$
$$(\text{for } i \in I)$$

Well-formedness of expressions

$$tenv \vdash f_i[tt] : tt \quad \text{if } tt \in T_i, \ \exists K : \emptyset \vdash tt : K$$

$$\frac{tenv \vdash te_1 : tt_1 \quad tenv \vdash te_2 : tt_2}{tenv \vdash \underline{(te_1, te_2)} : tt_1 \underline{\times} tt_2} \quad \text{if } \emptyset \vdash tt_1 : r, \ \emptyset \vdash tt_2 : r$$

$$\frac{tenv \vdash te_1 : tt_1 \quad tenv \vdash te_2 : tt_2}{tenv \vdash \overline{(te_1, te_2)} : tt_1 \overline{\times} tt_2} \quad \text{if } \emptyset \vdash tt_1 : c, \ \emptyset \vdash tt_2 : c$$

$$\frac{tenv \vdash te : tt_1 \underline{\times} tt_2}{tenv \vdash te\underline{\downarrow}i : tt_i} \quad \text{if } i \in \{1,2\}$$

$$\frac{tenv \vdash te : tt_1 \overline{\times} tt_2}{tenv \vdash te\overline{\downarrow i} : tt_i} \quad \text{if } i \in \{1,2\}$$

$$\frac{tenv \vdash te : tt_i}{tenv \vdash \underline{in}_i[tt]te : tt} \quad \text{if } i \in \{1,2\}, \ tt = tt_1 \underline{+} tt_2, \ \emptyset \vdash tt_1 : r, \ \emptyset \vdash tt_2 : r$$

$$\frac{tenv \vdash te : tt_i}{tenv \vdash \overline{in_i}[tt]te : tt} \quad \text{if } i \in \{1,2\}, \ tt = tt_1 \overline{+} tt_2, \ \emptyset \vdash tt_1 : c, \ \emptyset \vdash tt_2 : c$$

$$\frac{tenv \vdash te : tt_1 \underline{+} tt_2}{tenv \vdash \underline{is}_i \ te : \underline{A}_{bool}} \quad \text{if } i \in \{1,2\}$$

$$\frac{tenv \vdash te : tt_1 \overline{+} tt_2}{tenv \vdash \overline{is}_i \ te : \overline{A}_{bool}} \quad \text{if } i \in \{1,2\}$$

$$\frac{tenv \vdash te : tt_1 \underline{+} tt_2}{tenv \vdash \underline{out}_i \ te : tt_i} \quad \text{if } i \in \{1,2\}$$

$$\frac{tenv \vdash te : tt_1 \overline{+} tt_2}{tenv \vdash \overline{out}_i \ te : tt_i} \quad \text{if } i \in \{1,2\}$$

$$\frac{tenv[tt/x_i] \vdash te : tt'}{tenv \vdash \underline{\lambda}x_i[tt].te : tt \underline{\rightarrow} tt'} \quad \text{if } \emptyset \vdash tt' : r, \ \emptyset \vdash tt : r$$

$$\frac{tenv[tt/x_i] \vdash te : tt'}{tenv \vdash \overline{\lambda}x_i[tt].te : tt \overline{\Rightarrow} tt'} \quad \text{if } \emptyset \vdash tt' : c, \ \emptyset \vdash tt : c$$

$$\frac{tenv \vdash te_1 : tt \underline{\rightarrow} tt' \quad tenv \vdash te_2 : tt}{tenv \vdash te_1 \underline{\cdot} te_2 : tt'}$$

$$\frac{tenv \vdash te_1 : tt \overline{\Rightarrow} tt' \quad tenv \vdash te_2 : tt}{tenv \vdash te_1 \overline{\cdot} te_2 : tt'}$$

$$tenv \vdash x_i : tt \quad \text{if } x_i \in dom(tenv),\ tenv(x_i) = tt$$

$$\frac{tenv \vdash te : tt'[tt/X_i]}{tenv \vdash \underline{mkrec}[tt]te : tt} \quad \text{if } tt = \underline{rec}X_i.tt',\ \emptyset \vdash tt : r$$

$$\frac{tenv \vdash te : tt'[tt/X_i]}{tenv \vdash \overline{mkrec}[tt]te : tt} \quad \text{if } tt = \overline{rec}X_i.tt',\ \emptyset \vdash tt : c$$

$$\frac{tenv \vdash te : tt}{tenv \vdash \underline{unrec}\ te : tt'[tt/X_i]} \quad \text{if } tt = \underline{rec}X_i.tt'$$

$$\frac{tenv \vdash te : tt}{tenv \vdash \overline{unrec}\ te : tt'[tt/X_i]} \quad \text{if } tt = \overline{rec}X_i.tt'$$

$$\frac{tenv \vdash te : tt \underrightarrow{\ \ } tt}{tenv \vdash \underline{fix}[tt]te : tt}$$

$$\frac{tenv \vdash te : tt \Rightarrow tt}{tenv \vdash \overline{fix}[tt]te : tt}$$

$$\frac{tenv \vdash te_1 : \underline{A}_{bool} \quad tenv \vdash te_2 : tt \quad tenv \vdash te_3 : tt}{tenv \vdash te_1 \underrightarrow{\ \ } te_2, te_3 : tt}$$

$$\frac{tenv \vdash te_1 : \overline{A}_{bool} \quad tenv \vdash te_2 : tt \quad tenv \vdash te_3 : tt}{tenv \vdash te_1 \Rightarrow te_2, te_3 : tt}$$

Table 2: The syntax of **TML**$_e$

The types and expressions of **TML**$_e$ are subject to certain well-formedness conditions. Corresponding to the two notions of binding time considered here, we shall say that types have *kind* c (or $^-$) if they "live" at compile-time and that types have kind r (or $_-$) if they "live" at run-time. We formalize this by defining a syntactic category of kinds by the abstract syntax

$$K ::= c \mid r$$

The well-formedness relation for types then has the form

$$kenv \vdash tt : K$$

where *kenv* is a kind environment, i.e. a partial mapping from type variables to kinds such that the domain is finite. (If we had only had one sort of kinds, this would specialize to the form of the well-formedness relation for types in **DML**.) A type *tt* is *closed* if $\exists K : \emptyset \vdash tt : K$, where $\emptyset$ is the empty kind environment. For expressions the well-formedness relation has the form

$$tenv \vdash te : tt$$

much as for **DML**, and an expression *te* is *closed* if $\emptyset \vdash te : tt$ for some *tt*. The detailed definition of these relations may be found in Table 2, but in Section 3 we shall constrain the sets T_i of the allowed types of the f_i. For later reference we note that

Fact 2.4 If all $tenv(x_i)$ are closed and $tenv \vdash te : tt$ then *tt* is closed. $\square$

Fact 2.5 (Determinacy) If $tenv \vdash te : tt_1$ and $tenv \vdash te : tt_2$ then $tt_1 = tt_2$. $\square$

As in the case of **DML**, the proofs are by induction on the inference of $tenv \vdash te : tt$.

Example 2.6 Turning once again to the B combinator, we have a number of possible definitions in **TML**$_e$. We shall define B_0, B_1, B_2, and B_3 where the idea is that B_n takes all but the n last parameters at "compile-time" and the last n parameters at "run-time". We define

$$B_0 \equiv \overline{\lambda}x_1[\overline{A}_2 \Rightarrow \overline{A}_1].\overline{\lambda}x_2[\overline{A}_3 \Rightarrow \overline{A}_2].\overline{\lambda}x_3[\overline{A}_3].x_1 \;\overline{\cdot}\; (x_2 \;\overline{\cdot}\; x_3)$$

and it is straight-forward to verify that

$$\emptyset \vdash B_0 : (\overline{A}_2 \Rightarrow \overline{A}_1) \Rightarrow (\overline{A}_3 \Rightarrow \overline{A}_2) \Rightarrow \overline{A}_3 \Rightarrow \overline{A}_1$$

So any application of B_0 may be fully evaluated at compile-time. Next we define

$$B_1 \equiv \overline{\lambda}x_1[\underline{A}_2 \Rightarrow \underline{A}_1].\overline{\lambda}x_2[\underline{A}_3 \Rightarrow \underline{A}_2].\underline{\lambda}x_3[\underline{A}_3].x_1 \;\underline{\cdot}\; (x_2 \;\underline{\cdot}\; x_3)$$

and note that

$$\emptyset \vdash B_1 : (\underline{A}_2 \Rightarrow \underline{A}_1) \Rightarrow (\underline{A}_3 \Rightarrow \underline{A}_2) \Rightarrow \underline{A}_3 \Rightarrow \underline{A}_1$$

Here x_3 must have type $\underline{A}_3$, and due to the definition of the well-formedness relations we must then change the types of x_2 and x_1 to $\underline{A}_3 \Rightarrow \underline{A}_2$ and $\underline{A}_2 \Rightarrow \underline{A}_1$, respectively, and finally we must change $\overline{\cdot}$ to $\underline{\cdot}$. Turning to B_2, it is defined by

$$B_2 \equiv \overline{\lambda}x_1[\underline{A_2} \rightrightarrows \underline{A_1}].\lambda x_2[\underline{A_3} \rightrightarrows \underline{A_2}].\lambda x_3[\underline{A_3}].x_1 \underline{\cdot} (x_2 \underline{\cdot} x_3)$$

and we have

$$\emptyset \vdash B_2 : (\underline{A_2} \rightrightarrows \underline{A_1}) \overline{\rightarrow} (\underline{A_3} \rightrightarrows \underline{A_2}) \rightrightarrows \underline{A_3} \rightrightarrows \underline{A_1}$$

Finally B_3 is defined by

$$B_3 \equiv \underline{\lambda}x_1[\underline{A_2} \rightrightarrows \underline{A_1}].\lambda x_2[\underline{A_3} \rightrightarrows \underline{A_2}].\lambda x_3[\underline{A_3}].x_1 \underline{\cdot} (x_2 \underline{\cdot} x_3)$$

and we have

$$\emptyset \vdash B_3 : (\underline{A_2} \rightrightarrows \underline{A_1}) \rightrightarrows (\underline{A_3} \rightrightarrows \underline{A_2}) \rightrightarrows \underline{A_3} \rightrightarrows \underline{A_1}$$

so all computations in an application of B_3 must be deferred to run-time.

One may observe that the overlining or underlining of λ's in the definitions of the B_i is reflected in the overlining or underlining of $\rightarrow$'s in the types of the B_i. For this statement we are only considering the $\rightarrow$'s not appearing within parentheses, and the remaining $\rightarrow$'s are part of types that appear explicitly in the B_i's. This observation suggests that perhaps *most* aspects of the distinction between run-time and compile-time is reflected in the types. We shall return to this later. $\square$

We may use the types of the $\mathbf{TML}_e$ to express which parameters to some expression (in $\mathbf{DML}$ or $\mathbf{TML}_e$) are supplied before others. However, we do not claim that $\mathbf{TML}_e$ is the only possible choice for this. In particular a closed type of kind c (i.e. a compile-time type) can contain closed types of kind r (i.e. run-time types) only if the latter appear as part of a run-time function type. (See the definition of $kenv \vdash tt : K$ in Table 2.) This is in line with the point of view that a compiler may manipulate code, i.e. entities of run-time function types, but not actual run-time data, i.e. entities of other run-time types. On the same line of thought, a compile-time type cannot appear in a run-time type since compile-time takes place before run-time[*]. However, this point of view has the consequence that we cannot allow

$$B_2' = \underline{\lambda}x_1[\underline{A_2} \rightrightarrows \underline{A_1}].\overline{\lambda}x_2[\underline{A_3} \rightrightarrows \underline{A_2}].\lambda x_3[\underline{A_3}].x_1 \underline{\cdot} (x_2 \underline{\cdot} x_3)$$

as a well-formed expression of type

$$(\underline{A_2} \rightrightarrows \underline{A_1}) \rightrightarrows (\underline{A_3} \rightrightarrows \underline{A_2}) \overline{\rightarrow} \underline{A_3} \rightrightarrows \underline{A_1}$$

---

[*] This point of view may be found in [6,7,8,9,11]. Indeed the closed types of kind c correspond to the closed ct-types in [11] and the closed types of kind r correspond to the closed rt-types in [11].

If we wish to treat a function like B'_2, we must rearrange the order of its parameters and use

$$B''_2 = \overline{\lambda} x_2[\underline{A_3} \underline{\rightarrow} \underline{A_2}].\underline{\lambda} x_1[\underline{A_2} \underline{\rightarrow} \underline{A_1}].\underline{\lambda} x_3[\underline{A_3}].x_1 \underline{\cdot} (x_2 \underline{\cdot} x_3)$$

which is a well-formed expression of type

$$(\underline{A_3} \underline{\rightarrow} \underline{A_2}) \overline{\rightarrow} (\underline{A_2} \underline{\rightarrow} \underline{A_1}) \underline{\rightarrow} \underline{A_3} \underline{\rightarrow} \underline{A_1}$$

(A similar transformation is required in [5].) Turning to the well-formedness relations for expressions, this also disallows certain definitions. In particular we cannot allow

$$B''_1 = \overline{\lambda} x_2[\overline{A_3} \overline{\rightarrow} \overline{A_2}].\underline{\lambda} x_1[\underline{A_2} \underline{\rightarrow} \underline{A_1}].\underline{\lambda} x_3[\underline{A_3}].x_1 \underline{\cdot} (x_2 \underline{\cdot} x_3)$$

as a well-formed expression of type

$$(\overline{A_3} \overline{\rightarrow} \overline{A_2}) \overline{\rightarrow} (\underline{A_2} \underline{\rightarrow} \underline{A_1}) \underline{\rightarrow} \underline{A_3} \underline{\rightarrow} \underline{A_1}$$

The intuition behind this is that the ability to evaluate x_2 at compile-time does not necessarily imply the ability to generate code for x_2. If we do want to allow B''_1, we must change the definition of $tenv \vdash te : tt$ so that $tenv \vdash te_1 \underline{\cdot} te_2 : tt$ when $tenv \vdash te_2 : tt'$ even though $tenv \vdash te_1 : tt' \overline{\rightarrow} tt$. We shall return to this in Section 5.

3 Optimal Detection of Binding Times

Recalling the description we have given of partial evaluation, it is clear that it amounts to carrying out at compile-time some of those computation steps that do not depend on run-time data. Hence our treatment of partial evaluation in Section 4, and our comparison of the residual programs resulting from different partial evaluators, is intertwined with viewing (annotated) programs as expressions of $\mathbf{TML}_e$. Since our conception of program is that they are expressions of $\mathbf{DML}$, this motivates a study of the interplay between $\mathbf{DML}$ and $\mathbf{TML}_e$.

It is straight-forward to pass from $\mathbf{TML}_e$ to $\mathbf{DML}$ since one just removes all overlining and underlining. To be a bit more precise, we define mappings

$$\tau : \{tt \mid tt \in \mathbf{TML}_e\} \rightarrow \{dt \mid dt \in \mathbf{DML}\}$$

$$\varepsilon : \{te \mid te \in \mathbf{TML}_e\} \rightarrow \{de \mid de \in \mathbf{DML}\}$$

where e.g. $de \in \mathbf{DML}$ just means that de is an expression as given by the abstract syntax of $\mathbf{DML}$ so that de need not be well-formed. The definitions of τ and ε should be clear, and a few illustrative examples are

$$\tau(\underline{A_i}) = A_i$$

$$\tau(tt_1 \mathbin{\overline{\times}} tt_2) = \tau(tt_1) \times \tau(tt_2)$$

and

$$\varepsilon(\overline{fix}[tt]te) = fix[\tau(tt)]\varepsilon(te)$$

Returning to Examples 2.3 and 2.6, we note that $\varepsilon(B_i) = B$ and similarly for the types. Concerning well-formedness we shall feel free to index the $\vdash$ symbol with **DML** and **TML** as appropriate, and we then have

Fact 3.1 If $kenv \vdash_{TML} tt : K$ then $dom(kenv) \vdash_{DML} \tau(tt)$ □

Fact 3.2 If $tenv \vdash_{TML} te : tt$ then $(\tau \circ tenv) \vdash_{DML} \varepsilon(te) : \tau(tt)$ □

The proofs are by induction on the inference of $kenv \vdash_{TML} tt : K$ and $tenv \vdash_{TML} te : tt$. The proof of Fact 3.2 relies on the assumption that $\tau(tt) \in D_i$ whenever $tt \in T_i$.

It is less straight-forward to pass from **DML** to **TML**$_e$, and we first consider the types. Analogously to τ, one may of course define

$$\overline{\tau} : \{dt \mid dt \in \mathbf{DML}\} \to \{tt \mid tt \in \mathbf{TML}_e\}$$

$$\underline{\tau} : \{dt \mid dt \in \mathbf{DML}\} \to \{tt \mid tt \in \mathbf{TML}_e\}$$

by overlining, respectively underlining, the various symbols excluding type variables and periods. We shall write $\overline{\tau}[V]$, respectively $\underline{\tau}[V]$, for the kind environment that has domain V and maps $X_i \in V$ to c, respectively r. We then have

Fact 3.3 If $V \vdash_{DML} dt$ then $\overline{\tau}[V] \vdash_{TML} \overline{\tau}(dt) : c$ and $\underline{\tau}[V] \vdash_{TML} \underline{\tau}(dt) : r$.   □

Returning to Examples 2.3 and 2.6, the type of B_0 is obtained by applying $\overline{\tau}$ to the type of B and the type of B_3 is obtained by applying $\underline{\tau}$ to the type of B. In practice we are more likely to be interested in B_1 and B_2 and their types intuitively "lie between" the extremal types produced by $\overline{\tau}$ and $\underline{\tau}$.

To make this precise we define an auxiliary function Ξ that maps overlined symbols to c and underlined symbols to r. So we have

$$\Xi : \{tt \mid tt \in \mathbf{TML}_e\} \to \{c,r\}^*$$

and e.g.

$$\Xi(\overline{rec}X_i.X_i \mp \underline{A_1} \to \underline{A_2}) = ccrrr$$

In particular Ξ erases any trace of type variables and periods. The set $\{c,r\}^*$ may be partially ordered by

$$K_1 \ldots K_n \leq K_1' \ldots K_m' \text{ iff } n = m \wedge \forall i \in \{1, \ldots, n\} : K_i = c \Rightarrow K_i' = c$$

so that e.g. $r \leq c$. We may then define a partial order on the types of $\mathbf{TML}_e$ by

$$tt_1 \sqsubseteq tt_2 \text{ iff } \tau(tt_1) = \tau(tt_2) \text{ and } \Xi(tt_1) \leq \Xi(tt_2)$$

Fact 3.4 The relation $\sqsubseteq$ is a partial order on $\{tt \mid tt \in \mathbf{TML}_e\}$. $\qquad\square$

Writing tt_i for the types of the B_i in Example 2.6, and dt for the type of B, we thus have

$$\underline{\tau}(dt) = tt_3 \sqsubseteq tt_2 \sqsubseteq tt_1 \sqsubseteq tt_0 = \overline{\tau}(dt)$$

Clearly the types of B_i express different choices of how many parameters to supply at compile-time and how many to supply at run-time. We therefore view $\sqsubseteq$ as imposing an ordering upon the "degree" of partial evaluation possible.

For any positive integer n the set $\{c,r\}^n$ is a complete lattice under the partial order $\leq$. We shall write $\vee$ for the binary upper bound operator, and we may characterize it by

$$K_1 \ldots K_n \quad \vee \quad K_1' \ldots K_n' \quad = \quad K_1'' \ldots K_n''$$

where K_j'' is c if $c \in \{K_j, K_j'\}$ and r otherwise.

Furthermore, for all $dt \in \mathbf{DML}$ the set $\tau^{-1}(dt)$ defined by $\{tt \in \mathbf{TML}_e \mid \tau(tt) = dt\}$ is a complete lattice under $\sqsubseteq$ and the binary least upper bound operator $\sqcup$ satisfies $\Xi(tt_1 \sqcup tt_2) = \Xi(tt_1) \vee \Xi(tt_2)$. We shall be interested in extending this observation to closed types dt and tt. This motivates defining

$$\tau_{wf}^{-1}(dt) = \{tt \in \mathbf{TML}_e \mid \tau(tt) = dt \wedge \exists K : \varnothing \vdash_{TML} tt : K\}$$

By Fact 3.1 this set will be empty unless $\varnothing \vdash_{DML} dt$. The claim then is that for closed dt the set $\tau_{wf}^{-1}(dt)$ is a complete lattice with the least upper bound operator $\sqcup$ satisfying $\Xi(tt_1 \sqcup tt_2) = \Xi(tt_1) \vee \Xi(tt_2)$. (We have already seen that $\underline{\tau}(dt)$ will be the least element, and $\overline{\tau}(dt)$ will be the greatest element.) However, to prove this claim we shall need to encounter types that are not closed, and it is therefore helpful to consider formulae of the form $V|dt$ and $kenv|tt$. We shall write $\vdash_{DML} V|dt$ for $V \vdash_{DML} dt$ and $\vdash_{TML} kenv|tt$ for $\exists K : kenv \vdash_{TML} tt : K$. The partial order $\sqsubseteq$ may be extended by defining

$kenv_1|tt_1 \sqsubseteq kenv_2|tt_2$ iff

$tt_1 \sqsubseteq tt_2 \wedge dom(kenv_1) = dom(kenv_2) \wedge$

$\forall X_i \in dom(kenv_1) : kenv_1(X_i) \leq kenv_2(X_i)$

and we define a function σ by

$$\sigma(kenv|tt) = dom(kenv)|\tau(tt)$$

We then define

$$\sigma_{wf}^{-1}(V|dt) = \{(kenv|tt) \mid \sigma(kenv|tt) = (V|dt) \wedge \vdash_{TML} (kenv|tt)\}$$

and once again note that by Fact 3.1 this set will be empty unless $V \vdash_{DML} dt$.

Lemma 3.5 If $V \vdash_{DML} dt$ the set $\sigma_{wf}^{-1}(V|dt)$ is a complete lattice under $\sqsubseteq$, and the binary least upper bound operator $\sqcup$ satisfies that if $kenv|tt = (kenv_1|tt_1) \sqcup (kenv_2|tt_2)$, then

$$\Xi(tt) = \Xi(tt_1) \vee \Xi(tt_2)$$

$$dom(kenv) = V \wedge \forall X_i \in V : kenv(X_i) = kenv_1(X_i) \vee kenv_2(X_i) \qquad \square$$

Taking V to be empty we have our claim. The proof of the lemma is by structural induction on dt and may be found in the Appendix.

Lemma 3.5 will be the key in passing from the types of **DML** to the types of **TML**$_e$. Starting with a closed type dt of **DML** we must have some indications of which parts "live" at compile-time and which "live" at run-time as otherwise $\tau(dt)$ and $\bar{\tau}(dt)$ will be the only canonical candidates. We shall model this by a type t of the language L whose types are as indicated in

$$t ::= A_i \mid \underline{A_i} \mid \overline{A_i} \mid t \times t \mid t \underline{\times} t \mid t \overline{\times} t \mid \ldots$$

(One may view L as "the recursive union" of **DML** and **TML**$_e$.) We then extend the map Ξ to have functionality

$$\Xi : \{t \mid t \in L\} \rightarrow \{c, r, u\}^{\star}$$

where u means "uncommitted" and e.g. $\Xi(A_i) = u$. Similarly we extend the map τ to have functionality

$$\tau : \{t \mid t \in L\} \rightarrow \{dt \mid dt \in \mathbf{DML}\}$$

by e.g. $\tau(A_i) = A_i$. Also the relations $\leq$ and $\sqsubseteq$ may be extended by

$$K_1 \ldots K_n \leq K_1' \ldots K_m' \text{ iff } n = m \text{ and } \forall i : K_i' = r \Rightarrow K_i = r$$

and

$$t_1 \sqsubseteq t_2 \text{ iff } \tau(t_1) = \tau(t_2) \text{ and } \Xi(t_1) \leq \Xi(t_2)$$

but they no longer give partial orders. Our point of view then is that one must manually transform dt into t by giving some (possibly none) indications of what must take place at run-time. Clearly this t must satisfy that $\tau(t) = dt$. We can then obtain a best type in $\mathbf{TML}_e$ as follows. Define a function

$$\underline{\tau_{opt}} : \{t \in L \mid \emptyset \vdash_{DML} \tau(t)\} \rightarrow \{tt \in \mathbf{TML}_e \mid \vdash_{TML} (\emptyset|tt)\}$$

by

$$\underline{\tau_{opt}}(t) = \bigsqcup \{tt \in \mathbf{TML}_e \mid tt \sqsubseteq t \wedge \vdash_{TML} (\emptyset|tt)\}$$

Fact 3.6 $\underline{\tau_{opt}}$ is well-defined and satisfies $\underline{\tau_{opt}}(t) \sqsubseteq t$. $\qquad\qquad\square$

Proof. When $\tau(t) = dt$ is closed, the set $\{tt \in \mathbf{TML}_e \mid \vdash_{TML} (\emptyset|tt)\}$ is a subset of $\tau_{wf}^{-1}(dt)$ and a least upper bound $\underline{\tau_{opt}}(t)$ exists in $\tau_{wf}^{-1}(dt)$ by Lemma 3.5. Furthermore $\tau_{wf}^{-1}(dt)$ is finite, so by the classification of binary least upper bounds in Lemma 3.5 we have

$$\begin{aligned}
\Xi(\underline{\tau_{opt}}(t)) &= \bigvee \{\Xi(tt) \mid tt \in \mathbf{TML}_e \wedge tt \sqsubseteq t \wedge \vdash_{TML} (\emptyset|tt)\} \\
&\leq \bigvee \{\Xi(tt) \mid \Xi(tt) \leq \Xi(t)\} \\
&\leq \Xi(t)
\end{aligned}$$

as well as

$$\tau(\underline{\tau_{opt}}(t)) = \tau(t)$$

and this proves the fact.   □

So $\tau_{opt}(t)$ is the type of $\mathbf{TML}_e$ that allows as many parameters as possible to be supplied at compile-time although it does not supply things at compile-time that t says should be supplied at run-time*.

Example 3.7 Returning to the B combinators of Section 2, we let

$$t = (\overline{A}_2 \to \underline{A}_1) \to (A_3 \to \underline{A}_2) \to A_3 \to \underline{A}_1$$

Clearly $\tau(t)$ is the type of the B combinator. Then

$$
\begin{aligned}
\underline{\tau}_{opt}(t) &= \bigsqcup\{\ tt \in \mathbf{TML}_e \mid tt \sqsubseteq t \wedge\ \vdash_{TML} (\emptyset | tt)\} \\
&= \bigsqcup\{\ (\underline{A}_2 \rightrightarrows \underline{A}_1) \rightrightarrows (\underline{A}_3 \rightrightarrows \underline{A}_2) \rightrightarrows \underline{A}_3 \rightrightarrows \underline{A}_1 \\
&\quad ,(\underline{A}_2 \rightrightarrows \underline{A}_1) \rightrightarrows (\underline{A}_3 \rightrightarrows \underline{A}_2) \rightrightarrows \underline{A}_3 \rightrightarrows \underline{A}_1 \\
&\quad ,(\underline{A}_2 \rightrightarrows \underline{A}_1) \rightrightarrows (\underline{A}_3 \rightrightarrows \underline{A}_2) \rightrightarrows \underline{A}_3 \rightrightarrows \underline{A}_1\} \\
&= (\underline{A}_2 \rightrightarrows \underline{A}_1) \rightrightarrows (\underline{A}_3 \rightrightarrows \underline{A}_2) \rightrightarrows \underline{A}_3 \rightrightarrows \underline{A}_1
\end{aligned}
$$

Note that this is the type of the B_1 combinator and that the types in the set we take the least upper bound of are the types of the combinators B_1, B_2, and B_3. Also note that the $\overline{A}_2$ in t has become $\underline{A}_2$ in $\underline{\tau}_{opt}(t)$.   □

The passage from expressions of $\mathbf{DML}$ to expressions of $\mathbf{TML}_e$ follows the pattern we have just seen for types. So analogously to $\overline{\tau}$ and $\underline{\tau}$ we may define functions

$$\overline{\varepsilon} : \{de \mid de \in \mathbf{DML}\} \to \{te \mid te \in \mathbf{TML}_e\}$$

$$\underline{\varepsilon} : \{de \mid de \in \mathbf{DML}\} \to \{te \mid te \in \mathbf{TML}_e\}$$

that overline, respectively underline, the various symbols (excluding variables, constants, square brackets, periods and commas). An illustrative example is

$$\overline{\varepsilon}(fix[tt]te) = \overline{fix}[\overline{\tau}(tt)]\overline{\varepsilon}(te)$$

Assuming that $\underline{\tau}(dt) \in T_i$ and $\overline{\tau}(dt) \in T_i$ whenever $dt \in D_i$ we have

---

* Dually one might consider a function $\overline{\tau}_{opt}$ that would map t to the least tt satisfying $t \sqsubseteq tt$, but this is not necessary for the present purposes.

Fact 3.8 If $tenv \vdash_{DML} de : dt$, then $\overline{\tau} \circ tenv \vdash_{TML} \overline{\varepsilon}(de) : \overline{\tau}(dt)$ and $\underline{\tau} \circ tenv \vdash_{TML} \underline{\varepsilon}(de) : \underline{\tau}(dt)$. $\square$

As an example we note that for the B combinators of Section 2 we have $\underline{\varepsilon}(B) = B_3$ and $\overline{\varepsilon}(B) = B_0$. Intuitively the other B combinators lie in between the extremal cases $\underline{\varepsilon}(B)$ and $\overline{\varepsilon}(B)$. To formalize this we define a partial order on the expressions of $\mathbf{TML}_e$ by

$$te_1 \sqsubseteq te_2 \text{ iff } \varepsilon(te_1) = \varepsilon(te_2) \text{ and } \Xi(te_1) \leq \Xi(te_2)$$

where Ξ now also has functionality

$$\Xi : \{te \mid te \in \mathbf{TML}_e\} \rightarrow \{c, r\}^\star$$

and e.g.

$$\Xi(\overline{fix}[\underline{A_1} \rightrightarrows \underline{A_2}]\overline{\lambda}x_1[\underline{A_1} \rightrightarrows \underline{A_2}].x_1) = crrrcrrr$$

Fact 3.9 The relation $\sqsubseteq$ is a partial order on $\{te \mid te \in \mathbf{TML}_e\}$. $\square$

Clearly we have $\underline{\varepsilon}(B) = B_3 \sqsubseteq B_2 \sqsubseteq B_1 \sqsubseteq B_0 = \overline{\varepsilon}(B)$. This just confirms the intuition that $\sqsubseteq$ imposes an ordering upon the "degree" of partial evaluation possible.

Well-typing of expressions are relative to a type environment and in analogy with types it is helpful to consider formulae of the form $tenv|de : dt$ and $tenv|te : tt$. We shall write $\vdash_{DML} tenv|de : dt$ for $tenv \vdash_{DML} de : dt$ and $\vdash_{TML} tenv|te : tt$ for $tenv \vdash_{TML} te : tt$. The partial order $\sqsubseteq$ may be extended by defining

$$(tenv_1|te_1 : tt_1) \sqsubseteq (tenv_2|te_2 : tt_2) \text{ iff}$$
$$te_1 \sqsubseteq te_2 \land tt_1 \sqsubseteq tt_2 \land dom(tenv_1) = dom(tenv_2) \land$$
$$\forall x_i \in dom(tenv_1) : tenv_1(x_i) \sqsubseteq tenv_2(x_i)$$

and we define a function ω by

$$\omega(tenv|te : tt) = (\tau \circ tenv)|\varepsilon(te) : \tau(tt)$$

We then define

$$\omega_{wf}^{-1}(tenv|de : dt) = \{(tenv'|te' : tt') \mid \omega(tenv'|te' : tt') = (tenv|de : dt) \land$$
$$\vdash_{TML} (tenv'|te' : tt') \}$$

and note that by Fact 3.2 this set will be empty unless $tenv \vdash_{DML} de : dt$.

Theorem 3.10 If $tenv \vdash_{DML} de : dt$ then the set $\omega_{wf}^{-1}(tenv|de : dt)$ is a complete lattice under $\sqsubseteq$ and the binary least upper bound operator $\sqcup$ satisfies that if $(tenv'|te' : tt') = (tenv_1|te_1 : tt_1) \sqcup (tenv_2|te_2 : tt_2)$ then

$$\Xi(te') = \Xi(te_1) \vee \Xi(te_2)$$

$$tt' = tt_1 \sqcup tt_2$$

$$dom(tenv') = dom(tenv) \wedge \forall x_i \in dom(tenv) : tenv'(x_i) = tenv_1(x_i) \sqcup tenv_2(x_i) \qquad \square$$

The proof is by structural induction on de and may be found in the Appendix. It relies on the assumption that for all (closed) $dt \in D_i$ the set $T_i \cap \tau_{wf}^{-1}(dt)$ is a complete lattice that contains $\underline{\tau}(dt)$ and whose binary least upper bound operator is as characterized in Lemma 3.5. Actually, it is natural to take $T_i = \bigcup\{\tau_{wf}^{-1}(dt) \mid dt \in D_i\}$.

Remark 3.11 When considering the formula $kenv|tt$ for types we did not incorporate the kind of the type in the formulae. It is therefore interesting to observe that the presence of the type tt in the formulae $tenv|te : tt$ is not important. To see this define

$$(tenv_1|te_1) \sqsubseteq (tenv_2|te_2) \text{ iff}$$
$$te_1 \sqsubseteq te_2 \wedge dom(tenv_1) = dom(tenv_2) \wedge$$
$$\forall x_i \in dom(tenv_1) : tenv_1(x_i) \sqsubseteq tenv_2(x_i)$$

and define

$$\omega^\star(tenv|de) = \{(tenv'|te') \mid \tau \circ tenv' = tenv \wedge \varepsilon(te') = de \wedge \exists tt : tenv' \vdash_{TML} te' : tt\}$$

Given $tenv_j|te_j : tt_j$ in $\omega_{wf}^{-1}(tenv|de : dt)$ we have $tenv_j|te_j$ in $\omega^\star(tenv|de)$ and $(tenv_1|te_1) \sqsubseteq (tenv_2|te_2)$ if $(tenv_1|te_1 : tt_1) \sqsubseteq (tenv_2|te_2 : tt_2)$. If $\exists dt : tenv \vdash de : dt$ and $tenv_j|te_j$ are in $\omega^\star(tenv|de)$ there are unique dt and tt_j such that $tenv \vdash de : dt$ and $tenv_j \vdash te_j : tt_j$ and $\tau(tt_j) = dt$ (see Facts 2.2, 2.5, 3.2) and hence $tenv_j \vdash te_j : tt_j$ are in $\omega_{wf}^{-1}(tenv|de : dt)$. If $(tenv_1|te_1) \sqsubseteq (tenv_2|te_2)$, then $tenv_2|te_2 : (tt_1 \sqcup tt_2)$ is an element of $\omega_{wf}^{-1}(tenv|de : dt)$ by Theorem 3.10 and by Fact 2.5 we have $tt_1 \sqsubseteq tt_2$. So $\omega_{wf}^{-1}(tenv|de : dt)$ and $\omega^\star(tenv|de)$ are isomorphic in the domain theoretic sense. By way of digression we note that it easily follows that if de is a closed expression then

$$\varepsilon_{wf}^{-1}(de) = \{te \in \mathbf{TML}_e \mid \varepsilon(te) = de \wedge te \text{ closed}\}$$

is a complete lattice with $\Xi(te_1 \sqcup te_2) = \Xi(te_1) \vee \Xi(te_2)$. □

Theorem 3.10 will be the key in passing from the expressions of **DML** to the expressions of **TML**$_e$. For a closed expression de of **DML**, i.e. $\emptyset \vdash_{DML} de : dt$, it is probably most natural to express the binding time commitments by a type $t \in L$ such that $\tau(t) = dt$. However, in order not to be dogmatic we shall assume that L has expressions as indicated by

$$e ::= f_i[t] \mid (e, e) \mid \underline{(e, e)} \mid \overline{(e, e)} \mid \dots$$

and we shall then allow an arbitrary formula $tenv|e : t$ where each $tenv(x_i) \in L$. So we extend the relation $\sqsubseteq$ to expressions of L by

$$e_1 \sqsubseteq e_2 \text{ iff } \varepsilon(e_1) = \varepsilon(e_2) \text{ and } \Xi(e_1) \leq \Xi(e_2)$$

(where also the domains of ε and Ξ have been extended) and to the formulae $tenv \vdash e : t$ by

$$(tenv_1|e_1 : t_1) \sqsubseteq (tenv_2|e_2 : t_2) \text{ iff}$$
$$e_1 \sqsubseteq e_2 \wedge t_1 \sqsubseteq t_2 \wedge dom(tenv_1) = dom(tenv_2) \wedge$$
$$\forall x_i \in dom(tenv_1) : tenv_1(x_i) \sqsubseteq tenv_2(x_i)$$

We may then define a function

$$\underline{\omega_{opt}} : \{(tenv|e : t) \mid \vdash_{DML} \omega(tenv|e : t)\} \to \{(tenv|te : tt) \mid \vdash_{TML} (tenv|te : tt)\}$$

(assuming also the domain of ω has been extended) by

$$\underline{\omega_{opt}}(tenv|e : t) = \bigsqcup\{ (tenv'|te' : tt') \mid (tenv'|te' : tt') \sqsubseteq (tenv|e : t) \wedge$$
$$\vdash_{TML} (tenv'|te' : tt')\}$$

In analogy with Fact 3.6 we have

Fact 3.12 $\underline{\omega_{opt}}$ is well-defined and satisfies $\underline{\omega_{opt}}(tenv|e : t) \sqsubseteq (tenv|e : t)$ □

So $\underline{\omega_{opt}}(tenv|e : t)$ is the best way to complete the partial commitments expressed in $(tenv|e : t)$.

Example 3.13 To make this concrete we consider the B combinators of Section 2. We shall write dt for the type of B and tt_i for the type of B_i. We may then consider

$$t = (\overline{A}_2 \to \underline{A}_1) \to (A_3 \to \underline{A}_2) \to A_3 \to \underline{A}_1$$

so that $\tau(t)$ is the type of the B combinator. Then

$$
\begin{aligned}
\underline{\omega_{opt}}(\emptyset|B : t) &= \bigsqcup\{(\emptyset|te : tt) \mid te \sqsubseteq B \wedge tt \sqsubseteq t \wedge \emptyset \vdash_{TML} te : tt\} \\
&= \bigsqcup\{(\emptyset|B_1 : tt_1), (\emptyset|B_2 : tt_2), (\emptyset|B_3 : tt_3)\} \\
&= (\emptyset|B_1 : tt_1)
\end{aligned}
$$

so that B_1 is the combinator that performs as much as possible at compile-time given the commitments expressed in t. $\square$

We have said that a natural use of $\underline{\omega_{opt}}$ will be on formulae of the form $\emptyset|de : t$ where $\emptyset \vdash_{DML} de : \tau(t)$. However, it is important to note that although the result $\emptyset|te : tt$ of $\underline{\omega_{opt}}(\emptyset|de : t)$ must satisfy $tt \sqsubseteq \underline{\tau_{opt}}(t)$ we may have $tt \neq \underline{\tau_{opt}}(t)$. As an example let

$$
\begin{aligned}
de &= B \\
t &= (\overline{A}_2 \Rightarrow \overline{A}_1) \Rightarrow (\underline{A}_3 \xrightarrow{} \underline{A}_2) \Rightarrow (\overline{A}_3 \Rightarrow \overline{A}_1)
\end{aligned}
$$

so that

$$\underline{\tau_{opt}}(t) = t$$

but

$$\underline{\omega_{opt}}(\emptyset|te : t) = (\emptyset|B_1 : (\underline{A}_2 \xrightarrow{} \underline{A}_1) \Rightarrow (\underline{A}_3 \xrightarrow{} \underline{A}_2) \Rightarrow \underline{A}_3 \xrightarrow{} \underline{A}_1)$$

The explanation is of course that the expression de imposes additional constraints between various subparts of the type expression. This is the motivation behind the statement in Example 2.6 that *most* aspects of the distinction between run-time and compile-time are reflected in the types.

4   Comparison Relations

To be able to compare the residual programs resulting from different partial evaluators we must first clarify our understanding of *partial evaluation*. In general our approach towards *evaluation* of expressions of **DML** will be by means of the reduction rules of the λ-calculus [1] or the structural operational semantics of Plotkin [12]. This notion of evaluation may be extended to expressions of **TML**$_e$ by forgetting the binding time annotations, i.e. essentially by decreeing that te_1 evaluates to te_2 if $\varepsilon(te_1)$ evaluates to $\varepsilon(te_2)$. *Partial evaluation* of expressions in **TML**$_e$ then amounts to only performing reductions upon those parts of expressions that do not depend on run-time data. To make this explanation precise we define a relation

$te \ \triangleright \ te'$

intended to express when te evaluates to te' by one step of partial evaluation. The definition may be found in Table 3.

To motivate the definition of $\triangleright$ it would be helpful to consider evaluation of expressions in **DML** in more detail. We do not have the space to give a table containing the details, but such a table may easily be obtained from Table 3 by first applying ε to all expressions and then removing duplicate rules. This explanation is important because it allows to distinguish between those aspects of the definition of $\triangleright$ that are inherent in our formalization and those aspects that represent the author's rather unimportant decisions of how to approach evaluation of the monotyped λ-calculus. Among the latter aspects we may note the assumption that there are constants $f_{true}[\overline{A}_{bool}]$ and $f_{false}[\overline{A}_{bool}]$ for the compile-time truth values. The reduction relation is sufficiently flexible to be able to model call-by-name as well as call-by-value. To see this note that there are no conditions on the argument te for when

$$(\overline{\lambda} x_i[tt].te_1) \ ^{\dagger} \ te \ \triangleright \ te_1[te/x_i]$$

and concerning constants the condition for when

$$f_i[tt] \ ^{\dagger} \ te \ \triangleright \ te'$$

is that the pair (te, te') is in a set $F_{i,tt}$ that may be chosen rather freely.

Finally, the absence of explicit reductions of the form

$$\overline{out}_1 \ \overline{in}_2[tt]te \ \triangleright \ \ldots$$
$$\overline{in}_1[tt]\overline{out}_1 \ te \ \triangleright \ \ldots$$

are also due to the author's approach to the evaluation of a monotyped λ-calculus. If a different approach is desired, then Table 3 may be modified accordingly.

$$\frac{te_1 \ \triangleright \ te_1'}{(te_1, te_2) \ \triangleright \ (te_1', te_2)} \qquad\qquad \frac{te_1 \ \triangleright \ te_1'}{te_1 \ ^{\dagger} \ te_2 \ \triangleright \ te_1' \ ^{\dagger} \ te_2}$$

$$\frac{te_2 \;\rhd\; te_2'}{\underline{(}te_1, te_2\underline{)} \;\rhd\; \underline{(}te_1, te_2'\underline{)}} \qquad\qquad \frac{te_2 \;\rhd\; te_2'}{te_1 \bar{} te_2 \;\rhd\; te_1 \bar{} te_2'}$$

$$\frac{te_1 \;\rhd\; te_1'}{\overline{(te_1, te_2)} \;\rhd\; \overline{(te_1', te_2)}} \qquad\qquad (\overline{\lambda}x_1[tt].te_1) \bar{} te_2 \;\rhd\; te_1[te_2/x_i]$$

$$\frac{te_2 \;\rhd\; te_2'}{\overline{(te_1, te_2)} \;\rhd\; \overline{(te_1, te_2')}} \qquad\qquad (f_i[tt]) \bar{} te \;\rhd\; te' \text{ if } (te, te') \in F_{i,tt}$$

$$\frac{te \;\rhd\; te'}{te\underline{\downarrow i} \;\rhd\; te'\underline{\downarrow i}} \qquad\qquad \frac{te \;\rhd\; te'}{\underline{mkrec}[tt]te \;\rhd\; \underline{mkrec}[tt]te'}$$

$$\frac{te \;\rhd\; te'}{te\overline{\downarrow i} \;\rhd\; te'\overline{\downarrow i}} \qquad\qquad \frac{te \;\rhd\; te'}{\overline{mkrec}[tt]te \;\rhd\; \overline{mkrec}[tt]te'}$$

$$\overline{(te_1, te_2)}\,\overline{\downarrow i} \;\rhd\; te_i \text{ if } i \in \{1,2\} \qquad\qquad \frac{te \;\rhd\; te'}{\underline{unrec}\, te \;\rhd\; \underline{unrec}\, te'}$$

$$\frac{te \;\rhd\; te'}{\underline{in_i}[tt]te \;\rhd\; \underline{in_i}[tt]te'} \qquad\qquad \frac{te \;\rhd\; te'}{\overline{unrec}\, te \;\rhd\; \overline{unrec}\, te'}$$

$$\frac{te \;\rhd\; te'}{\overline{in_i}[tt]te \;\rhd\; \overline{in_i}[tt]te'} \qquad\qquad \overline{\overline{unrec}}\,\overline{mkrec}[tt]te \;\rhd\; te$$

$$\frac{te \;\rhd\; te'}{\underline{is_i}\, te \;\rhd\; \underline{is_i}\, te'} \qquad\qquad \frac{te \;\rhd\; te'}{\underline{fix}[tt]te \;\rhd\; \underline{fix}[tt]te'}$$

$$\frac{te \;\rhd\; te'}{\overline{is_i}\, te \;\rhd\; \overline{is_i}\, te'} \qquad\qquad \frac{te \;\rhd\; te'}{\overline{fix}[tt]te \;\rhd\; \overline{fix}[tt]te'}$$

$$\overline{is_i}\,\overline{in_i}[tt]te \;\rhd\; f_{true}[\overline{A}_{bool}] \qquad\qquad \overline{fix}[tt]te \;\rhd\; te \bar{} (\overline{fix}[tt]te)$$

$$\overline{is_i}\,\overline{in_j}[tt]te \;\rhd\; f_{false}[\overline{A}_{bool}] \text{ if } i \neq j \qquad\qquad \frac{te_1 \;\rhd\; te_1'}{te_1 \rightrightarrows te_2, te_3 \;\rhd\; te_1' \rightrightarrows te_2, te_3}$$

$$\frac{te \;\rhd\; te'}{\underline{out_i}\, te \;\rhd\; \underline{out_i}\, te'} \qquad\qquad \frac{te_2 \;\rhd\; te_2'}{te_1 \rightrightarrows te_2, te_3 \;\rhd\; te_1 \rightrightarrows te_2', te_3}$$

$$\frac{te \;\rhd\; te'}{\overline{out_i}\, te \;\rhd\; \overline{out_i}\, te'} \qquad\qquad \frac{te_3 \;\rhd\; te_3'}{te_1 \rightrightarrows te_2, te_3 \;\rhd\; te_1 \rightrightarrows te_2, te_3'}$$

$$\overline{out}_i\ \overline{in}_i[tt]te \ \rhd \ te \qquad\qquad \frac{te_1 \ \rhd \ te_1'}{te_1 \Rrightarrow te_2, te_3 \ \rhd \ te_1' \Rrightarrow te_2, te_3}$$

$$\frac{te \ \rhd \ te'}{\underline{\lambda}x_i[tt].te \ \rhd \ \underline{\lambda}x_i[tt].te'} \qquad\qquad \frac{te_2 \ \rhd \ te_2'}{te_1 \Rrightarrow te_2, te_3 \ \rhd \ te_1 \Rrightarrow te_2', te_3}$$

$$\frac{te \ \rhd \ te'}{\overline{\lambda}x_i[tt].te \ \rhd \ \overline{\lambda}x_i[tt].te'} \qquad\qquad \frac{te_3 \ \rhd \ te_3'}{te_1 \Rrightarrow te_2, te_3 \ \rhd \ te_1 \Rrightarrow te_2, te_3'}$$

$$\frac{te_1 \ \rhd \ te_1'}{te_1 \cdot te_2 \ \rhd \ te_1' \cdot te_2} \qquad\qquad f_{true}[\overline{A}_{bool}] \Rrightarrow te_2, te_3 \ \rhd \ te_2$$

$$\frac{te_2 \ \rhd \ te_2'}{te_1 \cdot te_2 \ \rhd \ te_1 \cdot te_2'} \qquad\qquad f_{false}[\overline{A}_{bool}] \Rrightarrow te_2, te_3 \ \rhd \ te_3$$

Table 3: The compile-time semantics of $\mathbf{TML}_e$.

To clarify the definition of $\rhd$ the following fact and example will be helpful.

Fact 4.1 If $tenv \vdash te : tt$ and $te \ \rhd \ te'$ then $tenv \vdash te' : tt$. $\qquad\qquad \square$

The proof is by induction on the inference of $te \ \rhd \ te'$ and merely amounts to checking the result for the axioms of Table 3 and checking that the result is preserved by the inference rules of Table 3. For this we shall assume that if $(te_1, te_2) \in F_{i,tt}$ then there are types tt_1 and tt_2 such that $\emptyset \vdash te_1 : tt_1$, $\emptyset \vdash te_2 : tt_2$, and $tt = tt_1 \Rrightarrow tt_2$.

Example 4.2 Following [5] we shall consider a program for computing z^5 by means of the observations that

$$z^n = (z^{n/2})^2 \qquad \text{if } n \text{ even}$$
$$z^n = z \times z^{n-1} \qquad \text{if } n \text{ odd}$$
$$z^0 = 1$$

The starting point is the **DML** expression p defined by

$$(fix[A_{int} \to A_{int} \to A_{int}] \; \lambda x_f[A_{int} \to A_{int} \to A_{int}].\lambda x_n[A_{int}].\lambda x_z[A_{int}].$$
$$f_{0?}[A_{int} \to A_{bool}] \cdot x_n \quad \to \quad f_1[A_{int}],$$
$$f_{even?}[A_{int} \to A_{bool}] \cdot x_n \quad \to \quad f_{square}[A_{int} \to A_{int}] \cdot$$
$$(x_f \cdot (f_{div2}[A_{int} \to A_{int}] \cdot x_n) \cdot x_z),$$
$$f_{mult}[A_{int} \to A_{int} \to A_{int}] \cdot x_z \cdot$$
$$(x_f \cdot (f_{sub1}[A_{int} \to A_{int}] \cdot x_n) \cdot x_z)) \cdot$$
$$f_5[A_{int}]$$

Hopefully the intention with the constants $f_{0?}$, f_{mult}, etc. will be clear without further explanation. Using Table 1 one may verify that

$$\emptyset \vdash_{DML} p : A_{int} \to A_{int}$$

We now assume that the value of z (i.e. x_z) will not be supplied until run-time, but that the value of n (i.e. x_n) is indeed available at compile-time. This motivates considering the formula

$$\emptyset | p : \underline{A}_{int} \to A_{int}$$

of L. We then get

$$\underline{\omega}_{opt}(\emptyset | p : \underline{A}_{int} \to A_{int}) = (\emptyset | p_1 : \underline{A}_{int} \rightrightarrows \underline{A}_{int})$$

where p_1 is the $\mathbf{TML}_e$ expression

$$(\overline{fix}[\overline{A}_{int} \rightrightarrows \underline{A}_{int} \rightrightarrows \underline{A}_{int}] \; \overline{\lambda} x_f[\overline{A}_{int} \rightrightarrows \underline{A}_{int} \rightrightarrows \underline{A}_{int}].\overline{\lambda} x_n[\overline{A}_{int}].\lambda x_z[\underline{A}_{int}].$$
$$f_{0?}[\overline{A}_{int} \rightrightarrows \overline{A}_{bool}] \; \overline{\cdot} \; x_n \quad \rightrightarrows \quad f_1[\underline{A}_{int}],$$
$$f_{even?}[\overline{A}_{int} \rightrightarrows \overline{A}_{bool}] \; \overline{\cdot} \; x_n \quad \rightrightarrows \quad f_{square}[\underline{A}_{int} \rightrightarrows \underline{A}_{int}] \; \underline{\cdot}$$
$$(x_f \; \overline{\cdot} \; (f_{div2}[\overline{A}_{int} \rightrightarrows \overline{A}_{int}] \; \overline{\cdot} \; x_n) \; \underline{\cdot} \; x_z),$$
$$f_{mult}[\underline{A}_{int} \rightrightarrows \underline{A}_{int} \rightrightarrows \underline{A}_{int}] \; \underline{\cdot} \; x_z \; \underline{\cdot}$$
$$(x_f \; \overline{\cdot} \; (f_{sub1}[\overline{A}_{int} \rightrightarrows \overline{A}_{int}] \; \overline{\cdot} \; x_n) \; \underline{\cdot} \; x_z)) \; \overline{\cdot}$$
$$f_5[\overline{A}_{int}]$$

This may be viewed as a result of partially evaluating de and thus corresponds to the result of the *trivial* partial evaluator. With respect to [5] it corresponds to their $resid_1$.

However, a more interesting result is obtained if the compile-time computations are carried out. We then get

$$p_1 \overset{*}{\triangleright} p_2$$

where we assume that e.g. $f_{sub1}[\overline{A}_{int} \Rightarrow \overline{A}_{int}] \vdots f_5[\overline{A}_{int}] \ \triangleright \ f_4[\overline{A}_{int}]$ and where p_2 is

$$
\underline{\lambda}x_z[\underline{A}_{int}].f_{mult}[\underline{A}_{int} \rightrightarrows \underline{A}_{int} \rightrightarrows \underline{A}_{int}] \vdots x_z \vdots (() \vdots x_z)
$$
$$
\overline{\underline{\lambda}x_z[\underline{A}_{int}].f_{square}[\underline{A}_{int} \rightrightarrows \underline{A}_{int}] \vdots (() \vdots x_z)}
$$
$$
\underline{\lambda}x_z[\underline{A}_{int}].f_{square}[\underline{A}_{int} \rightrightarrows \underline{A}_{int}] \vdots (() \vdots x_z)
$$
$$
\overline{\underline{\lambda}x_z[\underline{A}_{int}].f_{mult}[\underline{A}_{int} \rightrightarrows \underline{A}_{int}] \vdots x_z \vdots (() \vdots x_z)}
$$
$$
\underline{\lambda}x_z[\underline{A}_{int}].f_1[\underline{A}_{int}]
$$

This is not too readable due to the many run-time β-redexes, so if we incorporate the rule

$$(\underline{\lambda}x_i[tt].te) \vdots x_i \triangleright_{ext} te$$

we get

$$p_2 \overset{*}{\triangleright}_{ext} p_3$$

where p_3 is the $\mathbf{TML}_e$ expression

$$
\underline{\lambda}x_z[\underline{A}_{int}]. \ f_{mult}[\underline{A}_{int} \rightrightarrows \underline{A}_{int} \rightrightarrows \underline{A}_{int}] \vdots x_z
$$
$$
\vdots (f_{square}[\underline{A}_{int} \rightrightarrows \underline{A}_{int}]
$$
$$
\vdots (f_{square}[\underline{A}_{int} \rightrightarrows \underline{A}_{int}]
$$
$$
\vdots (f_{mult}[\underline{A}_{int} \rightrightarrows \underline{A}_{int} \rightrightarrows \underline{A}_{int}] \vdots x_z
$$
$$
\vdots (f_1[\underline{A}_{int}]))))
$$

Informally this may be written as $\lambda z. \ z \times ((z \times 1)^2)^2$ and is the result of *compiling* a specialized version of the original program. In particular one may note that *no* $\triangleright$-*redexes* remain, and one might define an *ideal* partial evaluator as one that performs all $\triangleright$-reductions. If we also had the rule

$$f_{mult}[\underline{A}_{int} \rightrightarrows \underline{A}_{int} \rightrightarrows \underline{A}_{int}] \vdots te \vdots f_1[\underline{A}_{int}] \ \triangleright \ te$$

we would have obtained $\lambda z.z \times (z^2)^2$ corresponding to $resid_2$ of [5].

To conclude the example we note that our $\triangleright$ relation corresponds well with the example of partial evaluation given in [5]. In particular the "need" to consider $\triangleright_{ext}$ does not indicate a shortcoming in our approach, but rather points to the fact that our notion of partial evaluation is slightly different from the notion of [5], and we expect no problems in adapting Table 3 to correspond more closely to [5]. □

We may now use our definition of partial evaluation, i.e. our definition of $\triangleright$, as a basis for comparing residual programs. We find it natural to regard residual programs as expressions of $\mathbf{TML}_e$ and so propose the following relations $te_1 \subseteq_i te_2$ for when te_1 is a "worse" residual program than te_2.

Definition 4.3 $te_1 \subseteq_1 te_2$ iff

$te_1 \overset{*}{\triangleright} te_2$ and te_1 and te_2 are closed $\hspace{2cm}\square$

Definition 4.4 $te_1 \subseteq_2 te_2$ iff

$te_1 (\triangleright \cup \sqsubseteq)^* te_2$ and $\exists tt : \emptyset \vdash te_1 : tt \land \emptyset \vdash te_2 : tt$ $\hspace{1cm}\square$

Definition 4.5 $te_1 \subseteq_3 te_2$ iff

$te_1 (\triangleright \cup \sqsubseteq)^* te_2$ and te_1 and te_2 are closed $\hspace{2cm}\square$

As usual $(\triangleright \cup \sqsubseteq)$ is the union of the relations $\triangleright$ and $\sqsubseteq$ and $(\triangleright \cup \sqsubseteq)^*$ is the reflexive and transitive closure of $(\triangleright \cup \sqsubseteq)$. The definition of $\subseteq_1$ merely says that te_1 is "worse" than te_2 if te_2 may be obtained from te_1 by performing $\triangleright$-reductions. With respect to the expressions p_i of Example 4.2 we have

$$p_1 \subseteq_1 p_2$$

and with respect to the B_i combinators of Section 2 we have

$$B_i \subseteq_1 B_j \text{ iff } i = j$$

The definition of $\subseteq_3$ is more liberal because it allows for the possibility that what is obtainable from te_1 may be less than what may lead to te_2. Hence

$$B_i \subseteq_3 B_j \text{ iff } i \geq j$$

and this is probably too liberal since the different B_i correspond to supplying a different number of arguments at compile-time. This is rectified by the second definition by constraining the type of the te_i to be the same. This is in accord with the arguments in Section 2 and 3 that it is really the type of an expression that should express the constraint on binding times. In particular we have

$$p_1 \subseteq_2 p_2$$

$$B_i \subseteq_2 B_j \text{ iff } i = j$$

The relationship between the three relations is given by

Fact 4.6 $te_1 \subseteq_1 te_2 \ \Rightarrow \ te_1 \subseteq_2 te_2 \ \Rightarrow \ te_1 \subseteq_3 te_2$ ☐

We have already seen that the second implication is proper in general, and this also holds for the first, e.g. when $te_2 = p_2$ and $te_1 = \underline{\varepsilon}(p)$.

Clearly one may define other relations than $\subseteq_1$, $\subseteq_2$, and $\subseteq_3$. Of the relations defined $\subseteq_1$ is a possible candidate, but $\subseteq_2$ is more in line with the general intuitions expressed in this paper. One may extend $\subseteq_2$ pointwise to partial evaluators, i.e.

$$Part_1 \ \subseteq_2 \ Part_2 \ \text{iff} \ \forall p : \forall d : Part_1(p, d) \ \subseteq_2 \ Part_2(p, d)$$

One may even extend the definition to expressions of **DML** by setting $de_1 \subseteq_2 de_2$ whenever $te_1 \subseteq_2 te_2$ and $de_i = \varepsilon(te_i)$, but it is not clear that this will be a useful definition. The relation $te_1 \subseteq_2 te_2$ is of course only semi-decidable, but this is already more tractable than the naive relation between programs, i.e. whether one program is no slower than another and that they are semantically equivalent, since the latter problem is not even semi-decidable.

5   Conclusion

We believe that the definition of $\subseteq_2$ formalizes the intuition behind when one partial evaluator is better than another. The main advantage of a formal definition is that different people's intuitions may be solved at the level of deciding the right definitions rather than by studying and discussing large and concrete residual programs. Hence it is hoped that the formalism will pave the way for a richer semantic theory of partial evaluation. (We have already seen that is a more tractable foundation than the "naive" relation.)

The main ingredient in our approach has been the study of a well-defined notation ($\mathbf{TML}_e$) for recording the binding times present in the "programming language" (**DML**). This has allowed us to perform the annotation of "programs" in a static way. While we have not given constructive algorithms — these may be found in [10] — it is clear (from the definition of ω_{opt}) that it is an effective process to transform a partly annotated formula into a fully annotated and well-typed formula. Hence our work generalizes previous work on the automatic binding time analysis of first-order recursion equation schemes [4] since we can handle the entire higher-order λ-calculus. (The methods are rather different, however, since we analyze a program statically whereas [4] prescribes an abstract interpretation.) The existence of a well-defined notation ($\mathbf{TML}_e$) to record the binding time information is also advantageous when formalizing the notion of *1 step of partial evaluation* ($\triangleright$) since it clearly distinguishes between those constructs that must be evaluated and those that must not. Alternatively, one would have to consider a relation upon the programs (expressions in **DML**) and let this relation incorporate a notion of when the required arguments are available. Hence it would need to perform in an implicit and dynamic way most of those distinctions that we perform explicitly and statically.

For some applications it is conceivable that one would be more interested in variants of $\mathbf{TML}_e$. It should be clear that the use of the terms "compile-time" and "run-time" is only intended as a possible interpretation of the kinds c and r and that the only important thing is that entities of kind c are supplied before entities of kind r. Also there is no need to consider only two kinds as one may have more than two binding times and in general one may let the kind structure represent an arbitrary (finite) partial order. On a more technical side we have already seen (in Section 2) that there might be reasons for using a less restrictive well-formedness relation. This also comes up when approaching the work in [4,5] on *binding time analysis* (corresponding to our ω_{opt}) and *function specialization* (corresponding to an evaluation strategy that is faithful to $\triangleright$). Here it is said that one should annotate the applications (our $\cdot$) rather than the function definitions [5] because an evaluator based on $\triangleright$ otherwise might loop too often. We actually annotate both function definitions and applications, but we require the annotations to match in that we have

$$\frac{tenv \vdash te_1 : tt \Rightarrow tt' \quad tenv \vdash te_2 : tt}{tenv \vdash te_1 \bar{\cdot} te_2 : tt'}$$

but we do not have

$$\frac{tenv \vdash te_1 : tt \Rightarrow tt' \quad tenv \vdash te_2 : tt}{tenv \vdash te_1 \underline{\cdot} te_2 : tt'}$$

To be able to subsume the development of [4,5] we would probably have to add the latter rule, or perhaps more generally to add

$$\frac{tenv \vdash te : tt}{tenv \vdash te \Downarrow tt' : tt'} \quad \text{if } tt' \sqsubseteq tt$$

However, as was said in Section 2, this presupposes that one works in a setting (such as LISP of [4,5]) where one can freely delay evaluation (as is clearly expressed by the rule above), and this is not always natural.

Acknowledgement

This research has been supported by The Danish Natural Science Research Council under the FTU-programme.

References

[1] H. P. Barendregt. *The Lambda Calculus, its Syntax and Semantics.* Volume 103 of *Studies in Logic*, North–Holland, 1984.

[2] A. P. Ershov. A Characterization of Partial and Mixed Computation. In the announcement of the Workshop on Partial and Mixed Computation, 1986.

[3] A. P. Ershov. Mixed computation : Potential Applications and Problems for Study. *Theoretical Computer Science 18*, pp. 41–67, 1982.

[4] N. D. Jones. Towards Automating the Transformation of Language Specifications into Compilers, Parts I & II. 1986. Unpublished manuscript.

[5] N. D. Jones, P. Sestoft, and H. Søndergaard. An experiment in Partial Evaluation : The Generation of a Compiler Generator. In *Proceedings of Rewriting Techniques and Applications*, 1985. Springer Lecture Notes in Computer Science, Vol. 202.

[6] F. Nielson. Abstract Interpretation of Denotational Definitions. In *Proceedings of STACS 1986*, 1986. Springer Lecture Notes in Computer Science, Vol. 210.

[7] F. Nielson. Strictness Analysis and Denotational Abstract Interpretation (Extended Abstract). In *Proceedings of the 1987 ACM Conference on Principles of Programming Languages*, 1987.

[8] F. Nielson. Towards a Denotational Theory of Abstract Interpretation. In S. Abramsky and C. Hankin, editors, *Abstract Interpretation of Declarative Languages*, Ellis Horwood, 1987.

[9] F. Nielson and H. R. Nielson. *Two-Level Semantics and Code Generation*. To appear in Theoretical Computer Science, 1988.

[10] H. R. Nielson and F. Nielson. *Automatic Binding Time Analysis for a Typed λ-Calculus (Extended Abstract)*. To appear in Proceedings of the 1988 ACM Conference on Principles of Programming Languages, 1988.

[11] H. R. Nielson and F. Nielson. Semantics Directed Compiling for Functional Languages. In *Proceedings of the 1986 ACM Conference on LISP and Functional Programming*, 1986.

[12] G. D. Plotkin. *A Structural Approach to Operational Semantics*. Computer Science Department, Aarhus University, Denmark, 1981.

[13] D. A. Schmidt. *Denotational Semantics : A Methodology for Language Development*. Allyn and Bacon, 1986.

[14] J. E. Stoy. *Denotational Semantics : The Scott-Strachey Approach to Programming Language Theory*. MIT Press, 1977.

Appendix

In this appendix we prove Lemma 3.5 and Theorem 3.10.

Lemma 3.5 If $V \vdash_{DML} d$: the set $\sigma_{wf}^{-1}(V|dt)$ is a complete lattice under $\sqsubseteq$, and the binary least upper bound operator $\sqcup$ satisfies that if $kenv|tt = (kenv_1|tt_1) \sqcup (kenv_2|tt_2)$ then

$$\Xi(tt) = \Xi(tt_1) \vee \Xi(tt_2)$$

$$dom(kenv) = V \wedge \forall X_i \in V : kenv(X_i) = kenv_1(X_i) \vee kenv_2(X_i)$$

Proof. By Fact 3.3 the set $\sigma_{wf}^{-1}(V|dt)$ contains $\underline{\tau}[V]|\underline{\tau}(dt)$ and it is straight-forward to verify that this is the least element. Since $\sigma_{wf}^{-1}(V|dt)$ is finite, the existence of binary least upper bounds then will ensure that $\sigma_{wf}^{-1}(V|dt)$ is a complete lattice. Our approach will therefore be to consider $kenv_1|tt_1$ and $kenv_2|tt_2$ in $\sigma_{wf}^{-1}(V|dt)$ and to *define* the not necessarily well-formed formula $kenv|tt$ by the demands that

$$\tau(tt) = dt$$

$$\Xi(tt) = \Xi(tt_1) \lor \Xi(tt_2)$$

$$dom(kenv) = V$$

$$\forall X_i \in V : kenv(X_i) = kenv_1(X_i) \lor kenv_2(X_i)$$

(It is straight-forward to verify that this defines a unique formula.)

To prove the Lemma it therefore suffices to show that $kenv|tt$ is well-formed, i.e. $\exists K : kenv \vdash_{TML} tt : K$. To do so it is helpful to observe that it follows from Table 2 that if $\exists K : kenv \vdash_{TML} tt : K$ then

$$kenv \vdash tt : r \quad \text{iff } tt = \underline{\tau}(\tau(tt)) \text{ and } kenv(X_i) = r \text{ if } X_i \text{ is free in } tt$$

$$kenv \vdash tt : c \quad \text{iff } tt \neq \underline{\tau}(\tau(tt)) \text{ or } kenv(X_i) \neq r \text{ for some } X_i \text{ free in } tt$$
$$\text{or } tt \text{ is of the form } \underline{\tau}(dt_1 \rightarrow dt_2).$$

It now remains to show the well-formedness of $kenv|tt$, and we do so by structural induction on dt.

If dt is A_i, we must have $tt_1 \sqsubseteq tt_2$ or $tt_2 \sqsubseteq tt_1$. We may without loss of generality assume that $tt_1 \sqsubseteq tt_2$ so that $tt = tt_2$. It is then straight-forward that $\exists K : kenv \vdash_{TML} tt : K$.

If dt is X_i, we must have $kenv_1(X_i) \leq kenv_2(X_i)$ or $kenv_2(X_i) \leq kenv_1(X_i)$. We may without loss of generality assume that $kenv_1(X_i) \leq kenv_2(X_i)$ so that $kenv(X_i) = kenv_2(X_i)$. It is then straight-forward that $\exists K : kenv \vdash_{TML} tt : K$.

If dt is $dt' \times dt''$ we must consider four combinations of tt_1 and tt_2.

If $tt_1 = tt_1' \times tt_1''$ and $tt_2 = tt_2' \times tt_2''$, then we have $kenv_1 \vdash tt_1' : r$, $kenv_1 \vdash tt_1'' : r$, $kenv_2 \vdash tt_2' : r$, and $kenv_2 \vdash tt_2'' : r$. Furthermore, tt must have the form $tt' \times tt''$ and by the induction hypothesis $\exists K : kenv \vdash tt' : K$ and $\exists K : kenv \vdash tt'' : K$. We may strengthen this to $kenv \vdash tt' : r$ and $kenv \vdash tt'' : r$. To see this suppose that $\neg kenv \vdash tt' : r$. Then $tt' \neq \underline{\tau}(tt')$ or some X_i that is free in dt' has $kenv(X_i) = c$. However, $tt_1' = \underline{\tau}(tt_1')$ and $tt_2' = \underline{\tau}(tt_2')$ and for all X_i that are free in dt' do we have $kenv_1(X_i) = r$ and $kenv_2(X_i) = r$. Hence the assumption of $\neg kenv \vdash tt' : r$ contradicts the definition of $kenv|tt$. It then follows that $kenv \vdash tt : r$.

Turning to the second combination we consider the case where $tt_1 = tt'_1 \overline{\times} tt''_1$ and $tt_2 = tt'_2 \overline{\times} tt''_2$. As before we have $kenv \vdash tt'_1 : c$, $kenv \vdash tt'_2 : c$, $kenv \vdash tt''_1 : c$, $kenv \vdash tt''_2 : c$, $\exists K : kenv \vdash tt' : K$ and $\exists K : kenv \vdash tt'' : K$ where $tt = tt' \overline{\times} tt''$. As before we may strengthen this to $kenv \vdash tt' : c$ and $kenv \vdash tt'' : c$ so that $kenv \vdash tt : c$. In the third combination we let $tt_1 = tt'_1 \underline{\times} tt''_1$ and $tt_2 = tt'_2 \overline{\times} tt''_2$. We then have $kenv \vdash tt'_1 : r$, $kenv \vdash tt'_2 : c$, $kenv \vdash tt''_1 : r$, $kenv \vdash tt''_2 : c$, $\exists K : kenv \vdash tt' : K$ and $\exists K : kenv \vdash tt'' : K$, where $tt = tt' \overline{\times} tt''$. We may strengthen this to $kenv \vdash tt' : c$ and $kenv \vdash tt'' : c$. It then follows that $kenv \vdash tt : c$. The fourth combination where $tt_1 = tt'_1 \overline{\times} tt''_1$ and $tt_2 = tt'_2 \underline{\times} tt''_2$ is similar.

If dt is $dt' + dt''$ the proof is analogous.

If dt is $dt' \to dt''$, the proof is also analogous as the possibility that $kenv \vdash tt' \underline{\to} tt'' : c$ does not complicate matters.

If dt is $recX_i.dt'$, we shall consider four combinations of tt_1 and tt_2. If $tt_1 = \underline{rec}X_i.ll'_1$ and $tt_2 = \underline{rec}X_i.tt'_2$, then tt will have the form $\underline{rec}X_i.tt'$. By the induction hypothesis we have $kenv_1[r/X_i] \vdash tt'_1 : r$, $kenv_2[r/X_i] \vdash tt'_2 : r$, and $\exists K : kenv[r/X_i] \vdash tt' : K$. We may strengthen this to $kenv[r/X_i] \vdash tt' : r$. It then follows that $kenv \vdash tt : r$. For our second combination we consider $tt_1 = \overline{rec}X_i.tt'_1$ and $tt_2 = \overline{rec}X_i.tt'_2$. Then tt has the form $\overline{rec}X_i.tt'$ and by the induction hypothesis we have $kenv_1[c/X_i] \vdash tt'_1 : c$, $kenv_2[c/X_i] \vdash tt'_2 : c$, and $\exists K : kenv[c/X_i] \vdash tt' : K$. We may strengthen this to $kenv[c/X_i] \vdash tt' : c$. It then follows that $kenv \vdash tt : c$. For our third combination we consider $tt_1 = \underline{rec}X_i.tt'_1$ and $tt_2 = \overline{rec}X_i.tt'_2$ where tt has the form $\overline{rec}X_i.tt'$. By the induction hypothesis we have $kenv_1[r/X_i] \vdash tt'_1 : r$, $kenv_2[c/X_i] \vdash tt'_2 : c$, and $\exists K : kenv[c/X_i] \vdash tt' : K$. We may strengthen this to $kenv[c/X_i] \vdash tt' : c$ from which $kenv \vdash tt : c$ follows. The last combination where $tt_1 = \overline{rec}X_i.tt'_1$ and $tt_2 = \underline{rec}X_i.tt'_2$ may be handled similarly. $\square$

Theorem 3.10 If $tenv \vdash_{DML} de : dt$, then the set $\omega_{wf}^{-1}(tenv|de : dt)$ is a complete lattice under $\sqsubseteq$ and the binary upper bound operator $\sqcup$ satisfies that if $(tenv'|te' : tt') = (tenv_1|te_1 : tt_1) \sqcup (tenv_2|te_2 : tt_2)$ then

$$\Xi(te') = \Xi(te_1) \vee \Xi(te_2)$$

$$tt' = tt_1 \sqcup tt_2$$

$$dom(tenv') = dom(tenv) \wedge \forall x_i \in dom(tenv) : tenv'(x_i) = tenv_1(x_i) \sqcup tenv_2(x_i)$$

Proof. By Fact 3.8 the set $\omega_{wf}^{-1}(tenv|de : dt)$ contains $(\underline{\tau} \circ tenv|\underline{\varepsilon}(de) : \underline{\tau}(dt))$, and it is straight-forward to see that this is the least element. Since $\omega_{wf}^{-1}(tenv|de : dt)$ is finite, the existence of binary least upper bounds then will ensure that $\omega_{wf}^{-1}(tenv|de : dt)$ is a complete lattice. Our approach will therefore be to consider $(tenv_1|te_1 : tt_1)$ and $(tenv_2|te_2 : tt_2)$ in $\omega_{wf}^{-1}(tenv|de : dt)$ and to *define* the not necessarily well-formed formula $(tenv'|te' : tt')$ by the demands that

$$\varepsilon(te') = de$$

$$\Xi(te') = \Xi(te_1) \ \vee \ \Xi(te_2)$$

$$tt' = tt_1 \ \sqcup \ tt_2$$

$$dom(tenv') = dom(tenv)$$

$$\forall x_i \in dom(tenv) : tenv'(x_i) = tenv_1(x_i) \ \sqcup \ tenv_2(x_i)$$

(By Lemma 3.5 it is straight-forward to verify that this defines a unique formula.) To prove the Theorem it therefore suffices to show that $(tenv'|te' : tt')$ is well-formed, i.e. $tenv' \vdash_{TML} te' : tt'$. The proof of this will be by structural induction on de.

If de is $f_i[dt]$, then it follows by Lemma 3.5 that $te' = f_i[tt']$. It also follows that $\exists K : \varnothing \vdash tt' : K$ so to establish that $tenv' \vdash_{TML} te' : tt'$ it suffices to assume that $tt' \in T_i$.

If de is (de_1, de_2), then te_1 must be of the form (te_{11}, te_{12}) or $\overline{(te_{11}, te_{12})}$, and similarly te_2 must be of the form (te_{21}, te_{22}) or $\overline{(te_{21}, te_{22})}$. It follows that there are four combinations to consider and let the first one be $te_1 = (te_{11}, te_{12})$ and $te_2 = (te_{21}, te_{22})$. Then $te' = (te_1', te_2')$ where $te_1' = te_{11} \ \sqcup \ te_{21}$ and $te_2' = te_{12} \ \sqcup \ te_{22}$. Since $(tenv_1|te_1 : tt_1)$ and $(tenv_2|te_2 : tt_2)$ are well-formed, we may write $tt_1 = tt_{11} \times tt_{12}$ and $tt_2 = tt_{21} \times tt_{22}$ and note that $\varnothing \vdash tt_{11} : r$, $\varnothing \vdash tt_{12} : r$, $\varnothing \vdash tt_{21} : r$, and $\varnothing \vdash tt_{22} : r$. It follows that $\varnothing \vdash tt_{11} \ \sqcup \ tt_{21} : r$ and $\varnothing \vdash tt_{12} \ \sqcup \ tt_{22} : r$ and since $tt' = (tt_{11} \ \sqcup \ tt_{21}) \times (tt_{12} \ \sqcup \ tt_{22})$ well-formedness of $(tenv'|te' : tt')$ follows by the induction hypothesis which asserts that $(tenv'|te_1' : tt_{11} \sqcup tt_{21})$ and $(tenv'|te_2' : tt_{12} \sqcup tt_{22})$ are well-formed. As the second combination let $te_1 = \overline{(te_{11}, te_{12})}$ and $te_2 = \overline{(te_{21}, te_{22})}$. Then $te' = \overline{(te_{11} \sqcup te_{21}, te_{12} \sqcup te_{22})}$ and $tt' = (tt_{11} \sqcup tt_{21}) \ \overline{\times} \ (tt_{12} \sqcup tt_{22})$ where $tt_1 = tt_{11} \ \overline{\times} \ tt_{12}$ and $tt_2 = tt_{21} \ \overline{\times} \ tt_{22}$. To show the well-formedness of $(tenv'|te' : tt')$ it suffices by the induction hypothesis to show that $\varnothing \vdash tt_{11} \ \sqcup \ tt_{21} : c$ and $\varnothing \vdash tt_{12} \ \sqcup \ tt_{22} : c$. This result follows much as before (using the characterization given in the proof of Lemma 3.5 for when $\varnothing \vdash \ldots : c$). As the third combination we take $te_1 = (te_{11}, te_{12})$ and $te_2 = \overline{(te_{21}, te_{22})}$. Then $te' = \overline{(te_{11} \ \sqcup \ te_{21}, te_{12} \ \sqcup \ te_{22})}$ and $tt' = (tt_{11} \ \sqcup \ tt_{21}) \ \overline{\times} \ (tt_{12} \ \sqcup \ tt_{22})$ where $tt_1 = tt_{11} \times tt_{12}$ and $tt_2 = tt_{21} \ \overline{\times} \ tt_{22}$. Again it suffices by the induction hypothesis to show that $\varnothing \vdash tt_{11} \sqcup tt_{21} : c$ and $\varnothing \vdash tt_{12} \sqcup tt_{22} : c$, and this follows because $tt_{11} \sqcup tt_{21} = tt_{21}$ and $tt_{12} \sqcup tt_{22} = tt_{22}$. The argument for the fourth combination is similar.

If de is $de_1 \!\downarrow\! i$, we again have four combinations to consider. The proof follows the lines of the previous case, but is slightly easier because the relevant inference rules in Table 2 have the same side conditions as the corresponding inference rules in Table 1. So we only treat the more interesting combination where $te_1 = te_{11} \!\downarrow\! i$ and $te_2 = te_{21} \overline{\downarrow} i$. Then $tenv_1 \vdash te_{11} : tt_{11} \times tt_{12}$ and $tenv_2 \vdash te_{21} : tt_{21} \ \overline{\times} \ tt_{22}$ for suitable types tt_{jk}. By the induction hypothesis $tenv \vdash (te_{11} \ \sqcup \ te_{21}) : tt_1' \ \overline{\times} \ tt_2'$, and the result follows by application of the relevant rule in Table 2.

If de is $in_i[dt]de_1$, there are type dt_1 and dt_2 such that $dt = dt_1 + dt_2$. Of the four combinations to consider we treat the one with $te_1 = \underline{in_i}[tt_1]te_{11}$ and $te_2 = \overline{in_i}[tt_2]te_{21}$. Then we may write $tt_1 = tt_{11} \pm tt_{12}$ and $tt_2 = tt_{21} \mp tt_{22}$, and we have $te' = \overline{in}_i[tt'](te_{11} \sqcup te_{21})$ where $tt' = (tt_{11} \sqcup tt_{21}) \mp (tt_{12} \sqcup tt_{22})$. By the induction hypothesis it suffices to show that $\emptyset \vdash tt_{11} \sqcup tt_{21}$: c and $\emptyset \vdash tt_{12} \sqcup tt_{22} : c$ and as usual this follows from the characterization of $\emptyset \vdash \ldots : c$ in the proof of Lemma 3.5.

If de is $is_i \, de_1$, the proof is similar.

If de is $out_i \, de_1$, the proof is similar.

If de is $\lambda x_i[dt_0].de_1$, then there is dt_1 such that $dt = dt_0 \to dt_1$. Of the four combinations to consider we treat the one where $te_1 = \underline{\lambda} x_i[tt_{10}].te_{11}$ and $te_2 = \overline{\lambda} x_i[tt_{20}].te_{21}$. There exists types tt_{11} and tt_{21} such that $tt_1 = tt_{10} \underline{\to} tt_{11}$ and $tt_2 = tt_{20} \overline{\to} tt_{21}$. By the well-formedness of $(tenv_1|te_1 : tt_1)$ and $(tenv_2|te_2 : tt_2)$ we have

$$tenv_1[tt_{10}/x_i] \vdash te_{11} : tt_{11}$$

$$tenv_2[tt_{20}/x_i] \vdash te_{21} : tt_{21}$$

By the induction hypothesis it follows that

$$tenv[tt_0'/x_i] \vdash te_1' : tt_1'$$

where $tt_0' = tt_{10} \sqcup tt_{20}$, $te_1' = te_{11} \sqcup te_{21}$, $tt_1' = tt_{11} \sqcup tt_{21}$, and $tt' = tt_0' \overline{\to} tt_1'$. To establish the desired

$$tenv' \vdash \overline{\lambda} x_i[tt_0'].te_1' : tt_0' \overline{\to} tt_1'$$

it therefore suffices to show that $\emptyset \vdash tt_0' : c$ and $\emptyset \vdash tt_1' : c$, and this follows from $\emptyset \vdash tt_{20} : c$ and $\emptyset \vdash tt_{21} : c$.

If de is $de_1 \cdot de_2$, there again are four combinations to consider, and we consider the one where $te_1 = te_{11} \underline{\cdot} te_{12}$ and $te_2 = te_{21} \overline{\cdot} te_{22}$. By the well-formedness of $(tenv_1|te_1 : tt_1)$ and $(tenv_2|te_2 : tt_2)$ there are types tt_{10} and tt_{20} such that

$$tenv_1 \vdash te_{11} : tt_{10} \underline{\to} tt_1 \quad tenv_1 \vdash te_{12} : tt_{10}$$

$$tenv_2 \vdash te_{21} : tt_{20} \overline{\to} tt_2 \quad tenv_2 \vdash te_{22} : tt_{20}$$

By the induction hypothesis we have

$$tenv' \vdash te_1' : tt_0' \overline{\to} tt' \quad tenv' \vdash te_2' : tt_0'$$

where $te_1' = te_{11} \sqcup te_{21}$, $tt_0' = tt_{10} \sqcup tt_{20}$, and $te_2' = te_{12} \sqcup te_{22}$. Since te' is $te_1' \cdot te_2'$, the result then easily follows.

If de is x_i, we have $tenv'(x_i) = tenv_1(x_i) \sqcup tenv_2(x_i) = tt_1 \sqcup tt_2 = tt'$, and the result is immediate.

If de is $mkrec[dt]de_1$, then there is X_i and dt_1 such that $dt = \widehat{recX_i.dt_1}$. We consider the combination where $te_1 = mkrec[tt_1]te_{11}$ and $te_2 = \overline{mkrec}[tt_2]te_{21}$ and note that $tt_1 = recX_i.tt_{10}$ and $tt_2 = \overline{rec}X_i.tt_{20}$ for suitable tt_{10} and tt_{20}. By the well-formedness of $(tenv_1|te_1 : tt_1)$ and $(tenv_2|te_2 : tt_2)$ we have

$$tenv_1 \vdash te_{11} : tt_{10}[tt_1/X_i]$$

$$tenv_2 \vdash te_{21} : tt_{20}[tt_2/X_i]$$

so that by the induction hypothesis

$$tenv' \vdash te_1' : tt_0'[tt'/X_i]$$

where $te' = \overline{mkrec}[tt']te_1'$ and $tt' = \overline{rec}X_i.tt_0'$. To prove the desired result

$$tenv' \vdash te' : tt'$$

it suffices to show that $\emptyset \vdash tt' : c$ and this follows from $\emptyset \vdash tt_2 : c$.

If de is $unrec\ de_1$, the proof is similar.

If de is $fix[dt]de_1$, we consider the combination where $te_1 = \underline{fix}[tt_1]te_{11}$ and $te_2 = \overline{fix}[tt_2]te_{21}$. By the well-formedness assumption we have

$$tenv_1 \vdash te_{11} : tt_1 \xrightarrow{} tt_1$$

$$tenv_2 \vdash te_{21} : tt_2 \Rightarrow tt_2$$

so that by the induction hypothesis

$$tenv \vdash te_1' : tt' \Rightarrow tt'$$

where $te' = \overline{fix}[tt']te_1'$. The desired result then follows by application of the inference rule for $\overline{fix}$.

If de is $de_1 \rightarrow de_2, de_3$, we consider the combination where $te_1 = te_{11} \xrightarrow{} te_{12}, te_{13}$ and $te_2 = te_{21} \Rightarrow te_{22}, te_{23}$. We may write $te' = te_1' \Rightarrow te_2', te_3'$, and the desired result follows from the induction hypothesis since $tenv' \vdash te_1' : \overline{A}_{bool}$ follows from $tenv_2 \vdash te_{21} : \overline{A}_{bool}$.   □

Partial Evaluation and Mixed Computation
D. Bjørner, A.P. Ershov and N.D. Jones (Editors)
Elsevier Science Publishers B.V. (North-Holland)
© IFIP, 1988

IMPLEMENTATION OF CONTROLLED MIXED COMPUTATION IN SYSTEM FOR AUTOMATIC DEVELOPMENT OF LANGUAGE-ORIENTED PARSERS

Boris N. OSTROVSKI

Altai Polytechnic Institute
Barnaul, USSR

1. INTRODUCTION

The key problem of mixed computation may be formulated as follows:

Let $P(x_1,...,x_n)$ be a program in algorithmic language L, if parameter x_1 is bounded by $a_1,...,$ parameter x_m is bounded by a_m ($m<n$), then a new program $P_{a1...am}(x_{m+1},...,x_n)$ must be constructed so that for arbitrary admissible values $b_{m+1},...,b_n$ of parameters $x_{m+1},...,x_n$ we have

$$P(a_1,...,a_m,b_{m+1},...,b_n) = P_{a1...am}(b_{m+1}...b_n)$$

A systematic development process of program $P_{a1...am}$ from program P and fixed values $a_1,...,a_m$ of its parameters is called mixed computation and program $P_{a1...am}$ itself we call a residual program. The residual program $P_{a1...am}$ is a specialization of program P to a narrowed domain of its application. Of course, $P_{a1...am}$ is more efficient than program P (by speed) because some of P's fragments by means of partial execution transform to program $P_{a1...am}$ in a simplified form or removed from P altogether.

In the framework of the key mixed computation problem the task of language-oriented parsing development is formulated as follows:

Let G be a class of grammars over alphabet T of terminal symbols. A program A(g,s) is called a universal parser for class G if, for any grammar $g \in G$ and source string $s \in T_*$, it returns either parsing of s in grammar g or a message of the error (inacceptability of s in grammar g). If argument g in A(g,s) is bounded by specific grammar $g_0 \in G$ and the program $A(g_0,s)$ is subjected to mixed computation, we get the residual program $A_{g0}(s)$ which further is supposed to be called a language-oriented parser.

Our research is devoted to the development of the mechanism of controlled mixed computation [8,13] to obtain efficient language-oriented parsers.

2. UNIVERSAL PARSERS

We outline a large class of universal parsers which encompasses most of used in practice parsing schemes for real programming languages. These parsers form the domain, in the framework of which we investigate the specializing possibilities of mixed computation.

2.1. Left and Right Parsing

The most widespread strategies of syntactic analysis are left and right parsing.

In the process of left parsing of source string $w \in T^*$ in grammar $G = \langle N, T, P, S \rangle$ there creates a sequence of left sentential forms $l_0, \ldots, l_n$ such that
  1. $l_0 = S$ (S is an axiom of grammar G);
  2. $l_i = x_i A_i \beta_i$, $l_{i+1} = x_i \alpha_i \beta_i$, $x_i \in T^*$, $A_i \to \alpha_i \in P$, $0 <= i < n$;
  3. $l_n = w$.

The key point of left parsing is choice of production by means of which in every left sentential form we realize a substitution (unfolding) the most left nonterminal symbol by the right hand side of production.

In the process of right parsing of source string $w \in T^*$ in grammar $G = (N, T, P, S)$ there creates a sequence of right sentential forms $r_0, r_1, \ldots, r_k$ such that
  1. $r_0 = w$;
  2. $r_i = \beta_i \alpha_i x_i$, $r_{i+1} = \beta_i A_i x_i$, $x_i \in T^*$, $A_i \to \alpha_i \in P$, $0 <= i < k$
       (α_i is called a handle of r_i);
  3. $r_k = S$ (S is an axiom of grammar G).

The key point of right parsing is to define the handle of right sentential form and substitute it (the handle) for the nonterminal symbol. Every substitution (reduction) takes place in accordance with the production from P where right hand side coincides with a handle of right sentential form and its left hand side is that nonterminal symbol to which this handle reduces itself.

Naturally, a sequence of productions used during left (or right) syntactic analysis characterizes the parsing unambiguously, therefore it is called a left (or right) parsing.

2.2. Abstract processor of parsing

Modelling of parsing is accomplished with the help of the DPD-transformer [1]. The latter consists of
    - an input tape upon which the string to be parsed is placed;
    - a finite control (a reading head);
    - a pushdown stack;
    - an output tape to write left or right parsing.

The system of commands drives the parser behaviour:
1. every step of parsing is to execute the command from the system, that is
    - to update the current parsing state;
    - to change contents of the stack;
    - to shift the reading head.
2. the choice of commands depends on the top of the stack and on the current state/the input symbol.

2.2.1. Left Parsers

In any current moment of left parsing of input string $w \in T^*$ in grammar G the concatenation of the part of input string w which has been read and contents of the stack (top is located to the left) is the left sentential form. The system of commands for left parsers consists of commands of three sorts: COMPARE, UNFOLD and COMBINED-UNFOLD. The meaning of these commands is explained in TABLE 1.

TABLE 1. Structure of Left Parsing Commands

Command	Command Code	Command meaning
COMPARE	C	The top is popped and the reading head is shifted one symbol right
UNFOLD	UN(A->α)	The top is substituted for α, production A->α is accumulated on the output tape
COMBINED-UNFOLD	CUN(A->aα)	The top is substituted for α, production A->aα is accumulated on the output tape and reading head is shifted

COMPARE command is executed iff the terminal symbol is located at the top of the stack.

UNFOLD/COMBINED-UNFOLD command is executed iff the top of the stack is the nonterminal symbol.

The LL(0)-, Regular, Simple, Weakly Divisible and LL(1)-grammars are processed by means of left parsers. There are special program constructors for all above-mentioned classes of grammars which generate a system of left parsing commands for every grammar from these classes.

2.2.2. Right Parsers

If we disengage ourselves from technical details we must state that at any given time of right parsing of input string $w \in T^*$ in grammar G the concatenation of stack contents (top is located to the right) and unreading part of input string w will represent a right sentential form. The system of right parsing commands contains four-type commands: SHIFT, POP, SUBSTITUTE and PUSH. The meaning of these commands is explained in TABLE 2.

SHIFT command is executed as the reading head hasn't achieved the right boundary of the handle yet.

POP command executes the search of the left boundary of the handle by means of popping symbols from the stack.

SUBSTITUTE command takes place if the left boundary of the handle is in the top of the stack.

PUSH command is executed after we have reached the left boundary.

In this paper we regard two widely spread families of the grammar classes processed by means of right parsing: Precedence Grammars (namely: Suffix-Free [12], Simple, Weak and Simple Mixed-Strategy Precedence Grammars [1]) and Knuth's Grammars (namely: LR(0)-, SLR(1)-, LALR(1)- and LR(1)-Grammars). The systems of commands

formed by appropriate grammar constructors allow to choise exactly
one of the possible commands.

TABLE 2. Structure of Right Parsing Commands

Command	Command Code	Command meaning
SHIFT	S(a)	Symbol "a" is pushed onto stack and the reading head is shifted one symbol right
POP	P(q)	The top is popped from the stack and the state transforms to q
SUBSTITUTE	St(A->α)	The top is substituted for symbol A and procedure A->α is accumulated on the output tape
PUSH	Ph(A->α)	Symbol "A" is pushed onto the stack and production A->α is accumulated on the output tape

2.3. Adaptation of Universal Parsers for the Mixed Computation

As is known, the traditional implementation of the above universal
parsers calls for a step-by-step execution of definite parsing
commands in accordance with the iterative scheme (see FIGURE 1).

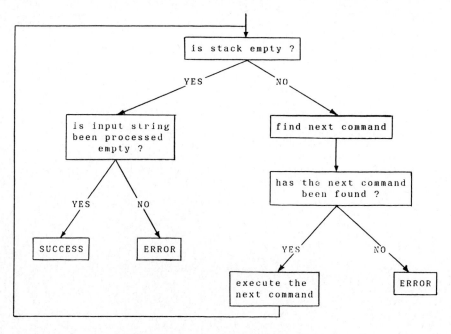

FIGURE 1. Scheme of Parser Behavior

Unfortunately, in the framework of this implementation, mixed computation can't use complete knowledge of the concrete system of commands (in accordance with a fixed grammar) to obtain efficient language-oriented parsers. Therefore we transform universal parsers to the standard form convenient for execution of mixed computation.

In our research we consider that the left parsers contain one recursive procedure R and the right parsers contain two recurcive procedures P and Q. All these procedures have one parameter which takes stack symbols as actual parameters. The conventional mechanism of handling for R-, P- and Q-calls is equivalent to the evident stack application in traditional parser implementations. Correspondence between these two parser versions (traditional and ours) is described in Table 3.

TABLE 3. Procedure Simulation of Parsing Commands

Command code	Procedure version of Command
C	Read
$UF(A\text{->}X_1...X_n)$	$Write(A\text{-->}X_1...X_n);\ R(X_1);...R(X_n)$
$CUF(A\text{->}aX_1...X_n)$	$Read;\ Write(A\text{->}aX_1...X_n);\ R(X_1);...R(X_n)$
$S(a)$	$Read;\ P(a);\ Q(X)$
$P(q)$	$k:=q$
$St(A\text{->}\alpha)$	$Write(A\text{->}\alpha);\ P(A)$
$Ph(A\text{->}\alpha)$	$Write(A\text{->}\alpha);\ P(A);\ Q(X)$

$Write(A\text{->}\alpha)$ is a statement for writing production $A\text{->}\alpha$ on the output tape,

Read   is a statement for shifting the reading head one symbol right,

k   is a state variable,

X   is a current stack top

3. THE DSP LANGUAGE AND ITS TRANSFORMATIONAL SEMANTICS

Taking the Pascal language [14] as a basis we have singled out a structured dialect of the language which is both convenient for a precise and effective programming of parsers and simple enough to keep mixed computation algorithms free of unnecessary details. We call the subset a DSP language (Description of Syntactic Parser).

3.1. THE DSP LANGUAGE

The DSP program consists of a heading (namely: program name, names of input and output files) and a body (block).

A block contains a declaration list (for named objects: constants, variables and procedures) and statement sequence.

The DSP- constants and variables are plain integers and structured objects: vectors and records (without variants). Initialization of named constant and variables is carried out by constant expressions or loading operations (from input files).

Procedure declarations consist of a heading (name and parameters) and a body (block). Parameters are plain integers called by value. Results are returned by assigment to global variables.

Basic statements are assigment, procedure calls, reads/writes, message prints and halts.

Composite statements are compound statements, if-statements and while-loops.

3.2. Transformational Approach

We adopt the transformational approach to the description of both conventional and mixed computation. According to [2,4] a transformational semantics is described as a collection of joint program-data transformations.

During computation program data are stored in an environment. Initially, the environment consists of input/output files, a print media and procedure declarations. Every initialized block attaches to the environment (in stack mode) a section storing data which are local to that block.

For every transformation, conditions of its applicability to each program fragment and data are known and effectively checkable.

Program (or fragment) p with corresponding data d is fixed point of transformational rule t if t is inapplicable to $<p,d>$ or $t(<p,d>)=<p,d>$.

Every language semantics must describe, in some or another way, a process of program execution. For transformational semantics, this process is a sequence of nondeterministic attempts to apply each of the transformational rules that form the semantics to program and its data. This process is either infinite or converges to a fixed point. For a correct semantics, such point is a pair: the degenerate (empty) program and the date from which the program result can be easily retrieved.

Mixed computation semantics is introduced as an extension of the conventional semantics for incomplete data. It means that, in an environment, some variables may have the status of inaccessible (undefined) variables. Undefined variables narrow the scope of transformational rules. As a result, the fixed point is not a degenerate program; rather it forms a non-trivial residual program corresponding to the initial incomplete data.

Semantics of conventional and mixed computation is formed from transformations of two sorts: reductions and expansions.

Reductions implement computational steps: they remove or simplify a language construct and change the environment.

Expansions "unpack" a composite language construct and make its constituents available to subsequent transformations. They ussually make the program longer.

Mixed computation semantics for DSP language is constructed from

conventional computation semantics by addition of spesial reductions, called suspensions, and special expansions (for if-statements and procedure calls).

Suspensions are applied to accessible constant/variable declarations and statements, provided that conventional reductions are
inapplicable to these constructs. Suspensions don't change the
program fragment to which they are applicated; and the variables
which are contained within complete result of a corresponding
fragment [8] get undefined values.

Special expansion for an if-statement is called polyvariant execution [8] and is performed, provided that boolean condition can't
be reduced to a logical constant. This transformation allows to
carry out mixed computation within the branches by duplicating
current environment.

Special expansion for a procedure call is called a projection and
allows to specialize procedure P to a new procedure Q provided
that every call to procedure P with definite fixed values of some
actual parameters will be substituted for the call to procedure Q.

For more detailed information about conventional and mixed computation semantics of DSP language the reader is refered to [8].

3.3. Transformational Machine

A transformational machine is an abstract device intended to
formally describe processing of programs and their data. A memory
of the transformational machine consists of pairs: program fragments and their data. We call these pairs operating elements. The
transformational machine operates as follows.

Initially its memory contains the only operating element formed
from the original program and its date. Every next step of the
transformational machine is
  - to modify a suitable operating element, either
  - to create a new operating element, or
  - to delete some operating element.

Each step of transformational machine is driven by DSP language
semantics (of conventional or mixed computation) so that these
semantics solves
  - what operating element may be modified and what transforma-
    tion from DSP language semantics must be applicated, either
  - from which a new operating element may be created and by
    means of which transformation it must be obtained, or
  - what operating element may be deleted from the memory.

The process is iterative and is finished provided that the memory
consists of the only fixed point operating element. This element
is regarded by us a result of the transformational computation
over the original program and its data.

It should be noted that modification and deletion of operating
elements are performed by means of reductions and creation of a
new operating elements is carried out by means of expansions.

3.4. Mixed Computation Control

Practical application of mixed computation confronts with a fundamental contradiction between, on the one hand, a desire to make as
deep a computation on the available data as possible and, on the
other hand, the necessity to provide a guaranteed termination of
mixed computation and to prevent an excessive growth of the residual program.

Universal mixed computation schemes [5,6] solve the problem by
imposing restrictions on expansion applications. Our approach to
the solution is to arrange the process of mixed computation. This
arrangement is called a control and consists of three components:
  - partial determination of computation process;
  - addition of conversions (reverse schematic program transfor-
    mations) into mixed computation semantics;
  - and the fact that specialization is a polyphased process.

Mixed computation control is an algorithm of a choise of the most
acceptable transformation between possible ones in order to obtain
an effective residual program. We determine an order for the
application of transformations as follows:
  - if any current moment transformations t_1 and t_2 are applica-
    tions to fragments F_1 and F_2 ($F_1 \subset F_2$) respectively then we
    must execute transformation t_1;
  - if transformations t_1 and t_2 belong to mixed computation
    semantics, t_1 belongs to conventional computation semantics
    in addition, t_1 and t_2 are applicated to a fragment F (F
    isn't a procedure call or loop) Then we execute transforma-
    tion t_1.

To specify the control means to formulate conditions of applicability for different variants of transformations:
  - to handle procedure calls by open substitution, projection or
    suspension;
  - to handle if-statements by polyvariant execution or suspen-
    sion;
  - to handle loops by expansion or suspension.

Conversions added to mixed computation semantics may be split into
two clusters: CATALYSTS and OPTIMIZERS.

CATALYSTS are those conversions which are applicated before
expansions of if- statements or procedure calls and rise the
efficiency of its execution;

OPTIMIZERS are those conversions which improve the residual program proper.

The control divides the entire specialization process into phases.
In each phase a specific scheme of mixed computation is applied
with a fixed control for that phase. The design of the overall
strategy of the specialization, which prescribes conversions, number of phases choise of a mixed computation scheme, is a non-
formal problem that requires creativity (taking into consideration
special features of the processes under specialization).

4. THE SYSTEM FOR AUTOMATIC DEVELOPMENT OF LANGUAGE-ORIENTED PARSERS

Our approach to obtain specialized programs has been implemented in the form of an experimental system for the automatic development of language-oriented parsers (SADLOP). In this section we describe the overall organization of the system. SADLOP has been implemented in the Pascal language and runs on the NORD-100 computer.

Our system consists of two parts.

The first part is called syntactical and is intended for experiments with universal parsers which are used into various programming languages. This part prepares the necessary data for the second part.

The second part is called specialized and is intended for generating language-oriented parsers. It allows to objectively evaluate the perspective of mixed computation for specialization of universal parsers.

4.1. The Syntactical Part

In this paragraph we outline the general structure and actions of the SADLOP-syntactical part. Its scheme is represented in Figure 2.

The description of the test language is formulated on two levels. The lower (lexical) level allows to split a program text into portions called tokens. The upper (syntactical) level allows the syntactical structure of the language which is defined by means of a suitable context-free grammar. The language tokens are terminal symbols of this grammar.

4.1.1. The Lexical Level of a Test Programming Language

We distinguish four sorts of tokens:
- RESERVED-WORDS which are sequences of symbols with the emphasis as the first symbol and the blank as the last symbol;
- SIMPLE-SEPARATORS which consist of the only symbol different from the emphasis, inverted commas, the blank, the letter or digit;
- COMBINED-SEPARATORS which consist of two symbols different from the emphasis, inverted commas, the blank, the letter or the digit;
- BASED-TOKENS such as identifiers, strings, blanks, integers, reals and so on.

The special program called LEXICAL-CONSTRUCTOR transforms the lexica of the test programming language (defined by the token list) to a lexical table by coding the tokens with integer values. The token can be uniquely recovered by means of the token code and of the constructed lexical table.

Another special program called SCANNER processes an input string in the test programming language and the lexical table to a chain of token codes. This program runs as the finite transducer [1] and its result (contents of output tape) is passed to the universal parser program as an actual parameter.

Language Description

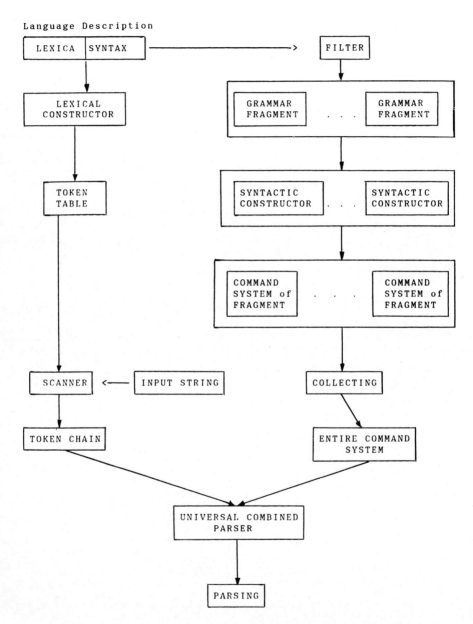

FIGURE 2. General Structure of SADLOP Syntactical Part

Although   our approach to a lexical description simplifies a   real
situation   taking   place in programming languages, however distinction   between our and real lexical form for   many   programming

languages is not very considerable. The main advantage of our method lies in the fact that it allows to construct the only lexical analyser for different programming languages.

Numeral characteristics of lexica for some languages are shown in Table 4.

TABLE 4. Example of lexical characteristics for some languages

Language	Reserved words	Simple separators	Combined separators	Based tokens
Algol-60	22	16	4	3
Snobol-4	4	20	1	4
Pascal	35	17	5	4

4.1.2. The Syntactical Level of a Test Programming Language

In order to make the test of mixed computation more severe, special care has been taken to make the universal parsers most efficient. To this end, the idea of a compound parsing (due to [10]) has been adopted. The essence of this idea is that a programming language grammar can always be fragmented in such a way that on some fragment a simpler parsing scheme can be applied. By partitioning the given grammar into a number of smaller parts we construct a corresponding parser for each part (using a suitable parsing constructor). After this operation we unite these individual parsers into a parser for entire grammar of the test language.

Every grammar fragment G' is a context-free grammar which may be obtained from given grammar $G=<N,T,P,S>$ provided that axiom S' (S' N) and quasiterminal set N' (N'$\subset$N) is defined in the following form $G'=<N-N'$, T$\cup$N',P',S'>, where P' contains only those productions from P left hand sides of which are not quasiterminal symbols or useless nonterminal symbols (in grammar G').

Partition $W=\{G_0,G_1,\ldots,G_n\}$ of given grammar G is called valid, provided that
 - the axiom of grammar G_0 coincides with the axiom of grammar G;
 - axioms of grammars cointained in W are disjoint;
 - for every quasiterminal symbol A from some grammar $G_i \in W$ there is grammar G_j the axiom of which coincides with A.

In our system there is a special procedure called FILTER which processes the given grammar and returns, as a result, the grammar list forming the valid partition.

The kernel of procedure FILTER is procedure COMPONENT. COMPONENT takes as a parameter some nonterminal symbol A of the given grammar and generates a definite grammar fragment with symbol A as an axiom. This grammar fragment contains a minimal number of productions sufficient for correct parsing by means of the simplest scheme mentioned above.

Procedure FILTER runs as follows. It builds an auxiliary list which consists of axioms of grammar fragments (marked and un-marked) forming the valid partition. Initially this auxiliary list contains the only unmarked symbol which is axiom of the given grammar. Then FILTER chooses arbitrary unmarked symbol A (if any) and generates grammar fragment G_A (with symbol A as an axiom). It is done by means of procedure COMPONENT and then added to the auxiliary list as unmarked symbols, those quasiterminal symbols of grammar G_A absent from this list. Symbol A is marked. FILTER is finished provided the auxiliary list consists only of marked symbols.

Numeral characteristics of the syntactical structure are shown in TABLE 5.

TABLE 5. Syntactic Characteristics for some Languages

	Languages								
	Algol-60			Snobol 4			Pascal		
	number of			number of			number of		
	frag ments	nonter minal sym bols	pro duc tions	frag ments	nonter minal sym bols	pro duc tions	frag ments	nonter minal sym bols	pro duc tions
LL(0)-				2	2	2	2	39	39
Regu- lar	3	3	6	6	6	12	20	20	40
Divi- sible	9	24	76	1	1	2			
Weakly divi- sible	6	6	30				4	4	8
LL(1)-				1	1	2	7	13	34
Suffix- Free				4	4	8	1	4	10
Simple Prece dence							2	4	10
LR(0)-				1	3	7			
SLR(1)-				1	23	55	5	61	100

4.2. The SADLOP Specialized Subsystem

The development of language-oriented parsers realized by the SADLOP specialized subsystem is divided in two stages.

During the first stage every grammar fragment together with suitable universal parser are subjected to mixed computation. Resulting residual programs are specialized parsers for individual grammar fragments of a test language.

During the second stage these fragments parsers are transformed into procedural form and united into language-oriented parser for the entire test language.

The mixed computation processor is the key component of the SADLOP specialized subsystem. Implementation of this processor is based on the transformation approach and the concept of mixed computation control.

According to transformational approach [2,4] mixed computation in DSP language is described as directed process of local program-data transformations. Every local transformation is defined by means of the appropriate procedure in implementation language (Pascal) and a set of these procedures forms transformational semantics of mixed computation in DSP language. The mechanism of activation of these procedures is based on the logic of a program being processed and state of its date. No special definition of this mechanism is required.

However some DSP construct (if-statements, loops, procedure calls) have different processing algorithms called variant transformations. For efficient use of these transformations we beforehand carry out the structural reorganization of of a program (by means of catalysts). Besides, obtained residual program is accessible for various optimizing transformations. All these transformations are described in procedural form and added to mixed computation semantics. Mixed computation semantics together with the special algorithm to choose variant transformations and conversions (catalysts and optimizers) is called controlled mixed computation (CMC).

In this section overall scheme of CMC in DSP language is described and our approach to program implementation of CMC (to obtain efficient language-oriented parsers) is formulated.

During mixed computation as well as conventional computation the program-data processing is divided into three stages: scanning, syntax directed translation and interpretation.

4.2.1. Scanning

Scanning is carried out in order check a correctness of program text being processed and to compress it by means of reducing symbol chains to appropriate tokens. The scanner for DSP language is an extended version of universal scanner which has been described above. This extensions is related to the processing of the based tokens and to construction of symbol and string tables.

4.2.2. Syntax Directed Translation

The purpose of translation is to transform a token chain formed by the scanner into structural form convenient to the following interpretation. This structural form of the program text resulted

from translation represents the abstract syntax tree and provides:
- compressed representation of programs to be processed;
- efficient allocation of main memory for further interpretation;
- obtaining structural listings of every program fragment and every program as a whole.

In our implementation the main memory intended for storage of processed programs is divided into some working domains. Most of this memory is alloted for statements (about 20K) and expressions (about 12K). Object code generated by the translator is formed as a by-product of parsing in the DSP language. DSP-translator processes only a small core (expressions) in Knuth's manner while the main body of DSP language it processes in LL-manner.

4.2.3. Interpretation

Interpretation of object code accompanied by obtaining a residual program is the main function of the specialized subsystem. The interpreter of the DSP language is the program version (in implementation language Pascal-NORD-100) of DSP transformational semantics. In our implementation DSP-constructs are handled by the interpreter in their textual order in the program. The choosing algorithm of variant transformations and conversions (control) described in the implementation language is inserted into the program of the interpreter.

The key items of program implementation of mixed computation in the DSP language should be noted:

1. Data Structure. Input and output data are stored in input and output files of the implementation language respectively. Every DSP program hasn't more than five input and/or output files. Values of simple data and structural data together with access information are stored in working domain which occupies about 2K. In order to reduce memory used during expansions of procedure calls and if-statements (for data copying and modification) we construct an auxiliary working domain. This domain occupies about 0.1K and is used for copying and modifying of those part of local date which ensures correct mixed computation. The allocation mechanism of this auxiliary working domain has a stack nature.

2. Choise and Modification of Local Data. The interpreter contains the special function (called ADDRESS) which returns address of memory where lies the current value of a constant/variable.

3. Processing of Program Constructs. Program constructs are handled during two stages:
   - pre-execution reduces program constructs to canonical forms by means of a substitution of appropriate expressions by their current values;
   - post-execution is applied to a program construct as a whole (after pre-execution) and completes its processing.

   For example, in the case of if-statement s we have
   pre-execution of s is that the conditional expression from s reduced;
   post-execution of s is that s is handled by means of the reduction (to such or another branch) provided that condi-

tional expression from s is a logical constant and by means of
the polyvariant execution or suspension otherwise

4. The Main Memory Allocation. DSP program and its data are stored
   in the main memory (occupying about 40K) and divided into
   several working domains. Every working domain is a vector and
   each element of the vector has a specific structure corresponding to appropriate program-data construct. During mixed
   computation these elements are created, modified and deleted
   from the memory. We use the same allocation mechanism for all
   working domains. Every working domain is divided into three
   subdomains (see FIGURE 3):
   - Information SubDomain (ISD) consists of elements which rep-
     resent program-data fragments to be processed;
   - Free SubDomain (FSD) consists of elements formerly created
     during mixed computation and then deleted from ISD;
   - Clear SubDomain (CSD) consists of elements not used for
     representation of program-data fragments.

   FSD has a list structure and CSD elements are successively
   stored at the memory. FSD and CSD have pointers to the head of
   the list and first element of CSD, respectively. Creating a
   new program-data fragment we store it into the head element of
   appropriate FSD (provided that FSD is not empty) or into the
   first element of the appropriate CSD, otherwise. Deleting a
   program-data fragment we append it to the appropriate FSD as a
   new head element. CREAT and DELETE operations require a corresponding modification of pointers to the FSD and/or CSD.

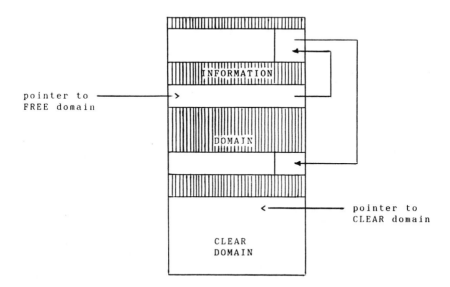

FIGURE 3. Structure of Working Domain

5. Mixed Computation Control. Polyphase nature of the interpretation ensures a possibility to obtain efficient residual prog-

rams. During each interpretation phase the entire program is processed. Modifying the control between successive phase we step by step generate more and more efficient residual programs. In the framework of this approach we realize profound mixed computation algorithms by means of a rather simple methods: we introduce into interpretation program so called control variables whose particular values are responsible for application of variant transformations and conversions.

The following conversions are used at various phases of the specialization process.

1. CODE MOVE IN

$$\text{if } R \text{ then } S_1 \text{ else } S_2 \text{ fi } ; S$$

$$\text{if } R \text{ then } S_1 ; S \text{ else } S_2 ; S \text{ fi}$$

2. FLIP-FLOP

$$\text{if } E_1 <> E_2 \text{ then } S_1 \text{ else } S_2 \text{ fi}$$

$$\text{if } E_1 = E_2 \text{ then } S_2 \text{ else } S_1 \text{ fi}$$

3. TAIL-RECURSION FACTORIZATION

$$\ldots P \ldots \text{ where proc } P = \\ \text{begin} \\ \text{if } R \text{ then } S_1; P \text{ else } S_2 \text{ fi} \\ \text{end}$$

$$\ldots P'; S_2 \ldots \text{ where proc } P' = \\ \text{begin} \\ \text{if } R \text{ then } S_1; P' \text{ fi} \\ \text{end}$$

4. PROCEDURE PAIRING

$$\ldots P_1; P_2 \ldots \text{ where proc } P_1 = \text{begin } S_1 \text{ end}, \\ \text{proc } P_2 = \text{begin } S_2 \text{ end}$$

$$\ldots P \ldots \text{ where proc } P = \text{begin } S_1; S_2 \text{ end}$$

5. CODE MOVE OUT (inverse to 1)

6. COMMON CODE ELIMINATION

$$\ldots P_1 \ldots P_2 \ldots \text{ where proc } P_1 = \text{begin } S \text{ end}, \\ \text{proc } P_2 = \text{begin } S \text{ end}$$

$$\ldots P \ldots P \ldots \text{ where proc } P = \text{begin } S \text{ end}$$

7. PROCEDURING

    ... S ...

     ... P ...   where <u>proc</u> P = <u>begin</u> S <u>end</u>

8. TAIL-RECURSION LOOPING

    ... P ... where <u>proc</u> P = <u>begin</u> <u>if</u> R <u>then</u> S; P <u>fi</u> <u>end</u>

       <u>while</u> R <u>do</u> S <u>od</u>

Interpreter generates left language-oriented parsers in one phase and uses the following control:

1. <u>Variant transformations</u>: loops are expanded; if-ststements are executed polyvariantly; procedures are projected.
2. <u>Catalyzers</u>: code move in; flip-flop.
3. <u>Optimizations</u>: code move out; proceduring; common code elimination; tail-recursion looping.

Our system generates right language-oriented parsers in three phases and uses the following control:

FIRST PHASE

1. <u>Variant transformations</u>: loops are expanded; if-statements are executed polyvariantly; procedures are projected.
2. <u>Catalyzers</u>: code move in; flip-flop.
3. <u>Optimizations</u>: common code elimination; code move out.

SECOND PHASE

1. <u>Variant transformations</u>: loops are reduced; if-statements are executed polyvariantly; procedures are projected.
2. <u>Catalyzers</u>: code move in; tail-recursion factorization.
3. <u>Optimizations</u>: code move out; common code elimination; proceduring.

THIRD PHASE

1. <u>Variant transformations</u>: loops are reduced; if-statements are executed polyvariantly; procedures are projected.
2. <u>Catalyzers</u>: code move in; tail-recursion factorization; procedure pairing.
3. <u>Optimizations</u>: code move out; common code elimination; proceduring; tail-recursion looping.

The system described above (SADLOP) has been used for the development of Algol-60 [11], Snobol-4 [3] and Pascal [14] parsers. The results of the computational experiments are given in Table 6. The total size of the system is about 12000 Pascal lines.

TABLE 6. Comparison of the Efficiency of Parsers

Language	Version	Parser size (in sourse code lines)	Ratio	Average parsing speed	Average speed-up ratio
Algol-60	language-oriented	1386	6.93	5036	2.14
	universal	200		2357	
Snobol-4	language-oriented	332	0.64	5297	3.68
	universal	520		1441	
Pascal	language-oriented	1226	1.45	5863	5.39
	universal	846		1088	

5. CONCLUSION

In this paper we consider the problem of obtaining, by means of mixed computation, specialized parsers (tailored to specific languages) from universal syntactic analyzer for a large class of programming languages.

Universal parsers forming the domain of our research reflect the most significant properties of practically used parsing algorithms. These algoritms represent evident interest for application, elaboration and implementation of mixed computation.

We constructed the specific language (DSP) intended for description of parser programs and for further study of specializing possibilities of mixed computation.

Specializing parsers are automatically developed by means of the programming system SADLOP. Machine experiments on obtaining of language-oriented parsers confirm the validity of our apptoach to mixed computation implementation (combined parsing, transformational method and concept of control).

REFERENCES

[1] Aho, A.V., Ullman, J.D., The theory of parsing, translation and compiling, v.1,2, Prentice Hall, 1972.
[2] Bauer, F.L., Program development by stepwise transformations, The Project CIP, in: Lect. Notes in Computer Sci., 1979, v.69, pp. 237-272.
[3] Griswold, R.E., Poage, J.F., Polonsky, I.P., The SNOBOL 4 programming language, Prentice Hall, 1968.
[4] Ershov, A.P., Transformational method in software technology, in: First All-union conference on software technology, (USSR, Kiev, 1979), pp. 12-26, (in Russian).

[5]   Ershov, A.P.,The organization of mixed computation for recur-
      sive programs, Sov. Math Dokl., 1979, v.20, No 2, pp.282-286.
[6]   Ershov, A.P., Mixed computation: potential applications and
      problem for study, Theoretical Computer Science, 1982, v.18,
      No 1, pp.41-67.
[7]   Ershov, A.P., Ostrovski, B.N., Systematic construction of
      program to solve a particular problem from a given class by
      method of mixed computation: the parser example, Sov. **Math**.
      Dokl., 1982, v.27, No 10, pp.787-789.
[8]   Ershov, A.P., Ostrovski B.N., Controlled mixed computation
      and its application to systematic development of language-
      oriented paesers, IFIP, TC 2 Working Conference on Program
      Specification and Transformation, April 15-17, Bad Tolz,
      F.R.G.
[9]   Futamura, J., Partial computation of programs,in: Lect. Notes
      in Computer Sci., 1983, v.147, pp.1-35.
[10] Korenjak, A.J., A practical method for constructing LR(k)-
      processors, Comm. ACM, 1969, v.12, No 11, pp.613-623.
[11] Lewis, P.M., Rosenkrantz,D.J., An Algol compiler designed
      using automata theory, Proc. Polytecnic Institute of Brooklyn
      Symp. on Computers and Automata, 1971, pp.75-88.
[12] Lewis, P.M., Rosenkrantz, D.J., Stearns, R.E., Compiler De-
      sign Theory, Addison-Wesley Publishing Company, 1976.
[13] Ostrovski, B.N., Controlled Mixed Computation Exemplified by
      Language-Oriented Parsers, in: Ershov, A.P., (ed.), Problems
      in Theoretical and System Programming (USSR, Novosibirsk,
      1984), pp. 30-49, (in Russian).
[14] Jensen, K., Wirth, N.,Pascal. User manual and report, Sprin-
      ger, 1978.

Partial Evaluation and Mixed Computation
D. Bjørner, A.P. Ershov and N.D. Jones (Editors)
Elsevier Science Publishers B.V. (North-Holland)
© IFIP, 1988

405

IMPORTING AND EXPORTING INFORMATION IN PROGRAM DEVELOPMENT

Alberto Pettorossi and Maurizio Proietti
IASI-CNR, Viale Manzoni 30
00185 Roma (Italy)

ABSTRACT

In order to derive efficient algorithms it is often useful during the process of program development, to perform *specialization steps* (see, for instance, [Scherlis 81]). Those steps can be viewed as partial computations by which the information content of some expressions is partially *imported* into the functions which take them as arguments.

We examine here a complementary approach which consists in *exporting* information from expressions, so that their values can be viewed as the result of applying suitably derived functions to appropriate arguments. Those pairs of functions and arguments realize the exports of information, while the corresponding function applications realize the associated imports.

The <functions,arguments> pairs are obtained using a strategy, called *lambda abstraction* [Pettorossi-Skowron 87]. Through some examples we will show that the program derivation process can indeed be viewed as a sequence of those exports and imports of information, and we will also see that some efficiency improvements can only be achieved by lambda abstractions, that is, exports of information.

1. INTRODUCTION

In the transformation approach the process of deriving programs from specifications can sometimes be viewed as a simplification process. Taking a simple example from elementary algebra, we may say, for instance, that from the initial program version (or specification) "$(x-1)*(x^2+x+1)$" we can derive the program "x^3-1", which is more efficient because fewer arithmetic operations are performed when computing the desired result.

Obviously, not all program transformations are simplifications. There are other transformations which are obtained either by methods for structuring computations, like the tupling strategy [Pettorossi 84], or by methods for defining 'more general' computations, like the generalization strategy [Aubin 76, Abdali-Vitopil 84].

Here we would like to consider one more transformation strategy, which is called lambda abstraction (or higher order generalization [Pettorossi-Skowron 87]), and analyze its properties with respect to the known techniques of partial evaluation and program specialization. Our attention will be focused on the derivation of both functional and logic programs.

In our study we have been stimulated by a technique for avoiding multiple traversals of data structures introduced in [Bird 84]. In that paper the author makes use of circular programs (also called local recursive programs) and lazy evaluation for achieving the desired performances.

In this paper we show that we do not need those techniques and that in a large number of cases call-by-value and lambda expressions are suitable tools for avoiding multiple traversals of data structures.

Related work has been presented in [Takeichi 87]. In that paper, although lambda expressions are used, no method has been proposed for the generation of the suitable lambda abstractions. On the contrary, we will give suggestions based on the *forced folding* idea [Darlington 81] for inventing the necessary auxiliary functions.

The examples we will present in Sections 2 and 3 also indicate that by using lambda abstraction we can efficiently manipulate data structures and simulate a clean and disciplined use of pointers within the framework of functional languages.

Section 4 will be devoted to the relation between various transformation strategies and the use of lambda abstraction. At the end of the paper we will present some preliminary ideas for a theory of program derivation strategies.

2. A COMPOSITIONAL VIEW OF COMPUTATIONS AND A PRELIMINARY EXAMPLE

The partial evaluation approach and the lambda abstraction strategy we will study in this paper, are methods for program development which are strictly related. We will now indicate the sense in which they can be considered as complementary approaches.

Let us first recall a formal correspondence between function application and function composition. It can be stated in the lambda calculus framework as follows (see [Church 37]).

Let $C_* \equiv \lambda xy.yx$, $B \equiv \lambda xyz.x(yz)$, and $\bullet$ denote function composition, that is, $x \bullet y \equiv \lambda z.x(yz)$. We have that [Barendregt 84, p. 533]:

i) $C_*(xy) = C_*y \bullet C_*x \bullet B$, because $C_*y(C_*x(Ba))$ β-reduces to $C_*(xy)a$, and

ii) $C_*x \bullet C_* = x$, because $(C_*x(C_*a))$ β-reduces to xa.

Therefore, $(xy) = C_*y \bullet C_*x \bullet B \bullet C_*$, and for any applicative term in $\{S,K\}^+$ we can derive a corresponding word in the monoid with generators $G=\{C_*K, C_*S, B, C_*, \bullet\}$, where the applications of the given term have been replaced by compositions. For instance, we have: $(SK)(KK) = C_*K \bullet C_*K \bullet B \bullet C_*K \bullet C_*S \bullet B \bullet B \bullet C_*$.

Notice that the above equations i) and ii) reverse the order of the occurrences of the combinators S and K. Despite this reversal of the order, in any composition $a \bullet b$ we will follow the terminological convention of referring to 'a' as 'the program' and to 'b' as 'the data'.

Church's result which we have recalled above, suggests two different, and yet equivalent, views of function evaluation:

i) the applicative view (as in the formalism of partial recursive functions), so that given the program p and the data d, the result of the computation is denoted by the application p(d), and

ii) the compositional view, so that given the program f and the data g the result of the computation is denoted by f•g.

Since composition is associative, in a word of the monoid **G** we can associate the basic symbols in the way we prefer, without changing its functional meaning. Thus, for instance, we have:

(SK)(KK) = C∗K• (λx.B(xK)K) •C∗S•B•B•C∗, because C∗K•B•C∗K= λx.B(xK)K.

The compositional view of function evaluation has the following advantage over the applicative view: it allows a uniform formalism for presenting the techniques of partial evaluation [Ershov 77], mixed computation [Ershov 82], program specialization [Scherlis 81], filter promotion [Darlington 81], and shifting of data boundaries [Jørring-Scherlis 86], in the way we will now explain.

Partial evaluation, filter promotion, and some kinds of program specialization techniques can indeed be formalized by the equality p•d = (p•d1)•d2, whereby the information in the data d≡d1•d2 has been partially *imported* into the program p, which becomes the new program (p•d1).

We may also say that the information in d has been divided into the composition of the two parts d1 and d2, and d1 has been left-associated to the program p.

In the sequel we will use the following terminology: in the composition a•b we will say that part of the information of "b" has been imported into "a" if a•b has been transformed into a•b1•b2 with b≡b1•b2 and a•b has been evaluated according to the bracketed expression (a•b1)•b2.

We will also say that part of the information of "a" has been *exported* to "b" when the opposite case occurs, namely a•b has been transformed into a1•a2•b and a•b has been evaluated according to a1•(a2•b).

Mixed computation [Ershov 82] can be viewed as the transformation of the program-data composition p•d, where p is p1•p2 and d is d1•d2, into the equivalent composition p1•(p2'•d1')•d2 for some suitable p2' and d1' such that: p2'•d1'=p2•d1. In most cases the mixed computation technique is applied when p1 and/or d2 are equal to the identity function λx.x.

Shifting of data boundaries can also be viewed as a method for exporting and importing information between the program p1•p2 and the data d1•d2, so that, instead of (p1•p2)•(d1•d2) we compute p1•r•d2 for some expression r such that r=p2•d1.

Finally, we can express the lambda abstraction strategy [Pettorossi-Skowron 87] as follows: in the program-data composition p•d we divide the program p (not the data d, as in the partial evaluation case) into the two program parts p1 and p2 such that p≡p1•p2. This division can be viewed as the extraction (or export) from a given program p of the data component p2. This is essentially the basic idea which underlines the lambda abstraction strategy, when we express it using the compositional paradigm of function evaluation.

Therefore, the abstraction strategy is complementary to the import of information realized by partial evaluation and program specialization methods, because when we apply it, we export information from programs (or expressions).

Another way of viewing the lambda abstraction strategy is to say that it consists in deriving from the expression "p[p2]" (which denotes the expression p where the subexpression p2 occurs) the application: "((λx.p[x]) p2)". We may also say that the lambda abstraction strategy consists in replacing the expression "p <u>where</u> x = p2" by the semantically equivalent expression "(λx.p[x]) p2".

Since the subexpression p2 occurring within p is replaced by the variable x, the application of the abstraction strategy may allow us to perform *folding steps* which otherwise cannot be performed. This increase of the folding capabilities makes it possible to derive better program structures and more efficient algorithms, as the examples given below will show.

Lambda abstraction also allows us to suspend computations, because in λx.p[x] the evaluation of the expression p is performed only when that lambda expression will be applied to its argument. This fact is very important, because often we may want to perform computations using call-by-value instead of call-by-need.

Let us now give a first example of application of the abstraction strategy. This example is important in itself because it shows that the abstraction strategy, together with the tupling strategy [Pettorossi 84], is powerful enough to often avoid the use of circular programs and lazy evaluation.

We will consider the problem (suggested in [Bird 84]) of testing whether or not a given list is palindrome. The difficulty resides in the fact that the list should be traversed only once and only the functions hd (or car) and tl (or cdr) should be used for accessing lists.

We will obtain a one-pass algorithm with the same time×space complexity of the one in [Bird 84], but our algorithm does not need either *local recursion* or *lazy evaluation*.

The bound variables generated in our program by the abstraction strategy, will play the role of the pointers which can be used in the corresponding Pascal-like program, and therefore, through our example, we show how to manipulate pointers within the framework of functional languages in a referentially transparent way.

As in [Bird 84] we start off from the following initial program version, where ':' denotes the 'cons' operation on lists, and [] denotes the empty list:

1. palindrome(*l*)   = eqlist(*l*,rev(*l*))
2. eqlist([],[])   = true
3. eqlist(a:*l*1,b:*l*2) = (a=b) <u>and</u> eqlist(*l*1,*l*2)
4. rev(*l*)   = acc-rev(*l*,[])
5. acc-rev([],y)   = y
6. acc-rev(a:*l*,y)   = acc-rev(*l*,a:y).

The function 'acc-rev' uses the second argument as an accumulator and in that way the need for list concatenation is avoided. This initial program requires for a given list of length n, 3n hd-operation, 3n tl-operations, and n cons-operations.

The transformation process begins by applying the *composition strategy* for the given expression of palindrome(*l*), that is, eqlist(*l*,rev(*l*)). After a few unfolding steps we get:

palindrome([]) = true

palindrome(a:*l*) = eqlist(a:*l*, acc-rev(a:*l*,[]))

$$= (a=hd(acc\text{-}rev(l,[a]))) \ \underline{and} \ eqlist(l, tl(acc\text{-}rev(l,[a])))$$
$$= (a=hd(x)) \ \underline{and} \ eqlist(l, tl(x)) \quad \underline{where} \ x=acc\text{-}rev(l,[a]).$$

But now a folding step, which is required for achieving a one-pass algorithm, is not possible. In fact, eqlist(l,tl(x)) does not match any instance of eqlist(l,rev(l)), because of the clash of the functions rev and tl. As in [Darlington 81] we may now use the *mismatch information* to perform suitable generalization steps. There are two ways of doing so:

(a) the traditional one (see [Aubin 76, Boyer-Moore 75]) by which the expressions tl(x) and rev(l) are generalized to the variable z, and we are suggested to look for the explicit definition of the expression: eqlist(l,z), and

(b) the application of our new generalization strategy by lambda abstraction [Pettorossi-Skowron 87]

by which we are suggested to define the function: $\lambda z.eqlist(l,z)$.

Let us now carry out the derivation of our program both in case (a) and (b) by applying the usual transformation techniques. The comparison of those derivations will give us a good understanding of the features and advantages of the lambda abstraction strategy with respect to the other generalization strategy.

Case (a). Both eqlist(l,z) and acc-rev(l,[a]) visit the same list l. We are suggested to use the *tupling strategy* and we get: $T(l,z) \equiv < eqlist(l,z), acc\text{-}rev(l,[a]) >$, whose explicit definition is:

$$T([],z) \ = \ < null(z), [a] >$$
$$T(b:l,z) \ = \ < eqlist(b:l,z), acc\text{-}rev(b:l,[a]) >$$
$$\qquad = \ < b=hd(z) \ \underline{and} \ eqlist(l,tl(z)), \ acc\text{-}rev(l,[b; a]) >$$

and again no folding step is possible, because acc-rev(l,[b; a]) does not match acc-rev(l,[a]). The mismatch information suggests the generalization of [a] to a variable, say y, so that we are required to find the explicit definition of the following function: $T1(l,z,y) \equiv < eqlist(l,z), acc\text{-}rev(l,y) >$.
We get:

$$T1([],z,y) \ = \ < null(z), y >$$
$$T1(b:l,z,y) \ = \ < eqlist(b:l,z), acc\text{-}rev(b:l,y) >$$
$$\qquad = \ < b=hd(z) \ \underline{and} \ u, \ v > \ \underline{where} \ <u,v>=T1(l,tl(z),a:y).$$

We also have: palindrome(l)=π1 T1(l,acc-rev(l,[]),[]). However, T1(l,acc-rev(l,[]),[]) visits the list l twice, the first time when computing acc-rev, and the second one when computing T1. Therefore the above program for palindrome(l) is not satisfactory, because it does not determine a one-pass algorithm.   ∎

Case (b). As in case (a) we apply the *tupling strategy* and we define the auxiliary function:

$$P(l) \equiv < \lambda z.eqlist(l,z), \ acc\text{-}rev(l,[a]) >.$$

Its explicit definition requires a generalization step, because we have:

$P(b:l) = < \lambda z.b=hd(z) \ \underline{and} \ eqlist(l,tl(z)), \ acc\text{-}rev(l,[b; a]) >$, and folding with P($l$) is not possible.
By generalizing [a] to the variable y, we get:

$$P1(l,y) \equiv < \lambda z.eqlist(l,z), \ acc\text{-}rev(l,y) >, \text{ whose explicit definition is:}$$

7. P1([],y) = < λz.null(z), y >   (by unfolding)

8. P1(a:l,y) = < λz.eqlist(a:l,z), acc-rev(a:l,y) >

            = < λz. a=hd(z) and eqlist(l, tl(z)), acc-rev(l,a:y) >

            = < λz. a=hd(z) and (u tl(z)), v >   where <u,v>=P1(l,a:y)   (by folding).

The final program consists of the above equations 7, and 8, together with:

9. palindrome(l) = (u v)   where <u,v> = P1(l,[]).   ∎

Notice that the abstraction strategy together with the tupling strategy allows us to express P1(a:l,y) in terms of P1(l,a:y) only. Therefore a linear recursive definition for P1(a:l,y) is derived, and the list l is visited only once. During that visit we test the equality of lists and, at the same time, we compute the reverse of the given list.

The above algorithm (equations 7,8,9) requires essentially the same time and space resources needed by the one presented in [Bird 84], which we rewrite here for the reader's convenience:

B1.   Bird-palindrome(l) = π1(p)   whererec p = eqrev(x, π2(p), [])

B2.   eqrev([], y, z) = < true, [] >

B3.   eqrev(a:l, y, z) = < a=hd(y) and u, v >   where <u,v>=eqrev(x, tl(y), a:z).

As usual, πi(p) denotes the i-th projection of p. Notice that the equation B1 is *locally recursive*, because the value of the pair p is defined in terms of second component of itself.

Now we would like to analyze the relationship between our program and Bird's program, and also to discuss the question whether or not our algorithm (equations 7,8,9) is truly 'one-pass'.

As for the first point, let us notice that pointers are a way of representing the circular structures occurring in a locally recursive program. Therefore, we can consider the following picture which shows the pointers situation when evaluating, for instance, Bird-palindrome([1,2,3]).

If the given list has length n then the computation of Bird-palindrome(l) requires 2n hd-operations, 2n tl-operations, and n cons-operations.

The same number of operations is required by our program (equations 7,8,9), as the reader may easily verify by considering the following figure:

step	l	y	P1(l,y)
(i)	[1,2,3]	[]	< λ z.1=hd(z) and u(tl(z)), v >
(ii)	[2,3]	[1]	< λ z.2=hd(z) and u(tl(z)), v >
(iii)	[3]	[2,1]	< λ z.3=hd(z) and u(tl(z)), v >
(iv)	[]	[3,2,1]	<λ z.null(z), [3,2,1] >

In our program n tl-operations and n hd-operations are performed at the time of the application (u v) of equation 9.

The program we have derived achieves the desired performances by means of *closures*, which are necessary for storing function-objects, and they are, in general, quite expensive data structures. However, in our case no free variables occur in the lambda abstractions, and therefore, closures can be implemented in a cheap way, using pairs of bound variables and functions bodies. Indeed, environments need not to be stored.

Let us now discuss the point of the one-pass feature of the derived program.

The final application (u v) could be considered as a second visit of the list rev(l) recorded in v, so that it seems a bit strange to say that we obtained a one-pass algorithm. However, since our algorithm performs the same number of structuring (cons) and destructuring (hd,tl) operations of the one given by Bird, we have followed his terminology. Perhaps one could say that the derived algorithm is *one-and-a-half pass*, because it reduces the number of hd and tl operations from 6n to 4n for any given list of length n.

Notice that the difficulty of obtaining a one-pass algorithm depends on the *access functions* which are available for the data structures under consideration. In fact, the derivation of a one-pass palindrome algorithm would have been straightforward if we also had the access functions 'last(l)' and 'begin(l)' computing the last element of a list l and the list l without its last element, respectively.

The theoretical results on the improvements of performances using our program (equations 7,8,9) are confirmed by the experiments we made on our ML implementation. Indeed, the derived program runs faster than the original one (equations 1,...,6) for lists of about 100 items or more.

We claim the following advantages over the program (B1,B2,B3) proposed in [Bird 84].

a) Bird needs circular programs for overcoming the difficulty of not having explicit pointers in the framework of functional languages. In his approach pointers are used in an implicit way, and that fact makes it difficult to understand the program behaviour. For instance, it is not immediate to see, as Bird himself says, that we get an infinite loop (even in a call-by-need mode) if the equation B3 is replaced by the following:

B3'. eqrev(a:*l*, b:y, z) = < (a=b) <u>and</u> u, v >   <u>where</u> <u,v>=eqrev(x, y, a:z).

The reason for the non-termination is that for equation B3' the evaluation of the second argument of eqrev is required more often than in the case of equation B3, because it has to be matched against the pattern b:*l*.

On the contrary, in our approach termination is guaranteed by straightforward application of structural induction on the input data.

Moreover, the program we have derived shows that:

- the bound variables in functional languages may play the role of pointers in data structures, and
- the bound variables behave like *restricted pointers*, because they can only be manipulated through function application. In that way the danger of their incorrect use is reduced and the referential transparency is preserved.

b) Through the Palindrome example we have also shown that call-by-value and lambda abstraction may avoid the need of circular programs and lazy evaluation, as suggested in [Bird 84, Takeichi 87].

c) In our approach the programmer need not to learn unfamiliar techniques, while the use of circular programs need "a little practice" [Bird 84, p. 246].

d) In the derivation of the program B1-B3, Bird does not provide any formal motivation for the definition of the auxiliary function 'eqrev'. Sometimes in his paper some other definitions are justified by "little foresight" [Bird 84, p. 245].

On the contrary, the aim of our program transformation strategies is to provide useful guidelines to the programmer in his search for suitable auxiliary functions. Thus, his task is made much easier.

3. EXAMPLES OF DERIVATIONS OF LOGICAL AND FUNCTIONAL PROGRAMS BY EXPORTING INFORMATION VIA LAMBDA ABSTRACTION

We will now consider some more examples of program derivation by *exporting information* from expressions, looking at other formalisms and languages. In particular, there is a way of realizing the lambda abstraction strategy also in the case of logical languages, like Prolog. We will see that it can be applied by adding extra arguments to suitable predicates. This point is best explained by the example we will give below.

Let us first recall the basic transformation strategies as they can be formulated in the case of Prolog programming. For expressing them, we will annotate the occurrence of a variable in an *atom* by "/i" (short for input) or "/o" (short for output) according to the case when it is bound before or after the satisfaction of the corresponding goal. Often in the literature that annotation is called the *mode* of the variable in that atom.

Those strategies are:

1. *Composition strategy.* When in the body of a given clause we have the goals p1(X/i, Y/o) and p2(Y/i, Z/o), where the variable Y occurs in p1 and p2 only, and the binding of Y produced by p1 is passed to the predicate p2, we can define the new predicate:

$$comp(X/i,Z/o) \leftarrow p1(X/i, Y/o), \ p2(Y/i, Z/o).$$

In that way, when comp(X/i, Z/o) is considered, the explicit binding for Y is not built. This strategy can also be applied when the variable X occurs in the predicate p2.

2. *Tupling strategy.* When in the body of a given clause we have the goals p1(X/i, Y1/o) and p2(X/i, Y2/o), where the variable X is visited by both p1 and p2, we can define the new predicate:

tuple(X/i, Y1/o, Y2/o) ← p1(X/i, Y1/o), p2(X/i, Y2/o).

In that way the data structure X is visited only once when computing the bindings of Y1 and Y2.

3. *Generalization strategy.* Suppose we have the clause:

$$a(X/i, Z/o) \leftarrow b(X/i, Y/o), c(X/i, Y/i, Z/o). \tag{$\bullet$}$$

3.1. We can generalize the input variable X to two distinct variables X1 and X2, and we define the new clause: gen1(X1/i, X2/i, Z/o) ← b(X1/i, Y/o), c(X2/i, Y/i, Z/o).

3.2. We can generalize the internal variable Y to two distinct variables Y1 and Y2, and we define the new clause: gen2(X/i, Y1/o, Y2/i, Z/o) ← b(X/i, Y1/o), c(X/i, Y2/i, Z/o). $(\bullet\bullet)$

The presence of distinct variables allows folding steps otherwise impossible. The example given below will clarify this point.

The reader may also realize the close correspondence between case (3.1) and the usual expression-to-variable generalization in functional programming [Aubin 76], while the case (3.2) closely corresponds to the lambda abstraction generalization. Indeed, the role of an internal variable like Y2 in $(\bullet\bullet)$, is similar to the one of a bound variable in functional programming, as we now informally indicate.

Let us assume that in $(\bullet)$ the evaluation of the predicate b(X,Y) binds Y to the value of a given expression $e_b[X]$ which depends on X, and that the evaluation of c(X,Y,Z) binds Z to the value of the expression $e_c[X,e_b]$, where e_b occurs as a subexpression. The generalization of the variable Y to the two variables Y1 and Y2 in $(\bullet\bullet)$ is like *exporting* the subexpression e_b from e_c and we derive (as for the lambda abstraction strategy) the equivalent application: $(\lambda Y2.e_c[X,Y2]\ Y1)$, corresponding to the predicate gen2(X,Y1,Y2,Z). The related application is simulated by the call of gen2 with Y1=Y2.

Let us now present an example of application of the lambda abstraction strategy, which realizes the export of information from expressions, in the case of a Prolog program.

Let us assume that we want to transform a given binary tree 'InTree' into a structurally equivalent one, called 'OutTree', by replacing all its leaves by their minimal value.

The term-constructors for binary trees are tip(-) and tr(-,-): tip(N) given an integer N creates a leaf with value N, and tr(L,R) given two binary trees L and R creates a new binary tree having L and R as left and right subtrees, respectively.

A two-pass Prolog program for realizing the required transformation, is as follows:

transf(InTree, OutTree) ← minleaves(InTree,MinLeaf), repl(InTree,OutTree,MinLeaf).
minleaves(tip(N), N).
minleaves(tr(L,R), Min) ← minleaves(L,MinL), minleaves(R,MinR), min(MinL,MinR,Min).

repl(tip(N), tip(Min), Min).

repl(tr(IL,IR), tr(OL,OR), Min) ← repl(IL,OL,Min), repl(IR,OR,Min).

The predicate minleaves(tr(L,R),Min) binds Min to the minimal leaf value in tr(L,R) and the predicate repl(tr(IL,IR),tr(OL,OR),Min) constructs the tree tr(OL,OR) from the tree tr(IL,IR) by making all its leaf values equal to Min. Obviously, the predicate min(X,Y,Z) binds Z to the value of X if X≤Y, otherwise it binds it to the value of Y.

We will derive a one-pass algorithm by applying first the composition strategy for the pair of goals "minleaves(InTree,MinLeaf), repl(InTree,OutTree,MinLeaf)" in the clause defining transf(InTree,OutTree). After a few unfolding steps, we obtain:

transf(tip(N),tip(N)) ← minleaves(tip(N),N), repl(tip(N),tip(N),N).

Thus, we get: transf(tip(N), tip(N)).   We also derive:

transf(tr(IL,IR), tr(OL,OR))← minleaves(IL,MinL), minleaves(IR,MinR), min(MinL,MinR,Min), repl(IL,OL,Min),   repl(IR,OR,Min).

Now, unfortunalety, we cannot fold "minleaves(IL,MinL), repl(IL,OL,Min)" with transf(IL,OL), because MinL ≠ Min. This mismatch information is then used for deriving a suitable generalization step. We make a generalization of type (3.2) and we define the predicate:

gentransf(InTree,OutTree,MinOut,MinIn) ← minleaves(InTree,MinOut), repl(InTree,OutTree,MinIn).

During the computation of the goal gentransf the variable MinOut is bound to the minimum leaf value found in the given tree InTree, and the variable MinIn is bound to the leaf value to be used for obtaining the output tree OutTree. After a few folding/unfolding steps we get:

G1. gentransf(tip(N), tip(Min), N, Min).

G2. gentransf(tr(IL,IR), tr(OL,OR), MinOut, MinIn) ← gentransf(IL, OL, MinOutL, MinIn), gentransf(IR, OR, MinOutR, MinIn),   min(MinOutL, MinOutR, MinOut).

G3. transf(InTree, OutTree) ← gentransf(InTree, OutTree, MinLeaf, MinLeaf).

The last clause is obtained by folding from the definition:

transf(InTree, OutTree) ← minleaves(InTree, MinLeaf), repl(InTree, OutTree, MinLeaf).

The algorithm we have derived is one-pass because of the recursive structure of the predicate gentransf. Computer experiments confirm the increase in efficiency.

It is interesting to notice that, while the two-pass Prolog program can easily be produced even by a beginner, the final program G1-G3 requires some familiarity with logic programming. We can say that the generalization strategy encapsulates the expertise necessary for writing the clauses G1-G3, and moreover, the transformation technique gives us for free the correctness proof of the derived program.

The example we have given also indicates that the generalization strategy has its power and flexibility across different languages. The improvements in efficiency it allows, are indeed related to a very abstract model of computation, and they are not dependent on the formalisms one uses for denoting computations.

The interested reader may also refer to [Pettorossi 87], where a similar algorithm for transforming trees has been derived using a functional language ML-like. Again the crucial strategies which produced the desired program, were the tupling and the lambda abstraction strategies. As in the Palindrome example, the one-pass algorithm cannot be obtained by using the tupling strategy alone.

The Prolog program G1-G3 shows that logical variables can behave as Pascal-like pointers. Its evaluation, in fact, can be understood as follows: when a tip has been found, we place in it a pointer to the location where the derived minimum leaf value will be stored at the end of the visit of the input tree. ∎

In [Bird 84] the author also proposes as a challenge, the following tree transformation problem, which again can be solved in a Pascal-like language using pointers. The difficulty resides in the fact that we are asked to use a functional language, and as Bird says, "no concept of tree addresses (or pointers) exists as individual entities in a functional framework" [Bird 84, p. 241].

Given a tree t, we are asked to construct a tree i) which is isomorphic to t, ii) it has the same multiset of leaves, and iii) its leaves occur in ascending order, when reading them from left to right. That construction should take place by making one traversal only of the given tree t.

Using the lambda abstraction strategy we will solve the proposed problem, without using locally recursive programs or lazy evaluation, and we will see again that the bound variables play the role of pointers. Moreover, the difficulty of pointer manipulations will be overcome by the recursive structure of the derived program itself.

A two-pass version of the program for realizing the required tree transformation is as follows:

T1.   TreeSort(t) = replace(t,sort(leaves(t))),

where: i) leaves(t) computes the list of the leaves of the tree t,

ii) sort(l) rearranges the list l of leaf values in an ascending order from left to right, and

iii) replace(t,l) uses the leftmost k values of the list l to replace the k leaf values of the tree t, in the left to right order.

We assume that 'sort' is a given routine defined in terms of the primitive function 'merge'. merge($l1,l2$) gives us back the sorted list whose elements come from the concatenation of the sorted lists $l1$ and $l2$. The definition of leaves and replace are as follows:

T2.   leaves(tip(n)) = [n]

T3.   leaves(t1^t2) = leaves(t1) @ leaves(t2)

T4.   replace(tip(n),l) = tip(hd(l))

T5.   replace(t1^t2,l) = replace(t1,take(k,l)) ^ replace(t2,drop(k,l))   <u>where</u> k=size(t1),

where size(t) computes the number of leaves in a given tree t, @ denotes concatenation of lists,

take(k,l) produces the list of the leftmost k elements of a given list l, and

drop(k,l) produces the list l without its leftmost k elements.

We assume that size(t) ≤ length(l) holds for any call of replace(t,l). We have:

T6.   size(tip(n)) = 1

T7. size(t1^t2) = size(t1) + size(t2)

T8. take(0,l) = []   T10. drop(0,l) = l

T9. take(n+1,l) = take(n,l) @ [hd(drop(n,l))]   T11. drop(n+1,l) = tl(drop(n,l))

We also assume that 0≤k≤length(l) holds for any call of take(k,l) and drop(k,l).

For instance, we have: size(tip(4)^tip(5))=2, take(4,[5,3,7,8,6])=[5,3,7,8], drop(4,[5,3,7,8,6])=[6], and if t ≡ ((6^3)^(4^3))^(1^(4^5)) (for simplicity we here write n instead of tip(n)) then TreeSort(t) = ((1^3)^(3^4))^(4^(5^6)).

The derivation of a one-pass algorithm from the equations T1-T11 proceeds by applying the composition strategy to the initial equation T1. However, it also requires the lambda abstraction strategy, while the tupling strategy alone is not successful.

Notice that the derivation we will present below, is different from the one presented in [Pettorossi 87], because different primitive functions are considered, and the suggested techniques are applied in a different way. From replace(t,sort(leaves(t))) we get (by function composition):

replace(tip(n),sort(leaves(tip(n)))) = replace(tip(n),sort([n])) = tip(n)

replace(t1^t2,sort(leaves(t1^t2))) = replace(t1,take(size(t1),x)) ^ replace(t2,drop(size(t1),x))

where x=sort(leaves(t1^t2)).

For making a folding step and deriving a recursive call to TreeSort(t) = replace(t,sort(leaves(t))) from replace(t,take(size(t),x)), we need to generalize the argument take(size(t),x) to a variable, say z, because there is a clash between the subexpressions sort(leaves(t)) and take(size(t),x). Therefore we obtain the expression replace(t,z). We then apply the tupling strategy for avoiding the repeated visit of the given tree t, and we define the function:

R(t,z) ≡ < replace(t,z), take(size(t),z), drop(size(t),z), sort(leaves(t)) >.

We may now continue the derivation process by looking for the explicit definition of R(t,z). It turns out that replace(t1^t2,z) is equal to replace(t1,take(size(t1),z)) ^ replace(t2,drop(size(t1),z)), and therefore, in order to get a recursive definition we need a locally recursive program because take(size(t1),z)) is the third component of R(t1,z) itself.

Using lambda abstraction we may avoid locally recursive programs. In fact, we consider the function:

R1(t) ≡ < λx.replace(t,x), λx.take(size(t),x), λx.drop(size(t),x), sort(leaves(t)) >.

The explicit definition of R1(t) can be derived by folding/unfolding steps and it is as follows:

R1(tip(n)) = < λx.tip(hd(x)), λx.hd(x), λx.tl(x), [n] >

R1(t1^t2) = < λx.(replace(t1,take(size(t1),x)) ^ replace(t2,drop(size(t1),x))),

          λx.take(size(t1)+size(t2),x),   λx.drop(size(t1)+size(t2),x),

          merge(sort(leaves(t1)),sort(leaves(t2))) >   (by definition)

        = < λx.(replace(t1,take(size(t1),x)) ^ replace(t2,drop(size(t1),x))),

          λx.(take(size(t1),x) @ take(size(t2),drop(size(t1),x))),

          λx.(drop(size(t2),drop(size(t1),x))),   merge(sort(leaves(t1)),sort(leaves(t2))) >

(by properties of take and drop)

$= < \lambda x.((A1\ (A2\ x))^{\wedge}B1(A3\ x)),\ \lambda x.((A2\ x)\ @\ (B2\ (A3\ x))),\ \lambda x.(B3\ (A3\ x)),$
$merge(A4,B4) > \underline{where}\ <A1,A2,A3,A4>=R1(t1)\ \underline{and}\ <B1,B2,B3,B4>=R1(t2).$
$NewTreeSort(t) = (A1\ A4)\ \underline{where}\ <A1,A2,A3,A4>=R1(t).$

The above program NewTreeSort(t) is a one-pass program in the sense that $R1(t1^{\wedge}t2)$ is defined in terms of $R1(t1)$ and $R1(t2)$ only. As in the Palindrome example, during the visit of the tree t, in the components of $R1(t)$ we collect the necessary information, so that one visit only need to be made. Computer experiments show that NewTreeSort(t) is indeed faster than TreeSort(t) for trees of about size 30 or larger.

A few words of comparison between our program and the one presented in [Bird 84]. Those programs have essentially the same time and space performances.

As we have already noticed, the major difference is that we use the ideas of the *forced folding* [Darlington 81] and *mismatch information* for deriving the suitable auxiliary functions. In [Bird 84] the related definitions are proposed without a satisfactory motivation, and from his presentation it is hard to see how a mechanized transformation system could be able to discover the required definitions. Minor differences with Bird's program are the following ones:
- he considers the function 'sort' as primitive, while we consider the function 'merge': we do so in order to perform the sorting of the leaves while the visit of the input tree is in progress; moreover, we can compute the four components of $R1(t)$ in parallel;
- he uses the function leaves(t,l) instead of the function leaves(t), for replacing the expensive concatenation operation of the equation T3 by a *cons* operation. We could have done the same without problems.

Notice also that in our program, as in the one in [Bird 84] (see, for instance, the definition of *combine*), we compute some components of the function R1 which we never use. This phenomenon sometimes occurs when applying the tupling strategy, and it can be avoided by adopting the call-by-need evaluation mode.

We finally notice that the nested applications occurring, for instance, in the first component of $R1(t1^{\wedge}t2)$, that is, $\lambda x.((A1(A2\ x))^{\wedge}(B1(A3\ x)))$, correspond in [Bird 84, p. 249] to the double recursion of the function 'repnd'. This situation also occurs in the analogous derivation given in [Pettorossi 87]. ■

4. COMPARING LAMBDA ABSTRACTIONS WITH OTHER STRATEGIES

In this section we would like to analyze the features of the lambda abstraction strategy with respect to other program transformation strategies considered in the literature. We will also discuss in more detail the ideas presented in Section 2.

Let us first look at the *composition strategy*. Similar comments will also apply to the *specialization strategy* for which the reader may refer to [Scherlis 81].

The composition strategy is applied by requiring the explicit definition of the function h = f•g when the expression f(g(x)) occurs in a given program. It corresponds to the *import of information* from g(x) within the function f. That import may avoid the explicit construction of the value of g(x). This fact is very important when g(x) is a potentially infinite structure (and its explicit computation may result in an infinite execution), while f can produce initial portions of its output when given initial portions of g(x) [Wadler 85].

Therefore, importing information from an argument to its corresponding function may save time and space during program execution. For that respect, the abstraction strategy may seem to be not useful because it does exactly the opposite: it exports information from an expression (or a function body) and it makes that expression to be the result of an application of a suitable function to an appropriate argument. More formally, from the expression e[e1] by abstraction we can produce the application ((λz.e[z]) e1). We see now the advantages one may obtain from an abstraction step.

The extra variable z occurring in λz.e[z] allows us to perform folding steps which may be otherwise impossible. This is exactly what happened in the Palindrome example given above. The efficiency improvement is due to the recursive structure which we can derive via folding, for the program that computes λz.e[z].

That point is very important. When transforming programs, in fact, the increase of program efficiency is obtained when we can make a folding step, which allows us to express the recursive computations in a more efficient way. As an example of that fact, the reader may recall the familiar derivation of a linear program for the Fibonacci function (see [Burstall-Darlington 77]). The transformation is successful simply because we can recursively express the function $g(n+1)=<fib(n+1),fib(n)>$ in terms of g(n).

The abstraction strategy makes use of higher order objects which, in general, may be difficult to store or manipulate. However, it is often the case that one can reduce those objects to low-order ones. The reader may see [Pettorossi-Skowron 87], where there is an example where functions are reduced to integers.

It should also be noticed that the functions which are created by lambda abstractions do not contain free variables, and therefore they can simply be represented via <bound variables, function bodies> pairs, without recording the environments.

Moreover, since lambda abstractions allow us to derive one-pass algorithms, we can improve the space performances of our algorithms by releasing *on the fly* the memory used for the input data structures while we visit them. For this technique one may refer to the destructiveness analysis in [Mycroft 81].

Let us now consider the relationship between lambda abstraction and *partial evaluation* [Ershov 82]. Similar comments can also be made when considering the abstraction strategy w.r.t. the *program divisions* techniques considered in [Jones 87].

Lambda abstraction can be viewed as an inverse strategy of the partial evaluation. In fact, using the partial evaluation strategy we import information from some given arguments to the corresponding functions, so that we can produce efficient code for their evaluation. When the remaining information about the arguments is available, the execution of the produced code will compute the desired results in a very efficient way.

The lambda abstraction approach does again the opposite: it exports information from a given expression. However, it determines, as we already mentioned, the following advantages w.r.t. the partial evaluation technique: i) the increase of the possibilities for folding, ii) the ability of simulating call-by-need using call-by-value, because function evaluations are suspended when lambda expressions are encountered, and iii) the derivation of one-pass algorithms, via the synergism between lambda abstraction and tupling strategy.

This last advantage can be obtained in the case when a given expression has two different, but not disjoined, subexpressions which both visit the same data structure. The Palindrome example we have given in Section 2 shows that point.

There is a less informal way of comparing the abstraction strategy with the partial evaluation technique. Following [Ershov 82], we can say that partial evaluation is defined via the function Part: Programs×Data $\rightarrow$ Programs, such that the semantics function, call it Sem: Programs×Data $\rightarrow$ Values, is preserved. Thus, the following equation, where p is a program and (d1,d2) a composite data, should hold: $Sem(p,(d1,d2)) = Sem(Part(p,d1),d2)$. The information of (d1,d2) has been partially imported into the program p by generating the new program Part(p,d1).

In the same way the abstraction strategy can be viewed as defined via the function Lambda: Programs $\rightarrow$ Programs × Data such that $Sem(p,d2) = Sem(\lambda x.p1, (d1,d2))$, where Lambda(p) = $(\lambda x.p1,d1)$. Using Lambda, from a program p we derive both a new program $\lambda x.p1$ and a data component d1. Since Lambda and Part have domain and codomain interchanged, we could consider the abstraction strategy as a kind of inverse of the partial evaluation.

Our experience in deriving programs by transformation is that we need both *import of information* (as done when using function specialization, function composition and partial evaluation) as well as *export of information*, which we advocate in this paper. Similar understanding of the program transformation process is also present in the literature, though in an implicit way (see, for instance, [Hughes 84, Takeichi 87]).

Finally, we will compare the lambda abstraction with the *lambda hoisting* strategy [Takeichi 87]. Both of them are variants of the generalization techniques and they both take advantage of the fact that higher order objects are available within functional languages.

The main differences are the following ones:

- lambda hoisting requires call-by-need and local recursion for achieving the desired improvement of program perfomances, while lambda abstraction does not;
- in the lambda hoisting approach no suggestion is given on how to derive the generalized functions

which are necessary for the transformation. Indeed, Takeichi himself says: "the generalization is heuristic" [Takeichi 87, p.63]. In the lambda abstraction strategy a mismatch information is used for finding the suitable generalizations one should make.

- The synergism between lambda expressions and tupling strategy is not considered when using lambda hoisting, while it is essential, as the Palindrome example shows, in the case of lambda abstraction, and we think that the use the two strategies together allows us a more flexible and powerful technique of program development. The example we will now give, based on a problem due to Hughes and taken from [Takeichi 87], illustrates that point.

We are required to find the list of the deepest leaf values in a given tree t. A naive two-pass algorithm is as follows:

deepest(tip(n)) = [n]

deepest(t1^t2) = if $d(t1) > d(t2)$ then deepest(t1) elseif $d(t1) < d(t2)$ then deepest(t2)

else deepest(t1) @ deepest(t2)

where the function d giving us the depth of a given tree t, is defined as follows:

d(tip(n)) = 1 $d(t1^t2) = max(d(t1),d(t2))+1$.

In [Takeichi 87, p.74] a one-pass program is derived by lambda hoisting. It is quite intricate and requires lazy evaluation, local recursion, and an ad-hoc application of the proposed general technique.

We can derive a one-pass algorithm by applying lambda abstraction and tupling as follows.

Since $d(t1)$ and $d(t2)$ occur within the body of deepest(t1^t2), we abstract them away from the expression defining deepest(t1^t2), and we get the function $\lambda xy.deepest(t1^t2,x,y)$.

This procedure is exactly the one we followed in the Palindrome example, where acc-rev(l,y) occurs in the expression eqlist(l,acc-rev(l,y)). By abstracting it away, we derived the function $\lambda z.eqlist(l,z)$.

We then apply the tupling strategy to the functions $\lambda xy.deepest(t1^t2,x,y)$, $d(t1)$, and $d(t2)$ because they all visit the same data structure t1^t2. Therefore we define the triple:

Z(t1^t2) $\equiv$ < $\lambda xy.deepest(t1^t2,x,y)$, $d(t1)$, $d(t2)$ >,

whose explicit definition, after a few simple fold/unfold steps, turns out to be:

Z(tip(n)) = < $\lambda xy.[n]$, 0, 0 >   (We used the value 0, which is the identity for +, because

the left and right subtrees of tip(n) are empty)

Z(t1^t2) = < $\lambda xy.$ if x>y then a1(a2,a3)   elseif x<y then b1(b2,b3) else a1(a2,a3) @ b1(b2,b3),

max(a2,a3)+1,   max(b2,b3)+1 >

where <a1,a2,a3>=Z(t1) and <b1,b2,b3>=Z(t2).

We also get: deepest(t) = a1(a2,a3) where <a1,a2,a3>=Z(t).

Obviously, the derived algorithm is one-pass. Computer experiments confirm the improvement in efficiency.

5. THE ORIGIN OF SOME PROGRAM TRANSFORMATION STRATEGIES

In this Section we would like to analyze the program transformation technique and study the idea of *isomorphism of data domains* as the origin of some transformation strategies.

When deriving programs we need to preserve semantics. In more formal terms, we say that when we derive program P1 from program P0, the following equation should be satisfied:

$$(\dagger) \quad Sem(P0) = Sem(P1).$$

However, this is not enough, because we also need P1 to be more efficient than P0 with respect to a given *cost function* C: Semantics×Programs → Costs, which tells us the cost of evaluating a given program according to a given semantics. Therefore, we also want the following inequation to hold: $(\dagger\dagger)$ C(Sem, P0) ≥ C(Sem, P1), because otherwise it would not be interesting to derive P1 from P0.

Unfortunately, the derivation of an improved program P1 from a given program P0 satisfying the relations $(\dagger)$ and $(\dagger\dagger)$ cannot be algorithmic, in general. Therefore, we may confine ourselves i) to consider particular classes of programs from which the program P0 is taken, and ii) to devise some derivation strategies which are successful for those classes.

Using the folding/unfolding rules [Burstall-Darlington 77] it turns out that the above equation $(\dagger)$ is always satisfied, but only in a partial sense, because we may loose termination. Thus, after deriving the final program, we need to show that both the initial program and the final one terminate for the same set of input data.

Unfortunately, no general method exists for ensuring the satisfaction of the inequation $(\dagger\dagger)$ when applying the folding/unfolding rules. However, in the literature there are suggestions for some strategies which are often successful. In the sequel we would like to give some preliminary ideas for the formal treatment of those strategies, hoping to contribute to their understanding and to stimulate the search for some more powerful ones.

The program derivation process from P0 to P1 can be considered as the construction of two *auxiliary programs*: Aux0 and Aux1 by: i) applying some transformation rules, and ii) introducing new data structures or function definitions using strategies. A pictorial view of that process is given by the following informal Diagram (A):

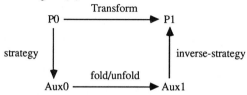

where the inverse-strategy relates the definition of the function computed by P0 to the one computed by Aux1, so that Sem(P0)=Sem(P1).

A given strategy and its inverse often derive from an *isomorphism of data domains*. More precisely, an isomorphism may produce two rules which relate a program 'with an abstract structure' (like P0 or P1 in the Diagram (A)) to a program with a corresponding 'concrete structure' (like Aux0 or Aux1, respectively). As we will see below, this is actually the case for the tupling strategy and the abstraction strategy, where the concrete structures are arrays and functions, respectively.

The *tupling strategy* is based on the isomorphism $(A{\to}B){\times}(A{\to}C) \cong A{\to}(B{\times}C)$, which produces the following two rules (corresponding to the left-to-right and right-to-left directions of the isomorphism):

Rule PI. (*pair introduction* or *tupling*)

$$f:\ A \to X,\ \ g:\ A \to Y$$
$$\overline{\qquad\qquad\qquad\qquad}$$
$$<f,g>:\ A \to X \times Y$$

with $<f, g>\ a = <fa, ga>$ for any $a \in A$. The array introduction (via iteration of pair introduction) comes from function pairing, as specified by Rule PI, by the associativity law of $\times$. An example of how tupling introduces arrays is again the function g(n) in the Fibonacci program (see [Burstall-Darlington 77]). Another one is our palindrome function given above. Many more exist in the literature.

Rule PE. (*pair elimination* or *projection*)

$$f:\ A \to X \times Y$$
$$\overline{\qquad\qquad\qquad\qquad\qquad}$$
$$f1:\ A \to X,\ \ \ \ f2:\ A \to Y$$

with $fj\ a = \pi j\ (f\ a)$ for any $a \in A$ and $j=1,2$. As usual, πj is the j-th projection function. Rule PE allows us to extract the components of a given array of values.

The informal Diagram (A) in the case of the tupling strategy becomes:

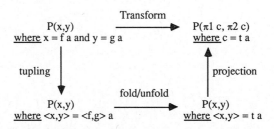

where the definition of t, which semantically depends on the functions f and g, is recursively given in terms of basic functions only (and possibly of itself). No explicit reference to f and g is made.

Let us now consider the *abstraction strategy*.

It is based on the isomorphism $((A{\times}B){\to}X) \cong (A{\to}(B{\to}X))$ which produces the following rules:

Rule FI. (*function introduction* or *lambda abstraction*)

$$f: \quad A \times B \to X$$
$$\overline{f^+: \quad A \to (B \to X)}$$

with $f^+ a = \lambda b.f(a,b)$ for any $a \in A$.

Rule FE. (*function elimination* or *application*)

$$g: \quad A \to (B \to X)$$
$$\overline{g^-: \quad A \times B \to X}$$

with $g^-(a,b) = (g(a)\ b)$ for any $a,b \in A \times B$.

In the case of the lambda abstraction strategy the informal Diagram (A) becomes:

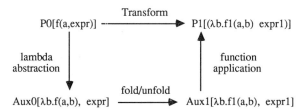

where p[e] denotes the program p where the subexpression e occurs, and f1 and expr1 are recursively defined in terms of basic functions only.

Notice also that the usual *expression-generalization* strategy [Aubin 76] (that is, the one from expressions to variables), can be viewed as a particular case of the lambda abstraction. The inverse-strategy of that generalization is the *substitution*. The corresponding instance of the Diagram (A) can be obtained from the one of lambda abstraction by deleting the λb's and replacing the function application by the substitution of expr1 for b in f1(a,b).

The reader should realize that strategies *come in pairs*, that is, in our diagrams we have both a descending arrow 'strategy' and an ascending arrow 'inverse-strategy'. We have seen that isomorphisms of data domains give us those pairs in a simple and straightforward way.

Here we would like to comment on Wirth's motto: "Algorithms + Data Structures = Programs" [Wirth 76]. The algorithms and their appropriate data structures are not always chosen *statically* at the beginning of the program derivation process; on the contrary, as our examples show, they can be *dynamically* constructed, and they are often suggested by the need of realizing efficient recursive schemata.

For instance, the pair $< \lambda z.\text{eqlist}(l,z), \text{acc-rev}(l,y) >$ (which is an array with two non-homogeneous components) in our Palindrome example derives from a folding requirement.

Finally, we would like to remark that the transformation from a given program P0 to a derived program P1 can be done by *language extension.*

It means that we are given two different semantics functions, say Sem0 and Sem1, and the equation which should be satisfied is: Sem0(P0) = Sem1(P1), where, as usual, the cost function C is such that: C(Sem0,P0) ≥ C(Sem1,P1). In this case we may get better run-time performances for P1 by adopting when evaluating Sem1, a more efficient evaluator than the one for Sem0.

6. CONCLUSIONS

We have considered the technique of program development using the transformation methodology. The increase in efficiency is often obtained by importing information from the arguments into their functions (see, for instance, the strategies of function composition and partial evaluation). We have considered here the complementary approach of developing programs by exporting information from expressions, and we have given various examples where that strategy is used to improve the performances of the derived programs.

We have called that transformation approach *lambda abstraction*, because it essentially produces functions, and we have also indicated how it can be applied in logic programming. The method we have presented is very powerful and it allows us to avoid multiple traversals of data structures. Other approaches to solve the same problems require circular programs and lazy evaluation [Bird 84, Takeichi 87].

At the end of the paper we have indicated that isomorphisms of data domains can be considered as the source of strategies for program transformation.

7. ACKNOWLEDGEMENTS

We would like to thank Richard Bird and Masato Takeichi who greatly stimulated our work through their papers. We also thank N. Jones, R. Paige, A. Skowron, and the colleagues of the IFIP Working Group 2.1. The suggestions of the referee were very useful.

This work was supported by the Institute for the Analysis of Sistems and Informatics of the Italian National Research Council and by an Esprit scholarship of Enidata.

8. REFERENCES

[Abdali-Vitopil 84]
    Abdali, K.S. and Vytopil, J.: "Generalization Heuristics for Theorems Related to Recursively Defined Functions" Report Buro Voor Systeemontwikkeling. Postbus 8348, Utrecht, Netherlands (1984).
[Aubin 76]
    Aubin, R.: "Mechanizing Structural Induction" Ph.D. Thesis, Dept. of Artificial Intelligence, University of Edinburgh (1976).
[Backus 78]
    Backus, J.: "Can Programming be Liberated from the Von Neumann Style?" Comm. A.C.M. 21(8) (1978), pp. 613-641.
[Barendregt 84]
    Barendregt, H.P.: "The Lambda Calculus. Its Syntax and Semantics" Studies in Logic, Vol.103, Revised Edition, North Holland (1984).
[Bird 84]
    Bird, R.S.: "Using Circular Programs to Eliminate Multiple Traversal of Data" Acta Informatica

21 (1984), pp. 239-250.

[Bird 86]
Bird, R.S.: "An Introduction to the Theory of Lists" Technical Monograph PRG-56, Oxford University Computing Laboratory, Oxford, England (1986).

[Boyer-Moore 75]
Boyer, R.S. and Moore, J.S.: "Proving Theorems About LISP Functions" J.A.C.M. 22, 1 (1975), pp. 129-144.

[Burstall-Darlington 77]
Burstall, R.M. and Darlington, J.: "A Transformation System for Developing Recursive Programs" J.A.C.M. Vol.24, 1 (1977), pp. 44-67.

[Church 37]
Church, A.: "Combinatory Logic as a Semigroup" Bull. Amer. Math. Soc. 43, pp. 333.

[Darlington 81]
Darlington, J.: "An Experimental Program Transformation and Synthesis System" Artificial Intelligence 16, (1981), pp. 1-46.

[Ershov 77]
Ershov, A. P.: "On the Partial Evaluation Principle" Info. Proc. Lett. 6, 2 (1977), pp.38-41.

[Ershov 82]
Ershov, A. P.: "Mixed Computation: Potential Applications and Problems for Study" Theoretical Computer Science Vol.18, (1982), pp. 41-67.

[Feather 86]
Feather, M.S.: "A Survey and Classification of Some Program Transformation Techniques" Proc. TC2 IFIP Working Conference on Program Specification and Transformation. Bad Tölz, Germany (ed. L. Meertens) (1986).

[Hughes 84]
Hughes, R. J. M.: "The Design and Implementation of Programming Languages" D. Phil. Thesis, Oxford University, England (1984).

[Jones 87]
Jones, N. D.: "Automatic Program Specialization: A Re-Examination From Basic Principles" IFIP TC2 Working Conference on Partial and Mixed Computation, Ebberup, Denmark, (D. Biörner and A. P. Ershov, eds.), (1987)

[Jørring-Scherlis 86]
Jørring, U. and Scherlis, W. L.: "Compilers and Staging Transformations" Thirteenth Annual A.C.M. Symposium on Principles of Programming Languages, St. Petersburgh Beach, Florida, USA (1986), pp. 86-96.

[Mycroft 81]
Mycroft, A.: "Abstract Interpretations and Optimising Transformations for Applicative Programs" Ph.D. Thesis, Computer Science Department, University of Edinburgh, Scotland (1981).

[Pettorossi 84]
Pettorossi, A.: "A Powerful Strategy for Deriving Efficient Programs by Transformation" ACM Symposium on Lisp and Functional Programming, Austin, Texas (1984), pp.273-281.

[Pettorossi-Skowron 87]
Pettorossi, A. and A. Skowron: "Higher Order Generalization in Program Derivation" Proc. Intern. Joint Conference on Theory and Practice of Software Development. Pisa, Italy. Lecture Notes in Computer Science n. 250, Springer Verlag (1987), pp. 182-196.

[Pettorossi 87]
Pettorossi, A.: "Program Development Using Lambda Abstraction" Proc. 7th Intern. Conference on Foundations of Software Technology and Theoretical Computer Science, Pune, India. (K. V. Nori, ed.) Lecture Notes in Computer Science n. 287, Springer Verlag (1987), pp. 420-434.

[Scherlis 81]
Scherlis, W. L.: "Program Improvement by Internal Specialization" A.C.M. Eighth Symposium on Principles of Programming Languages, (1981), pp. 146-160.

[Takeichi 87]
Takeichi, M.: "Partial Parametrization Eliminates Multiple Traversals of Data Structures" Acta Informatica 24, (1987), pp.57-77.

[Wadler 85]
Wadler, P.L.: "Listlessness is Better than Laziness" Ph. D. Thesis, Computer Science Department, CMU-CS-85-171, Carnegie Mellon University, Pittsburgh, USA (1985).

[Wirth 76]
Wirth, N.: "Algorithms + Data Structures = Programs" Prentice-Hall, Inc. (1976).

Partial Evaluation and Mixed Computation
D. Bjørner, A.P. Ershov and N.D. Jones (Editors)
Elsevier Science Publishers B.V. (North-Holland)
© IFIP, 1988

THE GENERATION OF INVERSE FUNCTIONS IN REFAL

Alexander Y. ROMANENKO

Institute of Phisical Chemistry
Academy of Sciences
Moscow,The USSR

Some problems of automatic generation of inverse functions are considered. Two approaches to inverse function
generation are compared: the transformational approach
and the configurational analysis. The possibilities to
invert non-injective functions are outlined. Related
extensions of the Refal language are proposed.

1. INTRODUCTION

Consider the following problem. Let $f,g:D^{n+1} \to D$ be the computable functions (D is the set of symbolic expressions); the program g is given in a language L_1 and equation

$$f(g(v,\bar{x}),\bar{x}) = v \qquad (1)$$

is written in the same language. Find a program in a language L_2
for the function f satisfying the equation (1). This is a formulation of the i n v e r s e   p r o b l e m. One of the proposed ways of solving it is a program transformation. (Note
that nothing prevents us from the generalization of the right
part in (1) to $h(v,\bar{x})$ with an arbitrary $h:D^{n+1} \to D$).

The language used by the author was REFAL - the REcursive
Function Algorithmic Language - as L_1, L_2 and an implementation
language [Tur79].

This approach has similarities with the use of other functional languages in [BuDa77,Bird84]: the d r i v i n g [Tur72] in
Refal corresponds to UNFOLD with INSTANTIATION, generalization -
to FOLD, but this similarity is not complete. By driving the
program in Refal we get not only syntactical program transformation but create a graph of states and transitions between possible configurations of the computing system. The generalization
permits to transform the infinite graph of states to a finite
one.

In the context of Refal the first results were obtained in
1972 [Tur72]. The formulation of the problem was as follows. Let
EQU(x,y) be the equality predicate and F(x) be a function. Find
an x such that EQU(F(x),C) is TRUE, where x is a variable and C
is a constant. For brevity s sake EQU(F(x),C) will be denoted by
P(x) and let DRIVE be the driving algorithm for Refal. When
applied to P, DRIVE tabulates it in the following way:

$$P(A1) \Rightarrow T$$
$$P(A2) \Rightarrow T$$

.   .   .   .   .

where A1, A2,.. are some constants or pattern expressions
(i.e. ones including variables!).

In general case this process is infinite but sometimes it may
terminate, the last sentence generated being:

$$P(x) \Rightarrow F.$$

Let EXTRACT be a function that extracts the argument (answer)
from the new definition of the predicate: EXTRACT(DRIVE(P)) The
evaluation of this expression yields such an A that P(A)=T, if
any exists. This algorithm was called the Universal Resolving
Algorithm (URA)[Tur72].

The first implementation of the URA was carried out by S.A.Ro-
manenko in 1973 and the next one was constructed in 1985 by
S.M.Abramov in the context of his dialogue URA-system. The programs from this system were used by the author for the generation of inverse functions.

Two approaches to inverse function generation are compared in
the next sections: the transformational approach and the configurational analysis. Some ways of solving related problems and
two extensions of Refal are proposed.

2. LANGUAGE

As was noted above we need to discuss three languages:
   - the input one on which the tasks for the system are described;
   - the output language intended for representing results - the
inverse functions;
   - the implementation language, the system is written in.
   Really we have used the only language - Refal - in all three
roles, although different versions of it. A short informal

description of the language is presented here in order for the
paper to be self-contained.

A program in Refal constists of a sequence of function definitions, a definition is a sequence of sentences. A sentence has
the form $\langle L \rangle = R$, where $\langle L \rangle$ is the left part and R is the right
part of the sentence. The left part is a pattern to be matched
against object expressions and the right part represents the
result to be produced in the case of successive matching.

Any pattern can contain variables of four types: s-variables
take symbols as values, t-variables, v-variables and e-variables
take as values correspondingly terms, nonempty expressions and
expressions. Note that parentheses are not symbols and cannot be
matched against symbol variables. The only variables can appear
in the right part of the sentence that are contained in the left
part of it. The nested function calls are not allowed in the
left parts. Angular brackets are used for description of control
structure.

A sentence is applicable if its left part can be matched
against the function call evaluated using some matching algorithm whose semantics can be expressed in the next words: to
find such a substitution S for variables in the left part $\langle L \rangle$ of
the sentence that applying S to $\langle L \rangle$ yields the given string,the
object expression to be matched [Tur86a]. The first applicable
sentence is selected on the every step. If an appropriate sentence is found the function call is replaced by the right part
of the sentence where all variables have been replaced by their
values. If such sentence is nct found the abnormal stop of program occurs.

Let us consider the reversing function as an example:

$$\langle \text{reverse } \rangle =$$

$$\langle \text{reverse } s_1 \ e_2 \rangle = \langle \text{reverse } e_2 \rangle \ s_1$$

$$\langle \text{reverse } (e_1)e_2 \rangle = \langle \text{reverse } e_2 \rangle(\langle \text{reverse } e_1 \rangle)$$

The first sentence describes the case of the argument being empty - the result is empty too. The second sentence is carrying
the next symbol recursively out of functional brackets, and the
last one prescribes what to do if the round brackets have been
met. The way "reverse" function works is obvious.

The next example illustrates the using of hidden recursion in
matching. The matching indeterminism is eliminated by selection

of the lexicographically first suitable substitution in each
case. "Make-set" function generates a set of terms, that are
contained in the argument on the top level of brackets (it
leaves the only instance of each):

$$\langle\text{make-set } e_1 \, t_x \, e_2 \, t_x \, e_3\rangle = e_1 \, \langle\text{make-set } e_2 \, t_x \, e_3\rangle$$

$$\langle\text{make-set } e_1\rangle = e_1$$

This version of Refal (so-called Refal-2 [KlRo87]) was used as
both an output and an implementation language.

It should be noted about various Refal extensions here. They
may be divided into two classes: purely pragmatical and regular.

Refal was developed as a universal metalanguage for the formal
description of problem-oriented algorithmic languages. Being an
algorithmic language itself, Refal may become an object of its
own manipulation. A powerfull system of equivalent transformations in Refal allows the implementation of directed program
optimization or transformation on computer. Consequently all
language extensions are estimated not only from the point of
view of the efficiency,programming convenience and so on, but in
the first turn in connection with a possibility of equivalent
program transformations in the language.

Regular extensions do not impede equivalent program transformations (though for all that they can be quite pragmatical)
whereas purely pragmatical extensions may not satisfy this criterion.

The s t r i c t R e f a l was selected as a basis of input
language, the above equivalence transformation system was developed for it [Tur72,Tur80].

The left parts of sentences in this version are restricted by
the following:

- the "open" expression variables are absent, i.e. there is no
more than one expression variable on each level of brackets;

- every expression or term variable can appear only once.

The first significant extension of strict Refal, intrduced to
represent the equation (1), is the possibility of nested function calls in the left parts of sentences. The semantics of
matching is modified properly: find such a substitution S for
the variables in $\langle L\rangle$ (the left part of the sentence) that applying S to L a n d e v a l u a t i n g the r e s u l t of it
yeilds the initial function call - the object expression to be
matched.

This extension modifies in some way the above restrictions:

- duplicate expression and term variables are permitted to appear in functional terms in the left part (they can duplicate the variables appearing outside the functional term);

- open expression variables are not allowed to appear if we replace the nested functional term by an expression variable.

3. TRANSFORMATIONAL APPROACH

Suppose, there is the equation (1) written in strict Refal and the function g defined in it. We need to construct a new definition of f not containing function calls in the left parts of the sentences.

Informally the algorithm producing the proper definition can be described as follows.

* Make one generalized step of the inner functional term g (driving).

* Substitute the result of it for this term and the results of the variables' contractions to the left and the right parts of the sentence.

* The residual functional calls in the left parts are substituted for some new expession variables.

* Old variables removed from the left part by previous substitution are substituted in the right part for the new function calls.

* Generate the unfold definition of the new functions by further driving.

* The process terminates when new function definitions on some step of algorithm are all matched against old ones. In this case the system becomes self-sufficient.

Consider the above "reverse" function, supposing for simplicity the argument can consist of symbols only and does not contain brackets:

$$\langle reverse \quad \rangle =$$

$$\langle reverse \ s_1 \ e_2 \ \rangle = \langle reverse \ e_2 \ \rangle \ s_1$$

$$\langle inv\text{-}reverse \ \langle reverse \ e_x \ \rangle \ \rangle = e_x$$

The function "inv-reverse" is defined implicitly (the last sentence we are calling the task for inversion). Making one generalized step of the inner functional term (driving) and substituting the results of contractions we obtain:

$$\langle inv\text{-}reverse\ \rangle\ =$$

$$\langle inv\text{-}reverse\ \langle reverse\ e_2 \rangle\ s_1\ \rangle\ =\ s_1\ e_2$$

The last sentence contains the inner functional term in the left part again. Replace the sentence with a new one:

$$\langle inv\text{-}reverse\ e_x\ s_1\ \rangle\ =\ s_1\ \langle new\text{-}fun\ e_x \rangle$$

where e_x is an expression variable, which stands for possible result of $\langle reverse\ e_2 \rangle$ function call, and "new-fun" is a new function such that $\langle new\text{-}fun\ e_x\ \rangle\ =\ e_2$ (compare with Hilbert's tau-symbol). By making a further step of driving the inner call in the second sentence of "inv-reverse" we get:

$$\langle inv\text{-}reverse\ s_1 \rangle\ =\ s_1$$

$$\langle inv\text{-}reverse\ \langle reverse\ e_3\ \rangle\ s_2\ s_1 \rangle\ =\ s_1\ s_2\ e_3$$

Comparing with the above definition of "new-fun" we obtain its instantiated description:

$$\langle new\text{-}fun\ \rangle\ \ =$$

$$\langle new\text{-}fun\ \langle reverse\ e_3 \rangle\ s_2\ \rangle\ =\ s_2\ e_3$$

which turns out to be identical to the description of "inv-reverse" if we substitute properly the variables in it. Thus we get the final definition of "inv-reverse":

$$\langle inv\text{-}reverse\ \rangle\ =$$

$$\langle inv\text{-}reverse\ e_x\ s_1 \rangle\ =\ s_1\ \langle inv\text{-}reverse\ e_x \rangle$$

This method works well for the class of Burstall's inductively defined functions [Bur85]. Consider the case of two variables, for instance (unary arithmetics):

$$\langle add\ (e_1)0 \rangle\ =\ e_1$$

$$\langle add\ (e_1)e_2\ 1 \rangle\ =\ \langle add\ (e_1)e_2 \rangle\ 1$$

$$\langle sub\ (\langle add\ (e_1)\ e_2 \rangle)e_2\ \rangle\ =\ e_1$$

Computer produces the result:

$$\langle sub\ (e_1)\ 0 \rangle\ =\ e_1$$

$$\langle sub\ (e_1 1)e_2 1 \rangle\ =\ \langle sub\ (e_1)e_2 \rangle$$

For the time being the available computer implementation works in the transformational area described, i.e. for functions with

the format of recursive call literally matching against their
initial format. The narrowly directed transformations comparing
with multiple ones in [Dar81,Fea82] allowed to automate the
above process completely.

The shortcomings of this approach appear in the case of accumulating parameters. Consider an example:

$$\langle \text{add-a } (e_1) \ 0 \rangle = e_1$$

$$\langle \text{add-a } (e_1)e_2 \ 1 \rangle = \langle \text{add-a } (e_1 \ 1 \ )e_2\rangle$$

$$\langle \text{sub-a } (\langle \text{add-a } (e_1)e_2\rangle) \ e_2\rangle = e_1$$

It differs from a previous one by the way of result being accu-
mulated - not out of a functional term but in one of function
parameters. Since the result can not be represented by one variable as in the above "add" function - the generated descriptions of new functions does not match against each other and the
generation process is infinite.

4. CONFIGURATIONAL ANALYSIS: EXTENSION OF POSSIBILITIES

The history of computations has played its role in all previous
examples, but it was not represented explitly: now we shall use
the whole graph of the computational histories - the graph of
configurations (the configuration is a set of states of the computing system, which can be represented by a Refal-expression
[Tur86a]).

Let us construct the finite graph of configurations for the
function "add-a". The initial configuration of the graph is the
inner functional term from the left part of the task for inversion. (We can always transform the infinite graph of configurations to a finite one by the proper generalization [Tur80]).
The vertexes of graph correspond to configurations, the verges
contain contractions and assignments of a computational history.
The dotted lines correspond to generalizations and contain the
assignments.

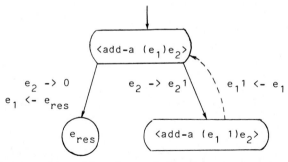

An arbitrary contraction is $v \to L$, where v is a variable and L
is an L-expression, i.e. an expression that is allowed in the
left part of a sentence in the strict Refal. An assignment has
the form: $E \gets v$, where v is a variable and E is an arbitrary
Refal-expression. For convenience of consideration we suppose
that all passive configurations in the graph are e_{res} and all
proper assignments are performed on the corresponding verges
(for instance, $e_1 \gets e_{res}$ here).

The common feature of all successfully inverted functions in
the previous section was the generation of their results out of
a functional term. It is necessary for successful inversion to
take into account not only a dynamics of direct function's arguments, but of their result too, since a result of a direct function corresponds to an argument of inverse one. Consequently
such functions must be replaced by their extended versions. To
do so the argument of a direct function is put in parentheses
and the function is redefined so, that result accumulates within the functional term, but out of the parentheses.

So, the function "add" from previous section is replaced by
the following new "add-ext":

$$\langle add\ (e_1)e_2\ \rangle = \langle add\text{-}ext\ ((e_1)e_2)\ \rangle$$

$$\langle add\text{-}ext\ ((e_1)0)\ e_{res}\rangle = e_1 e_{res}$$

$$\langle add\text{-}ext\ ((e_1)e_2 1)\ e_{res}\rangle = \langle add\text{-}ext\ ((e_1)e_2)1 e_{res}\rangle$$

the variable e_{res} is used for the result accumulation.
To obtain the inverse function having a graph of direct one we
have:

- to invert the graph of states with use of a task for inversion;

- to transform the "unlawful" contractions (if any exists) to
correct assignments producing the graph of states for an inverse

function;

  - to restore a definition of a function itself.

The main idea of the graph inverting is: to change the directions of all verges to the opposite and to replace all assignments by the proper contractions and vice versa - all contractions by the proper assignments.

More detailed algorithm for inverting a graph of a function is
follows.

* All variables of the graph (excluding e_{res}) are renamed and
  correspondence between the old and new names are stored
  (in our case e_1 and e_2 are renamed as e_a and e_b).
* The initial configuration of a new graph is produced from
  the left part of the task for inversion if we replace the
  nested function call by its argument (in the case of sub-a
  the initial configuration will be: <sub-a-ext $((e_a)e_b)$ e_2>,
  where sub-a-ext is a name of a new function: definition of
  sub-a will be obtained from it by a simple transformation).
* All verges change their direction on the opposite, all contractions are transformed to assignments and all assignments
  are transformed to contractions, and so every finishing
  verge with a passive configuration at the end is turned into
  initial one.
* All other vertexes of the graph are produced from the initial one applying the proper contractions and assignments.
* KU-annotation of the obtained so graph is performed i.e.
  all variables and expressions in contractions and assignments receive the attributes K (known) and U (unknown) according to the rules described below.

The purpose of a KU-annotation is the propagation of the information about the arguments given through the graph and discovering the "fixed point" of such propagation.
The rules of KU-annotation.

  (a) The annotation is made during the traversing of a graph
       from the input verges to the output ones with single
       passes of cycles.
  (b) An assignment of K<-U-type transforms an unknown variable
       to a known one.
  (c) The contraction of a known variable transforms it to an
       unknown one, if it is not contained in the expression on
       the right.

(d) Any constant is K-marked by definition.

(e) The variable e_{res} and the parameters corresponding to the
     arguments of the inverse function call (it is e_2 here)
     are annotated as "K" and the other parameters (they are
     e_a, e_b) - as "U".

(f) The contractions of K->K-type with function call are
     replaced by the corresponding assignment of K<-K-type.

(g) If all variables of an expression in an assignment are
     K-marked then the expression is K-marked and the whole
     assignment is K<-K-marked.

(h) If the left variable in a contraction is U-marked and the
     expression on the right is K-marked then this contraction
     is replaced by the opposite assignment.

(i) If the left variable in a contraction is K-marked and
     there is no more than one U-marked open expression va-
     riable on the right then the expression and all its va-
     riables are K-marked and the whole contraction receives
     the type K->K (Note, that the left variable may receive
     the type U due to (c)!).

If a variable which corresponds to some argument in the initial
configuration (it is e_b in our case) was annotated as K then we
add the contraction linking its value with the value of the argument to all output verges (e_b -> e_2 in our case). Otherwise if
such a variable was annotated as U, we add the assignment opposite to the above contraction to all input verges and update the
KU-annotation with respect to this information.

If in the graph produced the K->U-type, U->U-type contractions
and U->U-type assignments are absent the inverting of the graph
is complete.

For the last example we obtain (e_b is annotated as K, contraction e_b -> e_2 was added to the output verge):

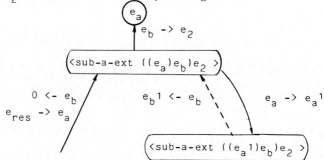

Restoring the definition of "sub-a-ext" on Refal:

$$\langle\text{sub-a-ext } ((e_a)e_2)\ e_2\rangle\ =\ e_a$$

$$\langle\text{sub-a-ext } ((e_a\ 1\ )e_b)\ e_2\rangle\ =$$
$$\langle\text{sub-a-ext } ((e_a)e_b\ 1)\ e_2\rangle$$

Adding the calling sentence of "sub-a-ext" (with the assignment $0 \leftarrow e_b$ and the needed transformation) we obtain the definition of "sub-a":

$$\langle\text{sub-a } (e_{res})e_2\rangle\ =\ \langle\text{sub-a-ext } ((e_{res})\ 0)\ e_2\rangle$$

It should be noted here the following.

A contraction is always can be transformed to a correct assignment but the opposite is not true. The criterion of the type $e_b \rightarrow e_2$ goes out of the limits of the strict Refal but not of Refal-2 (duplicate expression variables), while contractions $e_3 \rightarrow e_1 e_2$ or $e_3 \rightarrow \langle f(e_1)e_2\rangle$ are indeterminate if both e_1 and e_2 are unknown (they are annotated as K->U) and the last one is not correct for Refal-2 (at the same time the function itself may be injective and has the single-valued inverse one). What can we do if a function is not injective at all? What is the meaning of the inversion in this case? The result of the URA-program, as was mentioned above, may be a pattern expression containing variables (i.e. can represent sets). These questions are considered in the next sections.

5. CONCATENATION

As usually let us start from an example. The function "mul" describes the multiplication in unary arithmetics (0 is represented by emptiness):

$$\langle\text{mul } (e_1)\rangle\ =$$

$$\langle\text{mul } (e_1)e_2\ 1\rangle\ =\ \langle\text{mul } (e_1)e_2\rangle\ e_1$$

Compare the next two tasks for inversion:

$$\langle\text{div1 } (\langle\text{mul } (e_1)e_2\rangle)\ e_2\rangle\ =\ e_1$$

$$\langle\text{div2 } (\langle\text{mul } (e_1)e_2\rangle)\ e_1\rangle\ =\ e_2$$

Extended definition of "mul" is:

$$\langle\text{mul } (e_1)e_2\ \rangle\ =\ \langle\text{mul-ext } ((e_1)e_2)\rangle$$

$$\langle\text{mul-ext } ((e_1))e_{res}\rangle\ =\ e_{res}$$

$$\langle\text{mul-ext } ((e_1)e_2\ 1)e_{res}\rangle\ =\ \langle\text{mul-ext } ((e_1)e_2)e_1 e_{res}\rangle$$

Let us construct the graph of configurations for "mul-ext":

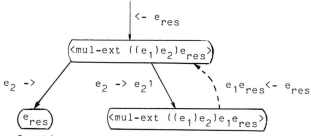

The inverse function graph generated (by the second argument):

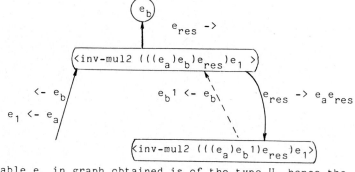

The variable e_a in graph obtained is of the type U, hence the assignment $e_1 \leftarrow e_a$ is added to the initial verge. The result of "inv-mul2" is a value of e_b. The definition of "inv-mul2" and hence, "div2" is easily restored from the graph. This solution is similar to the previous one. The inversion by the first argument is more complicated:

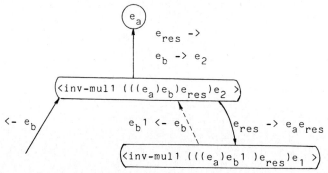

The variable e_b in graph obtained is of the type K, hence the contraction $e_b \rightarrow e_2$ is added to the output verge. The contraction $e_{res} \rightarrow e_a e_{res}$ has the type K->U because e_a and e_{res} on the right are unknown.

The semantics of this graph can be expessed in the words: find e_a such that sequential chipping e_a off e_{res} yields at the same time e_{res} = EMPTY and e_b = e_2. Hence we need a sequential search here and we can not restore "inv-mul1" using the above graph.

The suggested transformation of the graph leads to the explicit representation of the exhaustive search among the unknown variables.

If in some contraction e_i -> L of K->U-type on some level of brackets N expression variables of U-type appear then the search is arranged by N-1 of them: the initial values for N-2 of them are EMPTY , an arbitrary term is the initial value for the last variable (thus cycling is pevented) and we try to satisfy the known left e_i for all possible values of variables analogously to matching of open variables in Refal.

This graph transformation is needed if the above contraction is included in the cycle otherwise the built-in matching of Refal is sufficient.

The transformed graph of "inv-mul1" will be (the variable e_{res0} keeps the initial value of e_{res}, since the last one takes part in contractions and loses its initial value):

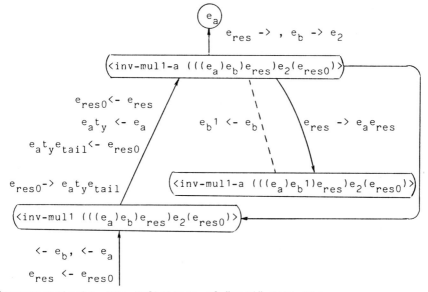

Correspondingly, the definition of "div1" will be:

$$\langle \text{div1 } (e_{res})e_2 \rangle = \langle \text{inv-mul1 } (((()))e_2(e_{res}) \rangle$$

$$\langle \text{inv-mul1 } (((e_a)e_b)e_{res})e_2(e_a t_y e_{tail}) \rangle =$$
$$\langle \text{inv-mul1-a } (((e_a t_y))e_a t_y e_{tail})e_2(e_a t_y e_{tail}) \rangle$$

$$\langle \text{inv-mul1-a } (((e_a)e_2))e_2(e_{res0}) \rangle = e_a$$

$$\langle \text{inv-mul1-a } (((e_a)e_b)e_a e_{res})e_2(e_{res0}) \rangle =$$
$$\langle \text{inv-mul1-a } (((e_a)e_b 1)e_{res})e_2(e_{res0}) \rangle$$

$$\langle \text{inv-mul1-a } (((e_a)e_b)e_{res})e_2(e_{res0}) \rangle =$$
$$\langle \text{inv-mul1 } (((e_a)e_b)e_{res})e_2(e_{res0}) \rangle$$

6. NESTED FUNCTION CALLS

Contractions $e_i \rightarrow \langle f \ldots \rangle$ appear as inversions of the assignments of $\langle f \ldots \rangle \leftarrow e_i$ when the nested function calls are
contained in the right part of a sentence in a function being
inverted.

If the call contains U-type variables then we replace the
contraction by the assignment of the form $\langle f_u^{-1} \ldots e_i \ldots \rangle \leftarrow e_u$,
where f_u^{-1} is a function inverse to f by the unknown argument.

To illustrate the last operation consider the Ackermann's
function (in unary arithmetics):

$$\langle \text{psi } (0)e_y \rangle = e_y 1$$
$$\langle \text{psi } (e_x 1)0 \rangle = \langle \text{psi } (e_x)01 \rangle$$
$$\langle \text{psi } (e_x 1)e_y 1 \rangle = \langle \text{psi } (e_x)\langle \text{psi } (e_x 1)e_y \rangle \rangle$$

The graph of states will be:

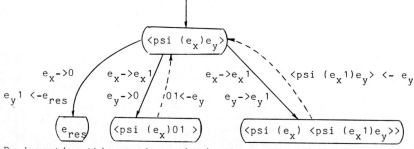

By inverting this graph we obtain the contraction:
$e_b \rightarrow \langle \text{psi } (e_a 1)e_b \rangle$, i.e. inversion of psi is needed again by
the second argument while the first one is known, the contrac-
tion is transformed to the assignment: $\langle \text{inv-psi2 } (e_b)e_a 1 \rangle \leftarrow e_b$.
Now we can easily restore both inverse functions:

$$\langle\text{inv-psi1 } (e_{res}1)e_2\rangle = \langle\text{inv-psi1-a } ((0)e_{res})e_2\rangle$$

$$\langle\text{inv-psi1-a } ((e_a)e_2)e_2\rangle = e_a$$

$$\langle\text{inv-psi1-a } ((e_a)01)e_2\rangle = \langle\text{inv-psi1-a } ((e_a1)0)e_2\rangle$$

$$\langle\text{inv-psi1-a } ((e_a)e_b)e_2\rangle =$$
$$\langle\text{inv-psi1-a } ((e_a1) \langle\text{inv-psi2 } (e_b)e_a1\rangle1) \ e_2\rangle$$

$$\langle\text{inv-psi2 } (e_{res}1)e_1\rangle = \langle\text{inv-psi2-a } ((0)e_{res})e_1\rangle$$

$$\langle\text{inv-psi2-a } ((e_1)e_b)e_1\rangle = e_b$$

$$\langle\text{inv-psi2-a } ((e_a)01)e_1\rangle = \langle\text{inv-psi2-a } ((e_a1)0)e_1\rangle$$

$$\langle\text{inv-psi2-a } ((e_a)e_b)e_1\rangle =$$
$$\langle\text{inv-psi2-a } ((e_a1) \langle\text{inv-psi2 } (e_b)e_a1\rangle1) \ e_1\rangle$$

They are very similar, but assimetrical.

7. EXTENSIONS OF THE LANGUAGE

Motivation of suggested extensions has appeared in a process of
functions inversion when we need to violate the limits of not
only the strict Refal but also Refal-2. These extensions are
useful in cases where the function to be inverted is not injective. So the result of inversion is not a value-to-value function.

The first extension of the language permits to hide into implementation a more powerful search cycle in comparison with the
matching of the open variables in the modern Refal. The projection of the extension on strict Refal does not contradict equivalent transformations.

The essence of this extension is so-called power expressions.
The base may be any pattern whereas the exponent must be a natural number or a variable whose values are natural numbers.
This construct means that the base is to be repeated as many
times as the exponent indicates.

In addition to usual Refal variables the base of power or the
left part itself can contain the so-called place-holder with the
type of symbol or term: $s_{?i}$ or $t_{?i}$. These variables can not be
used in the right parts of sentences.

The function "mul" then may be written in a form:

$$\langle\text{mul } (e_1) \ 1^{s_x}\rangle = e_1^{s_x}$$

the inverse functions are found immediately:

$$\langle div1 \ (e_1{}^{s_x}) 1^{s_x} \rangle = e_1$$

$$\langle div2 \ (e_1{}^{s_x}) e_1 \rangle = 1^{s_x}$$

The projection of this extension on the strict Refal:
- a base can not contain any e,v and ordinary t-variables;
- the replacement of a power by an expression variable does not entail the appearence of the open expression variables.

The generalized matching algorithm [Tur86a] may be extended easily for this linguage, and inverse functions in some cases become more explicit and of simpler construction. Place-holders in addition to ordinary ones are used naturally in power-expressions or may serve for length representation in Refal.

The second extension is related to the case of a U<-U-type assignment mentioned above. If on the right of the sentence a new variables can appear that were absent on the left (may be the place-holders also) then we can invert some non-injective functions. These new variables can not undergo contractions along the further computation process, otherwise the abnormal stop occurs.

Consider a function defining the length of an expression in terms.

$$\langle length \ e_n () \rangle = e_n$$
$$\langle length \ e_n (t_x e_y) \rangle = \langle length \ e_n 1 (e_y) \rangle$$

We can produce the inverse for it:

$$\langle inv\text{-}length \ (e_a) \rangle = e_a$$
$$\langle inv\text{-}length \ e_n 1 (e_a) \rangle = \langle inv\text{-}length \ e_n (t_{?i} e_a) \rangle$$

i is the new one on the every step here. "Inv-length" generates the expression consisting of a given number of t e r m   v a -
r i a b l e s, i.e. representing an arbitrary expression of the length given.

8.   CONCLUSION

The solutions of some problems related to function inversion have been presented. At the time being I am extending the computer implementation trying to include the algorithms described and to find the bounds of applicability and correctness of above methods.

In all above examples the sequence of the sentences in the inverse function has been inherited from the direct one. Indeterminism may be needed here in the general case: a calculus instead of algorithms.

In addition to the search of a "fixed point" in the class of functions I intend to translate all programs to new Refal-4 [Rom87a] which being absorbed in its own system of equivalent transformations and it is much more powerful for programming than Refal-2. Then all three languages of the system can be united in the one.

ACKNOWLEDGEMENTS

I gratefully aknowledge the early collaboration with Valentine Turchin who initiated my interests in this area, the invaluable help of Sergei Abramov, whose implementation of the URA-system was the main initial source of mine, the efforts of Andrei Klimov and Sergei Romanenko, who made numerous suggestions on this report and continuing support and discussions of this work by the other permanent participators of Refal-group seminar in Moscow - R.Gurin, Ark.Klimov,V.Kistlerov,N.Kondratyev, V.Rudnyi, A.Zibrov. I should like to thank the referee for giving many useful remarks on the extended abstract of this report.

REFERENCES

[Bird84] Bird, R.S., Promotion and Accumulation Strategies in Transformational Programming. - ACM Trans. on Prog. Lang. and Systems, 6(4),1984,pp.487-504.

[BuDa77] Burstall,R.M. and Darlington,J.,A Transformational System for Developing Recursive Programms. - JACM, 24(1), 1977, pp. 44-67.

[Bur85] Burstall,R.M.,Inductively Defined Functions.- LNCS,185, 1985, pp.92-96.

[Cut80] Cutland,N.,Computability. An Introduction to Recursive Function Theory. Cambridge Univ. Press, 1980.

[Dar81] Darlington, J., An Experimental Program Transformation and Synthesis System. Artificial Intelligence 16(1981), pp.1-46.

[Fea82] Feather,M.S.,A System for Assisting Program Transformation. - ACM Trans. on Prog. Lang. and Syst. 4(1),1982, pp.1-20.

[JSS85]   Jones,N.D.,Sestoft,P.,Sondergaard,H., An Experiment in
           Partial Evaluation: The Generation of a Compiler Gene-
           rator. - SIGPLAN Notices, 20(8),1985,pp.82-87.

[KlRc87]   Klimov,A.V.,Romanenko,S.A., REFAL-2 Programming System
           for ES-Computers. Input Language Description. Preprint,
           Keldysh Inst.of Appl.Math. Academy of Sciences,M.,1987.
           (In Russian)

[Rom87]   Romanenko,S.A.,A Compiler Generator Produced by a Self-
           Application of Specializer can have a Surprizingly Na-
           tural Structure.   - Preprint #26,M.,Keldysh Inst.of
           Appl.Math. Academy of Sciences,USSR,1987. (In Russian)

[Rom87a]   Romanenko,S.A., Refal-4 - The Extension of Refal-2 Sup-
           plying The Presentation of Driving Results.Preprint 147
           Keldysh Inst.of Appl.Math. Academy of Sciences,M.,1987.
           (In Russian)

[Ses86]   Sestoft,P., The Structure of Self-Applicable Partial
           Evaluator - Programs as Data Objects (Eds.H.Gauzinger,
           N.Jones), Lect. Notes on Comp. Science, V.217,1986,
           pp.257-281.

[Tur72]   Turchin,V.F., Equivalent Transformations of Recursive
           Functions defined in REFAL.   - in Teoria yazykov i me-
               dy postroenia system programirowania.   Trudy sympos.
           Kiev-Alushta,1972,pp.31-42.(In Russian)

[ur79]   Turchin,V.F.,Supercompiler System Based on the Language
           REFAL. - SIGPLAN Notices, 14(2),1979,pp.46-54.

[Tur80]   Turchin,V.F.,The Language REFAL, the Theory of Compila-
           tion and Metasystem Analisis.   - Technical Report#18,
           Curant Institute of Mathematics, NY,1980.

[Tur86a]   Turchin,V.F., The Concept of a Supercompiler.   - ACM
           Trans. on Prog. Lang. and Syst. 8(3),1986,pp.292-325.

[Tur86b]   Turchin,V.F.,Program Transformation by Supercompilation
           - Programs as Data Objects (Eds.H.Gauzinger,N.Jones),
           Lect. Notes on Comp. Science, V.217,1986,pp.257-281.

Partial Evaluation and Mixed Computation
D. Bjørner, A.P. Ershov and N.D. Jones (Editors)
Elsevier Science Publishers B.V. (North-Holland)
© IFIP, 1988

A COMPILER GENERATOR PRODUCED BY A SELF-APPLICABLE
SPECIALIZER CAN HAVE A SURPRISINGLY NATURAL AND
UNDERSTANDABLE STRUCTURE

Sergei A. ROMANENKO

Keldysh Institute of Applied Mathematics
Academy of Sciences of the USSR
Miusskaya Sq.4, SU-125047, Moscow, USSR

SUMMARY

This paper describes the structure of, and the ideas behind,
a self-applicable specializer of programs, as well as the
principles of operation of a compiler generator that has been
produced automatically by specializing the specializer with
respect to itself. It has been found that the structure of the
compilers produced can be improved by making use of such
devices as introducing different representations for the values
of K- and U-parameters, splitting the subject program into K-
and U-program, and automatically raising the arity of functions
in the residual program.

KEY WORDS AND PHRASES: Compiler generator, partial evaluation,
mixed computation, non-partial evaluation, self-applicability,
specializer, unmixed computation.

0. INTRODUCTION

Let Spec be a two-argument function specified by a program
and satisfying the equation $F(X,Y) = Spec(F,X)(Y)$, where F is
an arbitrary two-argument function specified by a program, X
and Y being inputs for F. Such a function Spec will be referred
to as a "specializer".
The idea that specializers can become a programming tool of
practical value dates back to the late 1960s [Lom 67], while it
seems that the term "specializer" appeared in the early 1970s
[Dix 71], [ChL 73].
In 1971 it was found by Y.Futtamura that compiling may be
carried out by specializing interpreters [Fut 71] in the
following way. Let Int be an interpreter of a programming
language, i.e. a two-argument function satisfying the equation
$Int(S,D) = S(D)$, where S(D) denotes the result of applying a
program S to an input D. According to [Fut 71], Spec(Int,S) can
be considered to be the result of compiling the program S into
the target language of the specializer, for $Spec(Int,S)(D) =
Int(S,D) = S(D)$.
In the same paper [Fut 71] Y.Futtamura pointed out that
interpreters can be automatically converted to compilers by
specializing a specializer with respect to the interpreters,
the reason being that $Spec(Spec,Int)(S) = Spec(Int,S)$. Of
course, this approach implies that the source language of the
specializer and the language it is written in are identical,
which makes the self-application of the specializer feasible.

Several years later it was realized [Bec 76], [Tur 77, 79, 80] that a compiler generator can be automatically produced by evaluating Spec(Spec,Spec). This compiler generator transforms interpreters into compilers, for Spec(Spec,Spec)(Int) = Spec(Spec,Int).

No matter how attractive this method of producing compiler generators may seem, for several years it remained a purely speculative possibility.

Although there are a few publications reporting success in compiling by specializing interpreters [Fut 71], [Tur 79], [TNT 82], [Tur 86], it is only recently that the group under the leadership by N.Jones succeeded in designing a non-trivial specializer that proved to be self-applicable not only in theory, but also in practice [JSS 85a], [JSS 85b], [Ses 86]. To the author's best knowledge, this specializer was the first to be used in practice to convert interpreters to compilers by Futtamura's method and to generate a non-trivial compiler generator Spec(Spec,Spec).

For brevity's sake, the specializer developed by N.Jones and coworkers will be, henceforth, referred to as the "Copenhagen" one.

It should be noted that the Copenhagen specializer is not a completely automatic one. It requires a hand-made annotation of the subject program. The user has to classify all function calls appearing in the subject program as "eliminable" or "residual". In the course of specialization, the eliminable calls are unfolded (i.e. replaced with the reduced equivalent of the called function's body), while the residual calls are suspended (i.e. replaced with a call to a residual variant of the called function). Thus, the actual execution of the residual calls is postponed up to the time when the residual program is run. Annotating the subject program is done by replacing the key word "call" with the key word "callr" for all residual calls.

Classifying all function calls as residual or eliminable proved to be a hard problem for the computer. This problem seems to be the main difficulty that impedes the self-application of completely automatic non-trivial specializers [Tur 86].

The paper [JSS 85a] describes the results obtained by means of the Copenhagen specializer as follows.

The compilers produced by evaluating Spec(Spec,Int) "have a surprisingly natural structure"; nevertheless, as far as the compiler generator Spec(Spec,Spec) is concerned, the situation is less satisfactory. Although, the compiler generator produced is "of reasonable size", "its logic is harder to follow" than the logic of the compilers generated. Furthermore, "it contains some unexpected constructions (like ''''nil!)".

In early 1986, by the courtesy of Neil Jones, the author received a detailed description of the structure and principles of the Copenhagen specializer. It inspired the author to make an attempt to reproduce the results obtained by the Copenhagen group. The original objectives of the project were:

* To modify the Copenhagen technique in order to make it applicable to programs written in Refal, rather than Lisp.

* To behold compilers generated this way, especially the compiler generator, and to examine their structure.

The availability of detailed information on the Copenhagen specializer enabled these objectives to be achieved without much difficulty. However, in the author's opinion, the compilers produced turned out to be unsatisfactory from the aesthitic point of view. Whereas the compilers were still within the human comprehension, the ugliness of the compiler generator prevented any attempt at reading it.

Nevertheless, a strong desire to fathom the mysterious principles of operation of the compiler generator made the author seek a way to improve the structure of residual programs produced by the specializer. As a result, the original specializer had been revised. For brevity's sake, the modified version of the specializer will be, henceforth, referred to as "the Moscow specializer".

The following sections discuss the differences and similarities of the two specializers. Finally, a description is given of the structure and principles of operation of the automatically generated compiler generator.

1. THE PRINCIPLES THE TWO SPECIALIZERS ARE BASED UPON

The main feature of the Copenhagen specializer that distinguishes it from those previously presented in the literature, and based on partial evaluation is that the specialization is done in several steps.

At the first step, the program is flow analyzed by a simple abstract interpretation over a domain consisting of the two symbols "K" and "U". "K" represents a value known at partial evaluation time, and "U" represents a value that may be unknown at partial evaluation time.

Partial evaluation is meta-evaluation with respect to ordinary evaluation, and KU-evaluation is meta-evaluation with respect to partial evaluation. Thus, KU-evaluation is meta-meta-evaluation.

The existence of a meta-meta-level is a peculiarity of the Copenhagen specializer, for the earlier specializers have only dealt with the basic level and the meta-level.

The correspondence between the three levels may be characterized as follows.

The basic level involves values, evaluation, interpreter.

The meta-level involves meta-values (terms of the semantic metalanguage), meta-evaluation (partial evaluation), meta-interpreter.

The meta-meta-level involves meta-meta-values ("K" and "U"), meta-meta-evaluation (meta-specialization), meta-meta-interpreter.

The first phase computes for each function in the subject program a description classifying the function's parameters as "known" K-parameters (eliminable) or "unknown" U-parameters (residual).

The information obtained by KU-interpretation is then used at the second step, when the subject program is transformed, i.e. annotated . The essence of annotation is in representing the global information obtained by meta-meta-interpretation locally. In the course of annotation the program is supplemented with additional directions meant for the meta-interpreter.

Thus, instead of being placed under the command of a supervisory device (as, for example, has been done in [Tur 80,

86]), the meta-interpreter is made to follow the directions
inserted into the annotated program. This is the second
principle the Copenhagen specializer is based upon. This
principle might be referred to as "the principle of self-
surveillence".
   The Moscow specializer is fully faithful to the two above
principles. It adheres to these principles even more thoroughly
and consistently than the Copenhagen specializer does. For this
reason, the Moscow specializer may be considered, in a sense,
to be a more "Copenhagen" one than the Copenhagen specializer
is.

2. THE SEMANTIC METALANGUAGE RL

   As has been pointed out by Y.Futtamura [Fut 71], a system
capable of producing compilers by self-application of a
specializer has to be based on a "semantic metalanguage"
satisfying a number of requirements. The specializer as well as
all interpreters to be transformed into compilers have to be
written in this language. As far as the Copenhagen specializer
is concerned, use is made of a dialect of pure Lisp, the
language L.
   The author's goal was to design a specializer capable of
accepting programs in the language Refal. Since Refal was
developed to serve as an "algorithmic metalanguage" [Tur 66],
[Tur 68], it may well be used as a semantic metalanguage. As a
matter of fact, it has been used this way [Tur 79], [Tur 80],
[Tur 86].
   Refal provides high-level facilities (such as pattern
matching), which enables symbolic manipulation algorithms to be
written in the form that is clear and simple from the human
point of view. However, as far as a specializer like the
Copenhagen one is concerned, these facilities tends to
complicate the operation of the specializer. This induced the
author to choose an alternative approach.
   The semantic metalanguage used by the Moscow specializer is
the language RL, which has been tailored by the author for this
purpose. For this reason, a Refal-program subject to
specialization has to be compiled into RL.
   RL is an intermediate language, which provides data
structures identical to those of Refal, but, as compared with
Refal, is a low-level language.
   The general structure of programs and the control constructs
provided by RL are similar to those of Lisp. For this reason,
the name "RL" may be interpreted as "Refal-Lisp".
   RL is less convenient for the human programmer than Refal,
though it is not low-level enough to prevent RL programs from
being written by hand. However, RL may well be, in some cases,
more suitable than Refal for automatic program generation and
transformation.
   RL is easier to implement than Refal, so an RL-program
automatically generated are hardly worth recompiling into
Refal.
   An RL-program is a non-empty list of function definitions.
The first function of the program is the goal function. Input
to the program is through the parameters of this function, and
output is the value returned by it.
   All functions used in RL-program may be classified as
"primitive" or "defined". A primitive function (or "operator")

can be called directly, whereas a defined function can only be called by means of the operator "call".

A defined function has a fixed arity, i.e. a certain number of arguments (which is allowed to be equal to zero). This is a peculiarity of RL in which it differs from Refal, as all functions defined in a Refal-program are formally one-argument. Any object expression (i.e. an arbitrary sequence of symbols and parentheses in which the parentheses are properly paired) can be taken as value by any parameter.

Any primitive function (i.e. operator) has a fixed arity. Nevertheless, in order to reduce the length of RL-program, a call of any unary operator is allowed to be given an arbitrary number of arguments, in which case the values of the arguments are concatenated to form an expression. This expression is then taken as value by the parameter of the operator.

An operator is either a function call, a conditional "if", a constant "quote", a constructor, a selector, or a predicate.

A constructor is a function that builds object expressions from object expressions. There are the following constructors: "br", which encloses its input in parentheses, and "expr", whose result is equal to its input. Since "expr" is a unary operator, it can be used to concatenate expressions.

A selector is a function that extracts a component from its input. There are the following selectors: "first", which takes the first term of an input expression, "last", which takes the last term of an expression, "bf", which takes all terms of an expression but the first one, "bl", which takes all terms of an expression but the last one, "cont", which takes the contents of a pair of parentheses.

A predicate is a function that tests the truth of a condition and produces either the symbol "true" or the symbol "false". There are the following predicates: "symbol", which tests whether its input expression is a symbol, and "equal", which tests whether its two inputs are equal.

The syntax or RL-programs may be described as follows (where <XXX>* is an abbreviation for the construction <XXX> repeated zero or more times).

```
<program> ::=
    <function-definition> <function-definition>*
<function-definition> ::=
    ( <function-name> ( <parameter>* ) <RL-term> )
<function-name> ::= <object-term>
<parameter> ::= <RL-variable>
<RL-variable> ::= <symbol>
<RL-term> ::=
    <RL-variable> |
    (abort) |
    (quote <object-expression> ) |
    (br    <RL-expression> ) |
    (expr  <RL-expression> ) |
    (first <RL-expression> ) |
    (bf    <RL-expression> ) |
    (last  <RL-expression> ) |
    (bl    <RL-expression> ) |
    (cont  <RL-expression> ) |
    (symbol <RL-expression> ) |
    (equal <RL-term> <RL-term> ) |
    (call  <function-name> <RL-term>* ) |
    (if    <RL-term> <RL-term> <RL-term> )
```

```
<RL-expression> ::= <RL-term>*
<object-expression> ::= <object-term>*
<object-term> ::=
    <symbol> | ( <object-expression> )
```

Here is given an RL-interpreter written in RL.

```
(RL-Int (Program Args)
  (call·Call (cont (first Program)) Args Program)
)

(Call (FnDef Vals Program)
  (callr Term
    (last FnDef)
    (cont (first (bf FnDef))))
  Vals Program
  )
)

(Term (Term Pars Vals Program)
  (if (symbol Term)
    (call LookUpV Term Pars Vals)
    (call Term-
      (first (cont Term))
      (bf (cont Term))
      Pars Vals Program
    )
  )
)

(Term- (Key Info Pars Vals Program)
  (if (equal Key (quote quote))
    Info
  (if (equal Key (quote abort))
    (abort)
  (if (equal Key (quote call))
    (call Call
      (call LookUpF (first Info) Program)
      (call Pars (bf Info) Pars Vals Program)
      Program
    )
  (if (equal Key (quote callr))
    (call Call
      (call LookUpF (first Info) Program)
      (call Pars (bf Info) Pars Vals Program)
      Program
    )
  (if (equal Key (quote br))
    (br    (call Expr Info Pars Vals Program))
  (if (equal Key (quote expr))
         (call Expr Info Pars Vals Program)
  (if (equal Key (quote first))
    (first (call Expr Info Pars Vals Program))
  (if (equal Key (quote bf))
    (bf    (call Expr Info Pars Vals Program))
  (if (equal Key (quote last))
    (last  (call Expr Info Pars Vals Program))
  (if (equal Key (quote bl))
    (bl    (call Expr Info Pars Vals Program))
  (if (equal Key (quote cont))
```

```
    (cont   (call Expr Info Pars Vals Program))
  (if (equal Key (quote symbol))
    (symbol (call Expr Info Pars Vals Program))
  (if (equal Key (quote equal))
    (equal
      (call Term  (first Info)      Pars Vals Program)
      (call Term  (first (bf Info)) Pars Vals Program)
    )
  (if (equal Key (quote if))
    (if
      (call Term  (first Info)           Pars Vals Program)
      (call Term  (first (bf Info))      Pars Vals Program)
      (call Term  (first (bf (bf Info))) Pars Vals Program)
    )
  (abort)
  )))))))))))))
)

(Pars (Terms Pars Vals Program)
  (if (equal Terms (quote))
    (quote)
    (expr
      (br (call Term (first Terms) Pars Vals Program) )
          (call Pars (bf Terms)    Pars Vals Program)
    )
  )
)

(Expr (Terms Pars Vals Program)
  (if (equal Terms (quote))
    (quote)
    (expr
      (call Term (first Terms) Pars Vals Program)
      (call Expr (bf Terms)    Pars Vals Program)
    )
  )
)

(LookUpV (Var Pars Vals)
  (if (equal Pars (quote))
    (abort)
  (if (equal Var (first Pars))
    (cont (first Vals))
    (call LookUpV Var (bf Pars) (bf Vals))
  ))
)

(LookUpF (FnName Program)
  (if (equal FnName (first (cont (first Program))))
    (cont (first Program))
    (call LookUpF FnName (bf Program))
  )
)
```

3. THE GENERAL STRUCTURE OF THE MOSCOW SPECIALIZER

In attempting to solve a problem, one should discern the difference between the end in view and the means to be made use of. In the context of the present work, specialization of programs is the end in view, whereas partial evaluation is merely one of the techniques applicable. There is thus no good reason to believe that partial evaluation is the only conceivable method of specializing programs. Other means may prove to be of value (e.g. the traditional optimization techniques).

In fact, the two major parts of the Moscow specializer are the arity reducer and the arity raiser, only the arity reducer being based on partial evaluation (or, as we prefer to say for reasons to be given below, on meta-evaluation).

The arity reducer is the part that roughly corresponds to the Copenhagen specializer. The peculiarity of the specialization technique based on partial evaluation is that any function appearing in a residual program has at most the same number of parameters as the function from which it has been produced. This accounts for the term "arity reducer".

A program produced by the arity reducer is then passed on to the arity raiser, which is based on optimization techniques that is fairly traditional.

The specializer is called as follows:

            (call Spec Prog Pars-Cl K-Vals U-Types)

where the the arguments have the following meanings:

> Prog is a source RL-program to be specialized;
> Pars-Cl is a sequence of symbols "K" and "U", which describes whether the corresponding parameter of Prog will be known (K) or unknown (U) in the course of meta-evaluation;
> K-Vals is a list of object expressions to be used as values of the K-parameters;
> U-Types is a description of types of the U-parameters.

The function Spec calls other two functions: the arity reducer Reduce-Ar and the arity raiser Raise-Ar.

```
(Spec (Prog Pars-Cl K-Vals U-Types)
  (call Raise-Ar
   (call Reduce-Ar Prog Pars-Cl K-Vals)
   U-Types
  )
)
```

4. THE ARITY RAISER

The operation of the arity raiser proceeds in three steps.

* First, the types of the parameters and results of all functions are determined. The information obtained is then used at the following steps.

* Secondly, the parameters of functions are splitted.

* Finally, local optimization is done.

For example, suppose that, according to the information obtained by the type analyzer, any value of the parameter X is bound to have the structure (e1) e2 t3

where e1 and e2 are object expressions, and t3 is an object
term. In this case X is splitted into three parameters X1, X2,
and X2, which are to contain the expressions e1, e2, and t3.
Then all occurrences of X in the function definition are
replaced with the RL-term

(expr (br X1) X2 X3)

Thus the principles upon which the arity raiser is based are
widely known. For this reason, they will not be discussed in
more detail in the present paper. However, there remains a few
remarks to be made.

* Being complementary in their purposes, the arity raiser
  and the arity reducer cooperate in a natural manner.

* Although the techniqes used by the arity raiser are
  straightforward, they considerably improve the readability
  and efficiency of programs generated by the specializer.

* The arity raiser is completely automatic, which, as far as
  the variable splitting is concerned [JSS 85b], [Ses 86],
  releaves the user of a hand-made annotation of the subject
  program.

From now on, when discussing the differences between the
Moscow specializer and the Copenhagen one, by the Moscow
specializer we, for the most part, shall understand the arity
reducer, because the Copenhagen specializer does not include any
automatic arity raiser.

5. THE ARITY REDUCER

The arity reducer removes the K-parameters of each function
appearing in the subject program to produce specialized
versions of the function. Its operation proceeds in several
steps.
First, the meta-meta-interpreter is called, which takes the
call annotated subject program and a description telling which
of the program's input parameters are known. Then the meta-
meta-interpreter computes for each function a safe description
of its parameters classifying them as K- or U-parameters.
Furthermore, the subject program's functions are classified
as K- or U-functions. In the course of meta-interpretation, K-
functions produce K-values, while U-functions produce U-values.

This is a feature of the Moscow specializer that
distinguishes it from the Copenhagen one, since the latter
classifies parameters, but does not classifies the functions
themselves.

Then the information is gathered about which of the subject
program's functions are <u>residual</u>, i.e. called by the operator
"callr" at least at one place in the program.
Secondly, on the basis of the information obtained, the U-
functions are annotated, i.e. transformed in order to

facilitate the operation of the meta-interpreter. A detailed
description of the way in which the program is annotated will
be given later.

The meta-meta-interpreter produces a three-term expression,
which is then decomposed and passed on to the meta-interpreter
in the form of three separate arguments. The meaning of these
arguments will be described later.

Thirdly, the meta-interpreter builds a specialized version
of the subject program, the actual values of the input K-
parameters being given by K-Vals.

Finally, the program generated is passed on to the function
Rename-Funcs, which invents new, shorter, names for the
functions appearing in the residual program.

Thus the arity reducer is defined as follows:

```
(Reduce-Ar (Prog Pars-Cl K-Vals)
  (call Reduce-Ar-
    (call MM-Int Prog Pars-Cl)
    K-Vals
  )
)

(Reduce-Ar- (Ann-Prog K-Vals)
  (call Rename-Funcs
    (call M-Int
      (cont (first Ann-Prog))
      (cont (first (bf Ann-Prog)))
      (cont (first (bf (bf Ann-Prog))))
      K-Vals
    )
  )
)
```

6. THE STRUCTURE OF AN ANNOTATED PROGRAM

An annotated program takes the form:

(R-Funcs) (K-Prog) (U-Prog)

where the expressions R-Funcs, K-Prog, and U-Prog have the
following meanings.

> R-Funcs is a list of the residual functions, i.e. the
> functions whose specialized versions can appear in a
> residual program.
> K-Prog is a K-program, i.e. definitions of functions
> which have only K-parameters and produce K-values.
> U-Prog is a U-program, i.e. definitions of functions
> which have at least one U-parameters and produce U-
> values.

The definitions appearing in the K-program are, without any
change, inherited from the source program.

The definitions appearing in the U-program are taken from
the source program and modified in the following way.

Let the source function definition be

(F (X1 X2 ... XL) T).

It is transformed into

(F (K1 K2 ... KM) (U1 U2 ... UN) AT),

where Ki are those Xi that belongs to the class K, and Ui are those Xi that belongs to the class U, M+N=L, and AT is an RL-term obtained by annotating T. Annotating an RL term is done as follows.

An RL-term involving neither U-parameters nor U-functions' calls will be referred to as a K-term. An RL-term that is not a K-term will be referred to as an U-term.

Let T be an RL-term. The result of annotating T will be denoted by AT.

AT is obtained from T by applying the following rules, with the precedence of the rules determined by the order in which they are listed.

If T=(quote C), then AT=(quote C).
If T=(abort), then AT=(abort).
If T is a K-term, then AT=(meta T).
If T is a variable, then AT=T.
If T=(call F T1 T2 ... TL), then AT=(call F (K1 K2 ... KM) (AU1 AU2 ... AUN)), where M+N=L, K1 K2 ... KM is the list of all Ti that correspond to the K-parameters of F, and AU1 AU2 ... AUN is the list of the terms that are obtained by annotating the terms Ti that correspond to the U-parameters of F.

If T=(callr F T1 T2 ... TL), then AT=(callr F (K1 K2 ... KM) (AU1 AU2 ... AUN)), where M+N=L, K1 K2 ... KM is the list of all Ti that correspond to the K-parameters of F, and AU1 AU2 ... AUN is the list of the terms that are obtained by annotating the terms Ti that correspond to the U-parameters of F.

If T=(if T0 T1 T2), where T0 is a K-term, then AT=(if-e T0 AT1 AT2).

If T=(if T0 T1 T2), where T0 is a U-term, then AT=(if-r AT0 AT1 AT2).

If T=(P T1 T2 ... TN), where P is one of the operators "br", "expr", "first", "bf", "last", "bl", "cont", "symbol", or "equal", then AT=(P AT1 AT2 ... ATN).

Consider the function

```
(Zipper (X Y)
  (if (equal X (quote))
    Y
  (if (equal Y (quote))
    X
    (expr
      (first X) (first Y)
      (call Zipper (bf X) (bf Y))
    )
  ))
)
```

On condition that X is a K-parameter, and Y is a U-parameter, the result of annotating Zipper is

```
(Zipper (X) (Y)
  (if-e (equal X (quote))
    Y
  (if-r (equal Y (quote))
    (meta X)
    (expr
      (meta (first X)) (first Y)
      (call Zipper ((bf X)) ((bf Y)) )
    )
  ))
)
```

7. THE META-INTERPRETER

The meta-interpreter is called as follows:

```
(call M-Int R-Funcs K-Prog U-Prog K-Vals)
```

The first three arguments contain an annotated program subject to specialization, and K-Vals contains values of the program's K-parameters. The meta-interpreter produces a residual program composed of functions, each function being a specialized version of a function appearing in U-Prog. More specifically, if the definition of a U-function is of the form

```
(F (K1 ... KM) (U1 ... UN) T),
```

it can give rise to function definitions of the form

```
((F (C1) ... (CM)) (U1 ... UN) T')
```

where C1, ..., CM are object expressions which are values of the K-parameters K1, ..., KM, and T' is the result of meta-evaluating T, with the K-parameters' values being C1, ..., CM, and the U-parameters' values being these parameters U1, ..., UN themselves. ((F (C1) ... (CM)) is the name of the function generated. This name is to be replaced with a shorter one at the next stage of specialization.

Thus, the principal task of the meta-interpreter consists in evaluating RL-terms. The result of meta-evaluating an RL-term is a U-value, i.e. an RL-term.

Consider, for example, the above function Zipper. It has the K-parameter X and the U-parameter Y. Suppose that the meta-interpreter has to evaluate Zipper, with the values of X and Y being

```
X = "ONE TWO";   Y = "VAR".
```

(From here on, variable values will be put in double quotation marks for fear that they might be confused with variable names.) The above conditions being met, the meta-evaluation of Zipper yields the RL-term

```
(if (equal VAR (quote))
  (quote ONE TWO)
  (expr
    (quote ONE) (first VAR)
    (if (equal (bf VAR) (quote))
      (quote TWO)
```

```
    (expr
      (quote TWO) (first (bf VAR))
      (bf (bf VAR))
    )
  )
 )
)
```

In the course of meta-evaluating the body of Zipper, the meta-interpreter has to carry out the recursive call of Zipper twice. When Zipper is called for the first time, the parameters take the values

X = "TWO"; Y = "(bf VAR)",

and when Zipper is called for the second time, they take the values

X = ""; Y = "(bf (bf VAR))".

Thus, the most complicated operation performed by the meta-interpreter consists in meta-evaluating RL-terms.

The basic principle followed in designing the Moscow specializer is that, in contrast to an ordinary interpreter, the meta-interpreter should deal with values of two kinds: K-values and U-values. These values are entirely different in nature, for they belong to different levels: K-values correspond to the basic level, whereas U-values correspond to the meta-level. U-values may, with respect to K-values, be regarded as meta-values, since they are RL-terms, which are to produce K-values only at the time the specialized program will be run.

Thus K-values and U-values have to be operated on in entirely different ways. For example, the application of the operator "bf" to the K-value "ONE TWO THREE" yields the K-value "TWO THREE", whereas the application of "bf" to the U-value "(expr X1 X2)" yields the U-value "(bf (expr X1 X2))", the "bf" being treated as a "meta-level" operator.

Hence, the meta-interpreter may take advantage of using entirely different representations for K-values and U-values. K-values, naturally, may be stored and operated on as "true" object expressions, the way they would be dealt with by an ordinary RL-interpreter, while U-values, naturally, may be stored as RL-terms.

Accordingly, K-values can be operated on "really", i.e. the way an RL-interpreter does, whereas U-values can be operated on "nominally", in a "meta" manner (which may be reduced to placing the operator applied before the RL-term).

Thus, the first principle the Moscow specializer is based upon is that, instead of being mixed, K-computation and U-computation ought to be soroughly separated. This principle may be referred to as the principle of unmixed computation.

The second basic principle is that any computation involving K- or U-values ought to be carried to completion. This is feasible since all K- or U-values dealt with by the meta-interpreter are completely known to the latter (although they are operated on differently). As there is no good reason to regard completed evaluation performed by the meta-interpreter as partial, the second principle may be referred to as the principle of non-partial evaluation.

The above considerations account for the author's preference for the term "meta-evaluation" over the term "partial evaluation" as far as the Moscow specializer is concerned.

The general structure of the meta-interpreter conforms to the above principles. The basis of the meta-interpreter is formed by two functions: Eval-Term and Spec-Term. Eval-Term computes the K-value of a K-term with respect to given K-parameters' values and a K-program. Spec-Term computes the U-value of a U-term with respect to given K-parameters' values, U-parameters' values, a K-program and a U-program.

Thus the meta-interpreter includes the K-interpreter, which is an ordinary RL-interpreter, and the U-interpreter, which is a meta-interpreter in the true sense of the word.

Having been called, the K-interpreter never calls the U-interpreter, whereas the U-interpreter calls the K-interpreter whenever the U-term under interpretation involves K-terms. This situation arises when the meta-interpreter runs into one of the following constructs:

```
(meta K)
(if-e K U1 U2)
(call  F (K1 ... KM) (U1 ... UN))
(callr F (K1 ... KM) (U1 ... UN))
```

As the class of any subterm is determinable from the context, there is no need for annotating operators appearing in the subject program by replacing each occurrence of an operator "p" either with "p-e" or "p-r" (as this is done by the Copenhagen specializer). The only exeption is the operator "if".

8. THE RESULTS OBTAINED BY APPLYING THE SPECIALIZER TO ITSELF

It is a peculiarity of both the Moscow specializer and the Copenhagen one that interpreters can be converted to compilers by evaluating Spec(M-Int,Ann-Int) instead of Spec(Spec,Int), where M-Int is the meta-interpreter, Int is an interpreter, and Ann-Int is the result of annotating Int. Similarly, a compiler generator can be produced by evaluating Spec(M-Int,Ann-M-Int), where Ann-M-Int is the result of annotating M-Int, the inputs of M-Int being classified as follows: R-Funcs, K-Prog, and U-Prog are K-parameters, and K-Vals is an U-parameter. This is feasible because the meta-interpreter is the only part of the specializer that has to know the value of the input parameter K-Vals (i.e. the values of the subject program's K-parameters) [JSS 85a], [JSS 85b], [Ses 86].

The autor succeeded in getting the specializer to produce several compilers from interpreters. Among the interpreters converted are a simple interpreter implementing an imperative two-register machine (which is essentially the same as the interpreter described in [JSS 85b]), an interpreter of finite automata, the RL-interpreter presented above, and an interpreter of the strict Refal [Tur 86].

The structure of all the compilers obtained turned out to be quite natural from the human point of view, the compilers being easy to read. The RL-compiler, as could be expected, proved to be an RL-optimizer, rather than a true compiler, its source and target languages being the language RL.

Then, by specializing the meta-interpreter with respect to the meta-interpreter, a compiler generator was generated. As could be expected, the names of functions appearing in the compiler generator proved to be, in many cases, rather insipid (for instance, the names Spec-Term-1, Spec-Term-2, ..., Spec-Term-45). Nevertheless, these names having been replaced by the author's hand with more suggestive ones, the compiler generator turned out to be quite readable.

A close examination of the compiler generator enabled its principles of operation to be fully understood. As a result, the way in which the interpreters mentioned above had been converted to compilers became apparent. Moreover, the compiler generator itself having been produced from the meta-interpreter in conformity with the same principles, the correspondence between the meta-interpreter and the compiler generator became clear.

9.THE WAY IN WHICH INTERPRETERS ARE CONVERTED TO COMPILERS

A compiler produced from an interpreter comprises two parts: the administrator and the generator. The administrator puts the compiler as a whole into operation, whereas the generator builds the residual program. The compilers produced by the Copenhagen specializer have a similar structure [JSS 85b], [Ses 86].

Being merely a slightly specialized version of the meta-interpreter's administrative part, the administrator has the structure that is almost independent of the source interpreter.

The structure of the generator is, on the contrary, completely dependent on the structure of the source interpreter, being entirely different for different interpreters.

As has been said above, an annotated interpreter takes the form

(R-Funcs) (K-Prog) (U-Prog)

The functions from the K-Prog are transferred to the compiler with insignificant alterations (such as local optimizations and renaming of functions and parameters).

The functions from U-Prog are transformed and then transferred to the compiler. The result of the transformation may be obtained by applying the following rules (modulo local optimizations and renaming of functions and parameters).

The functions from U-Prog will be referred to as "interpreting", and the corresponding functions from the compiler will be referred to as "compiling".

Let T be an RL-term appearing in the definition of an interpreting function. The result of transforming T, which corresponds to T in the compiling function, will be denoted by CT.

Let the definition of an interpreting function be

(F (K1 ... KM) (U1 ... UN) T).

It is transformed into the compiling function

    (F (K1 ... KM U1 ... UN) CT),

where CT is obtained from T by applying the following rules,
with the precedence of the rules determined by the order in
which they are listed.
    If T=(quote C), then CT=(quote (quote C)).
    If T=(abort), then CT=(quote (abort)).
    If T=(meta K), then CT=(br (quote quote) K).
    If T is a variable, then CT=T.
    If T=(call F (K1 ... KM) (U1 ... UN)), then CT=(call F K1
... KM CU1 ... CUN)).
    If T=(callr F (K1 ... KM) (U1 ... UN)), then CT=(br (quote
call) (br (quote F) (br K1) ... (br KM)) CU1 ... CUN).
    If T=(if-e K U1 U2), then CT=(if K CU1 CU2).
    If T=(if-r U0 U1 U2), then CT=(br (quote if) CU0 CU1 CU2).
    If T=(P U1 ... UN), where P is one of the operators "br",
"expr", "first", "bf", "last", "bl", "cont", "symbol" or
"equal", then CT=(br (quote P) CU1 ... CUN).

For example, the above function Zipper is transformed into
the compiling function

```
(Zipper (X Y)
  (if (equal X (quote))
    Y
  (br (quote if)
    (br (quote equal) Y (quote (quote)))
    (br (quote quote) X)
    (br (quote expr)
      (br (quote quote) (first X))
      (br (quote first) Y)
      (call Zipper (bf X) (br (quote bf) Y)
    )
  ))
)
```

    The above principles of transforming interpreting functions
into compiling ones appear to be quite natural. They, in all
probability, have been used in the hand-written compiler
generator reported in [Bec 76]. However, in our case, of
particular interest is the fact that these principles have been
automatically "discovered" by the computer in the course of
specializing a specializer.
    It should be noted that the above principles of producing
compiling functions are valid provided that the compiler
generator is dealt with in its integrity, with the inclusion of
the automatic arity raiser. Had the arity raiser been excluded
from the compiler generator, the compiling functions produced
would have had two parameters exactly. The first parameter, K-
Vals, would have contained K-values, whereas the second
parameter, U-Vals, would have contained U-values.

CONCLUSION

    The   main   feature of the Moscow specializer that
distinguishes it from the Copenhagen one is more strict and
static differentiation between K-values and U-values. It has
been achieved by the following means.

* In addition to the separation of K-parameters from U-parameters, the separation of K-functions from U-functions has been introduced.

* Subject programs are annotated in a different way, so that a program is divided into K-program and U-program. Thus, there is no need for replacing each occurrence of an operator "P" with either "P-e" or "P-r".

* The new method of annotation allowed the meta-interpreter to be divided into the K-interpreter and U-interpreter. Being an ordinary RL-interpreter, the K-interpreter deals only with K-values.

* The separation of the K-interpreter from the U-interpreter has made it possible to choose different representations for values of K- and U-parameters, such that a K-value is an object expression, whereas a U-value is an RL-term.

A considerable improvement in the structure of residual programs is, for the most part, due to the automatic arity raiser and the use of different representations for K- and U-values.

As far as the Copenhagen specializer is concerned, K- and U-values are treated in a different way: any value assigned to a K-parameter, instead of being an ordinary constant, is a representation of the constant in the form of a term of the semantic metalanguage. In other words, instead of a constant "C", use is made of the term "(quote C)". This has a disastrous effect on the size and readability of the compilers generated. Let, for instance, "(first X)" be a term appearing in a source interpreter, X being a K-parameter. Then, if K- and U-values had the same representation, this term would give rise to the term

        (br (quote quote) (first (bf (cont X))))

in the compiler, whereas the compiler generator produced by the Moscow specializer transfers this term to the compiler without any change.

Additionally, the separation of the K-interpreter from the U-interpreter eliminated the necessity of performing immediate local optimizations of the U-values being produced in the course of meta-interpretation, since these optimizations, in any case, is to be performed by the arity raiser. Besides, these optimizations can be done better by the arity reducer, because it can make use of the global information on the types of functions and variables.

Thus, it can be easily seen from the above considerations that making use of different representations of K- and U-values results in the more clear structure of the compiler generator and compilers produced from interpreters.

ACKNOWLEDGMENTS

The author expresses his appreciation and gratitude to Sergei Abramov, Andrei Klimov, Arkady Klimov, Nikolay Kondratiev, Victor Kistlerov, Alexandr Romanenko and other members of the Refal working group. While in progress, the present work has been regularly discussed at the meetings of the group. The advice and critical help recieved have been a permanent encouragement to the author's efforts.

In addition, the author wants to use this occasion to express his gratitude to Vsevolod S.Shtarkman, whose friendly and permanent support much contributed to the success of the work.

REFERENCES

[Bec 76]
L.Beckman, A.Haraldson, O.Oskarsson, E.Sandewall. A partial evaluator, and its use as a programming tool. Artificial Intelligence, Vol.7, No.4, 1976, pp.319-357.

[ChL 73]
Ch.Chang, R.Lee. Symbolic logic and mechanical theorem proving. - Academic Press, 1973.

[Dix 71]
J.Dixon. The specializer, a method of automatically writing computer programs. - Division of Computer Research and Technology, National. Inst. of Health, Bethenda, Maryland, 1971.

[Fut 71]
Y.Futtamura. Partial evaluation of computation process - an approach to a compiler compiler. - Systems, Computers, Controls, Vol.2, No.5, 1971, pp.45-50.

[JSS 85a]
N.D.Jones, P.Sestoft, H.Sondergaard. An experiment in partial evaluation: The generation of a compiler generator. - SIGPLAN Notices, Vol.20, No.8, 1985, pp.82-87.

[JSS 85b]
N.D.Jones, P.Sestoft, H.Sondergaard. An experiment in partial evaluation: The generation of a compiler generator. - In Proc. 1st Intl. Conf. on Rewriting Techniques and Applications, Dijon, France, 1985. Springer LNCS 202 (1985), pp.124-140.

[Lom 67]
L.A.Lombardi. Incremental computation. - Advances in Computers, 8, Academic Press, New York, 1967.

[Rom 87]
S.A.Romanenko. A compiler generator produced by a self-applicable specializer can have a clear and natural structure. Preprint, the Keldysh Institute of Applied Mathematics, the USSR Academy of Sciences, 1987, No.26.

[Ses 86]
P.Sestoft. The structure of a self-applicable partial evaluator. - In H.Ganzinger and N.D.Jones (Eds.): Programs as Data Objects, Copenhagen, Denmark, 1985. Springer LNCS 217 (1986), pp.236-256.

[TNT 82]
V.F.Turchin, R.N.Nirenberg, D.V.Turchin. Experiments with the supercompiler. - Conference Record of the ACM Symposium on Lisp and Functional Programming, 1982, pp.47-55.

[Tur 66]
V.F.Turchin. A metalanguage for the formal description of algorithmic languages. - In Tsyfrovaya Vychislitelynaya Tekhnika i Programmirovaniye, Moscow, Sovetskoye Radio, 1966, pp.116-124 (in Russian).

[Tur 68]
V.F.Turchin. The metaalgorithmic language. - Kibernetika, No.4, 1968, pp.45-54 (in Russian).

[Tur 77]
Basic REFAL and its implementation on computers. (Bazisnyi REFAL i yego realizatsiya na vychislitelynykh mashinakh.) - GOSSTROY SSSR TSNIPIASS, Moscow, 1977, pp.92-95 (in Russian).

[Tur 79]
V.F.Turchin. A supercompiler system based on the language REFAL. - SIGPLAN Notices, Vol.14, No.2, 1979, pp.46-54.

[Tur 80]
V.F.Turchin. Semantic definitions in REFAL and the automatic production of compilers. - In : Semantic Directed Compiler Generation (N.D.Jones Ed.). Springer LNCS 94 (1980),pp.441-474.

[Tur 86]
V.F.Turchin. The concept of a supercompiler. - ACM Transactions on Computer Languages and Systems, Vol.8, No.3, July 1986, pp.292-325.

Partial Evaluation and Mixed Computation
D. Bjørner, A.P. Ershov and N.D. Jones (Editors)
Elsevier Science Publishers B.V. (North-Holland)
© IFIP, 1988

Static Properties of Partial Evaluation

David A. Schmidt*
Computing and Information Sciences Dept.
Kansas State University
Manhattan, KS 66506 U.S.A.

Abstract:
We study the operational properties of call-by-value-style partial evaluation on typed lambda-calculus expressions. We prove that a reduction can be cleanly divided into a compile-time (partial evaluation) stage and a run-time stage. We also give a statically checkable condition which verifies that a type of data meant to be "compile-time reducible" does indeed reduce away completely at compile-time. The structure of the remaining "run-time reducible" values is preserved throughout compile-time reduction. Our method uses Nielson and Nielson's TML calculus to decorate the subexpressions of a lambda expression with compile-time type labels and run-time type labels. We also give an algorithm that decorates a lambda-expresssion with TML type labels, and we note that the algorithm supplies the minimal decoration for the expression.

0. Introduction

A fundamental problem in partial evaluation theory is *what* to reduce. The reducer must avoid (*i*) unbounded unfoldings of function calls [Jones et. al. 85, Mosses 79] and (*ii*) reductions that make the overall expression structure more complex [Jones et. al. 85, Paulson 82 84] or cause it to lose important structural properties [Raoult & Sethi 84, Schmidt 85a 85b 86a 86b, Sethi 82]. We study the second problem in this paper. We study it because it affects the generation of a compiler from a denotational definition of a programming language [Ershov 78, Mosses 79, Paulson 82 84, Raskovsky 82]. A denotational definition typically contains occurrences of environments, stores, and other semantic values that represent data structures. The denotational definition maps a source program into "lambda code," and the lambda code contains occurrences of the environments, stores, etc. If the store values in the denotational definition are used in a "structured" (single-threaded [Schmidt 85a, Sethi 82, Stoy 77]) way, the store values can be implemented as a single, global store variable [Appel 85, Mycroft 81, Raoult & Sethi 84, Schmidt 85a]. We do not want partial evaluation of the lambda code to destroy the

---

* This work was partially supported by NSF Grant DCR-8604080.

structure of the store values. On the other hand, the partial evaluator must not be too conservative, because we want to reduce other expressions, say the ones using environments, at partial evaluation-time. We need to distinguish the "compile-time reducible" parts from the "run-time reducible" parts, and we must prove that the compile-time reducible parts all reduce at compile-time (that is, at partial evaluation-time). Also, the run-time reducible parts must reduce only at run-time.

We use a typed lambda-calculus that attaches labels ("decorations") to the subparts of a lambda-calculus expression. The calculus is a minor variant of Nielson and Nielson's Two-level Metal Language (TML) for semantics definition [Nielson 86, Nielson & Nielson 86a 86b]. The decorations help to determine which redexes can be reduced without violating structural properties and to verify if a given type of data is completely "compile-time" reducible, that is, if all occurrences of its redexes can be partially evaluated. We also give an algorithm that decorates an unlabelled expression based on information about which primitives may not be partially evaluated. We note that the algorithm supplies the minimal decoration for the expression.

1. Background

We begin with the usual typed lambda-calculus [Curry & Feys 58, Hindley & Seldin 86]. The types in the calculus include first-order types (e.g., *Nat*, the natural numbers, *Tr*, the truth values, *Locn*, locations), and function space types:

$P \in$ *First-order-type*
$D \in$ *Type*
$E \in$ *Expression*
$x \in$ *Identifier*
$f \in$ *Operator*

$D ::= P \mid D_1 \rightarrow D_2$
$E ::= x^D \mid f^D \mid (\lambda x^{D_1}. E^{D_2})^{D_1 \rightarrow D_2} \mid (E_1^{D_1 \rightarrow D_2} E_2^{D_1})^{D_2}$

We often omit some or all of the type superscripts when we write expressions. Parentheses are often omitted as well.

The rewriting rule schemes are the usual ones:

β-rule: $(\lambda x.B)A \Rightarrow [A/x]B$
δ-rule: $(f A_1 \cdots A_n) \Rightarrow [A_n/a_n] \cdots [A_1/a_1]B$,
     where *n*-ary operator f is defined as $f a_1 \cdots a_n = B$
     and $(f A_1 \cdots A_n)$ abbreviates $((\cdots (f A_1) \cdots)A_n)$

For simplicity, we assume that an n-ary operator f has at most one rewriting rule. (If f requires more than one rule, then all the rules must take n arguments. An operator that has no rewriting rules is a *constant*.) The rewriting rules for δ-operators may be recursive, for example, $(fix f a) \Rightarrow f (fix f) a$. We treat the abstraction construction as *strict*, that is, $[\![(\lambda x. B)]\!]\bot = \bot$. Thus, a call-by-value reduction strategy must be used with the rewriting rules. This appears to be a harsh restriction, but semantic definitions of traditional sequential languages use strict abstractions. Also, efficient implementations use call-by-value reduction strategies.

1.1 Definition: *An expression is:*
(i) active if it is not properly contained in an abstraction.
(ii) a redex if it is active, closed, matches the left-hand side of a rewriting rule, and no proper, active, closed subexpression matches the left-hand side of a rewriting rule.
(iii)   in normal form if it is has no redexes.

Recall that a redex is reduced to an expression called its *contractum*.

The reduction strategy rewrites redexes until no more exist. It is a call-by-value (cbv) reduction strategy because a combination $(\lambda x.B)A$ is not a redex until A is in normal form. Note also that the body B of an expression $(\lambda x. B)$ can not be reduced until some expression is bound to x. This restriction gives an easy implementation [Landin 64] and preserves confluence [Berry & Levy 79, Plotkin 75, Rosen 73]. But it is too restrictive, because we may want to reduce some of B inside $(\lambda x.B)$ at partial evaluation-time. Shortly, we will relax the reduction strategy so this can occur.

Here is a sample reduction. We use the types *Nat* (natural numbers), *Locn* (storage locations), and *Store* (primary storage). Operators are *access*: $Locn \rightarrow (Store \rightarrow Nat)$, a binary operator that finds the number bound to a location in the store, *update*: $Locn \rightarrow (Nat \rightarrow (Store \rightarrow Store))$, a ternary operator that creates a store with a new binding, and *add*: $Nat \rightarrow (Nat \rightarrow Nat)$, a binary operator that adds its two arguments. Let n_0, n_1, and n_2 be hypothetical numbers, l_0 and l_1 be locations, and s_0 be a hypothetical store.

$$(\lambda s. \, add \, (access \, l_1 \, s) \, (access \, l_1 \, s))(update \, l_0 \, (access \, l_0 \, s_0) \, s_0)$$
$$\Rightarrow (\lambda s. \, add \, (access \, l_1 \, s) \, (access \, l_1 \, s))(update \, l_0 \, n_0 \, s_0)$$
$$\Rightarrow (\lambda s. \, add \, (access \, l_1 \, s) \, (access \, l_1 \, s)) \, s_1 \quad \text{where } s_1 = [l_0 \mapsto n_0]s_0$$
$$\Rightarrow add \, (access \, l_1 \, s_1) \, (access \, l_1 \, s_1)$$
$$\Rightarrow add \, n_1 \, (access \, l_1 \, s_1)$$
$$\Rightarrow add \, n_1 \, n_1$$
$$\Rightarrow n_2$$

The call-by-value strategy forces $(access \, l_0 \, s_0)$ to be reduced before $(update \, l_0 \cdots)$ is reduced before binding the updated store to s before reducing the two occurrences of $(access \, l_1 \cdots)$. In [Schmidt 85a, Stoy 77], this pattern of store handling is called *single-threading*. An expression that is single-threaded in its store can be implemented with a global store variable, and the operations on the store operate on the variable. Single-threading can be defined as a "structural property" of an expression [Schmidt 85a]. That is, if the expression is structured in a certain way, its call-by-value reduction will follow the single-threading pattern. If the semantic equations of the denotational definition are written so that each equation is single-threaded in the store argument, then the equations map any source program to a lambda expression that is single-threaded [Schmidt 85a].

Thus, we can detect the single-threading property in the denotational definition itself. See [Appel 85, Mycroft 81, Paulson 84, Raoult & Sethi 84, Schmidt 85a 85b 86a 86b] for more details on single-threading and other structural properties of expressions.

Redexes that use stores represent run-time computation steps, and their reductions are usually delayed until run-time. We say that the *Store* type is *frozen* [Ershov 78 82] or is a *run-time type* [Nielson 86, Nielson & Nielson 86a 86b]. If the *Store* type is indeed a run-time type, then the above example can not partially evaluate even a single step. All of the reduction steps are run-time reduction steps. Even the *add* operator must be delayed, because its arguments are run-time computed values.

Partial evaluation performs "compile-time" reductions. Within the framework of compiler generation, we perform partial evaluation after a source program is mapped to a lambda-expression and before the lambda-expression is translated to more efficient machine code. A good example of compile-time reductions are the reductions on environment ("symbol table") operations. For the type *Env* of environments, say that *find* : Identifier $\rightarrow$ *Env* $\rightarrow$ *Locn* extracts the location bound to an identifier in an environment, and *bind* : Identifier $\rightarrow$ *Locn* $\rightarrow$ *Env* $\rightarrow$ *Env* adds a new identifier, location binding to an environment. We call a type a *compile-time type* if its operations may be partially evaluated. Let *Store* be a run-time type and let *Env* be a compile-time type. The expression:

$$((\lambda e.\lambda s.\ access\ (find\ i_0\ e)\ s)\ (bind\ i_0\ l_0\ e_0))\ (update\ l_0\ one\ s_0)$$

contains three combinations that require partial evaluation: the combination $(bind\ i_0\ l_0\ e_0)$, the combination $(\lambda e.\ \cdots\ )(\ \cdots\ )$, and the combination $(find\ i_0\ \cdots\ )$. It is critical that we reduce all three combinations at compile-time. The reason is that values of type *Env* should appear exclusively at compile-time and not appear at run-time. A conventional, compiler-oriented programming language is designed so that *Env*-values, which correspond to a symbol table, are built and used at compile-time and are discarded at the end of compile-time. (In [Schmidt 86b], we show that a "structured" use of compile-time *Env*-values allows the values to be implemented as a global stack symbol table at compile-time.)

The first two combinations in the above example can be reduced by the call-by-value reduction strategy. But the third is embedded in the abstraction $(\lambda s.\ \cdots\ )$, whose reduction is delayed until run-time. Hence, the third abstraction can not be active and can not be a redex. Fortunately, if we relax the definition of "active," we can reduce the third combination. We plan to reduce compile-time-typed combinations even when they are embedded in an abstraction body, if the body has type $S \rightarrow T$, where S is a run-time type. We must be careful to precisely define the terms "compile-time type" and "run-time type," so that the reduction strategy is precisely defined.

We do this by labelling types as compile-time and run-time. A run-time primitive type P is "decorated" as $\underline{P}$. The type calculus for lambda-expressions now reads:

$P \in$ *First-order-type*
$D \in DType$
$ct \in$ *Compile-time-type*
$rt \in$ *Run-time-type*

$D ::= ct \mid rt$
$ct ::= P \mid ct \rightarrow D \mid rt \rightarrow rt$
$rt := \underline{P} \mid rt \xrightarrow{\sim} rt$

Types are now *compile-time* types or *run-time* types. Note the three versions of function types. An operation with type $ct \rightarrow D$ may be applied to a compile-time argument at compile-time. An operation with type $rt \rightarrow rt$ may not be applied at compile-time, but it can be used as an argument to a compile-time function; it resembles "object code," which can be built, but not applied, at compile-time. An operation with type $rt \xrightarrow{\sim} rt$ represents a value computed at run-time (a "closure"); it can be neither applied nor used as an argument at compile-time. An abstraction can be typed with any of the three versions of function types.

Like the original typed calculus, the type of an operator must match the type of its argument. For example, $((\lambda x^{\underline{A}}. x^{\underline{A}})^{\underline{A} \rightarrow \underline{A}} a^{\underline{A}})^{\underline{A}}$ is well-typed, but $((\lambda x^{\underline{A}}. x^{\underline{A}})^{\underline{A} \rightarrow \underline{A}} a^{A})$ is not. Also, $((\lambda x^{\underline{A}}. x^{\underline{A}})^{\underline{A} \xrightarrow{\sim} \underline{A}} x^{\underline{A}})^{\underline{A}}$ is well-typed. Types of identifiers in abstraction bodies must match the types of their binding identifiers. For example, $(\lambda x^{\underline{A}}. x^A)$ is not well-typed.

We call an expression that is typed with the new calculus a *decorated expression*. Let *DExpression* be the set of decorated expressions. The language of decorated expressions is a variant of Nielson and Nielson's Two-level Meta Language (TML) [Nielson 86, Nielson & Nielson 86a 86b]; our use of three kinds of function types is the main departure from standard TML.

Let S (for "*Store*") be a run-time type; all occurrences of S-typed expressions are decorated $\underline{S}$. Let I (for "Identifier"), N (for "*Nat*"), L (for "*Location*"), and E (for "*Env*") be compile-time types. Here are three examples of decorated expressions:

$(((bind^{I \rightarrow (\underline{N} \rightarrow (\underline{E} \xrightarrow{\sim} E))} i^I)^{\underline{N} \rightarrow (\underline{E} \xrightarrow{\sim} E)} ((access^{L \rightarrow (\underline{S} \rightarrow N)} l^L)^{\underline{S} \rightarrow N} \underline{s}^{\underline{S}})^{N})^{E \xrightarrow{\sim} E} \underline{e}^E)^E$
$(\lambda \underline{s}^{\underline{S}}. \underline{e}^E)^{\underline{S} \rightarrow E}$
$(((bind^{I \rightarrow ((\underline{S} \rightarrow \underline{N}) \rightarrow (E \rightarrow E))} i^I)^{(\underline{S} \rightarrow \underline{N}) \rightarrow (E \rightarrow E)} (access^{L \rightarrow (\underline{S} \rightarrow \underline{N})} l^L)^{\underline{S} \rightarrow \underline{N}})^{E \rightarrow E} e^E)^E$

The decorations show the consequences of the run-time S-values. The first example shows that the operation *bind* is forced to treat its second and third arguments as run-time values, because its second argument contains an $\underline{S}$-value. This implies that *bind* will not reduce at compile-time. The second example shows that the body of an abstraction must be a run-time value when the abstraction's argument is a run-time value. This shows that environment e must be retained until run-time. The third example shows that (*access l*) can be handled as an argument at compile-time, that is, run-time "code" can be saved in a compile-time environment.

We now restate some of the terms introduced in Definition 1.1 so that we may perform partial evaluation using the call-by-value reduction strategy.

1.2 Definition:

(i) *An abstraction $(\lambda x.B)$ is usable at compile-time if it has type $ct \to D$; otherwise it is unusable.*

(ii) *An n-ary δ-operator f is usable at compile-time if it has type $ct_1 \to ct_2 \to \cdots \to ct_n \to D$, $n > 0$. (If $n = 0$, then f is usable if it has type ct.) Otherwise, it is unusable.*

(iii) *An expression is active at compile-time if it is not contained in the body of a usable abstraction.*

Only usable operators may reduce at compile-time. The definition of "active at compile-time" allows us to reduce inside the bodies of not usable abstractions at compile-time.

We now define the term "compile-time redex." The definition matches the original, if the expression under consideration uses no run-time types.

1.3 Definition: *An expression is:*

(i) *compile-time reducible if it matches the left hand side of a rewriting rule and its operator part (that is, $(\lambda x.B)$ or f) is usable.*

(ii) *a compile-time redex if it is closed, active, compile-time reducible, and no proper, closed, active subexpression is compile-time reducible.*

(iii) *in compile-time normal form if it contains no compile-time redexes.*

Here is the decorated version of the expression that we encountered several pages ago:

$$(((\lambda e^E. (\lambda s^{\underline{S}}. ((access^{L \to (\underline{S} \to \underline{N})} ((find^{I \to (E \to L)} i_0^I)^{E \to L} e^E)^L)^{\underline{S} \to \underline{N}} s^{\underline{S}})^{\underline{N}})^{\underline{S} \to \underline{N}})^{E \to (\underline{S} \to \underline{N})}$$

$$(((bind^{I \to (L \to (E \to E))} i_0^I)^{L \to (E \to E)} l_0^L)^{E \to E} e_0^E)^E)^{\underline{S} \to \underline{N}}$$

$$(((update^{L \to (N \to (\underline{S} \to \underline{S}))} l_0^L)^{N \to (\underline{S} \to \underline{S})} one^N)^{\underline{S} \to \underline{S}} s_0^{\underline{S}})^{\underline{S}})^{\underline{N}}$$

The type superscripts show that *bind* and *find* are usable and can be reduced at compile-time. Furthermore, since β- and δ-reductions preserve types, *bind* and *find* will remain usable throughout all the stages of partial evaluation.

Here are the partial evaluation steps on the expression (some of the superscripts and brackets are omitted for clarity):

$$(\lambda e^E.\lambda s^{\underline{S}}. access^{L \to \underline{S} \to \underline{N}} (find^{I \to E \to L} i_0^I e^E) s^{\underline{S}}) (bind^{I \to L \to E \to E} i_0^I l_0^L e_0^E)$$
$$(update^{L \to N \to \underline{S} \to \underline{S}} l_0^L one^N s_0^{\underline{S}})$$

$$\Rightarrow (\lambda e^E.\lambda s^{\underline{S}}. access^{L \to \underline{S} \to \underline{N}} (find^{I \to E \to L} i_0^I e^E) s^{\underline{S}}) e_1^E$$
$$(update^{L \to N \to \underline{S} \to \underline{S}} l_0^L one^N s_0^{\underline{S}}) \quad \text{where } e_1 = [i_0 \mapsto l_0]e_0$$

$$\Rightarrow (\lambda s^{\underline{S}}. access^{L \to \underline{S} \to \underline{N}} (find^{I \to E \to L} i_0^I e_1^E) s^{\underline{S}}) (update^{L \to N \to \underline{S} \to \underline{S}} l_0^L one^N s_0^{\underline{S}})$$

$$\Rightarrow (\lambda s^{\underline{S}}. access^{L \to \underline{S} \to \underline{N}} l_0^L s^{\underline{S}}) (update^{L \to N \to \underline{S} \to \underline{S}} l_0^L one^N s_0^{\underline{S}})$$

The third reduction step becomes possible by the definition of "active at compile-time." Since the *Store* type is run-time, no *Store*-based operation is reduced. Hence, the structure of the *Store*-typed expressions is preserved.

2. Properties of Compile-Time Reduction

We first show that the splitting of a reduction into a compile-time stage (that is, a partial evaluation stage) and a run-time stage (that is, the remainder of the evaluation) does not hinder the discovery of normal forms.

2.1 Proposition: *If $E \Rightarrow^* E'$ by compile-time reduction, then $E' \Rightarrow^* E''$ iff $E \Rightarrow^* E''$, where E'' is a nonabstraction normal form.*

Proof: This claim and its proof are stated as Theorem A.2.6 in [Schmidt 86b]. □

Note that, if the E'' mentioned in Proposition 2.1 is an abstraction normal form, a two stage reduction can give a different result than a one stage reduction. Here is a simple example: $(\lambda s^{\underline{S}}. (\lambda n^N. two^{\underline{N}})one^N)$ is in normal form with respect to a one stage reduction, because the call by value reduction strategy does not reduce inside abstraction bodies. But a two stage reduction will reduce the expression to $(\lambda s^{\underline{S}}. two^{\underline{N}})$ at compile-time, because the abstraction body is active at compile-time.

The question of termination of compile-time reduction remains, and it is not an easy question to answer. At this point, we merely restate that well known result that, in the nonrecursively typed lambda-calculus with nonrecursive δ-operators, there exist no infinite reduction sequences [Hindley & Seldin 86 (Appendix 2), Schmidt 86b (Appendix 2)]. Of course, this property does not hold when a recursively defined δ-operator like *fix* is added to the calculus. We comment on this point at the end of the paper.

We next consider how effectively partial evaluation eliminates compile-time redexes. With a simple condition on the δ-operators, we can show that partial evaluation reduces all compile-time redexes.

2.2 Definition: *An n-ary δ-operator $f: D_1 \to \cdots \to D_n \to D_{n+1}$ is acceptable iff D_{n+1} is run-time-typed implies that the contractum of a redex $(f\, d_1 \cdots d_n)$ contains no compile-time redexes.*

Thus, an acceptable δ-operator is one that, if it produces a run-time value, it does not create any compile-time redexes in the process.

Say that an expression has been partially evaluated to an expression E that is in compile-time normal form. We show that no compile-time redexes arise during the run-time reduction of E.

2.3 Theorem: *Let all δ-operators be acceptable. If E is in compile-time normal form and $E \Rightarrow E'$, then E' is in compile-time normal form.*

Proof: The reduction of E to E' must occur due to a contraction of a redex that is not a compile-time redex. There are two cases:
(i) The redex contracted is a β-redex $(\lambda x.B)A$. Both A and B must have run-time types. Clearly, no compile-time redexes exist in those parts of E' disjoint from the contractum. By definition, B is active at compile-time, hence, it contains no compile-time redexes; nor does A. We use induction on the structure of B to show $[A/x]B$ has no compile-time redexes. The cases are:
   (a) B is an identifier or an operator: easy.
   (b) B is an abstraction. There are two subcases: (1) $[A\,/\,x](\lambda x.B') = (\lambda x.B')$,

which has no compile-time redexes because E had none. (2) $[A/x](\lambda y.B') = (\lambda y.[A/x]B')$, which has none by the inductive hypothesis for B'.

(c) B is a combination $[A/x]E_1[A/x]E_2$. By the inductive hypotheses for E_1 and E_2, the components of the combination have no compile-time redexes. Can the entire expression be a new compile-time redex? Let us consider the cases. For the expression to be a redex:

- $[A/x]E_1$ is some $(\lambda y.B')$ and $[A/x]E_2$ is compile-time-typed and in compile-time normal form. But we now proceed to show that, if the latter holds, then E_2 was itself compile-time-typed and in compile-time normal form. This implies that E_1E_2 was itself a compile-time redex, which is not possible.

Lemma: *If $[A/x]E_2$ is compile-time typed and in compile-time normal form, then so is E_2.*

Proof: Since substitution preserves typing, we need only show that E_2 must be in normal form. The proof is an induction on E_2:

(i) E_2 is an identifier: if it is x, then $[A/x]x = A$, which is run-time typed, so this is not possible; if it is $y \neq x$, then $[A/x]E_2 = y = E_2$.

(ii) E_2 is an abstraction: there are two cases: (a) $[A/x](\lambda x.B') = (\lambda x.B') = E_2$. (b) $[A/x](\lambda y.B') = (\lambda y.[A/x]B')$. Appeal to the inductive hypothesis for B'.

(iii) E_2 is a combination: if $[A/x]M[A/x]N$ is compile-time typed and in compile-time normal form, then $[A/x]M$ must have form $(f[A/x]M_1 \cdots [A/x]M_n)$, where all $[A/x]M_i$ are compile-time typed and in compile-time normal form. Now, appeal to the inductive hypothesis for each M_i and N. □

- $[A/x]E_1$ is a combination $(f[A/x]M_1 \cdots [A/x]M_n)$; all $[A/x]M_i$ are compile-time typed and in normal form, as is $[A/x]E_2$. Using the Lemma just proved, we know that all M_i and E_2 are compile-time-typed and in normal form. Hence, $(fM_1 \cdots M_n E_2) = (E_1 E_2)$ is a compile-time redex, which is not possible.

(ii) The redex contracted is a δ-redex $(fd_1 \cdots d_n)$. The parts of E' disjoint from the contractum has no compile-time redexes. Since the δ-redex itself is not a compile-time redex, d_n has a run-time type, implying that the contractum has one also. Since f is an acceptable operator, the contractum has no compile-time redexes. □

2.4 Corollary: *If $E \Rightarrow^* E'$ due to compile-time reduction and E' is in compile-time normal form, then no compile-time redex is contracted in the subsequent, run-time reduction of $E' \Rightarrow^* E''$.*

Proposition 2.1 and Corollary 2.4 tell us that any reduction can be cleanly split into a compile-time stage and a run-time stage. In particular, no abstraction or operator that is usable at compile-time will be the operator part of a redex at run-time. The "range" of compile-time reduction is indicated by the compile-time types in the lambda-expression.

The TML type information also warns us when a run-time expression can prevent an operation from reducing at compile-time. Consider this example (let *access* : *Locn* → *Store* → *Locn*):

$$(bind^{I\,\rightarrow\,\underline{L}\,\rightarrow\,(\underline{E}\,\rightarrow\,\underline{E})}\ i_0^I\ (access^{L\,\rightarrow\,\underline{S}\,\rightarrow\,\underline{L}}\ l_0^L\ s_0^{\underline{S}})^{\underline{L}}\ e_0^{\underline{E}})^{\underline{E}}$$

bind is meant to be a compile-time operation, but its second argument is run-time typed. This forces *bind*'s type to be $I \rightarrow \underline{L} \rightarrow (\underline{E} \xrightarrow{} \underline{E})$ which shows that *bind* is not usable. Also, environment e_0 has type $\underline{E}$, and it must be retained for run-time. So, we can not complete environment processing at compile-time. This ability to identify run-time dependencies is an important property of the TML calculus.

Under what conditions can we ensure that a type's expressions are completely reduced at compile-time? For example, if we define what we believe is a statically-typed language's semantics, we must verify that all *Env*-typed expressions "reduce away" (disappear) in the course of compile-time reduction.

2.5 Definition: *For a first-order type T, a decorated expression E is statically typed in T if no subexpression of E has type $\underline{T}$.*

We plan to show that if expression E is statically typed in T, then all potentially active T-typed values in E "reduce away" during compile-time reduction.

2.6 Definition: *An n-ary δ-operator $f : D_1 \rightarrow \cdots \rightarrow D_n \rightarrow D_{n+1}$ is acceptable to T iff*
(i) it is an acceptable operator;
(ii) if D_{n+1} is run-time-typed, then all T-typed and $\underline{T}$-typed subexpressions in the contractum of a redex $(f\,d_1 \cdots d_n)$ must be descendants of (that is, appear in) one of $d_1 \cdots d_n$;
(iii) if some $D_i = T$, $1 \leqslant i \leqslant n$, then $i = n$, and then any active combination $(f\,d_1 \cdots d_i)$ must be a compile-time redex when all of $d_1 \cdots d_i$ are closed and in compile-time normal form.

We like δ-operators that are acceptable to T because they do not create new T-values at run-time (condition (ii)), and they never retain a T-value for use at run-time, like a "closure" might do (condition (iii)).

2.7 Lemma: *If closed expression $E \notin T$ is statically typed in T, is in compile-time normal form, and all δ-operators are acceptable to T, then E has no active T-typed subexpressions.*

Proof: The proof is by an induction on the structure of E.
(i) E is an identifier or operator: immediate.
(ii) E is an abstraction $(\lambda x^{D_1}. B^{D_2})$: If $D_1 \in ct$, then B is not active, and the result holds. If $D_1 \in rt$, then B is active, implying that it is in compile-time normal form. Also, $D_2 \in rt$, implying that $B \notin T$. By the inductive hypothesis, B has no active T-typed expressions. So neither does E.
(iii) E is a combination $(E_1^{D_1\,\tau\,D_2}\,E_2^{D_1})$, $\tau \in \{\rightarrow, \xrightarrow{}\}$: if $D_1 \neq T$, appeal to the inductive hypothesis for E_1 and E_2 for the result. If $D_1 = T$, then $E_1 \in T \rightarrow D_2$. Since E_1 is in compile-time normal form, it must be either:
(a) an operator f: But f must be acceptable to T, implying that E is a compile-time redex.

(b) an identifier x: Since the overall expression is closed, x is bound to some binding identifier x with compile-time type $T \to D_2$. But this implies that E is inactive.

(c) an abstraction $(\lambda x^T. B^{D_2})$: but then E is a compile-time redex.

(d) a nested combination $(E_{10} \cdots E_{1n})^{T \to D_2}$, $n > 0$, such that E_{10} is not a combination. Say that each E_{1i} has type D_i', $0 \leqslant i \leqslant n$. Every $D_i' \in ct$, else E_1 would be typed $\underline{T} \overset{\cdot}{\to} D_2$. Further, each E_{1i} is in compile-time normal form. Reasoning similar to that in cases (b) and (c) above leads us to conclude that E_{10} must be an an operator f that is acceptable to T. But this means that E is a compile-time redex. $\square$

2.8 Lemma: *If E is statically typed in T and all δ-rules are acceptable to T, then $E \Rightarrow E'$ implies that E' is statically typed in T.*

Proof: A β-reduction preserves type information in its contractum. The contractum of a δ-operator acceptable to T contains no expressions typed $\underline{T}$, by condition (ii) of Definition 2.6. $\square$

2.9 Theorem: *If closed expression $E \notin T$ is statically typed in T, $E \Rightarrow^* E'$ due to compile-time reduction, and E' is in compile-time normal form, then E' has no active T-typed expressions.*

Proof: Lemmas 2.7 and 2.8. $\square$

Note that Theorem 2.9 mentions *active* T-typed expressions. Here is why: if $t_0 \in T$, then $(\lambda n^N. t_0^T)^{N \to T}$ is in compile-time normal form and contains no active occurrences of T-typed subexpressions. But it does contain an inactive occurrence. It is important that we verify that an inactive T-typed subexpression never becomes active during the run-time reduction stage. We do so now.

2.10 Theorem: *Let all δ-operators be acceptable to T. If closed expression E is statically typed in T, is in compile-time normal form, and has no active T-typed subexpressions, and if $E \Rightarrow E'$ due to a run-time reduction, then E' is statically typed in T, is in compile-time normal form, and has no active T-typed subexpressions.*

Proof: By Lemma 2.8, E' is statically typed in T. By Theorem 2.3, E' is in compile-time normal form. To show that E' has no active T-typed subexpressions, consider the redex contracted:

(i) a β-redex $(\lambda x.B)A$. Both x and A have a run-time type. Lemma 2.7 guarantees that no active T-typed expressions are in B or A. Hence, none are in $[A/x]B$.

(b) a δ-redex $(f d_1 \cdots d_n)$. The contractum must have a run-time type. No d_i contains an active T-typed subexpression, hence, by the definition of acceptable-to-T, the contractum has no active T-typed subexpressions. $\square$

2.11 Corollary: *If E is statically typed in T, $E \Rightarrow^* E'$ due to compile-time reduction, and E' is in compile-time normal form, then at no stage in the run-time reduction of $E' \Rightarrow^* E''$ does an active occurrence of a T-typed expression appear.*

If all the semantic equations of a denotational definition are statically typed in T, then any program that the definition maps into lambda code is statically typed in T. Thus, we show that a language uses a compile-time environment for all of its programs by verifying that the language's denotational definition is statically typed in *Env*.

We can also verify whether a structural property R of an expression is preserved by compile-time reduction. We develop an analogue to Lemma 2.8: "if E has R and $E \Rightarrow E'$, then E' has R." The proof of Lemma 2.8 suggests that property R be associated with the run-time types, because we wish to avoid reductions that destroy property R. So, expressions that preserve R are made "run-time" typed. This approach was taken in [Schmidt 86b], where the structure of *Store*-typed expressions was critical to single-threading. Hence, the *Store*-typed expressions were run-time typed.

In summary, the TML typing calculus is a simple, yet effective method for judging the power and safety of partial reduction. The static criteria imposed by the types proves useful to a language designer, for he can clearly see the division between static and dynamic features in the language definition. Also, the designer can detect trouble spots in binding times. Finally, he can direct the partial evaluator to avoid pitfalls like those mentioned in [Paulson 82 84].

3. An Algorithm for Decorating Expressions

The TML typing calculus is instructive and easy to use, but a language designer might prefer to write a language definition with undecorated types and let a type checker attach the decorations. In this section, we give an algorithm for decorating types and note that the algorithm produces a "minimal decoration," that is, starting with a list of the first-order types that must be run-time types, the algorithm decorates as few expressions as run-time typed as necessary to make the entire expression well-typed. We prove this result by placing a partial ordering on the decorated types and showing that the typing algorithm is the least fixed point of an appropriate functional. The complete development is too long to present here, so we give an overview. The complete presentation is in [Schmidt 87]. Similar presentations are in [Nielson 87, Nielson & Nielson 88].

We begin with the partial ordering.

3.1 Definition: *For all* $D_1, D_2 \in DType$, $D_1 \sqsubseteq D_2$ *iff*
(i) $D_1 = P$, *and* $D_2 = P$ *or* $D_2 = \underline{P}$.
(ii) $D_1 = \underline{P}$, *and* $D_2 = \underline{P}$.
(iii) $D_1 = D_{11} \tau_1 D_{12}$ *and* $D_2 = D_{21} \tau_2 D_{22}$; $\tau_1, \tau_2 \in \{ \rightarrow, \xrightarrow{\ } \}$; $D_{11} \sqsubseteq D_{21}$; $D_{12} \sqsubseteq D_{22}$; *and* $\tau_1 = \xrightarrow{\ }$ *implies* $\tau_2 = \xrightarrow{\ }$.

Hence, $D_1 \sqsubseteq D_2$ if D_2 has more run-time type information in it than D_1. In particular, it is easy to prove that $D_1 \sqsubseteq D_2$ and $D_1 \in rt$ imply $D_2 \in rt$.

3.2 Proposition: $\sqsubseteq$ *is a partial ordering.*

Let *forget* : $DType \rightarrow Type$ map a decorated type to its corresponding undecorated type by forgetting all underlining decorations. For example,

$forget(P \rightarrow (Q \rightarrow (\underline{R \xrightarrow{} S}))) = P \rightarrow (Q \rightarrow (R \rightarrow S)).$

3.3 Proposition: *For all $D_1, D_2 \in DType$, $D_1 \sqsubseteq D_2$ implies $forget(D_1) = forget(D_2)$.*

3.4 Proposition: *For all $D_1, D_2 \in DType$, if $forget(D_1) = forget(D_2)$, then $D_1 \sqcup D_2$ and $D_1 \sqcap D_2$ exist.*

From here on, we use $DType° = Dtype \cup \{\bot, \top\}$ as the set of decorated types. Our reason for working with $DType°$ instead of $DType$ is that the former is a complete lattice. (It is, in fact, a lattice with the finite chain property.)

We now formulate the algorithm. Let **R** be a set of first-order types that must be run-time types. Say that a decorated expression E is **R**-*consistent* if all occurrences of $P \in \mathbf{R}$ in E are decorated $\underline{P}$.

Function $make\text{-}rt(D)$ forces D to be a run-time type; $decorate\text{-}type_\mathbf{R}(D)$ decorates the type D with the minimum number of run-time types to make it **R**-consistent:

3.5 Definition: *For a set of run-time types* **R**, *$make\text{-}rt : DType° \rightarrow DType°$ is defined as follows:*

$make\text{-}rt(\bot) = \bot$
$make\text{-}rt(P) = \underline{P}$
$make\text{-}rt(\underline{P}) = \underline{P}$
$make\text{-}rt(ct \rightarrow D) = make\text{-}rt(ct) \xrightarrow{} make\text{-}rt(D)$
$make\text{-}rt(rt \rightarrow rt) = rt \xrightarrow{} rt$
$make\text{-}rt(rt \xrightarrow{} rt) = rt \xrightarrow{} rt$
$make\text{-}rt(\top) = \top$

$decorate\text{-}type_\mathbf{R} : Type \rightarrow DType°$ *is defined as follows:*

$decorate\text{-}type_\mathbf{R}(P) = $ if $P \in \mathbf{R}$ then $\underline{P}$ else P
$decorate\text{-}type_\mathbf{R}(D_1 \rightarrow D_2) = $ let $D_1' = decorate\text{-}type_\mathbf{R}(D_1)$ in
            let $D_2' = decorate\text{-}type_\mathbf{R}(D_2)$
            in $D_1' \rightarrow$ (if $D_1' \in rt$ then $make\text{-}rt(D_2')$ else D_2')

We draw the type structure of a decorated expression E^D, $D \in Dtype°$, as an (inverted) tree. Here is the "decoration tree" for the expression $((\lambda x^P. x^{\underline{P}})^{P \rightarrow \underline{P}} a^P)^\bot$:

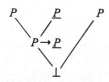

Note that the expression has a $\bot$-type in it. We call such expressions *partially well-typed* (*pwt*). A formal definition of "partially well-typed" is in [Schmidt 87]. A *well-typed* expression does not use $\bot$- or $\top$-types.

Let E be an expression that we wish to decorate. For simplicity, assume that each binding identifier λx in E is unique. We define a *type environment* to be a value in the set $TEnv = (\text{Operator} \cup \text{Identifier}) \rightarrow DType°$. A type environment gives the decorations for the operators and identifiers in E.

3.6 Definition: *For the set of run-time types* $\mathbf{R}$, *a type environment* $t \in TEnv$ *is* $\mathbf{R}$-*consistent iff for all* $a \in \text{Operator} \cup \text{Identifier}$, $t(a)$ *is* $\mathbf{R}$-*consistent.*

Further, if type environment t *is* $\mathbf{R}$-*consistent with respect to the set of run-time types* $\mathbf{R}$, *a pwt decorated expression* E^D *is* $\mathbf{R}$-t-*consistent iff for all* $a \in \text{Operator} \cup \text{Identifier}$ *occurring in* E^D, *if* a *is decorated as* a^{D_0}, $D_0 \neq \bot$, *then* $t(a) \sqsubseteq D_0$.

So a decorated expression E^D is $\mathbf{R}$-t-consistent if all types in $\mathbf{R}$ are decorated as run-time types, and all operators and constants are decorated with types that have as much run-time information as that specified by t.

We now define a function $Pass : TEnv \rightarrow DExpression \rightarrow DExpression$ that decorates the types of its expression argument. It uses its type environment argument to establish the types of operators and identifiers.

Figure 1 gives the definition. *Pass*'s definition is complex because both inherited and synthesized information is necessary to decorate an expression. Figure 2 shows how repeated uses of *Pass* determines a typing that uses no $\bot$ values for decorations.

3.7 Proposition: *If* E *is well-typed and* $\mathbf{R}$-t-*consistent, then* $(Pass\, t)(E) = E$.

If E' and E'' are two decorated versions of an undecorated expression E, we write $E' \sqsubseteq E''$ iff for every pair of homologous (corresponding) subexpressions $F'^{D'}$ in E' and $F''^{D''}$ in E'', $D' \sqsubseteq D''$. That is, each decorated type in E' is less run-time-typed than its corresponding decorated type in E''. The set $\{E' \in DExpression \mid E'$ is a decorated version of $E\}$, partially ordered as just described, is a complete lattice with the finite chain property because $DType°$ is a complete lattice with the finite chain property. The least decorated version of E is the one that uses $\bot$-type decorations for all subexpressions. Let us represent this decorated expression by $\bot_E$. Then, $fix(Pass\, t)$ is defined $\bigsqcup \{(Pass\, t)^i(\bot_E) \mid i \geqslant 0\}$, where f^i abbreviates $f \circ f \circ \cdots \circ f$, f repeated i times. By the finite chain property, $fix(Pass\, t) = (Pass\, t)^j(\bot_E)$, for some $j \geqslant 0$.

3.8 Proposition: *For any well-typed,* $\mathbf{R}$-t-*consistent expression* E, $fix(Pass\, t) \sqsubseteq E$.

3.9 Proposition: $fix(Pass\, t)$ *contains no* $\bot$- *or* $\top$-*type decorations.*

Unfortunately, $fix(Pass\, t)$ is *not* the minimally decorated, well-typed version of an undecorated expression. The problem is that *Pass* might not decorate all occurrences of the same identifier in the expression with the same decoration. For example, for $((\lambda x^P.\, (f^{P \rightarrow Q}\, x^P)^Q)^{P \rightarrow Q}\, a^P)^Q$, if a type environment t maps x to P and a to $\underline{P}$, then $fix(Pass\, t)$ is the decorated expression $((\lambda x^{\underline{P}}.\, (f^{P \rightarrow Q}\, x^P)^Q)^{\underline{P} \rightarrow Q}\, a^{\underline{P}})^Q$. Only the minimal number of run-time decorations were used to make the expression partially well-typed. But the expression is not well-typed, because x in the abstraction body has type P and not type $\underline{P}$.

Figure 1

Define $dom : DType° \rightarrow DType°$ as:
$\quad (D_1 \; \tau \; D_2).dom = D_1, \quad \tau \in \{\rightarrow, \underset{\sim}{\rightarrow}\}$
$\quad \top.dom = \top$
$\quad D.dom = \bot$, otherwise
Define $cod : DType° \rightarrow DType°$ as:
$\quad (D_1 \; \tau \; D_2).cod = D_2, \quad \tau \in \{\rightarrow, \underset{\sim}{\rightarrow}\}$
$\quad \top.cod = \top$
$\quad D.cod = \bot$, otherwise

Define $slet \; a = e_1 \; in e_2$ as:
$\quad slet \; a = \bot \; in \; e_2 \; = \; \bot$
$\quad slet \; a = \top \; in \; e_2 \; = \; \top$
$\quad slet \; a = e_1 \; in \; e_2 \; = \; (let \; a = e_1 \; in \; e_2), \quad$ otherwise

Define $Pass : Env \rightarrow DExpression \rightarrow DExpression$ as:

$Pass \; t \; E^D = traverse \; E^D \; D$

where $traverse : DExpression \rightarrow DType° \rightarrow DExpression$
is defined as:

$traverse \; expr \; inherit =$
$\quad$ cases $expr$ of
$\quad\quad is(f^{D_0}) : f^{\; inherit \sqcup t(f)}$
$\quad\quad is(x^{D_0}) : x^{inherit \sqcup t(x)}$
$\quad\quad is((E_1^{D_1} \; E_2^{D_2})^{D_0}) : ((traverse \; E_1^{D_1} \; D) \; (traverse \; E_2^{D_2} \; D.dom))^{D.cod}$
$\quad\quad\quad$ where $D = slet \; D_{11}' \; \tau \; D_{12}' = D_1$ in
$\quad\quad\quad\quad\quad\quad\quad\quad slet \; D_2' = D_2$ in
$\quad\quad\quad\quad\quad\quad\quad\quad let \; D_1'' = D_{11}' \sqcup D_2'$ in
$\quad\quad\quad\quad\quad\quad\quad\quad D_1'' \rightarrow (if \; D_1'' \in rt$
$\quad\quad\quad\quad\quad\quad\quad\quad\quad\quad\quad then \; make\text{-}rt(D_{12}' \sqcup inherit)$
$\quad\quad\quad\quad\quad\quad\quad\quad\quad\quad\quad else \; D_{12}' \sqcup inherit)$
$\quad\quad is((\lambda x^{D_1}. \; E_1^{D_2})^{D_0}) : (\lambda x^{\; D.dom}. \; (traverse \; E_1^{D_2} \; D.cod))^D$
$\quad\quad\quad$ where $D = slet \; D_1' = D_1 \sqcup t(x)$ in
$\quad\quad\quad\quad\quad\quad\quad\quad slet \; D_2' = D_2$ in
$\quad\quad\quad\quad\quad\quad\quad\quad (D_1' \rightarrow (if \; D_1' \in rt \; then \; make\text{-}rt(D_2') \; else \; D_2')) \sqcup inherit$

Figure 2

Let $\mathbf{R} = \{S\}$
and $t \in TEnv$ be defined such that:
$t(s) = \underline{S}$
$t(e) = \underline{E}$
$t(bind) = N \to (E \to E)$
$t(access) = \underline{S} \to \underline{N}$
$t(alter) = E \to E$

Let the trees below represent type decorations for the expression:
$((bind\ (access\ s))\ (alter\ e))$

$T_0 =$

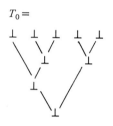

$T_1 = Pass(T_0)$

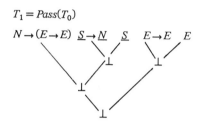

$T_2 = Pass(T_1)$

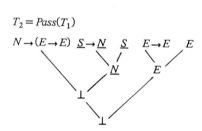

$T_3 = Pass(T_2)$

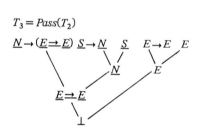

$T_4 = Pass(T_3) = Pass(Pass(T_3))$

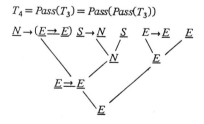

Fortunately, we can create a well-typed, decorated expression by building better and better approximations to a type environment t' that yields a well-typed expression $fix(Pass\,t')$. Here is our strategy: given an undecorated expression E and a set of run-time types $\mathbf{R}$, we define type environment t_0 to be $t_0 = \lambda a.\,decorate\text{-}type_\mathbf{R}(type\text{-}of\,a)$. (For an undecorated expression E, let $type\text{-}of : (\text{Operator} \cup \text{Identifier}) \to DType$ produce the type associated with an operator or identifier in E.) This is the minimal enviroment that is $\mathbf{R}$-consistent. Next, we compute $fix(Pass\,t_0)$, which propagates the decorations and environment information throughout the expression. We build the next approximate type environment t_1 by updating t_0 so that an identifier x maps to the join of all the decorated types that appear at all occurrences of x in $fix(Pass\,t_0)$. Then we compute $fix(Pass\,t_1)$. We repeat this process until a well-typed expression results.

3.10 Definition: *Define* $Refine : TEnv \to TEnv$ *as:*

$$Refine(t) = \{[x \mapsto \bigsqcup\{D \mid x^D \text{ occurs in } fix(Pass\,t)\}] \mid x \in \text{Identifier}\}t$$
$$\text{where } \{[a \mapsto v_a] \mid a \in A\}f \text{ represents the function } f' \text{ such that:}$$
$$f'(b) = v_b \quad if \ b \in A$$
$$f'(b) = f(b) \quad if \ b \notin A$$

When t is $\mathbf{R}$-consistent so is $Refine(t)$. Also, for no identifier x does $Refine(t)(x)$ equal $\top$.

3.11 Proposition: *For any well-typed, $\mathbf{R}\text{-}t_0$-consistent expression E, for all $i \geqslant 0$, $fix(Pass(Refine^i(t_0))) \sqsubseteq E$.*

It is important to note that the partially ordered set $TEnv$ has the finite chain property, because $Dtype°$ has it and the set $(\text{Operator} \cup \text{Identifier})$ is finite for any particular expression.

3.12 Theorem: *Let $t_k = \bigsqcup\{Refine^i(t_0) \mid i \geqslant 0\}$, which equals $Refine^k(t_0)$, for some $k \geqslant 0$. Then $fix(Pass\,t_k)$ is well-typed.*

3.13 Theorem: *For any undecorated expression E, run-time types $\mathbf{R}$, and type environment $t_0 = (\lambda a.\,decorate\text{-}type_\mathbf{R}(type\text{-}of\,a))$, $fix(Pass\,t_k)$ is the minimally decorated, well-typed, $\mathbf{R}\text{-}t_0$-consistent version of E.*

These results show that the minimally decorated, well-typed, $\mathbf{R}\text{-}t$-consistent version of an expression can be calculated in finite time with the functional in Figure 1 and the definitions in Definition 3.10 and Theorem 3.12.

4. Related Work

The results in this paper rely strongly on the efforts of Nielson and Nielson on TML. Nielson and Nielson also have developed an algorithm that attaches TML type decorations to an undecorated lambda-expression [Nielson 87, Nielson & Nielson 88]. Their algorithm runs in exponential time. Our subsequent effort, documented in Section 3, has not improved on that result.

5. Further Work

The termination question still confronts us. How do we use recursively defined δ-operations such as *fix*, where $(fix\,f\,a) \Rightarrow f(fix\,f)\,a$, and guarantee termination of compile-time reduction? The results in this paper shed little light on this problem. An extreme decision is to make any recursively defined δ-operator not usable at compile-time. Thus, compile-time reduction must terminate. But this step does not give the minimal TML-typing for the δ-operator, and it might clash with a static typing property of an expression. As the next stage of our research, we plan to use the TML calculus to develop useful conditions for reduction and termination of recursively defined δ-operations.

Acknowledgements

Thanks are due to: Hanne Riis Nielson and Flemming Nielson, for stimulating discussions and letters; Neil Jones, for discussions and encouragement; and the referees, for comments and criticisms.

References

[Appel 85] Appel, A. Semantics-directed code generation, *Proc. 12th ACM Symp. Princ. of Prog. Lang.*, New Orleans, 1985, pp. 315-324.

[Berry & Levy 79] Berry, G., and Levy, J.-J. A survey of some syntactic results of the lambda-calculus. *Proc. 8th Symp. Math. Foundations of Comp. Sci.*, LNCS 74, Springer, Berlin, 1979, pp. 552-566.

[Curry & Feys 58] Curry, H.B., and Feys, R. *Combinatory Logic, Vol. 1.* North-Holland, Amsterdam, 1958.

[Ershov 78] Ershov, A.P. On the essence of compilation. In *Formal Description of Programming Concepts,* E.J. Neuhold, ed., North-Holland, Amsterdam, 1978.

[Ershov 82] Ershov, A.P. Mixed computation: potential applications and problems for study. *Theoretical Computer Science* 18 (1982) 41-68.

[Hindley & Seldin 86] Hindley, J.R., and Seldin, J.P. *Introduction to Combinators and the Lambda-Calculus.* Cambridge University Press, Cambridge, 1986.

[Huet & Oppen 80] Huet, G., and Oppen, D.C. Equations and rewrite rules: a survey. In *Formal Language Theory,* R. Book, ed., Academic Press, New York, 1980.

[Jones et. al. 85] Jones, N.D., Sestoft, P., and Sondergaard, H. An experiment in partial evaluation: the generation of a compiler generator. In *Proc. Conf. on Rewriting Techniques and Applications,* LNCS 202, Springer, Berlin, 1985, pp. 124-140.

[Landin 64] Landin, P. The mechanical evaluation of expressions. *Computer*

Journal 6 (1964) 308-320.

[Mosses 79] Mosses, P.D. SIS— semantics implementation system: reference manual and user guide. Report DAIMI MD-30, Computer Science Dept., Aarhus Univ., Aarhus, Denmark, 1979.

[Mycroft 81] Mycroft, A. Abstract interpretation and optimizing transformations for applicative programs. Ph.D. thesis, Computer science department, University of Edinburgh, Scotland, 1981.

[Nielson 86] Nielson, F. Abstract interpetation of denotational definitions. In Proc. STACS 1986, Lecture Notes in C.S. 210, Springer, Berlin, 1986.

[Nielson 87] Nielson, F. A formal type system for comparing partial evaluators. Proc. Workshop on Partial Evaluation and Mixed Computation, Ebberup, Denmark, Oct. 1987.

[Nielson & Nielson 86a] Nielson, H.R., and Nielson, F. Pragmatic aspects of two-level denotational meta-grammars. In *Proc. ESOP,* LNCS 213, Springer, Berlin, 1986, pp. 133-143.

[Nielson & Nielson 86b] Nielson, H.R., and Nielson, F. Code generation from two-level denotational meta-languages. In *Proc. Workshop on Programs as Data Objects,* N.D. Jones, ed., LNCS 217, Springer, Berlin, 1986, pp. 192-205.

[Nielson & Nielson 88] Nielson, H.R., and Nielson, F. Automatic binding time analysis for a typed lambda-calculus. Proc. ACM Symp. on Principles of Prog. Languages, San Diego, CA, 1988.

[Paulson 82] Paulson, L. A semantics-directed compiler generator. in *Proc. 9th ACM Symp. on Prin. of Prog. Lang.,* 1982, pp. 224-233.

[Paulson 84] Paulson, L. Compiler generation from denotational semantics. In *Methods and Tools for Compiler Construction,* B. Lorho, ed., 1984, pp. 219-250.

[Plotkin 75] Plotkin, G. Call-by-name, call-by-value, and the lambda-calculus. *Theoretical Computer Science* 1 (1975) 125-159.

[Raoult & Sethi 84] Raoult, J.-C., and Sethi, R. The global storage needs of a subcomputation. In *Proc. 11th ACM Symp. on Prin. of Prog. Lang.,* Salt Lake City, Utah, 1984, pp. 148-157.

[Raskovsky 82] Raskovsky, M. Denotational semantics as a specification of code generators. *ACM SIGPLAN Notices* 17 (1982) 230-244.

[Rosen 73] Rosen, B. Tree-manipulating systems and Church-Rosser theorems. *J. ACM* 20 (1973) 160-187.

[Schmidt 85a] Schmidt, D.A. Detecting global variables in denotational specifications. *ACM Trans. on Prog. Lang. and Sys.* 7 (1985) 299-310.

[Schmidt 85b] Schmidt, D.A. An implementation from a direct semantics definition. In *Proc. Workshop on Programs as Data Objects,* N.D. Jones, ed., LNCS 217, Springer, Berlin, 1985, pp. 222-235.

[Schmidt 86] Schmidt, D.A. *Denotational Semantics.* Allyn and Bacon, Boston, 1986.

[Schmidt 86b] Schmidt, D.A. Detecting stack-based environments in denotational definitions. Technical report 86-3, Computer Science Department, Kansas State University, Manhattan, Kansas, 1986.

[Schmidt 87] Schmidt, D.A. Static properties of partial reduction (extended version), Report 87-9, Computer Science Dept., Kansas State University, Manhattan, Kansas, Sept. 1987.

[Sethi 82] Sethi, R. Pebble games for studying storage sharing. *Theoretical Comp. Sci.* 19 (1982) 69-84.

[Stoy 77] Stoy, J. *Denotational Semantics.* MIT Press, Cambridge, MA, 1977.

Partial Evaluation and Mixed Computation
D. Bjørner, A.P. Ershov and N.D. Jones (Editors)
Elsevier Science Publishers B.V. (North-Holland)
© IFIP, 1988

Automatic Call Unfolding in a Partial Evaluator

Peter Sestoft

DIKU, University of Copenhagen
Universitetsparken 1, DK-2100 Copenhagen Ø, Denmark

Partial evaluation of a functional language may be done by specialization of
functions, implemented by reduction of expressions and unfolding of
function calls. Expression reduction is fairly straightforward, but it is
difficult to decide when to unfold a function call and when to leave it in the
program produced by partial evaluation. A call unfolding strategy must be
adopted in order to make this decision in each particular case.

In the partial evaluators reported in the literature, this strategy is not
formalized, and the user of a partial evaluator must guide the call unfolding
by his own informal criteria. This is an obstacle to many applications of
partial evaluation.

In the present paper we describe a simple two-phase call unfolding
method which is fully automatic. The first phase is based on static call
annotations, obtained by a local analysis to avoid infinite unfolding and a
global analysis to avoid call duplication. The second phase does additional
unfolding based on a global analysis. The method has been employed in a
recent version of the partial evaluator mix, developed by Neil D. Jones,
Harald Søndergaard, and the author.

1. INTRODUCTION

The program transformation technique called partial evaluation has attracted much
attention in recent years and partial evaluators have been developed for a variety of
languages and purposes. Most partial evaluators however require some user
assistance, and so are not fully automatic program transformers. This is true also of
the early versions of mix, a partial evaluator for a small subset of pure Lisp
developed by Neil D. Jones, Harald Søndergaard, and the author.

In this paper we describe the problems that required user assistance in mix
and propose a rather simple way of automating their solution, thus achieving fully
automatic partial evaluation of a large class of programs. In particular, this class
includes the partial evaluator itself, and so the partial evaluator is self-applicable.

The setting of the problem we attempt to solve is this: the partial evaluator
produces a residual program from specializations of the given subject program's
functions. This is done by a function specialization phase which *reduces expressions*
and *unfolds function calls* in the subject program, making use of its known input.
Reduction of an expression depends only on the form of the expression and the
symbolic values of the variables occurring in it and so is quite straightforward. On
the other hand, the decision whether a call should be unfolded or not requires a

more global view of the program, in order to avoid infinite unfolding for example. For this reason, call unfolding was left to be decided by the user in the early versions of mix. This implied that the user had to understand the workings of mix as well as of the program to be partially evaluated. Naturally, this has provided an obstacle to its application in some cases. Therefore it would be desirable to automate the decision on call unfolding in the function specialization phase.

The solution described in this paper exploits the results of the binding time analysis (done by the first phase of mix) to find calls that may safely be unfolded (during the function specialization phase), and forbids unfolding of all other calls. Because of the simplicity of this strategy, the program produced by function specialization will have many very small functions and will hardly be readable to humans. Therefore a postprocessing phase is employed that unfolds calls to such small functions.

The structure of the rest of the paper is as follows. First, we briefly introduce partial evaluation and outline the structure of the partial evaluator mix in Section 2. On that background we discuss call unfolding in Section 3. The method we have developed is presented in Section 4, and results from its use are discussed in Section 5. The paper closes with a summary, acknowledgements, and a list of references.

2. BACKGROUND

In this section we first give a very brief introduction to partial evaluation and then describe the main features of the partial evaluator mix to provide background for the discussion in Section 3 and the description of our method in Section 4.

2.1 Partial Evaluation

Partial evaluation deals with specialization of programs. Suppose we are given a program p with two input parameters, and suppose that the value d_1 of the first parameter is available while that of the second parameter is not. Then obviously the program p cannot be evaluated to yield a result. It may however be *partially evaluated* with respect to the known value of the first parameter. This yields another program r, a so-called *residual program*. This program will compute the "rest" of p when given a value d_2 of the second parameter. That is, when evaluated on the remaining input, the residual program r will give the same result as the original *subject program* p when evaluated on all of its input, or in symbols,

$$\text{Eval } p\ (d_1, d_2) = \text{Eval } r\ (d_2) \quad \text{for all data } d_2.$$

A program that will produce a residual program r when given a subject program p and part of its input d_1 is called a *partial evaluator*. A partial evaluator that may be used to partially evaluate itself (letting the subject program p be the partial evaluator itself) is said to be *self-applicable*.

A partial evaluator may be used for many interesting purposes, for instance, to compile by partial evaluation of an interpreter with respect to a source program. This is useful for cheaply implementing special purpose languages such as the language of pattern expressions as interpreted by a general purpose pattern matcher. Furthermore, a self-applicable partial evaluator may be used for generating compilers (by partial evaluation of the partial evaluator with respect to an interpreter), and for generating a compiler generator (by partial evaluation of the partial evaluator with respect to itself).

Precursors to partial evaluation are found in Kleene's S-m-n theorem, in optimizing compilers, and in the paper [Lombardi 1967]. Futamura was the first to describe partial evaluation as a topic in its own right and to see its possible applications in compilation and compiler generation [Futamura 1971]. The first expositions of the possibility of generating a compiler generator are found in [Beckman *et al.* 1976], [Turchin 1979] and [Ershov 1982]. A partial evaluator for Lisp (with property lists and imperative features) is described in [Beckman *et al.* 1976]; partial evaluation of imperative languages is discussed in [Ershov 1978] and [Bulyonkov 1984].

2.2 The Structure of the Partial Evaluator Mix

The subject language (*i.e.*, language of subject programs) of mix is Mixwell, a small subset of pure Lisp with lexical scoping. A Mixwell program is a list of definitions of functions $f_1, ..., f_h$ with the first function f_1 as the goal function. Input to the program is through the variables of that function:

$$f_1 (x_1,...,x_{k1}) = e_1$$
$$...$$
$$f_h (y_1,...,y_{kh}) = e_h$$

The body e_i of function f_i is constructed from variables appearing in the variable list of f_i, from constants (quote ...), and operators atom, car, cdr, cons, equal (as in Lisp), a conditional if, and a function call call. The only data type is well-founded (*i.e.*, non-circular) S-expressions as known from Lisp. All operators except the conditional if are strict in all positions, and defined functions are called by value.

The partial evaluator is divided into two major phases:

- a binding time analysis phase, and
- a function specialization phase.

The *binding time analysis phase* takes as input a description of which parts of the program's input are known, and does a global analysis of the subject program to compute a description of each variable of each function as either Static or Dynamic. A variable is described as Static if it can take on only values dependent on the known input, and as Dynamic if it may possibly take on a value dependent on the unknown input. During the function specialization phase, a Static variable will have an ordinary value such as '(a b) whereas a Dynamic one will in general have a symbolic value, possibly containing variables, for example (cons '(a b) (car x)). The variable list of every function is split into two variable lists: one for Static variables and one for Dynamic variables.

The *function specialization phase* takes as input the actual values of the known input and produces a residual program built from specializations of the subject program's functions $f_1, ..., f_h$. A function f_i is specialized by symbolically evaluating its body e_i in a symbolic environment that binds each of its variables to an expression. Symbolic evaluation of other expressions than function calls is simple reduction, but for a function call (call f $se_1...se_m$ $de_1...de_n$) it must be decided whether it is to be unfolded or suspended (*i.e.*, not unfolded). Here $se_1...se_m$ are the argument expressions for the Static variables of f, and $de_1...de_n$ are the argument expressions for the Dynamic variables of f.

If the call is to be *unfolded*, then the call (call f $se_1...se_m$ $de_1...de_n$) is replaced by the body of f with the symbolic values of the argument expressions $se_1...se_m$ $de_1...de_n$ substituted for variable occurrences, and the resulting expression is symbolically evaluated. Hence a call that is unfolded during the function specialization phase disappears completely.

If the call is to be *suspended*, then the call expression is replaced by a call to an f-variant f*, the variables of which are f's Dynamic variables. Let $se_1*...se_m*$ be the (ordinary) values of the Static argument expressions $se_1...se_m$, and let $de_1*...de_n*$ be the symbolic values of the Dynamic argument expressions $de_1...de_n$. The resulting expression then is (call f* $de_1*...de_n*$). The variant f* is constructed by specializing the body of f to the values $se_1*...se_m*$ of its Static variables. So symbolic evaluation of a call (call f $se_1...se_m$ $de_1...de_n$) that is to be suspended will result in a specialized call (call f* $de_1*...de_n*$) to a specialized function f*.

The *difficult* point here is to decide whether a call met during symbolic evaluation is to be unfolded or to be suspended. To make good use of the known input, not too many calls should be suspended, whereas to make symbolic evaluation terminate, not too many calls should be unfolded. Unfolding the "wrong" calls may produce enormous residual programs, or may make them monstrously slow. In Section 3 we shall study the various pitfalls to avoid when developing a call unfolding strategy.

For a much more comprehensive description of mix, see [Jones, Sestoft, Søndergaard 1985], [Sestoft 1986], or [Jones, Sestoft, Søndergaard 1987].

3. PROBLEMS WITH CALL UNFOLDING

This section discusses call unfolding strategies and the various problems to be avoided when choosing a call unfolding strategy.

3.1 Call Unfolding Strategies

Call unfolding takes place in the function specialization phase of the partial evaluator as described in Section 2.2 above. The topic of this section is the various possible kinds of call unfolding strategies. Two obvious extremes as regards call unfolding strategies are:

- Never unfold any call
- Always unfold all calls

Neither of these is useful in general. The first alternative, never to unfold any call, will lead to trivial residual programs and bad partial evaluation results as shown in Section 3.2 below. On the other hand, the second alternative, always to unfold all calls, will cause the partial evaluator to loop in all but trivial cases as shown in Section 3.3 below.

We must look for a call unfolding strategy which is an intermediate between these two extremes: a decision on unfolding must be made for each particular call expression. There are two very different ways to make this decision:

- by a *dynamic strategy*, making the decision anew each time the call expression is met during the function specialization phase.
- by a *static strategy*, making the decision for each textual call in advance of the function specialization phase.

The difference is that by a dynamic strategy, if the same textual call expression is met several times during function specialization, it may be unfolded on one occasion and not unfolded on another. This does not happen with a static strategy; in this case either the call expression is unfolded every time it is met, or it is suspended every time. Dynamic strategies are more flexible and may give better results than static ones, and the class of dynamic strategies properly contains the class of static ones. Fuller and Abramsky describe a partial evaluator for Prolog employing a dynamic strategy based on loop detection [Fuller, Abramsky 1987].

The partial evaluator mix described in Section 2.2 above is restricted to the use of static strategies; this requires to decide on unfolding/suspension for each call appearing in the text of the subject program in advance of function specialization. This is mainly for reasons of simplicity: a dynamic strategy would require the function specialization phase of the partial evaluator to maintain some extra data structures to guide the dynamic unfolding decisions. The restriction to static strategies allows to represent the unfolding decision by a simple annotation of each call expression.

With static call unfolding strategies, four possible pitfalls can be clearly identified and will be discussed by means of examples below:

- too little unfolding, yielding trivial residual programs,
- too much unfolding, making partial evaluation loop,
- unfolding in the wrong place, yielding very slow residual programs,
- unfolding in the wrong place, yielding very large residual programs.

Furthermore, there are situations where no satisfactory decisions on call unfolding can be made in the (static) framework of mix. These have to do with infinite specialization. One such case will be discussed in Section 4.3 below.

3.2   Trivial Residual Programs

Too little unfolding happens only when we decide to suspend a call to a function with only Static variables. Consider the program

```
g (x z) = (if (call f x) then z else (cons z z))
f (y)   = (null y)
```

and assume x = 'nil to be known, z unknown. Then x and y are Static, z is Dynamic, and if the call to f were (wisely) unfolded, we would get the residual program

```
g (z)   = z
```

If however (stupidly) the call to f is suspended, then the only thing that can be done is to specialize f to the value 'nil of its Static parameter y, and so we would get

```
g (z)   = (if (call f) then z else (cons z z))
f ()    = 't
```

Moral: Calls to functions with only Static variables should always be unfolded. Note that this may still make the function specialization phase loop in case the subject program already contains a non-terminating loop that does not depend on Dynamic variables.

3.3 Infinite Unfolding

Too much unfolding may make function specialization loop infinitely. Consider the program

```
g (x z) = (if (equal x (car z)) then (cdr z)
           else (call g x (cdr z)))
```

and assume x = 'A to be known and z to be unknown. If we (wisely) choose to suspend the call to g, we will get g specialized to the value 'A of its Static variable x. The residual program would be

```
g (z)  = (if (equal 'A (car z)) then (cdr z)
           else (call g (cdr z)))
```

If on the other hand we (stupidly) attempted to unfold the call every time it is encountered during function specialization, then we would in effect try to build an infinite expression:

```
g (z)  = (if (equal 'A (car z)) then (cdr z)
           else (if (equal 'A (cadr z)) then (cddr z)
           else (if (equal 'A (caddr z)) then (cdddr z)
           else ...
```

The observable effect however is that partial evaluation will not terminate in this case. Moral: Every strategy for call unfolding must somehow ensure that infinite unfolding is not attempted. This may be done by imposing an arbitrary limit on the number of unfoldings that may take place, or (better) by allowing unfolding only where a bound on the number of unfoldings is known to exist. The latter idea is applied in our method as described in Section 4.1.1 below.

3.4 Call Duplication

Extremely slow residual programs may result from call duplication. This happens when an argument expression of a call to be unfolded contains a suspended call, and this (inner) call is duplicated by unfolding the outer call. Consider this program, the run time of which is linear in the length of (list) z:

```
g (x z) = (if (null z) then x
                else (call f (call g x (cdr z)))))
f (w)   = (cons w w)
```

with x = 'A known and z unknown. From the similarity to the previous example it should be clear that the call to g must be suspended, or else infinite unfolding will result. If we (wisely) suspend the call to f too, we will obtain the reasonable residual program

```
g (z)   = (if (null z) then 'A
                else (call f (call g (cdr z)))))
f (w)   = (cons w w)
```

which still has run time linear in the length of z. If however (stupidly) the call to f is unfolded, we will get

```
g (z)   = (if (null z) then 'A
                else (cons (call g (cdr z)) (call g (cdr z)))))
```

which has run time exponential in the length of z. The reason is that the call to g was duplicated and this happened because the body of f has two occurrences of the variable w in the argument position corresponding to the one with the call to g. We refer to this phenomenon as call duplication. Moral: A call to a function f with a suspended call to a function g in an argument expression should be unfolded only if the variable corresponding to that argument position appears at most once in the body of f. In fact, it is sufficient to require that the variable appears at most once in any conditional branch in the body of f.

3.5 Code Duplication

Extremely large residual programs may result from code duplication. This is a phenomenon similar to the above, but in this case the *size* (and not necessarily the run time) of the program explodes. This happens when an argument expression of a call to be unfolded contains a (sizeable) residual expression, and that expression is duplicated by unfolding the call. Consider the program

```
g (x z) = (if (null x) then z
                else (call f (call g (cdr x) z)))
f (w)   = (cons w w)
```

with x = '(A A A) known and z unknown. The call to g may be unfolded or suspended; neither will lead to trouble, so assume that it will be unfolded. If we (wisely) suspend the call to f, we get the residual program

```
g (z)  = (call f (call f (call f z)))
f (w)  = (cons w w)
```

and in general, if x is a list of length n, the body of g in the residual program will contain n nested calls to f. If however (stupidly) the call to f is unfolded, we will get (again for x = '(A A A)),

```
g (z)  = (cons  (cons (cons z z) (cons z z))
               (cons (cons z z) (cons z z)))
```

and in general, if x is a list of length n, the body of g will have 2^n-1 cons operators and 2^n occurrences of the variable z. Moral: A call with a sizeable residual argument expression should be unfolded only if the variable corresponding to that argument position appears at most once in the body of the unfolded function.

4. SIMPLE ANNOTATIONS AND POSTPROCESSING

In this section we describe our method for deciding on call unfolding. It has two phases. First, a *preprocessing* phase computes annotations to direct the call unfolding that takes place during the function specialization phase. This way a simple static call unfolding strategy is implemented. Secondly, the residual program resulting from the function specialization phase is improved by a *postprocessing* phase that eliminates simple functions by unfolding the calls to them.

These two phases are described in Sections 4.1 and 4.2 below. The section closes with a discussion of the limitations of the method in Section 4.3.

The preprocessing phase of our call unfolding method is based on the results of the binding time analysis done by mix and hence must be preceded by that. Thus the phases fit with the phases of mix in the way illustrated by Figure 4.1 on the next page.

4.1 Avoiding Infinite Unfolding and Call Duplication

The basic idea is to use a *static* call unfolding strategy, that is, to decide on call unfolding *in advance* of function specialization. Unfolding decisions are made for each individual call expression appearing in the subject program and are represented by annotations of the call expressions.

If the call is to be suspended every time it is met during function specialization, then it is annotated with an "r" yielding callr. This will be referred to as a *residual call*, that is, one to be left in the residual program. If the call is to be always unfolded during function specialization, then it is not marked, and will be referred to as an *eliminable call*. So by definition every residual call met during function specialization will be suspended, and every eliminable call met will be unfolded.

The annotations (representing call unfolding decisions) must satisfy at least two requirements as discussed in Section 3: there must be no infinite unfolding, and no call duplication. A set of annotations that satisfies these two requirements is found by two analyses done in separate subphases of the call annotation phase. In the first subphase, sufficiently many calls are made residual to ensure that infinite unfolding cannot take place during function specialization. In the second subphase, more calls are made residual to remove possible call duplication risks until there is no such risk anymore. Obviously, making more calls residual cannot reintroduce a risk of infinite unfolding.

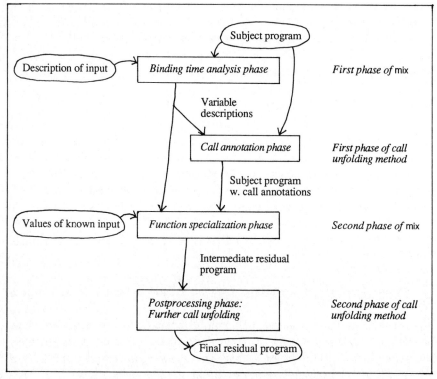

Figure 4.1: Structure of Mix with Call Unfolding

Both of the subphases are designed to avoid the pitfall of too little unfolding (when all variables in a call are Static), but no special care is taken of the risk of code duplication. Both of the subphases make use of the description of each variable as Static or Dynamic which is computed by the preceding binding time analysis phase of mix. The first analysis subphase, avoidance of infinite unfolding, is quite simple. It is based on the recognition of inductive variables and is described in Section 4.1.1 below. The second analysis subphase, avoidance of call duplication, is more involved. It alternates between a duplication risk analysis and a transformation that makes more calls residual. This second subphase is described in Section 4.1.2.

4.1.1 Simple Annotations Based on Inductive Variables

This first subphase of the call annotation phase makes call annotations that guarantee absence of infinite unfolding. When deciding on the annotation of calls, two cases are distinguished: a call to a function having only Static variables, and a call to a function with at least one Dynamic variable.

A call to a function with only Static variables is always made eliminable as was argued for in Section 3.2.

The decision for a call to a function with at least one Dynamic variable makes use of the concept of an *inductive variable*. The idea is to make a function call eliminable only if it can be ensured that it cannot be unfolded infinitely during function specialization. Infinite unfolding can of course happen only when a function calls itself recursively (possibly through calls to other functions).

To simplify the discussion (and the algorithm) we consider only the case of a direct recursive call from a function f to itself,

$$f (sv_1 \dots sv_m \ dv_1 \dots dv_n) = \dots (call \ f \ se_1 \dots se_m \ de_1 \dots de_n) \dots$$

Here the $sv_1 \dots sv_m$ are the Static variables of f, and the $dv_1 \dots dv_n$ are the Dynamic ones. Correspondingly, the $se_1 \dots se_m$ are the Static argument expressions, and the $de_1 \dots de_n$ are the Dynamic ones.

We shall say that a Static variable sv_i is *inductive* in the call from f to itself if and only if the corresponding argument expression se_i computes a value which is a proper substructure of the value of sv_i. For instance, se_i may be (car sv_i) or (cdr sv_i).

Let us define that a call satisfies the *structural induction condition* if there is at least one inductive Static variable in the call, and the remaining Static variables are either unchanged or inductive.

A call satisfying the structural induction condition cannot be unfolded infinitely often, and so it can safely be made eliminable. To see this, consider the totality of f's Static variables. In every call satisfying the structural induction condition, the total number of cons-cells in the values of the Static variables must decrease. Since only calls having no Dynamic variables or satisfying the structural induction condition will be unfolded, infinite unfolding during function specialization must involve only calls satisfying the structural induction condition. Hence infinite unfolding would imply decreasing the number of cons-cells infinitely many times, which is impossible, and therefore infinite unfolding cannot happen. Notice that it is crucial that the only kind of data in Mixwell is non-circular S-expressions, for with circular S-expressions there would be no bound on the "decrease" of cons-cells.

This technique could of course be extended to cover indirect recursive calls, *i.e.*, recursive call chains involving more than one function call.

In summary, a function call will be made residual by this subphase of the preprocessing unless

- it is a call to a function with only Static variables, or
- it is a direct recursive call satisfying the structural induction condition.

In these two cases it will be made eliminable.

4.1.2 Duplication Risk Analysis

This second subphase of the call annotation phase analyses the annotations produced by the first subphase to see whether there is a call duplication risk. If so, more calls are made residual until no call duplication risk remains.

The core of this subphase is a *duplication risk analysis* that checks every eliminable call in the following way. Each argument expression is checked to see whether its symbolic value (during function specialization) may be an expression containing a call as a subexpression. If there is an argument expression with this property for which the corresponding variable (in the function called by the eliminable call) appears twice or more in the same conditional branch of the called function's body, then there is a call duplication risk. Whenever such a risk is discovered, the eliminable call is made residual, and the duplication risk analysis is done over again. If no duplication risk is found in the program, the current set of annotations is accepted and is used by the function specialization phase. This is guaranteed to lead neither to infinite unfolding nor to call duplication.

Such a set of annotations will eventually be found by the algorithm for the following two reasons. First, the algorithm must terminate since there are only finitely many eliminable calls and at least one of these is made residual by every iteration. Second, if the boundary case is reached where every call (except those having only Static variables) has been made residual, no duplication can happen.

The duplication risk analysis outlined above is fairly straightforward except for the problem of deciding whether the symbolic value of an argument expression (during the function specialization phase) may contain a call expression. This requires a *call abstract interpretation* which is a global analysis of the subject program (including annotated calls), and which is quite similar to the binding time analysis used in mix.

The call abstract interpretation is an abstraction of the symbolic computation with expressions as data values that takes place during the function specialization phase of mix. It uses the abstract data values E and C, where E is the abstract value corresponding to symbolic expressions not containing a call, and C is the abstract value corresponding to expressions that may contain a call subexpression.

The call abstract interpretation will, for every function in the subject program, compute a description of its Dynamic variables and its result. A Dynamic variable dv of a function f is described as C if there is an eliminable (unfoldable) call to f in which the argument expression corresponding to dv has abstract value C. Otherwise the variable is described as E. Static variables are always described as E since the symbolic values of Static variables must be constant expressions; these cannot contain call subexpressions.

Given an assignment of abstract values to Dynamic variables (*i.e.*, an abstract environment), it is straightforward to compute the abstract value of an expression. The only non-trivial case is that of an eliminable call expression. In this case we define (slightly conservatively) that its abstract value is C if any of its argument expressions has abstract value C, or if the called function's body expression has abstract value C regardless of the abstract values of its Dynamic variables.

Below we describe the call abstract interpretation more formally for the sake of precision and brevity.

Let p be a Mixwell program with call annotations from the first call annotation subphase, $p = (f_i (sv_{i\,1} \dots sv_{im})(dv_{i\,1} \dots dv_{in}) = e_i)_{i=1,\dots,h}$, let
$$v \in D_{call} = \{E, C\}$$
be the domain of abstract values, let
$$\rho \in R = DVarnames \to D_{call}$$
be an environment assigning an abstract value to each Dynamic variable of a function, and let
$$\pi \in \Pi = FctNames \to R \times D_{call}$$
be a global environment assigning abstract argument and result values to every function in the program p. For $\pi \in \Pi$ and $f \in FctNames$ we will write
$$\pi_{arg}(f) \quad \text{for} \quad \text{let } (\rho, v_{res}) = \pi(f) \text{ in } \rho$$
$$\pi_{res}(f) \quad \text{for} \quad \text{let } (\rho, v_{res}) = \pi(f) \text{ in } v_{res}.$$
All the sets above are equipped with reflexive partial orderings as follows:
$$D_{call}: \quad E < C$$
$$R: \quad \rho_1 \leq \rho_2 \text{ iff } \forall dv \in DVarnames . \rho_1(dv) \leq \rho_2(dv)$$
$$\Pi: \quad \pi_1 \leq \pi_2 \text{ iff } \forall f \in FctNames . \pi_{1,arg}(f) \leq \pi_{2,arg}(f) \wedge \pi_{1,res}(f) \leq \pi_{2,res}(f)$$

We define two functions to do the call abstract interpretation using these ordered sets. The function F computes a new approximation to the final description of each function's Dynamic variables, whereas the function A computes the abstract value of an expression in a given abstract environment.

We want a final description $\pi \in \Pi$ that is consistent and has as few C's as possible. This must be the least fixed point for the simultaneous equations

$$
\begin{aligned}
\pi &= F[\![e_f]\!](\pi_{arg}(f))\pi && \text{for all f} \\
\pi_{res}(f) &= A[\![e_f]\!](\lambda\, dv{:}DVarnames_f \,.\, E)\pi && \text{for all f}
\end{aligned}
$$

Here e_f is the body of function f and $DVarnames_f$ is the set of its Dynamic variables. This fixed point exists, because for any given program p, Π is a lattice of finite height, and the functions A and F given below are monotonic in π. This fixed point can be computed by a standard algorithm.

F: Mixwell-expr $\times$ R $\times$ Π $\to$ Π

$F[\![\text{variable } v]\!]\rho\pi$ $\qquad = \pi$

$F[\![(\text{quote S-expression})]\!]\rho\pi$ $\qquad = \pi$

$F[\![(\text{car } e)]\!]\rho\pi$ $\qquad = F[\![e]\!]\rho\pi$ $\qquad\qquad$ same for cdr, atom

$F[\![(\text{cons } e_1\, e_2)]\!]\rho\pi$ $\qquad = F[\![e_1]\!]\rho\pi \sqcup F[\![e_2]\!]\rho\pi$ $\qquad$ same for equal

$F[\![(\text{if } e_1\, e_2\, e_3)]\!]\rho\pi$ $\qquad = F[\![e_1]\!]\rho\pi \sqcup F[\![e_2]\!]\rho\pi \sqcup F[\![e_3]\!]\rho\pi$

$F[\![(\text{callr } f(...)(de_1 \,...\, de_n))]\!]\rho\pi$ $\quad = \sqcup\, \{F[\![de_j]\!]\rho\pi \mid j{=}1,...,n\}$

$F[\![(\text{call } f(...)(de_1 \,...\, de_n))]\!]\rho\pi$ $\quad =$

$\qquad$ let $\quad \pi_{new} = \sqcup\, \{F[\![de_j]\!]\rho\pi \mid j{=}1,...,n\}$

$\qquad\qquad\quad \rho_{new} = [\, dv_j \mapsto A[\![de_j]\!]\rho\pi \text{ for } j{=}1,...,n\,]$

$\qquad$ in $\quad \pi_{new}[\, f \mapsto (\pi_{arg}(f) \sqcup \rho_{new},\, \pi_{res}(f))]$

$\qquad$ where the called function f has Dynamic variables dv_1, ..., dv_n.

A: Mixwell-expr $\times$ R $\times$ Π $\to$ D_{call}

$A[\![\text{variable } v]\!]\rho\pi$ $\qquad = E$ $\quad$ if v is Static

$\qquad\qquad\qquad\qquad\qquad\qquad\qquad \rho(v)$ $\;$ if v is Dynamic

$A[\![(\text{quote S-expression})]\!]\rho\pi$ $\qquad = E$

$A[\![(\text{car } e)]\!]\rho\pi$ $\qquad = A[\![e]\!]\rho\pi$ $\qquad\qquad$ same for cdr, atom

$A[\![(\text{cons } e_1\, e_2)]\!]\rho\pi$ $\qquad = A[\![e_1]\!]\rho\pi \sqcup A[\![e_2]\!]\rho\pi$ $\qquad$ same for equal

$A[\![(\text{if } e_1\, e_2\, e_3)]\!]\rho\pi$ $\qquad = A[\![e_1]\!]\rho\pi \sqcup A[\![e_2]\!]\rho\pi \sqcup A[\![e_3]\!]\rho\pi$

$A[\![(\text{callr } f(...)(...))]\!]\rho\pi$ $\qquad = C$

$A[\![(\text{call } f(...)(de_1 \,...\, de_n))]\!]\rho\pi$ $\quad =$

$\qquad$ let $(\rho',\, v_{res}) = \pi(f)$ in $v_{res} \sqcup (\sqcup\, \{A[\![de_j]\!]\rho\pi \mid j{=}1,...,n\})$

The call abstract interpretation realized by these functions is the basis of the duplication risk analysis. The duplication risk analysis used in this second subphase of the call annotation phase does not depend on the way annotations are made in the first subphase. It can be used with any call annotations as long as they are consistent with the Static/Dynamic classification of variables. Therefore the second subphase need not be modified in case the first subphase is improved to make better call annotations or is changed for other reasons.

4.2 Call Graph Analysis and Unfolding by Postprocessing

The annotations of every call as residual or eliminable produced by the call annotation phase are used by the subsequent function specialization phase. The simplicity of the first subphase of the call annotation phase implies that there will often be more residual calls than is in principle necessary to avoid infinite unfolding, call duplication and other anomalies. Every residual call encountered during function specialization gives rise to a (possibly new) residual function, and for that reason the residual program will often contain many very simple residual functions, some consisting of just a call to another function. This impairs readability and slows down execution of the residual program somewhat.

It is the purpose of the postprocessing phase described here to reduce the number of residual functions by doing further call unfolding in the residual program.

The postprocessing phase has two stages, or subphases. The first one does an analysis of the residual program to be processed to see which functions may be unfolded and which may not. The second subphase then does the unfolding of function calls (and some further reduction of expressions made possible by unfolding) while using the information gathered by the first subphase.

The important observation behind the analysis done by the first subphase is this: infinite unfolding must involve a recursive call chain from a function f (possibly through several others) back to itself, *e.g.*, f → g → h → f in

```
  ...
  f ( ... )  =   ... (call g ...) ...
  g ( ... )  =   ... (call h ...) ...
  h ( ... )  =   ... (call f ...) ...
  ...
```

By suspending all calls to at least one function in such a recursive chain, infinite unfolding of the chain will be prevented. The idea now is to select one function (to be called a *cutpoint*) in each recursive call chain, and then suspend calls to that function.

The two subphases of the postprocessing phase will be described in Sections 4.2.1 and 4.2.2 below. But first we give definitions of the concepts of call graph and recursive call chain. The *call graph* of a Mixwell program r is a directed multigraph that has the program's functions as nodes, and has an edge from function f to function g for each call to g in the body of f. A *recursive call chain* is a cycle in the call graph, that is, a non-empty sequence of edges (*i.e.*, calls) f → ... → f such that the first and last nodes are the same.

4.2.1 Call Graph Analysis

The call graph analysis of a Mixwell program r works by traversing the call graph of r to find its recursive call chains and then select a cutpoint for each of these.

The call graph analysis does a recursive depth-first traversal of the graph, starting with the goal function, and is an instance of a general scheme for depth-first traversal of directed graphs [Aho, Hopcroft, Ullman 1974].

The algorithm maintains a marking of the functions that have already been visited and keeps account of the current path from the goal function to the function currently being visited (inclusive). Furthermore, the algorithm records the cutpoints for the recursive call chains found so far. A *visit* to a function f consists of the actions

- mark f visited, then
- extend the current path by f, then
- for every function g called by f,
  - if g is on the current path, then
    - a recursive call chain has been discovered: make g a cutpoint
  - else if g is not already visited, then visit g,
- remove f from the end of the current path.

When the initial visit of the goal function is finished, (at least) one cutpoint has been found for every recursive call chain in the program. Note that the current path will never contain a recursive call chain, and that every function on the current path has already been marked visited.

Note that the algorithm visits each function once and does one traversal of its body. So provided the operations of marking and mark testing and the path manipulation operations each take constant time, the algorithm will run in time linear in the size of the program being analyzed.

4.2.2   Unfolding

The second subphase of the postprocessing phase traverses the residual program produced by the function specialization phase and unfolds calls to small functions while avoiding infinite unfolding, call duplication, and code duplication. The traversal starts with the goal function and consists in a symbolic evaluation (computing with expressions as values) in the same way as does the function specialization phase.

Again symbolic evaluation of expressions other than calls is straightforward, so we will discuss only the treatment of calls.

Consider a call (call g $e_1...e_n$) to a function g. First the reduced versions $e_1^*...e_n^*$ of the argument expressions $e_1...e_n$ are computed; the argument expressions may themselves contain calls that should be unfolded. Either the call to g will be unfolded, *i.e.*, replaced by the body e of g with the symbolic expressions $e_1^*...e_n^*$ substituted for occurrences of the corresponding variables $v_1...v_n$; or it will be left as it is, with $e_1...e_n$ replaced by $e_1^*...e_n^*$.

Which of these two actions to take will be decided as follows. If g has been chosen as a cutpoint by the preceding call graph analysis, then the call will not be unfolded. If g has not been chosen as a cutpoint, it will be checked whether there is a risk of call duplication or code duplication when unfolding the call. The check works like this: if the reduced form e_j^* of an argument expression in the call to g contains a call itself, or is a sizeable expression, then it is checked whether the corresponding variable v_j appears more than once in any branch of g's body expression e. If so, there is a risk of call duplication or code duplication for variable v_j. If there is such a risk for any of g's variables, then the call will not be unfolded; otherwise it will.

The transformations done by the unfolding phase are not fully semantics preserving. The errors are however on the "safe" side: a postprocessed program may terminate more often than the one input to the postprocessing. This is due to the call-by-name nature of unfolding.

4.3   Limitations of the Method

In this section we shall look at a case where the partial evaluator mix will not work with our call unfolding method (or any other for that matter).

Consider the example program

```
g (x z)   = (if (null z) then x
            else (call g (cons 'A x) (cdr z)))
```

and assume x = '() is known and z is unknown. We will see that in the framework of mix, no satisfactory call annotation is possible.

For if the call is made eliminable then clearly infinite unfolding will result. If on the other hand the call is made residual, an infinity of specialized versions of g will be produced, each specialized to a value of the Static variable x:

$$
\begin{aligned}
&g_{()} \quad (z) = (\text{if (null } z) \text{ then '() else (call } g_{(A)} \text{ (cdr } z))) \\
&g_{(A)} \quad (z) = (\text{if (null } z) \text{ then '(A) else (call } g_{(A\ A)} \text{ (cdr } z))) \\
&g_{(A\ A)}(z) = (\text{if (null } z) \text{ then '(A A) else (call } g_{(A\ A\ A)} \text{ (cdr } z))) \\
&\ldots
\end{aligned}
$$

It is a basic principle of mix to specialize each function to the possible values of its Static variables. For this to work, the number of possible values for each function must be finite, and in fact mix works well on programs satisfying this requirement. (The class of such programs has been called "analyzer programs with finitely defined memory" by Bulyonkov [Bulyonkov 1984, 1985].)

From the specialization point of view, the classification of x as Static by the binding time analysis is simply wrong. The set of possible values of x is not statically determined: it depends on the value of the Dynamic variable, and there is no statically determined bound on the size of the set of x's possible values.

These problems and related issues have recently been treated by Jones in a thorough reconsideration of the concept of binding time analysis [Jones 1988].

5. RESULTS AND ASSESSMENT

In this section we give some results from the use of our call unfolding method in the partial evaluator mix.

5.1 Simple Annotations Based on Inductive Variables

Partial evaluation using simple call annotations based on inductive variables gives residual programs that have a reasonable structure and a not too overwhelming size. These residual programs in general have very many small functions, which makes them quite unreadable to humans. On the other hand, they are usually almost as fast as and of approximately the same size as residual programs produced from subject programs that were carefully call annotated by hand. In particular, the method works well on the partial evaluator itself, and so it is fully automatic and self-applicable.

The method is very well suited for application to interpreters and other programs that "work by recursive descent": they decompose part of their input in the course of recursion or iteration. Such programs will often have several places where the structural induction condition is satisfied, and this will result in a fair number of calls being made eliminable. Satisfactory results for precisely this class of programs are important, because compilation by partial evaluation of an interpreter is a very interesting application of partial evaluation.

A great advantage of using call annotations that are generated automatically is that in contrast to human-made ones, they are *guaranteed* not to give trivial residual programs, infinite unfolding, or call duplication.

The call annotation algorithms are quite fast, in particular the first subphase which does only a local analysis of the program. The second subphase (which does one or more global analyses) is slower than the first, but still spends only approximately 5 cpu seconds on a 500 line Mixwell program.

As to future developments, it is tempting to improve on the first subphase so that it would recognize more situations where calls can safely be unfolded. This could be done without affecting the second subphase at all, as the second subphase does not depend on the way the call annotations are made. To make better call annotations, the first subphase would have to take a more global view of the program than it does presently. Information about the structure of the call graph of the subject program should be relevant, and so should information about the behaviour of Static variables along recursive call chains in the graph. This would allow to take into account also indirect recursive calls satisfying the structural induction condition. Call annotations that are of the same quality as those produced by an experienced user are probably very hard to make automatically.

5.2 Effects of Unfolding by Postprocessing

We briefly illustrate the effect of postprocessing on mix-produced residual programs. Below cocom is the compiler generator produced by mix, comp is a compiler for a tiny imperative language (produced by cocom), and target is a target program (produced by comp) for a program to compute x^y, *i.e.*, x raised to the y'th power.

First we give examples of the size reduction achieved by postprocessing. The number of lines is for prettyprinted Lisp listings. As can be seen, the effect on the size of the programs is considerable. Also the readability of the programs is improved, mostly because the plethora of calls to functions with non-telling names are replaced by the called functions' bodies substituted in-line.

Program		Before unfolding	After unfolding
target	No. of functions No. of lines No. of cons cells	37 112 474	6 36 253
comp	No. of functions No. of lines No. of cons cells	148 600 3387	24 303 2426
cocom	No. of functions No. of lines No. of cons cells	400 1904 11351	49 1062 8853

Figure 5.1: Size Improvement by Postprocessing

We have also found that reasonable speed-ups (running-time reduced by between 5 and 50 per cent) have been achieved by applying the postprocessing. For some larger programs, such as the compiler generator cocom, the speed-up achieved by postprocessing is negligible, and the main reason for applying it is the desire to get programs that are readable by humans.

The postprocessing phase itself is tolerably fast, taking 11 cpu seconds for processing the compiler generator cocom mentioned above. However, it is a drawback that, in contrast to the call annotation phase, it cannot be optimized by partial evaluation of the partial evaluator itself. For this reason it would be desirable to obviate the need for a postprocessing phase altogether, with the implication that a more sophisticated way to find call annotations would be needed. Such an improvement would concern the first subphase of the call annotation phase only, and is discussed above at the end of Section 5.1.

6. SUMMARY

We have discussed the problem of call unfolding in a partial evaluator for (first order) pure Lisp, and we presented an automatic two-phase call unfolding method. Some results from its use were reported and discussed.

We concluded that the method works well for a large class of programs, notably interpreter-like programs working by recursive descent. This class includes the partial evaluator mix, and this is crucial for self-applicability of the partial evaluator. For other programs, the method will fail due to problems with infinite specialization.

For programs on which the method works well, the second (*i.e.* postprocessing) phase mainly contributes by improving the readability of the resulting programs.

7. ACKNOWLEDGEMENTS

I am most grateful towards Neil D. Jones and Harald Søndergaard for introducing me to partial evaluation and for our exciting collaboration on the development of the self-applicable partial evaluator mix.

Thanks also go to Niels Carsten Kehler Holst and Olivier Danvy for suggesting, among other things, improvements to the call graph analysis, and to Torben Mogensen for discussions on call unfolding strategies.

8. REFERENCES

[Aho, Hopcroft, Ullman 1974]
  A. V. Aho, J. E. Hopcroft, J. D. Ullman. *The Design and Analysis of Computer Algorithms.* Addison-Wesley, 1974.

[Beckman *et al.* 1976]
  L. Beckman [*et al.*]. A partial evaluator, and its use as a programming tool. *Artificial Intelligence* **7**, 4 (1976) 319-357.

[Bulyonkov 1984]
  M. A. Bulyonkov. Polyvariant mixed computation for analyzer programs. *Acta Informatica* **21** (1984) 473-484.

[Bulyonkov 1985]
  M. A. Bulyonkov. Mixed computations for programs over finitely defined memory with strict partitioning. *Soviet Mathematics Doklady* **32**, 3 (1985) 807-811.

[Ershov 1978]
  A. P. Ershov. On the essence of compilation. In E.J. Neuhold (ed.): *Formal Description of Programming Concepts*, 391-420. North-Holland, 1978.

[Ershov 1982]
  A. P. Ershov. Mixed computation: Potential applications and problems for study. *Theoretical Computer Science* **18** (1982) 41-67.

[Fuller, Abramsky 1987]
  D. A. Fuller and S. Abramsky. Mixed computation of Prolog programs. In D. Bjørner, A. P. Ershov, and N. D. Jones (eds.): *Workshop Compendium. Workshop on Partial Evaluation and Mixed Computation, Gl. Avernæs, Denmark, October 1987*, 83-101. Department of Computer Science, Technical University of Denmark, Lyngby, Denmark, 1987.

[Futamura 1971]
  Y. Futamura. Partial evaluation of computation process - an approach to a compiler-compiler. *Systems, Computers, Controls* **2**, 5 (1971) 45-50.

[Jones 1988]
  N. D. Jones. Automatic program specialization: a re-examination from basic principles. In D. Bjørner, A. P. Ershov, and N. D. Jones (eds.): *Workshop on Partial Evaluation and Mixed Computation, Gl. Avernæs, Denmark, October 1987*. North-Holland, 1988. (This volume).

[Jones, Sestoft, Søndergaard 1985]
  N. D. Jones, P. Sestoft, and H. Søndergaard. An experiment in partial evaluation: The generation of a compiler generator. In J.-P. Jouannaud (ed.): *Rewriting Techniques and Applications*. *Lecture Notes in Computer Science* **202** (1985) 124-140. Springer-Verlag.

[Jones, Sestoft, Søndergaard 1987]
  N. D. Jones, P. Sestoft, and H. Søndergaard. MIX: A Self-Applicable Partial Evaluator for Experiments in Compiler Generation. DIKU Report **87/8** (June 1987). DIKU, University of Copenhagen, Denmark.

[Lombardi 1967]
  L. A. Lombardi. Incremental computation. In F. L. Alt and M. Rubinoff (eds.): *Advances in Computers* **8** (1967) 247-333. Academic Press.

[Sestoft 1986]
  P. Sestoft. The structure of a self-applicable partial evaluator. In H. Ganzinger and N.D. Jones (eds.): *Programs as Data Objects*. *Lecture Notes in Computer Science* **217** (1986) 236-256. Springer-Verlag.

[Turchin 1979]
  V. F. Turchin. A supercompiler system based on the language Refal. *SIGPLAN Notices* **14**, 2 (1979) 46-54.

Partial Evaluation and Mixed Computation
D. Bjørner, A.P. Ershov and N.D. Jones (Editors)
Elsevier Science Publishers B.V. (North-Holland)
© IFIP, 1988

Partial evaluation, higher–order abstractions, and reflection principles as system building tools [†]

Carolyn Talcott
Stanford University
CLT@SAIL.STANFORD.EDU

Richard Weyhrauch
IBUKI
RWW@SAIL.STANFORD.EDU

Abstract:

In this paper we take a look at partial evaluation from the point of view of symbolic computation systems, point out some challenging new applications for partial evaluation in such systems, and outline some criteria for a theory of partial evaluation. The key features of symbolic computation systems are summarized along with work on semantics of such systems which will hopefully aid in meeting the challenges. The new applications are illustrated by an example using on the concept of component configuration. This is a new idea for software development, based on the use of higer–order and reflective computation mechanisms, that generalizes such ideas as modules, classes, and programming in the large.

Keywords: components, configuration, partial evaluation, function abstraction, control abstraction, process abstraction, objects with memory.

1. Introduction

Existing symbolic computation systems have many features that are important for general software development environments. They are interactive, extensible, and dynamic with primitive but powerful facilites for managing data structures and developing code. What they lack is a clear mathematical semantics and tools for specifying and operating on programs. Our work is primarily focused on the problem of developing a semantics for such systems and providing a sound basis for developing programming tools. We believe that partial evaluation can contribute substantially as a technology for developing and maintaining programs and that it can benefit

---

[†] This research was partially supported by ARPA contract N00039-82-C-0250 and by IBUKI.

by interacting with other technologies including program transformation in general, debugging, and proving.

The systems we have in mind are interactive systems based on simple, expressive, extensible languages such as Lisp [Steele 1984], Scheme [Steele and Sussman 1975], and Actors [Hewitt 1977, Agha 1986] that use higher–order and reflective constructs. The computation tasks are symbolic. They involve transformation and modification of complex structures which may modify the meaning, or merely rearrange structures to provide easier access to certain information. Computation tasks may be carried out sequentially or in parallel. The sorts of interaction we have in mind include traditional activities such as use of the system to create, access, and modify symbolic information structures as well as to design, prototype, and implement application languages. They also include more advanced software development activities such as program specification, program modification (to meet modified or refined specifications of both behavior and implementation), and programming in the large (building components and assembling them into products) [Burstall 1984].

In this paper we take a look at partial evaluation in the context of symbolic computation systems and describe some challenges for the theory and application of partial evaluation that arise in this context. We interpret the term *partial evaluation* in a very general sense as meaning preserving transformations on programs and other computation structures based on partial specification of information about the parameters or context of use. If we want to use meaning preserving transformations then we must supply meanings to preserve and meanings to transform. We begin with an analysis of the key features of symbolic computation systems and of their underlying languages and we summarize some work on the semantics of such systems which provides a spectrum of meanings for programs and which will hopefully help in meeting some of the challenges raised.

To illustrate the applications of partial evaluation that we have in mind we present an example using the concept of component configuration. This is a new idea for software development based on a formalizm in which code, functional objects, and environments are all first class citizens. Component description and configuration are forms of programming in the large. They provide great flexibility in code reuse and in the configuring and reconfiguring of systems. In the spirit of Lisp, we take a somewhat *open*-structured approach.[1] Thus we impose a minimum of programming "style" restrictions on designers and programmers. However the traditional notions and

---

[1] We use open- rather than un- since there is in fact a great deal of structure, it is just not restricted to a single type system.

structures such as signatures, types, interfaces, modules, implementations, etc. play an important role. Our approach shares much in common with object oriented programming. However we formulate it in terms of components and function abstractions using meaning extending and meaning preserving operations and providing alternative views of objects to hide or expose internal structure as needed. In the main section of this paper we give an informal description of components and configuration. The concepts are illustrated by describing some components of a simple screen editor and giving a configuration scenario. The paper concludes with a summary of some of the challenges and opportunities for partial evaluation that arise in a symbolic computation system and with some critera for a theory of partial evaluation.

2. Background–where are we coming from?

In this section we set the stage with a discussion of general features of symbolic computation systems and of the underlying languages. We conclude the section with a summary of work on the semantics of such languages.

2.1. Symbolic computation systems

Our notion of symbolic computation system is derived from Lisp. It differs from, say, Common Lisp in that we imagine a simpler and more expressive underlying language with a clear mathematical semantics, and a system with more advanced tools for manipulating programs based on this semantics.

Symbolic computation includes AI-type programs and other programs that deal with symbolic information such as programs, mathematical expressions, logical formulae, rules of inference, models, situations, plans, schedules, and inventories. Practical symbolic computation has its origin in [McCarthy 1960], which is the beginning of the language Lisp. Some important aspects of Lisp are its data structures and the fact that it is interactive, customizable, and self-describing in a concise and natural manner.

- Lisp data structures are called S-expressions. They include numbers, symbols, and list structures. S-expressions were designed as a representation of symbolic information that is easy to read, print, and operate on. Lists are better than strings for representing programs and other symbolic information since they are pre-parsed and their structure is preserved internally. S-expressions are treated as abstract objects not just memory locations. They can be part of argument lists, bound in environments, returned as values, and stored in composite structures. S-expressions are more than a traditional algebraic structure. List structures may be dynamically extended and updated; they may be tree-like or or graph-like; and structure sharing is an important aspect of Lisp computation.

- Programming is an interactive and incremental process. The programmer interacts with the system via an interpreter — the *Read–Eval–Print* loop. Programs can be developed and compiled incrementally and modified dynamically. Compiled and interpreted versions of programs can be used interchangeably. There are simple but powerful tools for debugging including tracing, break points, single stepping, and the *baktrace* command which presents a brief summary of the events leading to the current computation state.

- Lisp is a creator's world. No programming dogmas are built in. Simple but powerful computation primitives are provided along with the means for using those primitives to create the computational environment and the programming style best suited to a given computation task.

- Programs and information about the computation state are represented as Lisp data. Lisp is defined in Lisp. Programs may operate on other programs to generate, edit, interpret, compile, trace, optimize, or expand macro definitions. Programs that operate on computation states can be used to provide extensions to the language and interactive debugging tools.

2.2. Languages for symbolic computation

The key to establishing a clear mathematical semantics for a symbolic computation system is to base the underlying language on a simple and expressive collection of primitives which include higher–order and reflective constructs.

By expressive, we mean that a wide variety of programming constructs and styles can be expressed directly in terms the primitives of the language using syntactic abbreviations. The lambda calculus is a mathematically well understood language, but it is not expressive in our sense of the word. For example one can program control abstractions using function abstractions by introducing an extra parameter whose value represents the current continuation. But this means writing complicated code and modifying all programs that interact with the given program to also use continuation passing style. Similarly, using a store variable one can simulate assignments — again with great sacrifice in clarity and modularity. Furthermore, when one considers programs describing processes that interact asynchronously, it becomes crucial to understand control and state in a local sense and not to sweep them under the extra parameter rug.

By higher–order constructs we mean constructs such as function, control, and process abstractions combined with the corresponding varieties of application (function call, context switching, and task creation) possibly acting on objects with memory. Such constructs are mathematically tractable computation primitives that allow one to express easily a wide variety of computation mechanisms and programming styles and to reason naturally about programs that employ these primitives [Landin 1964-66, Kahn and McQueen 1977, Talcott 1985, Mason 1986, Agha 1986, Felleisen 1987, Mason and Talcott 1987].

Function abstractions can be created by evaluating a lambda abstraction or other function expression. This fixes the interpretation of the free variables of the function expression to be that given by the evaluation environment, thus retaining some of the information present in the evaluation environment. Function abstractions can be used to represent structured (possibly infinite) data such as tuples and streams, to represent the continuation of a computation, and to describe delayed or lazy evaluation [Landin 1964–5, Friedman et. al. 1984].

Function abstractions acting on objects with memory can be used to represent objects in the object-oriented style of computation [Sussman and Steele 1975].

Control abstractions represent contexts built up in the process of carrying out a computation. They provide a means of suspending and resuming computations and can be used to program non-local control mechanisms such as escaping and co-routining [Landin 1965].

Process abstractions provide a means of expressing synchronous, asynchronous, and distributed computations such as CCS [Milner 1983], coroutines and networks of processes [Kahn and McQueen 1977], and Actors [Hewitt 1977, Agha 1986].

Reflection is a means of expressing and using the metamathematics of a formal theory within that theory. The idea of extending a formal theory by adding reflection principles has its orgin in formal metamathematics (see for example [Gödel 1931], [Kleene 1952]) and arithmetization of formal theories of arithmetic (see for example, [Feferman 1962], [Smorynski 1977]). Here reflection provides a tool for uniform extension of theories and for studying their proof theoretic power. This can be carried over to the use of reflection in automated theorem proving [Weyhrauch 1980, Boyer and Moore 1981]. Computational reflection principles provide the ability to convert computation state into data structures and conversely. The addition of computational reflection principles provides a mechanism for conversing with system about itself and for defining programming and debugging tools within the language. Some forms of reflection principles in computation are: Lisp primitives such as QUOTE, CATCH/THROW, and MACRO; Interlisp *environment descriptors* [Bobrow and Wegbreit 1973]; Zetalisp *stack groups* [Symbolics 1985]; Reflective Lisp [Smith 1982]; and metafunctions and reification [Talcott 1983] and [Friedman and Wand 1984].

2.3.   Towards a theory of symbolic computation

2.3.1.   An architecture of symbolic computation

In a dynamic interactive programming system such as Lisp it is necessary to be able to "discuss" the data structures used to represent computation and to "use" these structures within the same formalism. Thus programs and other parts of the computation state must be represented as data that can be operated on by programs. On the other hand we want to view programs abstractly as computing functions on the computation domain. In particular, we wish to consider two programs as "equal" if they compute the "same" function. These are not necessarily compatible requirements. It is easy to find theories of abstraction and application in which providing both programs as data and programs as functions is inconsistent (see for example [Feferman 1975]). To show how we can "have our cake and eat it too", we propose the following archictecture for a theory of symbolic computation. The main components are:

- an underlying model of computation;

- formal representation of the underlying computation model; and

- extension of the model by adding reflection principles.

The underlying model of computation determines a class of data structures (data domains and primitive operations); a computation domain (arguments and values for computations); programs; and an abstract machine with structures for representing computations and rules for carrying out computations [Talcott 1985]. We also require that the operational equivalence relation (equivalence as black boxes) derived from the operational semantics provide a reasonable basis for equational reasoning about programs [Morris 1968, Plotkin 1975].

Formal representation of the underlying model means representing objects of the model as data structures and representing operations and relations of the model as computable functions (programs) on these data structures. This provides an interpretation of programs and computations as data structures that can be operated on by programs; a basis for implementation of a programming system; a basis for programs that use procedural knowledge to building models or plans; and a basis for mechanization of reasoning about programs and operations on programs.

Reflection principles formalize the connections between the views of programs as functions, as descriptions of computation, and as data to be operated on. The addition of reflection principles provides a mechanism for conversing with system about itself and for defining programming and debugging tools within the language. Making reflection explicit provides a clear boundary between use and mention, allows one to maintain extensionality, and allows the same tools to be used for programming and operating on programs.

2.3.2. Semantics of higher–order constructs

We have advocated the use of languages with expressive constructs such as function abstractions, control abstractions, process abstractions, and objects with memory. If one is to apply transformation methods in general and partial evaluation in particular to programming in these languages then it is essential to have a clear understanding of what it means for programs to be equivalent and to have a theory of the equations satisfied by programs. In addition it is necessary to have a theory expressing when one program is better than another for a given purpose. In short, operations on programs need meanings to preserve and meanings to transform.

Traditionally the view has been that direct expression of control and store mechanisms and mathematical tractability are incompatible requirements. We believe it is important and possible to have programming languages that combine expressive power with mathematical cleanliness. Recent work of Talcott, Mason, and Felleisen establishes methods for attaining a better mathematical understanding of programming languages with function and control abstractions operating on objects with memory. This work extends work of Landin, Reynolds, Morris and Plotkin. [Landin 1964–5] and [Reynolds 1972] describe high level abstract machines for defining language semantics. [Morris 1968] defines an extensional equivalence relation for the classical lambda calculus. [Plotkin 1975] extends these ideas to the call–by–value lambda calculus defining *operational equivalence* as being indistinguishable in all contexts. Operational equivalence is the equivalence naturally associated with a pre–ordering we call operational approximation. [Talcott 1985] presents an intensional semantic theory[1] of function and control abstractions. Here programs are interpreted by computation

---

[1] terminology introduced in [Talcott 1986]

structures and transitions on these structures. Intensional properties of programs (meanings to transform) are properties of computation structures. A class of pre–orderings called comparison relations (meanings to preserve) is defined and the maximum comparison is proposed as an alternative to the methods of Scott[2] for obtaining extensional models of lambda calculi. [Talcott 1987] shows that in a language with function and control abstractions operational approximation is the maximum comparison relation. [Mason 1986] defines a relation called strong isomorphism in the first order fragment of destructive Lisp. [Felleisen 1987] defines reduction calculi for languages with function, control, and assignment abstractions and shows the relation to operational equivalence. Talcott, Mason, and Felleisen all apply their theories to expressing and proving properties of programs and program constructs.

3.   Configuring Components

The notion of *component* is an attempt to have descriptions of behaviors which are application and implementation independent and which allow for the instantition (binding) of parameters at any time: design time, coding time, compiling time, linking time, saving time, or run time. We will present our ideas informally. The main point is to show how partial evaluation can play a crucial role in increasing the automation and reliability of configuring activities and thus help make them a practical tool for software development. For this purpose, we describe some components of a simple character–oriented screen editor with windows and outline a configuring scenario. The example illustrates the variety of component and configuration options, the overlap and sharing of information and structure, and the use of the enriched parameter binding–time spectrum.

3.1.   About components

A component is an environment like object that provides (a possibly incomplete) description of some collection of objects which when taken together provide a coherent component of a software system. Components serve as an interface specifications in a manner that allows subsystems to be specified independently and later to be configured into complete systems. The term component was chosen to suggest the analogy to hardware components — devices are designed and built based on descriptions of components provided by the component manufacturers. Components are

---

[2] see [Barendregt 1981, ch. 18]

similiar to modules in Ada, and are related to the types in Amber [Cardelli 1985], to classes in traditional object oriented languages, and to modules for traditional linkers.

Components are more general than any of the traditional concepts. One difference is that a component may have a great variety of information associated with it. For example: type – basic type, function type, sequence type, ...; specification – code, constraints; value – should meet the specification; options – alternatives for implementation; status [of parameters] – required/optional, constant/assignable, private/shared/exported; and a history of the components development. The flexible structure of components means that intermediate optimization stages and their derivations can easily be saved thus increasing the opportunity for reuse of components and reuse of the methods used for development.

A second difference is that a component can be partial, and one of the important types of operation on components is successive refinement — filling in missing information. This filling in can occur at specification time, at configuration time, at compile time, or at run time. Even partial components will have information that is useful for some purposes and that will persist during the refinement process. From the object oriented view some components correspond to classes, some to instances, some to both, some to neither. Depending on the amount of information specified, a component might correspond to: a signature or interface — provides only type information and names of externally available operations; a specification — determines the behavior; an implementation — is executable; and many other intermediate and non–traditional forms.

3.2. About configuration

A long–term goal of our work on components is to develop an algebra of components and configuring operations. The algebra of component construction must contain full control over structure sharing. Creation time assignment and binding should be functionally the same as run–time assignment and binding. Just to get a flavor of what we have in mind assume that components are environment like objects associating symbols with values and other information. Since values may themselves be components we can refer to subcomponents by paths — the list of symbols that are accessed in order to reach the subcomponent. In this model, some of the primitive component operations are:

- $Cmpget(path)$;; gets the value of the symbol at the end of *path*

- $Cmpset(path, val)$;; assigns *val* to the symbol at the end of *path*

- *Abstract*(*cmp, path*)   ;; makes a function which when applied to v returns a component with the same bindings as *cmp* except that it binds v to the symbol at the end of *path*.

Components built up by straightforward combinations of components have the correct behavior but need optimization. In object oriented systems like Flavors and Portable Common Loops this optimization is the primary implementational difficulty. In forming different configurations, values can be given to parameters in different orders; various additional information can be specified in different orders and amounts; and optimizations on sub-configurations based on information available can be made at any stage. One of the important techniques in partial evaluation is the binding time analysis. Typically only two–binding times are considered – partial evaluation time and run time. The flexibility in choice of binding time for component parameters (as outlined above) provides high level control over system construction that allows for many of the kinds of optimizations that used to require assembly language to facilitate. This might be considered part of a long–standing interest of ours to elucidate high level constructs that are the analogs of the well known assembly language tricks. The philosophical point here is that if these optimizations are *principles* as opposed to *ad hoc* then high level languages should be able to accomodate them.

The complexity and variety of configurations that can be generated from a collection of components means it is essential to have interactive computer aided configuration and optimization tools to realize the full potential for code reuse. We propose to use partial evaluation in an interactive environment as one of the tools for configuring and optimizing.

A possible ambitious application of component configuration is distributed operating systems. Here there are many trade–offs between generality, robustness, and efficiency. One example is the representation of abstract data to be comunicated between processes on different machines. A description in terms of a common abstract representation and conversion functions (as part of a machine type description) can be optimized so that no conversion occurs when tranmitting between similar machines.

3.3.   Window editor example – introduction

A window editor manages the creation, positioning, selecting, and editing of windows on a display. A window editor can be considered to have the following parameters

(a) the type of terminal,

(b) the size and position of the allowable windows,

(c) the number of windows, and

(d) the available editing commands.

However, considered as formal parameters in the usual sense, this does not allow for many optimizations that would be natural if you were designing a particular editor. Note that each of these decisions can be made either at design time, at run time, or at intermediate times. We want to describe an window editor that is a fixed object with a well–defined semantics that can be configured with any of the above options. Examples of such editors might be:

(1) A simple screen editor in which the window covers the entire display screen. The terminal type is chosen at design time. The device driver is chosen at run time. The allowable commands are left for further configuration by whoever uses this component.

(2) An editor with several windows in fixed positions on the screen chosen at design time

(3) An editor which is initally a simple screen editor, but which has the capability of opening, closing, moving, and changing the size of windows, and which can determine what kind of terminal at run time.

(4) An editor of one of the types 1–3 in which the device driver [and terminal type] is fixed at design time (e.g. the computer console).

In the following, we define the behavior of an abstract character–oriented display. This behavior is to be used by designers of higher level components such as windows and editors. The behavior is independent of the particular implementation of the display. An implementation could simply simulate a display as a pair consisting of an array of characters and a cursor position, or it could connect to an actual physical display, or both. As examples we define an abstract display constructor and a VT100 display constructor. We then describe the construction of a window and of a window editor. In order to keep the example from becoming any longer, we describe only a few features of a rather rudimentary editor. We conclude the example by giving a possible scenario for configuring a window editor of type (2).

Functions are defined in a sugared form of the language Rum [Talcott 1985,7] extended by primitives for acting on objects with memory [Mason and Talcott 1987]. Familiarity with any applicative language such as Iswim or ML or Scheme should be sufficient to get the main ideas. $\leftarrow$ reads "is recursively defined by". $[a, b]$ is the sequence with elements a and b. We use some object–oriented syntax. msg.handlers$\{\ldots, lhs \Rightarrow rhs, \ldots\}$ abbreviates

"$\lambda(msg)$if msg has the form of lhs then execute rhs". If the last element of the message–handler list is a lambda expression, this function is to be applied to messages that do not match any of the lhs patterns.

3.4.   An abstract display

An abstract display is built from two components: a cursor and a screen. A cursor of dimension $m = [m_x, m_y]$ is a point $p = [p_x, p_y]$ constrained to be on a rectangular grid of dimension m — the set of points p such that $1 \leq p_x \leq m_x$ and $1 \leq p_y \leq m_y$. It responds to messages: Pos — return the coordinates of the point; and L, R, U, D — move cursor left, right, up, down (sticking at the boundaries). A screen s of dimension m is a map from the rectangular grid of dimension m to the set of printable characters. It responds to messages: $[\text{Get}, p]$ — get the character at p; and $[\text{Set}, p, char]$ — set the character at p to be $char$.

The messages a display responds to include: Dim — return the dimension; Pos — return the cursor position; $[\text{Charo}, char]$ — write $char$ at the cursor position and move the cursor right; Get — return the character at the cursor position; and L — move the cursor left. The behavior of a display is described formally by a function $DspBeh(m)(s, p)$ where m is a dimension, s is the behavior function of a screen of dimension m, and c is the behavior function of a cursor of dimension m. The display behavior function takes a message and returns a sequence whose first element is a function describing the new behavior and whose remainder [possibly empty] is the reply.

$\triangleright$ $DspBeh(m)(s, c) \leftarrow$
$\quad$ msg.handlers$\{$
$\quad\quad [\text{Dim}] \Rightarrow [DspBeh(m)(s, p), m]$
$\quad\quad [\text{Pos}] \Rightarrow \text{let}\{[c, p] \leftarrow c[\text{Pos}]\}[DspBeh(m)(s, c), p]$
$\quad\quad [\text{Get}] \Rightarrow$
$\quad\quad\quad \text{let}\{[c, p] \leftarrow c[\text{Pos}]\}\text{let}\{[s, x] \leftarrow s[\text{Get}, p]\}[DspBeh(m)(s, c), x]$
$\quad\quad [\text{Charo}, char] \Rightarrow$
$\quad\quad\quad \text{let}\{[c, p] \leftarrow c[\text{Pos}]\}\text{let}\{[s, x] \leftarrow s[\text{Set}, p, char]\}\text{let}\{c \leftarrow c[\text{R}]\}$
$\quad\quad\quad\quad [DspBeh(m)(s, c)]$
$\quad\quad [\text{L}] \Rightarrow \text{let}\{c \leftarrow c[\text{L}]\} DspBeh(m)(s, c)$
$\quad\quad \dots\}$

3.5. Abstract display construction

Given a behavior description such as *DspBeh* we can easily construct an object with that behavior by applying *Objmk* to the behavior function. *Objmk(beh)* puts the behavior function in a cell, passes messages to the contents of the cell, updates the contents of the cell with the new behavior that is returned and passes the reply on to the sender of the message. A cell is created by *Cellmk* and responds to messages Get — get the contents; and [Set, v] — replace contents by v.

▷ $Objmk(beh) \leftarrow$

      let$\{b \twoheadleftarrow Cellmk(beh)\}$

          $\lambda(msg)$let$\{[beh, rep] \twoheadleftarrow b[\text{Get}](msg)\}[b[\text{Set}, beh], rep]$

An alternative display constructor is *Dspmk* which uses cursor and screen constructors *Curmk* and *Scrmk*.

▷ $Dspmk(m) \leftarrow$ let$\{c \twoheadleftarrow Curmk(m)\}let\{s \twoheadleftarrow Scrmk(m)\}$

           msg.handlers$\{$

               $[\text{Dim}] \Rightarrow m$

               $[\text{Pos}] \Rightarrow c[\text{Pos}]$

               $[\text{Get}] \Rightarrow s[\text{Get}, c[\text{Pos}]]$

               $[\text{Charo}, char] \Rightarrow s[\text{Set}, c[\text{Pos}], char], c[\text{R}]$

               $[\text{L}] \Rightarrow c[\text{L}]$

               $\dots\}$

Remarks.

• The two display constructions produce objects with the same behavior and a theory of transformations on components should be able to produce the second construction systematically from the first.

• The display behavior function together with the constraints on its parameters and the display constructor are all part of the display component.

3.6. VT100 display

A character stream *cstm* is something that eats characters and passes them to the device connected to the other end. If *cstm* is connected to a physical display of type VT100 then *Vt100mk(cstm)* creates a VT100 display. It is necessary to maintain an image of the cursor and screen since one cannot read the cursor position and screen contents of a VT100 device.

▷ $Vt100mk(cstm)$ ←
    let$\{dsp \twoheadleftarrow Dspmk[80, 24]\}$
      msg.handlers$\{$
        $[\text{Dim}] \Rightarrow [80, 24]$
        $[\text{Pos}] \Rightarrow dsp[\text{Pos}]$
        $[\text{Get}] \Rightarrow dsp[\text{Get}]$
        $[\text{Charo}, char] \Rightarrow dsp[\text{Charo}, char], cstm[char]$
        $[\text{L}] \Rightarrow dsp[\text{L}], cstm[\chi_{esc}, \chi_L]$
          $\dots\}$

where χ_{esc} is the escape character and χ_L is the move-cursor-left character, etc.

3.7.   Window making

A window is a display imbedded in another display. It has an origin, a dimension, an a host display. It maintains an image of its abstract display since in general windows may overlap on the host. In addition to the normal display commands, a window also accepts the command to display itself.

▷ $Wdomk(o, m, host)$ ←
    let$\{dsp \twoheadleftarrow Dspmk(m)\}$
      msg.handlers$\{$
        $[\text{Pos}] \Rightarrow dsp[\text{Pos}]$
        $[\text{Get}] \Rightarrow dsp[\text{Get}]$
        $[\text{Display}] \Rightarrow Mapscr(dsp, host, o), Mapcur(dsp, host, o)$
        $[\text{Charo}, char] \Rightarrow dsp[\text{Charo}, char], Hcharo(host, o, m, char)$
        $[\text{L}] \Rightarrow dsp[\text{L}], Hcurl(host, o)$
          $\dots\}$

where $Hcharo(host, o, m, char)$ sends the character to the host and insures that the cursor remains in the window. For example, if the right window edge is not at the display edge and the cursor is at right window edge, then the display cursor must be moved left after printing the character. Similarly for $Hcurl$.

3.8. Window editor

A window editor has as parameters a host display *host* and a list of admissible editing commands *cmd*. It responds to messages: [Open, *n*] — open a new window with name *n* and select it and [Select, *n*] — select the window named *n*. Other messages are passed on the the current window if they are in the *cmds* list. *Wedmk* constructs a window editor. It uses a property–list object to keep track of the association between names and windows. A property list responds to messages [Get, *n*] – return the object associated with *n* and [Put, *n*, *v*] — associate *v* with *n*. *Plistmk* makes an empty property list.

▷ $Wedmk(host, cmds) \leftarrow$
               $\mathsf{let}\{wlist \twoheadleftarrow Plistmk()\}$
               $\mathsf{let}\{wcur \twoheadleftarrow Cellmk()\}$
            $\mathsf{msg.handlers}\{$
               $[\mathtt{Open}, o, m] \Rightarrow$
                  $\mathsf{let}\{w \twoheadleftarrow Wdomk(o, m, host)\}$
                     $w[\mathtt{Display}], wlist[\mathtt{Put}, n, w]), wcur[\mathtt{Set}, w]$
               $[\mathtt{Select}, n] \Rightarrow$
                     $wcur[\mathtt{Set}, wlist[\mathtt{Get}, n]], (wcur[\mathtt{Get}])[\mathtt{Display}]$
               $\lambda[t, v]\mathsf{if}(t \in cmds), (wcur[\mathtt{Get}])[t, v], Badmsg[t, v])\}$

3.9. Scenario: configuring a 2 window VT100 editor

In the following scenario we interactively configure and optimize an editor for a Vt100 display with two fixed windows. This is done by constructing an instance of such an editor, optimizing at various stages, and eventually abstracting to produce the desired product. In the scenario lines beginning with ▷ are commands to the system — some expressed formally, some expressed informally. Lines that begin with ;; are comments. := updates the interactive environment. We assume the environment initially contains all the functions defined above.

▷ specify *cstm* is connected to a Vt100 display.

▷ *host* := $Vt100mk(cstm)$

▷ *ed* := $Wedmk(host, cmds)$

;; *cstm* and *cmds* are uninstantiated parameters

▷ $ed[\mathtt{Open}, [41, 1], [80, 24]]$

▷ $ed[\mathtt{Open}, [1, 1], [40, 24]]$

▷ specify

    (i) no further **Open** commands

    (ii) *host* local to *ed*

▷ simplify *ed* by

    (i) removing **Open** message–handler

    (ii) replacing the property list *wlist* by variables w_1, w_2

▷ openup *ed* and expose screen and cursor components

▷ observe [and prove]

    (i) actions of w_1 do not effect image of w_2 and conversely

    (ii) the host cursor is computable from window cursors and window selection

▷ simplify *ed* by

    (i) aliasing window screens to host screen image

    (ii) omitting the host cursor

▷ specify $cmds = [\mathtt{Pos}, \mathtt{L}, \mathtt{U}, \mathtt{R}, \mathtt{D}, \mathtt{Charo}]$

▷ observe [prove] that host screen is not accessed

▷ simplify *ed* by omitting host screen

Abstracting we define a constructor for our Vt00 editor as follows:

▷ $Vt100wedmk(cstm)$ ←

       let$\{wcur$ ← $Cellmk()\}$let$\{wnum$ ← $Cellmk()\}$

       let$\{cmds$ ←$[$Pos, L, U, R, D, Charo$]\}$

       let$\{w_1$ ← $Vt100mk1(cstm)\}$let$\{w_2$ ← $Vt100mk2(cstm)\}$

       msg.handlers$\{$

          $[$Select, $1] \Rightarrow wcur[$Set$, w_1], wnum[$Set$, 1], w_1[$Display$]]$

          $[$Select, $2] \Rightarrow wcur[$Set$, w_2], wnum[$Set$, 2], w_2[$Display$]]$

          $\lambda[t, v]$if$(t \in wcmds, wcur[t, v], BadMsg[t, v])\}$

▷ $Vt100mk1(cstm)$ ←

      let$\{c$ ← $Curmk([1, 1], [40, 24])\}$

      msg.handlers$\{$

      $[$Pos$] \Rightarrow c[$Pos$]$

      $[$Charo, $char] \Rightarrow$ let$\{[p_x, p_y]$ ← $c[$Pos$]\}$

         $[cstm[char],$ if$(p_x < 40, c[$R$], cstm[\chi_{esc}, \chi_L])]$

      $[$L$] \Rightarrow c[$L$], cstm[\chi_{esc}, \chi_L]$

      $[$Display$] \Rightarrow$ move cursor to $[1, 1]$

      $\ldots\}$

▷ $Vt100mk2()$ ← $\ldots$

3.9.1.   What have we been doing?

In the above scenario we derived a specialized editor using a variety of operations on components. We created objects with uninstantiated parameters (partial application) and we sent messages to these objects in order to attain a given internal state. We specified some information about the context of use — restriction on commands and sharing of parameters — and made some simplifications based on that information. We opened up objects and flattened the internal environment structure to expose the representation of internal state. Using the context information some observations about the representation of internal state were made and proved. Simplifications in the representation of the combined internal state were made on the basis of these observations. The value of the *cmds* parameter was specified and this allowed further simplification. Finally we abstracted on the free *cstm* parameter to produce the desired specialized editor constructor. This abstraction process can be carried much further. For example having produced a prototype object (possibly with free parameters) we can abstract to produce a behavior description and derive other properties of the prototype, making distinctions as to which are properties of the behavior and which are properties of the implementation (prototype).

4.   Challenges and issues for partial evaluation

4.1.   Challenges

The configuring scenario illustrated two kinds of challenges. The first is the need to apply partial evaluation in situations where program text, function abstractions, and environments are first class citizens and where operations are provided to add and modify bindings, to abstract upon parameters occuring free in subcomponents, to open up closures, and to construct new closures. This raises a number of questions. Do existing partial evaluation methods apply? If not, what fails? What problems are unique to the richer languages? What new ideas are needed?

The second sort of challenge is the interleaving of the process of refinement (adding information to a component) and optimization. This gives rise to an important question — is partial evaluation or can it be made Church-Rosser? That is, does the order in which we do things matter? Suppose we specify some information, apply partial evaluation, specify some more information, apply partial evaluation, etc. If we change the order in which information is specified what effect does this have on the partial evaluation results. How do the results compare to those obtained by postponing partial evaluation until all the information has been added? Will doing things in the wrong order cause information to be lost and consequently prevent more important optimizations from being discovered? Would keeping more information correct this? Will it be useful or necessary to leave a trace of the tranformations for possible backtracking?

4.2.   Towards a theory of partial evaluation

A theory of partial evaluation should provide an analysis of basic concepts. It should specify the basic structures and operations on these structures and provide a language for expressing properties of the structures and operations. It should verify that the choices of primitives are adequate to account for exsisting methods and for developing new methods. It should address questions such as: are there meaningful notions of abstract partial evaluation step and strategy?

It seems likely that the choice of language will be important for providing a context where partial evaluation can be used most effectively. One of the by–products of a theory of partial evaluation should be guide lines for choice of basic computation constructs, criteria for intensional semantics (choice of operational semantics, design of abstract machines) and for the equational theory of the language. Conversely, developments in programming language theory and tools for reasoning about programs should provide valuable input and feedback to the theory and practice of partial evaluation.

As a component of an interactive system, partial evaluation should be usable by other components and should be able to make use of other components as they become available. It should also be able to interact with users, trading degree of automation for quality of result where appropriate. A theory of partial evaluation should provide a foundation for developing well understood modules with clearly specified interfaces. It should be provide an analysis that makes clear what aspects are unique to partial evaluation and what aspects are shared with other sorts of operations on programs such as proving properties; program specification, transformation, and modification; compiling; implementation of abstract machines and abstract data structures; intensional analysis; abstract interpretation; and debugging. It should identify data structures and operations that are common to various activities and can be shared among various tools or used as a basis of communication. Some candidates for sharing are - representations of programs, structures for annotation, user interfaces, and rewriting and other simplification tools.

References

Agha, G.

[1986] *Actors: A Model of Concurrent Computation in Distributed Systems*, (MIT Press).

Barendregt, H.

[1981] *The lambda calculus: its syntax and semantics* (North–Holland).

Bobrow, D. G. and B. Wegbreit

[1973] A model and stack implementation of multiple environments, *Comm. ACM*, **16**, pp. 591–603.

Boyer, R. S. and Moore J. S.

[1981] Metafunctions: proving them correct and using them efficiently as new proof procedures, in: Boyer, R. S. and Moore J. S. (eds.), *The correctness problem in computer science*, (Academic Press)

Burstall, R. M.

[1984] Programming with modules as typed functional programming in: *Proceedings of the international conference on fifth generation computer systems 1984, Tokyo*, pp. 103–112.

Cardelli, L.

[1985] Amber, in: *Combinators and functional programming languages, Proceedings of the 13th summer school of the LITP, France*

Feferman, S.

[1962] Transfinite recursive progressions of axiomatic theories, *J. Symbolic Logic*, **27**, pp. 259–316.

[1975] Non-extensional type-free theories of partial operations and classifications, I. in: *Proof theory symposium, Kiel 1974*, edited by J. Diller and G. H. Müller, Lecture notes in mathematics, no. 500 (Springer, Berlin) pp. 73–118.

Felleisen, M.

[1987] The calculi of lambda-v-cs conversion: A syntactic theory of control and state in imperative higher-order programming languages, Ph.D. thesis, Indiana University.

Friedman, D. P. and M. Wand

[1984] Reification: reflection without metaphysics, in: *Proceedings of the 1984 ACM symposium on Lisp and functional programming*, pp. 348–355.

Friedman, D. P., Haynes, C. T., and Wand, M.

[1984] Continuations and Coroutines: An Exercise in Meta-Programming (Summary) Computer Science Department, Indiana University.

Gödel, K.

[1931] Über formal unentscheidbare Sätz der *Principia mathematica* und verwandter Systeme I *Monatshefte für Mathematik und Physik*, **38**, pp 173–198.

Hewitt, C.

[1977] Viewing control structures as patterns of passing messages, *Artificial Intelligence*, **8**, pp. 323–363.

Kahn, G. and D. B. MacQueen

[1977] Coroutines and networks of parallel processes, *Information processing 77* (North-Holland, Amsterdam) pp.993–998.

Kleene, S. C.

[1952] *Introduction to metamathematics*, (North-Holland, Amsterdam).

Landin, P. J.

[1964] The mechanical evaluation of expressions, *Computer Journal*, **6**, pp. 308–320.

[1965] A correspondence between Algol60 and Church's lambda notation, *Comm. ACM*, **8**, pp. 89–101, 158–165.

[1966] The next 700 programming languages, *Comm. ACM*, **9**, pp. 157–166.

McCarthy, J.

[1960] Recursive functions of symbolic expressions and their computation by machine, Part I, *Comm. ACM*, **3**, pp. 184–195.

Mason, I.A.

[1986] *The semantics of destructive Lisp*, Ph.D. Thesis, Stanford University.

Mason, I. and Talcott, C.

[1987] Programming, transforming, and proving with function abstractions and memories, submitted to *Logic and computer science 1988*

Milner, R.

[1983] Calculi for Synchrony and Asynchrony, *Theoretical Computer Science*, **25**, pp. 267-310.

Morris, J. H.

[1968] *Lambda calculus models of programming languages*, Ph.D. thesis, Massachusetts Institute of Technology.

Plotkin, G.

[1975] Call-by-name, call-by-value and the lambda-v-calculus, *Theoretical Computer Science*, **1**, pp. 125–159.

Reynolds, J. C.

[1972] Definitional interpreters for higher-order programming languages, in: *Proceedings, ACM national convention*, pp. 717–740.

Smith, B. C.

[1982] *Reflection and semantics in a procedural language*, Ph.D. thesis, Massachusetts Institute of Technology.

Smorynski, C.

[1977] The incompleteness theorems, in: *Handbook of mathematical logic*, Barwise, J., (ed.), (North-Holland, Amsterdam), pp. 821–865.

Steele, G. L. Jr.

[1978] Rabbit: a compiler for Scheme, Artificial Intelligence Laboratory, Massachusetts Institute of Technology, Technical Report 474.

[1984] *Common Lisp: the language* (Digital Press).

Steele, G. L., and G. J. Sussman,

[1975] Scheme, an interpreter for extended lambda calculus, Artificial Intelligence Laboratory, Massachusetts Institute of Technology, Technical Report 349.

Symbolics Documentation Group

[1985] *Internals, processes, and storage management* (Symbolics, Inc., Cambridge Mass.)

Talcott, C.

[1983] Seus reference manual, Perseus internal memo.

[1985] The Essence of Rum: A theory of the intensional and extensional aspects of Lisp-type computation, Ph. D. Thesis, Stanford University.

[1986] Rum: An intensional theory of function and control abstractions, *Workshop on Functional and Logic Programming, Trento Italy, Dec 1986*, (to appear Springer Verlag, Lecture Notes in Computer Science Series).

[1987] Programming and proving with function and control abstractions. (Lectures given for the Western Institute of Computer Science, Stanford, Summer 1986) In preparation.

Weyhrauch, R. W.

[1980] Prolegomena to a theory of formal reasonin, *Artificial Intelligence*, **13**, pp. 133–170.

Partial Evaluation and Mixed Computation
D. Bjørner, A.P. Ershov and N.D. Jones (Editors)
Elsevier Science Publishers B.V. (North-Holland)
© IFIP, 1988

531

THE ALGORITHM OF GENERALIZATION IN THE SUPERCOMPILER[*]

Valentin F. Turchin

Computer Science Department
The City College of New York
New York, N.Y 10031 USA

The central problem of supercompilation is to find a finite set of
configurations (generalized states) of the computing system which
is, for a given initial configuration, self-sufficient in the
sense that the process of computation can be defined by a finite
graph of states and transitions using only these configurations
as nodes. Generalization over configurations is necessary for
this. The paper describes an algorithm of generalization in the
process of outside-in driving (forced unfolding of function calls
in the lazy evaluation semantics) which always terminates and
produces a finite graph of states and transitions with a self-
sufficient set of basic configurations.

1. INTRODUCTION. WHY TO GENERALIZE?

It may seem strange that the problem of generalization is raised
in the context of partial evaluation. Indeed, partial evaluation
is mostly used for, and therefore perceived as, program specialization, and this is something opposite to generalization.

However, we discuss here a special technique of function transformation, which is referred to as *supercompilation* (see [1-3]). When
supercompilation is used for the sake of partial evaluation (which
is not always the case, because supercompilation can do more) it
comes to the specialized program in a different way than the
straighforward partial evaluation.

In partial evaluation we have an original, general, program, and a
specialized function call. Then we make a global analysis of known
and unknown arguments, and specialize the original definition step
by step, watching that a certain limit is not overstepped. Thus
the loops in the specialized program are the old loops of the
original program, but (possibly) specialized. Partial evaluation
technique is, in a sense, monotonous with respect to specialization.

In supercompilation we, again, have an original, general, program,
and a specialized function call. Here, however, we never specialize the original program. We start from the ultimate specialization of the initial call, and then construct a program for it by
driving. If the program can be made self-contained without looping
back (a simple tree), there will be no generalization necessary.
Usually, however, we have to loop back, and these are *new* loops,
created *ad hoc* for current configurations. This may make it necessary to generalize configurations, because the former configura-

---

[*] This work was supported by the National Science Foundation under
grant DCR-8412986.

tion will not always be general enough. Thus the process of supercompilation is not monotonous: we first jump to the completely
specialized initial call, considered as the initial (degenerate)
graph of states and transitions, and then develop it into a self-
contained graph i.e. a program, using generalization when necessary.

While partial evaluation has the narrow goal of specializing
functions, supercompilation is a much wider framework for general
function transformations. We believe that it follows closer than
other techniques to the way we, human beings, think. Thinking is
creating mental models of the processes in the world around us.
How do we create those models? We watch the processes and try to
form some generalized states of the explored systems in terms of
which we can construct a self-sufficient model of the processes,
i.e. represent the processes as transitions between the basic
generalized states. But this is exactly what the supercompiler is
doing.

2. HOW TO GENERALIZE?

As an introduction to the problem of generalization, consider this
example. Suppose, two strings are given:

        'ABA'
        'ABXYABA'

and we are asked to write a generalization which is, in some
intuitive sense, the best. Then we should ask, before anything
else, what is meant by a generalization? The first step to define
a generalization is to notice that a generalization of a number of
objects is a set which includes all of these objects. This definition is not sufficient, however, because then the best generalization in our example would be simply the set of exactly the two
strings mentioned, and a similar trivial solution would exist in
any situation. Actually, when we speak of generalizations, we have
in mind a language in which sets of objects are defined, and we
want not just a set of objects, but an expression of this language
defining a set of objects which includes all the objects to be
generalized -- and, possibly, some other objects. Then the problem
of a "good" generalization is non-trivial.

Let the language to describe sets of strings be that of simple
patterns, as in Refal, where $s1$, $s2$ etc. stand for single symbols,
i.e., in our context, letters of the alphabet, and $e1$, $e2$, etc.
stand for arbitrary expressions -- here for strings, including the
empty string. Thus, 'A'$e1$ is the set of strings starting with 'A';
$e1$ $s2$ $s2$ is a string ending with two identical letters, etc. Then
for the two strings above, even after we exclude those generalizations for which we see obviously better (tighter) generalizations,
we still have quite a number of reasonable solutions, for example:

(1)   'AB'$e1$
(2)   'AB'$s1$ $e2$
(3) $e1$'ABA'
(4)   'AB'$e1$'A'

Which one to choose?

We faced this problem when working on the Refal supercompiler,
because intelligent generalization is the central problem of su-

percompilation. We do not discuss here the concept of a supercompiler in detail; the reader can address [1], or [2], or an
earlier and detailed (but not so easily available) publication
[3]. The objects to be generalized in supercompilation are function calls in Refal. Experimentation with different ways of generalization led us to the following principle, which we believe to
be of universal significance for symbolic objects:

The Generalization Principle. Generalization of objects has a
meaning only in the context of some processes of computation in
which the objects take part. Then the language of generalization
should have means to describe computation histories, and generalizations should be sets of objects which have common computational
histories up to a point.

According to this principle, we should not generalize unless we
know in what computational processes our two strings are taking
part. If we know, for instance, that the strings are scanned form
left to right, then the appropriate series of generalizations,
each next being tighter than (a subset of) the preceding, will be:

```
sl e2
'A'e2
'A'sl e2
'AB'e2
'AB'sl e2
```

Thus if we want the tightest generalization, we take the last one.
Should the strings be processed differently, the generalizations
would be defined differently. If no algorithmic processes are
defined over strings, there is no sense in generalization.

In the following sections of this paper we describe the algorithm
of generalization in the supercomiler based on this principle. In
the context of the language we use in the supercompiler, namely,
Refal, computation histories become tangible formal objects. It
should be noted that Refal fits the needs of generalization on two
counts. First, it has the concept of a pattern, which is, of
course, the simplest form of generalization, built into the language. Second, the functioning of the Refal machine is a simple
sequence of substitutions, which facilitates the formalization of
computational histories.

3. NEIGHBORHOODS

The objects we deal with in supercompilation are Refal graphs,
which are, essentially, graphs of states and transitions of the
Refal machine. The nodes of a Refal graph are Refal expressions,
the edges (directed) are transformations of two kinds: contractions and assignments. Both are pattern-matching operations over
variables, with the variables in the left-hand side having some
values, and the variables in the right-hand side being defined by
the operation. A contraction has a single variable in the left
side, and a pattern in the right side, e.g.

```
el  →  s2 el
```

is a conditional operation which checks that the value of el
starts with a symbol on the left, assigns that symbol to s2, and
redefines el as the remaining part of the original value. An
assignment has a single variable on the right and defines its new

value through constants and the variables of the left side, e.g.

        'A'eX s2(eY) ← eX

A Refal program can be represented as a Refal graph defining one
step of the Refal machine, e.g. the program:

        FAB {el = <FAB1 ()el>; }
        FAB1 {
                (el)'A'e2 = <FAB1 (el'B')e2>;
                (el)s3 e2 = <FAB1 (el s3)e2>;
                (el) = el;
                }

is, essentially, the graph:

    :(e0 → <FAB el>; <FAB1 ()el> ← e0
      + e0 → <FAB1 el> :(el → (el)'A'e2; <FAB1 (el'B')e2> ← e0
                         + el → (el)s3 e2; <FAB1 (el s3)e2> ← e0
                         + el → (el); el ← e0
)
)

Here we used the form $:(B_1+\ldots+B_n)$ to represent n branches B_1 ...
etc., which start from the same node. The nodes themselves are
left out in this graph; they can be restored when reading the
graph. Refal graphs are read as follows. The variable e0 stands
always for the content of the view-field (the current expression
being transformed) of the Refal machine. Our graph consists of two
subgraphs. The first begins with the contraction e0 → <FAB el>,
which corresponds to the case where the expression in the view-
field of the Refal machine is a call of the function FAB with a
completely unspecified argument represented by the free variable
el. The state of the view-field at this moment is, obviously,
<FAB el>; we skip it. The next operation is the assignment to the
view-field e0 of a new value, which is a call of FAB1; we can skip
the node again, without losing information. When we construct the
graph of states for an arbitrary expression in the view-field e0,
we need not write out nodes explicitly, because the current node
is always identical to the current value of e0.

The second subgraph is a definition of the function FAB1. Here we
separated the general configuration of the call of a given function, <FAB1 el>, from the detalization provided by sentences. This
gives us our first insight into the concept of a *neighborhood*. The
first thing the Refal machine does to perform a step is to identify a function symbol, which should follow the left evaluation
bracket <. Thus <FAB 'ABC'> and <FAB 'XY'> appear the same for the
Refal machine at this stage; they belong to the same neighborhood
<FAB el>. Any call of FAB1 belongs to a different neighborhood,
namely <FAB1 el>. Inside this neighborhood we see a further differentiation: <FAB1 ('X')'ABC'> and <FAB1 ('PQ')'AC'> are indistinguishable to the Refal machine as long as it executes one step on
them: in both cases the first sentence is used. The expression
<FAB1 ('XY')'BCD'>, however, will be distinguished in the first
step from those two. The former neighborhood is <FAB1 (el)'A'e2>,
the latter <FAB1 (el)s3 e2>, with the restriction that s3 is not
equal to 'A'.

Complex contractions which we find in the left sides of Refal
sentences can be decomposed into simpler contractions. In the
example above, the left side of the first sentence of FAB1 was

decomposed as follows:

    e0 → <FAB1 (e1)'A'e2> = e0 → <FAB1 e1>; e1 → (e1)'A'e2

We could go further and decompose it into

    e0 → <FAB1 e1>; e1 → (e1)e2; e2 → 'A'e2

Contractions are elements of computation histories. The more we decompose contraction, the more detailed the description of histories will be. This process comes to its natural close if we decompose all left sides of Refal sentences into *elementary* contractions. There are seven of these, namely:

    1.   eX → sY' eX

    2.   eX → (eY')eX

    3.   eX → eX sY'

    4.   eX → eX(eY')

    5.   eX →

    6.   sX → S

    7.   sX → sY

Here S stands for a definite (but arbitrary) symbol, and the primed variables sY' and eY' symbolize that the index Y' of the variable is *new*, i.e. was not used before.

The decomposition of the left side above into elementary contractions is:

    e0 → <FAB1 (e2)'A'e1> =

    e0 → <FAB1 e1>; e1 → (e2)e1; e1 → s3 e1; s3 → 'A'

(We renamed some variables in the left side; this, of course, changes nothing).

Definitions. An expression without free variables is a *ground* expression. We say that a contraction is executed *positively* over a ground expression, if the contraction is found applicable and applied; we say that it is executed *negatively* if it is established that the contraction is not applicable. The sequence of elementary contractions executed positively or negatively over a ground expression in n steps of the Refal machine is its *computation history* of n-th order. The set of all ground expressions with a common computation history of n-th order is a *neighborhoood* of n-th order.

Thus to every computation history a neighborhood corresponds. We shall denote neighborhoods by the same symbols as histories. If a history H_1 is a prefix of H_2, then the neighborhood H_2 is a subset of H_1. This relation between neighborhoods is a partial order.

A Refal program defines a system of partially ordered neighborhoods, in other words, a topology, in the space of ground expressions. The longer is the common part of computation histories

of two points in this space, the tighter is their common generalization to a neighbothood, in other words, the closer are these
points. Note that speaking of ground expressions we have in mind
only *active* ground expressions, i.e. those including at least one
pair of activation brackets. All *passive* expressions fall in one
big class with a zero-length computation history, and are of no
concern to us. This is, of course, a consequence of the generalization principle formulated above.

A compact representation of a neighborhood as a set can be obtained by folding the contractions of the corresponding history
into one pattern. With the program above, the system of first-
order neighborhoods is as follows:

    (a)   <FAB el>
    (b)   <FABl el>
    (c)   <FABl (e2)el>
    (d)   <FABl (e2)s3 el>
    (e)   <FABl (e2)'A'el>
    (f)   <FABl (e2)s3 el> (#s3 → 'A')
    (g)   <FABl (e2)>

The *restriction* (negative contraction) in (f) indicates that only
those ground expressions are in the pattern in which s3 is distinct from 'A'. These neighborhoods are partially ordered as
follows:

    b > c > d > e
            d > f
        c > g

where > denotes being a superset.

To compute the neighborhoods of the second order, we use *driving*
(see, e.g., [1]). Driving every active end-node in the graph for
FABl, we come to the graph that represents two steps of the operation of the Refal machine if it starts with any call of FABl. It
contains all possible computation histories of length two. Six new
neighborhoods will be added to the system. Three of them are
refinements of (e):

    (h)   <FABl (e2)'AA'el>
    (i)   <FABl (e2)'A's3 el>   (# s3 → 'A')
    (j)   <FABl (e2)'A'>

and the other three, analogously, develop (f).

Driving can be repeated as long as there are active end-nodes in
the graph. We refer to this process as *exhaustive driving*. It can,
and typically will, go on infinitely. Exhaustive driving defines
the set of *ultimate neighborhoods*, which correspond to terminated
computation histories. In the case of FABl the ultimate neighborhoods are:

    (1)   <FABl (e2) >
    (2)   <FABl (e2)'A'>
    (3)   <FABl (e2)s3>   (# s3 → 'A')
    (4)   <FABl (e2)'AA'>
    (5)   <FABl (e2)'A's3>   (# s3 → 'A')
    (6)   <FABl (e2)s3'A'>   (# s3 → 'A')
    (7)   <FABl (e2)s3 s4>   (# s3 → 'A') (# s4 → 'A')
    ... etc.

The expressions which belong to the same ultimate neighborhood
pass through the Refal machine in the exactly identical ways; the
machine has never a chance to discover the difference between
them.

4. WHEN TO GENERALIZE?

The idea of a supercompiler is to superwise the construction of
the full graph of states of the initial configuration, and at
certain moments loop back, i.e. reduce an end-configuration --
directly, or with a generalization -- to one of the previous
configurations, and in this way construct a finite graph on the
basis of a potentially infinite process. A direct reduction is
possible when the later configuration is a subset of the earlier
one. This is an easy case, when it is pretty obvious that the
reduction can be made and has sense. The difficult case is when
the later configuration is not a subset of the previous one, but
is "close" to it in some sense. If we simply ignore this closeness, and go on with driving, we may never loop back, and the
process will never stop.

Take a simple example with the functions we defined above. We want
to supercompile the configuration

(1)   <FAB el>

Nothing especially interesting is expected here. The supercompiler
must simply return the original definition. Our purpose is to see
that the supercompiler can indeed find the correct basic configurations for looping back whenever necessary to terminate the work.

The graph of states we construct in supercompilation must include
nodes, i.e. configurations of the Refal machine, explicitly,
because we want to compare and generalize configurations. Let the
nodes in graphs be represented by references to configuration
definitions. The first step of driving replaces (1) by the call of
FAB1, so the graph is the unconditional transition:

        (1) (2)

with the definition:

(2)   <FAB1 ()el>

Next step of driving results in the graph:

        (1) (2) :(el → 'A'el; (3)
                  + el → s2 el; (4)
                  + el → []; (5)

(3)   <FAB1 ('B')el>
(4)   <FAB1 (s2)el>
(5)   []

(For readability, we use [] to represent the empty expression).

The passive configuration (5) terminates the walk in the graph.
None of the new active configurations (3) and (4) is a subset of
any of the previous configurations (1) and (2). If this were our
criterion for looping back, we would go on with driving. After the

next steps we would have such configurations as

(6)   <FABl ('BB')el>
(7)   <FABl ('B's2)el>

etc., none of which, again, would loop back onto any of the previous configurations. In this way we would never come to a finite
graph.

To loop back properly, we must recognize that (3) and (2) are
close enough for looping back. Indeed, they belong to the same
first-order neighborhood

(N)   <FABl (e2)el>

If we set as a principle that belonging to the same first-order
neighborhood is a sufficient reason for looping back, we generalize (3) and (2) to (N), express (2) through (N):

         (2) = [] ← e2; (N)

and recompute the graph for the generalized configuration (N):

         (1) [] ← e2; (N) :(el → 'A'el; (3')
                            + el → s3 el; (4')
                            + el → []; (5)

(3')   <FABl (e2'B')el>
(4')   <FABl (e2 s3)el>

Now (3') and (4') are subsets of (N); reducing them to (N) we come
to the graph

         (1) [] ← e2; (N) :(el → 'A'el; 'B'e2 ← e2; (3')
                            + el → s3 el; e2 s3 ← e2; (4')
                            + el → []; (5)

Our algorithm of generalization is based on keeping in memory the
first-order neighborhoods of past configurations. We formulate it
first for the case where all function calls have passive arguments
only, i.e. there are no nested calls. Nested calls will be considered in the next section.

As the Refal machine applies to the function argument one elementary contraction after another, the neighborhood that describes
the function call becomes more narrow. Then the replacement is
executed, another descending sequence starts, etc. We have the
following row of neighborhoods in each branch of the graph:

$$f_1^1 \quad f_2^1 \ldots R^1 \quad f_1^2 \quad f_2^2 \ldots R^2 \quad \ldots \quad f_1^n \quad f_2^n \ldots f_m^n$$

They are partially ordered as follows:

$$f_1^1 > f_2^1 > \ldots$$
$$f_1^2 > f_2^2 > \ldots$$
$$\ldots$$
$$f_1^n > f_2^n > \ldots f_m^n$$

In a graphic form:

There are several variants of the algorithm, which place the
resulting program in different positions on the compilation-inter-
pretation axis (the more detailed is the set of basic configurations, the more compilative the program; the more general the
basic configurations are, the more interpretive the program, see
[1]). The most interpretive variant is as follows. Each time
before we make the next replacement, R^n, we compare each neighborhood of the current step, starting with the first one, f_1^n, with
all the previous neighborhoods, moving from R^{n-1} backwards, to the
beginning of the walk. If we find the same neighborhood, we loop
back to it. In this way we find the most general from the recurring neighborhoods. If we loop back, R^n is ignored and the step
due is not executed; reduction takes place instead. Since the
number of different first-order neighborhoods is finite, the algorithmic process is always finite.

This algorithm can be obviously generalized for neighborhoods of
an arbitrary order. The higher the order, the more compilative
will the resulting program be. The same effect can be achieved by
function iteration, using only the first-order neighborhood algorithm. If we define functions that correspond to two, three, etc.
steps of the Refal machine, and use the first-order algorithm with
them, then this will be equivalent to higher-order neighborhoods
for the original system of functions. We can control the process
of generalization by iterating some functions, while leaving alone
others. Therefore, the algorithm based on first-order neighborhoods has a certain property of completeness. If we accept the
principle that the closeness of expressions should be measured by
the length of the common part of their computation histories (the
program-induced topology), then all strategies of generalization
can be presented as refinements of an algorithm based on first-
order neighborhoods.

5. GENERALIZATION OF NESTED CALLS

If nested function calls are executed according to the inside-out
principle, known also as the applicative evaluation order, then
the computation of every active expression can be broken down into
a sequence of computations and substitutions, this sequence being
independent of function definitions. For example, the assignment

$$\langle F\ e1\ \langle G\ e2\rangle\ \langle H\ e3\rangle\rangle\ \leftarrow\ e\emptyset$$

will be decomposed into the sequence of assignments:

$$\langle G\ e2\rangle\ \leftarrow\ eX;\quad \langle H\ e3\rangle\ \leftarrow\ eY;\quad \langle F\ e1\ eX\ eY\rangle\ \leftarrow\ e\emptyset$$

We shall refer to such decompositions as *stacks*. Since the order
of execution is strictly left-to-right, computation histories --
and, therefore, neighborhoods -- for stacks break into pieces
corresponding to the first, second, etc. segments of the stack. If
a stack S_1 is a prefix of another stack, S_2, then the neighborhoods of S_1 are supersets (generalizations) of the neighbor-

hoods of S_2. There is no interaction between neighborhoods corresponding to different segments of the stack.

In the supercompiler, however, we use the outside-in (normal,
lazy) order of evaluation, because it provides one of the primary
means of optimization. In this case the situation is much more
complicated. A prefix of a decomposition is still a generalization
of a longer decomposition, of course. But we cannot decompose a
nested call into a stack without consulting function definitions.
The decomposition is still made, but it is made in the process of
moving from outside in, and it may depend on the values of variables. Computation histories may consist of alternating pieces
from different function calls. Indeed, suppose that the computation process starts with the all-embracing function call, but
after executing a number of contractions the Refal machine finds
that a not yet computed call inside is a hindrance for further
application of sentences. Then it will leave the unfinished function call as a *context*, and switch to the computation of that
internal call, which, in turn, may send the machine further inside. After computing the internal call -- completely or partially
- the process returns to the point in the outer function call
where it was interrupted.

Let us describe this in somewhat more detail. We call an expression *unitary active*, or just *unitary*, if it is of the form $\langle E \rangle$,
where E is any expression (possibly active, so that there are
nested function calls). If the result of replacement in the execution of a Refal step is unitary, we make it our next active
subexpression to compute. If it is not unitary, it is either
passive (completed computation), or non-unitary active (partially
computed, with some passive parts outside of activation brackets,
e.g. 'A'$\langle$FAB el$\rangle$). In both cases we substitute the result into the
context, and take the context as the next active subexpression to
compute. If there is no context (bottom of the stack call) and the
result of the step is passive, this is the end of driving. If the
result is partly passive, the passive part is kept in the view-
field of the Refal machine, and the unitary active part is driven
further.

We shall consider a few examples which typify different structures
of recursion. We shall demonstrate how we come to our algorithm of
generalization, and how it works. Then we shall prove that this
algorithm has a guaranteed termination.

The first example is the classical recursive definition of the
factorial:

```
     FACT {Ø = 1;
           1 = 1;
           sN = <MULT sN <FACT <SUB sN 1>>>;
          }
```

We assume that the arithmetic functions SUB and MULT are built-in
(not defined in Refal) functions which require their arguments to
be ready-for-use numbers. Then the inside-out and outside-in orders of evaluation will lead to the same sequnese of operations.
We see here three neighborhoods involved:

(f) $\langle$FACT s1$\rangle$
(m) $\langle$MULT s1 s2$\rangle$
(s) $\langle$SUB s1 s2$\rangle$

(To simplify things, we ignore such neighborhoods as <FACT e1>, <FACT s1 e2>, etc., which cause unique transitions). A stack will be denoted as a string of neighborhoods, e.g., sfm will stand for any of the nested calls like that in the definition of FACT.

When we simply drive <FACT s1> exhaustively we have, on one of the branches, the sequence of neighborhoods:

    f; sfm; fm; sfmm; fmm; sfmmm; fmmm; ... etc.

which goes on infinitely. Let us now apply the simple algorithm of comparing neighborhoods which we developed for the case of one-level function calls. We extend it by recalling that a stack is a specialization (subset of) its every prefix. At the third stage of the process above we recognize that fm is a subset of f. Thus we declare f basic, and come to the original algorithm.

This experience suggests to accept as the general criterion of generalization a situation where the current stack is of the form XY, where X is a previous stack. This criterion, of course, includes the one-level situation as a special case where Y is empty and X is one segment.

However, if we only slightly change our example, this criterion will not work. Let the factorial function be computed in the context of some other function, say,

(*)   <ADD 1 <FACT sN>>

If we denote by a the neighborhood corresponding to ADD, the sequence of stacks in driving will be:

    fa; sfma; fma; sfmma; fmma; sfmmma; fmmma; ... etc.

One can see that none of the previous stacks is a prefix of a subsequent one. Therefore, the process will never terminate.

The reason for this failure is that the algorithm, as it is at this point, does not draw a line between the part of stack that is recurrent, and the part that does not really participate in action, but is a passive context. We, therefore, modify the algorithm as follows. The stack will not be just a linear segment, but a structure of parenthesized segments, where the context part is taken outside of parentheses. Accordingly, the computation history will be written in such a way that the context is left outside of the parentheses as a common part to all the stages of the process as long as it has no impact on developments.

The nested call (*) will now be characterized by the formula (f)a. It results from outside-in driving, where we start driving from the call of ADD, an then see that before anything is done on this call, we must drive FACT. So, we leave ADD as a context, and FACT becomes the active subexpression.

After the first step of the Refal machine, the history of computation takes the form:

    (f; ((s)f)m)a

Then SUB is computed, and the next history record will be:

```
(f; (sf; f)m )a
```

We have followed here the Orwellian principle of permanently
rewriting the history. We have a better reason, though, than in
Orwell's novel. When s is computed, the result is substituted into
f; thus the real previous state to be used in comparisons should
now be seen as sf, not (s)f. Each time that a context enters the
play, we open the parentheses that separate it from the active
part at the current stage and all previous stages of history since
this context appeared.

As before, we compare the last stack with all the previous stacks
at every stage of development. When we exit context parentheses
while tracing the history backwards, we add the context to the
current stack before comparing it with next previous stacks. So,
after the first step of the Refal machine, we compare sfm with f.
After the second step we compare f with sf, and then fm with f.
The last comparison discovers that f is a repeated prefix, and the
algorithm successfully terminates.

Consider one more example. Let F be the function that scans the
argument from left to right and replaces each pair of identical
symbols by one symbol of the same kind:

```
F {
    s2 s2 el  =   s2 <F el>;
    s2 el  =  s2 <F el>;
       = ;
}
```

Let the initial configuration be

```
1.          <F <F <F el>>>
```

We want to supercompile it using, as always, the outside-in order
of evaluation, so that the final program performs in one pass the
job which is defined by the initial configuration as a three-pass
job. In this problem, it is easy to discover that the same function F is called again and again by itself, and declare it basic.
But if we do so, we, obviously, return to the original three-pass
program. The problem here is of just the opposite kind: how to
delay looping back in such a manner that the result is a one-pass
program. The algorithm must steer carefully between the Scylla of
looping back too early, and the Charybdis of never looping back at
all. We are going to show that our algorithm is capable of this
navigational feat.

Let us concentrate on the first branch in every step of driving.
Should we drive manually, we would produce this sequence of nodes:

```
2.          <F <F s2<F el>>>
3.          <F <F s2 s2<F el>>>
4.          <F s2<F <F el>>>
5.          <F s2<F s2<F el>>>
6.          <F s2<F s2 s2<F el>>>
7.          <F s2 s2<F <F<F el>>>
8.          s2 <F <F <F el>>>
```

At this stage, we would notice that the initial configuration re-
appears at the top level. We would separate it and terminate the
branch. We want now to see how the supercompiler will do this.

There are three neighborhoods at work in this example, which will be denoted as a, b, and c:

(a) <F eX>
(b) <F s2 eX>
(c) <F s2 s2 el>

Let us trace how the history changes while the supercompiler works. The initial history is

1.   ((a)a)a

There is no semicolon here, which signifies the fact that no step has yet been made. We simply decomposed the initial configuration into a stack. We shall now go through the stages 1 - 8 of driving above, using the stack-of-neighborhoods notation.

In the first step of the Refal machine, we use the contraction:

          el → s2 s2 el

The replacement results in s2<F el>. We now have the node

          <F <F s2 <F el>>>

Driving it outside-in, in order to decompose it into a stack, we find both the first, and the second call of F impossible to complete, so the active subexpression will be the third F again. The decomposition is:

          <F el> ← eX; <F s2 eX> ← eY; <F eY> ← e0

In the short notatation,

          ((a)b)a

Since the second F from outside (the context of the active third F) takes part in this transformation, we must open the corresponding parentheses: it is not just a which becomes b, but aa which becomes (a)b. Thus on the second stage the computation history is:

2.   (aa; (a)b)a

When we compare the current situation with every stage of history, we do not exit from the subgraph common to both. So, what we actually compare at this stage is ab with aa. The result is negative, and we go on. After the second step the node is

          <F <F s2 s2<F el>>>

Driving from outside in, we find the second F to be the active subexpression. The third F is not seen by the Refal machine; the neighborhood formula is (c)a. Since the context, which is now b, has taken part in the process again, we open the parentheses, and the history becomes:

3.   (aa; ab; c)a

Procedeing in this manner, we produce the further members of the "history of histories":

```
4.      aaa; aba; ca; ((a)a)b
5.      aaa; aba; ca; (aa; (a)b)b
6.      aaa; aba; ca; (aa; ab; c)b
7.      aaa; aba; ca; aab; abb; cb; c
8.      aaa; aba; ca; aab; abb; cb; c; ((a)a)a
```

Nowhere in the history before the last stage did we see a repeating context, so the process went on. At the last stage ((a)a)a
compares positively with aaa, and this combination is declared
basic. One can see that on all branches of the graph a similar
situations take place, so that in the end we have a finite graph.

Our last example is the merge-sort algorithm, which illustrates
one more pattern of recursion.

```
SORT { el = <CHECK <MERGE <PAIRS el>>>; };

MERGE {
  (el)(e2)eR = (<MERGE2 (el)(e2)>) <MERGE eR>;
  (el) = (el);
    =  ;
      };

CHECK {
  (el) = el;
  el = <CHECK <MERGE el>>;
      };
```

We shall not use the definitions of the functions PAIRS and
MERGE2. The former makes up the initial list of pairs from the
input list of items, which are assumed to be, syntactically, Refal
symbols (e.g., numbers). The latter merges two lists. We assume
that PAIRS has been executed, so that the initial configuration is

```
1.    <CHECK <MERGE el>>
```

where el is a list of pairs.

Driving this configuration outside-in, we have the following row
of configurations in the branch where el in the argument of MERGE
is not yet exhausted. We write C and M for CHECK and MERGE, and
put the ellipsis instead of MERGE2 calls, which make no impact on
driving:

```
2.      <C (...)<M el>>
3.      <C (...)(...) <M el>>
4.      <C <M (...)(...) <M el>>>
5.      <C (...)<M <M el>>>
6.      <C (...) <M (...) <M el>>>
7.      <C (...) <M (...)(...) <M el>>>
8.      <C (...)(...) <M <M el>>>
9.      <C <M (...)(...) <M <M el>>>>
10.     <C (...) <M <M <M el>>>>
```

The neighborhoods involved are:

```
(m)          <MERGE el>
(m₁)         <MERGE (e2) el>
(m₂)         <MERGE (e3)(e2) el>
(c)          <CHECK el>
(c₁)         <CHECK (e2) el>
(c₂)         <CHECK (e3)(e2) el>
```

The problem with this type of recursion is that the function CHECK is not a passive context, but one of the functions responsible for recursion; it cannot be taken outside of parentheses. If we look at the states of the stack at the moments when e1 is tested, i.e. 2, 5, 10, etc., we see the sequence:

$$mc_1; \quad mmc_1; \quad mmmc_1; \quad \ldots \text{ etc.}$$

where no stage is a prefix of any subsequent stage.

Nevertheless, our algorithm discovers the potential infiniteless of recursion, and declares <CHECK (e3)(e2)e1> a basic configuration. We leave it to the reader to verify that the computation history will develop as follows:

1. $(m)c$
2. $mc; \quad (m)c_1$
3. $mc; \quad mc_1; \quad c_2$
4. $mc; \quad mc_1; \quad c_2; \quad (m_2)c$
5. $mc; \quad mc_1; \quad c_2; \quad m_2c; \quad ((m)m)c_1$
6. $mc; \quad mc_1; \quad c_2; \quad m_2c; \quad (mm; \quad (m)m_1)c_1$
7. $mc; \quad mc_1; \quad c_2; \quad m_2c; \quad (mm; \quad mm_1; \quad m_2)c_1$
8. $mc; \quad mc_1; \quad c_2; \quad m_2c; \quad mmc_1; \quad mm_1c_1; \quad m_2c_1; \quad c_2$

At this stage the stack c_2 repeats itself, and the supercompiler declares it basic.

6. TERMINATION OF THE ALGORITHM

We want to prove now that the algorithm we have outlined and illustrated above always leads to a finite graph, because the driving of every branch of the graph will terminate, either because the resulting node is passive, or because the current stack has one of the previous stacks as its prefix (looping back). To formulate our algorithm in exact terms and to prove its termination, we must first review the formal objects which are used in the algorithm.

We represent the nodes of the graph of states by *stacks*, which consist of *neighborhoods* and are used in two forms: with and without parentheses. The current stack, as it appears from a step of the Refal machine, is represented in fully parenthesized form, which can be described by the following BNF:

$$\text{C-ST} \quad ::= \quad \text{empty} \quad | \quad \text{'(' C-ST ')' f}$$

Here quoted objects stand for themselves, and unquoted objects are classes of objects. The bar | separates alternatives. C-ST is a current stack, and f a neighborhood (function call). In our examples above, the neighborhoods were represented by letters.

When stacks stand for the past states, however, they are represented by strings of neighborhoods, which reflects the fact that these neighborhoods took part in the computation and must be considered together as representing one composite configuration of the Refal machine. Thus we introduce *past stacks*, which make up the class of objects STACK:

$$\text{STACK} \quad ::= \quad \text{empty} \quad | \quad \text{STACK f}$$

The consecutive members of computation histories are separated by semicolons, hence we need *history segments*, class H:

H ::= empty | H STACK ';'

As a result of maintaining the history records at every parenthesis level of the current stack, the overall record, which we shall designate as *the ongoing history*, ON-HIS, is from the class:

ON-HIS ::= H | H '(' ON-HIS ')' f

In a more reviewable form, the ongoing history is:

(*) $H_0(\ldots(H_{n-1}(H_n\ f_n)f_{n-1})\ldots)f_0$

where each H_i is a history segment, and f_i a neighborhood.

Now every branch of the graph of states which is being constructed by driving has a formal representation as an ON-HIS. The next thing to do is to formulate the rules according to which the ongoing history is transformed in driving, and define in exact terms the conditions under which a given branch is cut off, either because of the termination of driving, or because of looping back to a past stage. After that we shall be able to prove that under those condition no ON-HIS, i.e. no branch in the graph, can be infinite.

The starting point of driving is a current state C-ST which represents the initial configuration of the Refal machine. There are three transofrmation rules for ON-HIS. To put them as replacement formulas, we denote objects by the same symbols as the BNF classes to which they belong, adding subscripts when necessary.

Transformation Rules for ON-HIS

T1. Active replacement rule

$$H_n\ f_n\ \longrightarrow\ H_n\ f_n;\ C\text{-}ST$$

T2. Passive replacement rule:

$$H_{n-1}\ (H_n\ f_n)\ f_{n-1}\ \longrightarrow\ H_{n-1}\ H_n{}^*f_{n-1}\ f_nf_{n-1};\ C\text{-}ST$$

T3. Termination rule:

$$H_n\ f_n\ \longrightarrow\ H_n$$

Here f_n stands for the current active (top of stack) neighborhood, and H_n is the immediately preceding history segment. The active neighborhood in an ON-HIS is located as the one just before the first right parenthesis. The operation H*f in Rule T2 is the distribution of a neighborhood over a history segment defined by the formula:

$$H^*f\ =\ [STACK_1;\ STACK_2;\ \ldots\ STACK_k]^*f\ =$$

$$STACK_1f;\ STACK_2f;\ \ldots\ STACK_kf;$$

When a step of the Refal machine is performed in the process of driving, one rule must be applied to the ON-HIS representing the current branch. The three transformation rules correspond to the

three cases in the Algorithm of outside-in driving above. If the
result of the step is a unitary active expression, Rule T1 is
applied. According to this rule, the current active neighborhood
is added to the history of computation on its parenthesis level,
the context remains unchanged; a new Current Stack C-ST results
form the step. If the result of the step is passive or non-unitary
active, and there is a context (i.e. $n > 0$), Rule T2 is applied.
In this case one level of parentheses is eliminated; the context
neighborhood f_{n-1} is added to each stack in the history segment
H_n; one more History Stack, $f_n f_{n-1}$, is added to the history, and
followed by a semicolon; then new C-ST appears. If there is no
context and the result of the step is passive, Rule T3 is used. It
terminates the branch. In case of a non-unitary result and $n = 0$
(no context) Rule T1 is used.

The Cut-Off Rules

C1. Before applying the transformation rules, compare every STACK
of H_n with f_n, then every STACK of H_{n-1} with $f_n f_{n-1}$, etc. till the
STACKs of H_0 are compared with $f_n f_{n-1} \ldots f_0$. If in one of such
comparisons the first element is a prefix of the second, terminate
the ongoing history.

C2. Terminate the ongoing history if Rule T3 is used.

We now limit our attention to those ongoing histories only that
could have appeared in the process of driving, i.e. those which
can be constructed starting with a C-ST and applying Rules T1 and
T2, before Rule C1 is used.

<u>Lemma 1</u>. If a history segment is not empty then its last stack
consists either from one, or from two neighborhoods.

<u>Proof</u>. The lemma is true at the beginning of driving when all
history segments are empty. When Rule T1 is used, a STACK which
consists of one neighborhood f_n is added at the end of H_n. When
Rule T2 is used, H_n disappears, and H_{n-1} gets an addition which
ends with $f_n f_{n-1}$.

We shall refer to stacks of length one or two as *short* stacks.

<u>Lemma 2</u>. The situation where one of the history stacks in a seg-
ment is a prefix of a later stack in the same or a later segment
is impossible.

<u>Proof</u>. Suppose that such a situation exists. Let the earlier stack
(to become a prefix) be ab...z, where letters stand for neighborhoods. Each history stack starts at a certain moment when its
first neighborhood is the top element of the current stack. The
ongoing history at this moment can be seen as:

$$\ldots (\ldots \ ab \ldots z; \ldots \ (H_k \ \ldots (H_n \ f_n)' f_{n-1} \ \ldots) f_k \ ) \ldots$$

Here we left out the history segments and context neighborhoods
which are common to ab...z and the current stack $f_n f_{n-1} \ldots f_k$,
because they only add common endings to both strings. For the
earlier stack to be a prefix of the later, f_n must obviously be
identical to a. But it is also necessary that f_{n-1} be identical to
b. Indeed, f_n can be lengthened only if we open by Rule T2 the
internal parentheses marked by the prime '. The use of Rule T1
with any subsequent uses of both rules is irrelevant as long as

the marked parenthesis is not opened (it only creates history stacks subsequent to the stack of interest). This reasoning is also valid for all other elements of the earlier stack up to z; thus we conclude that ab...z must be a prefix of the string $f_n f_{n-1}...f_k$. This, however, is impossible, because Rule C1 (our algorithm of looping back) should have stopped the process at this stage.

Lemma 3 The number of different short stacks is finite.

Proof. The number of different neighborhoods of the first order is finite, because it is the number of paths in a finite tree. Therefore, the number of different stacks of length one or two is also finite.

Theorem. With the driving algorithm described above, no branch of the graph of states may be infinite.

Proof.. As shown above, to every branch in the graph, as long as it is not cut off, an ongoing history corresponds. We are now going to show that an infinite ongoing history is impossible.

First we construct yet another model, namely a model of the growth of the ongoing history (which itself is a model of the growth of a branch in driving). The general form of the ongoing history is given by (*). At every stage of the process it consists of a finite number of *levels* separated by parentheses. The part outside of all parentheses is counted as level 0. For $i > 0$, the i-th level is delimited by the i-th and the $i+1$-st nested pair of parentheses, and consists of a history segment H_i and the neighborhood f_i. We want a model which for each level i of the ongoing history will indicate a number of guaranteed short stacks in it. We shall denote this number as G_i. Thus the number of short segments in H_i must be at least G_i. The model describing the dynamics of the numbers G_i is as follows.

At each moment, the highest level n is the level on which an *action* is taken. There are two types of action, which correspond to Rules T1 and T2 above: A1, addition on the level n :

(A1) G_n becomes G_n+1

and A2, cancellation on the level n and addition on the level $n-1$:

(A2) G_n becomes 0, and

          G_{n-1} becomes $G_{n-1}+1$,   where $n > 0$.

Indeed, when we apply Rule T1 to the ongoing history, a stack of length 1 is added to H_n. When we apply Rule T2, the n-th level disappears, every term in H_n is lengthened by 1 and added to H_{n-1}. We do not know how many short (of length 2) stacks will be there after the operation, and we count it as zero. But one guaranteed stack of length 2 is added to H_{n-1}. After any of the two actions, a new C-ST is created according to both rules, which in our model means that the top level n is incremented by some positive number, and the values of G_i for the new levels are all set to zero.

Suppose now that there is an infinite branch, i.e. an infinite ongoing history. Then the number of levels in it is either limited by a finite number, or infinite. Suppose it is infinite. Some of the history segments may be empty, others non-empty. We want to prove that if the total number of levels is infinite, the number of levels with non-empty history segments must also be infinite. The total number of empty segments in the ongoing history increases when a new C-ST with at least one new parenthesis is created. Consider separately the cases when the number of parentheses is one, i.e. C-St is (f)g , or more: (...((f)g)...)h. In the former case, the use of Rule T1 transforms one empty segment into a non-empty segment (namely, f;). If Rule T2 is used then the only empty history disappears. In the case of more than one level in the C-ST, one of the empty segments on the level of f or g will be necessarily made non-empty, no matter which of the rules is used. We conclude that the number of empty segments cannot become infinite without making the number of non-empty segments infinite too. Therefore, if the total number of levels is infinite, the number of levels with non-empty history segments will be also infinite.

By Lemma 1 each non-empty history segment H_i ends with a short stack. Since the number of different short stacks is finite (Lemma 3), we must have a situation where two history stacks are identical. This is, however, impossible by Lemma 2.

Therefore, the number of levels must be limited by a finite number, even though the number of actions grows infinitely. Then there must be at least one level i such that an infinite number of actions takes place on that level. The actions, as we know, are of two types: A1 and A2. If the number of actions A2 at the i-th level were finite, then G_i would be infinite, because the number of additions would be infinite while the number of cancellations finite. But this would imply that there are two identical short stacks in H_i, and this is impossible. Therefore, the number of actions A2 must be infinite. However, each action A2 on level i creates an addition on level $i-1$, hence the number of cancellations, and, therefore, actions A2 on level $i-1$ must also be infinite. Reasoning in this way we come to the conclusion that the number of actions A2 on level 0 must also be infinite, but this is impossible, because only actions A1 can be performed on that level.

Thus the assumption of an infinite ongoing histoty leads to a contradiciton, which proves the theorem.

R E F E R E N C E S

[1]   Turchin, V.F. The concept of a supercompiler. ACM Trans. on Progr. Languages and Systems, vol. 8, No.3, 1986, pp. 292-325.

[2]   Turchin, V.F. Program transformation by supercompilation. In Programs as Data Objects, Lecture Note in Comp.Sci. No. 217, pp. 257-325, Springer Verlag, 1985.

[3]   Turchin, V.F. The language Refal, the theory of compilation, and metasystem analysis. Courant Institute Rep. #20, New York 1980.

Partial Evaluation and Mixed Computation
D. Bjørner, A.P. Ershov and N.D. Jones (Editors)
Elsevier Science Publishers B.V. (North-Holland)
© IFIP, 1988

A MODEL OF LANGUAGE SEMANTICS ORIENTED TO MIXED
EXECUTION OF PROGRAMS

Tatyana I. YOUGANOVA

ONTK "Soyuztsvetmetavtomatika"
Moscow, USSR

The problem stated in this work is to construct a model
of language semantics incorporating a possibility of
recursion and operation with the memory, and oriented
to a mixed execution of programs. The basic feature of
suggested approach resides in the fact that the mixed
computation is not built on a prefixed language but
introduced directly into it. This allows a possibility
to be considered and used in the program for its mixed
execution of the latter, for example, for organizing
various types of data processing depending on the degree
and nature of data suspension. The model offers means
for description and formal investigation of various
methods of suspension management.

1. PRINCIPLES OF MODEL CONSTRUCTION

The suggested approach is based on the ideas of L. Lombardi [1],
implemented in the INCOL language [2,3] . This language was
constructed before the creation of the mixed computation theory
and was intended for the programming support of one decision
making method under incomplete information [4]. When making computation in the INCOL language the residual program as a partial
solution of the problem is oriented to a perception by the human
being. Such orientation has caused an appearence in INCOL a set
of unusual means for suspension control allowing to decrease the
volume of partial solution and increase its informativity. Application of the mixed computation theory to the INCOL has allowed
to expose and to eliminate essential shortcomings of this language [5]. The suggested model is an attempt of the formalization, generalization and development of those features of INCOL
which can be useful in the others mixed evaluators.

The model represents a class of recursive schemes of programs
meeting requirements of the fixed point theory [6]. All the operations on suspension are realized by base functions which are
assigned to exact definitions, that is, a denotation semantics
of the mixed computation has been built. By altering the defini-

tions, as well as by introducing new functions one can model
various methods of the suspension management. In this case, it
is possible to investigate the model behaviour as a whole by
studying the properties of an obtained class of recursive schemes and consider separately its individual components by examin-
ing the properties of corresponding base functions.

Suppose we have an object domain $\mathcal{C}$ of the standard computation
and a set of primitives $\mathcal{P}$ on $\mathcal{C}$. The language to be modelled
must allow the construction of recursive programs on $\mathcal{C}$ and $\mathcal{P}$,
and in this case, enable the programmer to do the underfollow-
ing:

- Declare any initial data and functions suspended - an initial suspension.
- Recognize the operand suspension in the course of a program
  execution.
- Suspend the function reference depending on certain conditions, including on the suspension of arguments - a programmable
  suspension.
- Cancel the results of certain stage of computations by replacing them with a suspension of the corresponding function reference - a return suspension.
- Use both local and global variables in the function body (the
  latters are modelling computations with the memory).
- Generate and suspend the generation of names (primitives, global variables, functions and their actual parameters).

The algorithm of a standard computation on region $\mathcal{C}$ may be specified with the help of recursive schemes of the form as follows:

$$F_1(x_1, \ldots, x_n) \Leftarrow \tau_1[F_1, \ldots, F_m] \ (x_1, \ldots, x_n)$$
$$\ldots$$
$$F_m(x_1, \ldots, x_n) \Leftarrow \tau_m[F_1, \ldots, F_m] \ (x_1, \ldots, x_n) \qquad (1)$$

Here, the right sides in the definitions of function F_i contain
terms composed of base function references with the primitives
from $\mathcal{P}$ used as the such functions and defined functions F_k. In
order to execute the program corresponding to a scheme (1), we
build first the initial term $F_1(x_1^0, \ldots, x_n^0)$ basing on initial
data $x_1^0, \ldots, x_n^0$. Further, using any computation rule [6], we

obtain the result - element $\mathcal{C}$ or undefined value ω. If to suspend some data from x_1^0, ..., x_n^0 and definitions of some functions from F_1, ..., F_m the mixed execution of program should result in the general case in a certain scheme of the form (1) - a residual program. This program may be applied subsequently to the presuspended data with the use of functions suspended previously.

The mixed computation of recursive programs in [7] is realized by a special computation rule according to which a new definition of function - a projection of initial definition on the suspended arguments may be included into the residual program at any step of substitution. The mixed computation for programs with the memory [8,9] is also realized by complicating the interpretation algorithm, since all the language structures are assigned to a new extended semantics.

The model under consideration contemplates the use of a computation rule common for the theory of recursive schemes. The result of its application is an expression which may be interpreted as the body of a certain function. By connecting the corresponding definition to an initial scheme of the program as a head function, we obtain a residual program. Thus, in contrast to [7] we build a projection of only the first function of the scheme (1). Here however, other functions are also involved in the computation. When computing the reference, the latter is either suspended or recursively replaced with a partially computed body of the function - without constructing the new definitions.

The reason for reference suspension is an initial, programmable or return suspension of the function or a fact of the reference location in alternative of the suspended conventional structure. In other cases, a substitution is made, that is, the same computations are actually performed here as those done in the recursive algorithm [7] without a polyvariance.

Note, that when making computations in the INCOL language the concentration of computation result in one expression (including the references of customary initial functions) proves to be more convenient compared than the partial simplification (and multiplication - for various references) of a number of initial definitions.

In the suggested model, the mixed computation is realized by extending an object region $\mathcal{C}$, incorporating the suspended references into it. What is more, new base functions and additional definitions of functions like macrodefinitions are introduced. Thus, the complication of base operations semantics is maintained by extending the language - syntactic frames. This enables introduction into it of special aids to control a mixed computation with preserving the usual manner of executing recursive programs and the possibility for a direct application of recursive scheme theory.

The model is constructed in several stages. The first stage is used to build the model of a primitive program (consisting of one function without branchings and recursion) realizing the data suspension. Then possibilities are introduced for branching and recognizing the suspension. The third stage is used to construct the model of a recursive program with the abilities of initial and programmable suspensions of functions. Further, considerations are being given to the model extensions realizing the global variables, return suspension and the generation of names.

When selecting the method of suspension, account must be taken of the requirements on a mixed computation correctness and safety [9]. At the first stages of model construction, these requirements are considered as applied to primitive base functions. Here we obtain the necessary conditions of a mixed computation correctness in the form of constraints on the methods of suspending primitives. The introduction of new possibilities at the subsequent stages does not violate the correctness.

2. CONSTRUCTION OF PRIMITIVE FUNCTIONS

Let us refer to the elements of object domain $\mathcal{C}$ as constants.

〈constant〉 ::= 〈blank〉 / 〈 lexical token 〉 / 〈 normal constant 〉
〈normal constant 〉 ::= (〈 constants 〉)
〈constants 〉 ::= 〈 constant 〉 / 〈 constant 〉 , 〈 constants 〉

The lexical tokens do not contain brackets and commas and include logical constants *YES and *NO. As examples, use set $\mathcal{C}_o$, where

⟨lexical token⟩ ::= ⟨ integer number ⟩ /⟨identifier⟩/*YES/*NO

Confine set $\mathcal{P}$ to unary and binary primitives. Extend the primitives from $\mathcal{P}$ to set $\mathcal{C}^\omega = \mathcal{C} \cup \{\omega\}$, using the natural expansion only [6]: if even if one operand is equal to ω , then the primitive value also equals ω .

Consider set $\mathcal{E}$, whose elements will be referred to as expressions.

⟨expression⟩ ::= ⟨constant⟩ / ⟨suspended reference⟩
⟨suspended reference⟩ ::= ⟨suspended base reference⟩ /
                        ⟨suspended macroreference⟩
⟨suspended base reference⟩ ::=
        * ⟨ordinary function name⟩ (⟨ arguments ⟩)
⟨suspended macroreference⟩ ::=
        *⟨macrodefinition name⟩(⟨arguments⟩)
⟨arguments⟩ ::= ⟨ argument ⟩ / ⟨ argument ⟩ , ⟨ arguments ⟩
⟨argument⟩ ::= ⟨ expression ⟩
⟨ordinary function name⟩ ::=
        ⟨primitive name⟩/N/X/COND/PEXT/PINT
⟨macrodefinition name⟩ ::=F/FT/PR1/PR2

The ordinary base functions may be used in a program as opposed to special base functions whose references occur in macrodefinitions only. The primitive names are taken from $\mathcal{P}$. Assume that all of them differ from N, X, ..., PR2. Later on, we will reduce set $\mathcal{E}$ by defining more exactly the structure of suspended references.

We will begin the construction of base functions with the primitive functions - extensions of primitives of $\mathcal{P}$ from $\mathcal{C}^\omega$ to $\mathcal{E}^\omega$. While in those cases, when the value of primitive on $\mathcal{C}$ equals ω , the corresponding function may have a value from $\mathcal{E}$. The primitive function for each primitive from $\mathcal{P}$ with name z is constructed with an observance of the following mandatory rules: the name and number of arguments must be the same as of the primitive; if the function arguments represent constants and the value of primitive with such arguments is not ω , then the function takes the same value; function z is naturally extended to $\mathcal{E}^\omega$.

If there are arguments from $\mathcal{E}\backslash\mathcal{C}$ or if the primitive has value ω , then the function may be defined by various methods. For example, in INCOL the value ω is not allowed: a suspended reference is used instead of ω. Thus, PLUS(5,*NO)=*PLUS(5,*NO). In this case the computation is brought up to the end and the suspended incorrect references are well seen in a partial solution. Such a result is more informative than ω. Another example: at $a\in\mathcal{E}\backslash\mathcal{C}$ one may assume OR(*NO,a)=a instead of *OR(*NO,a).

Let us introduce ordinary function N (not primitive one) by predefining the concept of a normal expression:

⟨normal expression⟩::=⟨normal constant⟩/*N(⟨arguments⟩)

Function N has an optional number of arguments. If $a_1,\ldots,a_n\in\mathcal{C}$, then $N(a_1,\ldots,a_n)=(a_1,\ldots,a_n)$, and at $a_i\in\mathcal{E}\backslash\mathcal{C}$ $N(a_1,\ldots,a_n)=$ $=*N(a_1,\ldots,a_n)$. If there is an argument ω , then the value of function N is equal to ω. Function N makes possible to generate and analyse the structures with suspended components. For example, if $a=*N(a_1,\ldots,a_n)$, then $CAR(a)=a_1$ but not *CAR(a).

Apparently, the application of functions similar to OR and CAR is directed to an increase in the depth of a mixed computation. Note that in contrast to [10] all constructed functions remain natural extended.

3. SCHEME OF PRIMITIVE PROGRAM. DATA SUSPENSION

To construct the scheme of primitive program on $\mathcal{E}^\omega$, we will need unknowns - formal parameters of the defined function. To distinguish them from the object domain elements present the unknown in the form of an unsuspended reference to function X with the argument from $\mathcal{C}$ - name of the unknown.

Introduce the concept of a list of parameters.

⟨list of parameters⟩::=(⟨parameters-constants⟩)/(⟨parameters⟩)
⟨parameters⟩::=⟨expression⟩/⟨parameter⟩/⟨parameter⟩,⟨parameters⟩
⟨parameter⟩::=⟨name of parameter⟩,⟨meaning⟩
⟨name of parameter⟩::=⟨constant⟩   ⟨meaning⟩::=⟨expression⟩

The parameters-constants consist of constants only.

Introduce one more argument into function X. Let a∈𝒞,b be a
list of parameters. If there are parameters with name a in b,
then X(a,b) is equal to the value of the most left one of them.
If there is no parameter with name a in b, then X(a,b)=*X(a),
that is, the second argument at a suspension is removed.

Consider that the only argument of the function defined is a
list of parameters. It is precisely this argument that we'll refer to as a variable and denote it via $\mp$. The scheme of primitive program will be presented in the following form

$$S(\mp)<= \tau (\mp) \tag{2}$$

The right side of this definition is a term composed of unsuspended references to primitive functions, N and X. Variable $\mp$
may occur only at the place of the second argument of reference
X.

If to substitute any list of parameters, x, for $\mp$, then the
value of function S is calculated by usual simplifications of
the references composing term τ (x), starting with the most internal ones. The computation result will be ω or an expression
from $\mathcal{E}$, which may include the suspended references. The reason for their appearance may be the absence in list x of parameters for some of the unknowns, as well as the presence in a
program or generation of incorrect references (with unsuitable
arguments) in the course of computation. The suspension of these
references and references X may involve a forced suspension of
convolute references of base functions or remain unnoticed, if
these functions permit the processing of suspended arguments.

Thus, the initial list of parameters - value $\mp$ is an analog of
the initial state of memory in statement-type languages. The
suspended parameters are simply not included in this list, and
then the unknowns remained free are suspended. The refusal of
customary - positional method of specifying parameters has resulted from a need to formalize the value search. One may refuse
the key writing of parameters in the external representation of
the language.

Let us build a scheme of program computing the square of the
first element of the array M and adding the obtained number to

the value T: (for clarity, the comma is substituted by a colon):

$$S(\stackrel{\curlyvee}{})<=PLUS(X(T,\stackrel{\curlyvee}{}),SQ(CAR(X(M,\stackrel{\curlyvee}{})))) \qquad (3)$$
$$S((M:(1,12,5),T:0))=1$$
$$S((M:(1,12,5)))=*PLUS(*X(T),1)$$

4. ASSOCIATIVITY CRITERION FOR PRIMITIVE PROGRAM

Consider, how to obtain a residual program from the result of computations to the scheme (2). Suppose that x is a list of parameters-constants and $S(x)=\mathcal{T}(x)=e\in\mathcal{E}$. By removing in e the asterisks from all names of the suspended references and adding the second argument $\stackrel{\curlyvee}{}$ to all references X, we will obtain the term $t_e(\stackrel{\curlyvee}{})$. Now, let us construct the function definition $G(\stackrel{\curlyvee}{})<=t_e(\stackrel{\curlyvee}{})$ and declare it to be a scheme of the residual program. We will denote the transformation of expression e into term $t_e(\stackrel{\curlyvee}{})$ via $\mathcal{R}:\mathcal{R}(e)=t_e(\stackrel{\curlyvee}{})$ and refer to it as a resumption by analogy with [11].

It is possible to construct a function which overlap the resumption with a computation to the obtained program. Let us name it the interpretation function I, and define as follows. If $a,b\in\mathcal{E}$, term $t_a(\stackrel{\curlyvee}{})=\mathcal{R}(a)$, then $I(a,b)=t_a(b)$. Function I is not considered to be a base one. To make this definition to be quite correct, we will reduce set $\mathcal{E}$ up to set $\mathcal{D}$ $(e\subset\mathcal{D}\subset\mathcal{E})$ so that the resumption of elements $\mathcal{D}$ results in obtaining only correct (with respect to the number of arguments) references of ordinary functions. Then all introduced functions map $\mathcal{D}$ into itself.

Now, we can offer the strict rules for computing the value of function I. Let x is a list of parameters, $x,r\in\mathcal{D}$. Then
- if r is a constant, then $I(r,x)=r$;
- if $r=*z(a_1,\ldots,a_n)\in\mathcal{D}$, where z is a primitive name or N, $a_1\ldots,a_n\in\mathcal{D}$, then $I(r,x)=I(*z(a_1,\ldots,a_n),x)= z(I(a_1,x)\ldots,I(a_n,x))$;
- if $r=*X(a)$, where $a\in\mathcal{C}$, then $I(r,x)=I(*X(a),x)=X(a,x)$.
In the rest of cases $I(r,x)=\omega$.

In example (3), the result $*PLUS(*X(T),1)$ generates a residual program with the scheme $G(\stackrel{\curlyvee}{})<=PLUS(X(T,\stackrel{\curlyvee}{}),1)$ for function $S(\stackrel{\curlyvee}{})$. By executing this program with initial data $y=(T:0)$ we will get the result $G((T:0))=PLUS(X(T,(T:0)),1)=PLUS(0,1)=1$ and with the

help of function I have directly the following from the first
result I(*PLUS(*X(T),1) ,(T:0))=PLUS(X(T,(T:0)),1)=1=S((M:(1,12,
5),T:0)).

Thus, if to execute the residual program $G(\digamma) <= t_e(\digamma)$ with new
initial data y, then the result of computation $G(y)=t_e(y)$ may
be also written in the form of a value $I(e,y)=I(\mathcal{T}(x),y)$.

Suppose $\mathcal{T}(\digamma)=\mathcal{R}(r)$. In this case, the result $\mathcal{T}(x)$ of executing
the program (2) with initial data x may be written in the form
of I(r,x) and the result of residual program execution - in the
form of I(I(r,x),y).

Define the primitive function CONL. If a and b are the lists of
parameters, then the value CONL(a,b) is a merged list with the
unnecessary parameters removed from it (the most left one only
is out of similar parameters). When suspending the argument,
the CONL function reference is suspended.

Let us formulate the principle of partial computation for a
class of primitive programs. If $x,y,r \in \mathcal{D}$, x and y are the lists
of parameters-constants, then

$$I(r,CONL(x,y))=I(I(r,x),y) \qquad (4)$$

or $S(CONL(x,y))=I(S(x),y)$ in the designation of a source program, that is the result of one-fold execution of optional primitive program on $\mathcal{D}^{\omega}$ with a merged list of parameters is to
coincide with the result of a partitional computation, whose
first stage - obtaining I(r,x) or S(x) will be referred to as a
mixed computation and the second stage - as an execution of the
residual program. We will assume the computation with a merged
list of parameters to be a standard one (although its result may
also contain suspended references). Following L.A. Lombardi, the
property (4) will be identified as a strict associativity.

In some cases, the partitional computation may lead to a definite result (from $\mathcal{D}$), as well as in the case when the standard
computation produces ω . Therefore, instead of (4) we will consider more often the property

$$I(r,CONL(x,y)) \sqsubseteq I(I(r,x),y) \qquad (5)$$

and name it simply the associativity. (The sign $\sqsubseteq$ indicates a "less defined or equal" ratio [6]).

Suppose that $\widehat{\mathcal{D}} \subset \mathcal{D}$ is a set of values of function I. It can be shown that for a class of primitive programs the necessary and sufficient condition of computation associativity is the following requirement: for all unary primitive functions z1 and all binary primitive functions z2, optional list of parameters-constants y and $\forall p, q \in \widehat{\mathcal{D}}$ - an execution of

$$z1(I(p,y)) \sqsubseteq I(z1(p),y) \qquad (6)$$
$$z2(I(p,y),I(q,y)) \sqsubseteq I(z2(p,q),y) \qquad (7)$$

For a strict associativity it is necessary and sufficient to execute (6) and (7) with the replacement of sign $\sqsubseteq$ by equality.

We will refer to the properties of (6) and (7) as a commutativity of primitive function with I. In case of equality, a strict commutativity takes place. Function N is strictly commutative with I at any number of arguments.

Note that the class of primitive programs is a specific case for any models of programs. Therefore, the necessary conditions analogous to (6) and (7) should be true for other models of a mixed computation.

5.   PROGRAM WITH BRANCHINGS. SAFETY OF MIXED
      EXECUTION. SUSPENSION RECOGNITION

When introducing the possibilities of branching (without cycles) into a program, the mixed computation may prove to be unreliable even in case of using only "good" primitive functions - because of a possible emergency stop in the needless alternative. This means that ratio $\sqsubseteq$ in (4) may change to reverse. This problem in [12] is solved by using special recognizers which disable the execution of an emergency operation. In the suggested model, this is done at the level of base function definitions.

Let us add set $\mathcal{U}$ to references of the *COND(a,b,c) form for $a, b, c \in \mathcal{D}$ and define function COND with five arguments on $\mathcal{D}^{\omega}$: COND(*YES,b,c,d,e)=d; COND(*NO,b,c,d,e)=e; at $a \in \mathcal{D} \backslash \mathcal{C}, b, c \in \mathcal{D}$

COND(a,b,c,d,e)=*COND(a,b,c); in other cases COND(a,b,c,d,e)=ω
In this function under a logical condition use is made of argument d or e and at the condition suspension - arguments b and c.

Build a conjugate function for each primitive function from $\mathcal{P}$
with name z by replacing value ω with the suspended reference
in all cases when the arguments belong to $\mathcal{D}$. (When realizing
on a computer, instead of an additional analysis of arguments,
that is no always possible, one can use the interrupt processing
software and in case of an emergency suspend the reference).
Assign name $\bar{z}$ to the new function without introduced it into
language but its suspended reference preserves the *z name. In
the general case, function z is less defined or equivalent $\bar{z}$
 ($z \subseteq \bar{z}$). Construct also a conjugate function $\overline{COND}$ for function
COND.

Let us add a processing of references *COND to resumption trans-
formation $\mathcal{R}$: if a,b,c $\in \mathcal{D}$, then $\mathcal{R}$(*COND(a,b,c))=COND($\mathcal{R}$(a),
$\bar{\mathcal{R}}$(b),$\bar{\mathcal{R}}$(c),$\mathcal{R}$(b),$\mathcal{R}$(c)), where transformation $\bar{\mathcal{R}}$ differs from $\mathcal{R}$ by
and only by the fact that the names of suspended primitive re-
ferences z and references COND are replaced not with z and COND
but with $\bar{z}$ and $\overline{COND}$ respectively. In a similar way, function I
is extended and function $\bar{I}$ is introduced: if a,b,c$\in\mathcal{D}$, then
I(*COND(a,b,c),x)=COND(I(a,x),$\bar{I}$(b,x),$\bar{I}$(c,x),I(b,x),I(c,x)). In
this case, I$\subseteq$$\bar{I}$.

Consider a class of program schemes of the form (2) for which
$\exists r \in \mathcal{D}$ is such that τ($\bar{\digamma}$)=$\mathcal{R}$(r). It can be shown that the introduction of function COND and the corresponding change in functi-
on I do not violate (4) or (5).

With the introduction of function COND, the suspension recognition
becomes justified. Let us build the unary base function SUSP:
at a$\in \mathcal{C}$ SUSP(a)=*NO; at a$\in\mathcal{D}\backslash\mathcal{C}$ SUSP(a)=*YES. This function is
not suspended and not considered to be primitive one. The corre-
lation (6) is not executed for it, that is, its use violates the
computation associativity. This function enables the recognition
of an operand suspension and may be used depending on the result
to change the direction of a further computation. Examples of
using such a function is presented in [5]. We'll further assume
that function SUSP doesn't use.

6.   MODEL OF RECURSIVE PROGRAM. SUSPENSION OF FUNCTIONS

In order to build a program consisting of several functions and
in this case, have a possibility for suspending any of them we
will introduce a special function F for the realization of such
a suspension, similar to function X which was introduced to suspend the unknowns. However, the unknown processing terminates in
a substitution of the value, whereas the reference to function
requires a computation of its body and therefore, must be realized by a recursive construction. Consequently, function F
cannot be a base one. We will construct a macrodefinition F
which will be composed of references to special base functions
and functions to be defined, and introduce it into the program
scheme. The reference to any of definable functions in the program is made through function F only.

Let us introduce a new variable Ψ . Suppose the functions, we
want to use for building the program, have names $s_1, \ldots, s_m$. The
value of variable Ψ must be a normal constant, whose components
represent the names of unsuspended, that is accessible for computation, functions from $s_1, \ldots, s_m$. We will refer to the value
of variable Ψ as a list of functions names.

Then, we'll include the suspended references of the form *F(a,b)
in $\mathcal{D}$, where a - constant, b - list of parameters and add the
definition of transformation $\mathcal{R}$ to the following rule: $\mathcal{R}(*F(a,b))=$
$=F(a,\mathcal{R}(b),\Psi)$.

For each program function with name s_i, whose body represents
expression $r_i \in \mathcal{D}$, we construct the definition

$$F_i(\Psi ,\bar{\Psi})<= \tau_i[F](\Psi ,\bar{\Psi}), \qquad (8)$$

where term $\tau_i[F](\Psi ,\bar{\Psi})$ is obtained as a result of resumption
r_i, that is, $\tau_i[F] (\Psi ,\bar{\Psi})=\mathcal{R}(r_i)$. Macroreference F founded in
the right part of (8) means that it is necessary to refer with
a list of parameters, equalling the second argument value, the
function whose name is equal to the first argument value, if
this name is contained in the list - a value of the third argument. Otherwise. reference F must be suspended.

In order to make a definition of function F, realizing the stated actions, we will need a number of special base functions on

$\mathcal{D}^{\omega}$. The function IF(a,b,c) is analogous to a standard "if-then-
-else" function and will be used exactly in such a writing. The
IS(a,b) function performs the comparison of arguments irrespec-
tive of their possible suspension. The NOF(a,b) function realizes
the search in a list of names, if $a \in \mathcal{C}$,b - is a normal constant:
in the presence in b of a component equal to a, NOF(a,b)=*NO
(not suspended); otherwise NOF(a,b)=*YES. The SF(a,b) function
realizes the suspension of reference F: at $a,b \in \mathcal{D}$, SF(a,b)=
=*F(a,b).

Now, we can compose the macrodefinition of function F:

$$F(\alpha,\beta,\varphi) <= \underline{if} \; NOF(\alpha,\varphi) \; \underline{then} \; SF(\alpha,\beta) \qquad \underline{else}$$
$$\underline{if} \; IS(\alpha,s_1) \; \underline{then} \; F_1(\varphi,\beta) \qquad \underline{else}$$
$$\cdots \qquad\qquad (9)$$
$$\underline{if} \; IS(\alpha,s_{m-1}) \quad \underline{then} \; F_{m-1}(\varphi,\beta) \qquad \underline{else}$$
$$F_m(\varphi,\beta)\underline{end} \; \cdots \; \underline{end} \; \underline{end}$$

In a statement-type writing, this expression will take the form

$$F(\alpha,\beta,\varphi) = \tau_F[F_1,\ldots,F_m](\alpha,\beta,\varphi) \qquad (10)$$

Impose additional constraints on the bodies of defined functions
r_i. Require that $\forall i, 1 \leqslant i \leqslant m$ be present for each reference
*F(a,b) contained in r_i in which argument a coincides with any
of $s_j (1 \leqslant j \leqslant m)$ and argument b contains the names of all unknowns
occurred in r_j as names of the parameters. This constraint natural for functional programs means that the unknowns may be suspended only at the first computation of function F_1. For any
other function, the unknowns contained in its body are local,
therefore, suspending them beyond the function has no meaning.
They may, however, assume the suspended values.

Thus, the head function of a residual program may contain only
those unknowns which correspond to the suspended initial data,
that is, to the absent parameters of the initial program head
function. In other functions, there should be no free unknowns.
If the function contains a global unknown in essence, then we
require a formal transfer of its meaning from one function into
another with the help of parameter of the A:*X(A) form.

The introduced constraint is significant for ensuring the asso-

ciativity. There is no stated constraint in the INCOL language
[2] and L.A. Lombardi's project [1], that results in violation
of the computation correctness.

To check the initial values of variables, let us introduce one
more macrodefinition into the program scheme. The special functions TF and TX used in it check that all φ components are present in $(s_1,\ldots,s_m)$ and that $\check{\digamma}$ is a list of parameters-constants.

The definition of initial function of our scheme has the form

$H(\varphi,\check{\digamma})$ =<u>if</u> $OR(TF(\varphi,(s_1,\ldots,s_m)),TX(\check{\digamma}))$ <u>then</u> ω
<u>else</u> $F(s_1,\check{\digamma},\varphi)$ <u>end</u> (11)

or in the statement-type form

$$H(\varphi,\check{\digamma}) = \tau_H[F] \; (\varphi,\check{\digamma}) \tag{12}$$

To complete the scheme construction, it is necessary to define
the conjugate to function F. Function F is defined recursively
(via $\tau_F[F_1,\ldots,F_m]$ and F_i - via $\tau_i[F]$), therefore, in the
general case to construct such $\bar{F}$, as $F(a,b,c) \sqsubseteq \bar{F}(a,b,c)$ is not
possible algorithmically: to this end, we are to complete F by
suspended references in those cases when its computation is re-
cycled. Remind that for primitive and COND functions, it is precisely the $z \sqsubseteq \bar{z}$ property that ensured the associativity.

We will consider the simplest method of constructing function $\bar{F}$
by taking

$$\bar{F}(\alpha,\beta,\varphi) = SF(\alpha,\beta) \tag{13}$$

that is, we realize a regular tactics of prohibiting the defined
function references when a conventional construction is suspended. In contrast to primitive functions where the suspension
guarantees a commutativity with I, such a solution for recursive
function F will not allow the associativity to be ensured in all
cases. It is secured under a supplementary condition: if the
result of standard or partitional computation is a constant.

Require that the name of suspended reference *F in the definitions of transformation $\mathcal{R}$ be replaced with $\bar{F}$ instead of F. The

scheme of a recursive program composed from functions with names $s_1,\ldots,s_m$ and bodies $r_1,\ldots,r_m$ is built up from definitions (11), (8), (9) and (13) with an addition of argument $\bar{\bar{F}}$ to τ_i. In a statement-type writing, taking into consideration (10) and (12) this scheme has the following form

$$
\begin{aligned}
&H(\varphi,\bar{\varphi}) <= \tau_H[F]\ (\varphi,\bar{\varphi}) \\
&F_1(\varphi,\bar{\varphi}) <= \tau_1[F,\bar{F}]\ (\varphi,\bar{\varphi}) \\
&\ldots \\
&F_m(\varphi,\bar{\varphi}) <= \tau_m[F,\bar{F}]\ (\varphi,\bar{\varphi}) \\
&F(\alpha,\beta,\varphi) <= \tau_F[F_1,\ldots,F_m]\ (\alpha,\beta,\varphi) \\
&\bar{F}(\alpha,\beta,\varphi) = \tau_{\bar{F}}(\alpha,\beta)
\end{aligned}
\tag{14}
$$

The scheme (14) incorporates definitions $F_1,\ldots,F_m$ corresponding to initial functions $s_1,\ldots,s_m$, and macrodefinitions H, F and $\bar{F}$. The definitions F_i are composed by a formal transformation of the bodies of initial functions - expressions r_i and the macro-definitions H, F and $\bar{F}$ include the names of these functions. All statements $\tau_H,\tau_1,\ldots,\tau_m,\tau_F,\tau_{\bar{F}}$ are continuous [6], since they represent the superpositions of monotonic base functions and functional variables. This suggests that the constructed scheme has the least fixpoint.

7. PROGRAMMABLE SUSPENSION OF FUNCTIONS

The solution taken for function $\bar{F}$ enables the realization of possibilities to control the suspension of defined function references. Let us build an ordinary function PEXT(a,b,c) by adding first set $\mathcal{D}$ to references of the *PEXT(a,b) form for $a,b \in \mathcal{D}$. Suppose that PEXT(*YES,b,c)=c, at $a \in \mathcal{D}\backslash\{*YES\}, b \in \mathcal{D}$ PEXT(a,b,c)=*PEXT(a,b) and in other cases - ω.

Add the definition of transformation $\mathcal{R}$ to the following rule: if $a,b \in \mathcal{D}$, then $\mathcal{R}(*PEXT(a,b))=PEXT(\mathcal{R}(a),\bar{\mathcal{R}}(b),\mathcal{R}(b))$. This suggests that if the first argument is *YES, then the result of this reference computation will be a value of the third argument. Otherwise, the residual program will get the value of the same argument, but computed with a suspension of all references F, incorrect references to primitive functions and function COND. Thus, the PEXT function enables the blocking of references to functions when the specified conditions are violated, that is, it realizes the programmable suspension. Note that $\overline{\overline{PEXT}} \equiv PEXT$.

Let us give a new definition of the interpretation function I. Suppose that S - is a scheme of the form (14), $u,v \in \mathcal{D}$, u is a list of names of certain functions of the program to which scheme S is constructed, v - is a list of parameters. Then
- if $r \in \mathcal{C}^{\omega}$, then $I(r,u,v)=r$;
- if z - is the name of primitive function or N, $a_1,\ldots,a_n \in \mathcal{D}$, then
$I(*z(a_1,\ldots,a_n),u,v)=z(I(a_1,u,v),\ldots,I(a_n,u,v))$;
- if $a \in \mathcal{C}$, then $I(*X(a),u,v)=X(a,v)$;
- if $a \in \mathcal{C}$, b - a list of parameters, then $I(*F(a,b),u,v)=$
$=F(a,I(b,u,v),u)$;
- if $a,b \in \mathcal{D}$, then $I(*PEXT(a,b),u,v)=PEXT(I(a,u,v),\overline{I}(b,u,v),$
$I(b,u,v))$, where function $\overline{I}$ differs from I by and only by the fact that we take conjugate functions when computing the suspended references to primitive, COND and F functions;
- if $a,b,c \in \mathcal{D}$, then $I(*COND(a,b,c),u,v)=COND(I(a,u,v),\overline{I}(b,u,v),$
$\overline{I}(c,u,v),I(b,u,v),I(c,u,v))$.

Since function F is defined recursively via functions $F_1,\ldots,F_m$ of the S scheme, function I is also associated with the concrete scheme of a program. More exactly, function I is defined via components F and $\overline{F}$ of the least fixpoint of scheme S of the form (14).

8. PRINCIPLE OF PARTIAL COMPUTATION
   FOR CLASS OF RECURSIVE SCHEMES

A ratio $\sim\!|$ may be introduced on set $\mathcal{D}^{\omega}$, that will be referred to as a "less defined or like". Without giving the exact definition, we will note the basic property of this ratio. Suppose $a \sim\!| b$. In this case, if $a \in \mathcal{C}$, then a=b, and if $b \in \mathcal{C}$, then $a \subseteq b$.

Suppose S - a scheme of program of the form (14) on $\mathcal{D}^{\omega}$, h and g - lists of the names of some functions of this program, f=APP(h,g) - a merged list of names, x^o and y^o - lists of the parameters-constants, $w=CONL(x^o,y^o)$ - a merged list of parameters. Then

$$H(f,w) \sim\!| I(H(h,x^o),f,y^o) \tag{15}$$

Suppose x and y - lists of parameters, $t=CONL(I(x,f,y),y)$. Then

$$\forall r \in \mathcal{D}\ I(r,f,t) \sim\!\mid I(I(r,h,x),f,y) \qquad\qquad (16)$$

The statement (15) - is a principle of partial computation for a class of recursive programs on $\mathcal{D}^{\omega}$. The ratio (16) expresses the property of associativity of function I. It resembles (5), but the right side contains t=CONL(I(x,f,y),y) instead of CONL(x,y), that is, for a one-fold execution, it is necessary first to compute the list of parameters x.

Apparently, the conditions of (6) and (7) are required also for the execution of (15) and (16). The sufficient conditions are also obtained which impose some additional constraints on the methods of constructing primitive functions. Note that if a SUSP reference is used in a program only as a first argument of PEXT function, then the mixed computation of this program is associative.

9.   USE OF GLOBAL UNKNOWNS

Let us include the suspended references of *FT(a,b) form in $\mathcal{D}$, where a $\in \mathcal{C}$,b - a list of parameters. Add the program scheme to a definition of function FT.

$$FT(\alpha,\beta,\varphi,\widehat{\varsigma}) = \underline{if}\ NOF(\alpha,\varphi)\ \underline{then}\ SFT(\alpha,CONL(\beta,\widehat{\varsigma}))\qquad \underline{else}$$
$$\qquad\qquad if\ IS(\alpha,s_1)\ \underline{then}\ F_1(\varphi,CONL(\beta,\widehat{\varsigma}))\qquad \underline{else}$$
$$\qquad\qquad \bullet\bullet\bullet$$
$$\qquad\qquad \underline{if}\ IS(\alpha,s_{m-1})\ \underline{then}\ F_{m-1}(\varphi,CONL(\beta,\widehat{\varsigma}))\quad \underline{else}$$
$$\qquad\qquad F_m(\varphi,CONL(\beta,\widehat{\varsigma}))\quad \underline{end}\ \bullet\bullet\bullet\ \underline{end}\ \underline{end}$$

Here, the special base function SFT realizes the suspension of FT reference: SFT(a,b)=*FT(a,b). The macrodefinition of conjugate function $\overline{FT}$:

$$\overline{FT}(\alpha,\beta,\varphi,\widehat{\varsigma}) = SFT(\alpha,CONL(\beta,\widehat{\varsigma}))$$

A rule $\mathcal{R}$(*FT(a,b))=FT(a,$\mathcal{R}$(b),φ,$\widehat{\varsigma}$) is added to transformation $\mathcal{R}$. We have also I(*FT(a,b),u,v)=FT(a,I(b,u,v),u,v).

If during the computation of *FT reference for the value of an unknown no corresponding parameter is found in the *FT reference second argument value, the search is continued in the fourth argument value - in a list of parameters used to compute the preceding function. Because of this, there is no need to write

out the parameters relating to global unknowns. On the contrary,
an addition requirement is placed upon the *F(a,b) references so
that at $a=s_k$ the b list contains parameters for all unknowns
present not only in r_k but in the r_i bodies of all functions
transitively accessible from r_k via the *FT references. Now in
contrast to the scheme (14), the computation result may contain
unknowns not only from r_1 but from the bodies of other functions
of the program that are referred through function FT. The F reference in the initial function definition (11) is naturally replaced with FT.

The transit of parameters realized with the help of function FT
nears the recursive program execution to a computation with the
memory. The similar unknowns dynamically associated with the FT
references correspond to one global object. The list of parameters is analogous to a group assignment and plays a role of the
memory state but operates on a stack principle: on completing
the computation of a reference the assignments generated by the
latter are cancelled and the previous state of memory is restored. That is why there are no side effects. After resumption, the
*F reference does not contain argument $\frac{\zeta}{i}$, that is, it closes
the access to an old state of the stack of parameters until the
computation of this reference value is completed.

10.   RETURN SUSPENSION

The return suspension idea also has the sources in the INCOL
language and system. The language incorporates an aid for specifying the so-called internal threshold conditions, and in case
of violating them, the function computation is terminated and
its reference is restored in the solution. The system of programming also contains a means for abnormal termination of the
current function computation when the accessible working storage
is exhausted. In this case, provision is made for restoration of
initial reference in the solution and continuation of the computations.

Let us introduce a new ordinary base function PINT and special
base functions BACK and BACKT. The suspension fact is registered
with the help of a special value Θ by which we will extend the
region of function definitions: $\mathcal{D}^{\omega\Theta}=\mathcal{D}^{\omega}\cup\{\Theta\}$. This value is gene-

rated by the PINT function only and is consumed only by the
BACK and BACKT functions. When being an argument of any other
base function, Θ makes its value to be equal to Θ (provided
there is no ω among the previous arguments). After getting argument Θ, the BACK and BACKT functions restore the *F or *FT
references respectively. Note that with the introduction of value Θ, the base functions cease to be naturally extended but
remain monotonic.

Define function PINT(a,b): PINT$(\omega,b)=\omega$, PINT(*YES,b)=b; in
other cases, PINT(a,b)=Θ. Although the PINT function is not
suspended, we will include the *PINT(a,b) references in $\mathcal{D}$ for
a use when composing the program. Apparently, $\overline{PINT} \equiv PINT$.

The BACK and BACKT special functions absorb value Θ: at $a \neq \Theta$
BACK(a,b,c)=BACKT(a,b,c)=a; if $b \in \mathcal{C}$,c - a list of parameters,
then BACK(Θ,b,c)=*F(b,c),BACKT(Θ,b,c)=*FT(b,c). In macrodefinitions F and FT, the references of defined functions are enclosed
in the BACK and BACKT references:

... <u>if</u> IS(α,s_i) <u>then</u> BACK$(F_i(\varphi,\beta),s_i,\beta)$ <u>else</u> ...
... <u>if</u> IS(α,s_i) <u>then</u> BACKT$(F_i(\varphi,CONL(\beta,\overline{\varphi})),s_i,CONL(\beta,\overline{\varphi}))$ <u>else</u>...

Thus, if during the computation of the body of one of defined
functions F_i we execute the PINT reference in which the first
argument value differs from *YES, then the result of F_i function computation will be a suspended *F or *FT reference with the
first argument s_i which has generated the reference to function
F_i.

The introduction of value Θ results in a change of the associativity formula (16):

$$\forall r \in \mathcal{D} \ I(r,f,t) \sim |I(I(r,h,x),f,y) \vee I(r,h,x) = \Theta$$

11. GENERATION OF NAMES

Introduce the *PR1(a,b) form references where $a,b \in \mathcal{D}$ into $\mathcal{D}$ and
add the following macrodefinition to scheme S:

PR1(α,β) = <u>if</u> IS(α,z_{11}) <u>then</u> $z_{11}(\beta)$ <u>else</u>
$\qquad \bullet \bullet \bullet$
$\qquad$ <u>if</u> IS(α,z_{1k}) <u>then</u> $z_{1k}(\beta)$ <u>else</u>

$$\text{SPR1}(\alpha,\beta) \ \underline{\text{end}} \cdots \underline{\text{end}}$$

Here, $z_{11},\ldots,z_{1k}$ - the names of unary primitive functions from $\mathcal{P}$. Special base function SPR1 is realizing the computation of primitive with a suspended name: at $a \in \mathcal{D}\backslash\mathcal{C}$, $b \in \mathcal{D}$ SPR1(a,b)= =*PR1(a,b). The macrodefinition PR2(α,β,γ) and special function SPR2 are introduced analogously.

Now, apart from the standard primitive function references we can include into the program the *PR1 and *PR2 macroreferences ensuring the computation of a primitive function name. The macrodefinitions of conjugate functions $\overline{\text{PR1}}$ and $\overline{\text{PR2}}$ use the names of conjugate primitive functions.

To enable the generation of names of the unknowns, include all the *X(a) form references at $a \in \mathcal{D}$ in $\mathcal{D}$. Assume that $\mathcal{R}(*\text{X}(a))=$ $=\text{X}(\mathcal{R}(a),\widetilde{\varsigma})$; I(*X(a),u,v)=X(I(a,u,v),v). Extend function X for $a \in \mathcal{D}\backslash\mathcal{C}$ at $b \in \mathcal{D}$ by taking X(a,b)=Θ. Now, we can include the unknowns whose names represent expressions into the program. If during the computation of an unknown its name turns out to be suspended, it is performed a return suspension of the last *FT reference under processing in order to preserve the list of parameters where the value of unknown is to be retrieved for a subsequent restoration.

The possibility of generating the name of a function whose reference to be performed, as well as the list of parameters is realized during the computation by including all the *FT(a,b) form references where a,b$\in \mathcal{D}$ into $\mathcal{D}$. Such an extension for the *F reference is not allowed, since it would disable the completeness of a list of parameters to be checked until the program is executed. To simplify such an analysis in the bodies of functions for which there are *F type references in the program, one may prohibit the use of *FT and *X references with a suspended name, that is, the use of procedures - *F references is confined to the procedures-functions. Suppose that $\mathcal{R}(*\text{FT}(a,b))=\text{FT}(\mathcal{R}(a),$ $\mathcal{R}(b),\gamma,\widetilde{\varsigma})$ and I(*FT(a,b),u,v)=FT(I(a,u,v),I(b,u,v),u,v) and add checking the suspension of arguments to the macrodefinition of function FT:

$$\text{FT}(\alpha,\beta,\gamma,\widetilde{\varsigma})<=\underline{\text{if}} \ \text{OR(NOCF}(\alpha),\text{NOCL}(\beta)) \ \underline{\text{then}} \ \text{SFT}(\alpha,\text{CONL}(\beta,\widetilde{\varsigma})) \ \underline{\text{else}}\cdots$$

Here, special functions NOCF and NOCL check whether α is a constant and β is a list of parameters.

Note that introduced in sections 9-11 extensions of model do not violate (15).

12. NOTES ON REALIZATION

It follows from the definitions of function I and transformation $\mathcal{R}$ that functions F, FT and X ensure the substitution of parameters with a value. To realize the modelled language, one may construct an interpretation algorithm similar to [13]. As opposed to the rules for computing of recursive schemes theory, this algorithm is recursive and not iterative, and enables the computation of a defined function reference in one look through its body without resimplifications. It can be shown that this algorithm is equivalent to the call by value rule of computation.

13. CONCLUSIONS

The described model of language semantics provides various possibilities of the correct and safe mixed computation with the means for suspension control. The necessary conditions of the mixed execution associativity of primitive operations are given. The analogous means can be used in the other mixed evaluators for the optimization of residual programs.

REFERENCES

[1] Lombardy, L.A., Incremental Computation, in: Alt, F.L. and Rubinoff, M., (eds.), Advances in Computers (N.Y., Academic Press, 1967, Vol. 8) pp. 247-333.

[2] Babich, G.Kh., Shternberg, L.F. and Youganova, T.I., The INCOL Programming Language for Incomplete Information Computation, Programmirovanie (1976, No.4) pp. 24-32 (in Russian).

[3] Babich, G.Kh., et al., The INCOL Programming System for Incomplete Information Computation, Upravlayushchie sistemy i Mashiny (Control Systems and Machines. 1982, No. 4) pp. 97-101 (in Russian).

[4] Babich, G.Kh., Decision Making by Analysis of Decision Tree with Incomplete Information, Kybernetika (1986, No. 5) pp. 113-120 (in Russian).

[5] Youganova, T.I., Mixed Computation Correctness: INCOL Language Example, Programmirovanie (1987, No. 2) pp. 67-77 (in Russian).

[6] Manna, Z., Mathematical Theory of Computation (N.Y.; McGraw-Hill, 1974).

[7] Ershov, A.P., Mixed Computation in the Class of Recursive
     Program Shemata, Acta Cybernetica (1978, Vol. 4, No. 1)
     pp. 19-23.
[8] Ershov, A.P., and Itkin, V.E., Correctness of Mixed Computa-
     tion in Algol-like Programs, in: Gruska, J., (ed.), Mathe-
     matical Foundations of Computer Science (LNCS, Springer-Ver-
     lag, 1977, Vol. 53) pp. 59-77.
[9] Ershov, A.P., Mixed Computation: Potencial Applications and
     Problems for Study, Theoretical Computer Science (1982, No.
     18) pp. 41-67.
[10] Trakhtenbrot, M.B., On Transformations Which Complete Pro-
     gram Definition, Kybernetika (1980, No. 2) pp. 55-60 (in
     Russian).
[11] Henderson, P., Functional Programming: Application and Im-
     plementation (Prentice Hall, 1980).
[12] Itkin, V.E., Program Parallelization Algebra, in: Theoreti-
     cal and Applied Aspects of Parallel Information Processing
     (Novosibirsk, Computing Center, 1984) pp. 3-16 (in Russian).
[13] Shternberg, L.F., Economical Algorithms of INCOL Algorith-
     mic Language Interpretation, Kybernetika (1977, No. 1)
     pp. 69-74 (in Russian).

Partial Evaluation and Mixed Computation
D. Bjørner, A.P. Ershov and N.D. Jones (Editors)
Elsevier Science Publishers B.V. (North-Holland)
© IFIP, 1988

Experience with A Type Evaluator

Jonathan Young   Patrick O'Keefe
Yale University   ICAD, Inc.
Department of Computer Science

Abstract

In this paper we discuss our recent experience with a type evaluator for a lazy, side-effect-free language. We develop a type system for the language and define the properties of *safety* and *precision* for type evaluators. We exhibit a safe type semantics and increase the precision (and conciseness) of its implementation by means of such techniques as *depth bounding*, *fixpoint iteration*, *circularizing*, and *generalization*.

1 Introduction

For the past year, we have been developing a programming environment based on a side-effect-free, lazy dialect of Scheme [5]. We have written a type evaluator for this language which propagates constants and types through a program in the same way a partial evaluator does. In fact, many of the techniques we present in this paper are also used in the partial evaluator for the same programming environment.

The output of the type evaluator is a type which represents a subset of the value domain. In the presence of complete information, the type evaluator may act as an interpreter for the language, returning a type which corresponds to exactly one element from the value domain. The types output are useful for program optimization, testing user type assertions, and for presenting type information to programmers.

The primary goal of the type evaluator is to guarantee safety, that is, the type of an expression includes all values of the expression under the standard semantics. Another goal is precision; it tries not to lose information. Other goals of the type evaluator are conciseness, efficiency and termination. The language permits circular and infinite data structures; the type evaluator always produces finite type representations for such structures. For example, the type inferred for (map1+ x), where map1+ is the function which adds one to every element of an infinite list and x is unknown, is the (circular) type representing an infinite list of numbers. On the other hand, the type evaluator does not attempt to judge whether programs are "well-typed" – that is, it never rejects programs even if they contain run-time type errors.

Damas and Milner [2] propose a polymorphic type inferencing algorithm which is unsatisfactory for our purposes. Damas and Milner's system rejects programs which it cannot prove to be free from all run-time type errors. Variables bound in a lambda abstraction must receive the same type at all their occurrences, and both arms of a conditional must unify to the same type. This excludes some useful programming styles available in untyped languages. For example, a simple sort of object-oriented style could be achieved as follows:

```
(define make-automobile
  (lambda (color cylinders)
    (lambda (message)
      (case message
        (color color)           ;;; a symbol
        (cylinders cylinders)   ;;; a number
        ...
      ))))
```

Automobile objects could be created by expressions like

$$\text{(define my-car (make-automobile 'blue 4)),}$$

and messages sent with expressions like

$$\text{(my-car 'color).}$$

Objects such as my-car do not have a well-defined type in the Damas-Milner scheme. (See Wand [6] and Cardelli [1] for recent work in strongly typed object-oriented languages.)

In the rest of this paper we present the syntax and semantics of our lazy language, we develop a type domain and a safe type semantics, and we implement the semantics and augment the implementation by means of such techniques as *depth bounding*, *fixpoint iteration*, *circularizing*, and *generalization*.

2   Syntax and Standard Semantics

Our language, a lazy dialect of Scheme [5], includes as base values numbers, booleans, and *nil*. In addition, pairs of values are allowed, as well as functions from values to values. The abstract syntax of our language is as follows:

$$
\begin{array}{lll}
i & \in & Id \qquad\qquad\qquad \text{Identifiers}\\
e & \in & Exp \qquad\qquad\quad \text{Expressions}\\
n & \in & Num \qquad\qquad\; \text{Numerals}\\[2mm]
e & ::= & i\,|\,n\,|\\
  &   & \text{(IF e1 e2 e3)}\,| \qquad \text{Primitive conditional}\\
  &   & \text{(LAMBDA i e)}\,| \qquad\;\; \text{Lambda abstraction}\\
  &   & \text{(e1 e2)}\,| \qquad\qquad\;\; \text{Function application}\\
  &   & \text{(LETREC i e1 e2)}\,| \quad \text{Recursive definition}\\
  &   & \text{(CONS e1 e2)}\,| \qquad\; \text{Pair constructor}\\
  &   & \text{(FIRST e)}\,|\\
  &   & \text{(REST e)}
\end{array}
$$

In addition to the primitive syntax, we include several primitive functions, including NIL, FALSE, TRUE, PAIR?, NULL?, +, and NUMBER?. Note that this is not an exhaustive list; we expect that the meaning of the primitive functions we use will be clear from the context.

All functions in this language take one argument; operations such as + which usually take two arguments are *curried*. For convenience, we will write (f a b) for ((f a) b).

We now present a standard semantics for our language. Let *Bool* be the flat domain[1] of booleans containing *true* and *false*, *Nat* the flat domain of natural numbers, and *Nil* the flat domain containing *nil*. Then the domain of denotable values is $D = Tr + Nil + [Nat]_\perp + [D \times D]_\perp + [D \to D]_\perp$, where $+$ is the "smash" sum and $[D]_\perp$ is D "lifted" with a new element ($\perp$) attached to the bottom[2]. The semantic equations are written in a notational variant of the untyped lambda calculus in which $env[e/\mathbf{x}]$ represents the environment which maps $\mathbf{x}$ to e and otherwise behaves like env, $e = \langle e_1, e_2 \rangle$ is a pair satisfying the axioms $fst\ e = e_1$ and $snd\ e = e_2$, and WHEREREC denotes the least fixpoint of the the recursive definition which it introduces.

The derived domains and semantic equations are as follows:

$$
\begin{aligned}
env \in Env &= Id \to D \\
E &: Exp \to Env \to D \\
N &: Num \to Nat
\end{aligned}
$$

$$
\begin{aligned}
E[\![\mathbf{i}]\!]env &= env[\![\mathbf{i}]\!] \\
E[\![\mathbf{n}]\!]env &= N[\![\mathbf{n}]\!] \\
E[\![(\mathtt{IF\ e1\ e2\ e3})]\!]env &= \mathrm{IF}\ E[\![\mathtt{e1}]\!]env \\
&\quad\ \mathrm{THEN}\ E[\![\mathtt{e2}]\!]env \\
&\quad\ \mathrm{ELSE}\ E[\![\mathtt{e3}]\!]env \\
E[\![(\mathtt{LAMBDA\ i\ e})]\!]env &= \lambda d.E[\![\mathtt{e}]\!]env[d/\mathtt{i}] \\
E[\![(\mathtt{e1\ e2})]\!]env &= (E[\![\mathtt{e1}]\!]env)\ (E[\![\mathtt{e2}]\!]env) \\
E[\![(\mathtt{LETREC\ i\ e1\ e2})]\!]env &= E[\![\mathtt{e2}]\!]env' \\
&\quad\ \mathrm{WHEREREC}\ env' = env[(E[\![\mathtt{e1}]\!]env')/\mathtt{i}] \\
E[\![(\mathtt{CONS\ e1\ e2})]\!]env &= \langle E[\![\mathtt{e1}]\!]env, E[\![\mathtt{e2}]\!]env \rangle \\
E[\![(\mathtt{FIRST\ e})]\!]env &= fst\ (E[\![\mathtt{e}]\!]env) \\
E[\![(\mathtt{REST\ e})]\!]env &= snd\ (E[\![\mathtt{e}]\!]env)
\end{aligned}
$$

Note that fst, snd, and all the other functions used in the above semantic equations must be monotonic. Although type errors are ignored in the above semantics, our implementation in fact signals an error in this case.

3   Type System

In order to propagate values of different types, we construct the type domain by partitioning the values of D into disjoint sets. The reserved value "$*$" is used as a placeholder when no elements from the partition are present; "$\#$" is the token which represents all natural numbers. Our type domain is:

$$
T = [[\{true\}]_* \times [\{false\}]_* \times [\{nil\}]_* \times [Nat]_*^{\#} \times [T \times T]_* \times [T \to T]_*]_{\perp_T}^{\top_T}
$$

Define T_{true}, T_{false}, T_{nil}, T_{nat}, T_{prod}, and T_{fn} to be the appropriate projections from T. We also write in_T for the appropriate injection function into T, which should be apparent from the context.

Proposition 1 *The domain T is a complete lattice under $\sqsubseteq$ (induced from the domain equation), with $\vee$ as binary least upper bound and $\wedge$ as binary greatest lower bound.*

---

[1]All domains in this paper are pointed complete partial orders.

[2]We will also use the notation $[D]^\top$ for D "capped" with a new element $\top$ attached to the top.

Define $\tau : D \to T$ as follows:

$$
\begin{aligned}
\tau(\bot) &= \bot_T \\
\tau(true) &= \langle true, *, *, *, *, * \rangle \\
\tau(false) &= \langle *, false, *, *, *, * \rangle \\
\tau(nil) &= \langle *, *, nil, *, *, * \rangle \\
\tau(n) &= \langle *, *, *, n, *, * \rangle \\
\tau(\langle d_1, d_2 \rangle) &= \langle *, *, *, *, \langle \tau(d_1), \tau(d_2) \rangle, * \rangle \\
\tau(d) &= \langle *, *, *, *, *, t \rangle \\
&\quad \text{where} \quad t = \lambda t'. \bigsqcup_{\tau(d') \sqsubseteq t'} \tau(d\ d') \\
&\quad \text{if} \ \ d \in D \to D
\end{aligned}
$$

Extend τ to functions from $D^n \to D$ as follows:

$$
\tau(f)(t_1, \ldots, t_n) = \bigsqcup_{\tau(d_i) \sqsubseteq t_i} \tau f(d_1, \ldots, d_n)
$$

When $d \in D$ and $t \in T$ we say that $d :: t$ (d is represented by t) if $\tau(d) \sqsubseteq t$.

Proposition 2 τ is a homomorphism from D to T.

Proposition 3 (Downward Closure on D) If $d_1, d_2 \in D$, $t \in T$, $d_1 \sqsubseteq d_2$, and $d_2 :: t$, then $d_1 :: t$. In fact, the set $\{d | d :: t\}$ is an ideal[3] in D.

Proposition 4 (Upward Closure on T) If $d \in D$, $t_1, t_2 \in T$, $t_1 \sqsubseteq t_2$, and $d :: t_1$, then $d :: t_2$. Thus, $t_1 \sqsubseteq t_2$ just when $\{d | d :: t_1\} \subseteq \{d | d :: t_2\}$.

We are now ready to define the safety property for type evaluators.

Let $Tenv : Id \to T$. A *type evaluator* is a function $\mathcal{T} : Exp \to Tenv \to T$ which gives a type to every expression given the type information contained in *tenv*. A type evaluator is *precise* if it is correct on all inputs – that is, for all $\mathbf{exp}$ and *env*, $\tau(E[\![\mathbf{exp}]\!]env) = \mathcal{T}[\![\mathbf{exp}]\!]\tau(env)$. This is clearly impossible to achieve in the general case. Instead, we require only that our type evaluator be *safe*. A type t is *safe* for a value d if $d :: t$. Similarly, a type environment *tenv* is safe for *env* if for all $\mathbf{x}$, $tenv[\![\mathbf{x}]\!]$ is safe for $env[\![\mathbf{x}]\!]$. A type evaluator $\mathcal{T}$ is *safe* if for all $\mathbf{exp}$, when *tenv* is safe for *env*, $(\mathcal{T}[\![\mathbf{exp}]\!]tenv)$ is safe for $(E[\![\mathbf{exp}]\!]env)$. In other words, the type returned by the type evaluator must include the actual value returned by the standard semantics.

4   Type Semantics

The most trivial safe type evaluator is $\mathcal{T}[\![\mathbf{exp}]\!]tenv = \top_T$. We now present a type semantics which is in some sense the best (i.e. weakest) safe approximation to the type of the expression given the

---

[3]An *ideal* of D is a subset of D which is both downward closed and consistently closed. The concept of *types as ideals* has been developed by MacQueen and Sethi[4,3].

information in the type environment.

$$
\begin{aligned}
Tenv &= Id \rightarrow T \\
\mathcal{T} &: Exp \rightarrow Tenv \rightarrow T
\end{aligned}
$$

$$
\begin{aligned}
\mathcal{T}[\![\mathtt{i}]\!]tenv &= tenv[\![\mathtt{i}]\!] \\
\mathcal{T}[\![\mathtt{n}]\!]tenv &= in_T(N[\![\mathtt{n}]\!]) \\
\mathcal{T}[\![(\mathtt{IF\ e1\ e2\ e3})]\!]tenv &= (\text{IF}\ \ true :: (\mathcal{T}[\![\mathtt{e1}]\!]tenv) \\
&\qquad \text{THEN}\ (\mathcal{T}[\![\mathtt{e2}]\!]tenv)\ \text{ELSE}\ \bot_T) \\
&\quad \vee \\
&\quad (\text{IF}\ \ false :: (\mathcal{T}[\![\mathtt{e1}]\!]tenv) \\
&\qquad \text{THEN}\ (\mathcal{T}[\![\mathtt{e3}]\!]tenv)\ \text{ELSE}\ \bot_T) \\
\mathcal{T}[\![(\mathtt{LAMBDA\ i\ e})]\!]tenv &= in_T(\lambda v.\mathcal{T}[\![\mathtt{e}]\!]tenv[v/\mathtt{i}]) \\
\mathcal{T}[\![(\mathtt{e1\ e2})]\!]tenv &= T_{fn}(\mathcal{T}[\![\mathtt{e1}]\!]tenv)\ (\mathcal{T}[\![\mathtt{e2}]\!]tenv) \\
\mathcal{T}[\![(\mathtt{LETREC\ i\ e1\ e2})]\!]tenv &= \mathcal{T}[\![\mathtt{e2}]\!]tenv' \\
&\quad \text{WHEREREC}\ tenv' = tenv[(\mathcal{T}[\![\mathtt{e1}]\!]tenv')/\mathtt{i}] \\
\mathcal{T}[\![(\mathtt{CONS\ e1\ e2})]\!]tenv &= in_T\langle\mathcal{T}[\![\mathtt{e1}]\!]tenv, \mathcal{T}[\![\mathtt{e2}]\!]tenv\rangle \\
\mathcal{T}[\![(\mathtt{FIRST\ e})]\!]tenv &= fst\ (T_{prod}(\mathcal{T}[\![\mathtt{e}]\!]tenv)) \\
\mathcal{T}[\![(\mathtt{REST\ e})]\!]tenv &= snd\ (T_{prod}(\mathcal{T}[\![\mathtt{e}]\!]tenv))
\end{aligned}
$$

The proof that $\mathcal{T}$ is safe is by structural induction on *exp*. In the special case where everything is known (there is some *env* such that $tenv = \tau(env)$), $\mathcal{T}$ is also *precise*, and thus the weakest safe approximation.

The base type environment for our language includes, for example, assertions that NIL is of type $in_T(nil)$, and PAIR? is of type

$$
\begin{aligned}
\lambda t.\ &(\text{IF there exists a pair}\ \langle d_1, d_2\rangle :: t\ \text{THEN}\ \ in_T(true)\ \text{ELSE}\ \bot_T) \\
&\vee \\
&(\text{IF there exists a non-pair}\ d :: t\ \text{THEN}\ \ in_T(false)\ \text{ELSE}\ \bot_T).
\end{aligned}
$$

5 Implementation Considerations

A straightforward implementation of the above semantics, however, will diverge under many circumstances. For instance, if an expression denotes $\bot$, the implementation will sometimes diverge (rather than return $\bot_T$) since this is undecidable. In addition, it is not always possible to compute exactly the union or intersection of two infinite types. In order to ensure termination of our type evaluator, we increment a counter on recursive calls to $\mathcal{T}$ and when performing applications in the T domain. When the counter exceeds a threshold, we return $\top_T$ as the result of the whole computation. This is always safe, but compromises the precision of the type evaluator. The rest of this paper will be devoted to approximation techniques which continue to conserve termination and ensure safety but increase the precision and conciseness of the computed type.

When the initial type environment contains incomplete information, the implementation of the above type semantics often gets caught in an infinite (stopped only by the depth bound) loop, particularly when inferring the type of a recursive application. For instance, if we define **fac** by

```
(define fac
  (lambda (n)
    (if (zero? n)
        1
        (* n (fac (- n 1)))))))
```

then the computation of $T[\![(\text{fac } x)]\!]tenv$ where $tenv[\![x]\!] = in_T(\#)$ diverges.[4] We also place a depth bound on the number of recursive calls to a given function (e.g. `fac`) which will be expanded before we give up and approximate the result of that recursive call by $\top_T$. This is better than exceeding the global depth bound, because we continue to compute with the approximate value – in this case, we compute $T[\![(\text{fac } x)]\!]tenv = in_T(\#)$, a reasonable result.

Note that this is a *meta* argument - we are reasoning about the recursive nature of the type evaluator T. In practice, these depth bounds could be achieved in many ways: we could look at the stack and count the pending calls to T or we could pass an effective "stack" as another argument to T. The same is true of many of the techniques developed below.

5.1   Convergence

We can do even better in the case of `nth`, the function which returns the nth element of the list l. We represent the two arguments to `nth` as a pair; `(lambda (<n, 1>) ...)` is syntactic sugar for the appropriate destructuring operations.

```
(define nth
  (lambda (<n, 1>)
    (if (= n 0)
        (first 1)
        (nth <(- n 1), (rest 1)>))))
```

If we know that `n` is a number and `1` is an infinite list of numbers (i.e. that $tenv[\![n]\!] = in_T(\#)$ and $tenv[\![1]\!] = t$, where $t = in_T\langle in_T(\#), t\rangle$), then $T[\![(\text{nth } <n, 1>)]\!]tenv$ diverges. The recursion depth bound forces a returned value of $\top_T$ from the recursive application of `nth`, so the computed type for $T[\![(\text{nth } <n, 1>)]\!]tenv$ is also $\top_T$. By symbolic evaluation, however, we find that

$$T[\![(\text{nth } <in_T(\#), \ t>)]\!]tenv = in_T(\#) \lor T[\![(\text{nth } <in_T(\#), \ t>)]\!]tenv$$

This recursive type equation has the solution

$$T[\![(\text{nth } <in_T(\#), \ t>)]\!]tenv = in_T(\#).$$

We will try to solve this recursive equation if we discover *convergence* – if, in the process of evaluating the type of a function application, we encounter a recursive application *provably equivalent* to the previous application.

First, consider what would happen if we expand the application `(nth <n, 1>)` normally except that we return some type s whenever T is called recursively on an application provably equivalent to it. The value returned is a function of s, say $f(s)$. Now, as described in [7], it is safe for us to

---

[4]For the rest of the paper, we say that the type evaluator *diverges* when the global counter is exceeded and the value $\top_T$ is returned.

return any fixpoint of f as the type of the expression. The most desirable fixpoint is the one with the most constraints - the *least* one. We calculate the successive approximations of the Kleene chain $(\perp, f(\perp), f(f(\perp)), \ldots)$, until a fixpoint is found. We call this well-known method for computing the least fixpoint of a recursive equation *fixpoint iteration*.

Note that our type domain does not satisfy the ascending chain condition: there exist chains of infinite height. This means that fixpoint iteration may not terminate in a finite number of steps. In practice, if a fixpoint is not found in a small number of steps, then we attempt to create a circular type.

5.2 Circular Types

For certain recursive type equations, although fixpoint iteration does not terminate in a finite number of steps, there exists a concise circular representation for a fixpoint of the equation which is a more precise result than $\top_T$.

```
(define map1+
  (lambda (l)
    (cons
      (1+ (first l))
      (map1+ (rest l))))))
```

The function map1+, which adds one to each element of an infinite list, is one example. The computation of $T[\![(\text{map1+ 1})]\!]tenv$, with $tenv[\![1]\!] = \top_T$, converges, but the iterative technique does not find a fixpoint. The successive approximations are $\perp_T, in_T(\langle in_T(\#), \perp_T \rangle), in_T(\langle in_T(\#), in_T(\langle in_T(\#), \perp_T \rangle) \rangle), \ldots$. In this case, we are computing the fixpoint of the recursive type equation

$$T[\![(\text{map1+ 1})]\!]tenv = in_T(\langle in_T(\#), T[\![(\text{map1+ 1})]\!]tenv \rangle).$$

A solution to this equation is the circular type

$$t = in_T(\langle in_T(\#), t \rangle).$$

It is possible to construct this circular type: when a recursive application is encountered which is provably equivalent to a pending application, we may return the same value from both the recursive and the pending applications, thereby creating a cycle. Under certain circumstances, however, the value of the circular type may be needed in order to compute it. Since this would result in an infinite loop, we attempt circularization only when we can prove that a constructor (e.g. a pair or function abstraction) occurs within the cycle and that no strict primitive could access the circular value.

5.3 Generalization

It is still the case that some recursive functions do not converge – each recursive application is slightly different, and the above techniques do not apply. Consider tail-length, the tail recursive version of length, which counts the number of elements in a list l.

```
(define tail-length
  (lambda (l)
    (letrec tl
      (lambda (<l, n>)
        (if (null? l)
            n
            (tl <(rest l), (+ 1 n)>)))
      (tl <l, 0>)))))
```

When evaluating $\mathcal{T}[\![(\texttt{tail-length l})]\!]tenv$ with $tenv[\![\texttt{l}]\!] = \top_T$, we successively apply $\texttt{tl}$ to $in_T(\langle\top_T, in_T(0)\rangle)$, $in_T(\langle\top_T, in_T(1)\rangle)$, ..., etc. The global depth bound will be exceeded without convergence, so we cannot use any of the previous techniques for finding a fixpoint of a recursive equation. Before returning top, however, we attempt to find a type for a more general function application – in this case, $\texttt{tl}$ applied to $in_T(\langle\top_T, in_T(\#)\rangle)$. This is safe, since it must result in a more general type than the original application. In addition, it may result in convergence and a more precise type than simply $\top_T$. In this case, we compute the type of $(\texttt{tail-length l})$ to be $in_T(\#)$.

The more general function application is created from some of the pending applications of this function by heuristically combining the arguments of the applications to create a new "more general" argument. For example, if we generalize two types containing different numbers to a type containing $in_T(\#)$, then $in_T(\langle\top_T, n\rangle)$ and $in_T(\langle\top_T, n+1\rangle)$ are generalized to $in_T(\langle\top_T, in_T(\#)\rangle)$.

```
(define tail-reverse
  (lambda (l)
    (letrec tr
      (lambda (<l, acc>)
        (if (null? l)
            acc
            (tr <(rest l), (cons (hd l) acc)>)))
      (tr <l, nil>)))))
```

If we define the type constructor $list(t) = in_T\langle t, list(t)\rangle \vee in_T(nil)$ to be the type of a list of elements of type t of unknown length, terminated by nil, then when evaluating $\mathcal{T}[\![(\texttt{tail-reverse l})]\!]env$, where $env[\![\texttt{l}]\!] = list(in_T(\#))$, we successively apply $\texttt{tr}$ to

$in_T(\langle list(in_T(\#)), in_T(nil)\rangle)$,
$in_T(\langle list(in_T(\#)), in_T(\langle in_T(\#), in_T(nil)\rangle) \vee in_T(nil)\rangle)$,
$in_T(\langle list(in_T(\#)), in_T(\langle in_T(\#), in_T(\langle in_T(\#), in_T(nil)\rangle)\rangle)\rangle) \vee in_T(\langle in_T(\#), in_T(nil)\rangle) \vee in_T(nil)\rangle)$

etc. We generalize $in_T(\langle x, nil\rangle)$ and $in_T(nil)$ to $list(x)$, and as a result we converge when applying $\texttt{tr}$ to $in_T(\langle list(in_T(\#)), list(in_T(\#))\rangle)$. The computed type for $(\texttt{tail-reverse l})$ is $list(in_T(\#))$.

The proper choice of generalization function entails a trade-off between precision and successful convergence. If we overgeneralize, we may create a less constrained type than necessary. On the other hand, if the type we create is too constrained, the type evaluation still may not converge, and $\top_T$ may be the only safe answer.

6 Conclusions and Future Work

We have presented a safe type semantics, shown how to implement a type evaluator which always terminates and is faithful to the semantics, and extended the type evaluator in several ways. The techniques we use are primarily concerned with ensuring the termination of the evaluator in the presence of recursion and with the creation of concise, circular types. We have implemented all of these techniques and are generally pleased with the results.

There are several directions in which we would like to see this work extended. We anticipate extending the above type evaluator to do partial evaluation directly. In fact, the partial evaluator currently in use in our programming environment uses many of the same basic techniques presented in this paper. Other extensions include clarifying the formal basis of the type system, and improving our techniques for creating circular types and for generalizing types when we don't converge.

We would also like to extend our type evaluator to make use of *predicate* and *backward* information that may be available. Predicate information may be available when the predicate of a conditional constrains the types of variables within the consequent and alternate arms. For example, in the consequent of (IF (null? x) x 5), x is constrained to be null. Backward information occurs when an expression constrains the types of its sub-expressions. In (+ x 3), x is constrained to be a number. We are currently exploring ways to propagate this information.

References

[1] L. Cardelli. A semantics of multiple inheritance. *Information and Control*, to appear.

[2] L. Damas and R. Milner. Principle type schemes for functional languages. In *9th ACM Sym. on Prin. of Prog. Lang.*, ACM, August 1982.

[3] D. MacQueen, G. Plotkin, and R. Sethi. An ideal model for recursive polymorphic types. In *11th ACM Sym. on Prin. of Prog. Lang.*, pages 165–174, ACM, January 1984.

[4] D.B. MacQueen and R. Sethi. A semantic model of types for applicative languages. In *Sym. on LISP and Functional Progrmg.*, pages 243–252, ACM, August 1982.

[5] W. Clinger et al. *The Revised Revised Report on Scheme, or An UnCommon Lisp.* AI Memo 848, Massachusetts Institute of Technology, August 1985.

[6] M. Wand. Complete type inference for simple objects. In *Proc. 2nd IEEE Symp. on Logic in Computer Science*, to appear.

[7] J. Young and P. Hudak. *Finding fixpoints on function spaces.* Research Report YALEU/DCS/RR-505, Yale University, Department of Computer Science, November 1986.

Partial Evaluation and Mixed Computation
D. Bjørner, A.P. Ershov and N.D. Jones (Editors)
Elsevier Science Publishers B.V. (North-Holland)
© IFIP, 1988

Terminology

Ed.   Torben Mogensen.
       Carsten Kehler Holst.

Both at:
       Institute of Datalogy University of Copenhagen
       Universitetsparken 1
       DK-2100 København Ø
       electronic mail: ..!mcvax!freja!torbenm (kehler)

List of terms

Because of the small number of terms we have not tried to make a taxonomy.
Therefore what we present here is a list of terms with their definitions.The
definitions are as far as possible independent of any special programming
language. Auxilliary definitions that are specific to certain articles are not
included.

Notation

The notation L p v will be used for the result of executing the L-program p
with the input v. A language L is thus seen as a function that given a program
in that language and the input to it will produce its output. The notation
$<v_1,...,v_n>$ will be used to represent the tuple of the values $v_1,...,v_n$.

Autoprojector
   A synonym for a self-applicable partial evaluator.

Binding time
   The time at which a variable/expression is bound to a definite value. In
   partial evaluation variables bound (known) at partial evaluation time are
   called static as opposed to dynamic. (Alternativly the terms known and
   unknown are used)

Binding time analysis

> An algorithmic analysis that finds approximations of the binding times of variables/expressions in a program.

Call annotation

> Marking of calls to determine whether they should be suspended or unfolded.

Cogen

> Short for "Compiler Generator". Often used as the name of a compiler generator program.

Composition

> A strategy whereby an explicit definition of the composition of two functions is obtained from the definitions of these. That is, from the definitions (or programs) of f and g the definition of f o g is derived.

Computation of annotations

> A process that given a program and static characteristics (e.g. types) of some of its parts computes characteristics for other (or all) parts of the program.

Configuration

> An abstraction of a computation state, representing a set of states.

Constant folding / constant propagation

> Evaluating sub-expressions that only depend on constants.

Driving

> A strategy that force data structure selectors through a program. The purpose can be to move them to and cancel them with constructors, to collect them in groups or to move them into a configuration that is similar to a previous and by folding making a new recursive definition. The selectors are often in the form of patterns, so by instantiation the patterns will be forced through the program.

Dynamic

> A value or variable etc. which value is not known until a late binding time. See static.

Folding

Upon recognising that a configuration is similar to a previous configuration, a recursive definition can be made by defining a function or predicate denoting the previous configuration and making the new configuration into a call or reference to that definition. If the two configurations are not exactly identical a generalized definition encompassing both configurations can be made.

Futamura projections

The equations that specify how compilation and compiler generation can be done by partial evaluation of interpreters. Given an interpreter int for M written in L (defined by the equation M p v = L int <p,v>), an L program lp equivalent to the M program p can be obtained by the first Futamura projection: lp = L mix <int,p> . This is an easy consequence of the equation for partial evaluation (see there). By a similar reasoning a compiler m2l compiling from M to L can be obtained by the second Futamura projection: m2l = L mix <mix,int> $\Rightarrow$ lp = L m2l p . By the third Futamura projection you can make a compiler generator cogen that given an interpreter will produce a compiler: cogen = L mix <mix,mix> $\Rightarrow$ m2l = L cogen int .

Generalization

A strategy by which from the program (or definition) of the function f(x,a), where 'a' is a constant or a term occuring in the program, we derive the program for the function f(x,y). Often generalization allows recursive definitions where there would otherwise be infinite non-recursive definitions with different a´s.

Generating extension.

A generating extension of a program is a new program that given some input will produce the same residual program that is obtained by partially evaluating the original program with respect to this input. A generating extension of a program can be obtained by partially evaluating the partial evaluator with respect to the program. The generating extension of an interpreter is a compiler, as seen from the second Futamura projection.

Internal specialisation

Specialisation of components of a system to exploit their internal contexts of use while preserving overall system functionality.

Metasystem transition
>   Treating programs as data objects in a computation, thus going to a meta
>   level.

Meta Transformations
>   Program transformations for multi-level languages. Especially using
>   transformation rules that shift program fragments from the object/program
>   as data/run-time level to the meta/compile-time level.

Mixed Computation
>   A process that given a program and some data, will produce a new program
>   and new data, which will have the property that executing the original
>   program with the original data will give the same result as executing the new
>   program with the new data. As an equation: $L\ p_1\ v_1 = L\ p\ v$ where $<p_1,v_1>$
> $= L\ mc\ <p,v>$ where mc is a program that does mixed computation for the
>   language L.

Partial evaluation
>   A process that given a program and part of its input will produce a residual
>   program which when executed with the remaining input of the original
>   program will give the same result as the original program would if it was
>   executed with the complete input. Partial evaluation is also called projection.
>   Partial evaluation can be expressed by the equation $L\ (L\ mix\ <program,$
> $v_1,...,v_n>)\ <v_{n+1},\ ...\ ,v_m> = L\ program\ <v_1,...,v_n,v_{n+1},...,v_m>$ where mix is a
>   partial evaluator for the language L. A different way of stating the same is
>   that $resid = L\ mix\ <program,v_1,\ ...,v_n>$ implies $L\ resid\ <v_{n+1},...,v_m> =$
> $L\ program\ <v_1,...,v_n,v_{n+1},...,v_m>$.

Partially static value
>   A structured value that contains both static and dynamic parts.

Polyvariant
>   A term that is applied to algorithms for Partial evaluation, Mixed
>   computation and program specialisation, that produces the
>   residual/specialized programs a collection (poly) of variants of pieces of the
>   original program.

Program specialization

Transforming a program to exploit a stronger precondition. This is a special case of weakening. Partial evaluation can be expressed as a special case of program specialization.

Projection

Sometimes used as a synonym for partial evaluation.

Residual program

The program obtained by partial evaluation of the original program with respect to some of its input. Execution of the residual program will, given the remaining input produce the same result as execution of the original program would if it was given the complete input.

Roll-out

Successive unfoldings to obtain a (perhaps infinite) non-recursive tree equivalent to a recursive structure.

Stage of computation

A portion of a program distinguished from other parts of the program either by frequency of execution or by availability of parameter or environment values.

Staging transformation

Transformation techniques, such as partial evaluation, for shifting computations among stages to improve overall system performance. Examples include conventional frequency reduction, reduction-in-strength, and removal of interpretation levels (e.g. by reification or by partial evaluation).

Static

A value or a variable etc. which value is known at an early binding time. See dynamic.

Self-applicable partial evaluator

A partial evaluator that is written in the same language that it processes, giving the possibility of applying it to itself. Also called an autoprojector.

S-m-n theorem

> Theorem first stated by Kleene giving a key closure property of the class of
> (partial) recursive functions. Stated for programs (in a fixed language) it
> goes as follows: if p is a program with m+n arguments and a1 , ... , am are
> values then there is a program pa1...am of n arguments such that for any
> $b_1,...,b_n$: L p $a_1...a_m$ $<b_1,...,b_n>$ = L p $<a_1,...,a_m,b_1,...,b_n>$.

Supercompilation

> An algorithm combining driving, unfolding, folding and generalization.
> Supercompilation can perform partial evaluation, symbolic composition
> and other transformations.

Suspension

> In algorithms based on succesive unfolding, the unfolding will in some places
> be stopped (suspended). In such cases new definitions defining the suspended
> configurations must be made. Suspension can achieve results similar to those
> obtained by folding.

Tupling

> A strategy whereby the definition (or program) of $<f_1(x),...,f_n(x)>$ is
> obtained from the definitions of $f_1(x),...,f_n(x)$. The application of this
> strategy often improves efficency because the data x is visited only once, and
> common subcomputations are avoided.

Unfolding

> The substituting of a name by the structure it denotes. Most often used to
> describe the substitution of a function call with an instance of the definition of
> the function.

Variable splitting

> A transformation whereby a single variable from the original program may
> become several distinct variables in the residual program, each of which
> holds a part of the value of the original variable.

Weakening

> Program transformation induced by logical weakening of its postcondition
> and logical strengthening of its precondition.

Partial Evaluation and Mixed Computation
D. Bjørner, A.P. Ershov and N.D. Jones (Editors)
Elsevier Science Publishers B.V. (North-Holland)
© IFIP, 1988

589

Annotated Bibliography on
Partial Evaluation
and
Mixed Computation

Edited By

Peter Sestoft

DIKU, University of Copenhagen

Universitetsparken 1, DK-2100 Copenhagen Ø, Denmark

Alexander V. Zamulin

Computing Center, USSR Academy of Sciences

SU-630090 Novosibirsk, USSR

This bibliography originated as a literature list collected for the Workshop on Partial Evaluation and Mixed Computation. It contains references to all papers which are known to the editors and found closely relevant to the topic of this workshop. The bibliography includes papers in English, Russian, German, and Japanese; and it contains references to published papers as well as to theses and technical reports.

The English and German entries were collected primarily by Peter Sestoft and Harald Søndergaard, and the Russian ones by Alexander V. Zamulin. Dines Bjørner and Annie Rasmussen organized the solicitation of assistance from the authors of papers referenced. Most of the annotations are based on those suggested by the individual authors, while some were written by the editors. The editors want to thank the authors of papers and in particular the workshop participants for their help in the task of producing this bibliography.

References

[Abramov 82]   S.M. Abramov and N.V. Kondratjev. A Compiler Based on Partial
                  Evaluation. In *Problems of Applied Mathematics and Software Systems*,
                  pages 66–69, Moscow State University, Moscow, USSR, 1982. (in Rus-
                  sian).

                  The principles of a Refal optimizing compiler design based on mixed
                  computation methods are discussed. The configuration analysis module
                  which realizes mixed computation of a Refal program and checks for
                  infinite looping of the partial evaluator (i.e., the neighbourhood analysis)
                  is described in detail.

[Abramov 84]   S.M. Abramov. Using Neighbourhood Analysis for Software Testing. In
                  Various Aspects of Systems Programming, pages 125–129, Moscow State
                  Univ. Publ. House, USSR, 1984. (in Russian).

                  A method for software testing based on the use of the neighbourhood
                  analyzer vicon is described. The neighbourhood analyzer is in essence a
                  kind of monovariant partial evaluator which does metacomputation of
                  the given program on fully undefined data and usual computation on
                  fully defined data.

[Ambriola 85]   V. Ambriola, et al. Symbolic Semantics and Program Reduction. *IEEE
                  Transactions on Software Engineering*, SE-11(8):784–794, August 1985.

                  A class of symbolic constants is introduced to represent subsets of re-
                  cursively defined data domains. The data type operations are extended
                  to cope with symbolic constants, thus obtaining an intensional calculus
                  for sets. The ideas and results are exploited in a system for symbolic
                  evaluation of functional programs.

[Babich 72a]   G.Kh. Babich. DecAS — A Programming System for Simulation of In-
                  complete Information Processes. In *Computer Automation of Research*,
                  pages 41–45, Computing Center, Novosibirsk, USSR, 1972. (in Russian).

                  The design principles of the DecAS programming language are briefly
                  described.

[Babich 72b]   G.Kh. Babich and A.G. Arkadjev. Syntax and Interpretation Algo-
                  rithms for DecAS Algorithmic Language Primitives. *VNIKI "Tsvet-
                  metavtomatika" Woks*, (4):97–108, 1972. (in Russian).

                  The set of DecAS programming language primitives and the interpre-
                  tation algorithms in the programming system which implements this
                  language are described.

[Babich 74a]   G.Kh. Babich. An Algorithmic Language Interpreter. Author's Certifi-
                  cate N 446882. *The Official Journal of Discoveries, Inventions, Trade
                  Marks and Designs (USSR)*, (38), 1974. (in Russian).

                  The computer architecture which implements the DecAS programming
                  language interpretation algorithms in hardware is described. The lan-
                  guage is intended for mixed computation.

[Babich 74b]   G.Kh. Babich. The DecAS Programming Language for Decision Making in Incomplete Information Conditions and Its Interpretation Algorithms. *Kybernetika*, (2):61–71, 1974. (in Russian).

The syntax and semantics of the DecAS programming language, its interpretation algorithms, and the list-structure memory of the interpreter are described. An example of a DecAS program is given.

[Babich 75]   G.Kh. Babich. *Software for "Non-Ferrous Metallurgy" Management Information System with Incomplete Information.* Metallurgia Publ. House, Moscow, USSR, 1975. (in Russian).

The problems of constructing an automatic system which implements a man-machine dialogue for decision making under incomplete information conditions are discussed. The DecAS language for incomplete information systems and the programming methods for this language are described.

[Babich 76]   G.Kh. Babich, L.F. Sternberg and T.I. Youganova. The INCOL Programming Language for Incomplete Information Computation. *Programmirovanie*, (4):24–32, 1976. (in Russian).

The syntax and semantics of the programming language Incol are described. Incol is a descendant of the DecAS language previously published. An example of an Incol program is considered.

[Babich 82]   G.Kh. Babich, et al. The INCOL Programming Language for Incomplete Information Computation. *Upravlyayushchie Sistemy i Machiny (Control Systems and Machines)*, (4):97–101, 1982. (in Russian).

The development of a programming system for implementing the Incol language is described. Incol is intended for computation with incomplete information.

[Babich 86]   G.Kh. Babich. Decision Making by Analysis of Decision Trees with Incomplete Information. *Kybernetika*, (5):113–120, 1986. (in Russian).

A decision making method using a decision tree analysis is discussed. The method is intended for decision making with incomplete information. The design principles of the supporting programming system (written in Incol) are described.

[Barzdin 87]   G. Barzdin. Experiments with Mixed Computation. *Programmirovanie*, (1):30–43, 1987. (in Russian).

A method of compiler construction from an interpreter and the experiments with mixed computation which have led to this method are described.

[Barzdin 88]   G. Barzdin. Mixed Computation and Compiler Basis. In D. Bjørner, A.P. Ershov and N.D. Jones, editors, *Partial Evaluation and Mixed Computation*, North-Holland, 1988. (This volume).

A two-phase method of constructing a compiler from an interpreter is described. In the first phase, a so-called compiler basis is obtained, and in the second phase the compiler proper is obtained from the compiler basis by means of a global analysis.

[Beckman 76]   L. Beckman, et al. A Partial Evaluator, and Its Use as a Programming Tool. *Artificial Intelligence*, 7(4):319–357, 1976.

The paper describes partial evaluation as a practical tool in program development. It defines the concepts and discusses a number of applications. A partial evaluator program Redfun and a partial evaluator compiler Redcompile are described.

[Belostotsky 81]   A.N. Belostotsky and L.L. Sushentsov. Implementing Mixed Computation. In *Compilation Methods*, Computing Center, Novosibirsk, USSR, 1981. (in Russian).

The realization of mixed computation of programs in the stack computer Elbrus is described. The tagged memory of this computer is beneficial in making this procedure efficient.

[Belousov 78]   A.I. Belousov. On the Algorithm Parallelization Problem. *Programmirovanie*, (5):53–61, 1978. (in Russian).

A theorem about equivalent transformation from sequential composition of normal algorithms to parallel composition of these algorithms is proved on the basis of the notion of compatible normal algorithms.

[Belousov 82]   A.I. Belousov. An Analysis of Parallelism in Compilation Process for a Certain Language Family. In *Parallel Programming and High-Performance Systems*, pages 24–26, Naukova Dumka, Kiev, USSR, 1982. (in Russian).

A model of mixed computation (i.e., a model of compatible E-operators) is developed in which a special phase of 'unsuspending' of basic semantic items is inserted between parallel compilation and parallel implementation. The finiteness conditions of this phase which put certain topological constraints on the input domain are investigated.

[Bjørner 87]   D. Bjørner, A.P. Ershov and N.D. Jones (Editors). *Workshop Compendium, Workshop on Partial Evaluation and Mixed Computation, Gl. Avernæs, Denmark, October 1987*. Department of Computer Science, Technical University of Denmark, Lyngby, Denmark, 1987.

This Compendium is the preliminary proceedings of the workshop. Some papers appearing in the Compendium but not in these final Proceedings may later appear in a special issue of New Generation Computing (Springer-Verlag) on partial evaluation.

[Bloch 84]   C. Bloch. *Source-to-Source Tranformations of Logic Programs*. Report CS84-22, Weizmann Institute of Science, Rehovot, Israel, 1984.

A brief survey of the literature on partial evaluation and other optimization techniques for Prolog is given, and a restricted Prolog partial evaluator is presented. A number of transformations of Concurrent Prolog programs into Flat Concurrent Prolog are presented.

[Bondorf 87]   A. Bondorf. *Towards a Self-Applicable Partial Evaluator for Term Rewriting Systems*. Master's thesis, DIKU, University of Copenhagen,

Denmark, 112 pages, July 1987.

The subject of the paper [Bondorf 88] with the same title is dealt with in greater detail. In addition to this, efficient compilation of the pattern matching in the language Terse is discussed and implemented.

[Bondorf 88] A. Bondorf. Towards a Self-Applicable Partial Evaluator for Term Rewriting Systems. In D. Bjørner, A.P. Ershov and N.D. Jones, editors, *Partial Evaluation and Mixed Computation*, North-Holland, 1988. (This volume).

A fully automatic experimental partial evaluator is described. It handles partially static data and uses two-phase partial evaluation (binding time analysis and function specialization). It is based on a restricted term rewriting system language with call-by-value, Terse, and has been implemented in part. Partial evaluation of an interpreter and a self-interpreter is performed and the results are discussed.

[Bulyonkov 84] M.A. Bulyonkov. Polyvariant Mixed Computation for Analyzer Programs. *Acta Informatica*, 21:473–484, 1984.

An algorithm for mixed computation of low-level non-structured imperative programs is presented. The algorithm is shown to terminate and produce correct results when applied to the class of so-called analyzer programs, a definition of which is also given.

[Bulyonkov 85a] M.A. Bulyonkov. Mixed Computation for Programs over Finitely Defined Memory with Strict Partitioning. *Doklady Akademii Nauk SSSR*, 285(5):1033–1037, 1985. (in Russian).

The paper presents a new algorithm of mixed computation for the class of analyzer programs: those satisfying that the memory can be split into two parts — available memory and reserved memory — such that for every initial state of available memory, the number of states of the available memory does not depend on reserved memory.

[Bulyonkov 85b] M.A. Bulyonkov. Obtaining Object Code from a One-Loop Interpreter. In *Mathematical Theory of Programming*, pages 158–168, Computing Center, Novosibirsk, USSR, 1985. (in Russian).

A class of imperative programs, namely stack analyzer programs, is defined. It is shown that object code may be produced by projection and further optimizing transformations. In particular, it is shown how an interpreter stack can be split into compilation stack and run-time stack.

[Bulyonkov 85c] M.A. Bulyonkov. Mixed Computations for Programs over Finitely Defined Memory with Strict Partitioning. *Soviet Mathematics Doklady*, 32(3):807–811, 1985.

English translation of [Bulyonkov 85a].

[Bulyonkov 86a] M.A. Bulyonkov. A Computer Experiment with Mixed Computation Autoprojector. In *Automation of Programming System Production*, pages 11–13, Polytechnical Institute, Tallin, USSR, 1986. (in Russian).

The paper describes the results of computer experiments with an autoprojector. The object code of a program, a compiler for a toy language, and a compiler generator were automatically generated.

[Bulyonkov 86b]   M.A. Bulyonkov and A.P. Ershov. How Do Ad-Hoc Compiler Constructs Appear in Universal Mixed Computation Processes? In *Applied Logic, Computation Systems, Vol. 116*, Institute of Mathematics, Novosibirsk, USSR, 1986. (in Russian).

An autoprojector for a simple imperative language is described. The autoprojector is powerful enough to formally produce a compiler generator. The essence of specific compilation constructs such as symbol table, control stack, code generation patterns etc. is investigated.

[Bulyonkov 88a]   M.A. Bulyonkov. A Theoretical Approach to Polyvariant Mixed Computation. In D. Bjørner, A.P. Ershov and N.D. Jones, editors, *Partial Evaluation and Mixed Computation*, North-Holland, 1988. (This volume).

Different approaches to polyvariant mixed computation are described and their equivalence is proved. The method is based on the concept of an arbitrary (general) environment instead of partially known input data.

[Bulyonkov 88b]   M.A. Bulyonkov and A.P. Ershov. How Do Ad-Hoc Compiler Constructs Appear in Universal Mixed Computation Processes? In D. Bjørner, A.P. Ershov and N.D. Jones, editors, *Partial Evaluation and Mixed Computation*, North-Holland, 1988. (This volume).

English version of [Bulyonkov 86b].

[Codish 86]   M. Codish and E. Shapiro. Compiling Or-Parallelism into And-Parallelism. In E. Shapiro, editor, *Third International Conference on Logic Programming, London, United Kingdom*, pages 283–297, Lecture Notes in Computer Science, Vol. 225, Springer-Verlag, 1986. Also in New Generation Computing 5:45-61, Ohmsha Ltd. and Springer-Verlag, 1987.

A general method for compiling or-parallelism into and-parallelism is presented. An interpreter for an and/or-parallel subset of the language induces a source-to-source transformation from the full language into the and-parallel subset.

[Consel 88]   C. Consel. New Insights into Partial Evaluation: the Schism Experiment. In H. Ganzinger, editor, *ESOP'88, 2nd European Symposium on Programming, Nancy, France, March 1988*, pages 236–246, Lecture Notes in Computer Science, Vol. 300, Springer-Verlag, 1988.

A self-applicable partial evaluator called Schism is presented. It is written in a first-order subset of Scheme, with syntactic extensions and an extensible set of primitives, and can handle certain forms of side-effects. User-defined annotations control unfolding and specialization during partial evaluation. Work towards automating the annotations is presented.

[Coscia 86]   P. Coscia et al. Object Level Reflection of Inference Rules by Partial Evaluation. In P. Maes and D. Nardi, editors, *Workshop on Meta-Level Architectures and Reflection, Sardinia, Italy, October 1986*, North-Holland, (to appear).

A knowledge base management system built upon Prolog and a relational database is described. Metaprogramming plays a central role in the definition of the knowledge base structuring mechanisms and inference engines. Partial evaluation of metaprograms is used to drastically reduce the overhead of metaprogramming while preserving its flexibility.

[Danvy 88]   O. Danvy. Across the Bridge between Reflection and Partial Evaluation. In D. Bjørner, A.P. Ershov and N.D. Jones, editors, *Partial Evaluation and Mixed Computation*, North-Holland, 1988. (This volume).

The paper attempts to relate partial evaluation and procedural reflection on the basis that both require metalanguage and object language to be identical. This is necessary for self-application and for expressing simple and reflective procedures in a uniform way, respectively. It is shown that a partial evaluator collapses levels in a tower of interpreters because it is a program transformer rather than an evaluator.

[Darlington 88] J. Darlington and H. Pull. A Program Development Methodology Based on a Unified Approach to Execution and Transformation. In D. Bjørner, A.P. Ershov and N.D. Jones, editors, *Partial Evaluation and Mixed Computation*, North-Holland, 1988. (This volume).

The relationship between execution, symbolic execution and program transformation is discussed in the context of a functional programming language. A program development methodology is presented that allows a programmer to control both execution and transformation strategies by means of so-called scripts.

[Dybkjær 85]   H. Dybkjær. *Parsers and Partial Evaluation: An Experiment*. Student report no. 85-7-15, 128 pp., DIKU, University of Copenhagen, Denmark, July 1985.

An investigation of the practicability of applying a partial evaluator to the construction of specialized parsers (from Earley's general context free parser) is undertaken. The conclusion is drawn that the partial evaluator requires some development to become a good general purpose tool.

[Emanuelson 80a] P. Emanuelson. *Performance Enhancement in a Well-Structured Pattern Matcher Through Partial Evaluation*. Linköping Studies in Science and Technology Dissertations 55, Linköping University, Sweden, 1980.

An advanced general pattern matcher (including control structures such as backtracking and generators) written in Lisp is partially evaluated to obtain object code in Lisp. The partial evaluation system used is Redfun-2.

[Emanuelson 80b] P. Emanuelson and A. Haraldsson. On Compiling Embedded Languages in Lisp. In *1980 Lisp Conference, Stanford, California*, pages 208–215, 1980.

The idea of compiling Lisp embedded languages (iterative statements, pattern matching, etc.) by means of partial evaluation is described. Comparisons are made with specialized language compilers written in Interlisp.

[Emanuelson 82]   P. Emanuelson. From Abstract Model to Efficient Compilation of Patterns. In M. Dezani-Ciancaglini and U. Montanari, editors, *International Symposium on Programming, 5th Colloquium, Turin, Italy*, pages 91–104, Lecture Notes in Computer Science, Vol. 137, Springer-Verlag, 1982.

Partial evaluation is used to obtain efficient specialized pattern matchers from a cleanly structured extensible general pattern matcher.

[Ermakov 87]   G.V. Ermakov. *Symbolic Execution of Autocode-Type Programs in the MIX-System*. Preprint 2 (272), Institute of Mathematics, Minsk, USSR, 1987. (in Russian).

The concept of symbolic execution as realized in a integrated system designed for the development of Autocode-like programs is considered.

[Ershov 77a]   A.P. Ershov. On the Partial Computation Principle. *Information Processing Letters*, 6(2):38–41, April 1977.

A short note explaining the basic notions of partial (or mixed) computation. A number of traditional programming methods and techniques are considered as instances of partial computation.

[Ershov 77b]   A.P. Ershov and V.E. Itkin. Correctness of Mixed Computation in Algol-like Programs. In J. Gruska, editor, *Mathematical Foundations of Computer Science, Tatranská Lomnica, Czechoslovakia*, pages 59–77, Lecture Notes in Computer Science, Vol. 53, Springer-Verlag, 1977.

A formal treatment of mixed computation of programs in Algol-like languages. Three definitions of mixed computation are presented. The first one involves the smallest number of forcible suspensions but is incorrect in the general case. The other two are universally correct but require more forcible suspensions.

[Ershov 77c]   A.P. Ershov. On the Essence of Compilation. *Programmirovanie*, (5):21–39, 1977. (in Russian).

Some compiling algorithms including optimization and code generation are described on the basis of mixed computation analogues to partial binding of function arguments. The notion of generating extension is introduced and is used to demonstrate the transformation of an interpreter into a compiler. Comparisons with related work are made.

[Ershov 77d]   A.P. Ershov. On a Theoretical Principle of System Programming. *Doklady Akademii Nauk SSSR*, 233(2):272–275, 1977. (in Russian).

Russian version of [Ershov 77a].

[Ershov 77e]   A.P. Ershov and V.V. Grushetsky. An Implementation-Oriented Method for Describing Algorithmic Languages. In B. Gilchrist, editor, *Information Processing 77, Toronto, Canada*, pages 117–122, North-Holland, 1977.

Mixed computation is described as a way of connecting the interpretational and the translational semantics of algorithmic languages.

[Ershov 77f]   A.P. Ershov. A Theoretical Principle of System Programming. *Soviet Mathematics Doklady*, 18(2):312–315, 1977.

English translation of [Ershov 77d].

[Ershov 78a]   A.P. Ershov. On the Essence of Compilation. In E.J. Neuhold, editor, *Formal Description of Programming Concepts*, pages 391–420, North-Holland, 1978.

English version of [Ershov 77c].

[Ershov 78b]   A.P. Ershov. Mixed Computation in the Class of Recursive Program Schemata. *Acta Cybernetica*, 4(1):19–23, 1978.

A method of mixed computation of recursive programs based on the notion of a semi-bound call is described. The method involves rewriting (call unfolding) and simplification (symbolic expression reduction). Examples of mixed computation are given.

[Ershov 79a]   A.P. Ershov. Mixed Computation Organization for Recursive Programs. *Doklady Akademii Nauk SSSR*, 245(5):1041–1044, 1979. (in Russian).

Russian version of [Ershov 78b].

[Ershov 79b]   A.P. Ershov. The Organization of Mixed Computations for Recursive Programs. *Soviet Mathematics Doklady*, 20(2):382–386, 1979.

English translation of [Ershov 79a].

[Ershov 80]   A.P. Ershov. Mixed Computation: Potential Applications and Problems for Study. In *Mathematical Logic Methods in AI Problems and Systematic Programming, Part 1*, pages 26–55, Vil'nyus, USSR, 1980. (in Russian).

This is a survey paper presenting, summarizing, and integrating results from [Ershov 77b], [Ershov 77c], [Ershov 78b] and [Ershov 82c]. The paper is an overview of techniques, theory, and applications of mixed computation.

[Ershov 81]   A.P. Ershov. The Transformational Machine: Theme and Variations. In J. Gruska and M. Chytil, editors, *Mathematical Foundations of Computer Science, Štrbské Pleso, Czechoslovakia*, pages 16–32, Springer-Verlag, Lecture Notes in Computer Science, Vol. 118, 1981.

English version of [Ershov 82c].

[Ershov 82a]   A.P. Ershov. Mixed Computation: Potential Applications and Problems for Study. *Theoretical Computer Science*, 18:41–67, 1982.

English version of [Ershov 80].

[Ershov 82b]   A.P. Ershov. On Futamura Projections. *BIT*, 12(14):4–5, 1982. (in Japanese).

[Ershov 82c]   A.P. Ershov. Transformational Machine: Theme and Variations. In *Problems in Theoretical and Systems Programming*, pages 5–24, Novosibirsk State Univ., Novosibirsk, USSR, 1982. (in Russian).

A reduction-type transformational semantics for a simple imperative language is described. The notion of a transformational machine with base transformations as instruction set is introduced.

[Ershov 82d]   A.P. Ershov and B.N. Ostrovsky. Systematic Construction of a Program for Solution of a Particular Problem from a Certain Class Examplified by Syntactic Analyzers. *Doklady Akademii Nauk SSSR*, 266(4):803–806, 1982. (in Russian).

A method of producing language-oriented parsers by means of mixed computation in the framework of the transformational approach is described. The results of an experiment are given.

[Ershov 84]   A.P. Ershov. Mixed Computation. *V mire nauki (Scientific American, Russian Edition)*, (6):28–42, 1984. (in Russian).

A popular account of the basic ideas of mixed computation.

[Ershov 85]   A.P. Ershov. On Mixed Computation: Informal Account of the Strict and Polyvariant Computational Schemes. In M. Broy, editor, *Control Flow and Data Flow: Concepts of Distributed Programming. NATO ASI Series F: Computer and System Sciences*, Vol. 14, pages 107–120, Springer-Verlag, 1985.

An account of the general idea of mixed computation and a comparative analysis of results published in [Bulyonkov 84], [Itkin 83b], and [Ostrovsky 80b].

[Fujita 87a]   H. Fujita. *On Automating Partial Evaluation of Prolog Programs*. Technical Report TM-250, ICOT, Tokyo, Japan, 1987 (in Japanese).

An automatic partial evaluator for Prolog is presented. It uses information collected by preanalyses for ensuring termination of the partial evaluation process. The preanalyses are not formally described, but it is expected that they can be based on abstract interpretation.

[Fujita 87b]   H. Fujita. *An Algorithm for Partial Evaluation with Constraints*. Technical Report TM-367, ICOT, Tokyo, Japan, 1987.

A two-stage partial evaluation algorithm for Prolog is presented. In the first stage, a specialized program is built. In the second stage (called short-cutting and constraint evalaution) trivial one-clause predicates are unfolded and constraints are evaluated where possible.

[Fujita 88]   H. Fujita and K. Furukawa. A Self-Applicable Partial Evaluator and Its Use in Incremental Compilation. *New Generation Computing*, 6(2,3), June 1988. (to appear).

The paper presents an experimental implementation of a self-applicable partial evaluator in Prolog which is used for compiler generation, compiler generator generation, and incremental compilation.

[Fuller 88]   D.A. Fuller and S. Abramsky. Mixed Computation of Prolog Programs. *New Generation Computing*, 6(2,3), June 1988. (to appear).

The paper describes theoretical as well as implementation issues involved in mixed computation of Prolog programs. A self-applicable partial evaluator for Prolog is presented and a number of outstanding problems discussed.

[Furukawa 88]   K. Furukawa, A. Okumura and M. Murakami. Unfolding Rules for Guarded Horn Clause Programs. *New Generation Computing*, 6(2,3), June 1988. (to appear).

A set of rules for unfolding-based transformation of Guarded Horn Clauses (GHC) programs is presented. This set of rules is shown to preserve the set of solutions and absence from deadlock, and is expected to give a basis for partial evaluation of GHC programs.

[Futamura 71]   Y. Futamura. Partial Evaluation of Computation Process – An Approach to a Compiler-Compiler. *Systems, Computers, Controls*, 2(5):45–50, 1971.

This seminal paper defines partial evaluation and exposes its applications to (among other things) compilation and compiler generation. A brief discussion is given on the feasibility in practice and of some conceptual and engineering issues of partial evaluation.

[Futamura 83]   Y. Futamura. Partial Computation of Programs. In E. Goto, et al., editor, *RIMS Symposia on Software Science and Engineering, Kyoto, Japan, 1982*, pages 1–35, Lecture Notes in Computer Science, Vol. 147, Springer-Verlag, 1983.

Partial evaluation is formally defined, examples are given, and many applications are outlined. A partial evaluation method for a functional language is given, and a number of engineering problems are discussed.

[Futamura 88]   Y. Futamura and K. Nogi. Generalised Partial Computation. In D. Bjørner, A.P. Ershov and N.D. Jones, editors, *Partial Evaluation and Mixed Computation*, North-Holland, 1988. (This volume).

A partial evaluation method that makes use of a theorem prover to evaluate conditions in conditional expressions is proposed.

[Gallagher 86] J. Gallagher. Transforming Logic Programs by Specialising Interpreters. In *ECAI-86. 7th European Conference on Artificial Intelligence, Brighton Centre, United Kingdom*, pages 109–122, 1986.

Logic programs are transformed by partial evaluation of metainterpreters. Given an interpreter for a non-standard control strategy, a logic program that is to be executed using this control strategy can be transformed into an equivalent program to be executed using the standard strategy

[Gallagher 88] J. Gallagher, M. Codish and E. Shapiro. Specialisation of Prolog and FCP Programs Using Abstract Interpretation. *New Generation Computing*, 6(2,3), June 1988. (to appear).

An approach to specialization of logic programs is presented. Specialization takes place in two stages: an abstraction stage and a specialization stage. These are based on abstract interpretation of logic programs. The specialization technique is applied to sequential Prolog and Flat Concurrent Prolog.

[Ghezzi 85]   C. Ghezzi, D. Mandrioli and A. Tecchio. Program Simplification Via Symbolic Interpretation. In S.N. Maheshwari, editor, *Foundations of Software Technology and Theoretical Computer Science. Fifth Conference, New Delhi, India*, pages 116–128, Lecture Notes in Computer Science, Vol. 206, Springer-Verlag, 1985.

A program transformation technique called simplification is proposed. It is a specialization technique similar to partial evaluation but works with predicates to specify restricted domains of input values.

[Giannotti 87]   F. Giannotti, et al. Symbolic Evaluation with Structural Recursive Symbolic Constants. *Science of Computer Programming*, 9(2):161–177, 1987.

An extension of the class of symbolic constants introduced in [Ambriola 85] is presented. This allows to handle subsets of data domains represented via recursively defined predicates. The operational and denotational semantics of the new class of symbolic constants is given along with a few examples of its use.

[Goad 82]   C. Goad. Automatic Construction of Special Purpose Programs. In D.W. Loveland, editor, *6th Conference on Automated Deduction, New York, USA*, pages 194–208, Lecture Notes in Computer Science, Vol. 138, Springer-Verlag, 1982.

A technique for program specialization is presented and applied to the generation of efficient programs for use in computer graphics (hidden surface analysis specialized to a particular scene).

[Grokh 83]   A.V. Grokh, A.G. Krasovsky and V.F. Khoroshevsky. An Analysis of the Mixed-Computation-Oriented Meta-Language Description of Symbol Manipulation. In *Advanced Programming Technologies*, pages 69–75, MDNTP, Moscow, USSR, 1983. (in Russian).

A mixed computation based approach to the development of programming tools for automatic analysis of Refal programs is described. The notion of areal of a variable is introduced, and mixed computation on areals is defined.

[Grokh 87]   A.V. Grokh and A.G. Krasovsky. *Mixed Computation and an Analysis of Correctness of Symbolic Transformations*. Preprint 030-87, Moscow Institute of Physical Engineering, Moscow, USSR, 1987. (in Russian).

A definition of mixed computation in the class of recursive programs is given and its use for checking symbolic transformations is shown. The instrumental program system Areal designed for checking Refal programs is described.

[Guzowski 88]   M.A. Guzowski. *Towards Developing a Reflexive Partial Evaluator for an Interesting Subset of LISP.* Master's thesis, Dept. of Computer Engineering and Science, Case Western Reserve University, Cleveland, Ohio, January 1988.

Work towards partial evaluation of a minimally user-annotated dialect of full Scheme is presented. A non-selfapplicable partial evaluator is described which focuses on the general issues of control and environment, and admits a restricted form of side-effects.

[Haraldsson 77]   A. Haraldsson. *A Program Manipulation System Based on Partial Evaluation.* Linköping Studies in Science and Technology Dissertations 14, Linköping University, Sweden, 1977.

The system Redfun-2 for partial evaluation of Lisp is described. It works also for non-pure Lisp constructs, such as side-effects and assignments, and handles value ranges for parameters. Such value ranges can be automatically derived from predicates in conditionals.

[Haraldsson 78]   A. Haraldsson. A Partial Evaluator, and Its Use for Compiling Iterative Statements in Lisp. In *Fifth ACM Symposium on Principles of Programming Languages, Tucson, Arizona,* pages 195–202, 1978.

The paper describes an experiment in which an interpreter for iterative statements in Lisp is partially evaluated to obtain Lisp object code.

[Harrison 88]   P.G. Harrison. Function Inversion. In D. Bjørner, A.P. Ershov and N.D. Jones, editors, *Partial Evaluation and Mixed Computation,* North-Holland, 1988. (This volume).

A method for synthesizing recursive inverse function definitions for certain first order recursive functions is described.

[Hascoët 88]   L. Hascoët. Partial Evaluation with Inference Rules. *New Generation Computing,* 6(2,3), June 1988. (to appear).

The concept of partial evaluation of an inference system is defined, and the design of a partial evaluator for the language Typol of inference rules is described.

[Heering 86]   J. Heering. Partial Evaluation and ω-Completeness of Algebraic Specifications. *Theoretical Computer Science,* 43:149–167, 1986.

An investigation of omega-completeness of algebraic specifications suggests that for non-trivial languages, no partial evaluation algorithm can be devised that always makes 'maximal use' of the available input or 'performs as much computation in advance as possible'.

[Holst 88]   N.C.K. Holst. Language Triplets: The AMIX Approach. In D. Bjørner, A.P. Ershov and N.D. Jones, editors, *Partial Evaluation and Mixed Computation,* North-Holland, 1988. (This volume).

The theory of language triplets is presented. This theory describes partial evaluation and compiler generation in a natural way. It is further shown how using this theory it is possible to derive compiler generators which produce compilers in low level languages from high level language definitions by means of partial evaluation.

[Hughes 88]   J. Hughes. Backwards Analysis of Functional Programs. In D. Bjørner, A.P. Ershov and N.D. Jones, editors, *Partial Evaluation and Mixed Computation*, North-Holland, 1988. (This volume).

A framework for backwards analysis of functional programs is introduced. It is shown that backwards analysis can be extended to derive information about data structures and higher order functions in typed languages.

[Itkin 80]   V.E. Itkin. Characterization of Structured Control-Flow Graphs. *Doklady Akademii Nauk SSSR*, 250(2):1077–1080, 1980. (in Russian).

Some topological criteria for compositional structure of a flow graph are proposed in terms of mixed computation.

[Itkin 83a]   V.E. Itkin. Natural Modularity and Symmetry of Structured Programs. In *Compilation and Program Models*, pages 13–22, Computing Center, Novosibirsk, USSR, 1983. (in Russian).

Some compositional criteria for topological structure of a parallel flow graph are given.

[Itkin 83b]   V.E. Itkin. On Partial and Mixed Program Execution. In *Program Optimization and Transformation*, pages 17–30, Computing Center, Novosibirsk, USSR, 1983. (in Russian).

Dashed-line and polyvariant strategies of mixed computation are developed. The program graph node mark 'ignoring' and an indication of direction for a residual program representation is proposed. The thesis is advanced that the concept of a program being structured is similar to that of a program being suited to effective mixed computation.

[Itkin 83c]   V.E. Itkin. Incompleteness As an Attribute of Research Programs. In *Methodological Problems of Research Programs*, pages 54–64, Novosibirsk, USSR, 1983. (in Russian).

Incompleteness has been regarded as a motor of human constructive activities. Some criteria of effectivity of partial activity are investigated. A general definition of program and a concept of generator as a reflexive superstructure upon the program are given.

[Itkin 83d]   V.E. Itkin. Dynamic Program Parallelization Based on Mixed Computation. In *Theoretical Problems in Parallel Programming and Multiprocessor Computers*, pages 110–126, Novosibirsk, USSR, 1983. (in Russian).

Mixed computation of programs is defined in abstract terms as a set of interactions between a group of constant assignment statements and other program statements.

[Itkin 84a]   V.E. Itkin. Algebra of Mixed Program Execution. *Doklady Akademii Nauk SSSR*, 275(6):1332–1336, 1984. (in Russian).

An algebra of programs, deterministic memory states and subsets of the set of memory locations is given. By means of this algebra, the correctness of some superoperators of mixed computation is proved.

[Itkin 84b]   V.E. Itkin. Axiomatics of Complete and Partial Program Execution. In *Program Compilation and Transformation*, pages 69–93, Computing Center, Novosibirsk, USSR, 1984. (in Russian).

An axiomatic system for the concepts of completeness of input information, program input, and program output is proposed. This is used to prove the correctness of mixed computation.

[Itkin 84c]   V.E. Itkin. Program Parallelization Algebra. In *Theoretical and Applied Aspects of Parallel Information Processing*, pages 3–24, Computing Center, Novosibirsk, USSR, 1984. (in Russian).

The correctness of some superoperators of the dashed-line and polyvariant mixed computation is proved using algebraic and axiomatic tools.

[Itkin 85]   V.E. Itkin. On Algebra and Axiomatics of Program Parallelization. In *Theory of Programming and Representation of Discrete Systems Parallelism*, pages 38–53, Computing Center, Novosibirsk, USSR, 1985. (in Russian).

A method of two-step parallel execution of the superposition (concatenation) of two programs is proposed.

[Itkin 86]   V.E. Itkin. On Algebra and Logic of Parallelization of Function Superposition. In *Theoretical Aspects of Information Processing*, pages 18–33, Computing Center, Novosibirsk, USSR, 1986. (in Russian).

An algebra of deterministic memory states and subsets of the set of memory locations is transformed first into an algebra of non-deterministic memory states and then further into a quasi-boolean algebra of abstract 'information elements'. A method of parallel execution of superposition of programs is formulated in terms of this algebra.

[Itkin 88]   V.E. Itkin. An Algebra and Axiomatization System of Mixed Computation. In D. Bjørner, A.P. Ershov and N.D. Jones, editors, *Partial Evaluation and Mixed Computation*, North-Holland, 1988. (This volume).

An axiomatic system for the concepts of completeness of input information, program input and program output is proposed. It is used to prove the correctness of mixed computation and parallel execution of superposition of programs.

[Jones 85]   N.D. Jones, P. Sestoft and H. Søndergaard. An Experiment in Partial Evaluation: The Generation of a Compiler Generator. In J.-P. Jouannaud, editor, *Rewriting Techniques and Applications, Dijon, France*, pages 124–140, Lecture Notes in Computer Science, Vol. 202, Springer-Verlag, 1985.

A self-applicable partial evaluator for (first order) pure Lisp is described. It works in two phases and requires user-made annotations of calls in subject programs. The semi-automatic generation of experimental compilers and a compiler generator is reported, and the results of these generations are discussed.

[Jones 86]   N.D. Jones and A. Mycroft. Data Flow Analysis of Applicative Programs Using Minimal Function Graphs. In *Thirteenth ACM Symposium on Principles of Programming Languages, St. Petersburg, Florida*, pages 296–306, ACM, 1986.

The following problem is addressed: What is the natural analog for functional programs of Cousot's collecting semantics? An answer is given using the minimal set of (argument, result) pairs sufficient to compute on a given input set, and a framework for static program analysis including 'constant propagation' is developed.

[Jones 87a]   N.D. Jones, P. Sestoft and H. Søndergaard. *Mix: A Self-Applicable Partial Evaluator for Experiments in Compiler Generation*. DIKU Report 87/8, DIKU, University of Copenhagen, Denmark, 1987. Also in Lisp and Symbolic Computation, Kluwer Academic Publishers, Norwell, Massachusetts, (to appear).

A comprehensive discussion of partial evaluation, its applications to generation of compilers and compiler generators, and of engineering problems is given. A fully automatic version of the partial evaluator discussed in [Jones 85] is described and results from its use are reported.

[Jones 87b]   N.D. Jones. Towards Automating the Transformation of Programming Language Specifications into Compilers. Part I: DIKU Report 85/9, 60 pages, Part II: 74 pages. DIKU, University of Copenhagen, Denmark, 1987.

An overview is given of semantics-directed compiler generation including summaries of earlier work by others and by the author towards that goal. Part II deals with controlling complexity in semantics and compiler specfications and describes the then current state of the Mix partial evaluation project.

[Jones 87c]   N.D. Jones. Flow Analysis of Lazy Higher-Order Functional Programs. In S. Abramsky and C. Hankin, editors, *Abstract Interpretation of Declarative Languages*, pages 103–122, Ellis Horwood, Chichester, England, 1987.

A method is presented for static analysis of programs manipulating tree-structured data. An algorithm is given that constructs from a program in term rewriting system form a tree grammar safely approximating the program's variable bindings and intermediate results.

[Jones 87d]   N.D. Jones and H. Søndergaard. A Semantics-Based Framework for the Abstract Interpretation of Prolog. In S. Abramsky and C. Hankin, editors, *Abstract Interpretation of Declarative Languages*, pages 123–142, Ellis Horwood, Chichester, England, 1987.

A method resembling minimal function graphs is given for the static analysis of Prolog programs. It is based on the use of varying interpretations of a common core semantics for Prolog.

[Jones 88a]   N.D. Jones. Automatic Program Specialization: A Re-Examination from Basic Principles. In D. Bjørner, A.P. Ershov and N.D. Jones, editors,

Partial Evaluation and Mixed Computation, North-Holland, 1988. (This volume).

A careful formulation and investigation of fundamental problems involved in automatic program specialization, including the first precise description of the semantic issues underlying binding time analysis

[Jones 88b]   N.D. Jones. Static Semantics and Binding Time Analysis. 1988. Working paper, DIKU, University of Copenhagen, Denmark.

A working paper discussing the purpose and nature of static semantics and type checking, ending with some examples that suggest the possibility of automatically deriving a static semantics with the aid of binding time analysis.

[Jørring 86]   U. Jørring and W.L. Scherlis. Compilers and Staging Transformations. In *Thirteenth ACM Symposium on Principles of Programming Languages, St. Petersburg, Florida*, pages 86–96, 1986.

The so-called staging transformations are program transformations intended to exploit the fact that some data become available at an earlier stage than others. These transformations are used for the derivation of a compiler from an interpreter.

[Kahn 82]   K.M. Kahn. A Partial Evaluator of Lisp Programs Written in Prolog. In M. Van Caneghem, editor, *First International Logic Programming Conference, Marseille, France*, pages 19–25, 1982.

A partial evaluator for Lisp written in Prolog is briefly described. It is intended to be applied to a Prolog interpreter written in Lisp in order to achieve compilation of Prolog programs into Lisp. Work on this technique is in progress. Several small example uses of the partial evaluator are given.

[Kahn 83a]   K.M. Kahn. *A Partial Evaluator of Lisp written in Prolog*. Technical Report 17, UPMAIL, Uppsala University, Sweden, February 1983.

A slightly edited version of [Kahn 82].

[Kahn 83b]   K.M. Kahn. *Partial Evaluation as an Example of the Relationships between Programming Methodology and Artificial Intelligence*. Technical Report 23, UPMAIL, Uppsala University, Sweden, October 1983.

It is argued that programming methodologies and methodologies of artificial intelligence research depend on each other in important ways. Partial evaluation is presented as an example of this mutual dependency.

[Kahn 84a]   K.M. Kahn and M. Carlsson. The Compilation of Prolog Programs Without the Use of Prolog Compiler. In *International Conference on Fifth Generation Computer Systems, Tokyo, Japan*, pages 348–355, 1984.

A Prolog interpreter written in Lisp is presented. The partial evaluator described in [Kahn 82] is applied to this interpreter and Prolog source programs to obtain object programs in Lisp. It is reported that these object programs are one order of magnitude faster than interpretation of source programs.

[Kahn 84b]   K.M. Kahn. Partial Evaluation, Programming Methodology, and Artificial Intelligence. *The AI Magazine*, 5(1):53–57, 1984.

                  An expanded version of [Kahn 83b].

[Kaimin 85]   V.A. Kaimin. Functional Specifications, Mixed Computation and Systematic Construction of Algorithms. In A.P. Ershov, editor, *Mixed Computation*, Novosibirsk, USSR, 1985. (in Russian).

                  An approach to systematic construction of structured algorithms based on functional specifications is presented. A functional semantics of structured algorithms and a definition of functional specification based on mixed computation is given.

[Kasyanov 78]   V.N. Kasyanov. *A Practical Approach to Program Optimization*. Preprint 135, Computing Center, Novosibirsk, USSR, 1978. (in Russian).

                  An optimization method and its application to translation and other kinds of automatic programming are described. It is demonstrated how the method can be applied to reduce discrepancies between an program and its usage.

[Kasyanov 80]   V.N. Kasyanov. Mixed Computation and Program Optimization. *Kybernetika*, (2):51–54, 1980. (in Russian).

                  Mixed computation and program optimization are compared as two approaches to program concretization which preserve the meaning and improves the quality of a program for a given input subspace.

[Kasyanov 82a]   V.N. Kasyanov. Program Concretization Problems. In *Problems of Theoretical and Systems Programming*, pages 35–45, Novosibirsk State University, Novosibirsk, USSR, 1982. (in Russian).

                  Program concretization is defined as improving the quality without disturbing the correctness for a restricted and stable range of program applications, assumed to specify restricted sets of program input and outputs and a particular class of program quality properties.

[Kasyanov 82b]   V.N. Kasyanov and I.V. Pottosin. *Concretization Systems: Approach and Basic Concepts*. Preprint 349, Computing Center, Novosibirsk, USSR, 1982. (in Russian).

                  The notion of concretization systems as programming environments based on annotated program transformations is introduced.

[Kasyanov 83]   V.N. Kasyanov and I.V. Pottosin. *The Architecture of Concretization Systems*. Preprint 455, Computing Center, Novosibirsk, USSR, 1983. (in Russian).

                  The architecture of concretization systems with respect to three classes of users is described.

[Kasyanov 86]   V.N. Kasyanov. A Method for Constructing Qualitative Program Versions. In *New Methods for Program Construction*, pages 37–48, Novosibirsk State University, Novosibirsk, USSR, 1986. (in Russian).

Program concretization is considered as program optimization under given assumptions about their usage, represented by annotations. The problems of data flow analysis and reduction of annotated programs are solved. An example of a programming support system based on annotated program transformations is described.

[Katkov 84]   V.L. Katkov and G.V. Ermakov. Program Object Filtering Facilities in the MIX-system. *Upravlyayushchie Sistemy i Machiny (Control Systems and Machines)*, (4):59–63, 1984. (in Russian).

Tools for filtering of program objects in the Mix system, which is oriented to initial learning of assembler programming, are described. Main stages of implementation of the filter mechanism are considered and recommendations for their use in Mix-programs are given.

[Kistlerov 87]   V.L. Kistlerov. *The Basic Principles of the Algebraic Manipulation Language FLAC*. Preprint, Institute of Management Problems, Moscow, USSR, 1987. (in Russian).

The basic concepts of the language FLAC are described. It provides means for implementation of algebraic manipulation systems and is based on suspended evaluation. It is argued that all data structures commonly provided by algebraic manipulation systems can be represented as combinations of suspended function calls.

[Kleene 52]   S.C. Kleene. *Introduction to Metamathematics*. D. van Nostrand, Princeton, New Jersey, 1952.

A profound treatment of recursive function theory, this book studies properties of the class of partial recursive functions and operations on codes for functions in much detail. Among other things, the S-m-n theorem, enumeration, and the first and second recursion theorems are treated.

[Klimov 83]   A.V. Klimov. Applying the Idea of Mixed Computations to Construction of an Object-Oriented Functional Programming Language. In *Semiooticheskie Aspecty Formalicii Intellectualnoj Deyatelnosti*, pages 67–70, Shkola-Seminar 'TELAVI-83', Moscow, 1983 (in Russian).

[Klimov 87]   A.V. Klimov and S.A. Romanenko. *A Meta-Evaluator for the Language Refal. Basic Concepts and Examples*. Preprint 71, Keldysh Institute of Applied Mathematics, Moscow, USSR, 1987 (in Russian).

The paper describes a metaevaluator for specializing (partially evaluating) function calls in a Refal program provided that their arguments are partially known. It is argued that programs written in a simple language can be compiled into Refal if the semantics is described by an interpreter written in Refal.

[Komorowski 81] H.J. Komorowski. *A Specification of an Abstract Prolog Machine and Its Application to Partial Evaluation.* Linköping Studies in Science and Technology Dissertations 69, Linköping University, Sweden, 1981.

Partial evaluation of Prolog is investigated in depth. An abstract Prolog machine is systematically extended to an abstract Prolog partial evaluator, and an implementation of this partial evaluator is developed. Several examples of its use are given. Some directions of future research are pointed out.

[Komorowski 82] H.J. Komorowski. Partial Evaluation as a Means for Inferencing Data Structures in an Applicative Language: A Theory and Implementation in the Case of Prolog. In *Ninth ACM Symposium on Principles of Programming Languages, Albuquerque, New Mexico,* pages 255–267, 1982.

An abridged version of the above thesis [Komorowski 81].

[Kotlyarov 82] V.P. Kotlyarov, N.B. Morozov and A.V. Samochadin. Mixed Computation in Object-Oriented Languages for Microcomputer Software Development Systems. In *Microprocessor Programming,* pages 74–90, Valgus, Tallin, USSR, 1982. (in Russian).

The special requirements for mixed computation of object-oriented languages and microcomputer control-oriented programs are discussed. A mixed computation algorithm Omix that works on complicated multi-level structured programs is proposed. It processes programs in which part of type checking and some operations are delayed.

[Kotlyarov 83a] V.P. Kotlyarov and A.V. Samochadin. Use of Software Redundancy for Improving Its Quality. In *Proc. of the 7th Symp. on Information Systems Redundancy,* Vol. 2, pages 123–124, LIAP, Leningrad, USSR, 1983. (in Russian).

A method for increasing software quality by adapting it to concrete conditions of application is proposed. Adaptation is carried out by the mixed computation algorithm DMIX.

[Kotlyarov 83b] V.P. Kotlyarov and A.V. Samochadin. Mixed Computation of R-Programs. In *R-Technology of Programming, Part 1,* pages 62–63, Institute of Cybernetics, Kiev, USSR, 1983. (in Russian).

Some peculiarities of realization of a software development system for mixed computation of programs in the R-programming language for microcomputers are considered.

[Kotlyarov 83c] V.P. Kotlyarov, et al. Concretization Tools in Programming Technology for Special-Purpose Micro-Computers. In *R-Technology of Programming, Part 3,* pages 15–17, Institute of Cybernetics, Kiev, USSR, 1983. (in Russian).

An approach to the use of surplus information about intermediate results of a program (e.g., its variables' ranges) is described.

[Kotlyarov 84]   V.P. Kotlyarov and N.B. Morozov. Mixed Computation Algorithms Used in Control Programs of Micro-Computers. In *Program Compilation and Transformation*, pages 94–107, Novosibirsk, USSR, 1984. (in Russian).

Questions of microcomputer control-oriented program optimization by means of mixed computation are discussed. Some peculiarities of mixed computation algorithms for control-oriented programs are shown.

[Krasovsky 86]   A.G. Krasovsky and A.V. Grokh. State of the Art and Future Development of the ISKRA Instrumental System. In *Software Engineering, Part 2*, pages 185–187, Institute of Cybernetics, Kiev, USSR, 1986. (in Russian).

Results of experiments with a Refal program verifier are reported. The technology of development of multi-pass compilers based on designing the formal specifications for each pass and using them in the Refal verifier is described

[Krinitskii 87]   N.A. Krinitskii. An Algorithmic Analysis of Mixed Computation. *Programmirovanie*, (3):42–56, 1987. (in Russian).

The notion of mixed computation is studied and refined by means of the theory of algorithms. The roots of the main results have been found in the theory of algorithms.

[Kröger 81a]   H. Kröger. Static-Scope-Lisp: Splitting an Interpreter into Compiler and Run-Time System. In W. Brauer, editor, *GI-11. Jahrestagung, München, FRG, Informatik-Fachberichte 50*, pages 20–31, Springer-Verlag, 1981. (in German).

Using the concept of a phi-operator, it is demonstrated that an interpreter for Lisp can easily be divided into a compiler part and a run-time part.

[Kröger 81b]   H. Kröger. *Code Generation by Partial Evaluation*. Bericht 8105, Institut für Informatik und Praktische Mathematik, Universität Kiel, FRG, 1981. (in German).

The paper sketches fundamental aspects of partial and residual evaluation, distinguishing pure forms and phi-forms. A trial and error algorithm to label a program with phi-operators is outlined.

[Kröger 82a]   H. Kröger. *A Code Generating Formalization Operator and Its Use on a Lisp Interpreter*. Bericht 1/82, Institut für Informatik und Praktische Mathematik, Universität Kiel, FRG, January 1982. (in German).

The concept of a phi-operator is introduced to handle partial evaluation and residual evaluation. The method is applied to partial evaluation of an interpreter, i.e., compilation of programs, and is demonstrated to work for static-scope as well as dynamic-scope semantics.

[Kröger 82b]   H. Kröger. *Compiling of a Generalized LISP-Label-Concept by Partial Evaluation*. Technical Report, Institut für Informatik und Praktische Mathematik, Universität Kiel, FRG, February 1982.

The Label-concept of Lisp is extended to allow arbitrary nested and parallel declarations of functions, and static-scope as well as dynamic-scope interpreters are given for the extended language. The phi-operator concept is recapitulated and a detailed description of the compiler and run-time parts of the interpreters are described.

[Kröger 85]   H. Kröger. *A Summary of a System for Partial Evaluation, Residual Evaluation, Code Generation and Semantics Directed Compiler Generation.* Bericht Nr. 8505, Institut für Informatik und Praktische Mathematik, Universität Kiel, FRG, September 1985.

The phi-based partial evaluation method is implemented using Interlisp. Using the phi-operator concept, more detailed descriptions of Y. Futamura's equations for compiler generation etc. are given as well as some qualitative and quantitative remarks on the implemented system.

[Kröger 87]   H. Kröger. *Report on a ϕ-Based Method for Partial Evaluation and Residual Evaluation.* Bericht 8710, Institut für Informatik und Praktische Mathematik, Universität Kiel, FRG, May/August 1987.

This is an extended abstract of a planned comprehensive report on phi-operator based partial evaluation.

[Kursawe 86]   P. Kursawe. How to Invent a Prolog Machine. In E. Shapiro, editor, *Third International Conference on Logic Programming, London, United Kingdom,* pages 134–148, Lecture Notes in Computer Science, Vol. 225, Springer-Verlag, 1986. Also New Generation Computing 5:97-114, Ohmsha Ltd. and Springer-Verlag, 1987.

A partial evaluation based derivation of the unification instructions of the Warren abstract machine is given. Starting with a unification algorithm for terms, all parts that are executable when one term is known are evaluated.

[Kursawe 88]   P. Kursawe. Pure Partial Evaluation and Instantiation. In D. Bjørner, A.P. Ershov and N.D. Jones, editors, *Partial Evaluation and Mixed Computation,* North-Holland, 1988. (This volume).

Pure partial evaluation of declarative languages is defined as execution of interpretive steps according to a strategy different from interpretation. Proofs of correctness and completeness of the technique are given.

[Lakhotia 88]   A. Lakhotia and L. Sterling. Composing Recursive Logic Programs with Clausal Join. *New Generation Computing,* 6(2,3), June 1988. (to appear).

A family of methods for composing logic programs from simpler components is presented. The methods are based on clausal-join, a specific sequence of unfold/fold transformations. The transformations are straightforward to implement in Prolog, as is demonstrated in the paper.

[Launchbury 88]   J. Launchbury. Projections for Specialisation. In D. Bjørner, A.P. Ershov and N.D. Jones, editors, *Partial Evaluation and Mixed Computation,* North-Holland, 1988. (This volume).

The use of projections for splitting data into its static and dynamic parts is proposed. Several example domains of projections and some general constructions for finite domains of projections are given. These finite domains are useful in (say) binding time analyses to support partial evaluation.

[Lavrov 88] S.S. Lavrov. On the Essence of Mixed Computation. In D. Bjørner, A.P. Ershov and N.D. Jones, editors, *Partial Evaluation and Mixed Computation*, North-Holland, 1988. (This volume).

Some reflections on ordinary and mixed computation are given. A number of possible pitfalls in speaking about mixed computation are pointed out.

[Levi 88] G. Levi and G. Sardu. Partial Evaluation of Metaprograms in a Multiple Worlds Logic Language. *New Generation Computing*, 6(2,3), June 1988. (to appear).

A non-selfapplicable partial evaluator for Prolog (including cut and side-effects) is described, and several examples of its use are given. The partial evaluator is to be used as a compilation tool in a knowledge base management system based on Prolog.

[Lloyd 87] J.W. Lloyd and J.C. Shepherdson. *Partial Evaluation in Logic Programming*. Technical Report CS-87-09, Department of Computer Science, University of Bristol, England, 1987.

The paper gives a theoretical foundation for partial evaluation in logic programming. For both the declarative and the procedural semantics conditions are studied under which the partially evaluated program is sound and complete. A simple, syntactically checkable "closedness condition" is formulated and is shown to suffice for soundness and completeness wrt. the procedural semantics, and for soundness wrt. the declarative semantics.

[Lombardi 64] L.A. Lombardi and B. Raphael. Lisp as the Language for an Incremental Computer. In E.C. Berkeley and D.G. Bobrow, editors, *The Programming Language Lisp: Its Operation and Applications*, pages 204–219, MIT Press, Cambridge, Massachusetts, 1964.

It is argued that computer systems should be able to deal with incomplete information, that is, to do partial evaluation (this is probably the first paper to use that term). Partial evaluation of Lisp is studied as a means to this end, and a small partial evaluator for Lisp, unable to reduce conditionals, is actually presented in an appendix.

[Lombardi 67] L.A. Lombardi. Incremental Computation. In F.L. Alt and M. Rubinoff, editors, *Advances in Computers, Vol. 8*, pages 247–333, Academic Press, 1967.

The design of a system for dealing with incomplete information and for incremental data assimilation is discussed and described in great detail. The system incorporates facilities for partial evaluation.

[Margolin 79] M.S. Margolin and M.E. Nemenman. A Partial Evaluator for Macrodefinitions. In *Software Engineering*, pages 42–43, Institute of Cybernetics,

Kiev, USSR, 1979. (in Russian).

The feasibility of partial evaluation with restrictions on input data domains and without any initialization is stated. The first steps of the implementation of a partial evaluator (reducer) of macro definitions are presented.

[Margolin 80] M.S. Margolin. On a Method of Mixed Computation Implementation. In *Automation of Application Packages Production*, pages 111–113, Tallin, USSR, 1980. (in Russian).

The notion of areal as a set of acceptable data values is introduced. An algorithm for mixed computation using rough and fine reductions is reported

[Margolin 81] M.S. Margolin and T.P. Potapenko. Employment of Incomplete Input Data to Simplify Programs. *Upravlyayushchie Sistemy i Mashiny (Control Systems and Machines)*, (6):78–81, 1981. (in Russian).

A procedure for simplification of a program through the use of incomplete data is proposed. A mechanism of rough reduction in mixed computation is given in detail. The need for filters is shown.

[Margolin 83] M.S. Margolin. Reduction and Its Relationships with a Program Areal. In *Program Optimization and Transformation, Part 2*, pages 20–25, Novosibirsk, USSR, 1983. (in Russian).

The notion of data areal is suggested and the notion of program areal as the set of all input data areals is introduced. Reduction is defined as a process of bringing the program into correspondence with a given data areal. It is shown that mixed computations are reductions.

[Margolin 86] M.S. Margolin and T.P. Potapenko. Application of Residual programs to Source Program Debugging. In *Problems in Program Synthesis, Testing, Verification and Debugging, Vol. 2*, pages 24–25, Riga, USSR, 1986. (in Russian).

Residual programs are considered as results of adaptation of a source program to additional conditions. The benefits of using residual programs in the debugging process are shown.

[Mazaher 85] S. Mazaher and D.M. Berry. Deriving a Compiler from an Operational Semantics Written in VDL. *Computer Languages*, 10(2):147–164, 1985.

Mixed computation is used in deriving correct compilers from language definitions written in the Vienna Definition Language (VDL). An algorithm for mixed computation of VDL expressions is given.

[Mel'Nik 82] A.P. Mel'Nik. A Program Model of a Transformational Machine. In *Problems of System and Theoretical Programming*, pages 25–34, Novosibirsk, USSR, 1982. (in Russian).

A program model of a transformational machine has been implemented and is used for experiments in studying the transformational approach. The structure of the model is described.

[Mogensen 86]   T. Mogensen. *The Application of Partial Evaluation to Ray-Tracing.* Master's thesis, DIKU, University of Copenhagen, Denmark, 1986.

Partial evaluation is used to optimize ray-tracing (a computer graphics algorithm). A self-applicable partial evaluator is developed for this purpose, and significant speed improvements are reported to arise from its use.

[Mogensen 88]   T. Mogensen. Partially Static Structures in a Self-Applicable Partial Evaluator. In D. Bjørner, A.P. Ershov and N.D. Jones, editors, *Partial Evaluation and Mixed Computation*, North-Holland, 1988. (This volume).

The paper describes a self-applicable partial evaluator that uses the same basic methods as [Jones 85] but in addition gives good treatment of values that are not completely static or completely dynamic, but rather partially static. Thus it can do non-trivial partial evaluation for a larger class of programs.

[Mosses 79]   P. Mosses. *SIS — Semantics Implementation System, Reference Manual and User Guide.* DAIMI Report MD-30, DAIMI, University of Århus, Denmark, 1979.

A lambda expression reducer is used in a compiler-generating system to effectively compose a (denotational semantics) language definition and a source program to obtain an object program (as a lambda expression).

[Mycroft 86]   A. Mycroft and N.D. Jones. A Relational Framework for Abstract Interpretation. In H. Ganzinger and N.D. Jones, editors, *Programs as Data Objects, Copenhagen, Denmark, 1985*, pages 156–171, Lecture Notes in Computer Science, Vol. 217, Springer-Verlag, 1986.

The paper shows how logical relations may be combined with abstract interpretation for the purpose of static analysis of programs. An example applies the method to Hindley-Milner style polymorphic type checking.

[Nepejvoda 87]   N.N. Nepejvoda. Some Analogues of Partial & Mixed Computations in the Logical Programming Approach. In *[Bjørner 87]*, 1987.

The logical programming approach is a particular view of the process of algorithm and program development in which program transformations are used. A number of such transformations are compared to mixed computation concepts.

[Neumann 86]   G. Neumann. *Meta-Interpreter Directed Compilation of Logic Programs into Prolog.* Research Report RC 12113 (No. 54357), IBM, Yorktown Heights, New York, 1986.

[Nielson 88]   F. Nielson. A Formal Type System for Comparing Partial Evaluators. In D. Bjørner, A.P. Ershov and N.D. Jones, editors, *Partial Evaluation and Mixed Computation*, North-Holland, 1988. (This volume).

The lambda calculus is provided with a two-level type system for expressing binding time information. The concept of a best typing is defined, and an algorithm to compute it (i.e., a binding time analysis) is given. Finally, some relations for comparing partial evaluators are discussed.

[Ono 86]   S. Ono, N. Takahashi and M. Amamiya. Partial Computation with a
                Dataflow Machine. In E. Goto, K. Araki and T. Yuasa, editors, *RIMS
                Symposia on Software Science and Engineering II, Kyoto, Japan, 1983
                and 1984*, pages 87–113, Lecture Notes in Computer Science, Vol. 220,
                Springer-Verlag, 1986.

                A dataflow computation model is defined, and a restricted kind of partial
                evaluation for this computation model is presented.

[Ostrovsky 80a] B.N. Ostrovsky. Application of Mixed Computation to Automatic Gen-
                eration of Language-Oriented Parsers. In *Automation of Application
                Packages Production*, pages 172–173, Tallin, USSR, 1980. (in Russian).

                An experiment in automatic development of language-oriented parsers
                is described.

[Ostrovsky 80b] B.N. Ostrovsky. Application of Mixed Computation to Systematic De-
                velopment of Language-Oriented Parsers. In *Compilation and Program
                Models*, pages 69–80, Novosibirsk, USSR, 1980. (in Russian).

                The notions of strict and flexible mixed computation used for generation
                of language-oriented parsers are introduced.

[Ostrovsky 81]   B.N. Ostrovsky. A Sketch of a Transformational Machine Defining Se-
                mantics of a Pascal Subset. In *Methods of Compilation*, pages 121–124,
                Computing Center, Novosibirsk, USSR, 1981. (in Russian).

                A formalism for description of ordinary and mixed computation in a
                Pascal-like language is introduced.

[Ostrovsky 84]   B.N. Ostrovsky. Controlled Mixed Computation Examplified by
                Language-Oriented Parsers. In *Problems in Theoretical and System Pro-
                gramming*, pages 30–49, Novosibirsk, USSR, 1984. (in Russian).

                The concept of controlled mixed computation is introduced. An experi-
                ment on development of a top-down language-oriented parser for Algol
                60 is described.

[Ostrovsky 87]   B.N. Ostrovsky. Controlled Mixed Computation and Its Application
                to Systematic Development of Language-Oriented Parsers. *Program-
                mirovanie*, (2):56–67, 1987. (in Russian).

                The concept of controlled mixed computation is introduced. A descrip-
                tion of an automatic system for generation of language-oriented parsers
                is given. Results of computer experiments in obtaining language-oriented
                parsers for some real programming languages are given.

[Ostrovsky 88]   B.N. Ostrovsky. Implementation of Controlled Mixed Computation in
                System for Automatic Development of Language-Oriented Parsers. In
                D. Bjørner, A.P. Ershov and N.D. Jones, editors, *Partial Evaluation
                and Mixed Computation*, North-Holland, 1988. (This volume).

                English version of [Ostrovsky 87].

[Pagan 80]   F.G. Pagan. On the Generation of Compilers from Language Definitions. *Information Processing Letters*, 10(2):104–107, March 1980.

Partial   evaluation techniques are considered for transforming inter-preter-oriented language definitions into compilers.

[Pettorossi 88] A. Pettorossi and M. Proieth. Importing and Exporting Information in Program Development. In D. Bjørner, A.P. Ershov and N.D. Jones, editors, *Partial Evaluation and Mixed Computation*, North-Holland, 1988. (This volume).

Several examples of transformation of inefficient programs into efficient ones by hand are presented, and the proposed approach, called lambda abstraction, is compared to other approaches.

[Romanenko 83] S.A. Romanenko. *An Application of Mixed Computation to Assemblers and Loaders*. Preprint 27, Keldysh Institute of Applied Mathematics, Moscow, USSR, 1983. (in Russian).

Mixed computation is applied to the development of an assembler and a linking loader. The load module is considered to be a residual program produced by mixed computation of an assembler over a source module with frozen parameter values. When these are available, the load module can be executed to generate an absolute program.

[Romanenko 87a] S.A. Romanenko. *A Compiler Generator Produced by Self-Application of a Specializer Can Have a Clear and Natural Structure*. Preprint 26, Keldysh Institute of Applied Mathematics, Moscow, USSR, 1987. (in Russian).

The paper describes the structure of and ideas behind a self-applicable program specializer, and the principles of operation of a compiler generator produced automatically by specializing the specializer with respect to itself. The structure of the compilers produced is improved by means of some new devices suggested.

[Romanenko 87b] S.A. Romanenko. *Refal-4, an Extension of Refal-2, for Representing Results of Driving*. Preprint 147, Keldysh Institute of Applied Mathematics, Moscow, USSR, 1987 (in Russian).

The paper describes a number of constructs to be introduced into the language Refal-2. These will make it possible to represent the results of various optimizations that are performed by the Refal-compiler but cannot be represented in Refal-2 alone.

[Romanenko 88] S.A. Romanenko. A Compiler Generator Produced by a Self-Applicable Specializer Can Have a Surprisingly Natural and Understandable Structure. In D. Bjørner, A.P. Ershov and N.D. Jones, editors, *Partial Evaluation and Mixed Computation*, North-Holland, 1988. (This volume).

English version of [Romanenko 87a].

[Romanenko,A 88] A.Y. Romanenko. The Generation of Inverse Functions in Refal. In D. Bjørner, A.P. Ershov and N.D. Jones, editors, *Partial Evaluation and Mixed Computation*, North-Holland, 1988. (This volume).

Some problems in automatic generation of inverse functions are solved by means of configurational analysis: an analysis of the computation history. Some extensions of the Refal language are suggested to support function inversion.

[Safra 86a]   S. Safra. *Partial Evaluation of Concurrent Prolog and Its Implications.* Master's thesis, CS86-24, Weizmann Institute of Science, Rehovot, Israel, July 1986.

[Safra 86b]   S. Safra and E. Shapiro. Meta Interpreters for Real. In H.-J. Kugler, editor, *Information Processing 86, Dublin, Ireland*, pages 271–278, North-Holland, 1986.

Partial evaluation is defined and its applications to compilation and compiler generation are outlined. Several Prolog metainterpreters are described and it is argued that partial evaluation is useful for reducing the overhead incurred by metainterpretation.

[Sakama 88]   C. Sakama and H. Itoh. Partial Evaluation of Queries in Deductive Databases. *New Generation Computing*, 6(2,3), June 1988. (to appear).

The paper presents an application of partial evaluation to query optimization in a deductive database. The compilation approach to query processing is extended to multiple query processing using the generalization technique.

[Samochadin 82]   A.V. Samochadin. Optimizer for Structured Microcomputer Assembler Programs. In *Microprocessor Programming*, pages 89–99, Valgus, Tallin, USSR, 1982. (in Russian).

The mixed computation algorithms Smix and Dmix for structured assembly programs are described.

[Schmidt 88]   D.A. Schmidt. Static Properties of Partial Evaluation. In D. Bjørner, A.P. Ershov and N.D. Jones, editors, *Partial Evaluation and Mixed Computation*, North-Holland, 1988. (This volume).

Fundamental properties of call-by-value partial reduction of lambda-calculus expressions are stated and proved. A two-level type system plays an important role in the proofs. An algorithm for assigning a two-level typing to an expression is given.

[Schooler 84]   R. Schooler. *Partial Evaluation as a Means of Language Extensibility.* Master's thesis, 84 pages, MIT/LCS/TR-324, Laboratory for Computer Science, MIT, Cambridge, Massachusetts, August 1984.

A partial evaluator for an applicative subset of Scheme is developed. It can deal with side-effects, but does not try to optimize them. User-supplied annotations guide the partial evaluator which is intended to be used in a system for supporting language extensibility.

[Sestoft 86]   P. Sestoft. The Structure of a Self-Applicable Partial Evaluator. In H. Ganzinger and N.D. Jones, editors, *Programs as Data Objects, Copenhagen, Denmark, 1985*, pages 236–256, Lecture Notes in Computer Science, Vol. 217, Springer-Verlag, 1986.

The structure of the self-applicable partial evaluator reported in [Jones 85] is presented in detail. The problems arising from self-application are discussed, and experience from using the partial evaluator for generation of compilers and a compiler generator is assessed.

[Sestoft 88]   P. Sestoft. Automatic Call Unfolding in a Partial Evaluator. In D. Bjørner, A.P. Ershov and N.D. Jones, editors, *Partial Evaluation and Mixed Computation*, North-Holland, 1988. (This volume).

The partial evaluator described in [Jones 85] and [Sestoft 86] is extended with a mechanism to make automatic call annotations and hence avoid the need for human assistance. The problems with call unfolding are discussed, the new mechanism is described, and results from its use are reported.

[Shapiro 86]   E.Shapiro. Concurrent Prolog: A Progress Report. *Computer*, 19(8):44–58, August 1986.

In this survey paper on Concurrent Prolog, partial evaluation is mentioned as a technique to reduce metainterpreter overhead.

[Søndergaard 84]   H. Søndergaard. *A Primitive Autoprojector for a Simple Applicative Language*. Student Report 84-2-4, DIKU, University of Copenhagen, Denmark, November 1984.

This report is about work towards that presented in [Jones 85]. An analysis of the problems involved in partial evaluation is carried out, a one-phase self-applicable partial evaluator is presented, and the results are critically reviewed. Problems to be solved by future work are outlined.

[Stepanov 81a]   A.M. Stepanov. *Frames and Parallel Mixed Computation*. Preprint 297, Computing Center, Novosibirsk, USSR, 1981. (in Russian).

A parallel abstract machine based on the notion of frame is described. The notions of relation and scheme for depicting standard data structures are introduced.

[Stepanov 81b]   A.M. Stepanov. *Experimental Programming System*. Preprint 305, Computing Center, Novosibirsk, USSR, 1981. (in Russian).

The properties of a parallel abstract machine are discussed. It is shown that the proposed mechanism of data processing can be used as a universal computational tool. A simplified version of the external machine language is described, and the perspectives of development of the system are discussed.

[Sterling 86]   L. Sterling and R.D. Beer. Incremental Flavor-Mixing of Meta-Interpreters for Expert System Construction. In *Proc. 3rd Symposium on Logic Programming, Salt Lake City, Utah*, pages 20–27, 1986.

A partial evaluator is used for eliminating the inefficiency of use of metainterpreters in an expert system. Problems of how to guide a partial evaluator for Prolog are discussed.

[Sternberg 77]   L.F. Sternberg. Economical Algorithms of INCOL Algorithmic Language Interpretation. *Kybernetika*, (1):69–74, 1977. (in Russian).

Algorithms for interpretation of the Incol language are described. Common sublists and references are used in the algorithms. In this way, linearity is preserved.

[Takeuchi 86a]   A. Takeuchi. Affinity between Meta Interpreters and Partial Evaluation. In H.-J. Kugler, editor, *Information Processing 86, Dublin, Ireland*, pages 279–282, North-Holland, 1986.

An affinity between generality of metainterpreters and specialization by partial evaluation is noticed. Two open problems with this view are pointed out and discussed. One relates to the semantics of partial evaluation of non-deterministic parallel languages and the other concerns metalevel descriptions of parallel computation.

[Takeuchi 86b]   A. Takeuchi and K. Furukawa. Partial Evaluation of Prolog Programs and Its Application to Meta Programming. In H.-J. Kugler, editor, *Information Processing 86, Dublin, Ireland*, pages 415–420, North-Holland, 1986.

Partial evaluation of Prolog programs and its application to metaprogramming are presented. It is shown how the inefficiency incurred by metaprograms can be removed by means of partial evaluation without losing the expressive power of metaprogramming.

[Takeuchi 88]   A. Takeuchi and H. Fujita. Competitive Partial Evaluation – Some Remaining Problems of Partial Evaluation. *New Generation Computing*, 6(2,3), June 1988. (to appear).

Two case studies are presented that show how partial evaluation can improve efficiency. The many problems to be solved before partial evaluation can produce results comparable to those expert programmers produce are also discussed.

[Takewaki 85]   T. Takewaki et al. *Application of Partial Evaluation to the Algebraic Manipulation System and Its Evaluation*. Technical Report TR-148, ICOT, Tokyo, Japan, 1985.

The paper describes an application of partial evaluation to an algebraic manipulation system using metaprogramming.

[Talcott 88]   C. Talcott and R. Weyhrauch. Partial Evaluation, Higher-Order Abstractions, and Reflection Principles as System Building Tools. In D. Bjørner, A.P. Ershov and N.D. Jones, editors, *Partial Evaluation and Mixed Computation*, North-Holland, 1988. (This volume).

The paper describes interactive programming environments for symbolic computation quite generally and raises some challenging problems for partial evaluation in this context.

[Trakhtenbrot 80]   M.B. Trakhtenbrot. On Transformations Which Complete Program Definition. *Kybernetika*, (2):55–60, 1980. (in Russian).

A definition of correctness of program transformations is suggested. Transformations and program constructs are considered which permit to increase the quality and reliability of programs.

[Turchin 72]   V.F. Turchin. Equivalent Transformation of Recursive Functions Defined in Refal. In *Trudy Vsesoyuzn. Simpos Teoria Yazykov i Metody Progr.*, pages 31–42, Alushta-Kiev, 1972 (in Russian).

The basic rules of transformation of Refal programs are introduced. The rule of driving (forced instantiation with unfolding) is shown to be the most important tool. As an example of driving, it is shown how the algorithm of subtraction of binary numbers can be produced from the algorithm for addition.

[Turchin 74]   V.F. Turchin. Equivalent Transformations of Refal Programs. In *Automatizirovannaya Sistema Upravlenya Stroitelstvom, Vol. VI*, pages 36–68, TsNIPIASS, Moscow, 1974 (in Russian).

[Turchin 77]   V.F. Turchin (ed.). *Basic Refal and Its Implementation on Computers.* GOSSTROI SSSR, TsNIPIASS, 1977 (in Russian).

Treats the definition of Refal, its use, programming techniques and implementation on the main Soviet computers. The chapter on translation includes a discussion of the method of constructing compilers and compiler compilers by self-application of a supercompiler (a partial evaluator).

[Turchin 79]   V.F. Turchin. A Supercompiler System Based on the Language Refal. *SIGPLAN Notices*, 14(2):46–54, February 1979.

The paper describes a projected programming system in which the user will be able to create and define various specialized programming languages in Refal and to generate translators for them automatically.

[Turchin 80a]   V.F. Turchin. The Use of Metasystem Transition in Theorem Proving and Program Optimization. In J. De Bakker and J. van Leeuven, editors, *Automata, Languages and Programming. Seventh ICALP, Noordwijkerhout, The Netherlands*, pages 645–657, Lecture Notes in Computer Science, Vol. 85, Springer-Verlag, 1980.

The paper describes the use of a supercompiler as a theorem prover. Examples from recursive arithmetics are considered. When a direct supercompilation does not lead to a proof, it may be possible to do the proof by supercompiling the process of supercompilation itself (achieving a so-called metasystem transition).

[Turchin 80b]   V.F. Turchin. Semantic Definitions in Refal and Automatic Production of Compilers. In N.D. Jones, editor, *Semantics-Directed Compiler Generation, Aarhus, Denmark*, pages 441–474, Lecture Notes in Computer Science, Vol. 94, Springer-Verlag, 1980.

The operational semantics of a programming language can be defined in Refal. Then a compiler for the language can be built automatically by supercompilation and self-application. A simple supercompilation example is given.

[Turchin 80c]   V.F. Turchin. *The Language Refal, the Theory of Compilation and Metasystem Analysis.* Courant Computer Science Report 20, 245 pages, Courant Institute of Mathematical Sciences, New York University, New York, February 1980.

A detailed exposition of the language Refal and interpretation, compilation and transformation of Refal programs. The concept of metasystem transition is investigated using Refal.

[Turchin 82]   V.F. Turchin, R.M. Nirenberg and D.V. Turchin. Experiments with a Supercompiler. In *1982 ACM Symposium on Lisp and Functional Programming, Pittsburgh, Pennsylvania*, pages 47–55, ACM, 1982.

A dozen simple examples show how the supercompiler created at the City College of New York is working. The examples include partial evaluation, program specialization, problem solving, and theorem proving.

[Turchin 86a]   V.F. Turchin. Program Transformation by Supercompilation. In H. Ganzinger and N.D. Jones, editors, *Programs as Data Objects, Copenhagen, Denmark, 1985*, pages 257–281, Lecture Notes in Computer Science, Vol. 217, Springer-Verlag, 1986.

Driving is defined as forced instantiation of a function call for all possible value cases of the arguments, followed by unfolding. An algorithm for driving in Refal with a lazy evaluation semantics is given. Repeated driving with search for recurring configurations (supercompilation) becomes a method of program transformation.

[Turchin 86b]   V.F. Turchin. The Concept of a Supercompiler. *ACM Transactions on Programming Languages and Systems*, 8(3):292–325, July 1986.

The general principles and algorithms of supercompilation are described and compared with the usual approach to program transformation as stepwise application of equivalence transformations. Refal, used as the base language for supercompilation, is formally defined and compared with Lisp and Prolog. Examples are given.

[Turchin 88]   V.F. Turchin. The Algorithm of Generalization in the Supercompiler. In D. Bjørner, A.P. Ershov and N.D. Jones, editors, *Partial Evaluation and Mixed Computation*, North-Holland, 1988. (This volume).

The central problem of supercompilation is how to choose a self-sufficient finite set of configurations of the computing system. Generalization over configurations is necessary for this. The paper describes an algorithm of generalization in the process of driving (forced unfolding) which always terminates and produces a self-sufficient set.

[Vasey 86]   P. Vasey. Qualified Answers and Their Application to Transformation. In E. Shapiro, editor, *Third International Conference on Logic Programming, London, United Kingdom*, pages 425–432, Lecture Notes in Computer Science, Vol. 225, Springer-Verlag, 1986.

A metainterpreter for giving so-called qualified answers to Prolog queries is devised, and is shown to be useful for program transformation and program specialization.

[Venken 84] R. Venken. A Prolog Meta-Interpreter for Partial Evaluation and Its Application to Source to Source Transformation and Query-Optimisation. In T. O'Shea, editor, *ECAI-84, Advances in Artificial Intelligence, Pisa, Italy*, pages 91–100, North-Holland, 1984.

A partial evaluator for full Prolog is presented which relies on user-supplied annotations. It is intended for optimization of deductive database enquiries.

[Venken 88] R. Venken and B. Demoen. A Partial Evaluation System for Prolog: Some Practical Considerations. *New Generation Computing*, 6(2,3), June 1988. (to appear).

The operation principles of a Prolog partial evaluator are described, and some performance considerations are made. The conclusion is drawn that some 'natural' optimizations may be harmful to performance if they disturb the possibility of optimized implementation (by a compiler, say).

[Youganova 87] T.I. Youganova. Mixed Computation Correctness: Incol Language Example. *Programmirovanie*, (2):67–77, 1987. (in Russian).

The peculiarities of mixed computation in the language Incol by means of delay control are considered. Local correctness as a feature of computation is described and the reason for its failure are analyzed.

[Youganova 88] T.I. Youganova. A Model of Language Semantics Oriented to Mixed Execution of Programs. In D. Bjørner, A.P. Ershov and N.D. Jones, editors, *Partial Evaluation and Mixed Computation*, North-Holland, 1988. (This volume).

Features of mixed computation as incorporated into software to support decision making with incomplete information are discussed. The language Incol which is intended for mixed computation of programs and which contains suspension recognition and control facilities is also described.

[Young 88] J. Young and P. O'Keefe. Experience with a Type Evaluator. In D. Bjørner, A.P. Ershov and N.D. Jones, editors, *Partial Evaluation and Mixed Computation*, North-Holland, 1988. (This volume).

A type system for a lazy side-effect free language is developed, and the concepts of safety and preciseness of type evaluators are defined. A safe type semantics is presented, and various techniques for improving it and making it implementable are discussed.

[Zakharova 86a] N.T. Zakharova. Denotational Semantics of Mixed Computation in a Pascal Subset. In *Problems in Program Synthesis, Testing, Verification and Debugging, Vol. 1*, pages 132–134, Riga, USSR, 1986. (in Russian).

The process of mixed computation for a Pascal subset is briefly described. A criterion of functional correctness and a corresponding theorem are formulated.

[Zakharova 86b]   N.T. Zakharova and V.A. Petrushin. Denotational Semantics of Mixed
                  Computation in a Simple Structured Programming Language. In *Appli-*
                  cation of Mathematical Logic Methods, pages 74–76, Tallin, USSR, 1986.
                  (in Russian).

                  Two denotational models for mixed computation in a simple structured
                  programming language are briefly described. A theorem concerning func-
                  tional correctness of the models is formulated.

[Zakharova 87]   N.T. Zakharova, V.A. Petrushin and E.L. Yushchenko. Denotational Se-
                  mantics of Mixed Computation Processes. In *[Bjørner 87]*, pages 379–
                  388, 1987.

                  A denotational model of ordinary computation and two denotational
                  models of mixed computation in a simple structured programming lan-
                  guage are presented. A criterion of functional correctness of mixed com-
                  putation and the corresponding theorems are formulated.

[Zakharova 88]   N.T. Zakharova, V.A. Petrushin and E.L. Yushchenko. Denotational Se-
                  mantics of Mixed Computation of a Structured Programming Language.
                  Kybernetika, 1988 (to appear). (in Russian).

                  A denotational model of ordinary computation and two denotational
                  models of mixed computation in a simple structured language are pre-
                  sented. A criterion of functional correctness of mixed computation is
                  given and a theorem concerning the functional correctness is proved for
                  one of the models.

[Zamulin 86]   A.V. Zamulin and I.N. Skopin. Programming Language Constructs as
                  Data Types. In *Applied Informatics*, pages 93–110, Finansy i Statistika,
                  Iss. 2, Moscow, USSR, 1986 (in Russian).

                  The application of a unified data type constructor to the definition of
                  data processed at the compilation and execution stages is studied. The
                  approach permits to represent all programming language constructs as
                  an integrated data type system.

List of Participants

Barendregt, Henk	Nijmegen, The Netherlands
Barzdin, Jan M.	Riga, USSR
Beckman, Lennart	Uppsala, Sweden
Berglund, Eric	Stanford, California, USA
Bjørner, Dines	Lyngby, Denmark
Bonacina, Maria P.	Milano, Italy
Bondorf, Anders	Copenhagen, Denmark
Christiansen, Henning	Roskilde, Denmark
Codish, Michael	Rehovot, Israel
Consel, Charles	Saint Denis, France
Danvy, Olivier	Copenhagen, Denmark
Darlington, John	London, Great Britain
Demoen, Bart	Everberg, Belgium
Ershov, Andrei P.	Novosibirsk, USSR
Fujita, Hiroshi	Tokyo, Japan
Fuller, David	London, Great Britain
Furukawa, Koichi	Tokyo, Japan
Futamura, Yoshihiko	Tokyo, Japan
Gallagher, John	Rehovot, Israel
Guzowski, Mark	Solon, Ohio, USA
Haraldsson, Anders	Linköping, Sweden
Harrison, Peter G.	London, Great Britain
Hascoët, Laurent	Valbonne, France
Heering, Jan	Amsterdam, The Netherlands
Holst, N. Carsten Kehler	Copenhagen, Denmark
Howells, Gereth	Canterbury, Great Britain
Hughes, John	Glasgow, Great Britain
Jones, Cliff B.	Manchester, Great Britain
Jones, Neil D.	Copenhagen, Denmark
Jørring, Ulrik	Lyngby, Denmark
Kröger, Henner	Gießen, Germany
Kursawe, Peter	Karlsruhe, Germany
Lakhotia, Arun	Cleveland, Ohio, USA
Launchbury, John	Glasgow, Great Britain
Lavrov, S.S.	Leningrad, USSR
Levi, Giorgi	Pisa, Italy
Lucas, Peter	San José, California, USA
McCarthy, John	Stanford, California, USA
Maluszynski, Jan	Linköping, Sweden
Mogensen, Torben	Copenhagen, Denmark
Mosses, Peter	Aarhus, Denmark
Nepejvoda, N.N.	Izhevsk, USSR
De Niel, Anne	Leuven, Belgium
Nielson, Flemming	Lyngby, Denmark

Nielson, Hanne Riis	Aalborg, Denmark
Nilsson, Ulf	Linköping, Sweden
Nori, Kesav	Pune, India
Norman, Andy	Bristol, Great Britain
Ostrovski, Boris	Barnaul, USSR
Owen, Stephen	Bristol, Great Britain
Pettorossi, A.	Roma, Italy
Pull, Helen	London, Great Britain
Romanenko, Sergei A.	Moscow, USSR
Rosendahl, Mads	Cambridge, Great Britain
Ryčko, Marek	Warsaw, Poland
Sakama, Chiaki	Tokyo, Japan
Scherlis, William L.	Pittsburgh, Pennsylvania, USA
Schmidt, David A.	Manhattan, Kansas, USA
Sestoft, Peter	Copenhagen, Denmark
Sjöland, Thomas	Spånga, Sweden
Steensgaard-Madsen, Jørgen	Lyngby, Denmark
Takeuchi, Akikazu	Hoyogo, Japan
Talcott, Carolyn	Stanford, California, USA
Tribble, Eric	Palo Alto, California, USA
Turchin, Valentin F.	New York, USA
Waern, Annika	Spånga, Sweden
Young, Jonathan	New Haven, Connecticut, USA
Zamulin, Alexander V.	Novosibirsk, USSR

Author Index

Barzdin, G.J.   15

Bondorf, A.   27

Bulyonkov, M.A.   51

Bulyonkov, M.A.   65

Danvy, O.   83

Darlington, J.   117

Ershov, A.P.   65

Futamura, Y.   113

Harrison, P.G.   153

Holst, N.C. Kehler   167

Hughes, J.   187

Itkin, V.E.   209

Jones, N.D.   225

Kursawe, P.   283

Launchbury, J.   299

Lavrov, S.S.   317

Mogensen, T.   325

Nielson, F.   349

Nogi, K.   113

O'Keefe, P.   573

Ostrovski, B.N.   385

Pettorossi, A.   405

Proietti, M.   405

Pull, H.   117

Romanenko, A.   427

Romanenko, S.A.   445

Schmidt, D.A.   465

Sestoft, P.   485

Talcott, C.   507

Turchin, V.F.   531

Weyhrauch, R.   507

Youganova, T.I.   551

Young, J.   573